HARRY SCHWARTZ

SPECIALIST ON SOVIET AFFAIRS, NEW YORK TIMES
formerly PROFESSOR OF ECONOMICS
MAXWELL SCHOOL OF CITIZENSHIP, SYRACUSE UNIVERSITY

RUSSIA'S SOVIET ECONOMY

Second Edition

WITH APPENDIX

THE SOVIET ECONOMY: 1954–1958

PRENTICE-HALL, INC.

ENGLEWOOD CLIFFS, N. J.

L. C. Cat. Card No.: 54–11932

First printing...................................September, 1954
Second printing..................................January, 1958
Third printing...................................September, 1958

TO

Ruth, Billy, Johnny, and Bobby

PREFACE TO SECOND EDITION

THE APPEARANCE of a second edition of this study of the Soviet economy less than four years after publication of the first edition is the result of several factors. First, the swift pace of events since mid-1950 has illuminated many formerly obscure facets of the Soviet economy and — particularly since Stalin's death — raised a number of new major problems. Second, the almost unanimously kind reception given to the first edition by noncommunist reviewers has encouraged the author's belief that a comprehensive study of this type meets a real need. Third, government officials, college teachers, and others concerned with the Soviet economy have suggested that bringing the volume up to date would greatly increase its usefulness.

In preparing this second edition, the emphasis has been upon the inclusion of material dealing with developments from mid-1950 to mid-1954, as well as material dealing with earlier periods which became available only after the manuscript of the first edition had been completed. Though the basic skeleton of the volume has remained unchanged — having been found sound by the great majority of those who have been kind enough to communicate their opinions to the author — this present edition is able to report on the nature and progress of the Fifth Five-Year Plan, the changes in economic policy following Stalin's death, the struggle over East-West trade, Soviet progress in nuclear physics and other branches of weapons development, and the like. In addition, where appropriate, account has been taken of that rich source of data, the formerly secret Soviet Economic Plan for 1941.

The author must express his gratitude to Leon Herman, who has made many helpful suggestions in connection with this revision, as well as to other friends who have helped on particular points. The author's wife and children have once again uncomplainingly borne the burdens of family life, made most complicated by the exigencies of this revision.

v

Mrs. Lucy Earisman of Prentice-Hall has given generously of her time and energy to this revision. Aline E. Blumner has again excellently performed the onerous chores connected with typing the index. Ruth B. Schwartz, William D. Schwartz, and John L. Schwartz assisted in reading proofs. The author's thanks are extended to all these invaluable helpers.

PORT CHESTER, N. Y.   *Harry Schwartz.*

Economics of the Soviet Union

I   Introduction – Background in resources. –
     Chpt. ①; historical – (Von Rauch); ideological – chpt ③

II   Soviet Economic Growth & Development
     Development – Chpt. ④; labor productivity –
     Chpt ⑬; level of living & incentives – chpt ⑮

III   The National Economic Plan – Chpt. ⑤

IV   Organization & Operation of Soviet Industry
     Organization – Operation – Chpt. ⑥
     Growth of Industrial Production – Chpt ⑦

V   Soviet Agriculture
     organization – Chpt ⑧
     production development ⑨

VI   Transportation & Communication
                      – Chpt. ⑩

VII   Domestic Trade
     Trade, housing, services – Chpt. ⑪

VIII   Soviet Financial System – Chpt. ⑫

IX   Soviet Foreign Economic Relations – Chpt ⑭

TABLE OF CONTENTS

LIST OF MAPS

LIST OF FIGURES

LIST OF TABLES

CHAPTER I

THE RESOURCE BACKGROUND

MANY ELEMENTS COMBINE to fashion the economy of a large state such as the Soviet Union. This chapter will be concerned with some of the most fundamental of these elements. It will treat the physical setting of Soviet life, the availability and distribution of major natural resources, and the composition of the population. These are the basic physical and human resources at the foundation of the Soviet economy. Such other important factors as the economic development of Czarist Russia, the changing technology of production, the political and economic organization of the USSR, and so on, will be considered later in this volume.

The pattern of Soviet resources must be regarded from a dynamic rather than a static point of view. As do other modern industrial countries, the USSR regards limitations imposed upon it by terrain, climate, or soil as barriers to be removed or circumvented. Thus deserts can be irrigated, poor land fertilized, and mountains pierced by tunnels, where the required technologies are possessed, if the advantages to be gained outweigh the costs. Similarly the mineral wealth of a major nation is constantly changing in response to such factors as discoveries of new deposits, depletion of old ones, and scientific advances affecting the production or use of different minerals. Finally, human beings are perhaps the most changeable resource of all. Given the proper training, the ignorant shepherd boy can be turned into a skilled engineer, and within broad limits the location pattern of a country's population can be so altered as to shift workers to where they are needed most. These and other dynamic possibilities have been employed by the Soviet regime in

1

its economic development to date. Similar dynamism in resource utilization is to be expected in the future.

The Physical Setting

Two facts stand out in any consideration of the USSR's physical geography: the vast size of the country and the enormous variety of natural conditions contained within it. The Soviet Union forms the largest contiguous land and water area ruled by one government. Its area of about 8,436,000 square miles is almost three times as large as the continental area of the United States, comprising about one seventh of the total land surface of the earth; almost one sixth if we exclude areas covered by ice caps. North to south, Soviet territory stretches over 2,700 miles, and east to west about 7,000 miles. Occupying a large segment of Eastern Europe and all of Northern Asia, the USSR has land borders with countries from Poland to China and Korea as well as about 28,000 miles of coastline, mainly on the Arctic and Pacific oceans but also on the Baltic, Black, and Caspian seas.[1] Both its size and its location have played important roles in its political, economic, and military history.

The Soviet Union has an enormous variety of natural conditions. The range of climate permits both the raising of reindeer near the Arctic Circle and the growing of tea and citrus fruit in subtropical southern areas. Its mountains are among the highest in the world — Mount Stalin rises almost 25,000 feet above sea level — but it also has the great Caspian depression. Deserts cover large areas and must be irrigated to produce crops; bogs and swamps abound in other regions, requiring large-scale drainage projects before the land can be farmed. Such contrasts could be multiplied many times to illustrate the complexity of the physical geography.

In the following sections we shall consider specific aspects of the USSR's physical geography and natural resources from transportation, agricultural, and industrial points of view, in that order.

From the standpoint of transportation, the vital elements to be considered are topographical, that is, the pattern of mountains, plains, and other land forms; the extent and distribution of rivers,

---

[1] S. S. Balzak, *et al., Economic Geography of the USSR*, p. 1. New York: Macmillan, 1949. *Pravda,* May 2, 1954.

lakes, and other internal waterways; and land and water routes for foreign trade.

Soviet Topography

The dominating feature of the USSR's topography is the great plain — hilly in some parts, level in others — that stretches from the country's western borders in the heart of Europe eastward to the Yenisey River in the middle of Asia. Most of this plain is less than 1,000 feet above sea level. The Ural Mountains separate it into two parts, but they offer no more serious obstacle to land transportation than the Appalachian Mountains to movement from the Atlantic seaboard to the Mississippi Valley. On the west the Urals usually slope gently; they have many low passes; and their peaks seldom rise above 3,000 feet, though the highest is over 6,000 feet above sea level.

Obviously such a vast and relatively level area invites movement over it by men on foot or on horse. It offers tempting conditions for the building of roads and railroad lines, though the absence of rock for ballast is a handicap. In the Western Siberian Lowland, the Asiatic portion of this plain, height above sea level varies only a few hundred feet over distances of more than 1,500 miles. Little wonder that a major portion of Russian history is occupied with the sagas of great migrations, north and south, east and west, over this immense plain.

An important extension of the great Russian plain southward is the Central Asiatic Lowland, an area of deserts, oases, and irrigated sections. Historically the home of non-Russian Moslem peoples primarily engaged in pastoral livestock-tending, under the Soviet regime this territory has become an important region of settled agriculture and industry.

Land transportation is more difficult in the mountainous areas, which form roughly one fifth of the USSR's territory. Mountains and upland regions bound much of the central Russian plain and its extension in Central Asia. Most of these are in the southern and eastern portions of the country, though the Carpathian Mountains are in the southwest at the Czechoslovak border and the Karelian uplands adjoin Finland.

West of the Caspian Sea, the Caucasian and Crimean Mountains

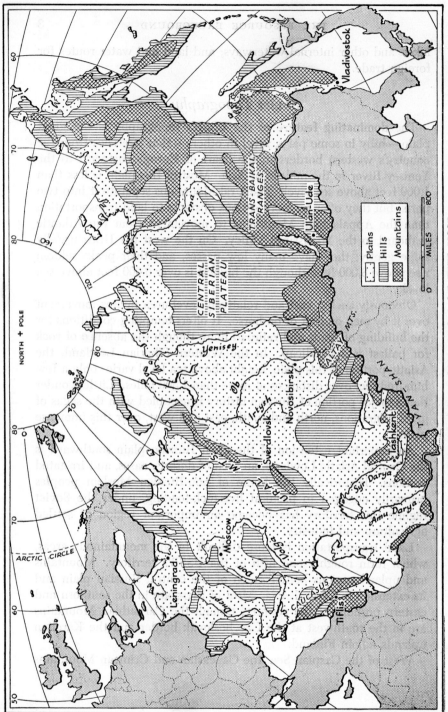

I. SURFACE CONFIGURATION OF THE USSR

are important terrain features. Farther east, beyond the Kara Kum Desert, most of the southern border of the USSR is fringed by mountain and highland areas, including the towering Pamir, Tyan-Shan, and Altay ranges among others. North of these mountains and stretching east from the Yenisey to the Pacific is an area with complex topography, most of it upland and mountain country with many plateaus and high hills. The Central Siberian Plateau, the Verkhoyansk Range, and the Northeastern Mountain Complex are among the main sectors of this vast area.

Bulky commodities can usually be moved more cheaply by water than by land, particularly over long distances; thus it is not strange that the extensive internal waterways of the USSR are an important link in its present transportation system and have much potentiality for greater use in the future. There are about 100,000 rivers with basins of more than 100 square kilometers, and thousands of lakes. In the main the most important rivers run north and south, a factor which limits their usefulness, since a very large proportion of Soviet freight is shipped east or west. Virtually all the Soviet Union's northern and eastern boundaries are formed by the Baltic Sea, the polar seas, and the Pacific Ocean. In the south the USSR has long coastlines on both the Caspian and Black Seas.

The usefulness of these waterways for transportation is limited, however, by the fact that the great majority of them freeze over during part of each year. In the extreme north, ice makes water passages unusable often for eight or nine months each year. Even the Amu Darya in Central Asia is frozen two to three months each year.

Economically, the most important river is the Volga, which annually carries the largest freight volume of any inland waterway. This river rises in the swamp country north of Moscow and empties into the Caspian Sea, after traversing some 2,300 miles. Among the major cities on the Volga are Gorky, Kazan, Kuibyshev, Saratov, and Stalingrad. Oil and food products are carried north up the river; timber and manufactured products are the main types of southbound freight.

Other major riverways in the European USSR include the Kama, a tributary of the Volga; the Northern Dvina, which reaches the White Sea at Archangel and carries much of Soviet timber; and, in the south, the Dnepr and Dnestr Rivers, which flow into the Black

Sea, and the Don, which flows into the Sea of Azov. The Soviet Union, like Czarist Russia before it, has been active in building canals and deepening river channels in order to connect many of the major rivers and lakes in this area. This has been done to make possible increased east-west water traffic and to permit ships entering ports in the north or in the south to penetrate deep into the continental plain. Thus Moscow is connected with the Volga basin by a major canal and linked with the Arctic Ocean and the Leningrad area by the Mariinsk Canal system and the Baltic-White Sea Canal.

The opening of the Volga-Don Canal in mid-1952 greatly increased the usability of the rivers of European Russia. It provided a direct water transport route connecting the Black Sea, the Sea of Azov, the Don and Volga Rivers, and the Caspian Sea. In addition, under favorable conditions of navigation along the Volga, this canal serves as the link — long dreamed of — which permits continuous water travel between the northern and southern sea frontiers of the Soviet Union, opening up great possibilities for the future. But much work will be needed to improve Volga navigation conditions before a dependable north-south water route across the heart of Russia will be available during all the months when the rivers are not frozen.

In Asiatic Russia the major rivers, the Ob, the Yenisey, and the Lena, together with their many tributaries, flow into the Arctic Ocean and are frozen much of each year. The opening of the Northern Sea Route along the polar seas in the mid-1930's not only permitted vessels to steam from Vladivostok to Murmansk or in the opposite direction each summer, but also made possible increased use of the major Siberian rivers as channels of distribution for the areas through which they flow. During World War II large amounts of Lend-Lease supplies were sent to the inhabitants of Northern Siberia over these waterways. The increased accessibility of this area has greatly facilitated the exploitation of its resources.

In the Soviet Far East the Amur River is most important. This river follows much of the boundary between the Soviet Union and China and then connects Khabarovsk with the ocean port of Nikolayevsk on the Tartar Strait. In Central Asia the Amu Darya and the Syr Darya, both of which flow into the Aral Sea, provide channels for ship transportation.

Important parts of the water transportation system are the lakes and seas entirely or partially in the USSR. The Black, Caspian, and Aral Seas in the south are the largest of these. Among the most important lakes are Ladoga and Onega near the Finnish border, Balkhash and Issyk-Kul in Central Asia near the border of Sinkiang, and Baikal in Southeastern Siberia. The Sea of Azov, between the Ukraine and the North Caucasus, is linked with the Black Sea by the Kerch Strait.

International Connections

Soviet imports and exports of goods move over both land and sea routes. The importance of land transportation in this trade has increased greatly since World War II, as the result of the great expansion of commerce between the USSR and the communist-dominated countries in Eastern Europe and Asia. Natural barriers do not significantly obstruct transportation toward the Atlantic Ocean from the USSR's western borders, and railroads carry a large portion of this trade. A man-made obstacle here is the difference between the "wide" gauge (5 feet) of Soviet railroads and the "standard" gauge (4 feet, 8½ inches) employed generally throughout Europe, which has usually made necessary unloading and reloading of goods at the Soviet border. This factor is becoming less important since some railroad lines in Soviet satellite areas appear to have been converted to the Soviet wide gauge, and since equipment has become available for quickly changing the undercarriage of rolling stock at the Soviet borders in Europe and Asia so cars can be used on both gauges.

Overland transportation facilities to the countries south of the USSR, in the Near East and Asia, are less well developed, both because of the mountain barriers frequent along these borders and because in the past the volume of trade has been small. In the future, as trade increases between Communist China and the Soviet Union, road and rail transport facilities will probably be improved.

The use of Soviet ports on major oceans and seas is usually hampered for some months of each year because of ice, which closes or slows down traffic in these ports. Among the few Soviet ports that are generally usable all year round, Murmansk, on the Barents Sea in the far north, and the Black Sea ports such as Odessa and Novorossiisk are outstanding. When winter loosens its grip, Soviet Baltic Sea ports from Kaliningrad to Leningrad, along with Archangel and Murmansk, offer outlets to Northern Europe and the Atlantic Ocean. Vladivostok, Sovetskaya Gavan, and Nikolayevsk are among the USSR's major ports on the Pacific Ocean for trade with the rest of Asia, Australia, and the western coasts of North and South America. Major Soviet ports on the Caspian Sea, such as Baku and Makhach-Kala, are used for maritime trade with Iran as well as for domestic commerce. In the south, however, the Black Sea ports are most important for trade with the Mediterranean area and across the Atlantic. From the USSR's point of view, a major weakness of its dependence upon Black and Baltic Sea ports for maritime access to the west lies in the fact that exit from both bodies can be cut off with comparative ease by other powers controlling the relatively narrow channels of egress. Soviet interest in the Turkish Dardanelles, for example, has been motivated by the desire to obtain more control over the vital passageway between the Black Sea and the Mediterranean.

In the discussion above, the nature of Soviet topography as well as the distribution of coastal and inland bodies of water has been considered primarily from the point of view of transportation. It must not be forgotten, however, that these features of the physical setting also exercise important influence upon the climate of the USSR and therefore upon its agriculture. In addition, as we shall see below, the complex terrain contains rich mineral deposits.

The Agricultural Setting

Climate and soil are the major natural factors determining the possibility of agricultural development in any area. Man may modify the effects of these factors by irrigation, fertilization, use of hothouses, and other techniques, but all these are expensive. Agriculture develops most easily where the conjunction of temperature, rainfall, sunlight, and quality of soil is favorable.

The great bulk of the USSR has a continental climate with very cold winters and relatively warm, though short, summers. Most of the land area of the Soviet Union lies in the same latitudes as Canada, between 45 degrees north latitude and the Arctic Ocean. Only the more southern portions of the USSR lie in latitudes corresponding to those of the northern and central areas of the United States. Most of the great land mass of the USSR is well inland, distant from the

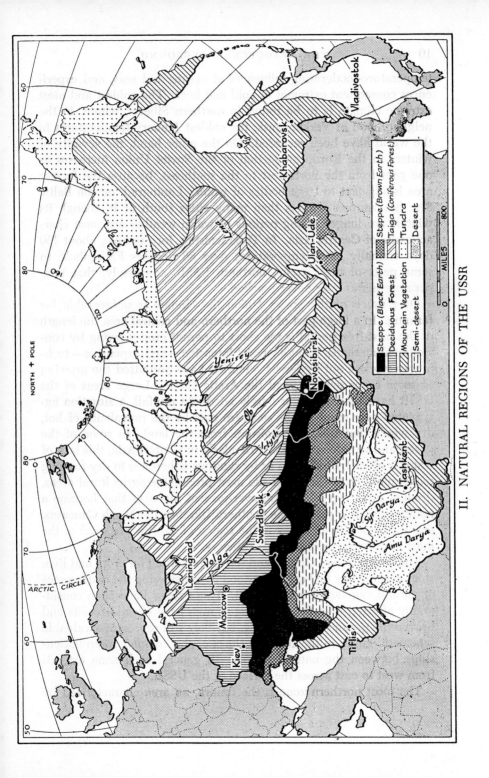

II. NATURAL REGIONS OF THE USSR

NORTH + POLE

ARCTIC CIRCLE

Vladivostok

Khabarovsk

Ulan-Ude

Lena

Yenisey

Novosibirsk

Ob

Irtysh

Sverdlovsk

Tashkent

Syr Darya

Amu Darya

Volga

Moscow

Leningrad

Kiev

Tiflis

Steppe (Black Earth)

Steppe (Brown Earth)

Deciduous Forest

Taiga (Coniferous Forest)

Mountain Vegetation

Tundra

Semi-desert

Desert

MILES

0   800

temperature-moderating influences of oceans and seas, and experiences consequent extremes of cold and heat. The coldest and most extreme climate is to be found in northern Siberia, where, in the neighborhood of Verkhoyansk, the coldest January temperatures in the world have been recorded. On the other hand, the severity of winters in the European section of the Soviet Union increases as one goes from the northwest to the southeast, because the former area is adjacent to large bodies of water. Leningrad, on the Baltic Sea, has warmer winters than many cities south of it, though its winters are longer. Long periods of warm weather are most characteristic of Central Asia. In Turkmenistan, for example, about 150 days annually have temperatures over 68 degrees Fahrenheit; in some parts of the extreme northern USSR, conversely, that temperature is rarely or never reached.

Over much of the Soviet Union the climate is unfavorable for farming. In a large part of the northern and central area the length of the frost-free period is too short to permit crop-growing by conventional methods, though special intensive — and expensive — techniques worked out by Soviet scientists have permitted the growing of some crops even beyond the Arctic Circle. Large areas of the USSR have inadequate or barely adequate rainfall, a situation aggravated over much of the southern part by the prevalence of hot, dry winds that suck the moisture from the land. In some of the desert and semidesert areas, particularly in Central Asia, this lack of water is offset by irrigation or by rigorous adherence to dry-farming techniques. But in many of the most productive agricultural areas, drought and crop failure are ever-present menaces that become a reality every few years. The Southern Ukraine, the North Caucasus, and the Volga River Valley in the region of Saratov are some of the most important regions in this category.

The interaction of climate and soil as the setting for crop- and livestock-raising may be best understood by considering the major zones of natural vegetation in the USSR. These zones have been considerably affected over the centuries, as men have cleared forests and broken the ground with the plow, but they still represent a valuable schematic guide to the broad outlines of the complex interrelationships between the natural factors. In general each zone extends from west to east across the surface of the USSR.

The most northern zone is the tundra, an area characterized by freezing or near-freezing temperatures almost all the year and permanently frozen subsoil. Waterlogged bogs and marshes cover much of this area during the brief summer, and moss, lichens, dwarf bushes, and flowers grow during this short respite. The raising of reindeer, fishing, and hunting are important occupations of the relatively small native tribes living in this bleak environment.

South of the tundra the predominant vegetation consists of coniferous trees, that is, evergreens such as fir, spruce, larch, and pine, which find the three- to four-month growing season adequate. This is the taiga area. In the European USSR it gradually gives way southward to a zone of broad-leaf deciduous trees such as the oak, maple, and elm. This region extends south beyond a line connecting Moscow and Kiev. It stretches east of the Volga below the latitude of Moscow. In these regions are the grey *podsol* soils, which cover about half the territory of the Soviet Union, including the great bulk of Soviet Asia. *Podsol* soils are usually stony, sandy, or clay-like, and are excessively acid; crops can be grown on them, but they are far from ideal for the purpose.

Over the centuries roughly half the forest area in North and Central European USSR has been cleared and replaced by settled agriculture, though the soil is relatively poor. On the other hand, rainfall is relatively adequate here compared with that in other agricultural areas. At Moscow the average annual rainfall is over 20 inches, as compared with 15 inches at Saratov on the Volga and 6 inches at Astrakhan, where the Volga enters the Caspian Sea.

The USSR still possesses enormous forest areas, particularly in the northern parts of European Russia and throughout Northern Siberia. Within the Soviet boundaries as of January 1, 1939, there were about 1,500,000,000 acres of forests, approximately one-third of all USSR territory at that time; they composed about 20 per cent of all forest areas in the world.[2] The exploitation of these forests is one of the most important industries of the USSR, providing not only a basic raw material for the domestic Soviet economy but also one of the most important export commodities. In addition, these forests abound in numerous fur-bearing animals, which are trapped or shot in large numbers annually, thus providing furs for domestic consumption and for export, particularly to the United States.

---

[2] *Ibid.*, pp. 67–68.

The steppe area, which is separated from the forest region by a transitional forest steppe belt, dominates the southern region of the USSR and covers about 14 per cent of the country. It extends from the Ukraine in the west through the Volga Valley south of Kazan into Siberia, beyond Novosibirsk but north of Lake Balkhash and the Aral Sea. In the north this region is a mixture of trees and grassland, but farther south grassland reigns supreme, the rainfall and ground moisture being inadequate for tree growth.

Much of the steppe consists of the richest soil in the world, the *chernozem,* or black earth, a somewhat alkaline soil with high humus content most favorable to crop growth. Variation in rainfall from year to year produces marked variation in the volume of crops grown in this area. With adequate rain, rich crops are gathered; but droughts occur every few years, resulting in partial or complete crop failure in this region of most fertile soil. Grass and crop growth are less luxuriant in the brown and chestnut soil areas immediately south of the black earth region, since rainfall is even sparser in these areas, the humus content of the soil is lower, and mineral salt concentration in the earth is higher.

In Central Asia, including Kazakhstan, desert and semidesert regions predominate; but where irrigation is employed, rich crops of cotton, rice, and other plants are grown. In parts of this area two and sometimes three crops a year can be grown on the same ground.

Besides Central Asia, there are only a few, very limited sections of the USSR, having long periods of warmth and abundant moisture, in which semitropical crops can be grown. One such area is in the Georgian Republic and the adjoining territory on the southeastern shore of the Black Sea, where tea, citrus fruits, and products requiring similar climatic conditions are raised. Since World War II the Soviet government has sponsored expansion of citrus and eucalyptus plantings in other southern areas of the European USSR. In the Soviet Far East, the Amur and Ussuri River valleys have semi-monsoon climates characterized by hot summers with abundant rainfall, permitting the raising of rice, soy beans, and corn, among other crops.

Livestock-raising is an important part of Soviet agriculture and is widely practiced over the USSR. Western Siberia's climate and soil have permitted the development of a large-scale dairy industry. In the black earth regions, particularly in the Ukraine, hog-raising has been well developed. Sheep and goats are abundant in the

Kazakh Republic and other areas with large regions of mountain pasture.

To combat frequent droughts in a vast area stretching from the Caspian Sea and the southern Urals to the Ukraine, the Soviet government in 1948 announced a large scale afforestation program scheduled to last almost two decades. By planting trees on almost 15,000,000 acres of farm fields, ravines, gulleys, and sand, as well as by planting eight giant continuous shelter belts of trees running north to south, it is hoped to check the hot drying winds from west of the Caspian and to permit greater retention of moisture in the soil. Other parts of this program include the building of ponds, the institution of crop rotation, and the large-scale planting of grasses, in order to create the agricultural regimen best suited for farming this large area of insufficient or barely sufficient rainfall. Fundamentally, the Soviet hope is so to change the climate of the area as to assure high and stable crop yields in the future.

In August and September 1950, the Soviet government announced a new series of projects aimed at combating the obstacles to a highly productive agriculture in these important areas with deficient or uncertain rainfall. Between 1950 and 1957 it planned to provide water for and irrigate well over 50,000,000 acres in the Volga River Valley, the area north and west of the Caspian Sea, the Southern Ukraine, and Crimea. At Kuibyshev and Stalingrad on the Volga, the USSR is building two of the largest hydroelectric stations in the world, along with dams, canals, and other installations to permit diversion of Volga River water for agriculture on both sides of the river. In the Turkmen Republic east of the Caspian, plans announced in 1950 called for building the Chief Turkmen Canal over a distance of almost 700 miles, so as to divert part of the Amu Darya from its present course to the Aral Sea and provide for irrigation and for pasture needs over an enormous arid area. In the same year, a similar large-scale project to build a sizeable canal and irrigation works through the Southern Ukraine and North Crimea was announced; an important part of this scheme was the project to build a hydroelectric station at Kakhovka on the Dnepr River.[3] Since these projects were all intended to be completed long before the afforestation program discussed above, their announcement indicated a

---

[3] *Pravda*, August 21 and 31, September 12 and 21, 1950.

need to improve natural conditions for agriculture in the areas affected well before any possible beneficial effects of the afforestation program could be important.

In the year after Stalin's death in March 1953, evidence seemed to accumulate that perhaps three of the major projects discussed above had been abandoned for the time being or given much lower priority and much less resources than originally planned. These projects are the Chief Turkmen Canal, the afforestation scheme, and the South Ukrainian-North Crimean Canal. No formal announcement that these projects had been abandoned was made public, but discussion of these efforts disappeared from the Soviet press, in sharp contrast with the publicity lavished on them earlier. Confirmatory evidence for the belief that the Chief Turkmen Canal project has been largely abandoned seems provided by the decree on cotton development in Turkmenistan published on April 23, 1954. This decree makes no mention of the Chief Turkmen Canal, but relies on the more modest Kara-Kum Canal project to provide additional irrigated land for cotton culture. The evidence indicates, however, that the hydroelectric stations at Kuibyshev, Stalingrad, and Kakhovka are being built.

Resources for Industry

The most spectacular feature of Soviet economic development since the Bolshevik revolution of 1917 has been the extremely rapid increase in the output of industry. Tractors, railroad locomotives, machine tools, and similar commodities are now produced in quantities permitting the USSR to rank as one of the foremost manufacturing nations of the world, clearly outdistanced only by the United States.

This rapid industrialization has been made possible in large part by the availability within Soviet borders of large quantities of fuel and raw material resources required by industry. Almost every significant mineral used in modern production is to be found in the USSR. Soviet supplies of many major metallic and nonmetallic raw materials are among the largest in the world. This fact, together with the abundance of water power and forest reserves, makes the Soviet Union comparable to the United States with respect to richness and variety of natural resources. And as we shall see later, this abundance of resources has permitted close approximation to the Soviet ideal of maximum self-sufficiency with respect to raw materials.

During the 1930's the Soviet government sponsored numerous geological surveys all over the country, but particularly in the area from the Urals to the Pacific. These studies revealed large and numerous mineral reserves whose extent had formerly been unsurveyed, and many of these have already begun to be exploited for Soviet industry and agriculture. By the beginning of 1945 about 73 per cent of Soviet territory had been geologically studied. Further intensive work of a similar nature is continuing, and it seems possible that additional important resources may be found in the future.

In the pages following we shall discuss the major industrial resources of the Soviet Union: their extent, location, and importance.

Water Power. The harnessing of swift-flowing streams to provide hydroelectric energy has been a significant source of the electrical power upon which Soviet industry has been built. In 1940 about 5 billion kilowatt hours of electrical energy were generated by hydroelectric stations, 10 per cent of the Soviet total; by 1950 about 16.5 billion kilowatt hours, 18.3 per cent of the nation's total electric supply, were obtained from this source.[4]

The water-power resources of the USSR are among the world's largest. In 1937 it was estimated that the potential capacity of possible Soviet hydroelectric sources was 280,000,000 kilowatts as against only about 82,000,000 kilowatts in the United States. In early 1954 Deputy Premier M. G. Pervukhin estimated that the total annual output of electric power from hydroelectric stations which could be built in the Soviet Union was over 1,700,000,000,000 kilowatt-hours, or almost 100 times as much hydroelectric power as was actually being produced at that time. The very large capital investment required for hydroelectric stations, however, has been a factor in Soviet internal disputes over the extent to which that country should rely upon hydroelectric power as against electricity generated in thermal stations using coal or other fuel, Mr. Pervukhin revealed.[5]

Coal. Soviet coal resources are among the greatest in the world,

[4] *Izvestia*, September 10, 1952.

[5] Y. A. Ioffe, compiler, *Ekonomicheskoye Sorevnovaniye Sotsialisma i Kapitalizma*, p. 22. Leningrad: Ogiz, 1939. *Pravda*, April 27, 1954.

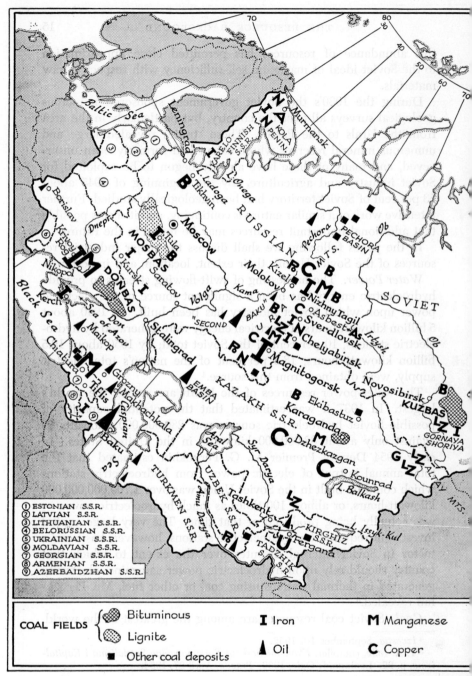

COAL FIELDS
- Bituminous
- Lignite
- Other coal deposits

I Iron   M Manganese

▲ Oil   C Copper

① ESTONIAN S.S.R.
② LATVIAN S.S.R.
③ LITHUANIAN S.S.R.
④ BELORUSSIAN S.S.R.
⑤ UKRAINIAN S.S.R.
⑥ MOLDAVIAN S.S.R.
⑦ GEORGIAN S.S.R.
⑧ ARMENIAN S.S.R.
⑨ AZERBAIDZHAN S.S.R.

III. MINERAL RESOURCE

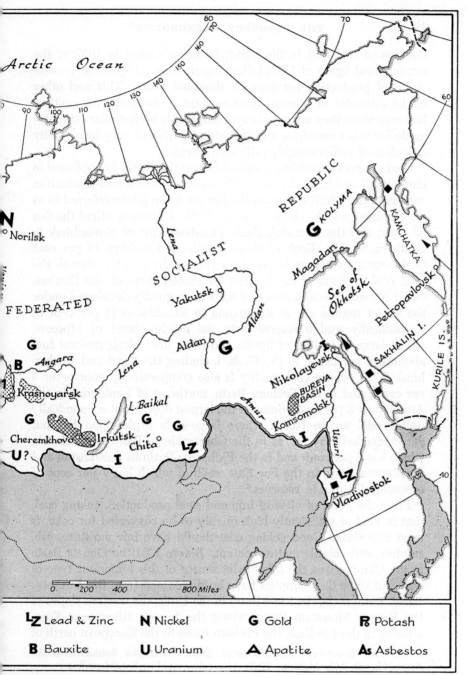

Arctic Ocean

Norilsk

N

FEDERATED

SOCIALIST

REPUBLIC

Lena

Yakutsk

Aldan

Aldan **G**

G

B *Angara*

Krasnoyarsk

Lena

G

Cheremkhovo Irkutsk *L. Baikal*

U?

Chita

I

G

LZ

KOLYMA

G

KAMCHATKA

Magadan

Sea of Okhotsk

Petropavlovsk

SAKHALIN I.

KURILE IS.

Nikolayevsk

BUREYA BASIN

Komsomolsk

Amur

Ussuri

I

LZ

Vladivostok

0.   200   400   800 Miles

LZ Lead & Zinc	**N** Nickel	**G** Gold	**P** Potash
B Bauxite	**U** Uranium	**▲** Apatite	**As** Asbestos

THE USSR

reserves of this fuel in the USSR being estimated in 1937 at the astronomical figure of 1,654 billion metric tons, adequate at present levels of production for over six thousand years. This and other Soviet estimates of mineral reserves must be treated with caution, however, since they are not always comparable with similar estimates made for other countries and include resources of very low quality as well as of rather roughly estimated extent.

Coal reserves are widely distributed over the USSR, being found in many small and large deposits. The most important coal-production centers in the USSR today are the Donets Basin (often referred to as the Donbas), which is located mainly in the Ukraine north of the Sea of Azov, and the Kuznetsk Basin (Kuzbas), east of Novosibirsk in Southern Siberia. Each of these is estimated to have 13 per cent of the economically usable coal reserves of the country, though the total coal deposits of the Kuzbas far exceed those of the Donbas. Other important coal basins that have been greatly developed under the Soviet regime are at Karaganda in Kazakhstan (4 per cent of economically usable reserves); in the neighborhood of Moscow, where large quantities of lignite and other low caloric content fuel abound (2 per cent); in the Urals, including the Kizel and Chelyabinsk fields, where coal quality is also comparatively poor (over 3 per cent); and in the Pechora Basin, northeast of Leningrad in the Arctic (over 3 per cent). Some of the largest deposits of economically usable coal are in basins where large-scale exploitation has not yet proceeded very far, as in the Cheremkhovo Basin near Irkutsk, which has 8 per cent; and in the Ekibastuz Basin in Kazakhstan and the Bureya Basin in the Far East, each of which has 7 per cent of economically usable reserves.[6]

From the point of view of iron and steel production, coking coal, that is, coal of sufficiently high quality to be converted for coke, is most important. Good coking coal should have low moisture, ash, sulphur, and volatile matter content. Before 1931 the Donets Basin in the Ukraine was the sole Soviet source of this important type of coal, but since then supplies have been obtained from the Kuznetsk Basin, Karaganda, the Kizel Basin in the Urals, the western slopes of the Bureya Mountain Range along the Bureya River near Komsomolsk in the Far East, the Pechora Basin in the European north of

[6] *Bolshaya Sovetskaya Entsiklopediya, Soyuz Sovetskikh Sotsialisticheskikh Respublik*, col. 245. Moscow: 1947. (Hereafter cited as *Entsiklopediya*.)

the USSR, and the Tkvarcheli and Tkvibuli deposits in Georgia. Karaganda coal tends to be high in ash content; Kizel coal has a high sulphur content, ranging up to almost 4 per cent, as well as a high ash content.[7]

A major problem facing the Soviet coal industry for the future is the fact that it is becoming necessary to go ever deeper into the earth in the older and most important coal areas, the Donets and Kuznetsk Basins. In the former, particularly, mining operations are being conducted at increasingly greater depths, where very serious safety problems, as well as higher costs, are encountered.[8] On the other hand, Soviet authorities are devoting ever greater efforts to obtain coal by relatively cheap methods, such as strip mining, underground conversion of coal into gas, and, most recently, hydroextraction of coal.

Iron Ore. Soviet iron-ore supplies of all kinds and grades are large, and the USSR claims to have had in 1938 a total of 53.5 per cent of all world iron ore reserves, including poor ores. This important raw material has been found at about 600 locations in the Soviet Union, of which about 100 have been exploited to some extent.[9] Total Soviet iron ore reserves as of January 1, 1938, were estimated to be about 10,900,000,000 metric tons, of which almost 4,500,000,000 tons consisted of reserves computed relatively accurately and available for immediate or not-too-distant use as required (the so-called A and B grades of reserves).[10] The chief ores used industrially are hematite, containing anhydrous ferric oxide (Fe_2O_3); magnetite, a magnetic ore containing ferrosoferric oxide (Fe_3O_4); and various so-called brown ores, containing hydrous ferric oxides, particularly limonite ($2Fe_2O_3 \cdot 3H_2O$). Soviet ores vary widely in richness of iron content and in kinds and amounts of impurities they contain. Both because of historical factors and because of the different technical characteristics of different ore bodies, the actual distribution of iron-ore mining differs rather sharply from the distribution of iron ore, as illustrated by the data below.

---

[7] M. Gardner Clark, *Some Economic Problems of the Soviet Iron and Steel Industry,* pp. 129–35. Cambridge: Harvard University Ph.D. thesis, March 1950 (hectographed).

[8] A. Bergson, ed., *Soviet Economic Growth,* p. 186. Evanston, Ill.: Row, Peterson and Co., 1953.

[9] *Entsiklopediya,* cols. 249–50.

[10] Clark, *op. cit.,* pp. 122 and 165.

TABLE 1. Geographic Distribution of Better Grade (A and B) Iron Ore Reserves in the USSR, January 1, 1938, and Distribution of Iron Ore Production in 1937.

Region	A and B Reserves		Production	
	MILL. METRIC TONS	PER CENT	THOUSAND METRIC TONS	PER CENT
NORTHWEST				
Komi ASSR	1	—		
Karelian ASSR	26	0.6	—	
Leningrad Province	107	2.4	—	
CENTER				
Tula Province	143	3.2	677.2	2.4
Gorky Province	2	—	—	
Kirov Province	7	—	26.2	0.1
Voronezh Province	103	2.3	710.2	2.5
Kursk Province	175	3.9	—	
SOUTH				
Crimean ASSR	1,638	36.5	771.2	2.8
Ukrainian SSR	668	14.9	16,414.1	59.0
Krasnodar Kray	15	0.3	—	
Kabardino-Balkar ASSR	22	0.5	—	
Stalingrad Province	148	3.3	—	
URALS				
Orenburg Province	98	2.2	85.6	0.3
Bashkir ASSR	71	1.6	176.4	0.6
Chelyabinsk Province	579	12.9	7,152.2	25.8
Sverdlovsk Province	395	8.8	1,247.5	4.5
WESTERN SIBERIA				
Novosibirsk Province	64	1.4	509.4	1.8
EASTERN SIBERIA				
Krasnoyarsk Kray	47	1.1	—	
Irkutsk Province	63	1.4	—	
Chita Province	2	—	—	
Far Eastern Kray	15	0.3	—	
Yakutsk ASSR	5	—	—	
Azerbaidzhan SSR	175	3.9	—	
Kazakh SSR	11	0.2	—	

Source: M. Gardner Clark, *Some Economic Problems of the Soviet Iron and Steel Industry*, p. 165.

Before World War II, the most important source of Soviet iron ore was the Krivoy Rog area in the Eastern Ukraine, which accounted for more than half of the USSR's output. Though badly devastated during World War II, this region has again become a major source of iron ore since then. Hematite, the chief ore here, has been exceptionally rich in iron content. The Ural Mountains have numerous scattered iron ore deposits, of which the most important and most intensively worked to date are those in the Magnetic Mountain at Magnitogorsk. In 1940 [11] over 22 per cent of all Soviet iron ore was produced here, and the area has undoubtedly grown in importance since that time. Ores are mined here by the relatively cheap open-pit method, and both basic and acid ores are found with iron content that has averaged in the past between 50 and 60 per cent. As we shall see later, the rich Magnitogorsk ores were the initial bases for the rapid development of the Soviet iron and steel industry in the Urals and Western Siberia during the early 1930's. Other important deposits in the general Urals area are at Bakal in Chelyabinsk Province, in the Komarovo district of Bashkiria, and in the Tagil-Kushvinsk region in Sverdlovsk Province in the Central Urals. There are also numerous other less important deposits. On the Kerch Peninsula in the Crimea, large quantities of iron ore are found, mainly composed of brown ores that contain usually between 30 and 40 per cent iron content, but with numerous harmful impurities that make the exploitation of these ores in iron and steel production relatively difficult and expensive. Other iron ore deposits significant for the current Soviet economy are in the Gornaya Shoriya area of Western Siberia, near the Kuznetsk coal basin; at Dashkesan in the southern Trans-Caucasus, not far from Lake Sevan; in the Kola Peninsula northwest of Leningrad; in the neighborhood of Tula and Lipetsk near Moscow; and at Nikolayevsk near the mouth of the Amur river in the Far East.[12] The Kursk area south of Moscow is the location of the so-called Kursk Magnetic Anomaly containing tremendous amounts of quartzite, which are apparently scheduled for intensive future exploitation.

Although Soviet iron ore reserves are abundant and widely distributed, their utilization has presented serious problems for more than a decade because of the rapid depletion of the richest ores. This has forced the USSR to resort to various costly expedients, among them the use of poorer-grade ores; preliminary processing of ores so as to concentrate iron content, agglomerate fine ores, and eliminate harmful impurities; and the reworking of large quantities of waste in dumps of low-grade ore previously not considered worth using. The latter practice has been particularly resorted to at

[11] *Entsiklopediya*, col. 250.
[12] Clark, *op. cit.*, pp. 144–64.

Magnitogorsk, where the higher-quality ores have been wastefully mined since 1747. In the 1920's at Krivoy Rog the USSR was able to restrict its consumption almost exclusively to high-grade ores averaging over 60 per cent iron content. More recently this area has been producing ore with as little as 48 per cent iron content. The postwar expansion in the use of Kerch ores, despite their poor chemical and physical properties, seems also dictated in large part by the depletion of better-grade reserves, although other factors also play a part.[13]

Petroleum. Soviet oil reserves, too, are believed to be among the largest in the world. Because of the complexity of petroleum geology, numerical estimates of reserves are most uncertain, but one such figure calculated in the later 1930's approached 5 billion metric tons. These reserves, which are only a small fraction of all Soviet fuel resources, are, however, highly localized in particular areas of the Soviet Union. As far as is known today, large regions of the USSR have no petroleum whatsoever, unlike the situation with respect to coal and iron ore.

Most oil production during the Soviet era has come from the Apsheron Peninsula on the southwest shore of the Caspian Sea adjoining the city of Baku. About 70 per cent of the 31 million metric tons of oil produced in the USSR during 1940 are believed to have been obtained in this region.[14] During World War II, however, production dropped considerably in this area, since the Baku region was threatened by German forces and new development was sharply curtailed. Renewed development of the area began after the war, and it continues to be the most important single supply region. Wasteful exploitation of Baku oil resources and inadequate geological prospecting during the 1930's created serious difficulties here in World War II and afterward. In recent years much energy has been devoted to sinking oil wells off shore under the Caspian Sea in the effort to raise output.

North of the Caspian Sea is the so-called "Second Baku," an oil-production area second in importance only to the Apsheron Peninsula, and one whose output grew considerably during World War

---

[13] *Ibid.* Cf. also Bergson, *op. cit.*, pp. 179–83, and D. B. Shimkin, *Minerals — A Key to Soviet Power*, pp. 44–46. Cambridge: Harvard University Press, 1953.

[14] A. D. Perejda, "Russia in the Oil Age," *American Review on the Soviet Union*, August 1946, p. 6.

II. Petroleum is obtained here over a relatively large area extending roughly along a diagonal from Saratov in the southwest to Molotov in the northeast. Production in this area is believed to have reached almost three million metric tons in 1945, almost 15 per cent of total Soviet output.

The Emba Basin, stretching northeast of the Caspian Sea in Western Kazakhstan is also increasingly important. Its reserves are estimated as second only to those of the Baku region. Other significant oil-producing areas are Maikop and Grozny in the Caucasus northwest of Baku, Sakhalin Island in the Far East, the Pechora Basin in the northern part of European Russia, the district southeast of Krasnovodsk in Turkmenistan, the Fergana Valley and the basin of the upper Amu Darya in southern Central Asia. There is petroleum in the Drogobych-Borislav area of the Western Ukraine, and oil was discovered during World War II near Makhach-Kala in the Dagestan area of the North Caucasus near the Caspian Sea.

Manganese. The Soviet Union is the leading source in the world for this vital steel-making element. More than 90 per cent of all Soviet industrial reserves are at Chiatura in the Georgian Republic and at Nikopol in the Ukraine. The loss of the Nikopol mines to German forces during World War II led to expansion of manganese output in Sverdlovsk Province in the Urals, though these ores are poorer. About 90 per cent of all Soviet manganese production in 1945 came from these three sources — more than half the total from Chiatura.[15] Smaller amounts are mined in Kazakhstan and in the Krasnoyarsk Territory in Eastern Siberia. Soviet manganese ores have relatively rich metal content, sometimes exceeding 50 per cent. In the past they have been an important factor in supplying the manganese needs of other nations, including the United States. The abundance of manganese in the USSR permits its use in place of other ferro-alloys, such as molybdenum, which either are not available domestically or are relatively expensive.[16]

Copper. About half of all Soviet copper reserves are in Kazakhstan, the most important sources being at Dzhezkazgan and Kounrad, west and north of Lake Balkhash respectively. Significant quantities of copper are also found in the Urals, particularly in

---

[15] *Entsiklopediya*, col. 254.
[16] Clark, *op. cit.*, p. 120. A most detailed account is given in Shimkin, *op. cit.*, pp. 60–68.

Sverdlovsk Province and the Bashkir Republic, as well as in the Monchegorsk area of Murmansk Province northwest of Leningrad and in the Norilsk region of Krasnoyarsk Territory in Eastern Siberia. In 1942 about 46 per cent of all Soviet copper output was in the Urals, primarily in Sverdlovsk Province, and about 40 per cent came from Kazakhstan.[17]

Lead and Zinc. Lead and zinc often occur together and in combination with other metals in complex polymetallic ores. About half of all Soviet reserves of these metals are in Kazakhstan, with the Altay region being particularly important. Other important reserves exist in the Asiatic USSR, including the Maritime Territory in the Far East, the Altay Territory, Chita Province, and Kemerovo Province in the Kuznetsk Basin. The Urals have important zinc reserves, particularly in Sverdlovsk Province.

Bauxite. This is the major raw material from which aluminum is extracted. Before the war about half of all Soviet bauxite came from Tikhvin, east of Leningrad. During World War II deposits in Sverdlovsk Province were intensively exploited. At the beginning of 1945 about 75 bauxite sources were known in the USSR, including reserves in the northern and central Urals, in the Bashkir, Uzbek, and Kazakh Republics, in Tula, Novosibirsk, and Kemerovo Provinces, and the Altay and Krasnoyarsk Territories. In 1945 over 96 per cent of all Soviet bauxite came from deposits in the eastern regions of the country, particularly from Sverdlovsk Province. These areas have continued to be exploited, although the Tikhvin area has regained much of its former importance.

Nickel. This important steel-making alloy is found in both sulfide and silicate ores in the USSR at a number of different points. The largest volume of Soviet nickel reserves is in the Norilsk region of Krasnoyarsk Territory in Eastern Siberia, followed by deposits at Monchegorsk in Kola Peninsula, and in the sourthern and central Urals. There are also important deposits in the Pechenga area of the Kola Peninsula, as well as in complex iron-chrome-nickel ores in the Kabardin ASSR in the North Caucasus. The great wealth of Soviet nickel resources and the progress made in their exploitation have made the USSR one of the very largest nickel producers in the world.

Uranium. This mineral, the great importance of which has be-

[17] *Entsiklopediya,* cols. 255–58.

come evident only in the last few years, is found in a number of places in the Soviet Union, including Tyuya Muyun in Central Asia's Fergana Valley and several other points in the same region, all within 250 miles of Tashkent.[18] Uranium may also be available in the Tannu Tuva area, north of Mongolia, incorporated into the USSR in 1944. The inadequacy of Soviet domestic resources is suggested by the intensive efforts made since World War II to obtain uranium from Eastern Germany and Czechoslovakia.

Gold. The Soviet Union is one of the world's largest producers of gold, although statistics on this output have not been published for many years. Two of the most important gold-mining regions in the USSR are in the Aldan Plateau in Eastern Siberia, southeast of the city of Yakutsk, and in the Kolyma area northeast of Yakutsk. Significant gold deposits are also found at other points in Asiatic Russia, including the Maritime Territory in the Far East, Kazakhstan, Buryat-Mongolia, and Irkutsk and Chita Provinces.

Other Metals. Soviet tin resources have not been plentiful in the past, requiring heavy reliance upon imports. Important new deposits have been discovered since 1933 and are being or will be exploited. The main tin deposits are found in Chita Province, on the upper reaches of the Kolyma River in Siberia, in the Maritime Territory of the Far East, Yakutsk, and in the Kirgiz and Kazakh Republics. Tin is found in polymetallic ores located on the northeast coast of Lake Ladoga and in the North-Osetian ASSR in the Caucasus. Reports of Soviet imports of tungsten and molybdenum suggest that domestic production is inadequate. Ores of these important ferro-alloying elements occur in a number of places in the USSR, including the North Caucasus, Kazakhstan, Chita Province, and the Buryat-Mongolian ASSR, among others. The USSR produces a significant amount of silver annually, but precise data have not been available for many years. Among the areas with major silver deposits, usually in polymetallic ores, are Kazakhstan, the Urals, the North Caucasus, and the Maritime Territory. The

---

[18] Shimkin, *op. cit.,* pp. 147–50, summarizes the scanty available information on Soviet and satellite uranium, radium, and thorium resources. An earlier work by the same writer summarizing the domestic Soviet uranium position is "Uranium Deposits in the USSR," *Science,* January 21, 1949, pp. 58–60. Some helpful information on Soviet uranium mining in Eastern Germany is given in R. Slusser, ed., *Soviet Economic Policy in Postwar Germany, passim.* New York: Research Program on the USSR, 1953.

USSR claims to hold first place among nations with respect to platinum reserves and produces relatively large quantities of this metal annually, in part from the Urals area near Nizhny Tagil. It is one of the world's major producers of chromium, at times exporting significant quantities abroad. Chromium ores are concentrated almost exclusively in the Urals and in Aktyubinsk Province in Kazakhstan. Mercury, antimony, bismuth, cobalt, arsenic, and various rare metals are mined in many different locations scattered throughout the USSR.

Nonmetallic Minerals and Fuels. The USSR has varied and rich resources of important industrial nonmetallic minerals, including among others asbestos, corundum (for abrasives), potassium salts, apatite (for fertilizers), phosphorites, borates, sodium chloride (common salt), and kaolin. Among the outstanding sources are the immense apatite works in the Kola Peninsula, beyond the Arctic Circle; the Solikamsk potassium region, north of the city of Molotov on the western slope of the Urals; and the asbestos-producing city of Asbest, in Sverdlovsk Province. Large deposits of peat are found in many parts of the Northern European USSR. Although of low caloric value, this fuel is used for many power stations, especially in the industrial region around Moscow. Oil shales are found in significant quantities in the Volga region and in Northeast Estonia. A shale-gas pipe line has been laid from the latter region to Leningrad, to provide that city with gas fuel. The deposits of natural gas in the Carpathian foothills and in the Saratov region are worth mentioning. Gas pipe lines have been laid from these deposits to Kiev and Moscow, respectively, so as to provide gas supplies for industry and household uses in those cities.

Population and Its Distribution

The human beings who constitute any society are its primary resource. In the USSR in early 1954 it is estimated that there were over 210,000,000 persons. This vast mass of human beings was composed of persons from many different cultural groups, speaking many different languages, and spread in most unequal densities over the vast expanse of Soviet territory. In the 1926 census members of more than 150 different ethnic groups are indicated as being citizens of the USSR, ranging from the major Slavic, Turkic, and Finnic groups to obscure and almost unknown peoples of a few thousand members each.[19] The distribution of the major national groups in the USSR in 1940 is indicated in Table 2.

TABLE 2. Estimated Size of Major Groups in the Soviet Population in 1940.

Group	Millions	Group	Millions
Great Russians	100.0	Georgians	2.3
Ukrainians	36.0	Estonians	2.3
White Russians	8.5	Lithuanians	2.2
Jews	5.0	Armenians	2.2
Uzbeks	5.0	Latvians	1.6
Tatars	4.5	Mordovians	1.5
Kazakhs	3.2	Chuvashi	1.4
Moldavians	2.5	Tadzhiks	1.3
Azerbaidzhans	2.4		

Source: Based primarily upon data in *Entsiklopediya*, col. 60.

This distribution was probably changed significantly, however, by the great mortality suffered during World War II by some peoples, particularly the Great Russians, Ukrainians, and Jews.

Even in the small number of groups shown in Table 2, there are major differences of religious background, economic history, language, and culture. To accomplish its goals, the Soviet regime has had to change radically the traditional modes of life of many of these and other ethnic groups as well, and to weld them together by requiring study of the Great Russian language by all peoples in the USSR.

A most important characteristic of the population change over most of the USSR's history has been the rapid natural increase achieved. The census of 1939 listed 170,467,000 persons within the boundaries existing at the beginning of that year, an increase of almost 23,500,000 persons over the 147,028,000 listed by the 1926 census. This not inconsiderable natural increase took place despite the famine of the early 1930's. It represents not only the high birth rates characteristic of rural areas in the USSR as well as elsewhere, but also the sharp excess of births over deaths in many Soviet cities. In 1938, for example, Moscow had 195 births for every 100 deaths, and Minsk — probably an extreme, unrepresentative example — had 252 births for every 100 deaths.[20]

[19] Frank Lorimer, *The Population of the Soviet Union: History and Prospects*, pp. 55–61. Geneva: League of Nations, 1946.
[20] *Entsiklopediya*, cols. 49–50.

By territorial acquisitions between 1939 and 1945, the USSR took over an area of 670,000 square kilometers, inhabited before World War II by 24,300,000 persons. This region included the Baltic States, Eastern Poland, the Carpatho-Ukraine of Czechoslovakia, Bessarabia, and Southern Sakhalin, among others.[21] If the population of the USSR within the previous boundaries had remained stable at the figure recorded by the 1939 census, these acquisitions would have raised the Soviet population to almost 195,000,000 persons. Actually, of course, between 1941 and 1945 the Soviet Union incurred tremendous casualties, both military and civilian, as the result of the struggle with Germany and Japan. Yet so great was the recuperative power of its people that by early 1954 the government set up election districts in such numbers as to indicate a total population of more than 210,000,000 inhabitants.[22]

One of the major factors explaining the reproductive vigor of the Soviet population considered as a whole is its relatively youthful composition. This factor also has important economic and military significance. In early 1939, for example, about 61,500,000 persons in the USSR, 36 per cent of the total, were under 15 years of age. About 81,000,000 persons, almost half the total, were in the 15 to 44 age group. About 29,000,000 persons or about 17 per cent of the total population, were 45 years or more old.

TABLE 3. Estimated Distribution of USSR Population, by Age and Sex, January 17, 1939.

Age	Male	Female	Total
0–9	19,764,850	19,543,013	39,307,863
10–19	18,564,267	18,840,758	37,405,025
20–29	15,100,740	15,719,003	30,819,743
30–39	11,870,386	13,612,016	25,482,402
40–49	6,733,299	8,592,423	15,325,722
50–59	4,924,984	6,006,518	10,931,502
60–69	3,085,551	4,053,350	7,138,901
70–79	1,372,403	2,011,427	3,383,830
80+	248,501	423,697	672,198

Source: Adapted from Frank Lorimer, *The Population of the Soviet Union: History and Prospects*, p. 143.

[21] Balzak, *op. cit.*, p. 544.

[22] *Pravda*, January 13, 1954. According to the Soviet Constitution, each district for the Council of the Union is to include 300,000 persons. The population estimate is obtained therefore by multiplying the number of districts by 300,000.

In the year 1950, one careful estimate indicates, the Soviet Union may have had about 68,000,000 persons under 16 years of age, about 120,000,000 between the ages of 16 and 59, and perhaps around 11,000,000 60 years of age and older. If this estimate is approximately correct, then the Soviet Union had in 1950 about 25,000,000 more persons in the productive age groups between 16 and 59 than it had in 1939 when both the Soviet population and the Soviet area were much smaller.[23]

In late 1951, Lavrenti P. Beria — then still a powerful Soviet figure — asserted that the net annual growth of the country's population exceeded 3,000,000 persons. Beria added that the Soviet death rate was half that of 1940.[24]

Analysis of Beria's statements in conjunction with Soviet data published before World War II suggests that in 1951 the Soviet death rate may have been about 13 per thousand, far lower than previously but still the highest in Europe. At the same time, however, his statements seem to imply also a sharp decline in the Soviet birth rate, probably to less than 30 per thousand as against 38.3 per thousand in 1938. That the Soviet birth rate should have dropped in the face of the great official encouragement, through subsidies for large families and the like, suggests that the Soviet Union, as it industrializes and becomes more urban, is following the population trends of other Western countries which industrialized earlier. Deputy Premier A. I. Mikoyan has claimed that in 1953 the Soviet death rate was only 8.9 per thousand, implying that the trends discussed above continued to operate during 1952 and 1953.[25]

The Soviet Union's population is distributed most unequally over its large land mass. The 1939 census, for example, found that 48 per cent of the USSR's population lived on 6 per cent of its territory. Conversely, only 6 per cent of its population lived on two thirds of its territory. The most densely populated area then was found to be roughly the southern half of the European USSR, from the upper reaches of the Volga to the shores of the Black Sea, an area throughout which the average density was no lower than 25 persons per

[23] These data are adapted from Warren W. Eason's estimates in Bergson, ed., *op. cit.*, p. 102.

[24] *Pravda*, November 7, 1951.

[25] Cf. E. M. Kulischer, "Russian Manpower," *Foreign Affairs*, October 1952, pp. 67–69. *Pravda*, April 27, 1954.

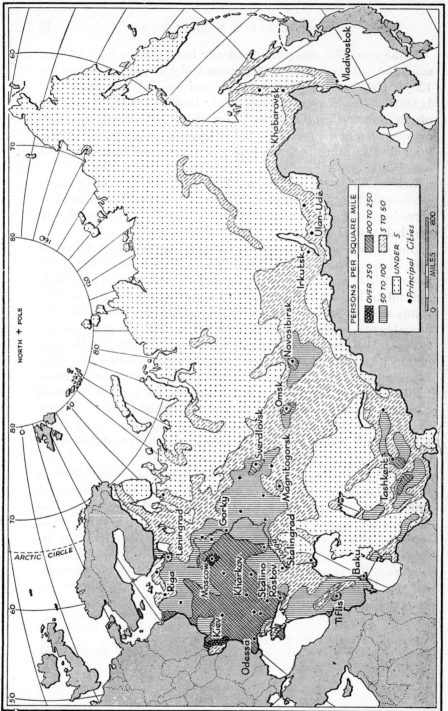

IV. POPULATION DENSITY IN THE USSR AND MAJOR CITIES

PERSONS PER SQUARE MILE

OVER 250   100 TO 250
50 TO 100   5 TO 50
UNDER 5
• Principal Cities

0   400   800
MILES

NORTH + POLE

ARCTIC CIRCLE

Vladivostok
Khabarovsk
Ulan-Ude
Irkutsk
Novosibirsk
Omsk
Sverdlovsk
Magnitogorsk
Tashkent
Leningrad
Riga
Moscow
Gorky
Kharkov
Kiev
Stalino
Rostov
Volga
Stalingrad
Baku
Tiflis
Odessa

square kilometer. In the most heavily populated heart of this area, stretching from the Donets Basin to the neighborhoods of Moscow and Ivanovo, population density varied from 50 to 100 persons per square kilometer, sometimes even exceeding the latter figure. On the fringes of the basic southern European area, population density usually declined to between 10 and 25 persons per square kilometer. Beyond these fringes, substantially lower densities were encountered. Thus in Archangel and Murmansk Provinces in the north, the 1939 census found densities of 1.8 and 2.1 persons per square kilometer, respectively, much of this population being concentrated in cities. In 1941, just before the Nazi attack on the USSR, there was only 9 per cent of the Soviet population in the Asiatic portion of the Russian Soviet Federated Socialist Republic beyond the Urals, a territory constituting 56 per cent of all Soviet land area. Here population was concentrated primarily in a few major areas, such as the Kuznetsk basin and along the Trans-Siberian Railroad. Northern Asiatic Russia has a very sparse population, as indicated by the fact that density in the Yakut Republic was only .13 persons per square kilometer. In Kazakhstan and Central Asia there is a very uneven distribution of population. Large areas of desert and semidesert territory in this region have very few inhabitants. The bulk of the population is concentrated about oases, major industrial installations, and along the northern, eastern, and southern boundaries of Kazakhstan. In the Caucasian republics, population density is high in the river valleys and industrial cities but very thinly distributed in the large mountainous areas. [26]

During World War II, major population movements took place as large numbers fled eastward before the Nazi invaders and much industry was relocated from western to eastern sites. After the war, it seems likely, some offsetting migrations took place as many people returned to their former homes. It is probable that the eastern portions of the USSR have retained much of their wartime population gains vis-a-vis the west. On the other hand, it also seems likely that the basic elements of the prewar population pattern still remain much the same; that is, people are still distributed most unequally throughout different parts of the Soviet Union, and the bulk of the population is still concentrated in the European portions of the

---

[26] *Entsiklopediya*, cols. 56–59.

USSR, particularly in the area between the Black Sea and the upper reaches of the Volga. Events since the invasion of June 1941 have not destroyed the basic climatic, soil, and economic factors that lay behind this basic pattern of population location.

That the general trends described are correct was indicated by the distribution of population implied in the election district data published in early 1954. These data, in which each election district presumably corresponds roughly to the legal requirement of 300,000 people per district, indicate that the Soviet population in European Russia and the Urals was 167,400,000 at that time, while there were 42,600,000 people east of the Urals. These data also indicated that the most rapid increase of population had taken place in Eastern Siberia. In Irkutsk Province alone, population had apparently shot up from 1,200,000 people in 1950 to 1,800,000 four years later, an increase of 50 per cent.[27]

With the increasing industrialization that has featured Soviet economic development, there has been a steady trend toward urbanization of the population. This movement of people from rural areas to the cities was apparent in the last decades of the Czarist regime, also a period of relatively rapid growth of industrial production and capacity. Though reversed during the chaotic civil war years following the 1917 Bolshevik revolution, the former trend toward growth of urban communities resumed in the early 1920's and has persisted since. As a result, both the absolute size and the percentage importance of the urban population in the total figure has risen sharply. This is illustrated by the data below, which apply to the boundaries of the USSR as of January 1, 1939. They show the pace of the movement that has been converting this once overwhelmingly rural nation into an urbanized country, though even in 1939 over two thirds of the population was still rural.[28]

	Millions of Urban Population	Per Cent of Total Population
Census of February 9, 1897........	15.8	14.8
Estimate for January 1, 1914.......	24.7	17.7
Census of December 17, 1926......	26.3	17.9
Census of January 17, 1939........	55.9	32.8

[27] Cf. *Pravda*, January 13, 1954.
[28] *Entsiklopediya*, col. 62.

In 1939 the proportion of the Soviet population living in urban areas, roughly one third, was somewhat less than the corresponding proportion for the United States in 1890. The 1926 percentage for the USSR was less than the percentage of persons living in communities of 2,500 or more in the United States in 1860.[29] During and since World War II, urban population has continued to increase still further, except perhaps in the Western USSR during the period of German occupation. As Soviet industry, commerce, and transportation activity increase in the future, the trend toward urbanization seems likely to continue.

In August 1953, Premier Georgi M. Malenkov revealed that the urban population of the Soviet Union at that time was about 80,000,000 persons, as compared with 61,000,000 in 1940.[30] Thus by 1953 almost 40 per cent of the Soviet population lived in towns and cities as against 17.9 per cent in 1926 and 32.8 per cent in 1939. There is perhaps no more vivid index of the economic revolution that has taken place in the Soviet Union in the past three decades than the growth of urban population from about 26,000,000 in 1926 to 80,000,000 in 1953. Implicit in this growth too, of course, is a major sociological revolution with consequences in every area of Soviet life.

Migration from rural to urban areas accounted for 62.5 per cent of the increase in city and town population in the USSR from 1926 to 1939. The rest was accounted for by natural increase, that is, the excess of births over deaths, and by the reclassification of rural villages into urban communities as the result of their growth or changed economic functioning.[31] The result was that in 1939 there were 174 cities with populations in excess of 50,000, as against only 90 such communities in 1926. There were 28 cities in 1939 with over 250,000 persons, as against only 9 in 1926.[32]

The fifteen largest cities of the USSR in 1939 are listed in Table 4, together with their populations as determined by the census in 1926 and 1939 and as estimated for 1954 on the basis of election district data.

---

[29] Lorimer, *op. cit.*, p. 147.
[30] *Pravda*, August 9, 1953.
[31] *Entsiklopediya*, col. 63.
[32] *Ibid.*, col. 64.

TABLE 4. Population of 15 Large Soviet Cities in 1926, 1939, and 1954.

City	1926	1939	1954
	(thousands of persons)		
Moscow	2,029	4,137	5,400
Leningrad	1,690	3,191	3,300
Kiev	514	846	900
Kharkov	417	833	900
Baku	453	809	over 600
Gorky	222	644	900
Odessa	421	604	under 600
Tashkent	324	585	under 600
Tiflis	294	519	under 600
Rostov	308	510	under 600
Dnepropetrovsk	237	501	600
Stalino	174	462	over 300
Stalingrad	151	445	about 300
Sverdlovsk	140	426	600
Novosibirsk	120	406	600

Sources: Lorimer, *The Population of the Soviet Union: History and Prospects*, p. 250, and calculations based on election district data in *Pravda*, January 13, 1954.

The data in the table above were based on the 15 largest Soviet cities as of 1939. In 1954 the 15 largest cities, as inferred from election district data, were somewhat different. Moscow and Leningrad were the only cities with populations over 1,000,000 persons each. Kiev, Kharkov, and Gorky had about 900,000 people each. The group of cities with populations between 600,000 and 900,000 people each included Baku, Dnepropetrovsk, Sverdlovsk, Novosibirsk, Kuibyshev, Kazan, Chelyabinsk, Omsk, Saratov, and Riga.

The great rise in the population of cities in the Urals and east of the Urals during and since World War II is indicated, not only by the increases shown in Table 4 above for Sverdlovsk and Novosi-

TABLE 5. Growth of Cities in Soviet Asia, 1939–44.

City	1939	1944	Increase	Per Cent Growth
Komsomolsk	71,000	127,000	56,000	79
Khabarovsk	199,000	250,000	51,000	79
Chita	103,000	170,000	67,000	65
Ulan-Ude	129,000	150,000	21,000	16
Irkutsk	243,000	300,000	57,000	23
Krasnoyarsk	190,000	300,000	110,000	59
Novosibirsk	406,000	600,000	194,000	48

Source: Henry A. Wallace, *Soviet Asia Mission*, p. 64.

birsk, but also by data for the city of Omsk. In 1939 Omsk had only about 281,000 inhabitants, but by 1950 election district data indicated it had about 600,000 persons, roughly double the 1939 total. The same trend is indicated by data given Henry Wallace during his 1944 visit to Soviet Asia.

Barring atomic warfare or similar catastrophe in the future, the continued rapid absolute numerical growth of the Soviet people seems certain, along with further gains in both the absolute number living in cities and towns and in the percentage importance of urbanites in the total Soviet population.

CHAPTER II

THE HISTORICAL BACKGROUND

FROM THE HISTORICAL point of view the present Soviet regime of the USSR is still very young in comparison with the state that preceded it. For hundreds of years before Lenin seized power in this area, the Russian Czars held sway. Under their dominion the tiny Moscow principality of the Middle Ages expanded into the massive geographical area inhabited by many diverse peoples that the Bolsheviks took over. The political, economic, and social institutions that evolved and changed during the centuries the Czars ruled created the setting in which Soviet power became possible, as well as the background for all subsequent development. Lenin and Stalin built on the foundation that existed before them. Any understanding of Soviet institutions is impossible without insight into the nature of the society and the economy from which they emerged.

The economic growth of Czarist Russia will be the focus of attention here, a growth that influenced and was influenced by political, social, military, and other noneconomic developments. Three factors may be singled out as particularly important in this evolution. These are, first, the frequent wars in which the Russian state was engaged; second, the tremendous expansion of the Russian territory and the Russian population; third, the relative isolation of this nation from the West, which led to its lagging behind Western Europe technologically, politically, and socially. These factors were themselves the results of many complex forces working over the centuries, but we single them out because they operated with great persistence over all or most of the time from before the beginning of the Romanov dynasty (in 1613) to its downfall in World War I.

36

War and the threat of war were frequent throughout the history of Czarist Russia, playing an important role in shaping its institutions and economy. Feudalism and its accompanying serfdom were in large part the products of early wars, which required an organization of society that would provide military manpower, permit satisfactory rewards for those who served as military commanders, and facilitate the transfer to the state of taxes required to pay the cost of these conflicts. Later, in the nineteenth century, the debacle of the Crimean War provided convincing proof that this form of societal organization had outlived its usefulness, thus helping to lay the groundwork for the historic reforms of the early 1860's. Military requirements for guns, ammunition, and ships provided much of the impetus for industrialization, particularly the development of metallurgy, mining, and related branches of production. Czarist Russia's military defeats in World War I and the accompanying disruption of its domestic economy set off the immediate chain of events that ended the Romanov dynasty.

The territorial growth of the Russian state from the fifteenth to the nineteenth centuries was the product both of successful wars against neighboring powers — the Tartars, Poles, Lithuanians, Swedes, Turks, and others — and of relatively peaceful colonization eastward to the Pacific that met varied opposition from the more primitive Asiatic peoples of Siberia. Most of this expansion took place in the sixteenth, seventeenth, and eighteenth centuries, but significant additions were also made in the nineteenth century, particularly in Poland, the Caucasus, Central Asia, and the Amur River basin of the Far East. Czarist dominion was thus extended over a host of different peoples with varied cultural backgrounds and at sharply contrasting stages of economic development. These conquests added rich new resources to the Russian Empire, but many of them remained unexploited until the Soviet period, in part because of the harshness of climate in Siberia and the lack of good transportation facilities between the European and Asiatic portions of the Czar's realm up to almost the end of the nineteenth century. These territorial gains, however, extended Russian power to the Pacific, to the Baltic, Caspian, and Black Sea coasts, and well into Eastern Europe, providing better access to markets in Europe, Asia, and the Near East.

In the eighteenth and nineteenth centuries the population ruled by the Russian Czar increased almost ten-fold. In 1725 about 13,000,000 people are believed to have been within Peter the Great's realm.[1] Less than two centuries later the census of 1897 listed over 125,600,000 people in the Russian Empire.[2] In part, of course, this population increase was the result of territorial expansion that had brought many new peoples under the Czar's rule. But the same period also saw a very rapid growth of the basic Slavic peoples (including Ukrainians and White Russians as well as Great Russians). Their numbers rose from about 17,900,000 in 1724, some of them outside Peter's realm, to about 94,300,000 in 1897, more than a five-fold increase. Along with this increase there occurred a major redistribution of this Slavic population, as here defined. In 1724 about 63 per cent lived in Northern and Central European Russia, but in 1897 only 32.5 per cent lived there. The trend of migration during these two centuries was to Southern and Southeastern European Russia as conquest of the Black Sea coast, the shores of the Caspian, the lower Volga basin, and the North Caucasus opened rich new territories for settlers. Only 35 per cent of the Russian population had lived in these southern regions in 1724; over 60 per cent lived there in 1897. There occurred also a significant though numerically less important movement to Asiatic Russia, which had only 400,000 Russians, 2 per cent of the total, in 1724, but almost 7,000,000 Russians, over 7 per cent of the total, in 1897.[3]

The reasons for Czarist Russia's relative technological and cultural isolation from the West are many and varied — the frequent wars after a long period of Mongol domination and the enmity of the Poles and other nations immediately to the west of Russia are among the major reasons usually given. Equally many and varied were the consequences. Absolute monarchy and feudal serfdom persisted in Russia long after they had vanished in England, France, and even Germany. Though many individual Russians contributed brilliantly to the progress of science — including such giants as the chemist Mendeleyev and the mathematician Lobachevsky — Russia did not enter into the main stream of the industrial and agricultural revolution of the seventeenth to nineteenth centuries until com-

---

[1] Cited from Miliukov in Witt Bowden, Michael Karpovich, and Abbott Payson Usher, *An Economic History of Europe since 1750*, p. 288. New York: American Book Company, 1937.

[2] Frank Lorimer, *op. cit.*, p. 10.

[3] *Ibid.*, and Bowden, *et al.*, *op. cit.*, pp. 288–90.

paratively late. When she did participate, it was largely under the influence of foreigners, who brought their technology — and in the late nineteenth century their capital — to help end the earlier isolation. Yet, curiously, the nobility of Russia prided itself upon being familiar with Western culture, particularly that of France; and Catherine the Great's court included at times many of the outstanding thinkers of her age. But the advanced ideas of the West did not percolate down to the masses until comparatively late, and those who sought to spread them were often exiled and their writings suppressed. The breaking down of this isolation in the late nineteenth and early twentieth centuries played a large part in setting the stage for the revolutionary overturns that followed.[4]

Against this brief background we shall attempt to trace the development of agriculture, industry, trade, and transport in greater detail, though here again it must be borne in mind that for most of the period under consideration we are dealing with a large area with relatively poor transportation and communication conditions. At no time were patterns uniform over the whole territory and for all its inhabitants, so that at most we can hope to sketch only the most typical and prevalent institutions and relationships, each subject to many exceptions under the influence of varied local conditions.

The Development of Agriculture

Agriculture was the chief occupation of the vast majority of people in Russia. It was agriculture based primarily upon the cultivation of grains — rye, wheat, barley, and oats, chiefly — and conducted with little change in technique and organization from at least the fourteenth and fifteenth centuries to the freeing of the serfs during our own Civil War, and even afterward. The techniques and implements employed were relatively primitive; livestock were comparatively few;[5] and the yields per acre was almost uniformly low. Famine was an all too common occurrence.

---

[4] The penetration of Western ideas into Russia and their effect and modification there are well summarized in Sir John Maynard, *Russia in Flux*, pp. 50–139. New York: Macmillan, 1948.

[5] P. I. Lyashchenko, *Istoriya Narodnogo Khozyaistva SSSR*, Vol. 1, p. 242. Moscow: 1947. An English translation of an earlier edition of this work has been published as *History of the National Economy of Russia to the 1917 Revolution*. New York: Macmillan, 1949. All references here are to the Russian edition cited.

Most frequently the system of cultivation employed was that known as the three-field system, the common primitive mode of cultivation under feudalism throughout Europe. Peasants lived together in small villages, forming communities known at various times as the *obshchina* or *mir*. In the classical three-field system, the land available is divided into three roughly equal parts. The first year, one field is planted in winter rye and winter wheat, another in spring crops, and the third is left fallow in order to permit it to accumulate moisture and regain fertility. Crops are shifted annually from field to field, and roughly one third of the land is left idle each year in a regular rotation.[6] Even more primitive agricultural organization in many areas was based upon a two-field system, in which each plot of ground was used for several years to grow small grains and then was left fallow for several years. Under this system, of course, an even larger fraction of the available arable land was left idle each year.[7]

Usually, the land was further subdivided into many small strips. Each peasant family's work area consisted of a number of strips scattered at random over all the fields. The number of strips worked by each family varied, depending usually upon the size of the family. For long periods in many areas there were periodic redistributions of the strips so as to adjust the amount of land each family had to its size or to the number of workers it had available. This system of scattered strips was inefficient, since much time was lost as workers went from one strip to another. The motivation for this distribution of the land was the desire to assure each family of having, on the average, the same quality of land as its neighbors. If each family's land had been concentrated into one area, the quality would have varied from family to family, with resultant bitterness and discontent.[8] Two foreign observers, Wallace and Haxthausen, commented on the great accuracy of the land divi-

---

[6] N. S. B. Gras, *A History of Agriculture in Europe and America*, pp. 28–29. New York: Crofts, 1940.

[7] Lyashchenko, *op. cit.*, pp. 240–41, 439. V. P. Timoshenko, *Agricultural Russia and the Wheat Problem*, pp. 45–46. Stanford University: Food Research Institute, 1932.

[8] A good description of how the land was divided is given in D. M. Wallace, *Russia*, pp. 136–37. New York: Holt, 1877. The comments of an earlier observer, Haxthausen, are reprinted in W. B. Walsh, *Readings . . . in Russian History*, pp. 274–75. Syracuse: Syracuse University Press, 1948.

sion achieved by illiterate peasants, and the latter noted that in some areas unequal amounts of land were given to different families, in compensation for the unequal qualities of different plots.

In this system of agriculture and community life, the *mir* played a most important role. It acted as an organizing agency of the peasantry, coordinating their farming activities by setting the dates at which sowing, harvesting, and other major crop operations were to be undertaken, and seeing to it that all followed the common crop pattern. Wallace noted that "the Communal land thus resembles to some extent a big farm. . . . A family may sow what it likes in the land allotted to it, but all families must at least conform to the accepted system of rotation. In like manner, a family cannot begin the autumn plowing before the appointed time, because it would thereby interfere with the rights of the other families, who use the fallow field as pasturage." [9]

As early as the fifteenth and sixteenth centuries the members of the peasant commune or *mir* were bound together by a common obligation to the state for taxes. Officers elected by the commune apportioned the total tax burden among its members, allotted land to new settlers, and represented the locality before courts and other government bodies. If some members of the community left it, the tax burden they escaped had to be met by the rest. [10] Throughout the history of Czarism the communal regulation of farming was one of the major institutions of the country.

In the fifteenth and sixteenth centuries, the land was tilled both by free peasants and by various categories of bondsmen. The distinguishing characteristic of the free peasant was his right to till the land whenever he made what he considered a satisfactory agreement with its owner, and to leave when he became dissatisfied. The earliest restrictions on this freedom aimed at preventing him from leaving his land in the middle of the crop year, forcing him to stay until the crop had been gathered. In some areas in the fifteenth century he could leave only on the fourteenth of November. Laws passed in 1497 and 1550 named the period in which he

---

[9] Wallace, *op. cit.*

[10] James Mavor, *An Economic History of Russia,* Vol. I, pp. 49–52. London and Toronto: Dent, 2nd Edition, 1925; Geroid T. Robinson, *Rural Russia Under the Old Regime,* pp. 10–12. New York: Macmillan, 1949.

could leave as the week before and the week after St. George's Day (November 26).[11]

The three major landowners in this period were the Czar himself, the *pomeshchiki* (the landholding nobility), and the monasteries. The *pomeshchiki* played the major role in creating the pressures that led to the mass enslavement of the agricultural population; yet in theory they themselves were the serfs of the Czar. They had received grants of land from the Czar as a reward for becoming and contingent upon their remaining "serving people," that is, those who functioned in one capacity or another at the royal court; or in return for providing and leading fully equipped troops as required in time of war or other emergency. When the "serving people" ceased to fulfill their obligations toward the sovereign, the estates reverted to the Czar — they were not intended to be the *pomeshchik's* property in the modern sense of that term. Ownership of an earlier form of Russian estate, the *vochina,* was not contingent upon service; such an estate was inherited from one generation to the next. In the fifteenth and sixteenth centuries, however, this distinction tended to become ever less important, and by the beginning of the eighteenth century the two types of estate had been fused into one. The noble owned his land in the sense that he could bequeath it, but both he and his heir were bound to give service; if the heir was a woman, she took a husband to serve the Czar.[12]

As successive and successful wars extended Moscow's domain, more and more land at the outskirts of the realm became available for bestowal upon the nobility, contingent upon their providing properly equipped soldiers in proportion to the size of their land grants. To till their land and secure the soldiers they were obligated to provide, the new groups of landowners needed peasants who would also perform military service as needed. To get these tenants they had to turn to the older areas nearer Moscow. Thus arose a competition between the older and the newer nobility, the latter trying to tempt peasants away from the former, who struggled to keep them.

Although the free peasant had the right to leave, even if only at a

---

[11] Lyashchenko, *op. cit.,* p. 260.
[12] Mavor, *op. cit.,* p. 40.

particular time of the year, this right was conditional upon his satisfaction of all obligations and indebtedness to his old master. But indebtedness was the normal state of the free peasant, since his obligations were heavy. He had to pay taxes to the state. He had to pay rent to the landowner, either in money or in farm products — the so-called *obrok* payment — or in a certain amount of labor each week on the noble's fields — the so-called *barshchina*. The low crop-yields in most years and the all-too-frequent crop failures not only prevented many peasants from reducing their past debts — incurred often for seeds, implements, livestock, and even for food to keep the family alive in the spring and early summer before the harvest — but resulted in mounting indebtedness. Fortunate indeed was the peasant who could add to his poor earnings from the land by other employment. The burden of debt was often so great that peasants sold themselves into personal bondage to cancel their debts and to get themselves off the tax rolls.

In these circumstances few peasants could meet their debts and leave. Sometimes those landowners who needed new settlers would offer to pay the accumulated obligations of those who would settle their land, and would make advances to enable the new settler and his family to live until their first crop had been gathered. More often, peasants and their families fled illegally, seeking to escape the crushing burden of debt upon them and make a new start. Sometimes they were aided and even enticed by their would-be new lords. Not infrequently, pitched battles occurred between the enticers and those whose peasants they were seeking to obtain. Peasants were sometimes terrorized or chained to make sure they would stay; often they retaliated by taking their master's valuables with them when they fled.[13]

The Czar and his government became increasingly concerned over this situation for a number of reasons. The flight of peasants from village communities in the older areas concentrated the debt burden upon an ever decreasing population. These remaining peasants could not pay the taxes, and by the end of the sixteenth century it seems likely that their obligations were completely beyond their ability to meet them. The reduction in tax payments that resulted was aggravated when the most debt-oppressed of the peas-

---

[13] *Ibid.*, pp. 62–64. Robinson, *op. cit.*, pp. 12–17.

antry voluntarily entered slavery, for by their doing so the number of taxpayers was further reduced. Added to these reasons for the state's concern was the agitation of the nobility for aid in securing the return of those who had fled.

An outstanding contemporary Soviet economic historian believes that the legislative enslavement of the free peasantry began about 1580, when so-called "forbidden years" were set up, during which peasants were simply forbidden to leave the land they occupied, even if they had paid their debts. The first such "forbidden years," he believes, were 1581–86; they were reinstituted in 1590–95, "after which the prohibition of departure had actually become a permanent measure." [14] Other historians believe that the first stage of enslavement was the *Ukaz* (decree) of 1597, which provided that if a peasant ran away from land he had settled after September 1, 1592, and the landowner brought suit, the courts had to authorize the compulsory return of the runaway debtor. The law apparently gave landowners no ground for action if a peasant had run away before 1592 and no suit had been entered before then.[15] Whatever the legality of the situation, however, it seems clear that by the beginning of the seventeenth century the heavy indebtedness of the great bulk of the peasantry had reduced large numbers to serf or near-serf status. Moreover, the legal machinery had been created to facilitate the return of those who had left illegally, as well as to hinder peasant procurement by labor-short nobles and monasteries.

The state further helped strengthen the nobility's legal position as serf-owners when it conducted censuses for tax purposes in 1627–28. A worker temporarily employed on an estate and registered as such by the census-takers automatically became a registered taxpayer and had to stay there. In taking the census of 1646 the government promised that all landed and landless peasants and their families registered in the census would be considered as bonded upon the estate where they were recorded and would be subject to return without any restriction. This promise was finally redeemed by a decree of 1649, which is usually regarded as one of the final legal steps in the establishment of serfdom. Thus the state sought to guarantee that its taxes should be paid and its nobility have cultivators of the soil as well as fighting men when the

---

[14] Lyashchenko, *op. cit.*, pp. 260–261.
[15] Mavor, *op. cit.*, p. 56.

need arose.[16] Even if a peasant should run away and remain un-apprehended, the decree protected the state's rights by requiring the landowner to pay the runaway's tax until the next census of his peasants for tax purposes.

During the eighteenth century the whole trend of law, custom, and practice tended to make the distinctions between different groups of slaves and serfs extremely tenuous. Serfs could be bought or sold, with or without the land they worked, like slaves. Legal differences and rights tended to become ever more submerged, since the enforcement of law on the estates was in the hands of the owners, the very persons who had most to gain from the bondage of their peasants and the abrogation in practice of any rights distinguishing them from slaves.[17] But, as might be expected, the creeping imposition of serfdom did not go unresisted, and peasants continued to flee as the opportunity arose. Mavor notes: "Toward the end of the seventeenth century there were epidemics of flights, 'Everyone was running.' . . . "[18] And periodically there were minor or major peasant revolts, the most noted of which was that led by Pugachev in 1773, when 30,000 armed rebels were rallied to show the serf's discontent with his unhappy lot.

In considering the situation of the agricultural serf, it must be remembered that he was primarily a small farmer who either tilled his strips of land full time and surrendered part of his produce to his master, or tilled his own strips part of the time and worked on the master's land the rest of the time. This was a different situation from that of the slave in America, who was employed primarily as an agricultural laborer on his owner's land, producing some valuable crop such as cotton. There were landless serfs in Russia who were employed full time on land recognized as the master's, but they were not in the typical pattern.

Perhaps the final perfection of the serfdom organization of agriculture came in 1762, when a royal decree abolished the service requirements that had formerly been the justification for the nobility's landholding. This decree left unchanged the bondage of the peasantry until its final abolition a century later.

Mavor estimates that at about this time (1762–66) some 14,800,000

---

[16] *Ibid.*, pp. 84–89. Robinson, *op. cit.*, pp. 19–20.
[17] Mavor, *op. cit.*, pp. 92–93.
[18] *Ibid.*, p. 93.

out of 19,000,000 persons living in the Russian Empire were serfs. Of these, almost 40 per cent were peasants belonging to the state itself; over 53 per cent belonged to *pomeshchiki*. Almost 80 per cent of the population lived in bondage.[19] The state peasants paid poll taxes, furnished recruits, and paid rent for the land they tilled. They were governed by the Czar's appointees, whose power resembled that of the landlords and was sometimes even more oppressive.[20]

What were the consequences of the institution of serfdom? First, it degraded the great bulk of the nation's people, keeping them in a subservient status and preventing most of them from rising above the illiteracy and blind adherence to tradition characteristic of this system of human relations. Second, it hindered improvement and experimentation in agricultural production. Bolder and more imaginative spirits among the peasants could not break the hold of the commune and primitive technique upon production, but had to follow the same pattern and practices as their less enterprising neighbors. Third, it bred ever increasing dissatisfaction among the serfs, most of whom had no hope of attaining freedom and resented bitterly having to share their meager produce with masters who often made no obvious — sometimes not any — contribution to production. Serfdom permitted the existence of a largely parasitic class of land- and serf-owners, while keeping the great mass of the population in abject poverty and alienating them from existing institutions. Little wonder the peasants believed firmly that the land was theirs by right and looked forward eagerly to the time when justice would be done them.

The Abolition of Serfdom

These and other deficiencies of serfdom were quite clear to many in the ruling circles of Russia. Even well before 1800, many government officials and intellectuals pondered the problem of how a more satisfactory organization of society could be achieved. How should the peasants be freed: by direct government order, or more slowly by government encouragement, making it easier for serfs to buy their freedom? Should the peasants simply be freed, or should

---

19 *Ibid.*, p. 192.
20 Robinson, *op. cit.*, p. 29.

provision also be made to assure them of some land? How were the serf-owners' interests and property rights to be treated in any project for mass liberation? Many proposals came up for consideration, and government committee after government committee struggled with the problem. All knew that serfdom had to end some day, but how could it be ended while maintaining the equilibrium of the state and — most important — preventing the peasantry from resorting to mass violence and bloodshed to gain revenge for past wrongs? A beginning was made as early as 1816–19, when the serfs in the Baltic provinces of Estonia, Kurland, and Livonia were freed, though they got no land and were forbidden to migrate from the rural areas.[21]

There were economic factors pressing for liberation. Some landowners in the first half of the nineteenth century found that they could work their land more profitably if they used hired labor. A free man worked much more satisfactorily than the unwilling serf, who did his duties perfunctorily and was often quite willing to get into a quarrel rather than obey orders properly. In bad years when crops were poor, landowners had to purchase bread for their serfs at high prices, in order to keep them alive. In the 1840's some landowners liberated their peasants rather than meet this obligation. In some areas, land on which no serfs were settled sold for higher prices than land inhabited by serfs. But in other areas, of course — for example, where labor was still scarce — economic conditions were such as to make the landowners favor continued serfdom.[22]

The final blow to serfdom was the disastrous Russian defeat in the Crimean War (1854-56). In the highest ruling circles and among the most influential intellectuals, this military catastrophe was recognized as primarily the result of the economic and political backwardness of Russia compared with the victors, England and France particularly. The leading element in this backwardness was recognized to be the outmoded institution of serfdom. Five years after this defeat, the peasants were emancipated; the institution that had met military needs in the sixteenth century had failed to meet them in the nineteenth.[23]

[21] Mavor, *op. cit.*, pp. 324–25.

[22] *Ibid.*, pp. 370–79.

[23] Lyashchenko, *op. cit.*, pp. 578–79. V. P. Timoshenko, "The Agrarian Policies of Russia and the Wars," *Agricultural History*, October 1943, pp. 192–94.

The reform of 1861 that deprived the nobles of their serfs, and the additional reforms in the next few years that freed the even larger number of state peasants, fell far short of meeting all the hopes of the peasantry. But these reforms were far more generous than many groups of landlords had wished. They represented compromises between the conflicting interests of the groups involved. The landlords in the black earth regions sought to keep as much of their land as possible; those in the less fertile northern regions sought maximum compensation for the profits they had made from serf labor. The peasants wished freedom and land without cost to themselves. Their expectations and hopes knew no bounds.[24]

The leading objective of the reforms of the 1860's seems to have been to create a new free class of peasants working the same amount of land they had worked before being freed, but leaving the landlords in possession of the land that had been worked for them by serfs doing *barshchina* or by landless agricultural laborers. To take account of the diverse conditions on different estates, maximum and minimum norms were set in different areas. Where actual serf holdings exceeded the maximum norms, landlords could demand that the excess remain their property. Where serfs had no land at all or less than the minimum norms, they were to be allotted additional land. In practice, however, the former serfs got little or no additional land, while losing perhaps as much as 20 per cent of the land they had worked before the reform, much of this loss taking place in the fertile black soil areas of the Ukraine and the middle Volga. Worst off from the point of view of land holdings were the more than half million peasants who chose to accept the so-called "beggarly allotments," equivalent to one fourth of the maximum norm, in order that their land might not be encumbered by any landlord claims for dues, services, or land payment.

The land allotted to the peasants was not a gift. It was to be paid for over a period of forty-nine years through redemption payments made to the state, which compensated the former landowners with redemption bonds immediately after the reform took place on each estate. Joint responsibility for meeting these payments was placed upon the members of the commune, and it was the commune, rather than the individual peasants, which was given title to the new

---

[24] Bowden, *et al., op. cit.,* pp. 599–600.

lands. Members could not leave the commune without its permission, a measure aimed at preventing peasants from fleeing their
obligations to redeem the land. Under the new laws the commune
became an even more formal unit of administration. It became a
basic component of the police system. It continued to levy taxes
for local needs and, often, to redistribute land periodically in order
to take account of the changing size and work force of each peasant
family.

From the peasants' point of view, one of the worst features of
these reforms was that the prices received by landlords for their land
were often far above its true market value. This gave many landlords a concealed but nonetheless real payment for the loss of their
serf property, though the law had specifically forbidden such compensation. Thus from the very beginning large numbers of former
serfs found themselves with inadequate amounts of land for which
they were heavily indebted, hardly an auspicious beginning for their
freedom.[25]

The reforms of the 1860's did not solve Russia's peasant problem,
as is evidenced by the prominent role of the peasantry in the disturbances of the second half of the nineteenth century and in the
revolutions of 1905 and 1917. After the reforms the plight of
millions of peasants grew steadily worse, as their debts piled up —
the result of the complete inadequacy of their land allotments to
provide income sufficient for the redemption payments, government
taxes, and subsistence needs. As early as the 1870's the government began to be alarmed about the mounting arrears in peasant
payments and sent investigators to the areas of greatest delinquency.
These investigators found the peasantry often near the edge of
starvation. The world-wide fall in grain prices during the last two
decades of the nineteenth century greatly worsened the situation; [26]
moreover, the rapid growth of population in this period intensified
peasant distress and made the inadequacy of their land holdings
ever more apparent.

Not all Russian peasants were poverty-stricken, however. By
1900 significant differentiation had arisen among them. The most
enterprising, those with better land, larger allotments, and a

---

[25] Timoshenko, op. cit., pp. 194–96, and Bernard Pares, A History of Russia,
pp. 353–55. New York: Knopf, 1944.
[26] Lyashchenko, op. cit., Vol. II, pp. 66–70.

favorable market situation, had become more prosperous and were raising themselves above the mass of their fellows. They were buying or leasing additional land and employing workers outside their families. Lenin estimated in 1905 that 10.5 million poor peasants had on the average about 19 acres each; 1 million "middle peasants" averaged about 40 acres each; 1.5 million farms, owned by the richest peasants and by capitalist entrepreneurs, averaged about 126 acres.[27] (The average-sized farm in the top group was, of course, of only moderate size by United States standards.) Lenin estimated too that 30,000 *pomeshchik* estates averaged over 6,200 acres apiece and had as much land in the aggregate as all the 1.5 million richer farmers, and almost as much land as the 10.5 million poor peasants, taken together.

The growth of peasant landholdings after the reform is summarized by comparing the approximately 300,000,000 acres they got originally in the early 1860's with the 500,000,000 acres they held on January 1, 1917.[28] In part this growth of peasant land was aided by the Peasant Bank, founded by the government in 1882, which lent money for land purchase and later was allowed to buy up estates for resale to peasants on easier terms.

Until the early years of the twentieth century, however, the commune often obstructed differentiation among the peasantry. This institution stood for equality of landholding in terms of manpower, an equality imposed by the periodic redistribution of land among members. And to the extent that the village community could force the observance of common crop patterns and cultivation practices on the strips of the three-field or the two-field system, it hindered technological improvement and higher agricultural production. The differentiation sanctioned by the *mir* was that resulting from the different sizes of peasant families. It is significant that the wealthiest 20 per cent of peasant families in the 1890's had 26 to 30 per cent of the peasant population.[29]

After 1860 Russian agriculture became increasingly commercial. More and more it produced for market sale rather than for peasant consumption and payment in kind to meet serf obligations. On the one hand, the peasants needed relatively large amounts of cash to

---

27 *Ibid.*, p. 84.
28 A. N. Antsiferov, *et al.*, *Russian Agriculture during the War*, pp. 20, 22. New Haven: Yale University Press, 1930.
29 Lyashchenko, *op. cit.*, p. 77.

meet their redemption payments and taxes. On the other, both domestic and foreign markets were expanding. From 1860–1914 industry grew rapidly, with consequent expansion in urban populations, for whom food had to be provided. The growth of the internal railroad network provided the means for moving food and agricultural raw materials from farms to urban markets and, most important, to seaports. This was the era in which Russian grain exports mounted sharply and became a major factor in international trade. The growth of these markets stimulated the development of large-scale production both on estates and on the holdings of the peasantry. The demand for sugar beets, dairy products, flax, hemp, and other agricultural raw materials stimulated expansion of the acreage devoted to them and consequently their production.

The unsuccessful Russo-Japanese War of 1904–5 and the accompanying revolutionary disturbances, both in the cities and the countryside, marked the next turning point in the development of Russia's agricultural institutions. The violently expressed resentment of the peasantry against the remaining large landholdings of the nobility raised the specter of more successful revolution in the future, the same specter that had played a potent part in the deliberations preceding 1861. Clearly the problem of making the peasantry, or at least a large section of it, a bulwark of Czarist rule rather than an opponent of it had not been solved.

In 1906 a new and radically different agrarian policy, the so-called Stolypin reforms, was adopted to accomplish this end, but important steps had been taken even earlier. In 1903 the collective responsibility for redemption payments had been ended, and in 1905 the redemption payments had been entirely wiped out, to quiet the revolutionary mood of the countryside. The Stolypin reforms went further. They aimed at ending the communal nature of Russian agriculture and substituting for it an agriculture composed of consolidated, individually owned farms on which modern farm technology could most easily be applied. On these the most enterprising and able could forge ahead, unhindered by the dead hand of traditional practice and egalitarianism as expressed in the *mir*.

To accomplish its objectives, the decree of November 9, 1906, divided all rural communities into two groups: those in which land had been redistributed among peasant families since the ending of serfdom, and those in which such redistribution had not taken place. Peasant allotments in the second group of communities were recognized as being the private property of the various peasant families involved. In those communities where redistribution had taken place, any member was permitted to leave the community when he wished. The community, upon his demand, was obligated to give him his land, not in the customary scattered strips, but, so far as possible, in one continuous piece. The regulations governing the breakup of communities by vote of members were revised so as to make such dissolution easier. The individual farms emerging from this reform could be sold or bequeathed to the owner's heirs. In some areas peasants were encouraged to move out of the old common villages into new homes, the so-called *khutors*, on the new consolidated areas they owned.[30]

These reforms obviously met a real demand from a significant section of the peasantry. Between 1907 and 1915, about 2.5 million peasants in European Russia, about 24 per cent of the total, were confirmed as individual owners of their own farms, a total area of about 45 million acres. In some parts of the Ukraine as much as 50 per cent of all peasant holdings had been turned into privately owned farms by 1915; but in areas where agriculture was less dependent upon market sale, the relative importance of this movement was much less. It was in the areas of commercialized agriculture that farmers were most apt to be dissatisfied with the hampering effects of *mir* control and to be aware of the possibilities in improved agricultural technique.[31]

In an effort to minimize peasant discontent in areas where the growth of population had intensified rural poverty, the Russian government encouraged migration to its Asiatic lands, subsidizing it in part and taking the responsibility of preparing land for new settlers. Between 1905 and 1914 alone, about 3 million persons moved from European to Asiatic Russia, thus practically completing the agricultural colonization of Siberia for several decades. The migration to Asia from 1906 to 1913 drained off about half the natural increase of the rural population in those parts of European Russia that were overpopulated.[32]

---

[30] Lyashchenko, *op. cit.*, p. 265, and Mavor, *op. cit.*, Vol. II, pp. 340–46.
[31] Lyashchenko, *op. cit.*, pp. 266–67.
[32] Timoshenko, *op. cit.*, pp. 202–3.

What the Stolypin reforms, the government-encouraged migration out of European Russia, and other steps taken by the Czarist regime to ease the peasant problem might have accomplished in time, we shall never know. The outbreak of World War I in 1914 required the concentration of energies upon other matters. In 1916 the Stolypin program had to be suspended because of fears among the soldiers that their interests at home might be damaged by its operation while they were away. Military defeats and peasant dissatisfaction helped overthrow first the Czar and then the parliamentary government that succeeded him. Thenceforth the development of Russian agriculture and of peasant organization were to be the concern of the new Bolshevik rulers. Thus history expressed its verdict that the reform of 1861, Stolypin's legislation, and the other steps taken by the Czarist regime had all fallen into the category of too little and too late.

Industry, Trade, and Transport

Before 1860 — and even decades later — the Russian village, like other preindustrial societies, met most of its own needs. The overwhelming majority of the population was engaged in agriculture, and the primal economic problem of most families was to produce enough food to feed its members and pay the required dues to the lord and the state. To a large extent each family was a self-contained unit, baking its own bread, making much of its own clothing, building and repairing its own abode, and otherwise meeting its own needs. A village typically had a few craftsmen and artisans — weavers, carpenters, blacksmiths, cobblers, and the like — who produced those items that the individual peasant family could not conveniently make itself. The number and variety of these craftsmen varied from village to village, both being greatest in those communities adjacent to a *pomeshchik* estate or a monastery. Here the greater demand and greater means for purchase enabled more craftsmen to make a living. To a very large extent, therefore, the needs of most people were met logically through their own and their neighbors' production.[33]

But even in the thirteenth and fourteenth centuries, when this picture was most typical, a certain amount of industry and trade

---

[33] Lyashchenko, *op. cit.*, Vol. I, pp. 201–4.

for comparatively large markets was carried on. In Moscow and other cities the number and variety of handicraftsmen and their products were much more extensive than in the peasant villages, and even those villages had to rely upon outside sources for salt, iron, wine, and other goods. The cities needed food for their inhabitants, which they obtained from the peasants, supplying in return weapons, clothing, shoes, and other products of urban production. As elsewhere in Europe, fairs, conducted annually or more often brought buyers and sellers together to exchange products produced over a wide area. Intercity and interareal trade were hindered by the poor condition, or complete absence, of roads, but goods were carried for long distances over the rivers of the Russian plain. Monasteries, princes, and large landowners often played important roles in this trade, either carrying it on directly with the help of agents located at widely distant points, or financing and protecting merchants engaged in this activity.[34]

The needs of war furnished a particularly important impetus for industry and trade in these years. Toward the end of the fifteenth century Ivan III called in foreigners to help inaugurate the production of artillery weapons for the Moscow state, thus hoping to end the earlier dependence of Russian armies upon imports of such heavy and relatively complex weapons. In general the needs of Russian armies for weapons, munitions, means of transport, and other commodities were on a scale that could not be easily satisfied by the production of the individual handicraftsman or by small groups. This gave an important impetus to the development of larger-scale industry.[35]

As the Moscow state expanded territorially from the fifteenth to the seventeenth century, it offered an ever-expanding domestic market for the products of industry and mining and an ever larger area for trade. Its cities grew both in size and in number, while the requirements of its armies rose too, as their numbers increased and military operations became more complex. In the sixteenth century the cities of the Moscow state had about 200 different types of artisans. Moscow and Novgorod had over 2,000 such workers each, while hundreds were to be found in smaller cities such as

---

[34] *Ibid.*, pp. 204–13.
[35] *Ibid.*, p. 273.

Mozhaisk and Tula. Bakers, fishermen, winemakers, leatherworkers, hatmakers, metal workers of diverse types, these were among the most important groups of artisans. Large-scale enterpreneurs and traders sprang up, organizing the production of varied commodities and trading over large areas. In the enterprises of the Stroganov family alone, 10,000 free workers and 5,000 serfs were employed.[36] In the seventeenth century the feudal lord Morozov had a large-scale potash works, as well as shops producing iron implements, leather, bricks, and other commodities. His own serfs composed a large part of his labor force, their work being the *barshchina* payment to him. He owned about 300 villages and tens of thousands of bondsmen, combining the activities of a large-scale landowner, industrialist, and trader.[37] During the sixteenth and seventeenth centuries the state owned mines, shops, and other enterprises, which supplied it with the weapons, currency, and other commodities it required. These production units employed state peasants directed by foreign technicians. About 1650 foreigners built glass, stationery, and iron-fabricating factories in Moscow and elsewhere. Foreign trade became an appreciable factor in the country's economy. Commerce with England and Holland flowed through the Barents Sea into Archangel and through non-Russian Baltic ports. Trade with Germany and Poland went overland through the Ukraine; and trade with Persia, China, and India, through Siberia and over the Caspian Sea.[38]

Peter the Great's Contribution

The reign of Peter the Great (1682–1725) saw the most concentrated and rapid progress in expanding industry achieved up to that time. Others before him had sent out prospectors to find mineral deposits; he sent out a veritable army of them, and was well rewarded by their findings. Two centuries before him, Ivan III had brought in an Italian cannonmaker, and small numbers of other foreign experts were brought in from time to time after that; Peter brought in foreign experts in wholesale lots and made his embassies throughout Europe virtual employment agencies. Moreover, he imported not only technicians but mathematicians and

36 *Ibid.*, pp. 267–72.
37 *Ibid.*, pp. 318–19.
38 *Ibid.*, p. 310.

other scholars to teach in his schools. He himself had visited Western Europe and England, learning at first hand the advanced nature of Western technology, and absorbing the mercantilist ideas of state economic policy prevalent at the time.[39]

In large part the motivation for Peter's economic policy was the desire to meet adequately the needs of his large armies and of the navy he hoped to build. His determination to build his new capital, St. Petersburg (now Leningrad), on the swamps where the Neva River joins the Gulf of Finland created additional great needs for commodities of the most diverse sort. Peter realized Russia's enormous resources and potentialities, and desired to make them actualities so far as he could. As absolute ruler of his country, he had the power to commandeer its wealth for the realization of his projects, much as the absolute rulers of the contemporary Soviet Union have been able to utilize the same nation's resources for their own ambitious goals.

To build a large-scale industry, one needs raw materials, technical knowledge, capital, and labor. For the first Peter could draw upon the varied agricultural and forest output of his realm, as well as upon the old and newly discovered mineral resources within it. Thus he intensively exploited the iron resources of the Ural Mountains. Almost 30,000 short tons of pig iron were smelted in Russia in 1718; England, usually regarded as the home of the industrial revolution, produced less than 20,000 short tons of iron in 1740. As a result of the beginnings made under Peter, by the middle of the eighteenth century Russia was the world's largest producer of iron and copper.[40]

Peter turned to the West, as we have seen, to obtain the most skilled technicians he could hire. These were brought to Russia under generous contracts, not only to work at their specialties, but also to teach Russians the new skills and methods that had been developed in France, Holland, England, and other Western countries. Moreover, Peter sent many young Russians abroad to study in the schools and the workshops of Western Europe, thus further adding to the technically and professionally trained personnel at his dis-

---

39 Mavor, op. cit., pp. 116–19.

40 Ibid., p. 129, and Lyashchenko, op. cit., p. 405. The pig-iron figure for Russia given here is cited by Lyashchenko as the conclusion of recent investigations invalidating the higher figure cited by Mavor. Cf. also Bowden, et al., op. cit., pp. 301, 385.

posal. More general, but not unimportant in its cumulative effect, was Peter's enthusiasm for education and his efforts to insure that at least the children of the "serving people" got an education. He required that they pass an examination before being admitted to public service.

Some of the most thorny problems Peter had to contend with were related to the obtaining of capital for starting new factories, mines, and other enterprises he desired to carry out. Much of this capital was provided by the state treasury, which initiated some productive units and partially subsidized others. Such financing of capital expansion was expensive, of course. Peter's wars and standing armed forces drained the treasury even more heavily and created a serious fiscal problem. To raise money for his treasury, Peter and his subordinates resorted to many devices. Not only were new taxes imposed upon the already heavily burdened peasantry, but excise taxes of every imaginable kind proliferated rapidly—beards, chimneys, water, baths, and cucumbers being a few of the things taxed. The state monopolized the production of many essential commodities such as salt, tobacco, fish, oil, oak coffins, and other items, and doubled or quadrupled their prices. Salt, for example, became a luxury, and poverty-stricken peasants died because they could not afford it. Peter ordered many of the country's church bells to be melted down to make cannon. In 1701 he confiscated the incomes from the large monastery estates. And like many another impecunious medieval ruler, he reduced the silver content of his currency. By the end of his reign the country had token money rather than a currency that was intrinsically valuable because of its silver content.[41]

Peter's exactions from his countrymen to pay for his military and economic activities served to reduce a low standard of living still further—again reminding us of the policies followed by the recent masters of the USSR; like them he abstained from obtaining foreign loans and other external financing that might have limited his freedom of action. Peter's generation, like Stalin's, paid for their country's progress by their own privation.

But treasury funds were not the only source of capital during this period. Substantial capital accumulations existed in the hands of the landowning gentry and the rich merchant families. Tax

41 Mavor, *op. cit.,* pp. 131–35.

exemptions, subsidies, high tariff protection, monopolistic privileges —these and other incentives were offered to those who would invest their means in enterprises as diverse as moose hunting in the forests of the north and silk manufacturing. The stick as well as the carrot was used to obtain such investment, and merchants were informed of their obligation to create industrial production units. Wealthy interests seeking to evade this "public duty" transferred their funds to England, Holland, and Italy, while others hoarded gold and silver. Many a potential entrepreneur was apparently frightened away by the close and arbitrary control exercised by the government over economic activity of any significant size. Those who invested did so because of the prospect of great profits, but their inexperience and incompetence often brought them to financial disaster, their enterprises collapsing unless additional government aid could be obtained.[42]

Since Russia, at the beginning of the eighteenth century, had no large body of free workers seeking employment for wages, the problem of recruiting an industrial labor force had to be solved primarily by the use of serfs belonging to either the state or the gentry. When the government set up factories, it typically assigned the residents of nearby villages on state land to work in them. In 1721 merchants owning factories were permitted to buy entire village populations, thus gaining the formerly denied right of owning serfs. These latter were associated with the enterprise and might not be diverted to other work. This was the origin of the class of "ascribed" or "possessional" peasants, who formed an important portion of Russia's nonagricultural labor force till the 1860's. Not all the industrial workers of this time were unfree, however. There were relatively small groups of urban free men—former handicraft workers, tradespeople, children of soldiers, beggars, and the like — who were recruited in such numbers as available. But the pressing need for a rapidly expanded labor supply could only be solved in this period by the use of forced labor, primarily that of the bonded peasantry, but also including convicts. Significantly, eleven years after Peter's death a decree of 1736 declared all free-men working in factories, together with their families, to be hence-forth bondsmen attached to the factories "forever." Russia's industrial proletariat, therefore, began as an unfree group, subject to

[42] *Ibid.*, pp. 127–28.

the same disabilities as the serfs of the countryside, from whose ranks most of these new proletarians were rudely taken by government fiat.[43]

Of the 195 largest factories established during Peter's reign, 26 produced linen and silk fabrics as well as cloth; 5 produced leather; 4, paper; and 3, weapons. In addition there were factories producing canvas for sails, about 20 iron and other metallurgical refineries, and other assorted enterprises.[44] Some of these production units employed well over a thousand workers each; others, several hundred. But these must not be thought of in terms of modern centralized factories, all of whose employees tend machinery in one building. Some of these "factories" were little more than organizations that united and coordinated the activities of hundreds of domestic workers, each in his own home, or small numbers working together in tiny workrooms. This tended to be the pattern in weaving and other branches of textile manufacturing. In metallurgical shops, on the other hand, the very nature of the production technique required that a fairly large number of workers be concentrated in one place. Their work was characterized by a fairly high division of labor, and some of them used machinery run by water power, bellows, furnaces, and the like, though many used only the simplest of tools, such as hammers. For some products, the manufacturing process involved both operations done in the central building and others done by artisans in small workrooms or at home.[45]

After Peter's death, industrial development continued, though at a slower pace for a time. In mining, for example, 31,383 ascribed peasants belonged to the work force in 1719. By 1741–43, the number had grown to 87,253; and 50 years later, in 1794–96, the number of these serf miners was 312,218, a tenfold growth within a century.[46] The growth of manufacturing was not nearly so rapid, however. Data for 1770, covering manufacturing plants outside of St. Petersburg that reported to the manufacturing collegium, show only 190 factories, employing a total of only 34,316 ascribed and

---

[43] *Ibid.*, pp. 125–26, and Lyashchenko, *op. cit.*, pp. 389–91.

[44] Lyashchenko, *op. cit.*, pp. 403–4.

[45] *Ibid.*, pp. 392–94.

[46] A. G. Rashin, *Formirovaniye Promyshlennogo Proletariata V Rossii*, p. 71. Moscow: 1940.

possessional peasants.[47] The growth thereafter was rapid, however, as is indicated by the following data:

TABLE 6. Number of Factories and Number of Workers in the Manufacturing Industry of Russia during Selected Years, 1770–1860.

Year	Number of Factories	Number of Workers (000 omitted)
1770	over 190	about 60
1804	2,399	95.2
1811	2,421	137.8
1820	4,578	179.6
1830	5,453	253.9
1840	6,863	435.8
1850	9,843	501.6
1860	15,338	565.1

Source: Rashin, *Formirovaniye Promyshlennogo Proletariata V Rossii*, p. 23.

The above data include many small enterprises of less than ten workers as well as larger plants, so they must be interpreted with care. In addition they reflect, not only the growth of old industries, but also the introduction and development of new ones over this period.[48] Despite the qualifications that must be attached to these data, the figures make it abundantly clear that industrial production grew significantly, and at times rapidly, in the century before the ending of serfdom. The Napoleonic wars cut Russia off from imports of English goods, stimulating the domestic production of substitutes; machinery of all kinds was slowly but steadily imported from abroad after 1800, so that Russia participated in part in the alteration of production methods that went on so rapidly in Western Europe, and particularly England. Cotton cloth production, based largely on the use of imported cotton, forged ahead very rapidly after 1830, as new technical developments made such cloth by far the cheapest clothing material and thus opened up a wide domestic market for its use. The government prohibited the import of many kinds of goods and put high tariff rates on many others, hoping to stimulate some industries by protecting them wholly or in part from the competition of cheaper production abroad. This protectionist policy lasted from 1822 to 1850, after which there was a turn toward freer trade.[49]

---

[47] *Ibid.*, p. 18.
[48] *Ibid.*, p. 24.
[49] Lyashchenko, *op. cit.*, pp. 462, 492.

But although the economic development during the first half of the nineteenth century was appreciable, it was relatively slow compared to the almost explosive increase of production elsewhere in Europe. Pig iron provides a striking, though not entirely representative, case in point. In 1800 Russia's pig-iron output was about the same as England's. By the 1850's Russia's production, which had much less than doubled, was far behind England's which had increased ten times over. By 1860, Russia stood in eighth place among the producers of pig iron, behind even Austria and Prussia.[50]

Such relative slowness of growth is not surprising in view of the political, social, and economic structure of the country at the time. Since the majority of the population consisted of poverty-stricken bonded peasants, mass markets existed for relatively few commodities. The existence of large areas of monopolized production hindered the increase of output that might have followed competitive price reductions. Effective Russian contributions to the rapid growth of industrial technology were few. The importation of more modern technology was hindered both by efforts of advanced powers to monopolize their discoveries—England's policy in the case of some types of textile machinery is illustrative—and by inertia and lack of mass markets in Russia. Not least important, the continuing role of unfree labor in large segments of Russia's nonagricultural economy hindered technical advance, since such workers could be relied upon to do only the simplest and least responsible tasks.

The inadequacies of an unfree labor force began to be realized soon after the introduction of automatic machinery and other displacement of simple hand methods in production. Thus in 1837 a group of manufacturers in Moscow Province wrote the Minister of Finance complaining that possessional peasants could not be used where thought and judgment, as well as mere physical exertion, were required. Moreover, they complained, these ignorant workers were an increasing burden, since they and their children had to be fed, regardless of their productive contribution.[51] Such sentiments were general and were acted upon by manufacturers. Data for most Russian industry, excluding mining and some food-processing branches, show that the proportion of free workers in the factory labor force rose from 32 per cent in 1770 to 50 per cent in 1812 and

---

[50] *Ibid.*, p. 537.
[51] Quoted in Rashin, *op. cit.*, p. 62.

87 per cent in 1860. As early as 1825, almost 95 per cent of all cotton textile workers and 93 per cent of leatherworkers were free, as were the great majority of workers in linen and silk manufacturing. Possessional peasants and serfs of the gentry formed the great bulk of the labor force in mining, in metallurgical manufacture, and in the branches of the textile industry controlled by the nobility, who used their own subject workers to process the flax, hemp, and wool their estates produced.[52] Long before serfdom was ended by the Czar's decree, much of Russian industry had learned that slavery and advanced technology were incompatible and made an unprofitable combination.

The term "free workers" as used above should not be interpreted in the modern sense, for the great majority of these were serfs too. But they had been given passports by their owners permitting them to travel and look for work under conditions that they negotiated with their employers. From their earnings they paid *obrok* money to their lord, keeping the remainder to provide for themselves. Their wages were low, far below the level of foreign workers. Nevertheless these serfs—and state peasants who could not find employment in agriculture—were termed a free labor force; they were relatively free compared to those who worked under usual feudal conditions. Moreover, as we have noted, the traveling serf-workman had an incentive to raise his earnings, and therefore his productive abilities, because he was permitted to retain the excess of his wages over the required *obrok* payment.[53]

Development after the End of Serfdom

The year 1861 marks a fundamental turning point in the history of the nonagricultural sectors of the Russian economy. The freeing of the serfs opened the way for recruitment of a free labor force on a scale never before known. For most peasants, the desertion of agriculture for other occupations was hindered by the collective obligations for land-redemption payments and the necessity for those so bound to obtain passports. But even in the first years of the postreform period, several million peasants found themselves with little or no land, and with no obligations for redemption payments. They were free to shift to other occupations.

---

52 *Ibid.*, p. 71, and Lyashchenko, *op. cit.*, pp. 535–36.
53 Rashin, *op. cit.*, pp. 79–82.

The land-redemption bonds issued the nobility by the government provided an important source of capital, since they could be liquidated at the owners' pleasure, though often only at a substantial discount. This capital could be, and often was, invested in the development of trade, industry, and transport. The land-redemption requirement, moreover, brought the mass of peasantry, more intimately than ever before, into a monetary economy, placing greater pressure upon them to raise crops for sale and, for many, creating a most potent incentive to earn money in occupations other than agriculture. In these and other ways the reform created a ferment and activity with the most momentous consequences.

The Russian revolutions of 1917 came, not at the end of a long period of stagnation and decay, but rather after more than a half century of the most rapid and comprehensive economic progress. The average annual rate of growth of industrial output in Russia between 1885 and 1889, and again between 1907 and 1913, substantially exceeded the corresponding rates of growth during the same period in the United States, Great Britain, and Germany. Between 1890 and 1899, industrial production in Russia grew on the average over 8 per cent each year.[54] In roughly two out of every three years between 1868 and 1919, 1,000 kilometers (621 miles) or more of railroad lines were completed. In 1908, 8,390 kilometers were finished; in 1899, 5,257 kilometers; in 1900 and 1901, over 3,000 kilometers each year. By the outbreak of the first World War, Western Russia was covered with a relatively dense network of railroad lines designed to serve both strategic military purposes and the domestic and foreign trade activities of the country.[55] Moreover, the Trans-Siberian Railroad had been completed, connecting Moscow and St. Petersburg with Vladivostok on the Pacific Ocean, and running through the heart of Siberia. This rapid development of industry and transportation did not proceed unchecked, of course, and was held back from time to time by crises and depression, as in 1873 and 1882; but the whole period 1861–1914 had rapid development as its key feature. The tempo of increased production of major commodities is shown in Table 7.

---

[54] A. Gerschenkron, "The Rate of Industrial Growth in Russia since 1885," *The Journal of Economic History*, Supplement VII (1947), p. 156.

[55] Edward Ames, "A Century of Russian Railroad Construction: 1837–1936," *The American Slavic and East European Review*, December 1947, *passim*.

TABLE 7. Production of Selected Commodities in Russia, 1860–1913.

Commodity	Unit	1860	1870	1880	1890	1900	1913
Coal	mil. puds*	18.3	42.4	200.9	367.2	995.2	2,214
Petroleum	mil. puds	—	1.8	34.0	241.0	632.0	561
Pig Iron	mil. puds	19.6	20.7	26.1	55.2	176.8	283
Iron and Steel ..	mil. puds	12.4	14.5	35.3	48.4	134.4	247

* One pud equals 36.1 pounds avoirdupois.
Source: Lyashchenko, *op. cit.*, Vol. II, pp. 151, 152, 410.

During the last half century of Czarist rule, the figures above clearly indicate, Russia went a good way toward ending its former economic backwardness. In this period was laid much of the foundation upon which the Soviet Union was later to build its own rapid economic expansion. The very rapidity of this movement created tensions and strains that produced social upheaval. But even the progress made by 1917 had far from closed the gap in economic development between Russia, on the one hand, and Western Europe and the United States, on the other.

What were the major factors behind this great unleashing of Russian energies? Among the most important were the expansion of domestic and foreign markets for Russian products, and the deliberate policy followed by the Russian government in consistently encouraging economic development in every way possible. Market expansion was in turn the product of many forces: the rapid rise of Russian population; the unifying of the country by railroad lines, which helped break down the old local barriers and created a true national market for the products of many industries; the continued weakening—though not elimination—of peasant village self-sufficiency under the impact of increased participation in a money economy and increased contact with urban living patterns; the particularly rapid growth of urban population, that is, of people accustomed to purchasing the bulk of their food and consumer goods; the requirements for rapid capital development of railroad lines, factories, shipbuilding, and other facilities, which, in turn, of course, represented a response in part to earlier market expansion. The growth of Russian exports, particularly of grain, was facilitated by the increasing industrialization of Central and Western Europe and the corresponding sharp increase of industrial populations seeking food at the lowest cost.

Government policy was most important in this development. Abolition of serfdom, itself, was perhaps the greatest single contribution, but other contributions were more direct. The state treasury itself financed much of the railroad building and factory construction, while the state bank helped other enterprises of nongovernment origin. A consistent policy of encouraging and facilitating foreign capital investment, and the import of technicians and technology from abroad, brought rich returns. To pay for heavy treasury expenditures the government kept the tax burden oppressive. This had the additional effect of forcing the peasantry to sell more grain and other agricultural products than they otherwise might have done, which in turn facilitated the grain exports that made it possible for Russia to have a favorable balance of trade and maintain interest payments on its huge capital imports. "Let us starve but export," was Finance Minister Vyshnegradsky's slogan [56] almost 50 years before Stalin let Ukrainians starve while shipping grain abroad to pay for American farm machinery. Through tariffs and other restrictions on international trade, the government sought on the one hand to protect domestic industry and on the other to cut down unnecessary imports that might endanger the favorable balance of trade needed to maintain the confidence of foreign investors. But this was not a policy of blind protectionism, and in the early years of railroad expansion, before the mid-eighties, the vast metallurgical and machinery requirements for this purpose were permitted to come in from abroad almost unhindered.[57]

Without the aid of foreign capital, technicians, and technology, this rapid development of productive forces and output could not have been attained. As early as 1890, over one third of all capital in Russian joint-stock companies was from foreign sources. By 1900 the ratio had risen to half the total. Of the more than 2.2 billion rubles of foreign capital so invested in 1916–17, 32.6 per cent came from France, 22.6 per cent from Great Britain, 19.7 per cent from Germany, 14.3 per cent from Belgium, and 5.2 per cent from the United States. In the mining industry the proportion of foreign capital was 91 per cent; in the chemical industry, 50 per cent; in metal fabricating, 42 per cent; in woodworking, 37 per cent; and in the textile industry, 28 per cent.[58] In addition a large part of the

[56] Gerschenkron, op. cit., p. 149.
[57] Mavor, op. cit., Vol. II, pp. 381–82.
[58] Lyashchenko, op. cit., pp. 161, 378.

cost of railroad construction was financed by foreign loans, particularly from France. Moreover, the foreigners did not merely content themselves with investing money to earn dividends and interest; they also provided the managerial, engineering, and other skills required for this development, as well as much of the modern machinery for Russia's new factories and railroads. The rapid development after 1870 of the Donets coal basin and Krivoy Rog iron mines for steelmaking and other purposes was to a large extent the result of the activities of the English entrepreneur John Hughes. Similarly, the Swedish firm of Nobel, backed by English and French capital, was responsible for the rapid increase in the production of oil at Baku, which soon became Russia's leading petroleum source, just as the Donbas-Krivoy Rog area became Russia's primary supplier of coal, iron, and steel. In the textile industry, Ludwig Knoop, a German, built and financed much of the rapid expansion that took place, utilizing many English technicians from Lancashire.

Along with the great expansion of industrial and mining output from 1860 to 1913 went a sharp increase in the labor force employed in these branches of the economy. In 1860 more than 800,000 workers were engaged in manufacturing and mining; in 1913 over 3,000,000 were so employed, a rise of almost 400 per cent.[59] In addition, Russia had over 1,000,000 construction workers about 1910,[60] and well over 400,000 railway employees of all kinds after 1900.[61] In total, therefore, over 4,500,000 Russians were engaged in the major branches of the nonagricultural economy before World War I.

Even in the last years of Czarist rule, however, the work of individual craftsmen, or small groups of artisans, working at home or in small village workshops, continued to play an important role in meeting the daily needs of the peasantry, who still constituted the bulk of Russia's population. Household utensils of all kinds, shoes and other leather products, some types of textiles, wood products, and other commodities were made on a wide scale throughout the country for predominantly local markets. The number of persons engaged in these occupations, either full time or in the off-season after the harvest, is not accurately known, but one

---

59 Rashin, *op. cit.*, pp. 23, 47, and 154.
60 *Ibid.*, p. 169.
61 Mavor, *op. cit.*, p. 386.

estimate—which may be much too high—is that seven or eight million such *kustar* workers were active about 1900.[62]

In the years after 1861 the workers in large-scale manufacturing came primarily from the peasant population. Large numbers of them shuttled annually between city and country, working in the fields at times of peak labor-need and in the cities at other seasons. But the trend in the last two decades before World War I was strongly in the direction of the formation of an urban proletariat permanently settled in the cities and towns near their places of employment. In studies made before 1917 only about 20 per cent of factory workers investigated were found to have land and to carry on agricultural production with the help of members of their families.[63] Nevertheless, it is also clear that family and other ties connected a very large proportion of industrial workers with the peasant villages, so that when the need came during the years 1917–20 many urbanites were easily able to leave the cities and return to familiar areas in the countryside.

The conditions of worker employment and daily life in the last decades of the Czarist regime were usually poor. Hours of work were long. Before 1897 men, women, and children often labored 12 or more hours daily, though later the 10-hour day became common. Wages were low and permitted workers to enjoy little more than a subsistence livelihood. Housing was markedly inadequate, with great overcrowding the rule rather than the exception. Proper medical facilities and adequate safeguards against industrial accidents were all too often lacking. The conditions of the Russian proletariat in these years, in short, were not unlike those of the corresponding group in England during the first half of the nineteenth century.[64]

Occasionally, progressive employers provided better conditions, but these were not typical. The government from time to time sought to improve matters by legislation. As early as 1866 an act required employers to provide a minimal amount of free hospital

---

[62] L. C. A. Knowles, *Economic Development in the Nineteenth Century*, p. 182. London: Routledge, 1947. Lyashchenko, *op. cit.*, pp. 98–102, argues that such small-scale household production declined considerably in the later years of the Czarist period as large-scale manufacturing conquered ever wider markets with cheap machine-made products.

[63] Rashin, *op. cit.*, p. 417.

[64] Mavor, *op. cit.*, pp. 389–409.

and medical care. A decree of 1862 prohibited the work of children under 12 and limited the hours of work for adolescents. Night work in textile factories by persons under 17 years of age was forbidden in 1885, and a year later another law required that wages be paid at least once a month, while banning payment in kind. In 1897 a decree limited factory work to 11½ hours in the daytime and to 10 hours at night, while prohibiting work on Sundays and holidays. Beginning in 1882 a system of periodic factory inspection was set up to enforce these laws, and it achieved some important results, particularly in reducing the number of child workers. Legislatively, the Czarist state was one of the pioneers in providing protection for workers. Inadequate enforcement, however, vitiated the actual benefits resulting from these laws, and after 1897 some of the most "extreme" protective legislation was nullified by repeal or amendment under pressure from employers.[65]

The prevailing poor working and living conditions created much resentment among those affected, but the legal expression of this discontent through the formation of unions was forbidden for a long time. Before 1900, however, bitterly contested strikes had taken place, and trade unions had been repressed through arrests and other coercion. Worker discontent expressed itself fiercely during 1903–5 in many strikes, some of which, in 1905, were general strikes and carried the threat of leading to revolutionary overthrow of the regime.[66] Despite both concessions and periodic repression during 1905–14, the union movement and consciousness of solidarity among workers grew stronger, as did the influence of the Social Democratic Party, whose aim was the end of Czarism and the establishment of socialism. In each of the years 1912, 1913, and 1914, there were well over 2,000 strikes. The annual number of strikers approximated 1,000,000, or over 20 per cent of the number of workers estimated above as engaged in manufacturing, mining, railway transport, and construction. Most ominous for the Czarist state was the fact that a large number of these strikes—two thirds of them, in 1914—had political as well as economic objectives.[67]

On the eve of World War I the tensions and strains in Russia's social and economic organization were obviously great. The stage was set for the world-shaking events that were to follow.

[65] Ibid., pp. 408–12. Manya Gordon, Workers Before and After Lenin, pp. 18–24. New York: Dutton, 1941.

[66] Mavor, op. cit., pp. 443–571.

[67] Lyashchenko, op. cit., p. 405.

CHAPTER III

THE IDEOLOGICAL BACKGROUND

T HE SOVIET UNION has been led from its inception by men who have proclaimed their belief that they were wiping out a hateful order of society and building a new civilization in which all men could enjoy abundance and security without oppression or injustice. This combination of condemnation for the old ways of human organization with their many defects and of assurance that a new and better world can be built is the essence of the dynamic ideology of communism today, giving it an appeal that has won it millions of adherents in all countries. This ideology has been one of the important elements whose interaction has produced the contemporary Soviet economy.

The communist ideology, usually called Marxism or Marxism-Leninism, after its principal formulators, is by no means the first doctrine men have composed to expose the iniquities of existing society and to show the way to a better future. The philosophers of Ancient Greece, the Biblical prophets, Thomas More and the long line of Utopian Socialists who succeeded him—all these and others attacked the injustices of their times, and many of them drew more or less detailed outlines of a future society. In contemporary times, however, it is Marxism that has won the greatest following among all revolutionary and reform movements and that inspired the Bolsheviks, who set up the Soviet regime.

The body of doctrine that we call Marxism is the composite work of two men, Karl Marx (1818–83) and Friedrich Engels (1820–95). Marx was born in Trier, Germany, the son of a far-from-proletarian Jewish lawyer who converted himself and his family to Christianity when his famous son was but six years old. After an early career as a student, journalist, and revolutionary organizer in Germany, France, and Belgium, Karl Marx settled in London, where he spent long years in research, writing his epoch-making works and exerting an important influence upon the developing socialist and union movements of the nineteenth century. Engels was also a member of the bourgeoisie, the scion of a wealthy textile-manufacturing family, who ran cotton mills in England for much of his life. He earned the income to support not only himself, but also Marx and his family, making possible the latter's long years of financial unremunerative research in the British Museum. But Engels' contribution to Marxism also included important additions to its doctrine.

The most influential single statement of socialist doctrine ever written, *The Communist Manifesto,* was the joint product of Marx and Engels in 1848. Within brief compass it contains the core of the ideas that they propagandized throughout their lives and developed in much longer works. The monumental structure of Marxian economic doctrine is most fully elaborated in the three-volume work, *Capital,* by Marx, the first volume of which appeared in 1867. The second volume, in 1893, and the third, in 1894, were published posthumously under Engels' editorship. Engels' most important work is generally conceded to be his *Anti-Dühring,* or more fully, *Herr Eugen Dühring's Revolution in Science,* first issued in 1878. Here, in the process of demolishing an intellectual opponent's comprehensive system of thought, Engels elaborated what has now become canonical Marxism on many topics that were relatively slighted in Marx's own writings. Both men wrote a large number of other books as well, and carried on a voluminous correspondence; their collected works fill many volumes. The two wrote so much, indeed, that different varieties of socialists have found support for many variants of the basic ideology in passages scattered through their works, a fact that reflects also the changes in their views over the almost half century of their active, adult years.

At the risk of some injustice to its abundant and complex content, Marxism may be divided into four interrelated branches: a general philosophy of all phenomena; a theory of human history; a critique of capitalism; and a vague forecast of the future development of human society into its ultimate perfection. We shall treat the first three of these briefly and center our attention on the fourth, since official Soviet ideology maintains that the Soviet Union is in process of realizing the ideal future foreseen by Marx.

Dialectical Materialism

Marxian philosophy centers about the concept of *dialectical materialism.* The dialectics portion of this concept was borrowed from the German philosopher Hegel. It conceives of the world and all phenomena in it as in constant process of change and motion according to a certain tripartite pattern. As Engels says, "Dialectics is nothing more than the science of the general laws of motion and development of Nature, human society, and thought." [1] The dialectical pattern was defined by Hegel as consisting of thesis, antithesis, and synthesis of the original thesis and its antithesis. Engels illustrates the pattern by reference to elementary mathematics. If we take a quantity a as our thesis, its antithesis is $-a$. The synthesis, or negation of the negation as he calls it, is obtained, he claims, by multiplying $-a$ by itself to get a^2, which he terms "The original positive magnitude, but at a higher degree. . . ." [2] Just why the negation of the negation should be obtained by such multiplication— and not, for example, by dividing $-a$ by itself or subtracting $-a$ from itself, and so on—is not explained.

The materialism aspect of dialectical materialism was used by Marx and Engels to differentiate their philosophic system from the idealistic dialectics of Hegel. According to Marx:

> My dialectical method is not only different from the Hegelian, but is its direct opposite. To Hegel the life-process of the human brain, i.e., the process of thinking, which, under the name of "The Idea," he even transforms into an independent subject, is demiurgos of the real world, and the real world is only the external, phenomenal form of "The Idea." With me, on the contrary, the ideal is nothing else than the material world reflected in the human mind and translated into forms of thought. [3]

According to Engels, ". . . materialism conceives nature as the sole reality," and believes that "Nature exists independently of all philosophy. . . . Nothing exists outside nature and man, and the

---

[1] Friedrich Engels, *Herr Eugen Dühring's Revolution in Science,* p. 155. New York: International Publishers, 1939.

[2] *Ibid.,* p. 150.

[3] Karl Marx, *Capital,* Vol. I, p. 25. Chicago: Kerr, 1906.

higher beings our religious fantasies have created are only the
fantastic reflection of our own essence." [4]

Dialectical materialism, therefore, would seem to be the doctrine
that the world of our senses is "the sole reality," and that all things
in it are in constant development and change in the dialectical
pattern of thesis, antithesis, and synthesis. In the Soviet Union
today this philosophic view is the only correct one, with important
repercussions upon the views scientists are permitted to hold regarding even the subject matter they study. Elsewhere, where men
have the right to reach independent conclusions, dialectical materialism has some supporters, including even a few noted scientists,
but is rejected by what is probably the large majority of philosophers and scientists.

Historical materialism is the name usually given to the Marxian
theory of history, which applies dialectical materialism to uncover
what are claimed to be the laws of development of human society.
Engels gave this definition:

> The materialistic concept of history starts from the proposition that
> the production of the means to support human life and, next to pro-
> duction, the exchange of things produced, is the basis of all social
> structure; that in every society that has appeared in history, the
> manner in which wealth is distributed and society divided into
> classes or orders is dependent upon what is produced, how it is pro-
> duced, and how the products are exchanged. From this point of
> view the final causes of all social changes and political revolutions are
> to be sought, not in men's brains, not in man's better insight into
> eternal truth and justice, but in changes in the modes of production
> and exchange. They are to be sought, not in the *philosophy*, but in
> the *economics* of each particular epoch. [Engels' italics.] [5]

In much of the later discussion it has been assumed that the
Marxian theory was one of pure economic determinism, that is,
embodying an insistence that all human phenomena are directly
caused by economic factors. A notable clarification, therefore, is
one made by Engels in a letter written in the last years of his life:

> According to the materialist conception of history the determining
> element in history is *ultimately* the production and reproduction in

---

[4] Friedrich Engels, *Ludwig Feuerbach*, p. 28. New York: International Publishers, 1935.

[5] Friedrich Engels, *Socialism Utopian and Scientific*, p. 54. New York: International Publishers, 1935.

real life. More than this neither Marx nor I have ever asserted. If therefore somebody twists this into the statement that the economic element is the *only* determining one, he transforms it into a meaningless, abstract, and absurd phrase. . . . We make our own history, but in the first place under very definite presuppositions and conditions. Among these the economic ones are finally decisive. But the political, etc. ones, and indeed even the traditions which haunt human minds, also play a part, though not the decisive one.[6]

The historical mechanism through which the material conditions of life result in dialectical change of human organization is the class struggle, the conflict between the exploiters and the exploited in every society. This is how *The Communist Manifesto* states the matter:

> The history of all hitherto existing society is the history of class struggles. Freeman and slave, patrician and plebian, lord and serf, guild master and journeyman, in a word, oppressor and oppressed, stood in constant opposition to one another, carried on uninterrupted, now hidden, now open fight, a fight that each time ended, either in a revolutionary constitution of society at large or in the common ruin of the contending classes. . . . The modern bourgeois society that has sprouted from the ruins of feudal society has not done away with class antagonism. It has established new classes, new conditions of oppression, new forms of struggle in place of the old ones. Our epoch, the epoch of the bourgeoisie, possesses, however, this distinctive feature; it has simplified the class antagonisms. Society as a whole is more and more splitting up into two great hostile camps, into two great classes directly facing each other: Bourgeoisie and Proletariat.

Capitalism, *The Communist Manifesto* argues, served the world well for a time, having "created more massive and more colossal productive forces than have all preceding generations together." Admiringly, Marx and Engels ask, ". . . what earlier century had even a presentiment that such productive forces slumbered in the lap of social labor?" But true to the dialectical process, capitalism in its triumph had forged the weapons for its own destruction and formed the men who would "wield those weapons—the modern working class—the proletarians." Marx and Engels conclude this section of the *Manifesto* with the brave words "What the bourgeoisie therefore produces above all, are its own grave diggers. Its fall and the victory of the proletariat are equally inevitable."

---

[6] *Marx-Engels Selected Correspondence*, p. 475. New York: International Publishers, 1935.

It was the conviction of Marx and Engels that they had for the first time uncovered the laws of historical development and could predict, therefore, the inevitable future development. This conviction led them to call their socialism "scientific" in contrast to the "utopian socialism" of others. Ultimately, however, their own system was based on an alleged insight into "eternal truth" of a sort not qualitatively different from the alleged insight of others whom they ridiculed. And as prophets their record is not too impressive. They looked to the proletariat of Western Europe to lead the way to socialism, but it was in overwhelmingly agrarian and peasant Russia that their followers first seized state control. In more recent times it has been in the farming districts of China that the communist movement gained the strength that finally enabled it to capture the great cities in which the bulk of the Chinese proletariat lives. They wrote in 1848 as though capitalism had exhausted its capacities for growth and progress, and the revolution were near at hand. The Bolshevik revolution did not come until seventy years later, and the achievements of capitalism in raising standards of living in the century after 1848 make the achievements the *Manifesto* praised so seem modest indeed. Few scholars would deny that the materialist conception of history helped increase our insight into the importance of the economic forces among the *entire complex of forces* that have shaped man's destiny. But the subsequent record would hardly seem to justify the grandiose claims for this doctrine advanced by Marx and Engels, and later by their followers to this day.

Marxian Economic Theory

Marx's critique of capitalism is contained in the elaborate economic theory worked out in the three volumes of *Capital*. His conclusion that labor was exploited and must eventually act to end capitalism had been stated long before this work was written, in *The Communist Manifesto* and other writings. In *Capital* he attempted to supply the missing proof for his conclusions. In this major work, therefore, he worked out what he regarded as a complete deductive theory of the nature and internal operations of the capitalist economy. He supported his theoretical propositions by reference to the abundant literature available in the mid-nineteenth century on the abuses suffered by workers during the early stages of the English industrial revolution. For his starting point, he took the labor theory of value as propounded by David Ricardo and earlier English economists, but elaborated this theory along quite different lines, lines more suitable to the revolutionary views he held at the initiation of his studies.

The main points of Marx's economic theory may be summarized briefly: The exchange value of a commodity, that is, how much a given amount of cloth, say, will be exchanged for in terms of other commodities, is determined by the amount of socially necessary labor required for its production. The qualification "socially necessary" is added because obviously a commodity that is made inefficiently is not more valuable than the same commodity made with the most modern technique. Marx recognizes that different grades of labor are employed in production, but says that, by applying suitable coefficients, the value of each superior grade of labor relative to common unskilled labor may be obtained; consequently he claims that his argument need only be carried out in terms of the latter type of labor.[7]

Having established this proposition to his satisfaction, Marx argues that the typical feature of capitalistic economic activity is the use of money to buy commodities that are in turn sold for a larger amount of money; or, in Marx's notation, the process is $M\text{-}C\text{-}M'$, where M' is the larger sum at the end. Marx asks where this excess of M' over M comes from.[8] After arguing at length that all the usual explanations for this phenomenon are false, he presents his own solution: The businessman is able to buy a special commodity, *labor power,* or a worker's capacity to work, which, when consumed (that is, employed), produces more value than is paid for it . Labor power, in other words, is a worker's ability to work, and this is what the employer pays wages for. The worker in working produces commodities that obtain value because his labor—that is, work already done, something Marx distinguishes sharply from labor power—is embodied in them. The businessman gains, or makes *surplus value* in Marx's terminology, because the value of the product turned out by the worker and obtained when goods are sold is greater than the value of the labor power the employer has paid for in wages. The value of labor power, Marx says, "is the

[7] Marx, *Capital,* Vol. I, pp. 41–48, 51–52.
[8] *Ibid.,* p. 173.

value of the necessaries required to produce, develop, maintain, and perpetuate" that labor power.[9] By the last requirement, Marx allows also for the cost of raising children to replace the worker later. The secret of surplus value, therefore, is that the capitalist for whom a worker labors, say, ten hours, pays him a value equal only to what he produces in, say, five hours, retaining the production of the remaining five hours for himself as surplus value. Obviously such a theory is finely contrived to "prove" the necessity and inevitability of exploitation of worker by employer.

It is in surplus value that Marx sees the origin of all capital. In his view the thirst for additional surplus value is the driving motivation of capitalism. To increase surplus value employers may lengthen the work day or they may increase the efficiency of their workers so that the latter can produce the value of their wages in a shorter amount of time, leaving a larger residue of surplus value to be pocketed by the employer.[10]

Marx and Engels discerned that the simple theory as outlined above produced conclusions that varied from the facts of real life. All other things being equal, it would appear from the above, industries using relatively large amounts of labor and relatively small amounts of machinery and other capital should make more surplus value or profit than industries using relatively small amounts of labor and relatively large amounts of machinery and other capital. Yet it is a well-known fact that businessmen always seek to invest their money where the most profit is to be made. At any one time the tendency is for all industries to make roughly equal rates of profit, rather than markedly unequal rates according as they use relatively much or relatively little labor power. To get around this difficulty, Marx, in volume III of *Capital*, abandoned the notion that commodities actually exchange in proportion to the amount of labor contained in them, and substituted, without proof, the following proposition: "the sum of all the prices of production of all commodities in society, comprising the totality of all lines of production, is equal to the sum of all the values." [11] This in effect abandons all effort to explain the actual market exchange rates in terms of labor, since it implicitly recognizes that commodities sell for more or less

---

[9] Karl Marx, *Value, Price and Profit*, p. 40. New York: International Publishers, 1935.
[10] Marx, *Capital*, Vol. I, pp. 342–45.
[11] *Ibid.*, Vol. III, p. 188. By "price of production," Marx means the actual cost price plus the average rate of profit prevailing.

than their value, as Marx defined it. Consequently it destroys much of the justification for the theory of surplus value as the sole explanation of the internal workings of capitalism.

On the basis of this theoretical foundation, Marx reaches a number of important and interesting conclusions:

1. *The Doctrine of Increasing Misery of the Working Classes.* One version of this doctrine offered by Marx follows:

> All methods of the production of surplus value are at the same time methods of accumulation; and every extension of accumulation becomes again a means for the development of these methods. It follows therefore that in proportion as capital accumulates, the lot of the laborer, be his payment high or low, must grow worse. . . . Accumulation of wealth at one pole is, therefore, at the same time accumulation of misery, agony of toil, slavery, ignorance, brutality, mental degradation, at the opposite pole.[12]

The increase of real wages, educational opportunity, and length of life, together with the decrease in hours worked in industry during the long period since Marx wrote, hardly seems to confirm this pessimistic forecast. One recent study, for example, estimates that the average real earnings of nonfarm workers in the United States approximately doubled between 1890–94 and 1945–46, and that even in the none-too-prosperous period of 1935–39 average real earnings were 15 per cent above those in 1890–94. They were almost 25 per cent above the base period in 1925–29.[13]

2. *The Doctrine of the Industrial Reserve Army.* As the use of machinery and other fixed capital rises, the amount of total capital increases, but the proportion used to pay wages decreases. Hence the number of workers available for employment increases more rapidly than the opportunities for employment. Thus arises the industrial reserve army of unemployed, whose representatives at every factory gate, vainly seeking employment, always help the capitalists keep wages down to the subsistence level. As Marx says:

> The industrial reserve army, during the periods of stagnation and average prosperity, weighs down the active labor army; during the periods of over-production and paroxysm, it holds its pretensions in check. Relative surplus-population is therefore the pivot upon which the law of demand and supply of labor works.[14]

---

[12] *Ibid.,* Vol. I, p. 708.

[13] Stanley Lebergott, "Earnings of Non-Farm Employees in the U.S., 1890–1946," *Journal of the American Statistical Association,* March 1948, p. 75.

[14] Marx, *Capital,* Vol. I, p. 701.

If Marx's statement is interpreted simply as a prediction that capitalism is often characterized by the presence of a significant number of unemployed persons, he has often been correct, though the United States and other countries have had substantial full employment at various periods in their history. It is quite true, however, that the problem of assuring full or nearly full employment is still one of capitalism's major dilemmas. What Marx did not foresee here, and elsewhere in his writings, was the rise of strong mass unions and the institution of various types of unemployment insurance, which have tended often to insulate wage rates from the decreases that would otherwise have been brought about by increased unemployment and keener competition for jobs.

3. *The Law of the Falling Rate of Profit.* Marx argued that the tendency under conditions of increasing capitalist accumulation was for the rate of profit to fall, except as counteracted by various factors. This argument arose from his view that the ratio of the amount of surplus value (which, according to him, can arise only from labor), or profit, to the total amount of capital also fell. The decline could be counteracted, however, by increasing the intensity of exploitation, by getting cheaper raw materials from abroad, by depressing wages below the real value of labor power, and by other measures.[15]

4. *Marx's Theory of Crises.* Marx regarded the crisis or depression as an inevitable feature of capitalist development, and one that would help cause its eventual collapse. His explanation for this phenomenon, however, is somewhat ambiguous, containing different strands, so that even his followers are not sure which one, among the different factors he discussed, he considered most important.[16] At least two important ideas, however, seem basic in his thinking. First, there is the notion that crises are the result of the falling rate of profit and that the events during the depression phase of the business cycle lay the groundwork for future revival by making possible later increases in the rate of profit.[17] Quite another view is given in this passage from *Capital:*

> The last cause of all real crises always remains the poverty and re-
> stricted consumption of the masses as compared to the tendency of
> capitalist production to develop the productive forces in such a way

15 *Ibid.*, Vol. III, ch. XIII.
16 Paul M. Sweezy, *The Theory of Capitalist Development*, pp. 147–48. New York: Oxford University Press, 1942.
17 See the quotation cited in Sweezy, *op. cit.*, pp. 152–53.

that only the absolute power of consumption of the entire society would be their limit.

Here the emphasis is upon the inadequate purchasing power of the exploited masses as compared with the boundless productivity of capitalist production. But despite the lack of an integrated, clear theory of crises in Marx's work, it should be recognized that he was one of the first to emphasize many elements in the explanation of business cycles, particularly their depression phases, which have been later developed by other writers, both Marxists and non-Marxists.

We may summarize Marx's views as follows: The essential feature of capitalism is the extortion of surplus value by employers from their workers. The accumulation of surplus value permits the increase of the productive powers of society through the building of more factories, more machinery, and so on. But in turn this accumulation tends to create an ineradicable and often increasing army of unemployed whose pressure on wage rates contributes to the increasing misery of the masses. Moreover, the very accumulation of capital tends to work against the capitalists by forcing the rate of profit to go down, or by requiring ever greater exertion to prevent such decline. Further, the very pace and nature of capitalist development prevents it from being an even process, bringing on frequent depressions in which the lot of the masses becomes worse and the value of much previously accumulated capital vanishes. As this process continues over time, society is more and more divided into two classes, a small group of incredibly wealthy capitalists and the remainder of the population, which has been forced into the proletariat. At the end the great mass of the population will dispossess their exploiters and take over the reins of economic control and political power themselves, in order to do away with the misery caused by the inexorable functioning of capitalism. Here, certainly, is a comprehensive indictment of the existing order, calculated to hasten its doom. The propaganda effectiveness of this theory is best indicated by the millions of converts it has won, despite the fact that many of its forecasts have been proved wrong over time.

The Future Society

When we turn to the writing of Marx and Engels for information regarding the nature of the society they expected would inevitably supplant capitalism, we find relatively little, compared to the huge volume of material denouncing capitalism. Perhaps as a reaction against the extremely detailed descriptions of future ideal societies given by Fourier and other utopians, Marx and Engels give in general only vague indications of the kind of human organization they so vehemently argued had to come. Almost all these indications are contained in a few passages of *The Communist Manifesto* and in a letter written by Marx in 1875 to a German socialist, commenting on the proposed program of the German Worker's Party at that time. In all their voluminous writings, there is apparently not even a single independent pamphlet, by either Marx or Engels, treating at all systematically the questions that were to become all-important when their supporters gained power.

In order to comprehend the specific details given, however, we must first remember that Marxist theory views the state in capitalist society as merely the organization by which the bourgeoisie oppress the workers. In the words of *The Communist Manifesto,* "The executive of the modern State is but a committee for managing the common affairs of the whole bourgeoisie," and "Political power, properly so called, is merely the organized power of one class for oppressing the other." The *Manifesto* made clear the communists' objective of overthrowing "bourgeois supremacy," that is, the existing state, and achieving "conquest of political power by the proletariat." In 1875 Marx wrote:

> Between capitalist and communist society lies the period of the revolutionary transformation of the one into the other. There corresponds to this also a political transition period in which the state can be nothing but *the revolutionary dictatorship of the proletariat.* [Marx's italics.] [18]

As early as 1852, Marx had used the phrase "dictatorship of the proletariat" in a letter, and had added, "this dictatorship itself only constitutes the transition to the *abolition of all classes and to a classless society.*" (Marx's italics.) [19]

A somewhat different view of the transformation is given by Engels:

> The proletariat seizes the state power, and transforms the means of production in the first instance into the state power. But in doing

---

[18] Karl Marx, *Critique of the Gotha Programme,* p. 18. New York: International Publishers, 1938.

[19] *Marx-Engels Selected Correspondence,* p. 57.

this, it puts an end to itself as the proletariat, it puts an end to all class differences and class antagonisms, it puts an end also to the state as the state. . . . As soon as there is no longer any class of society to be held in subjection . . . there is nothing more to be repressed which would make a special repressive force, a state necessary. The first act in which the state really comes forward as the representative of society as a whole—the taking possession of the means of production in the name of the society—is at the same time its last independent act as a state. The interference of the state power in social relations becomes superfluous in one sphere after another, and then ceases of itself. The government of persons is replaced by the administration of things and the direction of the processes of production. The state is not "abolished," *it withers away.* [Engels' italics.] [20]

It seems likely from the above quotations, one of which does not even mention the dictatorship of the proletariat in describing the transition, that Marx and Engels thought of this transitional period as relatively short and perhaps were even somewhat naive in their thinking regarding the difficulties of this transitional period. The state and the alleged dictatorship of the proletariat have continued to exist in the Soviet Union for more than thirty years now, with no end in sight. Stalin, speaking in 1939, made this extremely significant comment on the quotation from Engels above:

. . . Engels' general formula about the destiny of the socialist state in general cannot be extended to the partial and specific case of the victory of socialism in one country only, a country which is surrounded by a capitalist world, is subject to the menace of foreign military attack . . . consequently, must have its own state, strong enough to defend the conquests of socialism from foreign attack.

We have no right to expect of the classical Marxist writers, separated as they were from our day by a period of forty-five or fifty-five years, that they should have foreseen each and every zigzag of history in the distant future in every separate country. It would be ridiculous to expect that the classical Marxist writers should have elaborated for our benefit ready-made solutions for each and every theoretical problem that might arise in any particular country fifty or one hundred years afterwards, so that we . . . might calmly doze at the fireside and munch ready-made solutions. . . . we now have an entirely new, socialist state without precedent in history and differing considerably in form and functions from the socialist state of the first phase.

But development cannot stop there. We are going ahead, towards communism. Will our state remain in the period of communism also?

[20] Engels, *Herr Eugen Dühring's Revolution in Science,* pp. 306–7.

Yes, it will, unless the capitalist encirclement is liquidated, and unless the danger of foreign military attack has disappeared. Naturally, of course, the forms of our state will again change in conformity with the change in the situation at home and abroad.

No, it will not remain and will atrophy if the capitalist encirclement is liquidated and a socialist encirclement takes its place.[21]

The Communist Manifesto gives the following program for the transformation of society once the proletariat has won power:

The proletariat will use its political supremacy to wrest, by degrees, all capital from the bourgeoisie, to centralize all instruments of production in the hands of the state,—that is, of the proletariat organized as a ruling class; and to increase the total productive forces as rapidly as possible. Of course, in the beginning, this cannot be effected except by means of despotic inroads on the rights of property, and on the conditions of bourgeois production; by means of measures, therefore, which appear economically insufficient and untenable, but which in the course of movement outstrip themselves, necessitate further inroads upon the old social order, and are unavoidable as a means of revolutionizing the mode of production.

These measures will of course be different in different countries. Nevertheless in the most advanced countries the following will be pretty generally applicable:

1. Abolition of property in land and application of all rents of land to public purposes.
2. A heavy progressive or graduated income tax.
3. Abolition of all right of inheritance.
4. Confiscation of property of all emigrants and rebels.
5. Centralization of credit in the hands of the state, by means of a national bank with state capital and exclusive monopoly.
6. Centralization of the means of communication and transport in the hands of the state.
7. Extension of factories and instruments of production owned by the state; the bringing into cultivation of waste lands, and the improvement of the soil generally in accordance with a common plan.
8. Equal liability of all to labor. Establishment of industrial armies, especially for agriculture.
9. Combination of agriculture with manufacturing industries; gradual abolition of the distinction between town and country

---

[21] J. Stalin, "Report on the Work of the Central Committee to the Eighteenth Congress of the C.P.S.U. (B)," *The Land of Socialism Today and Tomorrow*, pp. 47–51. Moscow: Foreign Languages Publishing House, 1939.

by a more equable distribution of the population over the country.

10. Free education for all children in public schools. Abolition of children's factory labor in its present form. Combination of education with industrial production and so forth.

It is interesting to note, however, that much of the program has been peacefully realized in nonsocialist countries. Free public education and a heavily progressive income tax are commonplace in the United States and Western Europe. The right of inheritance in the upper brackets has been sharply limited by high inheritance taxes. Most advanced nations have a central bank that exercises a high degree of control over their credit structure; and many governments own all or much of their communication and transportation systems. Government ownership of factories is now common—even in this country the state owns important arms-manufacturing plants, as well as the multibillion dollar atomic energy industry—as is government support of measures to improve and expand agriculture. The progress of transportation and the spread of radios, telephones, and mail-order catalogues have done much to lessen the difference between town and country. There seems to be no evidence in the *Manifesto* that its authors felt that their objectives could be gained without fundamental and revolutionary changes, although this has actually happened in large part. In a preface to the 1872 edition of the *Manifesto*, however, Marx and Engels indicated that they would have altered this prescription if they had been writing it for the first time then.

Marx's anticipations with regard to the economics of the future society were stated in the 1875 letter mentioned above. Here he pointed out that even when capitalism is overthrown workers will not receive directly the value of all they produce. From the "total social product," he argues, must be deducted: (1) an allowance for replacement of means of production used up in current output; (2) amounts set aside to permit expansion of production, that is, an increase in capital; (3) allowances for insurance or reserves for protection against poor harvests, natural catastrophes, and the like; (4) an allowance for the general costs of administration; (5) an allowance for those unable to work. The first three deductions Marx calls "an economic necessity"; presumably they must be provided in any economic system. Only that which is left over from the total social product, he points out, is available for distribution among the workers, and this he terms the "diminished proceeds" of the community's work.[22] Since Marx defined surplus value as the difference between what the worker produces, in value terms, and what he is paid, it is apparent from the above that Marx envisaged the continued existence of such a difference or surplus value even after capitalism had been overthrown.

How are these "diminished proceeds" to be distributed among the workers when they are the masters? Marx's answer is this:

> . . . the individual producer receives back from society—after the deductions have been made—exactly what he gives to it. What he has given to it is his individual amount of labor. For example, the social working day consists of the sum of the individual labor hours; the individual labor time of the individual producer is the part of the social labor day contributed by him, his share in it. He receives a certificate from society that he has furnished such and such an amount of labor (after deducting his labor for the common fund), and with this certificate he draws from the social stock of means of consumption as much as the same amount of labor costs. The same amount of labor which he has given to society in one form, he receives back in another.[23]

But Marx makes clear that the system of distribution outlined above is not that for the eventual ideal society; it is only that which is to prevail in the transition period. For, he points out, the rewards of different workers under this system would be unequal, since individuals differ in talents and abilities to contribute to production. Moreover, the needs of different workers vary, since one may be single and another married, with ten children to support; yet these varying needs are not taken into account in the above distribution system. He regards these features as "defects" that "are inevitable in the first phase of communist society as it is when it has just emerged after prolonged birth pangs from capitalist society." The ultimate distribution system and the prerequisites for its attainment he describes in this key paragraph:

> In a higher phase of communist society, after the enslaving subordination of individuals under division of labor, and therewith also the antithesis between mental and physical labor, has vanished; after labor, from a mere means of life, has itself become the prime neces-

---

[22] Marx, *Critique of the Gotha Programme*, pp. 6–8.
[23] *Ibid.*, p. 8.

sity of life; after the productive forces have also increased with the all-round development of the individual and all the springs of cooperative weatlh flow more abundantly—only then can the narrow horizon of bourgeois rights be fully left behind and society inscribe on its banners: from each according to his ability, to each according to his needs! [24]

What is perhaps most noteworthy about this quotation is the stringency of the prerequisites set up for the final attainment of the "higher phase of communist society." The division of labor and the differences between mental and physical work must be done away with; people must come to have an attitude that requires them to work voluntarily rather than because they have to earn a living; and social production must be so enormously productive that all needs can be satisfied — the word "needs" being left undefined, thus raising all sorts of questions as to whether the worker's needs in such a society would be determined by him or would be more in the nature of some arbitrary subsistence, or more than subsistence, standard set by society. Certainly there seems to be enough vagueness in this prescription to justify almost indefinite postponement of its attainment after capitalism has been overthrown, as in the Soviet Union. It leaves unanswered the basic question of whether such changes in human nature are ever attainable at all, merely assuming that they will occur. Here again Marx shows himself to have been far more influenced by the despised "utopians" than one would judge from his and Engels' diatribes against them.

Some additional clues regarding the system of distribution of the future are given by Engels when he argues that the higher wage paid for "compound labor" — the work of persons with special education — in bourgeois society arises from the fact that such training has to be paid for by these workers or their families and is therefore part of the cost of labor power met by wages. But, Engels writes, "In a socialistically organized society, these costs are borne by society, and to it therefore belongs also the fruits, the greater values produced by skilled labor. The laborer himself has no claim to extra payment." [25] Marx, we saw above, recognized that in the first stage of the postcapitalist world individuals with different natural endowments would be paid differently, and Engels here

---

[24] *Ibid.*, p. 10.
[25] Engels, *Herr Eugen Dühring's Revolution in Science*, p. 222.

argues that so far as differences are the results of training or education, they should not be paid for differentially.

Marx's sneering reference above to "the enslaving subordination
of individuals under division of labor" seems clarified by further
material in Engels' writings:

> . . . distribution, in so far as it is governed by purely economic con-
> siderations, is regulated by the interests of production, and produc-
> tion is most encouraged by a mode of distribution which allows *all*
> members of society to develop, maintain and exert their capacities
> in all possible directions. It is true that, to the mode of thought of
> the educated classes which Herr Dühring has inherited, it must seem
> monstrous that in time to come there will no longer be any profes-
> sional porters or architects, and that the man who for half an hour
> gives instructions as an architect will also push a barrow for a period,
> until his activity as an architect is once again required. It is a fine
> sort of socialism which perpetuates the professional porter! [26]

As we shall see from the discussion later, important modifications
have already been made in the original picture of future communism
as envisaged by Marx and Engels. During their lifetimes, Lenin
and Stalin did not hesitate to alter the shape of Soviet life away
from the Marxist blueprint where that was necessary to retain power.
Judging by the tone and content of the statements of Stalin's
successors, particularly Malenkov, during the first year after Stalin's
death, it seems likely that they also do not regard themselves as
prisoners of Marxist Utopian dogma, and are ready to depart from
the dogma as is necessary to make Soviet society function.

Marxism Penetrates Russia

How did Marxism, a doctrine elaborated in Western Europe and
Great Britain and based upon the experiences of relatively industrialized countries, penetrate into and win a following in overwhelmingly rural and despotic Czarist Russia? The main initial
channel seems to have been through Russian students and exiles in
Western Europe, particularly in Switzerland, who were in contact
with the rising socialist movement there and became acquainted
with Marxian doctrine. These expatriates translated Marx's writings
into Russian so as to make them available for readers in the Czar's

[26] *Ibid.,* p. 221.

domain. They spread the doctrine personally when they returned home, forming, at first, discussion and education groups and, later, after they had gathered strength, the Social-Democratic Party.

The spread of Marxist ideas in Russia started slowly at first but then picked up in intensity. Mikhail Bakunin published a Russian translation of *The Communist Manifesto* in the early 1860's, and in 1872 the first Russian translation of *Capital* appeared. George Plekhanov published the first systematic exposition of Marxist ideas in Russian in two books, which appeared in 1883 and 1884; and by 1894 Peter Struve's book on Marxism had been passed by the Russian censor, the first volume in support of Marxian doctrines to be legally published. As early as 1887, one writer maintains, the Russian translation of *Capital* was the book most widely read by Russian students.[27]

During the 1880's and 1890's the Russian Marxists, both in and out of the country, busied themselves with propaganda aimed at spreading the master's ideas. They formed study groups for intellectuals and workers, spread literature, and engaged in polemics with those who held opposed political and economic views. In the 1890's, after the police had permitted publications supporting Marxism, books and journals appeared to popularize the doctrine, and groups of Marxists began to function effectively in various cities throughout the country. The increasingly rapid industrialization of Russia in these years provided ever more fertile soil for their propaganda, as the number of factories and workers increased and made the relevance of Marx's concern with the proletariat more obviously apparent. As the number of Marxists increased, divisions of opinion appeared among them. Some, the so-called "Economists," emphasized the importance of fighting for the improvement of workers' conditions. Plekhanov's "Emancipation of Labor" group emphasized primarily that the working class must be organized to take over political power, rather than merely to struggle for short-term gains in its working conditions. A third group, headed by Lenin, wished to create an organization to overthrow Czarism, based on a conspiratorial nucleus or "general staff" directed in highly centralized fashion and providing leadership for the workers as they became more restive. But all trends of Marxist thinking united at

---

27 Maynard, *Russia in Flux*, pp. 118–28. Mavor, *An Economic History of Russia*, Vol. II, p. 153.

Minsk in March 1898 to form the "Russian Social Democratic Working Men's Party."[28]

It was on the subject of party discipline that the Social-Democratic Party split into two groups, Mensheviks and Bolsheviks, at its second Congress in 1903. Lenin won control of the party and backing for his view that what was required was, in the words of Maynard, "a disciplined order of devoted adherents more nearly resembling the Society of Jesus than any of the lax aggregations of political sympathisers to which we are accustomed to apply the name of political party."[29]

In this way was formed the Bolshevik group, which seized power in November 1917 and laid the groundwork for the USSR of today. Since Lenin provided its leadership both before and for the first few years after the revolution, it is his doctrines that we shall examine now to gain some insight into the preconceptions of those who formed the Soviet regime.

Lenin and Leninism

Vladimir Ilyich Ulyanov (1870–1924) — better known to history as Lenin — spent most of his life as a professional revolutonary and revolutionary leader, though born the son of a minor Czarist school official in Simbirsk (now Ulyanovsk), on the Volga River. Along with Karl Marx, he is credited by the Soviet Union with being the co-founder of the Marxism-Leninism that is the official ideology. Though Lenin wrote no one major work such as *Capital,* the total volume of his writing is tremendous, ranging from brief newspaper articles and polemical tracts to scholarly studies of economic and philosophic subjects based on intensive research.

Lenin built his doctrines on the foundations laid down by Marx and Engels, applying the notions of Marxism to the analysis of the international political and economic situation of his time, and also emphasizing certain aspects of Marxism that had tended to be obscured in the development of the Social-Democratic movement after Marx's death. Stalin's well-known definition of Leninism emphasizes some key points:

> Leninism is Marxism of the era of imperialism and of the proletarian revolution. To be more exact, Leninism is the theory and tactics of

---

[28] Mavor, *op. cit.,* pp. 143–61. Bertram D. Wolfe, *Three Who Made a Revolution,* pp. 99–117. New York: Dial Press, 1948.

[29] Maynard, *op. cit.,* pp. 128–29.

the proletarian revolution in general, the theory and tactics of the dictatorship of the proletariat in particular.[30]

We shall consider here briefly Lenin's contribution to the critique of capitalism and his views on the nature of the postrevolutionary workers' state as he expressed them before the Bolshevik Revolution. The development of his views on the socialist state as he encountered the practical problems of heading the Soviet Union after attaining power will be considered in later chapters.

Lenin's view — as expressed in his pamphlet *Imperialism* — is that by about 1900 the capitalism of Europe and America had entered a new stage, that of imperialism or monopoly capitalism, which had replaced the relatively free competition of about 1860–70. Production had become highly concentrated in a relatively small number of enterprises having great quantities of capital. A financial oligarchy controlled the complex structure of production through its hold over the banks, which kept the purse strings and determined the distribution of capital and credit, granting them to some producers and denying them to others. Concrete bank control of industry is exercised through corporation directors, who represent the financial oligarchy. In this stage of finance capital there is pronounced separation between the *rentier,* who provides capital and lives off the unearned income, and the *entrepreneurs* who actually use and manage this capital.

Because of the uneven development of capitalist countries, he argues, imperialism is marked by the great export of capital from highly developed countries, where rates of profit are relatively low, to backward countries, where profits are high because land, wages, and raw materials are cheap. The export of commodities is greatly facilitated by these capital exports, since loan agreements often stipulate that money may be spent only in the country where capital has been obtained. In this period world markets are characteristically divided into spheres of exclusive influence by the huge corporations of the advanced powers. By the time Lenin wrote, in the early twentieth century, he believed that the partition of the world between the major advanced capitalist nations had been completed, and that in the future only repartition could take place, as the result of armed struggles inspired by each capitalist power's desire for a larger share of the world to dominate. Under this view imperialism

---

[30] Joseph Stalin, *Problems of Leninism,* p. 2. Moscow: Foreign Languages Publishing House, 1940.

is therefore necessarily the era of imperialist wars between the nations that are exploiting the rest of the world.

One result of this situation, Lenin argued, was the existence of an upper stratum of workers who had been corrupted by being allowed to share in the profits of the *rentier* class and in those arising from exploitation of backward nations. It is this bribed group of workers who give rise to social reform movements that seek to divert the energies of the working class from the revolutionary over-throw of capitalism.[31]

Lenin emphasized the necessity of a violent revolution, to be followed by a dictatorship of the proletariat, a new state succeeding the smashed capitalist state and existing for the purpose of putting down the former oppressors. He argued most vigorously against those who drew the conclusion from Engels' words about the withering away of the state that the dictatorship of the proletariat would exist for only a short time, writing:

> . . . we have a right to speak solely of the inevitable withering away of the state, emphasizing the protracted nature of this process and its dependence upon the rapidity of development of the *higher phase* of Communism; leaving quite open the question of lengths of time, or the concrete forms of withering away, since material for the solution of such questions is *not available*. [Lenin's italics.] [32]

Lenin lays great stress upon Marx's teachings in the *Critique of the Gotha Programme* in formulating his own statement of the shape of the postrevolutionary society, particularly Marx's distinction between the first and the higher phases of communism. The state will only disappear, he maintains, in the higher phase, when the prerequisites set down by Marx, such as the transformation of work into a first necessity of life, and so on, have been realized. Lenin notes that ". . . the great Socialists in foreseeing its [the higher phase's — H.S.] arrival, presupposed both a productivity of labor unlike the present and a person not like the present man in the street, capable . . . of demanding the impossible." But until the far-off time comes:

> . . . the Socialists demand the *strictest* control, *by society and by the state*, of the quantity of labor and the quantity of consumption; only

---

[31] V. I. Lenin, *Imperialism, the Highest Stage of Capitalism*, pp. 105–7. New York: International Publishers, 1939.

[32] V. I. Lenin, *State and Revolution*, p. 79. New York: International Publishers, 1932.

this control must *start* with the expropriation of the capitalists, with the control of the workers over the capitalists, and must be carried out, not by a state of bureaucrats, but by a state of *armed workers.* [Lenin's italics.] [33]

Here was foreshadowed the actual severe control of labor and income distribution — and therefore of consumption — that has taken place in the USSR.

Lenin's ideas on the internal organization of the economy of a victorious socialist state are of particular interest, both for later comparison with what has actually been done and because they were publicly expressed in a pamphlet finished in August 1917, almost on the very eve of his seizure of power. Because of their importance we shall present Lenin's views, in his own words, at some length:

. . . capitalism, as it develops, itself creates prerequisites for "every one" *to be able* really to take part in the administration of the state. Among such prerequisites are: universal literacy, already realized in most of the advanced capitalist countries, then the "training and disciplining" of millions of workers by the huge, complex, and socialized apparatus of the post-office, the railways, the big factories, large scale commerce, banking, etc., etc.

With such *economic* prerequisites it is perfectly possible, immediately, within twenty-four hours after the overthrow of the capitalists and bureaucrats, to replace them, in the control of production and distribution, in the business of *control* of labor and products by the armed workers, by the whole people in arms. (The question of control and accounting must not be confused with the question of the scientifically educated staff of engineers, agronomists, and so on. These gentlemen work today, obeying the capitalists; they will work even better tomorrow, obeying the armed workers.)

Accounting and control—these are the *chief* things necessary for the organizing and correct functioning of the *first phase* of Communist society. *All* citizens are here transformed into hired employees of the state, which is made up of the armed workers. *All* citizens become employees and workers of *one* national state "syndicate." All that is required is that they should work equally, should regularly do their share of work, and should receive equal pay. The accounting and the control necessary for this have been *simplified* by capitalism to the utmost, till they have become the extraordinarily simple operations of watching, recording, and issuing receipts, within the reach of anybody who can read and write and knows the first four rules

[33] *Ibid.,* p. 80.

of arithmetic. The whole of society will have become one office and one factory, with equal work and equal pay.

But this "factory" discipline, which the proletariat will extend to the whole of society after the defeat of the capitalists and the overthrow of the exploiters, is by no means our ideal, or our final aim. It is but a *foothold* necessary for the radical cleansing of society of all the hideousness and foulness of capitalist exploitation, *in order to advance further.*

*   *   *

For when *all* have learned to manage, and independently are actually managing by themselves social production, keeping accounts, controlling the idlers, the gentlefolk, the swindlers and similar "guardians of capitalist traditions," then the escape from this national accounting and control will inevitably become so increasingly difficult, such a rare exception, and will probably be accompanied by such swift and severe punishment (for the armed workers are men of practical life, not sentimental intellectuals, and they will scarcely allow any one to trifle with them), that very soon the *necessity* of observing the simple, fundamental rules of every-day social life in common will have become a *habit.*

The door will then be wide open for the transition from the first phase of Communist society to its higher phase, and along with it to the complete withering away of the state. [All italics by Lenin.] [34]

Lenin's anticipations on this subject seem so clearly expressed above that little comment is necessary, except to point out that he grossly underestimated the actual difficulties he and his comrades were to face when they seized power, shortly after these words were written. True, those difficulties were greatly aggravated by the civil war and the foreign intervention that followed the November revolution. These were perhaps extraneous factors, though the civil war at least might have been anticipated. But even without these military factors, taking control and operating even a relatively simple economy, such as that of Russia in 1917, is a far more complex job than Lenin's reference to "the first four rules of arithmetic" suggests. This lesson had to be learned the hard way, in practice, but has been well learned, as we shall see below.

Lenin's mention of equal pay for all is a puzzling point, since at first sight it seems to contradict Marx's assertion that in the first phase of communism individuals with unequal natural endowments would be compensated unequally. But elsewhere in the same

---

[34] *Ibid.,* pp. 83–85.

pamphlet Lenin remarks on the socialist principle, "for an equal quantity of labor, an equal quantity of products." [35] Consequently, what he may have had in mind was equal pay for the same unit of labor, defined in some fashion, which would not preclude unequal earnings among individuals, because some can work longer, that is, earn more units of labor, or work more intensively, than others, as Marx noted in his original formulation of this thesis.

Stalin's Contributions

More a man of action than a theoretician, Joseph Stalin made contributions to communist ideology which were not usually the result of academic deliberation but rather his response to the different problems facing the Soviet regime during the period of his dictatorial rule from the mid-1920's to the time of his death in 1953. As indicated above in the discussion of the proposition of the withering away of the state under communism, Stalin did not hesitate to depart from and to revise the doctrines of his predecessors when he deemed such action necessary or expedient. In a very real sense, Stalin's major contribution to communist ideology was incorporated in the organization and doctrinal orthodoxy of the Soviet state as it developed during his rule. This organization and this doctrine are key factors of the Soviet economy which is the subject of this volume.

Though Stalin's particular contributions to communist ideology are discussed as pertinent in the latter chapters of this study, it seems desirable to summarize here the one work he prepared which came nearest of all his writings to being a general exposition of his views in the field of economics. Titled "Economic Problems of Socialism," this work was written at various times in 1952 and touches on a wide variety of questions of domestic and foreign policy. It consists of four parts. The first contains his comments on the discussions of Soviet economists regarding the draft of a comprehensive textbook on the Soviet economy. The other three parts are his answers to three letters from Soviet economists raising questions with respect to points made in the first part. Published at the beginning of October 1952, this work became the leading topic of discussion and, in a sense, the chief document of the 19th

---

[35] *Ibid.*, p. 78.

Communist Party Congress which opened in Moscow shortly thereafter.[36] After Stalin's death, five months later, his successors soon
indicated that they felt no more obliged to abide by Stalin's dogma
in all particulars than Stalin had felt bound by the works of his
predecessors. Nevertheless this work must be regarded as one of the
basic communist writings in the field of economics.

We may summarize Stalin's views as a series of propositions regarding the main points he discusses. His own discussion is not
systematic, so that the order of the points made below is not always
the same as that in which these matters occur in the original. It
should be borne in mind, too, that Stalin probably intended this
work partly to serve Soviet propaganda goals — as in his statements
of the "basic laws" of capitalism and socialism. In addition, as the
dictator of the Soviet Union, he felt no need to establish his propositions by adequate rational argument supported by objective evidence. His main propositions follow:

1. Economic laws, like laws of nature, are "reflections of objective
processes taking place independently of people's will." These laws
may be discovered, recognized, studied, taken into account, and
used in the interests of society, but they cannot be changed or
negated. Most economic laws, if not all, "operate for a definite
historic period, after which they give way to new laws." Soviet
economic plans are not economic laws, as many Soviet economists
had argued, since these plans are merely attempts to apply what
Stalin calls the "objective economic law of planned, proportional development of the national economy" under socialism. Stalin gives
no precise statement of this last "law" but he uses this insistence on
the "objective" nature of economic law to warn his associates against
imagining that they "can do anything," that is against setting goals
beyond the actual ability of the Soviet economy.

2. The main feature of the basic economic law of contemporary
capitalism, Stalin argues without even the pretense of proof, is
"roughly as follows: to secure the maximum capitalist profit through
the exploitation, ruin and impoverishment of the majority of the

---

[36] This was originally published in *Bolshevik*, No. 18, September 1952, and
then reprinted widely in the Soviet press, particularly in *Pravda*, October 3 and
4, 1952. A good English translation is given in *The Current Digest of the Soviet
Press*, October 18, 1952, as a separate pamphlet. The same translation is reprinted in Leo Gruliow, ed., *Current Soviet Policies*, pp. 1–20. New York:
Praeger, 1953.

population of a given country, through the enslavement and system-atic robbing of the people of other nations, especially backward nations, and finally through the militarization of national economy, [all means] which are used to guarantee the highest profit." This is sheer propaganda, as is the next point.

3. The main feature of the basic law of socialism is "approxi-mately as follows: to assure maximum satisfaction of the constantly growing material and cultural requirements of all society through steady growth and improvement of socialist production employing the most advanced technology." The actual history of the Soviet economy, as we shall see below, is far from proof that this idyllic picture of Soviet economics is true, but suggests a rather different set of objectives as ruling.

4. At least three basic conditions must be attained in order to prepare the transition to ideal communism: (a) the over-all growth of production, particularly the growth of production of capital goods (means of production); (b) the conversion of collective farm property into state property and the elimination of commodity turnover — that is, the purchase and sale of goods for money in the market — in favor of direct exchange of goods (changes which must be made gradually so that ultimately "the central power or some other social-economic center might direct the output of all social production in the interests of society"); (c) the attainment of such a high cultural level of development that each citizen can get enough education to make a free choice of occupation and not be forced to stay in one type of work all his life. Subordinate to this is the necessity to re-duce the work day to six and then five hours, greatly to improve housing conditions, and to raise real wages at least 100 per cent.

5. The most important economic consequence of World War II was the disintegration of the single world market, and its replace-ment by two parallel world markets, one consisting of communist-ruled states, the other of non-communist states. This has greatly intensified the crisis of world capitalism because of the loss of great markets such as the Soviet Union and China.

6. Wars among capitalist nations, because of rivalries among them, are still inevitable. Stalin hints here that such wars among capitalist nations are more likely than war between the communist and non-communist nations, and he denies that the capitalist na-tions have learned from past history to avoid destructive wars

among themselves. Here he seems to be giving implicit instructions that the policy of seeking to set non-communist nations against each other, primarily by taking account of their economic rivalries, must be a basic communist tactic in the effort for world domination. That the goal of eliminating capitalism remains fixed, he indicates somewhat circuitously, but clearly, by saying, "In order to eliminate the inevitability of wars imperialism must be destroyed."

There are many other subordinate points made in this last major theoretical pronouncement of Stalin. These will be considered when appropriate later in this volume.

Since Stalin's death, his successors — particularly Premier Georgi M. Malenkov — have made important changes in Soviet economic practice and to a lesser extent in professed doctrine. But these are more in the nature of tactical moves, it would seem, than basic expressions of doctrinal change. Most of the leaders who succeeded Stalin were, of course, before his death, in his immediate entourage, and contented themselves with quoting him and praising his wisdom, being too wise themselves to attempt any doctrinal innovations which might rouse his wrath against them.

CHAPTER IV

SOVIET ECONOMIC DEVELOPMENT

THE PURPOSE of this chapter is to present a bird's-eye view of the development of the leading features of the Soviet economy, from the Bolshevik revolution to the middle of the Fifth Five-Year Plan period in 1954, a time span of thirty-seven years. In this summary treatment, the emphasis will be upon the most important events and the most enduring trends.

Our concern here is with the chain of events and policies that transformed the Soviet economy from the chaos and weakness of November 1917 to its present situation, in which its strength is second only to that of the United States. Much of this history is the account of the destruction of the capitalistic institutions and property relations of old Russia as they had developed during the fifty-six years following 1861. The other side of the story is that of the introduction of new institutions and new relationships, and of the ways in which new forms of economic organization were tested and modified over more than thirty years of Soviet rule.

It will be helpful to begin by pointing out the chief features of the Soviet economy as of 1954. First, we may note the economic predominance of the state, which owns all land and other natural resources and owns and operates virtually all industry and means of communication and transport; all banks and other financial institutions; most urban retail and wholesale distribution facilities, housing, and municipal utilities; and a relatively small but significant portion of all farms, as well as the postal system, military installations, and other facilities that are customarily in state possession even in capitalist countries.

Second, the only owners or operators, other than the state, of significant amounts of means of production are cooperatives, organizations that are completely under the state's domination, with little freedom of action. Such cooperatives are most important in agriculture, where in the form of collective farms they help produce most Soviet farm output on land belonging to the state. Industrial producers' cooperatives, including cooperatives of invalids, exist in towns and cities throughout the country. They are significant mainly as producers of consumer goods or suppliers of miscellaneous services. Cooperative consumers' organizations dominate wholesale and retail trade in the countryside. State property and cooperative property are legally considered merely different forms of socialist property.

Third, purely private property consists in the main of personal possessions such as clothing and household utensils. Private ownership of means of production is limited to such implements, instruments, and livestock as are needed by an independent craftsman or by a peasant working a small plot of land with his own and his family's labor. Many small homes are owned by their occupants. The right to transmit personal possessions (including savings) through inheritance is recognized.

Fourth, virtually all economic activity of the country is coordinated through the government plan, which sets future production objectives for all major commodities and directs the growth of the economy with a view of attaining the objectives set up.

Fifth, all able-bodied citizens of the USSR are required to work, in accordance with the principle "He who does not work, neither shall he eat." In practice this seems to be interpreted to mean that no one may live solely on the basis of unearned income, such as interest on government bonds. But a wife may be supported by her husband. The Soviet Union today is legally regarded as being a socialist society operating in accordance with the slogan "From each according to his ability, to each according to his work." An individual must work for himself alone, for a cooperative organization, or for the state. The employment of workers for the private profit of another individual is forbidden.[1]

What is this Soviet state that exercises such all-embracing economic power, far exceeding that of the Czarist regime in, say,

---

[1] The economic features of the Soviet state are laid down in articles 4–12 of the Soviet constitution.

1914, or of any single capitalist or group of capitalists before the Bolshevik revolution? The Soviet constitution declares that the USSR "is a socialist state of workers and peasants," and that "all power in the USSR belongs to the working people of town and country as represented by the Soviets of Working People's Deputies." (Articles 1 and 3.)

Nominally, according to the constitution, "the highest organ of state power in the USSR is the Supreme Soviet of the USSR." (Article 30.) This legislature consists of two chambers, the Soviet of the Union and the Soviet of the Nationalities, members of which are elected by popular vote. (Articles 33 and 34.) The Supreme Soviet performs certain functions of a legislative body in the brief periods when it is in session, and elects a Presidium of 33 members that acts for it between sessions, that is, most of the time. (Articles 48 and 49.) Executive and administrative power is in the hands of the Council of Ministers, composed primarily of the heads of the various government ministries, which "issues decisions and orders on the basis and in pursuance of the laws in operation, and verifies their execution." (Articles 64 and 66.) This is the organizational structure of the national government of the USSR. Each of the sixteen constituent republics, such as the Ukraine, has a similar organization. (Articles 57–63.)

The sixteen Soviet republics are the Russian Soviet Federated Socialist Republic (RSFSR), the Ukrainian Soviet Socialist Republic (Ukrainian SSR), the Belorussian SSR, the Uzbek SSR, the Kazakh SSR, the Georgian SSR, the Azerbaidzhan SSR, the Lithuanian SSR, the Moldavian SSR, the Latvian SSR, the Kirgiz SSR, the Tadzhik SSR, the Armenian SSR, the Turkmen SSR, the Estonian SSR, and the Karelo-Finnish SSR.

To get at the real locus of Soviet power, however, we must look at Article 126, which states that "the most active and politically conscious citizens in the ranks of the working class and other sections of the working people unite in the Communist Party of the Soviet Union, which is the vanguard of the working people in their struggle to strengthen and develop the socialist system and is the leading core of all organizations of the working people, both public and state."

In practice the Soviet state is a dictatorship of the Communist Party, which in turn is completely dominated by the Presidium of its Central Committee, headed by Premier Malenkov. The basic

decisions of Soviet policy are made by the Presidum and then put
into effect by government action. Important economic decrees are
often promulgated jointly by the Council of Ministers and the
Central Committee of the Communist Party,[2] but sometimes the
most important ones are first promulgated solely by the Central
Committee.[3] There is internal democracy neither in the Soviet
state nor in the ruling Communist Party.

This rule of the state by the Communist Party is made possible
in large part by the fact that the most important state offices are
usually reserved exclusively for party members, throughout all levels
of the complex governmental hierarchy. Government and other
officials who are not party members hold their posts at the sufferance
of the Communist Party and may be removed whenever the appropriate party group so decides. Moreover, party groups and members
have extraordinary powers to intervene in state matters, directing
or criticizing the work of governmental or economic organizations
as may be required. Stalin described this party direction in these
terms:

> The Party verifies the work of the organs of government and the
> organs of authority, correcting unavoidable mistakes and shortcom-
> ings, helping them develop the decisions of the government and
> trying to guarantee them support of the masses; and *not a single
> important decision is taken by them without corresponding directions
> of the Party.*[4] [My emphasis—H.S.]

Recalcitrance, protest, or revolt against the party's decisions in
economic or political matters is punished according to the severity
of the offense, punishments ranging from mere reprimands to imprisonment in forced-labor camps for long periods and, at times,
in the past, even death. As in all dictatorships, it is the coercive
power of the regular police, secret police, and armed forces that
assures the ultimate execution of the party's commands.[5]

---

[2] For example, the three-year plan for livestock development; *Pravda*, April
19, 1949.

[3] This was the case with respect to the comprehensive program for expanding
agricultural production in the post-Stalin era; *Izvestia*, September 13, 1953.

[4] Quoted in Andrei Y. Vyshinsky, *The Law of the Soviet State*, p. 160. New
York: Macmillan, 1948. Cf. also Julian Towster, *Political Power in the USSR
1917–1947*, pp. 119–20. New York: Oxford University Press, 1948.

[5] Abundant evidence on the use of such coercion will be found in J. Gliksman,
Tell the West. New York: Gresham, 1948; *The Dark Side of the Moon*. New
York: Scribner's, 1947; and Victor Kravchenko, *I Chose Freedom*. New York:
Scribner's, 1946.

The Problem of Motivation

Against the background we have sketched earlier, the most obvious motivation for the economic policies of the Soviet regime has been the desire to remold the old Russia into the new pattern called for by Marx and Lenin. *The Communist Manifesto* of 1848 had called for the abolition of private landownership; nationalization of credit, transport, and communications; extension of state-owned factories; and equal liability of all to labor. Marx had pointed out that for the final stage of communism to be reached, the "productive forces" must be increased so that "the springs of cooperative wealth flow more abundantly," thus pointing the way to a policy of intensive development of agricultural and industrial output. Other hints for policy were available elsewhere in the classics of Marxism-Leninism.

But these ideological imperatives alone are inadequate to explain the pattern of development, and what is more, at times the suggestions made in Marxist literature have even been ignored: *The Communist Manifesto*, for example, calls for "abolition of all right of inheritance," but inheritance exists in the USSR today. The true importance of the prerevolutionary blueprints is that they provided the leaders of the Soviet state primarily with objectives; on the vital questions of tactics, forms of organization, and rate of development they gave little or no guidance. Lenin and his successor, Stalin, were therefore ideologically free to choose among their many options on a wide range of questions.

For more adequate insight into the motivations of Soviet policymakers, we must turn to the problem that has been their basic preoccupation since they took power: the problem of insuring the continued existence of the Soviet state and therefore of their own rule. Lenin was able to seize power and retain it during the first critical months because he adopted the un-Marxist slogan "All Land to the Peasants!" and actively supported the "Black Partition" that raged in the countryside as the peasantry took over the lands of the nobles and wealthier farmers.[6] But what the peasantry had given it could take away. Throughout the 1920's the Soviet government struggled with the problem of enabling a proletarian-oriented regime to retain power in a primarily agrarian, small-peasant nation. Aside

---

[6] Alexander Baykov, *The Development of the Soviet Economic System*, pp. 16–18. New York: Macmillan, 1947.

from the potential threat of the peasants, the Soviet regime has been constantly haunted by the fear that it would be overthrown by force of arms. Shortly after its birth, it had to struggle for survival against the armies of Czarist sympathizers and the military intervention of foreign powers, including England, Japan, and the United States. After the new state had won its right to exist by military victories, its leaders continued to believe that they were surrounded by a hostile capitalist world that would sooner or later attempt to crush them. To obtain the means to resist such invasion successfully, they built up Russia's economic strength at frantic speed and high cost. Thus they obtained the resources that — together with American Lend-Lease aid and other outside help — enabled the USSR to absorb the first Nazi onslaughts in World War II and later to push on from Stalingrad to Berlin. From 1928 on this economic preparation for war was a leading element in Soviet policy making, and it has been evident in the strained international atmosphere since World War II.

The Soviet fears that they might be defeated by foreign military intervention were clearly expressed by Stalin in 1931, addressing a group of business executives:

> To slacken the tempo would mean falling behind. And those who fall behind get beaten. But we do not want to be beaten. No, we refuse to be beaten! One feature of the history of old Russia was the continual beatings she suffered for falling behind, for her backwardness. She was beaten by the Mongol Khans. She was beaten by the Turkish beys. She was beaten by the Swedish feudal lords. She was beaten by Polish and Lithuanian gentry. She was beaten by the British and French capitalists. She was beaten by the Japanese barons. All beat her—for her backwardness: for military backwardness, for cultural backwardness, for political backwardness, for industrial backwardness, for agricultural backwardness. She was beaten because to do so was profitable and could be done with impunity. . . . In ten years at most we must make good the distance we are lagging behind the advanced capitalist nations.[7]

The problem of historical motivation is always complex, and the specific case of the Soviet Union considered here is no exception. The desire to strengthen the economic base of Soviet military strength has played a role throughout the history of the USSR, but the specific force of this factor has varied from time to time

---

[7] Stalin, *Problems of Leninism*, p. 365.

in accordance with changes in the international situation. Soviet policymakers have also realized that internal discontent was a factor to be reckoned with, one that could be at least partially alleviated by raising the standard of living. The emphasis upon consumer-goods industries has therefore shifted from time to time, depending upon both the internal and the external situation. The sense of rivalry with capitalist powers abroad has also played a significant role, as Soviet leaders have sought to equal and surpass the economic power of Germany, Great Britain, and the United States. In short many elements have a part in the motivation of Soviet economic policy, but the preservation and expansion of communist power has been the dominant theme.

When ideology and the need for survival clashed, it was the former that gave way throughout this era. We have noted before Stalin's remarks that the state could not "wither away," despite Engels' prediction, because the Soviet Union faced the threat of war. In 1921 Lenin gave way before peasant opposition and instituted the New Economic Policy, whose concessions insured a period of relative domestic tranquillity, though at the cost of temporarily strengthening capitalist elements in the countryside and city. And even the concern for the proletariat, so central a feature of Marxist ideology, did not deter Soviet leaders from holding down their people's standard of living while concentrating resources in capital investment and the increase of military-economic strength.

The Spread of State Control

At the very outset of Bolshevik rule, Lenin does not seem to have intended any immediate widespread nationalization of the economy. The existing disorganization of normal life and production was already great. His preoccupation was to insure the smoothest operation possible, under the circumstances, of remaining industrial and transport facilities. Moreover the Bolsheviks knew that they lacked technically trained people to replace the old managers and directors of the economy, despite Lenin's earlier brave words about the simplicity of modern control and accounting. Dobb has described the policy contemplated as "a controlled or directed Capitalism, steered by such measures of economic control as had come to be the common stock-in-trade of belligerent governments." [8]

But the Bolsheviks had rather natural suspicions about the extent to which they could trust the owners and managers of industry, whose sympathies were likely to be with the old regime. On November 14, 1917, a decree was published providing for Worker Control, or, more accurately, participation, in the direction of industry. Factory committees were given the right to supervise management, to determine minimum production levels, and to have access to all correspondence and accounts, but the right of proprietors to give orders was explicitly upheld. In this way the Soviet government sought to continue to use the knowledge and skill of production managers, while keeping them under the scrutiny of workers' groups, which, presumably, would seek to guard against sabotage.[9] On December 5, 1917, another decree was published setting up a Supreme Council of the National Economy, which had the function of providing centralized coordination for the economy. Direct nationalization was still regarded as a minor element of policy, for use in special cases only.

The current of events, however, pushed the government ever further along the path of nationalization. On December 27, 1917, for example, banking was made a state monopoly, and all existing banks and their assets were merged into the state bank. Lenin declared that he had wished to permit the private bankers to continue their activity, provided they cooperated with the regime, but that their hostility prevented this.[10] More ideological in its inspiration was the decree of February 19, 1918, nationalizing all land, since the practical impact of this order upon actual events in the countryside was slight. An earlier decree on the second day of the Soviet regime, November 8, 1917, had abolished land ownership by estate owners without compensation and had ordered all such land and the agricultural capital on it to be held in custody of local peasant committees. But before and after these decrees, the peasantry simply took over by force of numbers, taking the land and livestock of the estates and distributing them among the mem-

---

[8] Maurice Dobb, *Soviet Economic Development since 1917*, p. 83. London: Routledge and Kegan Paul, 1948.

[9] *Ibid.;* Baykov, *op. cit.*, p. 5.

[10] Arthur Z. Arnold, *Banks, Credit, and Money in Soviet Russia*, pp. 58–61. New York: Columbia University Press, 1937.

bers of the peasant communities.[11] With regard to foreign trade, a system of import and export permits was first introduced, but on April 22, 1918, a government monopoly of foreign trade was instituted.[12] In domestic trade, it was first intended to permit private merchants, checked by workers' control committees, to co-exist alongside a state monopoly of trade covering only the important goods. Such monopolies — covering successively farm machinery, textiles, food, matches, candles, and so on — were set up in late 1917 and early 1918, as goods shortages created more and more distribution difficulties. On November 21, 1918, finally, nationalization of all trade was decreed.[13] Most of the country's railroad lines, it may be noted, had been built by the state or nationalized under the Czarist regime and were therefore automatically taken over upon the Bolshevik assumption of power.[14]

In industry the policy was initially to nationalize only particular large firms, either because of their importance or because of sabotage by owners who refused to continue production or work under the system of workers' control. By June 1918, some 521 large factories had been taken over by the state, most of them by order of local authorities in various areas rather than by order of the central government. During this period the situation became ever more anarchic, as increasing shortages of materials, transport disorganization, and currency chaos made their effects felt on production. In addition strong syndicalist tendencies became evident at many factories, where workers acted under the impression that under the new regime they could take over the factories and operate them as they saw fit for their own benefit. The functioning of such privately owned enterprises was becoming increasingly impossible, and the resulting production decline harmed and endangered the new state. The result was the decree of June 28, 1918, nationalizing all large-scale industries. After it had became evident that the operation of the nationalized plants depended on the functioning of small enterprises, these latter were also nationalized by a decree of December 29, 1920. Direction — and weak direction it was at first —

---

11 Baykov, *op. cit.*, pp. 16–18.
12 Alexander Baykov, *Soviet Foreign Trade*, p. 8. Princeton: Princeton University Press, 1946.
13 Baykov, *The Development of the Soviet Economic System*, pp. 24–25.
14 Margaret S. Miller, *The Economic Development of Russia, 1905–1914*, p. 208. London: King, 1926.

of these new state industries was entrusted to the Supreme Economic Council, which was thus transformed from a coordinating and planning group into an operating agency with greatly expanded functions and personnel.[15]

This period of attempted direct state control and operation of the entire nonagricultural economy, usually termed the era of War Communism, lasted from 1918 to 1921. Market relationships virtually ended. Food was requisitioned forcibly from the peasants, often with little or no payment of any kind. Connections between different segments of the state-operated economy were maintained by means of orders and allocations. Inflation mounted steadily throughout the period, while production fell precipitously. Money lost much of its significance, both for exchange and economic calculation. Administration was inept and haphazard, as the untrained and inexperienced personnel of the Supreme Economic Council sought to operate the economy on the basis of inadequate and often faulty information. Yet somehow enough was produced to supply the Red Army with essentials and to keep the economy behind the lines functioning, though at minimal levels. But the shortages of food and consumer goods, the arbitrary and often brutal requisitioning techniques, and the confused economic administration had their inevitable effect: peasant dissatisfaction mounted, breaking out even in armed rebellion. In the cities industrial discipline declined, while absenteeism, strikes, and even anti-Soviet sentiment rose. The Kronstadt naval rebellion against Bolshevik rule in early 1921 showed the temper of the people and the peril to the Soviet regime.[16]

To save the Soviet regime the New Economic Policy (NEP) was initiated. It sought to appease the peasantry and to revive the economy by permitting the legal activity of private entrepreneurs in specific fields. Instead of the former ruthless requisitioning—often amounting simply to confiscation—of peasant grain, a new tax was introduced: one that required farmers to surrender only part of their produce to the state, leaving them free to sell the remainder on the open market for any price they could get. The tax rate was fixed so as to obtain for the state only about half the amount formerly requisitioned, being calculated on the basis of the amount needed to feed the Red Army and workers in the vital government enter-

---

[15] Baykov, *op. cit.*, pp. 4–7; Dobb, *op. cit.*, pp. 82–96.
[16] Dobb, *op. cit.*, pp., 112–24.

prises. Private trade was once again permitted, and a new class of retail merchants sprang up immediately in all areas of the economy, quickly dominating retail distribution and playing a very important role as wholesalers. Illegal private trade had existed during War Communism, when thousands of "bagmen" trudged between city and country, bartering food for consumer goods and playing a significant role in what limited exchange of goods took place. During 1922–23, about 75 per cent of the retail trade volume of the Soviet Union was accounted for by private merchants; state and cooperative stores did only about 15 and 10 per cent of the business, respectively.[17] In industry, too, the state relinquished some of its former primacy, keeping the largest and most important factories and branches of industry, but leasing many smaller plants to cooperatives and private operators and restoring others to their original owners. Foreign concessionaires were allowed to take over some enterprises. A few others were given over to companies based on both state and private capital investment. A study published in 1923 found that only 8.5 per cent of all industrial enterprises in the USSR belonged to the government; but these employed over 84 per cent of all industrial workers, indicating clearly the small and often minuscule size of cooperative and privately run enterprises.[18]

Thus was instituted a "mixed economy," in which the state held firmly to the "commanding heights" through its continued control of the government, large industry, the credit and banking machinery, transport, and all foreign trade, as well as part of the domestic trade network. In agriculture, on the other hand, the pattern consisted overwhelmingly of millions of small farms operated on anything but socialistic principles. In the cities private enterprise flourished in retail and wholesale trade, and in small-scale manufacturing units, many of them consisting of no more than an artisan and his assistant. Even financial exchanges were organized in Moscow and several other cities to provide a market for buying and selling government bonds and foreign currencies.[19] Trade, of course, meant the reinstitution of markets for all commodities and an end to the old system of moneyless transactions between

---

[17] Baykov, *The Development of the Soviet Economic System*, p. 65.
[18] *Ibid.*, pp. 106–7.
[19] Lancelot Lawton, *An Economic History of Soviet Russia*, Vol. I, p. 197. London: Macmillan, 1932.

state organizations, which were later completely reorganized. Industry remaining in government hands was divided into 486 trusts, each with the legal status of an independent economic entity operated for profit and free to buy from and sell to all customers, including other state organizations and private businessmen.[20] Lenin termed this new economic system "state capitalism," but said that it was a state capitalism that had never before been envisaged because it existed in a state ruled by the proletariat. He recognized that there were dangers implicit in this new economic organization, because of the potential strengthening of hostile capitalist elements within Russia. But he felt confident that it was "capitalism which we shall know how to restrict and to which we shall be able to set limits." [21]

Lenin's confidence proved to be justified. Within a decade private trading and industrial production based on the use of hired labor had been virtually wiped out. Against the traders who had proliferated so quickly after the NEP was announced the government proceeded on two fronts. It made the need for such private enterprise ever less pressing by encouraging and achieving a tremendous expansion in the state and cooperative wholesale and distribution networks, rapidly increasing the number of buying and selling points of these organizations and augmenting their personnel as required. Conversely, it discouraged private traders by imposing high taxes on their profits, sharply restricting the commodities they could buy from state enterprises, and making it difficult or impossible for them to move their goods over the state-owned railroads.[22] The results were soon apparent. From about 75 per cent in 1922–23, the share of private traders in retail volume fell to 22.5 per cent in 1928, 5.6 per cent in 1930, and became negligible thereafter.[23] In 1932 private trading by merchants was forbidden. A provision of the Criminal Code adopted that year provided prison terms of five years or more for those guilty of "speculation," that is, buying or reselling goods for private profit.

Private industry—confined largely to small-scale handicraft production, except for a few large concession enterprises operated by

---

[20] *Ibid.*, pp. 193–94.
[21] Quoted in Baykov, *op. cit.*, p. 50.
[22] L. E. Hubbard, *Soviet Trade and Distribution*, pp. 19–23. London: Macmillan, 1938.
[23] *Sotsialisticheskoye Stroitelstvo SSSR*, p. 607. Moscow: 1936. Hereafter cited as *Sot. Stroi.*

foreign investors—succumbed similarly within a decade after the beginning of NEP tolerance. Denied raw materials and credit, discriminated against in use of transport facilities, taxed far more heavily than their state-supported competitors, these small independent producers rapidly gave up at the end of the 1920's. In 1925–26 they accounted for 19.9 per cent of all industrial production; by 1930, only 5.6 per cent; and by 1932 an infinitesimal 0.5 per cent.[24] By 1931 the state and its subservient cooperatives were in complete control of all Soviet industry and trade and the NEP concessions had been ended.

In agriculture the transformation to complete state control was largely accomplished in the early 1930's, but strong resistance had to be overcome at heavy cost. There were almost 26,000,000 separate peasant farms in the Soviet Union in 1928.[25] To the Soviet leaders it was obvious that such an unwieldy mass of individual small producers was incompatible with the centrally directed, large-scale industrial economy they hoped to build. So long as the peasant remained his own master, the state would have to meet his terms if it wished to get the grain required to feed the city masses. To meet those terms, the state would have had to be in a position to deliver the abundant supply of consumer goods farmers wanted. This would have put serious brakes on the state's goals for capital investment and rapid heavy industrial expansion. Only by smashing the peasants' independence could the state regain its freedom of action.

The first few years of the NEP period, however, were years of appeasement. The Soviet leaders were trying to renew the *smychka* or collaboration between the proletariat and the peasantry—particularly the poor and middle peasantry—that had been so brutally destroyed by the grain confiscation policies of the preceding period. The shift to a grain tax and peasant freedom to sell surplus production, mentioned above, created a notable incentive for increased farm production. These moves once again linked the peasant's welfare to the volume of his output. As elsewhere private enterprise was given greater freedom, and peasants were permitted to lease land, farm machinery, and other items of production capital as well as to hire a limited number of workers per farm. Soon differentia-

---

[24] Baykov, *op. cit.*, pp. 124–25; *Sot. Stroi.*, p. xlii.
[25] Baykov, *op. cit.*, p. 135.

tion made itself evident among the peasantry, as the more enterprising and those with above-average capital took advantage of the new opportunities. In 1927 the Soviet government estimated that there were about 5,000,000 poor peasants, 14,300,000 middle peasants, and 896,000 labor-employing farmers. Few even of the upper group would have been regarded as anything but poor in the United States, but in a country where millions had to eke out a living on farms of 10 acres or less, the ownership of a few head of livestock or the capital adequate to permit hiring of machinery or labor were enough to classify a farmer as an affluent *kulak*.[26]

Before it had had a chance to become cemented, however, the alliance between workers and peasants that the Soviet regime sought to attain during the 1920's was almost wrecked, as a result of the famous "scissors crisis" of late 1922 and 1923—the sharp reversal of price relationships that took place at that time.

Both 1922 and 1923 were years of general inflationary price rises. Superimposed upon the general rise in prices during the first half of 1922 was a relative rise of agricultural prices and a relative decline in industrial prices. By May 1, 1922—when this gap was widest—the purchasing power of agricultural commodities in terms of industrial commodities was much greater than it had been in 1913. The "terms of trade" between city and country had shifted in favor of farmers, in part as a result of the frantic dumping of industrial goods on the market by industrial organizations desperate for working capital. After May 1922 industrial prices increased much more rapidly than did farm prices so that by August 1, 1922, the ratio of agricultural to industrial prices was virtually the same as in 1913. This reverse movement continued for another year, however, with the result that through most of 1923 industrial goods were far more expensive in terms of agricultural commodities than they had been in 1913. The "terms of trade" had shifted violently against the rural population. When these price changes are plotted on a graph, the shifting relationship between the two price curves suggests the blades of an open pair of scissors. This is the origin of the name by which this phenomenon is known.

The price disparity against agriculture in 1923 had serious consequences. Peasant demand for high-priced urban consumer goods

---

[26] *Ibid.*, pp. 135–38. There were also 2,560,000 very small farmers classified as belonging to the rural proletariat.

fell off sharply, producing serious gluts and overstocked warehouses in the cities; however, monopolistic price control by industrial trusts prevented prices from falling. The decline in peasant purchases carried along with it the threat of a decline of peasant sales of food and industrial raw materials, with consequent disastrous results for the urban population and industry dependent upon these supplies. The government might have solved the crisis by resorting once again to compulsory requisitioning and by abandoning a market economy, but this would have removed any hope of attaining the worker-peasant cooperation aimed for by government policy. Instead of using force, therefore, the government moved to lower industrial prices and raise agricultural prices. The ability of industry to hold goods off the market and raise prices monopolistically was attacked by reducing bank credits so as to force the goods-hoarders to unload. Maximum selling prices were set for some goods. On the other hand the government altered its grain purchase policy so as to raise prices paid farmers. The result was a substantial closing of the relative disparity between industrial and agricultural prices, as measured against their 1913 relationship. But the entire gap was never closed. Throughout the remainder of the 1920's, the peasantry enjoyed a less favorable position vis-a-vis industry than they had before the outbreak of World War I.[27]

Despite the vigorous measures that alleviated the 1923 "scissors crisis," the government experienced increasing difficulty during the middle and late 1920's in getting the agricultural supplies it required. Of central importance here was the fact that the percentage of the total grain supply sold shrank sharply in the 1920's, being only 13.3 per cent in 1926–27 as against 26 per cent before World War I. The key factor was that the poor and middle peasants, who produced 85.3 per cent of all Soviet grain in 1926, marketed only 11.2 per cent of their output. The *kulaks*, whose fields gave only 13 per cent of the harvest, sold 20 per cent of their grain; while the relatively unimportant state and collective farms, which produced only 1.7 per cent of all grain, marketed 47.2 per cent of their grain.[28] In 1927 and 1928 sharp difficulties again began to be encountered by the government in its efforts to secure adequate grain. Once more it had to resort to emergency measures such as confiscating

[27] Dobb, *op. cit.*, pp. 149–76, 215–16; Baykov, *op. cit.*, pp. 54–61.
[28] Stalin, *Problems of Leninism*, p. 208.

grain from rich peasants who refused to deliver it at prices fixed by the state. The government's needs for grain had increased with the increase in urban population, while the peasants were becoming less eager to grow and sell grain, at the government-fixed price, since other crops could be raised more profitably. It was also more profitable to feed grain to livestock and sell the resulting meat and dairy products than to sell grain itself at the state price. Yet the government could not adequately raise its price for grain. It did not want to increase peasant purchasing power when it had no intention of correspondingly increasing the supply of manufactured goods—mainly consumer goods—available for peasant purchase.[29]

Three major lines of development merged in determining the final outcome of this struggle. First, the government need for grain increased rapidly in 1928 and 1929 as its program of rapid industrialization got under way, with a corresponding increase in industrial and construction workers who had to be fed from government-controlled supplies. With even greater supplies to be required in the future as industrialization proceeded still further, the pressure for a solution satisfactory to the regime mounted sharply.

Second, the government regarded the struggle as primarily one against the kulaks, the wealthier farmers, who, as we saw earlier, had relatively large surpluses of grain. They were the peasants, moreover, who were most concerned with maximizing their money income by shifting their production from grain to nongrain crops or by feeding grain to livestock. To combat the growing influence of the kulaks, the state had reversed its earlier tolerance, raising taxes imposed upon them sharply during the late 1920's. But these measures were not enough, and in 1929 the government, in Soviet phraseology, "passed from the policy of restricting the exploiting proclivities of the kulaks to the policy of eliminating the kulaks as a class." [30]

Third, as early as March 1919, the Eighth Congress of the Communist Party had laid down the policy that the eventual organization of Soviet agriculture would be based upon two institutions: large-scale state farms, owned and operated by the government; and collective farms, formed by amalgamating the lands of many

[29] L. E. Hubbard, The Economics of Soviet Agriculture, pp. 105–9. London: Macmillan, 1939.

[30] Stalin, Problems of Leninism, p. 323. Stalin's italics.

peasants, who would then work the larger area cooperatively.[31] Both these types of farms were of only minor importance in the 1920's. As late as 1929 they accounted for less than 7 per cent of all sown acreage. In 1928 and 1929, however, the formation of new collective farms and the entrance of peasants into them increased sharply, as the poorest farmers, destitute of virtually all capital required for production, were attracted by promises of generous government aid, including credit, machinery, and technical assistance. The higher rates of collectivization prevailing in these years is indicated by the fact that whereas in November 1927 there were only 14,832 collective farms with 195,000 peasant members, by June 1, 1929, there were 57,000 such farms with 1,003,000 families.[32] Being dependent upon the government for subsidies and other aid, these collectives provided the regime with a much higher percentage of the grain they produced than did individual peasants. From the government's point of view, therefore, this organizational form was much preferable. The state farms, on the other hand, had proved disappointing because of their high costs. Moreover the Soviet leaders realized that the bulk of the peasantry would not take kindly to any government effort to convert them into out-and-out hired hands on such "factories in the field." All these considerations were influential in persuading the government in the late 1920's that its only way out of the ever more menacing grain crisis was the collectivization of the great bulk of Soviet agriculture and the wiping out of the independent kulaks.[33]

The actual process of mass collectivization in early 1930 was one of the most tempestuous periods in Soviet history. A decision of the Communist Party Central Committee in November 1929 ordered that 25,000 trusted industrial workers be sent to the countryside to lead the campaign. Plans were set in motion to build large-scale farm machinery plants to supply the large new collective farms that were to be formed. Regional and provincial authorities were empowered to use "all requisite measures to fight the kulaks, including

---

[31] Entsiklopediya, col. 842.

[32] Sotsialisticheskoye Stroitelstvo SSSR (1933–1938 gg.), p. 96. Moscow-Leningrad: 1939. Hereafter cited as Sot. Stroi. (1933—38). Baykov, The Development of the Soviet Economic System, p. 191.

[33] A. Yugow, Russia's Economic Front for War and Peace, pp. 61–62. New York: Harper, 1942.

the total confiscation of *kulak* property and their deportation beyond the boundaries of individual districts and regions (provinces)." [34] The tempo of collectivization was ordered speeded up far beyond that originally envisaged in the First Five-Year Plan.

Events moved rapidly thereafter. On February 20, 1930, there were 59,400 collective farms with about 4,400,000 families, already a very considerable increase over the preceding spring. Six weeks later, in March, there were reported to be 110,200 collective farms with almost 14,300,000 peasant households, 55 per cent of all peasant families. The most rapid agricultural transformation in history had apparently been accomplished.

But the reality behind these swiftly mounting figures was something quite different. Collectivization was often literally jammed down the peasants' throats by the urban workers sent to the countryside together with party and government functionaries. Instead of winning the peasants' voluntary consent to the merger of their property and land, these overenthusiastic collectivizers often simply informed the peasants that they had been collectivized willy-nilly, or threatened them with dire punishment if they did not vote to form collectives. *Kulaks* and others who resisted were shot, beaten up, or deported to forced labor camps. Those who opposed this new reign of terror responded by killing their livestock and destroying other assets that would otherwise have gone to the hated collective farm. The struggle and disaffection so roused in the countryside assumed such proportions that they threatened to disrupt the whole 1930 spring-sowing campaign, with disastrous results for the crop of that year.[35]

Stalin sounded the alarm with a famous statement, titled "Dizzy With Success," published in *Pravda*, March 2, 1930. He asked: "Who benefits by these distortions, this bureaucratic decreeing of a collective-farm movement, these unseemly threats against the peasants? Nobody, but our enemies. What may these distortions lead to? To the strengthening of our enemies and the discrediting of the idea of the collective-farm movement." [36] To ease the tension, peasants were allowed to withdraw from collective farms imposed upon

---

[34] Quoted in Baykov, *op. cit.*, p. 194.

[35] Dobb, *op. cit.*, pp. 228–29; Baykov, *op. cit.*, pp. 192–97; Yugow, *op. cit.*, p. 45.

[36] Stalin, *Problems of Leninism*, p. 336.

them. As a result, between March 1, 1930, and May 1, 1930, the number of collective farms dropped from 110,200 to 82,300, while the number of member peasant households declined from about 14,300,000 to about 5,800,000.

But this temporary retreat did not mean that the government had dropped its collectivization campaign. The regime had merely changed its tactics. Greater emphasis was placed upon special privileges, such as exemptions from taxation, given collective farms. They were aided also by being given machinery, seed, and credit, while the burdens on individual farmers were increased. The struggle against the *kulaks* was also continued energetically. Moreover, many of the peasants who withdrew from the collectives got back only a small fraction of their original capital. In the end the government had its way. By July 1, 1931, there were 211,100 collective farms, including over half of all peasant households and embracing two-thirds of the peasant-sown acreage. Two years later, 64.4 per cent of the peasantry and over 83 per cent of the peasant-sown area had been collectivized. By 1936, almost 90 per cent of the peasantry and virtually all the peasant-sown area were included in 245,700 collective farms.[37]

The government had won. But the cost had been heavy, being estimated by one competent observer to have included the loss of half the nation's livestock, much of its other agricultural capital, and a disruption of agriculture that helped bring on the poor harvests of 1931 and 1932 with their accompanying famine. Perhaps as many as five million *kulak* families may have been deported to Siberia and the Far North for their resistance.[38] Only by importing large numbers of American tractors was the Soviet government able partially to replace the large number of horses slaughtered during its struggle with the peasants.

With this victory over the independent peasantry, the Soviet state won complete control of the economy of the USSR, a control that has not been seriously challenged since. When Eastern Poland, Latvia, Lithuania, Estonia, Bessarabia, and Northern Bukovina were annexed during 1939–41, private trade and industry in these areas were liquidated, and a land reform was carried through that broke up all farms above a modest maximum. After Soviet control

[37] *Sot. Stroi.*, p. 278.
[38] Hubbard, *The Economics of Soviet Agriculture,* pp. 117–19.

was regained in these areas during and after World War II, a new campaign for collectivization was begun and rapid extension of the system was made in 1948 and 1949.[39] By 1950 the economies of these areas had been transformed into the same pattern as the remainder of the USSR.

The Planning System

Every economy of any significant size rests on the everyday cooperation of many individuals and groups of individuals engaged in both production and consumption. Such cooperation is not random, but is coordinated in some fashion through a mechanism that decides or helps to decide such basic questions as: What commodities and services shall be produced? How much of each shall be produced? How shall the community's total production be distributed among its individual members? How much of the community's total production shall be consumed for current needs, and how much shall be set aside to increase production capacity and provide reserves against emergencies or future needs? In an economy such as that of the United States these questions are answered—and economic activity is thereby coordinated—on the basis of decisions made by many individuals and groups of individuals acting under the guidance of signals given by the behavior of prices set in the many markets for different commodities, as well as on the basis of other information. In the Soviet Union such coordination is achieved primarily on the basis of decisions made by a relatively small group of persons at the head of the government and incorporated in a central economic plan that has the effect of law in guiding the economic activities of the citizens of the USSR. This is what we mean when we say that the Soviet Union is a "planned economy." We do not thereby imply—as is sometimes mistakenly argued—that other economies are "unplanned" and therefore chaotic; we imply merely that other economies achieve coordination through some kind of market mechanism rather than by a centrally determined and imposed plan.

The contemporary type of Soviet economic plan, whether it covers

---

[39] Cf., for example, the data on the Baltic States in *Pravda* and *Izvestia*, July 21, 1949. On the methods employed, see the letter from a Latvian journalist in *The New York Times*, August 23, 1949.

the next five years or the next year, or some shorter future period, is a directive to the different parts of the economy to produce certain quantities of different commodities—250,000,000,000 tons of coal or 500,000 automobiles, or 2,000,000 tons of cotton, and so forth. Commodities and resources available to the USSR—labor, machinery, raw materials — are allocated to the different parts of the economy in amounts intended to permit fulfillment of state goals. Paralleling the plans expressed in physical units of different commodities and resources are financial plans, which help coordinate the planned production program in terms of the monetary measurement of value. Soviet economic plans, therefore, are extremely complex documents resting upon a very detailed and extensive factual knowledge of the existing productive mechanism and its future possibilities in operation. How did this come to be? [40]

Lenin wrote in 1917 that society would become "one office and one factory," a statement implicitly assuming that the economic system of the future would be operated in accordance with one centralized set of objectives, that is, a plan. The Supreme Economic Council, formed shortly after the Bolshevik revolution, was at one time regarded as the body that would produce a unified economic plan, but its energies were soon mainly absorbed in the work of administering nationalized industry. Actual coordination of the Soviet economy during the years of War Communism seems to have been practically accomplished through the activities of the Council of Defense. This body did not issue carefully balanced blue prints, but solved urgent problems as they arose by concentrating all available resources upon their solution. Many of the government economic bureaus of the period had their planning groups, which produced detailed plans for their own sectors, but there was no one over-all directing plan coordinating the economy. [41]

The first approach to a comprehensive Soviet plan was the work of the GOELRO (State Commission for Electrification) group founded in March 1920 to prepare a program for the electrification of the Russian Soviet Federated Socialist Republic. This plan, as presented to and adopted by the Eighth Congress of Soviets, in

---

[40] Questions of how plans are prepared and how they operate in practice will be discussed in a later chapter on planning and the planning system.

[41] Dobb, *op. cit.*, pp. 313–14; *Planovoye Khozyaistvo*, No. 1 (1946), pp. 37–39.

December 1920, presented a list of goals in the production of different commodities to be achieved over a ten- or fifteen-year period, during which some thirty electric power stations were to be constructed in different parts of the country. Among the objectives set were the output of 62.3 million tons of coal, 19.6 million tons of iron ore, 8.2 million tons of pig iron, 6.5 million tons of steel, and the raising of all industry to a level of output 80 to 100 per cent above the prewar level.[42] Both in scope and in adequacy of the factual data upon which it was based, this initial effort had little in common with the complex plans of today.

In February 1921 the State Planning Commission, or *Gosplan*, was set up, the organ that is still today the chief planning agency of the USSR. The *Gosplan* was charged with working out a unified economic plan for the country, together with the means and order of its realization; with reviewing plans drawn up by various departmental and areal authorities; and with carrying out studies required for the realization of the plan. The GOELRO plan was to be the basis of its work.[43] Initially *Gosplan* consisted of 40 economists, engineers, and other personnel. By 1923 these had increased to 300, and by 1925 a network of subordinate planning offices had been set up throughout the Soviet Union. Many planning groups also existed in the various People's Commissariats (now called Ministries) and individual enterprises of the country. In its earliest years *Gosplan* confined itself largely to making studies and reports on particular problems, such as reconstruction of the Donbas coal basin, while it slowly gathered the information and personnel required to enable it to draw up a comprehensive plan. It also tried to coordinate the activities of different departments by acting as an umpire in deciding between their rival claims for resources, but this was hardly planning in the true sense.[44]

A closer approach to a comprehensive plan came with the publication of the annual Control Figures for 1925–26. These set up approximate goals for the major areas of the economy, based on an over-all view of the resources available and the possibilities for further progress. These were followed by similar Control Figures for

[42] A. Rothstein, *Man and Plan in Soviet Economy*, pp. 16–18. London: Muller, 1948.

[43] *Planovoye Khozyaistvo*, No. 1 (1946), pp. 27–28.

[44] Dobb, *op. cit.*, pp. 316–18.

1926–27 and then for 1927–28, each year's effort being based on better and more comprehensive data. The first two sets of Control Figures for 1926–27 were rejected by the government; the goals set were bitterly resisted by the various economic divisions, which wished to proceed in accordance with their own conceptions. Moreover, the Control Figures were challenged on the ground that some of their most strategic components, based upon faulty and inadequate statistical information, particularly with regard to agriculture, were inaccurate. The work of drawing up these goals and the criticism they received at the hands of party officials and economic leaders contributed, however, to improving the planning work and making possible further progress.

A historic controversy took place in this period that was to have major importance for the future development of Soviet planning. A number of the chief economists in *Gosplan* viewed planning as essentially an effort at forecasting the *probable future development* of the economy. These economists regarded the most essential task of economic planning as the maintenance of the equilibrium between supply and demand on the market. They believed that the growth of the Soviet economy was essentially limited by the preponderant importance of agriculture, that area of the Soviet economy in which individualism reigned supreme at the time and in which the planned direction of the government was least effective. In addition they believed that once the Soviet economy had made good the losses of World War I and the civil war that followed it, the rate of growth of the economy as a whole would necessarily decline. These economists were very much influenced by the techniques of economic forecasting and business cycle analysis then in vogue among economists in the West, and these they tried to apply to the problems of the Soviet Union. Such an approach, which denied the possibility of extremely rapid economic development as desired by the leaders of the Soviet state, was naturally most unacceptable to the government. In addition these economists warned against government efforts to secure grain from the peasantry by coercive methods. They argued that state attempts to get increasing quantities of grain while keeping grain prices relatively low could lead to a diminution of farm output with disastrous consequences for the economy. These warnings too were unpalatable to the ruling group. A thorough purge of *Gosplan* and associated bodies was conducted to remove these economists and their sympathizers, who were accused of being "wreckers" and "opportunists" trying to sabotage the Soviet economy. This controversy helped focus attention upon the absolute necessity for the Soviet government to overcome the individualism and lack of planned control of agriculture if economic progress was to proceed at the rate desired.[45]

Speaking in May 1928 of the difficulties encountered by the government in securing adequate grain, the central problem of the time, Stalin described the root of the Soviet government's difficulties, and the relative importance of planning at the time, in these words:

> At the first glance it might appear that our grain difficulties are of a fortuitous nature, the result merely of faulty planning, the result merely of a number of mistakes committed in the sphere of economic coordination. But that might appear so only at the first glance. . . . To attribute everything to faulty planning and chance mistakes would be a gross error. It would be a still greater error to exaggerate the part played by the planning principle, in the belief that we have already reached a stage of development when it is possible to plan and regulate everything. It must not be forgotten that in addition to elements which lend themselves to planning there are elements in our national economy which do not as yet lend themselves to planning; and that, apart from everything else, there are hostile classes which cannot be overcome simply by the planning of the State Planning Commission.[46]

Only when agriculture had become completely collectivized could it be brought more adequately within the sphere of Soviet planning and control, apart of course from the vagaries of nature and the resultant fluctuations in harvests, always a source of difficulty for economic planners in all countries.

In December 1927 the Fifteenth Congress of the Communist Party directed that a five-year plan for the development of the Soviet economy be prepared. Even earlier, in January 1927, a draft of such a plan, putting major emphasis upon the growth of heavy industry, had been prepared by the Supreme Economic Council. *Gosplan* had also been working on a similar project, one in which the possible goals for the future were viewed rather cautiously, in

---

[45] *Ibid.*, pp. 320–30; Baykov, *The Development of the Soviet Economic System*, pp. 431–35; Boris Brutzkus, *Economic Planning in Soviet Russia*, pp. 118–25. London: Routledge, 1935.

[46] Stalin, *Problems of Leninism*, p. 205.

line with the reasoning described above. A great deal of public debate took place about the several variants of the Five-Year Plan released by *Gosplan*, the final choice put before the government being between the "minimal" and the "optimal" variants. The latter was the bolder program, premised on such uncertain assumptions as that there would be no crop failure during the five years and that foreign trade with the outside world, as well as foreign credits to the USSR, would increase sharply. It was the "optimal variant" that was finally adopted in April 1929 by the Sixteenth Communist Party Congress, though execution of the plan had been begun in late 1928.[47]

The period of execution of the First Five-Year Plan had originally been set as the five years following September 30, 1928; but it was officially announced as completed in four and one-quarter years, that is, as of December 31, 1932. Several of the basic assumptions behind the "optimal variant" were far from realized during these years. The crops of 1931 and 1932 were poor; the Soviet Union did not receive extensive foreign credits. Nevertheless, during these years, substantial progress was made, but it was very uneven progress. Behind the reported fulfillment of the plan was the fact that while, in terms of ruble value, output of machinery and electrical equipment in 1932 was 157 per cent of the 1932–33 goal, that of heavy metallurgy was only 67.7 per cent, and that of consumer goods only 73.5 per cent, of their goals.[48] Where the plan had envisaged that less than 25 per cent of all peasant households would be collectivized by its end, the actual percentage in 1932 was over 60. The plan had provided that, in 1932, 106,000,000 metric tons of grain would be produced; actual output was less than 70 million tons. Steel production in 1932–33 was to be 10,400,000 tons; in 1932 it was under 6,000,000 tons.[49] Many other similar examples might be cited, but the basic situation is clear: The First Five-Year Plan may be considered to have been fulfilled, if one defines fulfillment solely in terms of some over-all indicator that balances failures in one area

[47] Dobb, *op. cit.*, pp. 231–36.
[48] Baykov, *op. cit.*, p. 166.
[49] Goals for the First Five-Year Plan are given in State Planning Commission of the USSR, *The Soviet Union Looks Ahead*. New York: Liveright, 1930, *passim*. A convenient source in English for data on Soviet economic conditions in 1932 is State Planning Commission of the USSR, *The Second Five-Year Plan*, p. 545 ff. New York: International Publishers, n.d.

with unexpectedly good performance in another. In retrospect, however, there can be no doubt but that the First Five-Year Plan gave only a poor forecast of what actually did happen after its adoption, except, in the most general sense, that the plan did call for an intensive program of capital investment and greater socialization in all major areas of the economy.

To understand the real significance of a Soviet plan, one must abandon any notion that such a plan is a device for securing orderly economic growth, that it is at all analogous to a railroad timetable, for example. Such a timetable predicts that a certain sequence of events will happen at certain times. Those who work on the railroad attempt to make the trains leave and arrive on time. If a train is late, that is considered a violation of the timetable; but so is the arrival of a train well ahead of schedule. An engineer who brought in a train from a five-hour journey in three hours might well be disciplined for skipping stops en route, for exceeding safe speeds, and for endangering lives by being out of step with the rest of the railroad. Not so with the Soviet plan. The objective of such a plan is primarily to secure the maximum possible rate of development of the economy in a given time period. If a branch of the economy progresses more rapidly than originally envisaged, that is, overfulfills its plan, its manager and other personnel are rewarded. It is only when progress lags behind the plan that the directors of the Soviet economy become concerned.

Oscar Lange, who later became a leading official of the communist-dominated Polish government, expressed the point this way several years ago:

> In a truly planned economy the output of different industries and plants as well as the inter-temporal structure of the investment program must be balanced against each other and coordinated with each other. Thus overfulfillment of the plan, not less than underfulfillment, must be considered as a disturbance which upsets the plan. This argument, however, holds true only if the military objectives of economic planning are left out of account. The Soviet economy was planned not for the harmony of its different branches, but for one single purpose, namely the most rapid industrialization and preparation of effective national defense. The industrialization program was considered by the Soviet government as a race against time. . . . The fact that overfulfillment of the production plan is regarded as a virtue, instead of as an upsetting of the general economic plan, shows clearly that Soviet economic planning did not

serve the objectives of a harmonious socialist welfare economy, but served political and military objectives to which all other aspects of economic planning were sacrificed.[50]

From this point of view, it is clear that the plan is a set of goals or a forecast; it is not an end in itself, but merely the means to an end. If conditions change, the plan is changed, as was the case with regard to collectivization in the early 1930's. Moreover, the Soviet leaders regard the actual formulation of a plan as only the first step in real planning. Supervision of the execution of the plan is the major task, they believe. The day-to-day development of the economy must be watched so as to avoid bottlenecks, foresee impending difficulties and avert them, and modify the plan in accordance with the actual experience of the earlier work in achieving its goals.

The Second Five-Year Plan, covering the years 1933–37, was adopted at the Seventeenth Congress of the Communist Party in early 1934. The railroad portion of this plan was announced as fulfilled in four years, and the industrial portion in four and a quarter years.[51] But again this fulfillment was of a curiously uneven kind, though somewhat more even than the fulfillment of the First Five-Year Plan. In 1937 output of steel was 4 per cent above the amount planned for that year, but pig iron production was 10 per cent below; petroleum output 30 per cent below; and woolen textiles 50 per cent below.[52]

The Third Five-Year Plan, originally intended to cover the years 1938–42, was adopted by the Eighteenth Congress of the Communist Party in March 1939. This plan showed the influence of the direct threat of war existing in the late 1930's. As its execution proceeded, it was more and more modified to take account of the increasing possibility of Soviet involvement. This plan was, of course, rudely interrupted by the Nazi invasion of the USSR in June 1941. A week after the invasion a "mobilizational economic plan" for the third quarter of 1941 was adopted by the government. In August 1941

---

[50] Oscar Lange, "The Working Principles of the Soviet Economy," in *USSR Economy and the War*, p. 43. New York: Russian Economic Institute, 1943.

[51] *Planovoye Khozyaistvo*, No. 1 (1946), pp. 57–61.

[52] Cf. the interesting and more extensive comparison between plan figures and actual accomplishment in W. W. Leontief, Sr., "Soviet Planning: The Problem of Economic Balance," *The Russian Review*, Autumn 1946, pp. 28–29.

the Soviet government adopted the "war economic plan" for the last quarter of 1941 and for 1942.[53] Other plans were subsequently adopted for the later years of the war, through 1945. The Fourth Five-Year Plan, originally presented as covering the years 1946–50 and providing a program for the reconstruction and development of the Soviet economy after World War II, was adopted as a law by the Supreme Soviet of the USSR in March 1946. Debate over this comprehensive program was most perfunctory, being limited to a small number of speeches by members of the Supreme Soviet— most of the speeches devoted simply to praising the plan completely —after a long explanatory and summary speech by N. A. Voznesensky, head of the *Gosplan* which had made up the document.

The Soviet government's official report on the fulfillment of the Fourth Five-Year Plan, published April 17, 1951, claimed that this plan "has been successfully fulfilled and the most important plan goals have been considerably exceeded." The impression given by this statement is misleading, unless it is understood that the latter phrase implies a very uneven pattern of fulfillment and nonfulfillment. While objectives for 1950 production of many key industrial raw materials—coal, petroleum, and electric power among others— were exceeded, the objectives for production of important types of civilian machinery, consumer goods, and farm products were not reached. From 1946 to 1950, the data suggest, Soviet heavy industry grew more rapidly than originally envisaged, while production of many types of consumer goods and food lagged behind, in part because of the diversion of resources from the civilian areas of the economy to those areas of the economy more directly related to military-economic potential. Not least among the latter, in all probability, was the production of nuclear weapons.

Though V. M. Molotov had indicated as early as March 1950 that a Fifth Five-Year Plan, for the years 1951–55 inclusive, was under preparation, the actual text of this plan has not been published. Brief "Directives" for such a plan, covering many of its main features, were published in August 1952, and then approved, with minor modifications, at the Nineteenth Communist Party Congress the following October. Phrased largely in terms of percentage increases, rather than absolute numbers, as target goals, these

53 N. A. Voznesensky, *The Economy of the USSR During World War II*, pp. 20–22. Washington: Public Affairs Press, 1948 (mimeographed).

"Directives" constitute the smallest and least satisfactory body of information ever made available regarding a Soviet Five-Year Plan. The fact that the Korean War raged from 1950 to 1953 may have played a role both in the delay in announcing any details of the Fifth Five-Year Plan, and also in the minimal amount of information made public regarding that plan. The Korean War, of course, was sustained because the USSR delivered military supplies to the communist troops, while also posing the possibility of eventual direct participation.

After Stalin's death, the later pronouncements of his successors—particularly Premier Malenkov's speech of August 1953 and N. S. Khrushchev's speech on farm policy delivered a month later—indicated that the 1952 Directives had been changed in some major particulars, with more emphasis on consumer goods and agricultural output than originally envisaged. If the promises made in this regard during 1953 are actually fulfilled, it may be that in the perspective of history, the death of Stalin may appear to have been another major turning point in Soviet economic history. Developments during the first months of 1954, however, suggested that the changes introduced by the post-Stalin rulers were more the result of expediency than of any long-term shift from Stalin's goals. On the one hand, the ambitious program for expanding grain acreage and output announced in March 1954 clearly had not been envisaged either in the original Fifth Five-Year Plan or in the first farm program enunciated by Khrushchev in September 1953. On the other hand, the speeches of Malenkov and Khrushchev at the Supreme Soviet session in late April 1954 seemed to make it clear beyond doubt that the new regime intended to continue the old emphasis on heavy industry and on military production. The revelation, during the air parade of May 1, 1954, that the Soviet Union was building giant intercontinental jet bombers made it crystal clear that the Soviet economy was not making the satisfaction of consumer needs its primary objective.

The five-year plans discussed above are of course not the only kinds of Soviet plans. The Control Figures issued first in 1925–26 were an initial attempt to formulate annual economic plans for a year ahead, plans that could be more concrete and specific than the longer-range five-year plans. Control figures continued to be issued annually for a time after the beginning of the First Five-Year Plan, but in 1931 these guides were dropped. Instead it became the practice, beginning with that year, to prepare a comprehensive annual economic plan, in which developments that had occurred since the formulation of the original five-year plan could be taken account of.[54] For the most important branches of the economy, as well as for individual enterprises, quarterly, monthly, and sometimes even bimonthly or ten-day plans are also prepared, so as to get the greatest maneuverability of economic direction over the year.

Longer-range planning for periods in excess of five years has been relatively slow to develop, though the first GOELRO plan had looked ahead ten to fifteen years. Some work on such longer-range planning was apparently done in 1938 and early 1939. Stalin, in his report to the Eighteenth Communist Party Congress, referred to the necessity of reaching a pig-iron output of 50 to 60 million tons in order to exceed the per capita United States output of pig iron in 1929, obviously a matter of several five-year plans.[55] Writing in 1940, a Soviet economist gave detailed figures showing that a considerable amount of thinking had been done about major objectives to be reached by the Soviet economy by 1947 or 1952, that is, at the end of the Fifth or Sixth Five-Year Plan, had there been no World War II.[56] That such interest in long-range planning has been carried over to the postwar period was indicated by Stalin in February 1946. He spoke then of tripling Soviet prewar industrial production and reaching specified output goals for pig iron, steel, oil, and coal, far beyond the 1950 goals of the Fourth Five-Year Plan. Stalin's tentative time schedule—and the period over which long-range planning was probably being carried—was indicated by his statement, "That will take three more Five-Year Plans, I should think, if not more. But it can be done and we must do it."[57]

The Growth of Production

No aspect of Soviet economic development has been more spectacular than the rapid growth of production in all fields during the 1920's and 1930's. This growth was interrupted by the Nazi invasion in June 1941, which resulted in great losses of industrial

---

[54] A. Kursky, *Sotsialisticheskoye Planirovaniye Narodnogo Khozyaistva SSSR*, p. 20. Moscow: Gosplanizdat, 1945.

[55] Stalin, *Problems of Leninism*, pp. 633–34.

[56] *Planovoye Khozyaistvo*, No. 10 (1940), pp. 30–43.

[57] Quotation from the translation of his speech issued by the Soviet Embassy.

and agricultural capital, with consequent sharp declines in production. But a revival followed after 1945, when sights were set for output levels exceeding any achieved before.

A number of obstacles make it difficult to present a satisfactory statistical picture of the development of Soviet national income, industrial production, and farm output since 1917. Data for some years have never been officially published, while for other years they have only been implied. More serious even, the available Soviet indexes are highly suspect as tending to exaggerate the pace of Soviet economic growth. The technical reasons for these suspicions are discussed later in this chapter. With these cautions in mind, we shall look first at the official picture of over-all Soviet economic development, and then at the results reached by some non-Soviet scholars who have attempted independent evaluations of Soviet economic growth. The data in Table 8 give what is essentially

TABLE 8. National Income, Gross Industrial Output, and Gross Farm Output of the USSR for Selected Years, Based on Soviet Data.

Year	National Income*	Gross Output of Industry	Gross Farm Output	National Income*	Gross Output of Industry	Gross Farm Output
	BILLIONS OF RUBLES †			PER CENT OF 1913		
1913	21.0	16.2	12.6	100	100	100
1921	8.0	‡	‡	38.1	‡	‡
1926	21.7	16.0§	‡	103.3	98.8	‡
1929	28.9	25.7	14.7	137.6	158.6	116.7
1932	45.5	43.3	13.1	216.6	267.3	104.0
1937	96.3	95.5	20.1	458.5	589.5	159.6
1940	128.3	138.5	23.2	611.0	854.9	184.1
1942	‡	103.0	‡	‡	635.8	‡
1945	‡	127.5	‡	‡	787.0	‡
1946	‡	105.5	‡	‡	648.1	‡
1950	211.1	239.6	26.4	1,005.1	1,479.0	210.0
1952	260.6	310.6	25.5	1,241.0	1,917.3	203.2
1953	281.4	347.2	‡	1,340.0	2,143.2	‡
1955 goal** .	337.8	407.3	‡	1,608.6	2,514.2	‡

* National income is a net output concept and is therefore not the sum of the gross output of various branches of the economy.
† These data are in terms of "constant" 1926-27 prices through 1950 and thereafter are calculated from percentages as though the use of these "constant" prices had been retained. See text for fuller discussion.
‡ Data unavailable.
§ 1926-27.
** Based on directives adopted in October 1952 at Nineteenth Communist Party Congress.
Sources: Data taken from or calculated on basis of Soviet statistical handbooks published in the 1930's; writings and speeches of N. A. Voznesensky, G. M. Malenkov, and N. S. Khrushchev; and various postwar official Soviet government statements.

the official picture of Soviet economic development, using figures actually published by the Soviet government or implied in official statements.

The official data in the table above indicate that, up to about 1926, the Soviet Union was engaged in recovering from and restoring the damage and production loss caused by World War I and the following Civil War. These conflicts had reduced national income to 38 per cent of 1913, agricultural output to probably about half the prewar level, and industrial output to 20 per cent or less of 1913 figures.[58] Between 1926 and 1940, the official data above indicate, national income increased about sixfold, largely the result of an almost ninefold rise in industrial output.[59] Agricultural output in 1940 apparently had increased less than twofold over the level of 1913. Moreover, it had actually decreased significantly during the early 1930's as the result of peasant resistance to collectivization, drought, and related factors. In the first year or two of World War II, Soviet industrial production dropped 25 per cent or more, while agricultural production probably dropped much more sharply since much of the country's most productive farm area was lost to the enemy. By 1945, industrial output had regained part of the lost ground, as had agricultural output. The first full postwar year, 1946, saw a significant decline in non-agricultural output as the result of partial reconversion from military to civilian output. In 1946, however, agriculture suffered a serious drought which set back its recovery markedly. Thereafter official reports indicated that both industrial and agricultural production climbed. By 1953, there could be no doubt, Soviet industrial production and capacity were at record levels far above the highest marks achieved before World War II. Agriculture's postwar progress, though far from negligible, was much slower, and total Soviet farm output reported for 1952 was approximately 15 per cent less than the original production goal for 1950 set in the Fourth Five-Year Plan.

More generally, the data above show clearly the great discrepancy between the growth of agricultural production and of indus-

---

[58] The statements on industrial and agricultural production are based on *The Soviet Union*, pp. 69, 76. Washington: Soviet Union Information Bureau, 1929.

[59] The Soviet definition of national income, it should be borne in mind, includes primarily only material production, excluding many services whose value is included in the definition of national income employed in the United States and other Western countries.

trial production under the Soviet regime. Taking the official figures at face value for the moment, these show that between 1913 and 1952 gross industrial production increased almost twenty times while farm output barely doubled. Though both of these Soviet indicators probably require extensive revision downward, the overall discrepancy they indicate is clearly a basic fact of Soviet economic development. The difficulties caused by this discrepancy were confessed openly for the first time only after Stalin's death, in the major policy speeches of Malenkov and Khrushchev during the summer of 1953, speeches followed by the announcement of major programs aimed at improving the situation of agricultural production.

Even within the area of industrial production, the advance made has not been an even one. On the contrary, the pattern of development during the late 1920's, the 1930's, and World War II was one of most rapid expansion for capital goods of all kinds, machines, transport equipment, industrial raw materials, and the like. But output of consumer goods, even as reflected in official data, has lagged behind. This is the essence of what Stalin has called the Communist Party's industrialization policy. As he said in his speech of February 9, 1946:

> The Party knew that a war was looming, that the country could not be defended without heavy industry, that the development of heavy industry must be undertaken as soon as possible, that to be behind with this would mean to lose out. . . . Accordingly the Communist Party of our country . . . began the work of industrializing the country by developing heavy industry.

Deficiencies of Soviet Statistics

Up to this point our discussion of Soviet production growth has been in terms of the official Soviet statistics. As indicated above, there are grave doubts about the accuracy with which these data represent the actual course of development. There is no doubt that Soviet industrial production has grown far beyond that of Czarist Russia. But the rate of growth shown by the Soviet data, and consequently the aggregate magnitude of the country's total output, seem patently exaggerated. There have been grave technical defects in the construction of the production indexes, and these data have often been published with a view to exploiting their propaganda value. The Soviet index of total agricultural production also seems open to the same objections, even though the rate of growth it shows is much more modest than in the case of industrial production. In addition, it must be remembered, Soviet farm production data in the postwar period have included the output of annexed areas, such as Eastern Poland and the Baltic States, so that these figures are not strictly comparable with the earlier statistics for the more limited territory of the country before 1939.

Gross industrial production data for the Soviet Union now available are nominally based on the joining of two indexes. Up to and through 1950, they are calculated in terms of so-called "constant 1926–27 prices." For the years thereafter they are supposedly based on constant wholesale prices of January 1, 1952. It should be noted that no absolute figures in terms of the latter prices have been published, only percentage data. In the table above, an attempt has been made to overcome this difficulty by applying the percentage growth claimed for the years after 1950 to the earlier data expressed in terms of 1926–27 prices. This linkage of the two indexes is similar to the practice used by Soviet statisticians in computing percentage growth of industrial output between years up to 1950 and years thereafter.

Official Soviet data give an illuminating summary of the lopsided development of Soviet industrial production, with output of means of production, including armaments, far outstripping that of consumer goods. The output of means of production grew from 8.5 billion rubles in 1928 to 84.8 billion in 1940, a tenfold increase, and to over 240 billion rubles in 1953, a thirtyfold rise in a quarter of a century. Consumer goods production, on the other hand, rose from 12.9 billion rubles in 1928 to 53.7 billion rubles in 1940, or only about four times, and to about 100 billion rubles in 1953, an eightfold gain in twenty-five years. Though these data, which are in terms of "constant" 1926–27 prices or their equivalent, are subject to much question, the over-all differential rates of production they portray constitute one of the basic features of the pattern of Soviet economic growth.

The discrepancy may also be indicated in another fashion. In 1928, Soviet data claim, means of production constituted 46.2 per cent of industrial production and consumer goods 53.8 per cent. In 1953, G. M. Malenkov revealed, means of production were planned to constitute about 70 per cent of industrial output and consumer goods only about 30 per cent. In some years of World War II, consumer goods accounted for only 20 per cent of Soviet industrial production.

This sort of unequal development, both as between agriculture and industry and as between heavy industry and light (consumer goods) industry, was made possible by government policy which allocated resources primarily to the favored branches of the economy. Of all government investments for capital construction and plant in the Soviet economy between 1929 and 1952, measured in current prices, about 64 per cent or 638 billion rubles, went to heavy industry; about 20 per cent or 193 billion rubles went to transport; about 7 per cent or 72 billion rubles went to light industry; and about 9 per cent, or 94 billion rubles, went to agriculture.[60] With this pattern of investment, a pattern repeated also in other areas of resource allocation, there need be no wonder that Soviet military-economic strength increased so rapidly from 1928 to 1953 while Soviet consumers received relatively little benefit from the over-all progress of the economy.

Too little has been published by the Soviet Union about the index based on 1952 prices to permit intelligent evaluation of its adequacy or inadequacy. Even if this new index is a satisfactory one, however, the failure to recalculate earlier production data—for 1950 and before—in terms of these new prices, means that the exaggeration caused by the defective 1926–27 price technique has been "frozen into" the system of Soviet historical statistics. This exaggeration must be understood for accurate use of Soviet aggregative statistics.

The basic technical factor resulting in the exaggeration of the growth of the physical volume of production in the official Soviet data arose from the rapid development of the Soviet economy after 1926–27, the year whose prices were nominally taken as constant weights in measuring production. Already by 1930, and in much greater degree thereafter, the USSR was producing many products never before made in the country, as well as improvements and new

---

[60] The above discussion is based largely on data from N. A. Voznesensky's book, *The Economy of the USSR During World War II* and on G. M. Malenkov's speech of August 8, 1953. Cf. also *Planovoye Khozyaistvo*, No. 4 (1946), p. 4.

models of goods made in 1926–27 or earlier. In measuring production as a whole, prices had to be assigned for valuing these new products, improvements, and new models, since they had not been produced in the USSR in 1926–27. Very often these new items were valued at the price they sold for in the first year of their large-scale output, 1930, or 1932, or other years. Because of Soviet price inflation after 1926–27, fixed quantities of labor and other economic resources usually cost much more in the 1930's and after than they had in 1926–27. New goods, valued at later prices in measuring industrial production, received a much higher weight than if the labor and raw materials used to make them had been obtained in 1926–27. Thus the more new products turned out in the USSR and the farther the Soviet economy progressed from the base year, 1926–27, the greater was the inflationary bias imparted to the official index for measuring the physical volume of production. After 1935, some effort was made to curb this source of statistical inflation, but the available evidence suggests that the attempt was inadequate, so that the whole system of 1926–27 prices had eventually to be scrapped after 1950. As early as the middle and late 1930's, Soviet economists had understood the deficiencies of the valuation of industrial output in terms of 1926–27 prices and had written publicly about the need for a more accurate technique of measurement. Presumably these protests went unheeded because of the valuable propaganda material provided by the inflationary bias these prices introduced into the statistics of industrial production.

With regard to consumer goods, an additional influence toward exaggeration arises from the fact that the output of small, private production was inadequately measured in the 1920's and earlier. It was extremely difficult to count and evaluate the output of many small producers scattered over the country. In the late 1920's these producers had great incentive to hide the volume of their output from government statistics gatherers. Thus in discussing a Soviet census of small business in late 1929, a Soviet statistical source speaks of the "tendency of private producers to hide the actual volume of their production. . . ." [61] As a result it seems clear that part of the increase in consumer-goods production recorded in

[61] *Narodnoye Khozyaistvo SSSR Statistichesky Spravochnik* 1932, p. 647. Moscow-Leningrad: 1932.

statistics for the 1930's was not a real increase. It reflected mainly the growth of output in large government factories and state-sponsored cooperatives, while neglecting to take account of the counter-balancing decline in production of consumer goods caused by the extinction of many small individual producers or groups of producers who had formerly turned out a very large fraction of this production. Furthermore, the quality of much factory-made Soviet consumer goods has been very poor, yet it is dubious that anything like adequate allowance has been made for this fact in official calculations. Finally, with the increased urbanization of the Soviet population, there has been a significant shift of production from the home to the factory. Whereas a peasant family normally bakes its own bread and makes its own clothing, a city family usually expects to buy these and other goods ready-made in bakeries and other workshops. But whereas bread baked or clothes made in the home do not enter statistical records of production, the same goods made commercially outside the home do. The very process of urbanization results in an *apparent* rise in consumer-goods output though there has been no real increase, only a transfer in function. For these and other reasons, the fivefold rise in consumer-goods output by 1940 shown in official Soviet statistics is a very misleading clue as to actual changes in the standard of living in the USSR, which was probably little if any improved over that of the late 1920's.

Measures of agricultural production have been artificially inflated by shifting the accounting of crop output from a net basis, that is, omitting losses in harvest and transport, to a gross basis, where such losses—which are quite significant in the USSR—are counted in crop production as though they were available for consumption of any kind.[62] After mid-1953, however, there may have been a return to a net crop basis.

Against this background, it can be seen that the introduction of

[62] For further discussion of problems connected with Soviet production statistics, see Harry Schwartz, "On the Use of Soviet Statistics," *Journal of the American Statistical Association*, September 1947; Alexander Gerschenkron, "The Soviet Indices of Industrial Production," *Review of Economic Statistics*, November 1947; Naum Jasny, "Intricacies of Russian National Income Indexes," *Journal of Political Economy*, August 1947. For a contrary point of view, see Maurice Dobb, "A Comment on Soviet Statistics," *Review of Economics and Statistics*, February 1948, pp. 34–38.

the new index based on 1952 prices may well be an important advance, assuming that this index is properly constructed, a point on which we cannot be certain. Over time, of course, this method of calculation will also tend to become defective because of the introduction of new commodities after January 1, 1952. There is some suggestion in Soviet sources of an intention to meet this problem in the future by changing the price system every five years or so.[63]

The introduction of this new index does not however, eliminate by itself the other difficulties related above: the continuance of the biased index calculated for the years before 1951 as the base for comparisons with later years; the inflation of the consumer goods production index because of incomplete coverage in the earlier years; the exaggeration of the agricultural output index because of the use of the "harvest in the field" concept without allowance for losses, though on this latter point the critical remarks made by Premier Malenkov in August 1953 suggest that there may be some change toward a more realistic basis of agricultural accounting. Finally, however, we still have no assurance that the Soviet price system as of January 1, 1952, the basis of the new index, represents an economically valid price system, one which actually reflects the true supply, demand, and cost conditions at that time.

The remarks above about the deficiencies of the 1926–27 prices in the calculation of industrial output apply also to the use of these prices for national income data. The Soviet index of national income has also been shifted to a 1952 price basis since 1950, apparently at the same time and in the same fashion as the industrial output index.[64]

Other Approaches to the Problem

The deficiencies of the Soviet data, as described above, have induced various non-Soviet scholars to attempt independently the construction of production indexes which would be free of the difficulties in the official statistics. A wide variety of techniques has

---

[63] The first description of the index based on 1952 prices was given in G. Drampyan and N. Fedotov, "O Planirovanii Valovoi Produktsii Promyshlennosti v Sopostavimykh Tsenakh," *Planovoye Khozyaistvo*, No. 1 (1952), pp. 75–79. A translation appeared in *The Current Digest of the Soviet Press* April 12, 1952, pp. 3–5. Other material on this subject appeared in *Vestnik Statistiki*, No. 2 (1952).

[64] A. I. Petrov, ed., *Kurs Ekonomicheskoi Statistiki*, p. 435. Moscow: 1952.

been used by these scholars, among whom Colin Clark, Julius Wyler, Paul A. Baran, Naum Jasny, Abram Bergson, Alexander Gerschenkron, and Donald R. Hodgman have been pioneers.[65]

Some writers have attempted to measure Soviet national income or industrial production in terms of the prices of another country, the United States for example. A second group has attempted to calculate such figures in terms of current Soviet ruble prices for different years—rather than any one set of "constant" prices—with the eventual hope that, after the development of a satisfactory Soviet price index, the data for different years in terms of rubles of different purchasing power may be deflated so as to eliminate the impact of price changes and produce a series actually measuring the physical growth of production or national income. Other miscellaneous techniques have been tried as well. Space limitations make it impossible to review all these attempts here, so what follows will be a brief illustrative sampling of some of the methods employed.

Prof. Abram Bergson and his colleagues have attempted to measure Soviet Gross National Product for a number of different years in ruble prices of each year. Their results have been adjusted in an effort to remove the distorting influence of certain features of the Soviet price system, but these results have not been reduced to rubles of uniform purchasing power. These results, in billions of "adjusted rubles," are as follows for four years:

$$1937 \ldots\ldots\ldots\ldots\ldots\ldots 223.9$$
$$1940 \ldots\ldots\ldots\ldots\ldots\ldots 366.1$$
$$1944 \ldots\ldots\ldots\ldots\ldots\ldots 408.5$$
$$1948 \ldots\ldots\ldots\ldots\ldots\ldots 616.7$$

The approximate tripling of gross national product shown above reflects the inflation of Soviet prices over this period as well as the undoubted growth of production. The price indexes needed to deflate these data are unavailable at this writing.[66]

---

[65] For historical material on these efforts cf. Abram Bergson, *Soviet National Income and Product in 1937*, pp. 2–11. New York: Columbia University Press, 1953. Naum Jasny, *The Soviet Economy During the Plan Era*, pp. 7–9. Stanford: Stanford University Press, 1951. Alexander Gershenkron, *A Dollar Index of Soviet Machinery Output, 1927–28 to 1937*, pp. 7–10. Santa Monica: The RAND Corporation, 1951.

[66] Abram Bergson and Hans Heymann, Jr., *Soviet National Income and Product 1940–48*, p. 70. New York: Columbia University Press, 1954.

Prof. Donald R. Hodgman has constructed a Soviet industrial production index for 1927–28 to 1950 in which the relative importance of the different components "is measured by the net value-added per unit of product" in 1934. He approximates the value-added weights for the commodities involved on the basis of Soviet wages and salary for different branches of industry. Though this raises important questions of concept and methodology, it is interesting to compare Hodgman's index with the official picture of the growth of Soviet gross industrial output as below: [67]

Year	Hodgman's Index	Official Index
	1927–28 = 100	
1927–28	100	100
1932	172	234
1937	371	551
1940	430	768
1946	304	582
1950	646	1332

It is worthy of note that where the official index claims industrial production grew more than 13 times between 1927–28 and 1950, Prof. Hodgman's calculations suggest a growth of only about 6.5 times. Put another way, over this entire period the official index implies an average annual percentage growth of 12.5 per cent, where Prof. Hodgman's results suggest a growth of only 8.9 per cent annually on the average. Even the latter, of course, is a very rapid rate of development, but the difference is highly significant, not least for efforts to project the speed of future Soviet industrial expansion.

Similar confirmation of the belief that official Soviet aggregative data exaggerate the speed of industrial output growth is given by Prof. Gerschenkron's construction of a Soviet machinery index, in terms of United States 1939 dollar prices, for the years from 1927–28 to 1937. Taking 1927–28 as 100, the Soviet machinery production index indicates that output in 1937 should be represented by an index number of 1,415. Prof. Gerschenkron's index suggests instead that the appropriate 1937 index on the same base should be only 525, a far more modest estimate of growth.[68] Machinery production,

---

[67] A summary description of his techniques and results is given by Hodgman in his article, "Industrial Production," included in Abram Bergson, ed., *Soviet Economic Growth*, pp. 225–44. Evanston: Row, Peterson, 1953.

[68] Gerschenkron, *op. cit.*, p. 29.

of course, is one of the main areas of the Soviet economy in which the introduction of new items after the mid-1920's resulted in distortion and exaggeration of the official index based on "constant 1926–27 prices."

The Sources of Soviet Economic Expansion

The economic expansion and development achieved by the USSR since 1928 was made possible by the creative drive and organizing power contributed by the communist leadership. Capital investment of the sort that took place on such a large scale during this period consists essentially of the application of labor and other resources for purposes that are not immediately productive of goods for consumption. Even when one builds a shoe factory, for example, one does not obtain any shoes from it during the period of construction. In the case of the Soviet Union, of course, it was not primarily shoe factories that were being built, but rather installations for increasing the "roundaboutness" of production. In oversimplified fashion one might say that steel mills were constructed to provide the steel to make machine tools that would be used to make tractors that would finally be applied in agriculture to increase food output; or machine tools to make weapons for the armed forces.

In any economy where all resources are being fully employed at a given time, an increased rate of capital investment requires diversion of resources from output of current consumption goods and services and thus must lead at least for a time to reduced consumption.[69] The case is different in an economy where large quantities of labor, factories, machinery, raw materials, and other resources are unemployed or only partially employed. These can be applied to capital investment purposes without reducing the previous total of goods and services being made available for consumption. When the five-year plans were begun in 1928, there were significant reserves of unemployed or only partially employed resources, particularly in agriculture. Some additional capital investment could therefore have been obtained without extracting significant sacrifices from the population's consumption. But the volume and the tempo of the capital investment program desired by the First Five-

---

[69] Assuming, for simplicity's sake, that there are no reserves to cushion the shock of resource diversion.

Year Plan and its successors were so great that they more than took up the slack in the economy provided by available unemployed resources. They required in addition significant diversion of employed resources from production of consumer goods and services, with consequent sacrifices imposed upon the population. Thus private trade and private industrial production were wiped out during the First Five-Year Plan. During the same period, too, large quantities of grain were exported abroad to pay for new machinery and technical aid, though food was rationed in the cities and famine stalked the Ukraine and adjoining areas. The fact that there were great losses of agricultural capital, particularly livestock, during this period as the result of the struggle over collectivization added to the deprivations suffered.

To the extent that resources needed for capital investment can be obtained from abroad in the form of loans or other aid, the immediate domestic diversion of resources for a given volume of investment can be lessened. But, as we shall see below, such external aid played only a minor role in Soviet economic development before World War II.

In the paragraphs below we shall consider in turn the sources of capital, labor, technical knowledge, and raw materials employed by the USSR in its rapid industrialization after 1928.

Capital. Almost all the capital expended for Soviet economic development has been obtained internally, that is, by restricting the consumption of the Soviet people below what it might have been and devoting an extraordinarily large percentage of their national income for investment purposes, such as building new factories, new railroad lines, and the like. Since the peasantry has been the dominant group in the Soviet population until comparatively recently, this element has borne the brunt of the burden. Once the farms had been collectivized, the government was able each year to get a large fraction of the agricultural produce, particularly grain, at very low prices. This was then resold, in original or processed form, at much higher prices. Putting the matter more generally, the Soviet government during most of its existence has imposed very high rates of taxation on foods and consumer goods, thus obtaining a large amount of income that it could and did convert into investment funds for use throughout the economy. This so-called turnover tax—similar to our sales and excise taxes—also cut down the consumption of the urban population by forcing its members to pay the relatively high prices that resulted from the inclusion of this tax in the prices of goods they bought. From 1931 to 1940 this source accounted for between half and two-thirds of all Soviet government income annually. [70] The Soviet government also levies income and other taxes on the population and sells billions of rubles worth of bonds annually, all providing it with additional funds that can be and are used for capital investment and other purposes.

In such years as 1933, over 60 per cent of Soviet government expenditures went for the financing of the national economy.[71] Of course, as the national income increased following earlier heavy state investment, it became possible to loosen somewhat the restrictions upon consumption while still diverting huge sums for capital expansion. Thus, while strict rationing had to be resorted to in the early 1930's to supplement fiscal devices used to reduce consumption, this rationing was ended in the middle 1930's and not resumed till the invasion of the USSR in 1941. In the late 1930's increasing military expenditures were added to the desire for further investment as motivations for restraining the population's consumption and the growth of its standard of living. Military requirements were dominant, of course, during World War II and continued to be a very significant drain upon the national income after 1945, as the result of the tense international situation.

Before 1941, Soviet acquisitions of capital from abroad were relatively minor. During the 1920's the USSR did permit foreigners to obtain concessions to operate mining, manufacturing, trading, and other enterprises; and as of June 1, 1928, over 97 foreign concessions were in operation. About $30,000,000 was invested in 39 concessions operating in July 1927; [72] this sum was estimated to be less than one per cent of all the capital invested in the USSR. As late as 1929 the Chief Concessions Committee of the USSR was seeking to interest foreign investors in building such important projects as the Magnitogorsk and Taganrog metallurgical works.[73] But foreign capitalists

---

[70] Baykov, *op. cit.*, p. 397.

[71] *Ibid.*

[72] *The Soviet Union*, pp. 170–71.

[73] Cf. the references to the publications listed in Harry Schwartz, *The Soviet Economy: A Selected Bibliography of Materials in English*, p. 38. Syracuse: Syracuse University Press, 1949. *The Soviet Union*, issued in 1929, lists over 150 concession possibilities drawn up by the State Planning Commission to fit in with the first Five-Year Plan. As late as September 1928 the Soviet government announced a policy of extending and liberalizing the conditions on which concessions were granted. Cf. *ibid.*, pp. 173–74.

could hardly be expected to be enthusiastic about investing their money in the economic development of the USSR, a country whose leaders made no secret of their opposition to world capitalism. It is not surprising that no really significant influx of foreign capital voluntarily reached the Soviet Union. By about 1930 the Soviet government had decided to accept the hardships of financing its capital expansion from domestic sources, except to the extent it could get credits abroad for the purchases of various products it required. In 1931 it owed about $1,400,000,000 to foreign governments and exporters for goods bought, but by April 1938 these debts had been wiped out.[74]

When the Soviet government annexed Eastern Poland, the Baltic States, and other areas during 1939–40, it took over the capital and other resources of these areas. When Soviet troops occupied Eastern Europe, Eastern Germany, Eastern Austria, Manchuria, and Northern Korea at the end of World War II, they seized large quantities of machinery, livestock, and other capital, which were moved to the USSR on the ground that they were war booty, reparations, and property stolen from the USSR. These capital acquisitions have undoubtedly facilitated the rebuilding of the war-devastated areas of the country. During World War II the USSR received machinery, equipment, and other capital goods from the United States, Great Britain, and France, under the Lend-Lease and Mutual Aid Programs. These acquisitions of capital from abroad during the past 15 years far exceed the value of foreign investments in the USSR during the 1920's.

Labor. The rapid expansion of production, particularly industrial production, during most of the period of Soviet rule would have been impossible without drastic changes in the size and distribution of its working population. In part the increased number of workers required came from the rise in population. Thus the 1926 census recorded about 147,000,000 individuals in the USSR; the census of January 1939 found almost 170,500,000 living within the same boundaries. The areas annexed by the Soviet Union during 1939–40 are estimated to have had about 22,000,000 inhabitants, so that by 1940 approximately 193,000,000 persons lived under Soviet rule, a rise of more than 30 per cent as compared with 1926. From the point

---

[74] M. V. Condoide, *Russian-American Trade*, p. 63. Columbus: Ohio State University, 1946.

of view of recruitment of industrial labor, the most important phenomenon has been the shift of millions of persons from agricultural to nonagricultural employment to provide labor for the rapidly growing number of factories, mines, transport lines, construction projects, and government agencies. Such a shift of labor, without perilous reduction of agricultural production, was possible because of the rapid rate of increase of farm population before World War II, because much of the farm population had previously been far from fully employed, and because collectivization and mechanization of Soviet agriculture in the 1930's helped further reduce farm labor requirements.

The restoration of the labor force for large industry is indicated by data for so-called census industry. This branch of production had employed 2,885,000 workers in 1913 but was down to 1,602,000 by the beginning of 1922, when some degree of stability had been regained. By 1928 census industry exceeded the 1913 mark and employed almost 3,100,000 workers.[75] A more general indicator of the early growth of the nonagricultural labor force is provided by data showing that the number of persons employed outside agriculture increased from 5,843,000 in 1923–24 to 9,545,000 in 1928.[76]

It was after 1928 that the great expansion of the nonagricultural labor force occurred, as the tremendous construction and production activity of the five-year plans pushed ahead. By 1938 the number of workers and employees in the national economy — a term roughly equivalent to the number of persons employed outside of agriculture — had increased to 27,800,000, almost three times the approximately corresponding figure for 1928.[77] By 1940, after the annexation of Eastern Poland, the Baltic States, and parts of Rumania, the number of workers and employees in the Soviet national economy reached 31,200,000. This number fell sharply during the first years of World War II, to 19,300,000 in 1943, re-

---

[75] *Narodnoye Khozyaistvo, SSSR,* pp. 112, 113, 410, 411.

[76] *Ibid.,* p. 411.

[77] Figure cited by Abram Bergson, "A Problem in Soviet Statistics," *Review of Economic Statistics,* November 1947, p. 236. The term workers and employees in the national economy includes also government employees in agriculture, such as those on state farms, but these are believed to have been less than 10 per cent of the total. Cf. the discussion in Harry Schwartz, "A Critique of 'Appraisals of Russian Economic Statistics,'" *Review of Economics and Statistics,* February 1948, p. 40. Since the expansion of M.T.S. staff in late 1953, the percentage is somewhat larger.

covering in 1945 to 27,200,000 and to the new high of 33,400,000 in 1948.[78] By the end of 1953, the total had reached 44,800,000 workers and employees.

Technology. As had been done so often before in earlier Russian history, the leaders of the Soviet Union turned to the West for many of the technically trained personnel and much of the advanced machinery they required in the vital first stages of their economic development program. During most of the 1920's and 1930's, large numbers of American, British, French, German, and other foreign technicians were brought to the USSR to superintend the construction of new plants, mines, and dams, or the introduction of new production processes, as well as to teach Russians their technical skills. The great Dnepr River hydroelectric system, for example, was built under the supervision of the American engineer Hugh Cooper, and received its original basic equipment from the General Electric Company's plants in Schenectady, N. Y., and elsewhere. Such examples could be multiplied.[79] A significant number of Russians were sent abroad, as in the time of Peter the Great, to study in foreign schools and to work in foreign factories and other enterprises where they could learn the advanced technology of the West. Many of the Soviet Union's major new plants erected in the late 1920's and early 1930's were equipped with foreign-made machinery, for in many cases such equipment had never been made in the USSR before. Russia's agriculture, threatened with a catastrophic shortage of draft power when peasants slaughtered their horses and cattle in the period of forced collectivization, was substantially aided by imports of tens of thousands of tractors during 1929–31, before Soviet tractor plants had come into full operation. It seems correct to say that every or almost every major branch of the Soviet productive system received substantial technical aid from abroad and had much of its rapidly expanding corps of native engineers and technicians of all kinds trained directly or indirectly by foreigners.

The above should not be interpreted to mean that the Soviet Union could not have forged ahead economically without this help from abroad. Even in 1928 the USSR had a significant corps of

[78] Harry Schwartz, "Soviet Labor Policy 1945–1949," *The Annals of the American Academy of Political and Social Science*, May 1949, p. 75.

[79] Much valuable material on the American contribution to the Soviet Union's technical progress is provided in Hans Heymann, *We Can Do Business With Russia, passim.* Chicago: Ziff Davis, 1945.

technically competent personnel of all kinds; and if the need had arisen, these might have struggled alone with the tasks set by the central government, and perhaps eventually fulfilled them. But the progress achieved under such conditions could not have been nearly so rapid as that actually attained.

Since the late 1930's the USSR has employed relatively few foreign technicians, except for Germans brought eastward after World War II. In part this has been the result of the fact that those who worked in the USSR earlier did their work well and trained a tremendously enlarged army of Soviet citizens who could take over their tasks. Also, the beginnings had been well made in most areas where the USSR had originally been backward. In part, however, the cutting of direct ties with Western specialists resulted from the political tension and international distrust that affected all areas of Soviet policy after the purge trials of the late 1930's in which many of the outstanding Soviet political and military figures were condemned as foreign agents. In the postwar period, the role of foreigners in stimulating the growth of the Soviet economy before World War II has been systematically ignored, while the virtues and preëminence of Soviet science and technology are boasted about at all opportunities. Nevertheless the Soviet Union still keeps sharp watch upon the advances in technology in other countries so that it may appropriate them, as well as the advances made by its own citizens, for its future economic growth.

Raw Materials. In an earlier chapter, we have noted the great natural wealth of the USSR, and particularly its large-scale resources of most major industrial raw materials. Much of the present knowledge of this wealth has been obtained in detail only during the Soviet era, during which large numbers of geologists, prospectors, and related personnel have been sent forth to find all possible deposits of useful metals and minerals. As we shall see in more detail later, where the USSR did not have needed raw materials in adequate quantity, vigorous steps were taken to remedy the situation so far as possible. Long before the United States undertook its wartime synthetic rubber production program, the USSR had gone in for such production, as well as for the growing of rubber-bearing plants such as *kok-sagyz* in order to make up for the deficiency of rubber trees in the USSR. Raw cotton, long one of the major imported raw materials of the Soviet and Russian economies, is now for the most part obtained from domestic production, as the result of sharply expanded plantings of this crop in Central Asia and elsewhere.

The examples cited above illustrate one of the most important aspects of Soviet economic policy both before and after World War II — the effort to obtain maximum self-sufficiency. This attitude, of course, was born as the result of the Soviet preoccupation with what they regarded as the certainty of future war, one that they have felt might see the entire noncommunist world arrayed against them. Under these circumstances shortages of key raw materials could lead to the same fatal consequences as technological backwardness or inadequate industry. Spurred on by this motivation, the Soviet leaders have been willing to bear the higher costs of producing at home commodities that could be bought more cheaply abroad.

The Making of Major Decisions in Economic Policy

At the beginning of this chapter, it was pointed out that supreme power in the field of economic policy — as in all areas of Soviet policy—is today in the hands of Premier Malenkov and his Presidium colleagues. It is they who make the fundamental decisions regarding the direction and tempo of Soviet economic development. Whatever disagreements and debates may take place among them are carefully kept from the outside world, which is presented merely with the decisions reached, decisions from which no dissent is permitted. Since the later 1920's, therefore, we know little of the actual course of argument behind the making of economic policy, though we know the broad factors — such as the fear of war — that must have been vital determinants. Before Stalin died, much economic policy was baldly presented to the world as wholly the result of Stalin's inspiration and suggestion, with little or no credit to others.

Matters were not so, however, in the first decade of the Soviet regime. Debate was vigorous, and opinion varied publicly among Soviet leaders in those early years. Their disputes were conducted in public congresses and by means of polemics in the press and in pamphlets or books. At various times in those early years, the "Right" faction lead by Bukharin and others urged that the solution of the Soviet government's economic problems be sought by means of greater concessions to the wealthy peasantry to induce them to increase their production and make it available to the government voluntarily, even if such concessions slowed down the pace of industrialization. A "Left" faction headed by Trotsky argued that the concessions made to the *kulaks* and the peasantry in general were already excessive and should be revoked, urging in the mid-1920's that an intensive program of rapid industrialization be undertaken, the means to be procured through exploitation of the peasantry. These debates were only in part arguments about economic policy, for paralleling them were titanic struggles for the leadership of the Communist Party after Lenin's death. Stalin, who won this bitter contest and became the unchallenged ruler of the Soviet Union, headed a faction whose policy fluctuated between the "Right" and "Left" extremes, and he himself conducted notable polemics against Trotsky, Bukharin, and other oustanding proponents of divergent economic and political policies. Once Stalin had achieved a clear-cut victory over his opponents, the five-year plans were carried out in a way resembling the policy sought by Trotsky and his supporters several years earlier. Maurice Dobb, the noted English student of the Soviet economy, who is an admirer of Stalin, argues that while Trotsky's policy was wrong in 1925 when he fought for it, it was correct under the different conditions of 1928 when Stalin began putting it into effect.[80]

But these open debates belong to the historical record only, so far as our public knowledge goes. For the past two decades Soviet economic policy has been decided in secret and then approved in public after only the most cursory and superficial semblance of debate, so far as essentials are concerned. But it would seem contrary to human experience to assume that such debates no longer go on, even if only within the inner circle.

[80] Maurice Dobb, *op. cit.*, pp. 206–7. A summary, but also somewhat partisan, review of these debates is given in this book, Ch. 8. Cf. also Alexander Ehrlich, "Preobrazhenski and the Economics of Soviet Industrialization," *Quarterly Journal of Economics*, February 1950, pp. 57–88.

CHAPTER V

THE NATIONAL ECONOMIC PLAN

T HE NATIONAL ECONOMIC PLAN is the central coordinating mechanism of the Soviet economy. This plan outlines the tasks to be accomplished during the period it covers and directs the allocation of all resources toward the achievement of the assigned goals. On the production side, it prescribes the total national income objective and the physical volume of production for all major commodities. The plan specifies the division of the national income between investment and consumption and assigns the relative share in consumption to be enjoyed by each significant group of the population. The volume and composition of both internal and foreign trade are governed by the plan, as are the prices of most commodities bought and sold. All money in circulation is taken into account in this document, which estimates how much of the population's income will go for purchases of consumer goods, for bank savings, for buying government bonds, and for direct taxes. The annual government budget is an important component of the financial portions of the plan. In short, the Soviet economic plan is a gigantic, comprehensive blueprint that attempts to govern the economic activities and interrelations of all persons and institutions in the USSR, as well as the economic relations of the USSR with other countries. To the extent that the plan actually controls the development of events, all the manifold activities of the Soviet economy are coordinated as if they were parts of one incredibly enormous enterprise directed from the central headquarters in Moscow.

The Soviet Union uses several different types of national economic plans. Once these are adopted by the Communist Party's leadership

Amer. Econ. Review - Dec. 1959
"Planning with material balance."

and the government, they have the force of law and must be carried out, or exceeded, except as changes in original plans are made by the proper authorities. The most widely publicized have been the five-year plans, which chart the major lines of future economic development for that period, and cover the entire national economy. Similar comprehensive plans looking fifteen years or more into the future are believed to have been prepared, though they have never been published in detail. Each year the State Planning Committee prepares an annual plan in extremely great detail to govern economic development during the twelve months ahead. Quarterly plans and monthly plans for major areas of the national economy are also prepared, based upon the annual and five-year plans covering each period but taking account of developments since formulation of the original programs.

Besides plans for the national economy as a whole, development programs are drawn up for each significant sector and region of the USSR's productive machine. Most of these are merely part of a five-year or one-year plan and are prepared as part of the work on drawing up the comprehensive document. But from time to time special plans have been drawn up providing that extraordinary attention be given to some particularly important sector of the economy. Such special plans may cover a span of several five-year-plan periods, as in the case of the long-range afforestation program announced in 1948, or may begin in one five-year-plan era and end in the next, as in the case of the three-year plans for raising consumer goods and food output announced in late 1953. Such extraordinary partial plans are presumably woven into the fabric of annual and five-year plans for the national economy after their adoption.

Despite the fact that they have the force of law, Soviet economic plans are not regarded as inflexible, but rather as subject to such change as is found necessary during the period of their operation. The classic formulation of this attitude was given by Stalin:

> For us, for bolsheviks, the five-year plan is not something finished and given once and for all. For us the five-year plan, like any other plan, is only a plan accepted as a first approximation, which must be made more exact, changed, and completed on the basis of experience. . . . No economic plan can take into account all the possibilities which are hidden in the depths of our society and which are discovered only in the course of work, in the course of realizing the plan at the

factory, at the mill, in the collective farm, in the state farm, in the county, etc.[1]

Stalin might have added that Soviet plans are changed to take account of new developments in the field of foreign relations and to meet problems caused by unforeseen domestic events, such as the poor harvest of 1946. His admission that Soviet planners have neither perfect foresight nor perfect insight should be borne in mind in considering the material that follows.

Over the years since the beginning of organized planning, Soviet plans have become progressively more complete and detailed. The GOELRO plan accepted in 1920 covered only about 15 industries, while the First Five-Year Plan promulgated less than a decade later set targets for some 50 industries, as well as for agriculture and the major aspects of the country's financial system. The Second Five-Year Plan covered about 120 branches of industry and had a much more detailed construction program, while providing for agricultural development in terms of specific crops. Only rather sketchy outlines of the Third, Fourth, and Fifth Five-Year Plans were published, but it seems likely that the basic unpublished documents reflected improvement over the earlier efforts. One indication of this improvement is the fact that during the last war planning authorities allocated the most important commodities directly to 120 major claimants. They prepared quarterly supply plans every three months, each containing over 30,000 separate planned figures.[2]

Since the first beginning of Soviet planning efforts, the amount of information upon which the planners could draw has increased many times, while they have accumulated a large fund of valuable experience. A very complete and complex statistical reporting mechanism has been built up that provides current data on the progress of work in every part of the economy, as well as basic data for further planning.[3] Scientists and technicians of every specialty have been en-

[1] Quoted in G. Sorokin, *Sotsialisticheskoye Planirovaniye Narodnogo Khozyaistva SSSR*, pp. 35–36. Moscow: 1946.

[2] *Ibid.*, pp. 38, 46, 60.

[3] Harry Schwartz, "The Organization and Operation of the Soviet Statistical Apparatus," *The American Statistician*, April–May 1953. The Central Statistical Administration of the Council of Ministers is the chief statistical agency, but many other agencies participate as well. A Soviet source stated early in 1952 that over 2,000,000 bookkeepers, statisticians, accountants, and economists were engaged in the work of providing needed data. *Vestnik Statistiki*, No. 2 (1952), p. 65.

APPROXIMATE ORGANIZATION OF THE
STATE PLANNING COMMITTEE IN LATE 1946

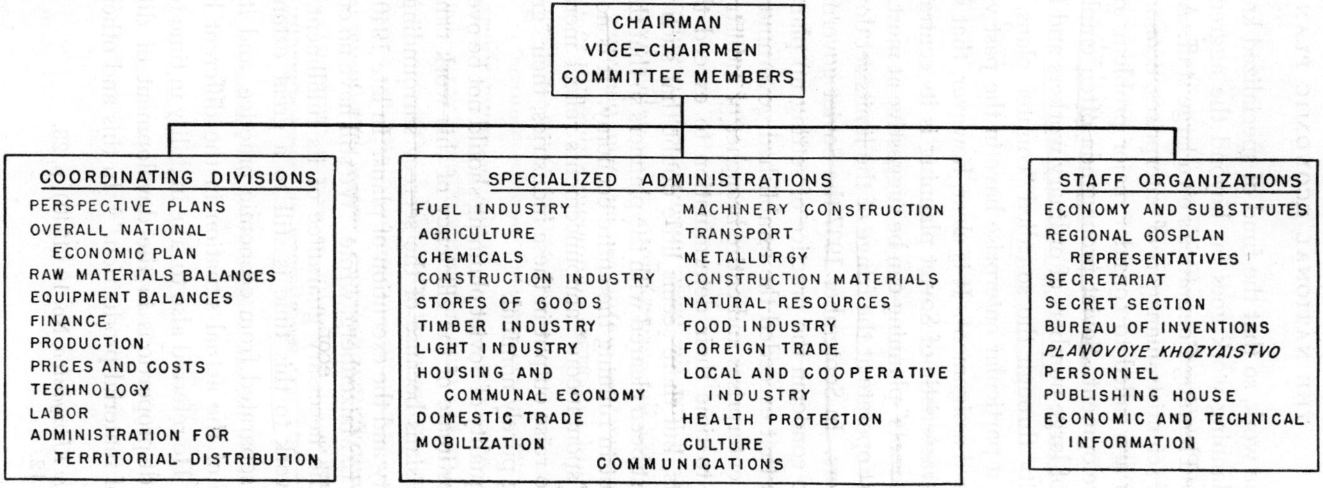

CHAIRMAN
VICE-CHAIRMEN
COMMITTEE MEMBERS

COORDINATING DIVISIONS
PERSPECTIVE PLANS
OVERALL NATIONAL ECONOMIC PLAN
RAW MATERIALS BALANCES
EQUIPMENT BALANCES
FINANCE
PRODUCTION
PRICES AND COSTS
TECHNOLOGY
LABOR
ADMINISTRATION FOR TERRITORIAL DISTRIBUTION

SPECIALIZED ADMINISTRATIONS
FUEL INDUSTRY
AGRICULTURE
CHEMICALS
CONSTRUCTION INDUSTRY
STORES OF GOODS
TIMBER INDUSTRY
LIGHT INDUSTRY
HOUSING AND COMMUNAL ECONOMY
DOMESTIC TRADE
MOBILIZATION
MACHINERY CONSTRUCTION
TRANSPORT
METALLURGY
CONSTRUCTION MATERIALS
NATURAL RESOURCES
FOOD INDUSTRY
FOREIGN TRADE
LOCAL AND COOPERATIVE INDUSTRY
HEALTH PROTECTION
CULTURE
COMMUNICATIONS

STAFF ORGANIZATIONS
ECONOMY AND SUBSTITUTES
REGIONAL GOSPLAN REPRESENTATIVES
SECRETARIAT
SECRET SECTION
BUREAU OF INVENTIONS
PLANOVOYE KHOZYAISTVO
PERSONNEL
PUBLISHING HOUSE
ECONOMIC AND TECHNICAL INFORMATION

FIGURE 1. *Organization of the State Planning Committee.*

149

listed in the work, so that the fund of specialized knowledge drawn upon in planning work goes far beyond the aggregate capabilities of the State Planning Committee's own large staff. As required, conferences of scientists, managers of enterprises, economists, engineers, and others are called to consider major problems of planning and future development. Soviet propaganda often emphasizes the participation of large numbers of ordinary workers and farmers in planning activity through the so-called "counter plans," by which the workers in a particular enterprise have in the past vowed to exceed their planned assignment. It is clear, however, that since the fundamental characteristic of Soviet planning is its centralized character, such "grass roots" planning can be suggestive at most, and by its very nature must operate at the fringe of the limits set down by the Moscow planners. In September 1937 the Soviet government had to go so far as to condemn the practice of setting up plans for individual enterprises that exceeded the established government assignments.[4] Individual enterprises and entire branches of industry still announce from time to time their determination to exceed their productive assignments, but there seems little doubt that such announcements have at least been cleared with the planners so that they can be taken into account in running the entire economy. It is not at all unlikely that such "spontaneous" announcements reflect merely government decisions to raise output in these industries, their "grass roots" character being purely nominal.

But the quality of Soviet planning should not be overestimated. An adequate estimate of the efficiency of this work cannot be reached by non-Russians because of the secrecy surrounding detailed planning activity and the execution of plans. In late 1940, a noted Soviet economist, L. Maizenberg, wrote, "We still have no current economic plan and the necessary guarantee of its fulfillment," adding, "Our planning work to this time is still to a great extent bureaucratic-statistical, separated from economic practice, and it lacks concrete knowledge of the actual situation in the different branches of the economy." He referred also to "the inability in time to prevent penetration of disproportions in the development of different decisive branches of material production."[5] In this and other comment that

---

[4] *Planovoye Khozyaistvo*, No. 10 (1940), p. 23.
[5] *Ibid.*, p. 12.

has come forth from Soviet sources at various times are strong hints that behind the complex calculations and enormous tables of Soviet plans there may be strong elements of ignorance and confusion.[6]

In evaluating Soviet planning, it must be borne in mind that no single blueprint could encompass all the economic activities of more than 200,000,000 people spread over that country's vast area. Economic planning is most detailed and most influential in those branches that the government considers most important, particularly heavy industry. It is less detailed and less influential in many parts of the economy serving consumers or producing for them, for example, local and cooperative industry. The problems of making the far-flung agriculture of the USSR completely subservient to planned direction of production activities is probably still far from entirely solved. Moreover, the plan must be translated into reality by human beings, not automatons. An energetic factory manager, for example, may take the risk of breaking out of planned restrictions if he thinks it necessary in order to attain his assigned goals. If he has powerful friends in the Communist Party, government, or economic hierarchies, he will have more freedom of action and more opportunity to exercise initiative than another official with less powerful connections. Corruption and graft are not unknown in the Soviet economy, and those who profit by such malfeasance often do so at the expense of, or by evading, planned assignments. Soviet novels and plays, often sources of valuable insight into the realities of life in the USSR, have shown time and again that the interrelationships between economic plans and those whom they direct are complex rather than simple.

The Nature of Soviet Economic Plans

To understand the nature and objectives of Soviet economic plans, it is helpful to visualize a complex economy in operation during some period of time, say a year. At the end of this time a complete recording of these operations would note the following factors:

First, physical production of goods would have been carried out and these goods would have been utilized or stored in different ways. Let us take the case of steel. The total supply of steel would ob-

---

[6] On this point cf. *Pravda*, April 18, 1940, and N. A. Voznesensky, "Stalin's Three Five-Year Plans," *Bolshevik*, No. 1 (1940). Russian text.

viously consist of the steel in storage at the beginning of the year plus the production during the year plus any imports. At the end of the year it would be found that there was a certain amount of steel in storage while the rest of the steel had been consumed in various ways or exported. A complete accounting of steel would have to account both for the total supply and for its utilization, as in the following equation:

Supply	*Utilization*
Amount in storage at the beginning of year + Production + Imports	Amount in storage at end of year + Amount consumed in the steel industry itself +
=	Amount consumed in the tractor industry + Amount consumed in construction+Amount consumed in making locomotives + Amount consumed in making freight cars + (and so on for all the many industries using steel) + Exports.

This equation can be stated more simply in symbols if we call the amount in storage at the beginning of the year S_o, the amount in storage at the end of the year S_e, production P, exports E, imports I, and the amounts consumed in different industries, $c_1, c_2, c_3, \ldots c_n$, where n is simply the number of different industries using steel. We then have the above equation in words translated into the symbolic form:

$$S_o + P + I = S_e + c_1 + c_2 + c_3 + c_4 + c_5 + \ldots + c_n + E$$

If there were 100 industries using steel, there would be 100 different c quantities; if 1,000 industries, 1,000 c's; and so forth. The equation above simplifies the actual situation for steel considerably. Steel is stored in many different places; in any one industry it will be used at different plants; and it may be exported to many different countries. If the above equation were written out in its full complexity, each term would have to be replaced by the various terms of which it is composed. Thus the amount in storage at the beginning of the year, S_o, might be replaced by $S_o' + S_o'' + S_o''' + S_o''''$ and so on for as many terms as there are steel storage centers. To write down the equation above in full detail for a country like the Soviet Union would undoubtedly require thousands of terms.

Even the detail suggested in the preceding paragraph does not really represent the situation fully, since it implicitly assumes that steel is a homogenous commodity, which is not. For example, ordinary low-grade carbon steel cannot be used where stainless steel is required. In actuality there are many different kinds of steels, meeting different needs, each of which would have to be accounted for separately if we required complete detail. Thus even the simplified form of the general steel equation above would have to be broken down into a series of different equations, at least several hundred in number, each one showing the supply and distribution of each different kind of steel. And if these equations were to be written in the detailed form suggested above, a full description of the production and distribution of steel would require several hundred equations, many of which would have hundreds and thousands of terms.

It should be clear, however, that the number of equations required to represent the equality of the total amount of steel available and the total amount distributed between storage, consumption, and exports will depend upon the degree of precision and detail desired. On this factor too will depend the number of terms explicitly contained in the equation. But even in the simplest form, a summary statement, such as the first equation above stated first in words and then in symbols, must rest upon a complete accounting of all stocks, production, international trade, and consumption. The complexity described is inherent in the nature of the steel industry, its widespread geographic distribution, and its many customers; this complexity cannot be escaped.

But steel, or rather each variety of steel, is only one commodity. A similar supply and distribution equation would have to be prepared for each commodity in the economy, and considerations similar to those suggested for steel above would apply. A full accounting for all production would have to include supply and distribution equations for tractors, shoes, ball bearings, bread, sugar beets, printing presses, paper, and so on. This would require thousands of equations, which, if presented in the full detail outlined above, would include millions of terms. Even the simplest formulation, based on groups of commodities, such as all kinds of steel taken together, all kinds of motor vehicles taken together, and so forth, would require at least several hundred equations containing many thousands of terms.

An important feature of such an accounting record is the fact that if it were available we should be able to see in detail all the commodities utilized in the making of each product. For the automobile industry, for example, the system of equations described above would supply us with the information on the steel, copper, rubber, leather, gears, spark plugs, and other materials and parts utilized in the manufacture of automobiles. The kinds and amounts of these different commodities so employed would of course be determined by the types of cars being made and the technology of their production. For any product, the relationship between the volume of output of that product and the amounts of different complementary goods required to produce that output is termed the *production function*. The system of equations we have described above, therefore, would supply us with the production functions of different industries or products, depending upon whether the consumption items in those equations applied to industries or to individual products. Obviously, for fullest detail, the c's in our equation should be the consumption of each material in the making of a particular product.

Analogous to the equations we have been discussing for commodities would be one showing the supply of human labor available in that economy during a particular year, and its distribution among different employments. For full precision, such an accounting of labor resources would have to take into account the fact that a carpenter cannot be used where a skilled machinist is required. The full record would have to contain a large number of equations showing the supply and utilization of all the many different types of skilled, semiskilled, and unskilled workers. Moreover, since human beings grow old and retire, or die, our accounting record would have to show what progress was made during the period studied in training new workers for all the different kinds of jobs that must be done. Service workers of all kinds, from barbers to doctors, would also have to be included in this accounting of labor use.

So far our discussion of this accounting of an economy's operation has been conducted in purely physical terms, and our equations have involved tons of steel, thousands of tractors, millions of nails, and numbers of workers. But if we confined our records to this material, we should have a very inadequate knowledge of what had happened during the period studied, because we should have ignored the fact that goods are bought and sold for money. Even in the Soviet economy, both consumers and producers make decisions regarding what to buy or sell, at least in part, in the light of the prices of different goods and the amount of monetary resources they have available. Thus the full accounting would have to include a series of financial equations.

We can see their form if we recall our remarks about the automobile industry and its purchase of many different goods and labor services for use in production, using this term broadly to cover all activities of the industry. In any given period, the automobile industry has an income derived from the sale of cars. This income is equal to the cost of production plus profit or minus loss, as the case may be. To state this relationship symbolically, let us suppose for the sake of simplicity that all cars sell at the same price, p, and that q cars have been sold. Income during our period will then be simply the product pq. Let us suppose that in the various supply and distribution equations for different products discussed above, c_4 in each case represented the amount of that product going to the automobile industry. Let us use a system of primes to denote different materials. Thus c_4' might be the amount of steel, c_4'' the amount of rubber, c_4''' the amount of leather, and so on. And let us suppose that the unit prices of these commodities are p', p'', p''', and so on, respectively.[7] Then the total cost or expenditure of the automobile industry can be represented as the sum of the products of each c multiplied by the corresponding p. If we introduce the quantity D, defined simply as the difference between income and cost, the relationship between the industry income and cost can be expressed in equation form. We then have:

$$pq = p' c_4{}^1 + p'' c_4'' + p''' c_4''' + \ldots + p^k c_4{}^k + D$$

Here $p^k c_4{}^k$ represents simply the cost of the kth or last commodity purchased. It will be seen from this equation that if D is zero, income equals cost. If D is positive, income exceeds costs, and a profit has been made that can be used for savings or other purposes. If D is negative, costs have exceeded income. This loss may simply be due to uneconomic management or other factors. But costs may exceed income too if they include the expenses of new investment in the making of automobiles, such as the building of new factories or the expansion of old ones.

The hypothetical accounting record we have been discussing

---

[7] Depreciation can be fitted into this scheme by defining a unit of depreciation as that amount worth one dollar, so if the industry's depreciation allowance is $1,000,000, it may be said to have used 1,000,000 units of depreciation (the c in our formulation) at the price of one dollar each. Here as elsewhere in this discussion the writer has leaned heavily upon the exposition of Prof. W. W. Leontief in his *The Structure of the American Economy 1919–1929*, pp. 33 ff. Cambridge: Harvard University Press, 1941.

would contain a similar cost-income equation for each product or industry in the economy — for the making of tires, the growing of grain, the production of motion pictures, and so on. Since there are hundreds of industries and thousands of products, the number of such cost-income equations would be large and the number of terms in these equations enormous. The financial aspects of capital-construction projects could be handled as above by substituting the amount allocated for each project instead of the income term, pq.

The discussion above has been in terms of the costs and income of a product or an industry, but the concepts involved are more general. Our hypothetical record would contain an equation showing the sources of income of the government and its expenditures for different purposes. Since the Soviet Union has national, provincial, and local governments, the number of such governmental financial equations could easily reach several thousand. A similar tabulation would presumably be available for the money incomes and expenditures of the population as a whole, and for major groups in the population, such as urban dwellers, farmers, and other groups.

The most summary data of our hypothetical record would show the total value of all goods and services (the gross national product, or the national income, or some similar over-all measure), and the breakdown of this production between consumption, investment, and reserves. The record would show too all the investment projects inaugurated, continued, or ended during the year, including all new factories, railroads, roads, houses, schools, and so forth. If any human mind could encompass all these data, it would have a bird's-eye view of all economic activity in the nation during the period studied.

The above discussion has been in terms of a quantitative history of economic activity *after* the period in which this activity has taken place. Economic planning, on the other hand, is the effort to prepare such a detailed scheme of economic activity *before* a particular period, and then to assure that the economy actually follows the path blueprinted by the planners. With regard to Soviet economic planning, it must be added that in the course of executing the plan the authorities have often altered the original blueprint in order to facilitate the fulfillment or overfulfillment of certain goals of major importance, even at the expense of nonfulfillment of other goals that are regarded as less important. Such alteration of original plans is the result either of poor planning that failed to provide for a future course of economic activity compatible with the real possibilities, or of the appearance of new factors affecting over-all policy — such as a major change in the state of international tension — which requires the substitution of new goals for those sought when the original plan was drawn up. Even in their most elaborate form, however, economic plans do not attain the most detailed and comprehensive coverage suggested above.

In an economy dominated by private enterprise, there is little or no organized, collective effort made *in advance* to fix the the equations of physical production and financial equilibrium for the entire economy, at least during peacetime.[8] The economic activity that takes place in such a society is the resultant of the activities and decisions of many different individuals and groups of individuals who act on the basis of current economic information and their anticipations regarding future prices, supply, and demand. These individuals and groups of individuals are free to attempt to maximize their profits, or to serve other ends, so long as their activities remain within the legal framework provided by the laws governing contracts, prohibiting certain types of monopolies, regulating wages and hours, and so on. Our economy relies upon the *force of competition* among the participants in economic activity to assure that the welfare of the community will be served. Our government acts to help certain groups assumed legally to be too weak to fend for themselves, and it intervenes from time to time in an effort to help maintain or restore competition. But the rights of private property and the right to seek private profit through economic activity are still fundamental to our way of life, despite some important peripheral modifications in our ideas on these subjects in recent years. Increasingly in the past two decades the United States government has become a direct participant in economic activity through

---

[8] In the United States, one exception, however, is the government budget, which is prepared in advance in an effort to anticipate and govern future government revenues and expenditures. And presumably in the present strained postwar situation, government agencies keep sharp watch over supplies and utilization of the most important raw materials, but such activity, before the Korean conflict, was mainly observational and was not planning in the sense used above. A closer approach to economic planning was begun in this country after United States involvement in the Korean conflict and subsequent stepped-up mobilization.

such agencies as the Atomic Energy Commission and the Reconstruction Finance Corporation. These and other instruments of government action have important influences upon many different markets for goods and services, but they do not replace markets in peacetime as the major coordinating agencies of our economy.

Soviet planners are in a completely different situation. All economic activity is legally subservient to the plan and must be performed in accordance with its instructions. In carrying on their work, therefore, Soviet planners make in advance the decisions — such as the division of national income between consumption and investment — that in a free enterprise society are simply the resultants of the independent decisions of competing individuals and groups. The equations discussed above in our hypothetical sketch of quantitative economic history are explicitly formulated in advance by Soviet planners, who call them "balances" — natural balances if they are expressed in commodity terms, synthetic balances if they are financial equations or deal with labor distribution. The composition of these advance balances is one of the most important steps in the drawing up of Soviet plans, since it is at this point that the problems of economic coordination are explicitly faced. Each figure in these balances — amounts stored, produced, imported, exported, consumed, and so on — is the subject of consciously planned decisions. In a capitalist economy, prices are fixed in the market and act as among the most important indicators and guides for economic activity. In the USSR, prices are fixed by Soviet planners, and the entrepreneurs of the Soviet economy are explicitly instructed that the plan's instructions, not price or profit considerations, are to guide their activities whenever there is conflict between the two.

The difficulties of constituting consistent balances are clear. The discussion above has pointed out how large must be the number of different quantities to be set by the planners, even if the number of balances is restricted by consolidating related commodities. Balancing the economy in advance requires both prediction of future output, that is, the setting of attainable, ever increasing goals, and the allocation of commodities produced. For example, the amount of sulphuric acid to be made in a year is determined and is then divided among its different uses. But the making of sulphuric acid must be assigned enough raw materials, labor, machinery, and financial means to make possible the production of the amount set as the goal. In turn, the amount of sulphuric acid allocated to the making of fertilizer, for example, must be sufficient to meet that industry's needs for this chemical in order that the production objective for fertilizers may be met. The consistency of the production function for each product or industry must be assured in advance, for the output of any commodity is limited to the amount made possible by the supply of the most scarce complementary goods required. The planners may have provided enough steel, copper, rubber, and other materials for 500,000 automobiles. But if they have allocated only enough bearings for 100,000 cars, only 100,000 properly working automobiles can be produced. The planners' problems are further complicated by the fact that the output of some commodities is highly variable and outside their control to a large extent. A bad harvest can work havoc upon the best-made plan, unless reserves of food and agricultural raw materials are large enough to cushion Nature's niggardliness effectively.

But mere consistency of the natural and synthetic balances in a plan — even though a difficult enough goal to achieve — is far from enough. A properly operated economy should employ its resources efficiently, getting the maximum return from its input of labor, raw materials, and other resources. The planners must strive to insure that their balances and plans provide for production at minimum expenditure of input. But how is such minimum expenditure to be measured in the USSR? Money costs do not necessarily reflect real costs there, since most prices are set arbitrarily by planners and have remained fixed for long periods at a time, though the underlying supply and demand conditions for the commodities involved changed markedly.[9] Economists have long debated whether it is possible for a socialist state to be managed rationally. Those who have denied this possibility have done so precisely on the ground that arbitrary prices in such an economy would offer no guide for in-

---

[9] At the beginning of 1949 a general increase of wholesale prices for the products of heavy industry and of railroad freight rates took place, the first since before the Nazi invasion of the Soviet Union in 1941. These prices had remained constant all through the war years and immediate postwar years, though the structure of costs for these commodities and the level of costs had changed considerably. Many of these prices were lowered at the beginning of 1950, and later as well. Cf. Naum Jasny, *Soviet Prices of Producers' Goods*, pp. 12–17. Stanford: Stanford University Press, 1952.

telligent choice among alternatives. Many of the economists who have affirmed the possibility of rational use of resources in a socialist state have done so on the premise that a meaningful price system would be set up and that prices would *not* be set arbitrarily.[10] This consideration must be kept in mind in considering Soviet planning. The USSR's price system will be considered in more detail later in this volume.

Drawing Up the Plan

The information available to foreigners on how the plan is actually drawn up in detail is rather scanty. Citizens of countries other than the Soviet Union have not in general been encouraged to visit the State Planning Committee and study its activities from the inside, nor does that committee usually publish its detailed worksheets or other essential material. It seems desirable, therefore, to present what is essentially a Soviet economist's account of how a Soviet plan is drawn up. The material that follows is largely based on, and in part translated from, a Soviet planning textbook issued in 1946.[11] Other Soviet sources are used as well, as indicated. The vagueness of part of this discussion is typical of that encountered in many Soviet expositions of this topic.

Four stages may be distinguished in working out a national economic plan: preparing directives for the plan; composing a proposed plan on the basis of the directives and making a balanced check of the proposed development of the branches of the economy; approval of the plan by the government; organization and control of plan fulfillment. In organizing the composition of the plan, the Gosplan (now known as the State Planning Committee[12] of the Council of Ministers) works out a system of indexes, that is, a list of tasks during the planned period for ministries, republics, territories, and provinces, and also a list of measures aiding fulfillment of the planned tasks.

10 Cf. F. A. Hayek, ed., *Collectivist Economic Planning.* London: Routledge, 1935; and the essays by Oscar Lange and Fred M. Taylor in Benjamin E. Lippincott, ed., *On the Economic Theory of Socialism.* Minneapolis: University of Minnesota Press, 1938. A sharply different third point of view, however, is that of Maurice Dobb, *Political Economy and Capitalism,* Ch. VIII, especially pp. 271–76. New York: International Publishers, 1945.

11 Sorokin, *op. cit.,* pp. 61 ff.

12 *Gosplan* was formerly known as the State Planning Commission.

The economic plan includes first the production tasks of each branch of industry and agriculture, and also technical-economic conditions of production, such as indexes of quality, technological organization, and norms for expenditure of materials and labor. It usually contains a very voluminous construction program aimed at increasing facilities for expanding production and meeting public needs.

The plan provides for the distribution of the total output, on the following scheme: from the total output is drawn, first, resources to cover expenditures for restoring means of production that have been used up. Second, part of the product goes for new investment. Third, there is formed a reserve or insurance fund against unexpected contingencies. Besides this there are formed funds for administration, for maintaining the armed forces, for meeting social needs (schools, sanitary institutions, and so on). The remaining part of the total output is available for purchase by consumers. The plan also defines the magnitude and means of the circulation of goods as well as the work of transport and mercantile organizations.

Measures in the field of labor include the distribution of the work force among branches of the economy, efforts to raise labor productivity through appropriate wage policy and mechanization of work, and expansion of the skilled labor force. The plan also allocates resources for housing, education, medical care, and other facets of consumption.

Finally the plans contain a financial program (budget, credit, measures regarding monetary circulation). The financial plan reflects the activity projected in production, distribution, and consumption. A system of financial incentives actively aids the entire process of economic activity.

A more concrete list of the plan's divisions follows:

1. Summary division, including basic indexes *(list of tasks)* of economic development.

2. Industry, including gross and marketed production in value terms, physical production, technical economic indicators.

3. Agriculture, including data on sown area, tractor work, agronomic measures, yields, number of livestock, indicators of livestock productivity.

4. Transport and communications, including average daily traffic,

work of all kinds of transport, repair and utilization of rolling stock, the development of communications.

5. Capital investment, including the volume of capital construction; the program for putting new productive capacity, new houses, and other capital projects into use; development of the construction industry; geological and prospecting work.

6. The technological plan, including the plan for introducing new techniques into the national economy.

7. The plans for supplying branches of the economy with raw materials, fuel, and equipment.

8. Plans for cultural and welfare construction, including children's institutions, health centers, schools, universities, movies, theaters, municipal utilities.

9. Labor, including the number of workers, their productivity, wages, and the training of specialists and supervisory workers.

10. Domestic trade and the requisitioning of agricultural products.

11. The plan for lowering costs in branches of the economy.

12. The state budget, credit, monetary circulation.

13. The plan for development of the economies of the union republics and major economic regions.

14. Foreign trade plans providing for exports and imports.

The plan and its indicators must be maximally exact, concrete, and directed specifically toward those individuals charged with each responsibility. As a result of these requirements, the plan or its most important divisions are worked out in branch and inter-branch sections in breakdowns according to forms of property, ministries, and regions. The branch breakdown includes the tasks assigned to industry as a whole, agriculture as a whole, all machine construction industries, all woodworking industries, and so on. The interbranch functional breakdown of the plan consists of the program for guaranteeing the economy with labor, equipment, metals, fuel, construction materials, and other necessities; the program for lowering costs and organizing savings; and so on.

Building the plan up by sections into a whole permits solution of certain general problems. Do the tempos of development of branches of consumption in the economy correspond to each other? What are the links between the branches with regard to raw materials, fuel, labor, monetary resources? It is impossible, for example, to say whether all construction projects will have equipment if there is no summary plan for machine construction. The problem of guaranteeing the population bread and livestock products is approached through the summary production plan for all collective farms, state farms, and other subordinate agricultural producers. The plan for supplying the national economy with fuel may be constructed only by taking into account the production of all kinds of fuel by all producers.

Consistency among the requirements of different branches for equipment, fuel, raw materials, labor, and financial means from state resources is attained by planning inter-branch linkages on the basis of the corresponding balances and distribution plans that have been worked out.

The economic plan takes into account the existence of state property and collective farm-cooperative property. The production of state enterprises and the wages of their employees are fully regulated by the national economic plan. The distribution of collective farm products is only partially covered by the state plan, since part of this production is disposed of at the farmers' discretion, including sale of some products on the free market at prices prevailing there. The plan takes account of the differences between state and cooperative enterprises.

The organizational or ministerial breakdown of the branch plan guarantees that the plan will give direct assignments to those who are responsible for each production task, thus bestowing on the plan an operative character. All tasks of the national economic plan are distributed by ministries. The 1945 plan gave industrial production assignments to more than 100 government organizations.

The plan for each ministry is part of the general national plan. Indicators and indexes are the same for all ministries, a fact that gives these figures a unifying role. Thus the indicators for the plans for industrial production are basically the following: gross production; marketed production in wholesale prices; physical output of the most important products; capital repair; expansion and new construction of enterprises; the number of workers and labor productivity; wages fund; provisions for guaranteeing enterprises raw materials, fuel, and semifabricated products; estimates of expenditures and incomes; costs of production; estimates of profits.

Besides fixing the list of indicators, the *Gosplan* establishes exact definitions of them, so as to avoid confusion and inconsistency in their calculation. The indexes of the national economic plan are used by the ministries as the basis for establishing the indexes on which to plan the activities of individual enterprises within their jurisdiction.

Regional Planning

The national economic plan is also broken down geographically, by regions. Goals for industry and agriculture, construction plans, and the work of transport cannot be determined exactly if they do not take into account the actual territorial distribution of the productive forces. The regional breakdown of the plan contains specific measures for proportional development of productive forces, for eliminating economic and cultural backwardness of some national republics, for special development of some regions in accordance with the interests of strengthening the military power of the country. Territorial breakdown of the plan is needed to guarantee the complete complex development of economic regions. Only a plan broken down geographically can give specific assignments as regards what to build, what to produce, and what organization is responsible for construction and production. Territorial breakdown not only is obligatory for the general government plan, but must be carried further. In each province the plan must be broken down by administrative districts, by villages, and by enterprises. The plan for the country as a whole is broken down into tasks for union republics; and inside them for autonomous republics, adminstrative territories, and provinces. Such administrative and territorial division is necessary to make the plan operative; otherwise much of it would lose practical significance.

As late as November 1940, a Soviet economist wrote: "It is necessary to note that up to recently almost all attention in the work of the *Gosplan* and the People's Commissariats has been paid to planning in terms of branches of industry. But the division of regional planning of the *Gosplan* did not comply with the work of territorial planning. . . . It is necessary to emphasize that until this time there has been no careful analysis of the distribution of each branch of industry, no analysis of inter-regional connections. Therefore there is also no clearly worked out material regarding the distribution of the different branches of the national economy and regarding the perspective complex development of the economic regions of the country. . . ." He indicated further that great confusion, duplication, and bureaucratic incompetence existed in the whole area of regional planning and geographic distribution of economic activity.[13] It seems likely, however, that strong measures were taken in 1940 and afterward to improve this aspect of Soviet planning.

For each republic or administrative province, the following basic plan indicators are worked out: output of industrial production (with separate indication of local industrial production not included in the output of all-union ministries); size of sown area; number of livestock; a titular list of new construction projects; volume of trade turnover and requisitions of agricultural products; network of schools, education, and medical institutions; municipal and housing economy; budget.

Not only is the plan worked out in a breakdown based on administrative-territorial units (province, territory, republic); it is also broken down on the basis of a series of large regions that do not coincide with administrative boundaries. In planning the coal industry, separate blueprints are drawn up for the southern coal region (Donbas), the central region (Mosbas), the Urals region, Kazakhstan, Siberia, and so forth. Planning by coal basins permits the definition of the zones supplied by each basin, of the rational boundaries for consumption of coal from specific minor local sources, of locations of new mines, of points for geological investigation. In planning the iron and steel industry, each of the following regions is examined separately: South, Center, Urals, Siberia, and Far East. Planning on the basis of such enlarged regions not only facilitates rational distribution of metal consumption but makes it possible for each region to solve the problems of metallurgical raw materials, fuels, types of output, and so forth.

Complete complex regional planning permits the fullest and most economical utilization of regional resources. It helps provide for the development of production so as to satisfy local needs in maxi-

---

[13] *Planovoye Khozyaistvo*, No. 11 (1940), pp. 39–46. Quoted material is on pp. 40–42. Continued serious inadequacies in Soviet planning are implied in a later issue, No. 2 (1953), p. 7.

mum degree and to end unnecessary transport of raw materials, fuel, and consumer goods over distances. The Eighteenth Congress of the Communist Party gave directives for the complex economic development of basic major economic regions. It showed the necessity of organizing in these areas the output of fuel, cement, alabaster, chemical fertilizers, glass, and consumer goods in amounts meeting local requirements. The *Gosplan* does this planning for such enlarged regions. In working out the majority of problems of territorial distribution of production in the Third Five-Year Plan, all the union republics were taken as major economic regions, but the RSFSR was divided into the following areas: European North, Northwest, Center, Volga, North Caucasus and Crimea, Urals, Western Siberia, Eastern Siberia, Far East.

The system of accounting indexes is built on the basis of indexes employed in the plan. Statistics and accounting in the USSR are at the service of plan fulfillment. The organs of accounting and statistics systematically report to the government and also to the *Gosplan* on the course of realization of planned tasks by ministries, enterprises, and provinces.

Directive on Composing the Plan

(defining basic economic lines)

The detailed working out of the national economic plan is preceded by the drawing up of directives for the plan, defining the basic line of economic development for the forthcoming period. These directives come from the directing party organs. The Presidium of the Central Committee of the Communist Party is presumably the highest authority in making the decisions regarding these directives.

In the making of plan directives, all the concrete possibilities of the plan period are considered. These emerge from study of the existing level of internal productive development, the relationships of classes in the USSR, and the international situation. Analysis of the existing level uncovers future possibilities regarding such matters as tempos for production growth, reserves for raising labor productivitiy, increased utilization of existing equipment, introduction of new techniques, reserves for reducing costs. Analysis of the existing level uncovers bottlenecks, disproportions, defects in economic work, which must be removed. Thus the analysis of the existing level provides a starting point for the composition of the plan.

Since the Soviet economy has been a planned economy for most of its existence and one plan period follows another, the analysis of the existing level for the composition of a new plan is primarily the analysis of the execution of the plan of the preceding period.

The directives for composing the plan formulate the basic political tasks during the planned time segment. To these political tasks all plan goals are subordinate, and from them they flow. Further directives distinguish the leading branches of the national economy. Determining the leading branches, the directives establish their tempos of development and the levels of production of individual products.

The problem of tempos is decided in directives by taking account of all the intricacies of social-economic conditions. In general, Soviet leaders seek to attain the highest levels of production increase practicable in each given period, as determined by the existing condition of the productive apparatus.

Formulating the general tasks of the future period, the directives for plan composition predetermine the development of the leading branches of the national economy. They contain instructions regarding the direction of planning the remaining branches and regarding the basic measures for guaranteeing plan fulfillment (principles of labor organization, price policy, and so on). Thus directives determine the plan's basic profile. They compose its skeleton and shape the work of the planning system.

In prescribing the basic outlines of future economic development, the plan directives also establish policy on the nature and amount of future capital investment. The decisions in this area are in part based upon political and military considerations, which frequently have priority over purely economic factors. Insofar as these decisions are economic in nature, they are based on a large amount of staff work and research concerning the national economy, its needs and its possibilities. The volume of capital investment desired in a particular field, say steel, is decided by comparing the volume of production desired at some future date — frequently the last year of a five-year-plan period — with the volume of production to be expected at that date from existing plants and from plants under construction at the time the decision is being made. The difference must be made up by building new capacity, taking account of the drain this new investment imposes upon current production. One of the most important functions of the long-range plans stretching fifteen years or more into the future is presumably to provide production targets for guiding long-range capital investment policy. At the beginning of each five-year plan's composition, very detailed studies are made of the makeup of existing capital and of the highest level of existing technique. The technical experience of foreign countries is studied carefully, with a view to applying their experience to the Soviet economy. It is on the basis of this enormous amount of staff work, presumably, that the members of the Presidium and other decision-making officials of the USSR reach their conclusions, taking into account, often, non-economic as well as economic factors.[14]

Mere determination of the volume of capacity that must be built in a future period does not exhaust the problems in a given field. Thus if 10,000,000 tons of steel-making capacity must be constructed in a given period, it could be provided by two plants of 5,000,000 tons capacity each, or by 10 mills of 1,000,000 tons capacity each, or by some other combination of plants of varying capacities. If a railroad must be built between two points, there are frequently several different alternative routes it can follow, each with its own advantages and disadvantages. Should the railroad be electrified, or should it use diesel or steam locomotives? These questions are typical of the kinds of major decisions that must be made in planning capital investments. The rational bases on which such decisions should be made so as to secure most effective utilization of resources have been a subject of warm debate among Soviet economists.[15] The problem is further complicated for Soviet planners by the fact that they reject the appropriateness of taking into account interest on capital investments, a theoretical position that corresponds to the practice followed by the state in not charging interest to enterprises given funds for long-term investment. A private entrepreneur in a capitalist economy can make such decisions by comparing the expected rate of return from an investment (more precisely, the marginal efficiency of capital) with the interest rate that he has to

---

[14] *Planovoye Khozyaistvo*, No. 9 (1940), pp. 51–67.

[15] Cf., for example, *Voprosy Ekonomiki*, No. 6 (1949), pp. 78–95 and 96–115, or the translations of these articles in *The Current Digest of the Soviet Press*, February 18, 1950, pp. 3–11, and March 4, 1950, pp. 12–19.

pay for borrowed capital or that his own capital could earn if invested elsewhere. This private entrepreneur will seek to invest his capital in such a way as to get the highest rate of return (or marginal efficiency of capital). In any case he will not invest his capital in a project where it is expected to earn less than the prevailing rate of interest. This type of explicit use of the rate of interest in making decisions is barred to Soviet economists by their ideological opposition to the concept and employment of interest.

For many years, however, Soviet economists have employed a rather analogous procedure, using different terminology and somewhat different methods of calculation. In railroad transport, for example, the concept of "Coefficient of Relative Effectiveness" was much used until at least the middle or late 1940's. To illustrate the use of this device, let us suppose that in building a new railroad the problem of electrification versus steam traction is being considered. Let us assume that to electrify the road might cost 90,000,000 rubles and that annual operating expenses thereafter would be 2,500,000 rubles; to use steam power would require a capital investment of only 70,000,000 rubles but would result in annual operating expenses of 5,000,000 rubles. In comparing the two alternatives, therefore, it is seen that a saving of 2,500,000 rubles annually in operating expenses can be obtained by a larger initial capital expenditure of 20,000,000 rubles. Dividing the annual economy in operating costs by the additional capital expenditure, we find the coefficient of relative effectiveness of the more expensive capital investment to be 12.5 per cent. In practice, apparently, Soviet economists have made decisions by setting an arbitrary minimum coefficient of relative effectiveness — 10 per cent was customarily employed in railroad planning before World War II — and comparing this with the coefficients obtained from sets of alternatives. In the example cited above, the 12.5 per cent coefficient obtained would have indicated that it was wise to go ahead with the more expensive capital investment project, electrification, if the arbitrary criterion employed had been 10 per cent. On the other hand, if the arbitrary criterion employed had been 15 per cent, steam traction would presumably have been employed, since the relative effectiveness of electrification, 12.5 per cent, would have then been less than the criterion. The formal analogy of this technique with the use of the interest rate in capitalist economy is obvious, but the criterion employed is so arbitrary that it can be only a crude guide at best. Moreover the technique is essentially based on average costs and returns, so that it is inferior in precision to techniques based on marginal notions.[16]

This procedure and others similar to it were roundly denounced in the late 1940's on the ground that this is using the rate of interest under a new name,[17] and the issue has been widely discussed among Soviet economists. By early 1954 no definitive solution seems to have been reached, those participating in this discussion usually suggesting that decisions may be made by considering many different relevant factors rather than one particular mechanical measure of the relative effectiveness of different alternatives.[18] But while this discussion raged, Soviet planners continued to make capital investment decisions, their practice presumably reflecting the confusion and differences of opinion expressed by those discussing the issue in published articles.

The confusion that exists in Soviet capital investment decision-making was concretely illustrated by the remarks of Deputy Premier M. G. Pervukhin published in *Pravda*, April 27, 1954:

> In comparing the expenditure on the construction of hydroelectric stations and of thermal electric stations, the cost of equipping coal mines is sometimes not taken into account. The latter must be taken into account to the extent that mine construction is necessary to provide fuel for thermal electric stations. Such omission leads to the incorrect conclusions that the construction of hydroelectric stations is always dearer than of thermal electric stations. If one compares state expenditures on hydroelectric station construction with that for thermal electric station construction, taking account in the latter case of the corresponding expansion of the national fuel base, then the cost of one established kilowatt at a hydroelectric station is not higher than at a thermal station, and in some cases it is even lower.

What is remarkable about the above statement by one of the highest officials of the Soviet government is not only that it should

[16] Holland Hunter, "The Planning of Investments in the Soviet Union," *The Review of Economics and Statistics*, February 1949, pp. 54–62.

[17] *Voprosy Ekonomiki*, No. 10 (1948), pp. 34–48; J. M., "Some Recent Developments in Soviet Economic Thought," *Soviet Studies*, October 1949, pp. 119–27. Cf. also Norman Kaplan, "Investment Alternatives in Soviet Economic Theory," *Journal of Political Economy*, April 1952, pp. 133–44, and Gregory Grossman, "Scarce Capital and Soviet Doctrine," *Quarterly Journal of Economics*, August 1953, pp. 311–43.

[18] *Current Digest of the Soviet Press*, February 8, 1950, pp. 3–11, and March 4, 1950, pp. 12–19.

have to be made at so late a time as April 1954, but that the statement should reveal the official's ignoring of a key point. If Soviet coal prices included interest on capital investment required for coal mines, then the factor Mr. Pervukhin puts so much emphasis on would have been taken care of automatically. Certainly the statement quoted above suggests that debate about and uncertainty regarding how capital investment decisions should be made have by no means ceased among Soviet leaders and economists.

The Method of Balances in Planning

The goals given in directives regarding rates and levels of production for the most important branches of the economy permit the calculation of tempos of expansion and the level of production of the national economy as a whole. All branches of labor, as the result of earlier assigned levels of technique, are connected by definite relationships. Thus, for example, in the iron and steel industry we have these relations among branches: for a ton of ingot steel, 0.6 to 0.7 tons of pig iron and about 1 ton of other materials are required; for one ton of pig iron, about 1.7 to 1.8 tons of iron ore, 0.9 to 1.1 tons of coke, and so forth. These kinds of technical and labor proportions, along with the existence of assigned tempos for the leading branches of production, permit calculation of the required volume of production of these branches. The plan of development for industry in the main predetermines the program of agricultural production. In correspondence with the preassigned standard of living for the workers, there is worked out the plan for goods turnover, the plan for development of health protection, the plan for housing and municipal utilities.

The method of balances helps determine the quantitative relations between different branches of the economy, in particular the amounts of their material needs arising from the tasks posed them during the given planned period by the party and the government. In correspondence with the decisive tasks of socialist planning, particular significance in practice attaches to the balances of ferrous and nonferrous metals, fuels, electric power, equipment, chemicals, grains, cotton, leather, and semifabricated commodities, as well as to the balances of the labor force, specialized personnel, monetary incomes and expenditures of the population, incomes and expenditures of the state budget, national income. The complete system of balances is utilized for the solution of questions of inter-branch linkages in the plan.

The following schematic arrangement was used in making the economic plan for 1950: [19]

Total Supply	*Total Utilization*
1. Production listed by producing agencies	1. Production requirements
2. Imports	2. Construction requirements
3. Supplies from state reserves	3. Supplies utilized in the production of that commodity itself
4. Supplies in the hands of distributors at the beginning of the period, listed by distributors	4. Supplies for retail sale
	5. Exports
	6. Additions to state reserves
	7. Supplies in the hands of distributors at the end of each period, listed by distributors

For 1950 material balances of this sort were apparently prepared for all funded commodities, that is, those directly allocated by the government, more than 1,500 in all. These included many different kinds, shapes, and forms of metals, electric power, coal, peat, lumber, all basic types of petroleum products, many different kinds of machinery and equipment, the most important construction materials, basic chemicals and rubber products, other basic industrial and food commodities, and agricultural raw materials.[20]

In making up the balance of a particular type of steel, for example, the requirements of the machinery industries and of capital construction are carefully checked. Special attention must be paid to economizing on metal by reducing the amount of waste production and by introducing more economical norms of metal expenditure per unit of product, through replacing metals by other materials. In making up the distribution part of the balance there must first be guaranteed the satisfaction of the needs of those branches of the economy that are most important at the given moment.

An extremely important task in composing the balance of rolled metals is the formation of state reserves, which permit the government to increase the supplies of one industrial branch during the

---

[19] *Planovoye Khozyaistvo*, No. 2 (1950), p. 50.
[20] *Ibid.*, pp. 46–47.

year without disrupting the plan for supplying metal to other branches.

The economy's metal requirements must be satisfied chiefly from production. Thus the balance of metals is most directly connected with the determination of the production program of metallurgical enterprises. The balances of metals and other commodities are termed material (natural) balances. There are also balances that measure more complex proportions in the economy, as, for example, the relation between supply and demand, between savings and consumption; these are called synthetic balances. An example is the balance of money incomes and expenditures of the population, which is built thus:

Income ⟵ Balance of ⟶ *Expenditures*

A. CITY	A. CITY
Wages and money incomes like wages	Purchase of goods
Incomes from bonds and savings	(a) in state stores
Other incomes	(b) on collective farm market
Reserves from past years	Noncommodity expenditures
Total Income	(taxes, transport and mail expenditures, and so forth)
	Savings (bond purchases, deposits in savings banks)
	Total Expenditures

B. RURAL	B. RURAL
Money incomes from work on collective farms	Purchase of goods
Incomes from collective farm trade	Noncommodity expenditures
Incomes from renting horses and seasonal work	(taxes, transport, mail, and so forth)
Incomes from bonds and savings	Savings (bond purchases, deposits in banks)
Other incomes	Total Expenditures
Reserves from past years	
Total Income	

The balance of money incomes and expenditures is needed first of all to establish proportionality between demand and supply, for planning the volume of merchandise turnover. At the given level of prices, savings, and noncommodity expenditures, the volume of retail trade turnover must correspond to the money incomes minus noncommodity expenditures and savings. In other words, supply must equal the planned demand. The balance of money incomes and expenditures is also needed for making the financial plan. At a given level of expenditures for goods, there may be determined what part of the monetary means of the population may be mobilized through financial institutions (government bonds, savings in banks, taxes). The balance of money incomes and expenditures is necessary also for planning and regulating monetary circulation.

Other major financial plans that are coordinated with the other parts of the national economic plan are the state budget, which is essentially the financial balance of government expenditures and incomes, and the cash and credit plans of the State Bank. Financial plans balancing incomes and expenditures are prepared for all economic ministries. These are linked with the production programs of the ministries as expressed in physical terms, as regards both quantities of output and quantities of labor, materials, and other input. The financial balance for each ministry is further broken down at a later stage into balances for each of its major divisions and enterprises.[21]

Labor balances similar to the above are worked out with a view to insuring that all requirements for workers, both for all workers as a whole and for different types of specialized workers, will be covered by the supply. These balances take into account the needs of different branches of the economy, the number of persons being trained in vocational and technical schools of all kinds, the possibilities of recruiting persons not actually employed outside their households, and so on. A similar balance is made up separately for labor on the collective farms, with the aim of determining the number of workers who can be shifted from agriculture to nonfarm occupations without endangering fulfillment of agricultural production goals.[22]

The National Balance as a Whole

Full linkage of all the different parts of the economy can be attained by working out a balance of the national economy as a whole. Such a balance must reflect all the most important aspects of

---

[21] N. N. Rovinsky, *Gosudarstvenny Byudzhet SSSR*, pp. 78-86. Moscow: Gosfinizdat, 1944.

[22] A. Kursky, *Sotsialisticheskoye Planirovaniye Narodnogo Khozyaistva SSSR*, p. 45.

economic development in the planned period. It must encompass all resources for strengthening the tempo of economic development, while stimultaneously safeguarding the plan from bureaucratic excesses. The chief components of the balance of the national economy must be the balance of labor, of social product and national income, of national wealth, and of finances.

The labor balance shows the distribution of the chief productive forces of society between branches of production and regions of the country, the productivity of labor in the planned period, and the preparation of skilled workers. The balance of social product and national income shows the size of the social product produced and the directions in which it is distributed; it shows how the national income is divided between saving and consumption. The balance of national wealth shows how, during the productive cycle, the masses of fixed capital, working capital, reserves, and consumption funds are increased. The financial balance exposes the movement of financial resources, reflecting the corresponding movement of material resources and labor force. The balance of the national economy does not replace the system of partial balances described above, but on the contrary is based on them and caps them all.

The balanced working out of a plan makes more exact and sometimes modifies the initial projections in the fields of production and distribution, depending upon the requirements that have been ascertained for the national economy and also upon the available resources.

A noted Soviet economist, S. Turetsky, has summarized the final coordination problem faced in making up the national economic plan as follows:

> The final balanced links and checks of planned proposals are the last stages of work over composing the plan. True, already in the very directives and limits for composing the plan the bases for balanced links have been laid down. In the very process of working over plans before the final balanced linkage of different parts, it is necessary to work out a series of different rough balances. In the process of working out plans it is impossible to establish full linkage of all indexes at once. On the basis of established directive limits work unfolds simultaneously over different partial plans, each of which is part of a unified whole. It is impossible to represent the matter as being that first one part of the plan is worked out, then work goes over to the following, and so on. The unity of work over the plan is guaranteed by directives and limits for composing

the plan. But the limits give only basic indicators and orientation, since they themselves in the very process of planning often undergo a series of stages from rough orientating drafts to final balanced plans. A simple sum of blueprints for different parts of the national economy (metal, coal, fuel, machine building, objects of individual consumption, etc.) worked out simultaneously on the basis of directives still does not give one a unified national economic plan, does not by itself guarantee balanced connections. In the process of working out different parts of the plan it is often necessary to work out, to compose several variants for guaranteeing balanced connections in the national economic plan. These variant approximations are worked out from the point of view of a unified economic plan. A change in any one indicator requires changes in numerous indicators, since in a plan we have to deal with a unified system of indicators. If in the process of working out a plan we make more exact the volume and structure of machine construction output, then it is necessary to make corresponding changes in the blueprints for metallurgy, coal, etc.; in determining the assortment of cotton textiles there is required the more exact specification of the proposed raw material base and on the reverse: the blueprints for trade turnover are corrected which changes the proposals for consumption, making proposed prices more exact introduces corresponding changes in the financial plan, etc.[23]

Even this discussion oversimplifies the problems involved in making sure that changes, sometimes radical changes, in one part of the plan correspond with the rest of the plan. The balance equations may be compared to a complex electrical network, a change in any part of which alters the balance of forces throughout the network. A change in the tractor-production program makes itself felt in the balance for every one of the many materials going into the making of tractors and in the labor balance, and then reciprocally has its effects upon the agricultural program, which was drawn up on the assumption that the initial number of tractors planned would be produced. In turn these secondary changes require other changes in a complex and ever widening series of chain reactions upon the entire plan. The difficulties involved when there are so many equations and variables are truly stupendous, and it is questionable whether more than rough allowance can be made throughout the system of balances. The difficulties involved are suggested by W. W. Leontief in discussing a related matter:

> While in the case of partial analysis, which operates simultaneously with only two or three variables, the interrelations among these few

[23] *Planovoye Khozyaistvo*, No. 2 (1936), pp. 159–60.

elements can often be perceived directly, such intuitive inference becomes practically impossible as soon as the number of variables increases up to four or five, not to say ten or twenty. A doubtful reader of these lines can ascertain the limitation of his own common-sense intuition by trying to hazard at least an approximate solution of a system of three simple linear equations with three variables; or after having found the right answers mathematically, by trying to guess out intuitively what effect a change in one of the constants would have on the value of all three unknowns.[24]

The system of Soviet economic balances, it may be added, involves hundreds of variables, not any mere ten or twenty.

During the years of the five-year plans, the methodology of working out balances has improved significantly. In working out the distribution side of material balances, technically based norms are employed. Regional breakdowns are widely applied in projecting natural and synthetic balances. A regional breakdown of the labor balance permits a property based plan for recruitment of workers; a regional breakdown of the balance of the population's money incomes and expenditures helps set up a plan for the distribution of merchandise by provinces; the regional balances of production and consumption give materials for forming rational transport plans, cutting down cross hauls and superfluously distant carriage of freight.

Together with the working out of the projection of the national economic plan, work is carried on in other directions: the technical profile of the plan and measures for introducing advanced technique are determined. Norms for utilizing equipment, for expenditure of raw materials and labor, and for labor productivity are established, being based on the experience of outstanding workers; there are calculated estimates of production, plans for lowering costs, financial plans. The results of these calculations are utilized for correcting the balances; on the other hand, the balance data determine the direction of work regarding norms. For example, the strain of the fuel balance requires every possible rationalization of the fuel expenditure norms.

Some Observations on Soviet Planning

We have now concluded the description of Soviet planning procedure as presented in idealized form by Soviet sources. Certain

---

[24] Leontief, op. cit., p. 34.

matters ignored or glossed over in this description now require comment.

First, we may point out the nondemocratic nature of this planning, the complete absence of what has come to be called "consumers' sovereignty." Plans are drawn up on the basis of directives from the leadership of the Communist Party, which also controls the government. These directives reflect the judgment of these leaders as to the relative importance of different economic ends attainable during the period for which the plan is being formulated. If these leaders decree that the rapid development of transport is the most important task of a given year, that will be given top priority, regardless of consumer wishes or needs for food, clothing, shelter, or luxuries. The needs of consumers set limits upon the discretion of planners, however, since consumers are also producers, and if the people are not fed, clothed, and housed at or above minimal requirement levels, this will react upon production. As a general principle, Soviet leaders have always avowed their interest in raising the standard of living of their people, and such interest can be granted even if only because such a rise in the standard of living would minimize domestic political tension and disaffection. But the crucial point is that, within the wide limits set by the minimal quantities required to permit workers to keep on working and to keep dissatisfaction within controllable bounds, those who frame the plan directives can largely give second priority to consumer wishes.

Second, the principle of concentration on the most important objectives of each period emerges as the basic principle of Soviet planning. All the balance calculations are subordinated to the "leading links" set by the directives. In 1935, for example, the development of transport was set as the primary objective. In that year, consequently, a much greater percentage of Soviet metal consumption was permitted railroads than had been true in 1932.[25] Thus it would appear that the Soviet economy progresses in a series of fits and jerks, as different areas of it are successively made the "leading link" for each period while the others are forced to get along as best they can on what is left after the full needs of the top priority branches have been met. For the most part branches of heavy in-

---

[25] *Planovoye Khozyaistvo*, No. 2 (1936), p. 163.

dustry have enjoyed top priority, while consumer-goods production has had to get along on the resources left over.

Third, in predicting future output, that is, in setting goals for such output, a congeries of factors must be considered. On the one hand, estimates of future output, outside of agriculture, can be made by taking account of existing capacity of plants and by assigning resources adequate to keep these plants operating at 100 per cent, or at some other fraction, of capacity. This will be the dominating factor for short-run prediction. In the longer run, account must be taken of new capital investment, the period it requires, and the speed with which the new facilities will come into operation. The capital investment program and medium- and long-range production goals are therefore intimately connected. But even in the short run, important complications must be taken into account. Plant capacity is not an eternally fixed constant, but will vary depending upon labor productivity, coefficients of utilization of machinery, adequacy of raw material supply, and other factors. Soviet planners, in making their short-run goal determinations, presumably have information regarding these factors in the latest plan period and make provision for improved performance. But actual realization of that improved performance depends in turn upon progress made in improving the standard of living, the effectiveness of propaganda for higher labor productivity, smoothness of the work of transportation, and other factors. In view of these complexities Soviet planning must require a large degree of guesswork, with all the inaccuracy that even the best guesswork implies.

Fourth, the arbitrary nature of Soviet prices, which frequently in the past have failed to reflect the supply and demand situation of each commodity, imposes many crudities and inefficiencies upon Soviet planning and operation of the economy. In seeking to decide between alternative investment possibilities, Soviet planners can only grope in deciding which is the most economical, because comparisons of money costs and returns are probably of questionable validity in many cases, as a result of the arbitrary character of Soviet prices. Thirty-six years after the Bolshevik revolution Soviet planners have still been unable to find a satisfactory technique for making investment decisions, although they are keenly aware that the techniques they have employed have been unsatisfactory. Another result of this confused price structure is that Soviet managers often find it profitable, in terms of the costs and prices with which they are faced, to disobey the assignments given by the plan and to produce products that differ in quality, amount of production, and other characteristics from those set by the planners. We shall go into this point in more detail later.

Fifth, it should not be thought that the State Planning Committee is the sole agency concerned with planning. The *Gosplan* has its representatives in the organizations of all different branches of the Soviet economy as well as at key places throughout the USSR. They work with ministerial and provincial (or other geographical unit) planning groups as well as with economic and government administrators in preparing the partial plans for each sector of the economy or each area of the country. These partial plans are submitted to *Gosplan* for integration into the master plan and for necessary revision. In the process of give and take between *Gosplan* and various sectional or branch interests, there is probably a good deal of heated conflict, as each particular interest seeks to secure the maximum resources for its own development. As is inevitably the case in such situations, the outcome must often reflect the relative bargaining skill and power of the different participants rather than the actual patterns of economic needs. The fact that consumers' wishes impose no final check upon the arbitrariness of most economic decisions facilitates the dominance of such bureaucratic higgling in the making of plan decisions.

Speaking to the Supreme Soviet on April 26, 1954, Premier Malenkov gave this characterization of the state of Soviet planning at that time and of needed changes in it:

> Together with the working out of basic assignments, our planning organs often try to define from the center numerous detailed indicators of the economic activity of enterprises, building projects, railroads, state and collective farms, trading enterprises, and other organizations. Since this is done without the necessary knowledge of varied local conditions and possibilities, it is consequently done with insufficient skill. It is completely evident that such planning creates difficulties in the work at the grass roots, binding the initiative of local organs.
>
> The state has taken measures to reduce the list of assignments approved in the annual plans, both in industrial and agricultural production. This has already given positive results. But the demands

of the national economy on planning work are growing and becoming more complex. Therefore our central planning organs, primarily *Gosplan*, must concentrate their attention first of all on the most important national economic problems — on establishing the correct proportions in the development of different branches, on liquidating bottlenecks, on the maximum utilization of existing reserves in the national economy so as to obtain great results with least capital investment.

Execution of the Plan

In Soviet ideology, drawing up an economic plan is considered only the first step in planning. Supervising the execution of this plan is considered the decisive test. Such supervision consists of checking on the way in which different industries are meeting their assignments, anticipating and preventing materials shortages or other developments that may interrupt production, finding possibilities for increasing output above that actually planned for, and making such changes in the original plan as are called for by domestic or foreign developments after the preparation of the initial document. Such supervision is done by a great number of agencies and persons. *Gosplan* and the Central Statistical Administration both scrutinize current output data and prepare regular reports for higher authorities on the progress being achieved and the difficulties being met. Each unit of the economic administration watches the performance of the production units under its jurisdiction and takes such action as it deems necessary from time to time to correct deviations from the plan. Communist Party units all over the country exercise similar watchfulness and are expected to intervene and order changes made where performance is poor. The government maintains its own separate control and inspection personnel to check on plan fulfillment; through the system of criticism and self-criticism, ordinary workers, farmers, and other citizens are expected to help show up inadequacies by speaking out in open meetings, writing letters to newspapers, reporting to government authorities, and so on.

As indicated earlier, difficulties often do arise in the execution of economic plans, causing them to be changed materially and often to be fulfilled in lopsided fashion. The guiding principle in such changes seems often to be an extension of the "leading link" notion used in planning, that is, where goals on top priority objectives are in danger of not being fulfilled, still further concentration of resources upon these objectives is often ordered. It is this type of plan revision that helps to explain the frequent failure of Soviet production to attain goals set for consumer-goods output, although objectives in heavy industry have often been attained or even more than attained.

Since planning is all-pervasive throughout the Soviet economy, we shall have frequent occasion in the following chapters to refer to the role of planning and economic plans in different sectors of the Soviet economy.

— union, republican **Ministry** (*Council of Ministers*)

Subdivisions below ministry

2) Glavk: Chief administration (subministry in a given area)

3) Trust or Combine - group of plants combined in one administrative organization. Some combines in charge of related enterprises

4) Enterprise in either a trust, a combine, or an individual factory

CHAPTER VI

ORGANIZATION AND OPERATION OF SOVIET INDUSTRY

INDUSTRIAL PRODUCTION in the Soviet Union is carried on by three types of enterprises: those owned by the state, industrial cooperatives, and individual artisans working alone. Of these the state factories and mines are by far the most important, producing the overwhelming bulk of all industrial commodities. Cooperative production is significant only in the output of consumer goods. Individual artisans, who are prohibited under Soviet law from employing even one assistant, produce only an infinitesimal fraction of all Soviet goods.

The state-owned and -operated industry of the USSR is the largest single centrally-directed productive apparatus in the world, far dwarfing such individual giants of American industry as United States Steel or General Motors. It is composed of thousands of factories and mines of every description, spread throughout the vast territory of the Soviet Union. About forty million persons are employed in these state enterprises. They produce a tremendous variety of commodities, ranging from tanks and jet airplanes to buttons and soft drinks.

The organization and operation of such a vast productive mechanism obviously presents difficult problems. The Soviet government has attempted to solve these problems so as to secure an organizational structure and operating technique that would insure maximum production at minimum cost. The history of the Soviet government's efforts to secure the most efficient organization and operation of its industry is a long and complex one. We shall be concerned here primarily, however, with the current situation, referring to earlier arrangements only in so far as they help to illuminate and explain the existing situation.

Organization of State Industry

The highest executive body of the Soviet government, the Council of Ministers, is the apex of the organizational pyramid of Soviet industry. This group supervises the over-all work of Soviet industry, issues necessary orders, and approves the annual and quarterly economic plans directing the operations of industry during each time period. The Council of Ministers consists of the ministers who head each major section of the Soviet government. Some ministries, like the Ministry of Foreign Affairs, deal primarily with noneconomic matters, but most of them are economic ministries operating major branches of Soviet production. The Council of Ministers, in practice, is subordinate to the Presidium of the Central Committee of the Communist Party. The Presidium makes the fundamental decisions that are executed by the Council of Ministers. Most Presidium members are also in the Council of Ministers. In early 1954, G. M. Malenkov was Chairman of the Council of Ministers, or Premier, while V. M. Molotov, N. A. Bulganin, and L. M. Kaganovich were First Deputy Chairmen. A. I. Mikoyan, Maxim A. Saburov, and M. G. Pervukhin were Deputy Chairmen.[1]

Within the Council of Ministers there is a small supercabinet, the Presidium of the Council of Ministers, consisting of Malenkov and the Deputy Chairmen. This group apparently has major coordinating functions and presumably also policymaking power. Nikita S. Khrushchev, First Secretary of the Communist Party, who seems to be in charge of agriculture, too, though he has no formal ministerial post, also probably sits in with this group. Thus the nine members of the Presidium of the Party's Central Committee make up an interlocking directorate occupying the chief places in both the Communist Party and the Soviet State, and exercising oligarchical control over the Soviet Union.

Attached to the Council of Ministers and reporting to it are a number of subgroups. The most important of these are the Central Statistical Administration, the Committee on State Security, the

[1] *Pravda*, April 28, 1954.

State Planning Committee (*Gosplan*), and the State Committee on Construction Affairs. Other groups deal with the Northern Sea Route, the Civil Aviation Fleet, Hydro-Meteorological Services, Weights and Measures, the TASS news agency, and the like.[2]

The detailed, everyday operation of Soviet industry is organized and supervised by individual ministries, each directing a major segment of production. In the early years of the Soviet regime, virtually all state industry was directed by one central body, the Supreme Economic Council. During the 1930's this council was broken down successively into a large number of individual ministries. After World War II, the trend was toward consolidation of ministries, and the greatest reduction in their number took place in the governmental reorganization immediately following Stalin's death. Thirteen months after Stalin's death, in April 1954, the number of ministries was again raised sharply.

Soviet ministries are of two kinds: all-union and union-republican. The all-union ministries, primarily in heavy industry, direct their particular segments of the economy without regard for the internal administrative organization of the country, particularly its division into 16 nominal republics. The union-republican ministries, on the other hand, have a dual organization consisting of an over-all ministry in Moscow, under which are republican ministries in the different republics of the Soviet Union. For these latter the Moscow organization usually acts as the republican ministry for the largest Soviet republic, the RSFSR, as well as a national ministry.

The ministerial organization of the Soviet government created in late April 1954, reflecting the reversal of the consolidation policy adopted in March 1953, was as follows: [3]

Aviation Industry	Defense Industry
Trade	Food Products Industry
Automobile Transport and Roads	Consumer Goods Industry
Foreign Trade	Radiotechnical Industry
Higher Education	Communications
State Control	State Farms
Health Protection	Construction and Road Machinery
Lumber Industry	Construction of Metallurgical and
Maritime and River Fleet	Chemical Plants

[2] *Ibid.*, March 16, 1953, and F. M. Marx, *Foreign Governments*, p. 471. New York: Prentice-Hall, 1949.

[3] *Pravda*, April 28, 1954.

Transport Machine Building
Finance
Heavy Machine Building
Nonferrous Metallurgy
Electric Power Stations
Justice
Automobile, Tractor, and Farm
    Machinery Building
Medium Machine Building
Paper and Woodworking Industry
Internal Affairs
Geology and Conservation
Procurements
Culture
Machine and Instrument Building

Oil Industry
Meat and Dairy Products Industry
Building Materials Industry
Transport
Fish Industry
Agriculture
Machine Tool and Instrument
    Industry
Construction
Ship Construction Industry
Coal Industry
Chemical Industry
Ferrous Metallurgy
Electrotechnical Industry

The minister in charge of each ministry has power to issue orders to all plants and organizations in his jurisdiction and to appoint or dismiss the major officials subordinate to him. While the organization of each ministry differs somewhat from that of others, ordinarily a ministry will have technical, planning, finance, supply, sale, construction, manpower, and accounting divisions. These help the minister coordinate and direct the activities of the production units under his supervision.[4] Each minister is undisputed chief of his organization, though he consults regularly with his collegium, an advisory group composed usually of his chief assistants.

The chain of command within each ministry, from the minister at the top to the individual plant or mine doing the actual production, depends on conditions and problems in that ministry. A complete organizational chart of Soviet industrial organization would be extremely complex therefore, since there are many different patterns in chains of command in the different ministries. Fundamentally, however, there are three types of subdivisions below the ministerial level. The first is the *chief administration* (*Glavk,* plural *Glavki*). The chief administration is a sort of subministry, controlling plants in a given area producing a given type or types of products, as the case may be. Under the chief administration there may be either a *trust* or a *combine.* Each of these is usually a group of plants combined in one administrative organization. Typically, a combine

---

[4] G. Bienstock, S. M. Schwarz, and A. Yugow, *Management in Russian Industry and Agriculture,* p. 7. New York: Oxford University Press, 1944.

consists of a group of related plants and other enterprises producing one or a group of related products. Thus, the Magnitogorsk Combine is in charge of iron mines, steel mills, and coke chemical plants in and near the city of Magnitogorsk. In the past decade the trend in Soviet industrial organization has been towards simplification and elimination of intermediate administrative organizations between the ministry and the final enterprise actually engaged in production. As a result, many of the most important plants in the USSR are directly subordinate to and controlled by the corresponding ministry. In many other cases, however, plants are subordinate directly to a chief administration, or to a trust, which is in turn subordinate to a chief administration. The proliferation of administrative links can be even more complex in some cases.[5]

The ultimate Soviet production unit, from the administrative point of view, is the enterprise, which may be a trust, a combine, or simply an individual factory. The enterprise is headed by a director who has full power of administration and control over it, within the limits set by higher authority. The enterprise is a legal entity that may sue or be sued in the courts. It operates on the basis of a separate charter registered with the government and approved either by the appropriate minister or by the Council of Ministers. Each enterprise operates on the basis of cost accounting and has certain fixed capital — buildings, machinery, and so on — conferred upon it by the government, as well as its own supply of working capital in the form of raw materials and of money in the bank, also received originally from the state. In addition, each enterprise has its own production plan. It has a separate account in the State Bank. It has an individual accounting existence, that is, an independent balance sheet and profit-and-loss statement. The State Treasury is legally free of any liability for an enterprise's debts, though these enterprises are all state-owned and -operated.[6]

Throughout the hierarchy of Soviet industrial administration, the principle of one-man control is paramount, though each head is expected to consult with his collegium. The principle of organization is production-territorial, that is, by production units in a specific area, not along functional lines. Functional activities at each level

[5] V. Gsovski, *Soviet Civil Law*, Vol. I, pp. 403–5. Ann Arbor: University of Michigan Law School, 1949.
[6] *Ibid.*; Savinsky, *Kurs Promyshlennoy Statistiki*, p. 38.

are subordinate to the over-all head, who directs orders down and reports up the ladder of command.

Two interesting developments affecting industrial management manifested themselves after Stalin's death. On the one hand the public stress on the principle of "collective leadership" as opposed to "one-man rule" seemed to be contrary to the chief trend in Soviet management since the early 1930's. This seemed to require that ministers, plant managers, and similar executives attribute much more importance to their associates' opinions than had earlier been customary. On the other hand, the power of individual ministers to shift capital funds and otherwise to allocate resources among the plants under their jurisdiction was increased. That these reforms did not solve the problems of the overgrown Soviet bureaucracy is suggested by Premier Malenkov's statement, April 26, 1954:

> The Government has considerably increased the powers of ministers, heads of departments, and directors of chief administrations of ministries, with a view to raising the responsibility of ministries, achieving a higher level of efficiency, and ensuring timely solution of economic problems. This has already produced positive results and undoubtedly there will be still more as time goes on. But we cannot close our eyes to the fact that many heads of ministries and departments, insteal of taking action and solving the problems that arise, indulge in unnecessary correspondence in order to escape responsibility and shift it on to others.

Communist Party Secretary Khrushchev commented similarly the same day:

> Experience has shown that it is difficult for large ministries which embrace many branches of the economy and large numbers of diverse enterprises to give them proper and effective guidance. . . . Some ministers seem to think their job is to build up a large and cumbersome apparatus. They have to be corrected . . . we must drastically cut down correspondence and inflated record-keeping and mercilessly root out bureaucracy and guidance by correspondence.

One glimpse into the extent and working of Soviet bureaucracy was given in a *Pravda* editorial, May 10, 1954, describing the past organization of the Ministry of Construction:

> . . . the ministry had 514 administrations, divisions, and sectors; 194 of these had 2-3 workers each. The ministry's incoming and outgoing mail during the past year and January 1954 was over one and a half million documents, or about 5,000 daily. During the same

period the ministry daily sent its construction enterprises 2,350 instructions, circulars, and letters.

An Organizational Example

The general schemata of Soviet industrial organization within a ministry sketched above may be illustrated by reference to the early postwar organization of the Ministry for Ferrous Metallurgy. At the top level was the minister, assisted by some twenty-eight functional groups. Among these were twelve functional chief administrations, handling such matters as personnel and pay, purchase of production supplies (*Glavsnab*), labor force procurement (*Glavurs*), sale of ferrous metals produced (*Glavmetallosbyt*), capital construction, industrial equipment, electric power, transport, geological research, scrap-metal procurement and processing, and schools. In addition there were sixteen smaller functional groups, dealing with planning, finances, bookkeeping, housing, legal problems, archives, office administration, metallurgical journals, and so on.

Production units immediately subordinate to the ministry fell into three groups: (1) Chief administrations for Metallurgical Industry of the South and Center; special steels; steel pipe; Urals metallurgy; ferro-alloys; metal articles; construction of ferrous metallurgical machinery; firebrick; iron ore; coke; and timber for ferrous metallurgy. (2) A special production department directly under the minister included the nine most important plants in the ministry immediately after World War II, including the Magnitogorsk and Kuznetsk combines among others. This production department was essentially the most important chief administration in the ministry. (3) Production trusts for ferrous metallurgical timber (Moscow); ferrous metallurgical electric power; Donets Basin water; ferrous metallurgical timber in the south.

Of the twelve chief administrations listed above, all but two — those for iron ore and metallurgical timber — directly operated all enterprises subordinate to them. These ten illustrated a three-link chain of command: ministry — chief administration — enterprise. The Chief Ore Administration had five major production trusts under it, for Urals iron ore, Krivoy Rog iron ore, Chiatura manganese, Nikopol manganese, and USSR fluorspar. Each of these trusts had mine administrations as the enterprises under it, so that in this case the four-link chain of command was: ministry — chief administration — trust — enterprise. A similar pattern existed in the Chief Administration for Ferrous Metallurgical Timber, which consisted of six trusts: one for metallurgical woodworking and five for timber production. Under these trusts were enterprises such as timber camps, woodworking factories, and mechanized timber centers, the bottom units in a similar four-link chain of command.[7]

The organizational structure sketched above is that of an almost completely integrated iron and steel industry under one management, producing, except for coal, almost all its significant basic raw materials, iron ore, manganese, ferro-alloys, fluorspar, coke, timber, and so on, as well as much of the machinery required for its operations. The ministry provided housing for its workers and sold them consumer goods in enterprise stores. It operated newspapers, trained technicians, and carried out numerous other varied activities contributing in one way or another to final output of all types of iron and steel products. It was an empire in itself, with the minister at the top holding undisputed sway over this vast complex of activity spread throughout the Soviet Union. — all-union industry

Other Types of State Industry

The Ministry of Ferrous Metallurgy sketched above was at that time an example of an all-union industry. Other types of industry in the USSR are organized on a republic or local basis, or are operated incidentally to the major activities of a nonindustrial ministry or other organization. Republican industry includes primarily ministries producing consumer goods, food, and construction materials. Republican governments, say in the Ukraine or Uzbekistan, play important roles in directing these branches of industry, though ultimate control and coordination still remain in Moscow. Soviet local industry consists of small enterprises in particular localities, serving the needs of consumers in that region by processing raw materials obtainable there. Thus a small coal deposit may be worked by a unit of local industry to supply the needs of a nearby town, or

[7] A. Arakelian, *Industrial Management in the USSR*, pp. 108–9. Washington: Public Affairs Press, 1950. A more extensive discussion of this point is given in David Granick, *Management of the Industrial Firm in the USSR*, pp. 14–21. New York: Columbia University Press, 1954. The entire volume is relevant to the matters discussed in this chapter.

a group of workers may turn timber obtained nearby into furniture sold only locally. There is a Minister of Local Industry in each union republic (but none at the national level) who supervises the operation of these many small enterprises in his area. There is a hierarchy of control going down to each lower territorial level. At each stage (province, territory, city, village, or small district) the local industry there is subordinate both to the appropriate official or government department and to the local government as a whole in a system of dual subordination to functional and administrative-territorial authorities. Nonindustrial ministries' industrial operations include such enterprises as the repair shops of the Transport Ministry. These subordinate industrial enterprises produce about 10 per cent of all output of state industry.[8]

Control Mechanisms

While primary responsibility for everyday operation and supervision of Soviet industry is in the hands of the appropriate ministries and their subordinate bodies, a large number of other control organizations are constantly active. The State Planning Committee, through its representatives throughout the country, keeps constant check on the fulfillment or lack of fulfillment of the industrial output plans. The Ministry of Finance, through the State Bank and its tax collection officials, also constantly checks the financial aspects of industrial operations, and through them the actual conduct of enterprises. The Communist Party, at all levels — from the Presidium to the local party group in a factory — is constantly engaged in similar checking, and frequently intervenes to order changes or even to replace unsatisfactory personnel. The higher Communist Party bodies, such as republican, provincial, and city party committees, frequently have elaborate organizations paralleling the ministerial organizations to keep constant check on the course of output.

Not least important among these control mechanisms is that directly subordinate to the Central Committee of the Communist Party. The Production Departments of the Committee's "apparatus" make special investigations of industrial operations and coordinate the activities of subordinate party groups in exercising economic controls.[9]

8 *Arakelian, op. cit.,* pp. 104, 110–11.
9 Louis Nemzer, "The Kremlin's Professional Staff . . .," *The American Political Science Review,* March 1950, pp. 64–85.

The Ministry of State Control "exercises a general watchdog role over state property and administration. Like the Ministry of Finance, it is charged with strict control over expenditures of state funds, and it also has a broader mandate to check the fulfillment of all governmental decisions." Its organization parallels that of the state administration, and it has control personnel in all important factories, warehouses, and other units. These controllers have the right of access to all administrative records and may undertake documentary audits. The ministry may issue reprimands, levy fines up to the amount of three months' salary, order the removal of offending personnel, or submit charges against administrative personnel before courts. The ministry works closely with Communist Party groups at all levels.

The secret police of the Ministry of Internal Affairs (MVD) also exercise important control functions. Secret police agents permeate the entire fabric of Soviet society, with representation in all enterprises and at all levels of industrial administration. The secret police apparently not only make arrests where necessary, but also try and sentence individuals to banishment from particular localities or to serve sentences at forced labor in "correctional labor camps." The secret police also work closely with the Communist Party organization, and their members are usually required to be party members.[10]

An informal but frequently important type of control is that known as criticism and self-criticism (*kritika i samo-kritika*). In theory all persons in the Soviet Union are encouraged to complain publicly about derelictions of duty, poor work, violations of government orders, and so forth. These complaints may be voiced in shop meetings, in letters to the newspaper or to a government organization, or in other ways. Newspapers frequently print articles of criticism based on information gathered by their reporters in a particular factory or ministry. Those criticized are expected to defend themselves and to acknowledge their errors preliminary to correcting them if the charges are true. This criticism and self-criticism, however, are limited to revealing defects in the way in which government orders are being executed. Basic government

---

[10] Merle Fainsod, *How Russia is Ruled*, chaps. 13 and 15. Cambridge: Harvard University Press, 1953. The Central Statistical Administration also has an important control and inspection system. Cf. *Vestnik Statistiki*, No. 3 (1953), p. 67.

policy and the highest officials in the Presidium are immune to such criticism from below, and any effort by subordinate personnel to subject them to it publicly would meet with swift punishment as sedition. The salutary effect of this criticism and self-criticism is tempered, however, by the fact that those who engage in it — say ordinary workers in a factory — expose themselves to the vengeance of those they have attacked. Frequently, study of the Soviet press suggests, those who attempt to avail themselves of this privilege suffer grievous consequences, though the government tries to protect them if it becomes aware of such illegal punishment. Sometimes, too, there is collaboration between party, government, and industrial officials in an area to protect one another against the barbs of criticism and self-criticism.

It is clear from the above that those who direct Soviet industry (as well as other sections of the Soviet economy and society) are constantly under surveillance from many quarters and are under extreme pressure to fulfill the orders they receive from above, no matter what the obstacles. Punishment for wrongdoing is severe, and mere failure to fulfill one's plan — even because of factors beyond the control of the "culprit" — may be punished by superiors who refuse to recognize what are sneeringly referred to as "objective" causes. In the 1930's failure to achieve production plans was sometimes interpreted as sabotage, and dire punishment was administered to those found guilty. Since World War II there have been no such publicized sabotage trials, but reports have been published from time to time saying industrial chiefs have been sent to prison for various offenses, particularly for production of poor-quality goods.[11] The heads of Soviet industry at all levels undoubtedly work under great tension and strain, as a result of the multiple checks upon them and the possible penalties they may incur. They undoubtedly transmit the impact of this tension to all those working under them, so that it affects all engaged in production.

The fear of punishment in case of failure to meet government plans is so great that industrial managers, not infrequently, are driven to perform grossly illegal acts so as to meet their plans or to cover up their failure. Thus many reports have been published of officials' having illegally required workers to work overtime or to work on their days off at the end of a month so as to meet the pro-

[11] Cf., for example, *Moskovskaya Pravda*, April 9, 1950.

duction plan. Managers sometimes falsify their reports to the state on production and reserves in an effort to hide their failure.[12] Many managers apparently try to secure minimal production plans, to hoard scarce materials and labor, or otherwise to serve their own or their organizations' immediate ends at the expense of the economy as a whole.[13] They put their own bureaucratic and sectional interests first to avoid punishment for failure and to gain rewards for accomplishment.[14]

Enterprise Organization and Operation

The organization of an industrial enterprise will depend upon its size and complexity. The basic chain of command is from the director to the shop chiefs to the foremen to the brigade leaders. The director has a number of functional departments — for planning, finance, payroll, personnel, technical control, supply and sales, and so on — and a number of assistants, of whom the most important is the chief engineer. The latter is directly in charge of production and has under him such functionaries as the chief designer, chief mechanic, and chief electrician. The enterprise is divided into a number of workshops, each with its own chief. Under him is a shop planning and dispatching bureau, a technical bureau, a shop mechanic, shop office manager, bookkeeper, and others. The bureaus are headed by assistant shop chiefs. Small workshops have less complex organizations. Foremen have messengers, order-bearers, and instructors under them.[15]

In theory, the enterprise director has complete charge of all activities and personnel under him. This nominal position he enjoys is the result of a long, complex development and is not always true in practice. In the 1920's and early 1930's a brisk conflict was waged over the best method of control in Soviet industry. For a time there was a triumvirate in charge, consisting of the plant manager, the plant's Communist Party chief, and the plant's trade-union head. But this three-man control was done away with about two decades

---

[12] *Pravda Ukrainy*, November 11, 1949; *Pravda*, November 23, 1949.

[13] *Bolshevik*, July 15, 1949, p. 4.

[14] Excellent general discussions of these points are to be found in J. S. Berliner, "The Informal Organization of the Soviet Firm," *Quarterly Journal of Economics*, August 1952, and *Fortune*, February 1953.

[15] Arakelian, *op. cit.*, pp. 126–27.

1920's + early '30's

ago. In part this disolution of "triangle" control was the result of the complete subordination of the Soviet trade-union movement to the Soviet drive for production. Union leaders do not now usually try to protect the interests of workers too strongly where the possibility exists that such action might interfere with the growth of production. The problem of the relationship between the plant manager and the local communist cell in his plant or the local Communist Party authorities in his area is, however, still far from adequately solved. Readers of the Soviet press find frequent articles dealing with this subject. These articles sometimes berate communists in a given plant or area for interfering excessively with the operation of particular industrial plants or mines. At other times these articles attack local factory or other communist units for not keeping close enough check on economic activity and not acting sufficiently vigorously to help or force plant managers to end deficiencies. Undoubtedly Communist Party officials still play important roles in the direction of production at many enterprises.[16]

Within the limits of the directives sent down by higher authorities, the management of each enterprise works out the so-called technical-industrial-financial plan for that enterprise (*tekhpromfinplan*). This technical-industrial-financial plan covers the following matters in great detail for each enterprise: estimated number of workers to be employed; estimated payroll; production cost plan; estimated requirements for fuel, electric power, raw materials, semifinished products, and equipment; norms for utilization of plant equipment; organizational and technical measures to be employed for most efficient utilization of plant resources; and the financial results to be sought by the management during the annual, quarterly, or monthly period covered by the particular technical-industrial-financial plan. In addition, this plan covers such matters as the distribution of the plant's products, introduction of new processes, details of plant expansion, production other than that of the main items turned out at the plant, cooperation with other enterprises, and other matters. The program for cooperation of an enterprise with other enterprises is based upon information supplied it regarding the availability of supplies it needs and the requirements of the enterprises to which it sells its products. The technical-industrial-financial plan for each enterprise is submitted to higher

[16] Bienstock, Schwarz and Yugow, *op. cit.*, pp. 35–38.

authorities. When approved by them it becomes the concrete program of action guiding the management of that enterprise. In the
course of working out this plan, the management of each enterprise
has an opportunity to suggest changes in the directives given it by
higher authorities. These changes are welcomed particularly if they
permit greater production or lower-cost output.[17]

Most Soviet industrial enterprises operate in accordance with
the principles of economic accountability (khozraschet). By economic accountability is meant essentially that each enterprise is
considered as an independent, quasi-corporation endowed with certain resources. The enterprise must use its resources in accordance
with its plan and with the objective also of attaining maximum profit
within the framework of the plan's goals. Relationships between
enterprises are commercial relationships, that is, they are sales or
purchases for money at prices fixed by higher authorities. Each
enterprise is empowered to enter into legally binding contracts with
other enterprises. It may be sued in court and made to pay damages
for nonfulfillment of a contract. All transactions entered into by a
plant are measured in money terms as well as in units of physical
product. The over-all success of a plant or enterprise is judged in
terms of its ability to fulfill or overfulfill its production goals and
to lower its material and money costs. The legal fiction of the
independence of each enterprise is maintained, though each such
enterprise is purely a creature of the state. The transactions in
which it engages with other state-owned enterprises are really in
the nature of bookkeeping transactions.[18]

It is clear from the above that a Soviet enterprise resembles in
some respects an ordinary commercial production unit in our society.
An American company, like its Russian counterpart, buys and sells;
has only a limited amount of resources with which to work; is legally
responsible for observance of contracts; may borrow from the banks
for additional working capital needs; and so on. But there are also
important differences. A Soviet plant director, for example, cannot,
in general, sell any important part of his fixed capital — a building,
a machine, or the like — without specific instructions or permission
from higher authorities. He may not sell at prices other than those

---

[17] Ibid., pp. 53–54.
[18] A. V. Venediktov, Gosudarstvennaya Sotsialisticheskaya Sobstvennost, pp.
513–16. Moscow-Leningrad: 1948.

set by his superiors, even if selling at those prices requires him to take a loss. He is not expected to adjust his production so as to emphasize the output of most profitable items and minimize the output of the least profitable items. Instead, he is required to produce an assortment of goods in the quantity and quality called for by his plan. From time to time the Soviet press complains that directors of enterprises in the USSR have violated these prohibitions, that is, have sold items of fixed capital or adjusted their production so as to maximize profit in violation of the plan. The practice appears to be widespread although persons guilty of such offenses are liable to dismissal or more severe punishment, including imprisonment.[19]

In his direction of everyday activity, the enterprise head is very severely limited. The prices he may charge; the unit expenditure of materials, fuel, electric power; the total number of workers he may employ; the total amount of payroll he may pay out; and other key facets of the economic environment are set for him by higher authorities, and he must stay within those limits. Usually he is not responsible for buying the equipment and materials he needs, or for the sale of the commodities he produces, all these important functions being performed by organs of the ministry or chief adminstration superior to him. All these restrictions limit most seriously his area of discretion and the flexibility with which he can use the resources put at his command for productive purposes.[20]

The need to give enterprise directors greater powers, so that they may have more flexibility in their operations and more opportunities to exercise their initiative has been recognized by the Soviet government. Thus in 1940, *Pravda* published a letter by four Leningrad plant managers complaining of the restrictions put on them that prevented them from using their resources to best advantage.[21] *Pravda* and other periodicals responded sympathetically to these complaints and denounced the excessively strict control exercised by chief administrations and ministries over subordinate bodies. The Soviet government has complained about the excessive turnover of directors and engineers, who have often been shifted from post to post before they could really get started running their en-

---

[19] Some interesting examples of cases where Soviet plant directors have attempted to act like the owners of capitalist enterprises by selling items of fixed capital are given in Venediktov, *op. cit.*, pp. 405–8.

[20] Bienstock, Schwarz, and Yugow, *op. cit.*, pp. 9, 10.

[21] *Pravda*, September 10, 1940.

terprises.[22] Presumably progress has been achieved in giving these
supervisory enterprise officials more power and greater stability
in their positions. Yet it is significant that in May 1950 a Leningrad
factory director still found it necessary to complain in these terms:

> . . . It is impossible to evade the question of the rights of the direc-
> tor, which has long been a sore point. The existing control by
> ministries and chief administrations now binds enterprise directors
> hand and foot. The director's activities are bounded by all kinds of
> limitations, often contradictory ones. He does not have the right to
> strengthen one part of the work at the expense of another. He must
> strictly maintain the official staff table of organization, which is long
> since obsolete and by its very nature is distinguished by its inertia,
> failing to correspond to the dialectical character of production,
> which is always changing and putting forward new requirements.
> The director may not deviate by an iota from the general sum of
> wages and even within its limits he may not reward, for example,
> the most talented constructors or technologists.[23]

Another important means of control over the activities of the
manager of an enterprise or higher organ in the industrial hierarchy
is the so-called "control by the ruble" exercised by the Soviet banking system. All enterprises are compelled to have accounts in the
State Bank, and virtually all short-term credit available to them
comes from this source alone. In the case of a purchase or a sale
by an enterprise or other production unit, the financial transaction is
handled by the State Bank. The bank credits the account of the
seller and debits the account of the purchaser after the purchaser
has accepted the goods or otherwise given specific authority for
payment.

Short-term credit is extended to an enterprise only for strictly
determined goals, usually set down in advance by the enterprise's
credit and financial plan. These objectives are primarily the financing of goods in transit, financing seasonal processes of production,
and financing the accumulation of seasonal reserves of raw materials,
fuel, finished products, and so on. Loans are usually made for
three-month periods, and interest is paid on them. Credit is extended outside that provided for in an enterprise's financial plan in
the event of emergencies creating unforeseen credit needs. Banks
also supervise strictly the number of workers employed by in-

[22] Bienstock, Schwarz, and Yugow, *op. cit.*, p. 11.
[23] *Leningradskaya Pravda*, May 12, 1950.

dividual enterprises and the payment of wages. In general, the banking system acts as the state's financial overseer, insuring that financial discipline is maintained by a plant. This includes seeing to it that the plant's expenditures are kept within its plan and making sure that it meets its obligations to other plant, in other parts of the economy. The fact that enterprises are forbidden to make settlements of any significant size between each other by means of cash payments helps a good deal in assuring the adequacy of this bank control of financial discipline.[24]

The Leningrad factory director quoted above on the limitations of directors' powers complained at the same time about the mechanistic, bureaucratic way in which the State Bank controlled enterprises' funds. An enterprise can fulfill or overfulfill its production plans, yet it may fall into serious financial difficulties and have trouble buying raw materials or meeting its bills because its customers are delinquent in their payments. In such cases, he added, bank officials should take account of the peculiarities of the situation rather than operating purely on the basis of the financial picture presented by the enterprise's bank account.

The other side of the picture in the controversies between enterprise directors and their superiors or controllers is often presented by complaints in the Soviet press. It is not unusual, for example, to read denunciations of plant managers who regard themselves as the "boss" of their establishment and who refuse to take advice or suggestions from any source, even the local Communist Party group. Many managers, apparently, also care about little but meeting their production goals and are indifferent as to how they achieve this end. In many branches of Soviet industry it is apparently common practice each month to work at a leisurely tempo during the first ten days, speed up a bit in the middle of the month, and then work frantically in the last ten days to meet the month's output objective. The practice is apparently motivated by the desire for overtime pay at the end of the month.[25]

---

24 *Finansy SSR Za XXX Let*, pp. 119–20. Moscow: 1947. Arnold, *Banks, Credit, and Money in Soviet Russia*, pp. 375–79. Bienstock, Schwarz, and Yugow, *op. cit.*, pp. 89–90.

25 Cf. the typical complaints in *Moskovskaya Pravda*, August 3, 1950 and *Planovoye Khozyaistvo*, No. 4 (1950), p. 88. Also cf. L. M. Herman, "The Pattern of Soviet Industrial Expansion," *Problems of Communism*, No. 6 (1953), p. 19.

Purchase and Sale

Purchases and sales of industrial commodities are handled through a complex set of organizations directed by an annual distribution plan prepared by the State Planning Committee and approved by the Council of Ministers. The organ of procurement for each ministry is usually a Chief Administration of Supply (*Glavsnab*), which has regional offices and local agencies. There are also supply divisions in individual enterprises. The chief organ of sale in each ministry is usually the Chief Administration for Sale of Products (*Glavsbyt*). This body usually also has local offices and affiliates that work with the sales divisions of individual enterprises. In general, the Chief Administrations of Supply and Sale have primary responsibility for purchasing or selling the commodities required or produced by the plants subordinate to them.

The activities of these organizations are particularly important with regard to the most scarce commodities, the so-called "funded" commodities and "quota" commodities. Funded commodities are not sold by their producers directly, but are distributed by direct orders of the central government under strict allocation. These allocations specify the amount of each such commodity to be supplied each particular user. Such strict allocation is deemed necessary because of the great scarcity and importance of these funded commodities. Quota commodities are supplied by the ministries producing them to any individual user, provided that the quota allocated to the user's industry or area in the procurement plan has not all been used up. The third major group of commodities bought by Soviet plants are obtained by the so-called "decentralized" purchases. These are largely agricultural raw materials and products of local industrial plants, such as building materials. They are bought locally throughout the country by the local offices of Chief Administrations of Supply, as well as by the purchasing officers of individual enterprises.[26]

The Chief Administration for Supply or Sale of each ministry exercises rigid control over the enterprises and offices subordinate

---

[26] One writer has suggested that the system of quota commodities has been abandoned since World War II and all commodities are now either "funded" or obtained through decentralized purchases. Cf. Barrington Moore, Jr., *Terror and Progress USSR*, p. 43. Cambridge: Harvard University Press, 1954.

to it and keeps detailed accounts of their activities. That these organs do not operate with maximum efficiency is suggested by the frequent complaints in the Soviet press regarding the proliferation of needless procurement and sales agencies throughout the country. These apparently often duplicate each other's efforts and, striving to justify their existence in any way, sometimes go far beyond the activities nominally allocated to them by their home organizations.[27]

Despite the great abundance of organizations devoted to arranging for the flow of materials and parts, complaints in the Soviet press suggest that the industrial supply system does not operate satisfactorily. In the summer of 1950, the central press carried articles denouncing the fact that parts for plants in the Urals, for example, are obtained from supply sources in all parts of the country and have to be moved great distances. Failure to integrate production of parts and raw materials properly with the work of assembly plants results in work interruptions or the necessity of resorting to airplane delivery to keep plants operating. On May 10, 1950, *Moskovskaya Pravda* denounced the poor organization for consumer-goods plants in and around Moscow. It revealed that a class of unofficial middlemen had sprung up. These make a living, apparently, by searching out plants that have surpluses and deficits of different materials and arranging barter deals among them, receiving fees or commissions for their work. Some of these deals are reported to be quite complicated, requiring exchanges among four or five different plants at one time. All this is quite illegal, but is apparently resorted to by enterprise managers — and tolerated by their superiors — because of the failure of official supply channels to meet their needs. Related to this is the widespread use of "pushers" or expediters (the so-called *tolkachy*) to speed up materials delivery. The Soviet economics magazine *Voprosy Ekonomiki* (No. 7, 1953, p. 11) reported in late 1953 that one Urals plant had diverted more than 1,000 workers from production in the preceding two years so they might act as "pushers." It is probably only because of the use of these extralegal and semilegal expedients that the supply system manages to work with tolerable satisfaction. That corruption thrives under these conditions seems unquestionable.[28]

---

[27] Bienstock, Schwarz, and Yugow, *op. cit.*, pp. 58–65.
[28] Cf. Joseph S. Berliner, " 'Blat' is Higher than Stalin!" *Problems of Communism*, No. 1 (1954), pp. 22–31.

The Industrial Price System

In a free-enterprise economy, prices are sensitive barometers of supply and demand, changing in response to bids and offers on the market and also in response to more general factors, such as the supply of money. They are among the primary determinants of decisions by producers and consumers. In the Soviet economy, prices have played a secondary role, and the basic decisions embodied in economic plans have often been based on other considerations, such as the government's desire to attain a given level of production or the physical availability of different raw materials. Nevertheless, within the circumscribed area in which industrial managers or consumers are free to make decisions, prices play an important role. The enterprise director is expected to produce at lowest cost and make maximum profit consistent with the plan; and where he has freedom of choice he will seek to buy at the lowest price and sell at the highest one.

To the extent that prices do not reflect underlying demand and supply conditions, they tend to produce changes that worsen a given situation. Thus in the postwar period immediately after 1945, petroleum was in very short supply in the USSR. In a freely competitive economy this would have resulted in a price rise to the point where demand was reduced to the available supply. This apparently did not happen in the USSR, and the Soviet government was obliged to apply other pressures to induce enterprises of all types to convert from petroleum to other fuels and to exercise maximal economy in utilizing gasoline, lubricating oils, and other petroleum products. Moreover, apparently, the price pattern before 1949 was such as to encourage overproduction of some commodities in excess of planned quantities and underproduction of others, as hard-pressed enterprise directors sought to maximize their profits by producing the most advantageous commodities in terms of cost-price relationships. Complaints appeared frequently in the Soviet press that enterprises were violating their orders regarding the assortment and relative proportions of different items in their output, although exceeding their production plan in terms of the value of total production.

For planning purposes, Soviet enterprises and other organizations used three different sets of prices before January 1, 1949. These were the constant 1926–27 prices, officially fixed wholesale prices, and so-called current planning prices. The character and deficiencies of 1926–27 prices have been discussed earlier. The fixed wholesale prices are those at which goods are actually bought and sold between enterprises. The current planning prices seem to be closely linked with the wholesale prices and would perhaps be the same except for state subsidies. They are used in planning the volume of investment in the national economy.[29]

The utilization of these different sets of prices introduced difficulties in planning work, both because of the deficiencies of the 1926–27 quotations and because of the significant differences in the relative proportions of the prices for different commodities from one set of prices to another. Thus (to take an example from the petroleum industry), in terms of 1926–27 prices, petroleum coke of the second grade was more than seven times as expensive as fuel oil. In terms of 1948 wholesale prices, petroleum coke of the second grade was only little more than twice as expensive as fuel oil. In terms of the third set of 1948 prices — labeled "new corrected prices" — this grade of coke was only about two thirds as expensive as fuel oil![30] Such discrepancies must undoubtedly have resulted in much confusion before planning was shifted entirely to a current wholesale price basis, beginning in 1949.

For our study of Soviet industrial organization and operation, the most important prices are those actually employed in transactions, the wholesale prices. These are set on the following basis: The government estimates total planned cost, that is, the cost of raw materials, wages, and other items, set at the level desired by the state. To this is added the planned profit allocated to that firm, whatever it may be. Finally, where applicable, there is added the turnover tax (a sales tax applied to many commodities). The sum of planned costs, planned profit, and turnover tax, if any, is the final price. It will be noted that the planned costs set need have no relation to the actual costs of a given plant. Planned costs may even be uniform for all plants in a given branch of industry, though these plants may have sharply different actual costs. The function of a plant manager may be defined in part as the maximization of

[29] M. C. Kaser, "Soviet Planning and the Price Mechanism," *Economic Journal*, March 1950, pp. 84–86.

[30] *Ibid.*, p. 88n.

profit from his sales at government fixed prices by lowering his costs as far below the planned costs as possible. It is only in this sense that maximization of profit is a primary goal of Soviet industrial management. This is obviously a much more limited sense than that in which the same notion of profit maximization is used in our own and other capitalist societies.[31]

Data published in the June 1950 issue of *Voprosy Ekonomiki* shed important light on the difficulties facing Soviet price fixers because of the great variations in costs among different plants producing the same product. In the third quarter of 1949, for example, the actual cost of producing pig iron was 70 per cent greater in Ukrainian metallurgical plants than at Magnitogorsk. Similarly in the case of petroleum the cost of obtaining one ton of petroleum from Baku in 1941 was 16.6 rubles. At the same time in the Syzran oil field the equivalent cost was 39.7 rubles, more than twice as much. In the case of coal, data for 1940 show that the cost of production in the eastern regions of the USSR was 58–71 per cent less than the average cost for the entire country. The cost differential was even wider when comparison was made between the low cost eastern areas and the very high cost Donbas region. These prewar differentials were apparently broadened in the postwar period. To meet this problem of sharply differing costs, Soviet planners have apparently set markedly different prices for similar products at least in some cases. Thus in 1940 the wholesale price of a ton of coke made from Kuznetsk coal was 47 rubles 80 kopeks, while Donets coke was priced at 67 rubles per ton. This differential was apparently preserved as late as 1950.

Soviet planners considered that the power of fixing prices is one of the most important weapons in their hands, permitting them to stimulate attainment of the objectives of maximum production at constantly decreasing costs. By reducing planned costs they apply pressure on enterprise directors to lower the actual costs of production in order to make a profit. Moreover, the Soviet government has sometimes adjusted prices in order to stimulate the growth of various parts of the economy. Thus, in the early 1930's the government maintained extremely low prices for coal, wood, ores, metals, and a number of other products. These low prices were intended to make possible the rapid development of the machinery industries

[31] *Planovoye Khozyaistvo*, No. 6 (1945), p. 60.

buying these raw materials on which prices were kept down below cost. The losses sustained by the industries whose prices were thus kept down were made up through direct subsidies from the government budget. As the machinery industries succeeded in reducing their own costs substantially, so that they could begin to make a profit, the government, beginning in 1936, adjusted prices of raw materials and other products upward so as to bring them more closely into line with their actual costs. The objective throughout, however, was to maintain a price structure that would stimulate growth of production. Once this growth of production had been achieved, prices began to be brought into line with costs, in order to encourage greater efficiency and economy in the use of resources.[32] It is evident that sometimes the Soviet government plans prices so as actually to make what we may term a planned loss, that is, it deliberately orders goods sold at a net price below their cost of production. The rate of profit or loss planned for different industries or products may vary widely, the available evidence indicates. Thus, in 1937 it was planned for the oil industry to make over 27 per cent profit, and for the cement industry to lose more than 7 per cent, other branches of heavy industry having profits or losses in between the two.

Rates of profit on individual commodities also vary widely. Thus, in early 1938, spare parts for autos were bringing the automobile industry about 39 per cent profit, while spare parts for tractors were bringing the tractor industry a profit in excess of 150 per cent. Rubber shoes were bringing in an average profit of about 200 per cent, but auto tires were being sold at an average loss of 30 per cent. Some farm machines were sold for 25 per cent over cost; others were sold at a loss. In the cotton textile industry, some products were sold for profits of 20 to 30 per cent, while others were sold at losses ranging up to 10 or 15 per cent. A Soviet economist, commenting on these vagaries in the prices and profits set by the Soviet government, urged that economically unjustified differences in profits be eliminated. He did not go so far, however, as to urge that one uniform level of profit be set throughout all state industry, arguing merely that profits be adjusted in each branch to the situation and needs existing there.[33]

---

[32] *Planovoye Khozyaistvo*, No. 10 (1938), p. 60; and No. 1 (1939), p. 118.
[33] *Ibid.*, No. 10 (1938), pp. 57–64.

During World War II the Soviet government apparently maintained most prices for raw materials, fuel, industrial equipment, and other goods at constant levels, despite the fact that many of these industries suffered increased costs due to the dislocations and changes of wartime. Prices were altered somewhat so as to establish comparatively high profits for some urgently needed goods, such as spare parts and some instruments. In these cases the government established prices at twice the normal rate for deliveries in excess of the plan. Increased prices were also established where it was necessary to stimulate production of products requiring relatively large amounts of labor. In the iron and steel industry, for example, the government established differential profits for different groups of products, based on the laboriousness of their production. On the whole however, the effort was made to keep industrial prices stable or to reduce them, as in the case of war-equipment items, whose output rose tremendously while their costs fell during the conflict.[34]

This policy was apparently continued in the early postwar years. A necessary consequence of it, however, was the fact that many branches of heavy industry lost substantial sums and had to be reimbursed through government subsidy. Not until 1948 did many of these plants begin to become profitable, as government pressure was exerted for lower costs and improved operation under more normal peacetime conditions. On January 1, 1949, a new price system was put into effect for a number of branches of heavy industry. This provided increases in the wholesale prices of metals, fuel, electricity, timber, cement, and bricks, as well as in railroad freight rates, in order to help eliminate the losses being suffered and to remove the need for government subsidies. As one Soviet economist explains the matter:

> The system of government subsidies which was necessary in the years of the patriotic war and in the conditions of postwar reconstruction of the economy, became a hindrance to the path of further development of the national economy. It destroyed the basis of economic accountability—the coincidence of expenditures and the results of production, the guaranteeing of expenditures through the means of enterprises themselves. The system of government subsidies tends to make enterprises live from government budgetary sub-

[34] *Ibid.*, No. 6 (1945), pp. 61, 62, 67.

sidies, it weakens the stimulus to struggle for lower costs, and it contradicts the task of strengthening the Soviet ruble.[35]

In the new prices set in 1949, account was apparently taken of the disproportions between prices of different commodities and their relative cost, supply, and demand situations. This is suggested by a comment in *Ugol,* the coal industry journal: "The new prices have been fixed to reflect grades and quality. . . . These differences will make sorting work worth while and make the coal industry directly interested in supplying the national economy with those types and grades it most needs." [36]

At the beginning of 1950 general reductions were announced in wholesale prices for metals, machines and equipment, chemicals, electric power, lumber materials, and paper; and in railroad freight rates.[37] It will be noted that this list excludes fuel, cement, and bricks, items on which prices were raised at the beginning of 1949. The list does include machines and equipment, major categories of commodities that went unmentioned in the list of 1949 price increases. On July 1, 1950, prices for building materials and construction equipment, and freight rates on these commodities, were lowered in a government move aimed at reducing construction costs by 25 per cent.[38] There were also later reductions.

The frequency with which wholesale prices of many industrial commodities were changed in 1949–1953 is in sharp contrast with the great rigidity and infrequent changes of prices in the two preceding decades. The more recent practice suggests that the experience of Soviet planners has impressed them with the importance of a meaningful price system as an aid in carrying out their economic plans and securing most efficient utilization of resources. But even the apparently changed policy since 1949 leaves Soviet wholesale prices far more rigid than the corresponding quotations in a free-enterprise economy. Moreover the accuracy with which Soviet planners can adjust prices to supply and demand conditions is open to question. The new Soviet practice seems to reflect ideas of economic theorists in the non-Soviet world, who have suggested that in socialist economies prices could be used as guides to produc-

---

[35] *Voprosy Ekonomiki,* No. 8 (1948), p. 31.
[36] Quoted by Kaser, *op. cit.,* p. 90.
[37] *Pravda,* April 27, 1950.
[38] *Pravda,* June 14, 1950.

tion if planning authorities changed them periodically, lowering them where supply exceeded demand and raising them where demand exceeded supply.[39] But unlike these theorists, Soviet planners still do not put their main reliance upon prices, using them only as important secondary aids and stimuli to realization of the specific production goals ordered in economic plans.

The present philosophy behind Soviet industrial price policy is summarized by this statement of the principles on which the price changes of 1949 and 1950 were based:

> a. The new wholesale prices must guarantee that enterprises will work without losses. They must give practical possibilities for doing without subsidies and guarantee the receipt of profits according to plan.

> b. Prices must be established so as to stimulate increased output of deficit or especially necessary products and simultaneously limit their consumption in production.

> c. Changes in rates must be directed toward guaranteeing railroad operation without loss, stimulating transport by waterways, combating baseless distant transport of freight, and promoting better utilization of rolling stock.[40]

Whether these principles have actually been strictly applied since 1949, it is difficult to decide due to the present serious lack of necessary price and cost data. Certainly it must be hard for Soviet planners to overcome the tradition and practice of fairly arbitrary price-setting, which has historically been dominant in their activities.

The preceding discussion may be made somewhat more concrete by considering the changes in the prices of a number of industrial commodities from 1926–27 to 1949 or 1950, depending upon the last date for which data are available. The prices in Table 9 are for a metric ton of each commodity, in rubles.

Several facts are clearly apparent even from the limited sample of prices given above. First, the general upward trend of wholesale prices over the entire period is obvious, the increases introduced on March 1, 1949, having been particularly sharp. Second, it is clear that prices remained constant or almost constant over long periods when economic conditions fluctuated very much, most notably

[39] Cf. Lippincott, ed., *On the Economic Theory of Socialism, passim.*
[40] *Izvestia Akademii Nauk SSSR, Otdeleniye Ekonomiki i Prava*, No. 3 (1950), p. 170.

TABLE 9. Changes in Prices of Selected Commodities, 1926–27 to 1949 or 1950.

Commodity	1926–27	1930	July 1, 1936	Dec. 31, 1940	Dec. 16, 1947	Mar. 1, 1949	July 1, 1950
Coal	11.61	10.63	21.78	36.25	36.25	120.50	120.50
Fuel Oil	48.10	48.10	48.10	137.00	137.00	355.00	†
Steel Rails	110.00	112.00	259.00	318.00	318.00	951.00	†
Timber *	17.36	13.89	17.40	17.40	23.00	104.50	75.24
Cement	29.00	25.23	57.16	89.00	89.00	190.00	121.60
Sulphuric Acid .	53.06	43.72	100.00	152.00	152.00	270.00	172.80

* Cubic meter is unit priced.
† Not available.
Source: Naum Jasny, *The Soviet Price System*, p. 168. Stanford: Stanford University Press, 1951.

between 1940 and 1947, during which World War II alone must have drastically altered supply and demand relationships. Third, the data for July 1, 1950, suggest strongly that the radical price reform of March 1, 1949, was too steep a change for the Soviet managerial group to adjust to easily, forcing a very substantial lowering of many of these prices in little more than a year; it seems doubtful that these 1949–50 price reductions are actually explainable in terms of increased productivity or other forces making for lower costs.

This section may perhaps best be concluded by pointing out that Stalin, in his last major theoretical work released in 1952, scathingly said:

> The trouble is that our managers and planners, with few execeptions, are poorly acquainted with the results of the law of value. They fail to study these results and do not know how to reckon with them in their calculations. Speaking strictly, it is this that explains the confusion which still reigns in our country in the matter of price policy. Some time ago it was decided, in the interests of cotton cultivation, to correlate the price of cotton and grain, to define carefully the price of grain sold to cotton raisers and to increase the price of cotton delivered to the state. Our managers and planners made a suggestion which astonished the members of the Central Committee. Under this proposal the price suggested for a ton of grain was virtually equal to that for a ton of cotton. The price of a ton of grain was equated, moreover, with that of a ton of bread. The authors of this suggestion found nothing rational to say to the statements of members of the Central Committee that the price of a ton of bread should be higher than that of a ton of grain because of the additional cost of milling and baking, that generally cotton costs far more than grain as is evidenced also by world prices of cotton and

grain. As a result, the Central Committee had to take matters into its own hands, cut the grain price and raise the cotton price. What would have happened had the proposal of these comrades gone into effect? We would have impoverished the cotton raisers and have been left without cotton.

It seems illuminating that thirty-five years after the Bolshevik Revolution, Stalin could find no better guide to price policy within the Soviet Union than price patterns obtaining in the world capitalist market. The Soviet experience, this suggests, does not so far support those economic theorists who believe a socialist economy could evolve in practice a rational price system, efficiently guiding the allocation of resources in line with changing demand, supply, and cost conditions.

Profit Sharing in Industry

Along with coercive controls aimed at securing compliance with its production plans, the government of the USSR also uses incentives, one of the most important of which is a form of profit-sharing known as the Director's Fund.

In both 1939 and 1940, about 60 per cent of all the profits realized by Soviet industry were returned to the Soviet government as part of its budgetary income.[41] These government receipts from industrial profits were mingled with the general incomes of the Soviet treasury and then expanded for the various purposes provided in the budget, including the expansion of fixed and working capital of Soviet industry. The profit remaining in industry went for a number of purposes. Part of it went for the expansion of capital investment and working capital within the enterprises and ministries that had realized the profits. In addition, however, part of this profit, then and at present, goes to the Director's Fund.

The Director's Fund was inaugurated in 1936, suspended during World War II, and revived after 1945. In the early years after the war, industries were divided into three groups, by regulations governing contributions to Directors' Funds. One group, comprising mainly consumer-goods industries, formed its Director's Fund by contributions to it of 2 per cent of planned profits and 75 per cent of profits in excess of plan. The other two groups contributed 4

---

[41] A. K. Suchkov, ed., *Dokhody Gosudarstvennogo Byudzheta SSSR*, p. 86. Moscow: Gosplanizdat, 1945.

per cent and 10 per cent of planned profits, and 50 and 25 per cent of profits above plan, respectively. In 1950 the Soviet press revealed that a new set of percentages was in effect for the Director's Fund. Coal, metal mining, petroleum, metallurgical production, and other labor-intensive industries allocate 5 per cent of their planned profit and 45 per cent of their unplanned profit to this Fund. A second group of industries, including machinery and textiles, allocates 2 per cent of planned profits and 30 per cent of unplanned profits. Most consumer goods industries put in 1 per cent and 15 per cent, respectively.[42]

The Director's Fund is expended in the following ways: Fifty per cent of it must be spent for expanding production and for constructing and repairing housing for the plant's workers in amounts above the planned capital investment. The rest is spent for the improvement of living conditions of workers, for bonuses to outstanding employees, for financing vacations and trips for outstanding workers, and for related uses.

The Director's Fund is primarily a means of sharing any excess profits or savings with those responsible for the achievement of these above-plan financial gains. In this way the Soviet government seeks to increase the personal interest of workers and managers in the individual productive units to attain greater reductions in costs than originally envisaged by their plans.

Cooperative Industry

Three main types of cooperative industry exist in the USSR: industrial cooperatives, consisting of artisans and handicraft workers; cooperatives of invalids, consisting of disabled war veterans and other handicapped persons; and the subordinate industrial cooperatives of some consumer cooperatives. In addition there are industrial cooperatives ancillary to hunting and fishing cooperatives, which produce commodities needed in these activities. There are also industrial cooperatives on some collective farms, composed of members of those farms. The industrial cooperatives first listed above are by far the most important group, producing over 80 per cent of all cooperative industrial production.[43]

[42] Venediktov, *op. cit.*, p. 519. Gsovski, *op. cit.*, vol. I, pp. 385–87. *Trud*, May 26, 1950. *Trud*, Sept. 16, 1950.
[43] Arakelian, *op. cit.*, p. 111.

These cooperatives produce a wide variety of consumer goods. Furniture, kitchen equipment, boots and shoes, barrels and baskets, textiles, toys, leather goods, artistic wood and iron work, pottery, and similar goods are their chief products. During World War II, industrial cooperatives, like other parts of the Soviet production apparatus, concentrated primarily on the output of goods required by the war effort. The number of workers employed in these cooperatives was about two million in 1931 and about a million and a half at the end of the 1930's.[44]

Cooperative industry is considered a form of socialist industry in the USSR because all means of production are owned in common by the members, all of whom participate in the joint enterprise. A Soviet citizen may join and work in an industrial cooperative by paying admission dues and buying a share of the enterprise. These dues and share payments go into the capital fund used to provide the fixed and working capital of the organization. The cooperative is governed by a charter that defines its activities and organization. The highest authority in the organization is the general meeting of members, who are also the workers. The general meeting elects an administration, which directs the enterprise between general meetings. Cooperative workers are paid wages, which are their primary source of income. In 1946 a government decree permitted distribution of up to 20 per cent of a cooperative's profits among members. If there are losses, these are taken out of the members' share payments.[45]

These cooperatives operate in a fashion generally similar to that of the state-owned industrial plants. Their work is governed by the master plan drawn up for the nation as a whole by the State Planning Committee.

Industrial cooperatives purchase equipment and raw materials from state enterprises and are also expected to meet as much of their material needs as possible through local purchases. Waste products of state industry are sold to them for further processing and sale. They can receive short- and long-term loans from government banks to finance their activities. In November 1946 the Soviet government

[44] One of the most comprehensive descriptions of Soviet industrial cooperatives is given in Sidney and Beatrice Webb, *Soviet Communism: A New Civilization?* vol. I, pp. 219–33. New York: Scribner's, 1936.
[45] Arakelian, *op. cit.*, p. 114. Schwartz, *Russia's Postwar Economy*, p. 44.

adopted a decree to stimulate cooperative production of consumer goods, ordering that superfluous machinery and tools of state enterprises be turned over to them and instituting some reductions in taxes on their income. The same decree ordered the expansion of both the number of producers' cooperatives and of the number of stores through which they sell their products to the state. In January 1948 industrial cooperatives, together with invalids' cooperatives, operated 3,288 stores; 12,717 stalls, kiosks, and the like; 1,336 restaurants; and 3,236 refreshment stands. These had a total retail sales volume of 7,650,000,000 rubles.[46]

Cooperatives of invalids were first set up legally in 1921 to permit the utilization of disabled persons in productive activity. Their number expanded over the years, increasingly greatly as a result of the large numbers incapacitated in World War II. In 1946, the RSFSR alone had 2,500 such cooperatives, employing 245,000 workers. These cooperatives are active in providing repair services, such as for sewing machines, typewriters, watches, as well as in direct commodity production. The administration of each cooperative is elected by the general meeting of members, while the heads of republican, provincial, and city cooperative unions are elected by representatives of local cooperatives.[47]

Though their organizational form differs from that of state-owned industrial enterprises, the industrial cooperatives and newer invalids' cooperatives are both completely under the control of the state. They operate only in accord with the directives of the state. At times, however, the government has been sharply concerned because of the efforts of various individuals to engage in private entrepreneurial production and trade, using the mask of cooperatives to hide their profit-seeking activities, which are punishable under Soviet law.[48]

In mid-1953 the formerly separate national adminstrative organizations of industrial cooperatives and invalids' cooperatives were abolished. Instead both types of organizations were combined and put under the newly formed USSR Central Council of Producers' Cooperatives at the national level, with corresponding councils at the republic and provincial levels.

---

[46] Arakelian, *op. cit.*, pp. 119–20. *Planovoye Khozyaistvo*, No. 4 (1948), p. 52.
[47] Arakelian, *op. cit.*, p. 117.
[48] *Planovoye Khozyaistvo*, No. 4 (1948), p. 58.

Speaking in August, 1953, Deputy Premier A. I. Mikoyan revealed that these cooperatives operated 126,000 enterprises and workshops employing 1,865,000 workers. He said that in 1953 these cooperatives were scheduled to produce 47,000,000,000 rubles worth of consumer goods as compared with 42,000,000,000 rubles in 1952 and 28,000,000,000 rubles in 1940. Cooperatives produce 40 per cent of all Soviet furniture, up to 35 per cent of ready-to-wear clothing, 40 per cent of knitted outerwear, over 35 per cent of felt footwear, and roughly half of all carts and drays. They operate 45,000 repair shops which earn 5,000,000,000 rubles annually repairing household goods. Mikoyan sharply criticized the poor quality of much of the cooperatives' output, their lack of proper working arrangements and equipment, and their frequently outmoded technology. It is the intention, apparently, to increase sharply the importance and output of these cooperatives as part of the post-Stalin effort to improve the Soviet standard of living.[49]

---

[49] The full text of Mikoyan's important speech is given in *Pravda*, August 26, 1953.

CHAPTER VII

THE GROWTH OF INDUSTRIAL PRODUCTION

THE MOST SPECTACULAR aspect of Soviet economic development has been the growth of industrial production. Basically, it is this rapid rise in manufacturing, mining, and related activities which has produced the great enhancement of Soviet world political and military power since the 1920's. As late as 1930, the popular foreign stereotype of the Soviet Union and its people saw a land of illiterate peasants, ignorant of machinery and modern technology. Though exaggerated, this stereotype had more than a grain of truth in it then. Yet by 1954 the outside world had to reckon with the fact that the Soviet Union had produced the most complex of modern weapons, atomic and hydrogen bombs, as well as warplanes which had proved in Korea to be technically on a level with United States jet fighters.

With typical boastfulness, Soviet propaganda described this industrial revolution's results by 1953 in these terms:

If in 1924–25, our country could produce only 1,868,000 tons of steel, 16,520,000 tons of coal, less than 3 billion kilowatt-hours of electric power, then in 1953 there will be produced over 38,000,000 tons of steel (21 times more than in 1924–25), over 320,000,000 tons of coal (19 times more), 133 billion kilowatt-hours of electric power (45 times more than in 1924–25). During the 28 years since the Fourteenth Party Congress, industrial output has grown 29 times, with production of the means of production growing approximately 55 times. Production of consumer goods has grown approximately 12 times in the last 28 years. Not in one country of the world has industry developed at such a quick tempo as it has developed and is developing in the Soviet land.[1]

[1] *Pravda,* November 6, 1953.

215

Yet even after one allows for the propaganda exaggeration in such statements as the above, the magnitude of the Soviet production feat still commands attention as one of the fundamental events in modern history.

It was pointed out in Chapter IV that the Soviet measure of the growth of the physical volume of industrial production in terms of 1926–27 prices has been so constructed that it exaggerates this growth. Nevertheless, reference to data or estimates regarding production of individual commodities such as will be given throughout this chapter makes clear certain major conclusions:

1. Soviet industrial production has grown very sharply over most of the years since the Bolshevik revolution. This growth has been made possible by the construction of literally thousands of new factories, power stations, and mines using modern machinery and techniques. The Soviet Union now has many times the production and the production capacity that it had in 1928 or that Czarist Russia had in 1913. The chief characteristic of Soviet industrial development has been the growth of heavy industry, that is, the increase in facilities for and output of industrial raw materials, machinery of all kinds, industrial chemicals, electric-power generating and transmission facilities, armaments, transportation equipment, and so on. The factory production of consumer goods has increased appreciably, too, but a major part of this rise has been simply the replacement of manufacture by artisans or in peasant households. It is illustrative of the utilitarian nature of Soviet industry that manufacture of motor vehicles in the USSR consists primarily of truck production. Passenger-car output is only a relatively small fraction of the whole, a situation the reverse of that in the United States automotive industry.

2. Along with the rise in physical *volume*, the *variety* of goods produced by Soviet industry has increased greatly. Complex machine tools, automatic production machinery, jet airplanes, many types of chemicals, rare metals, and other products never made in the USSR before 1928 or 1930 have been brought into production. Subsequent expansion has made the Soviet Union one of the world's leading producers of many of these new commodities. Much of Soviet industrial development has been activated by the desire to build up the nation's military strength through achieving maximum self-sufficiency as well as maximum output. Hence, frequently, the

relatively high cost of domestic manufacture compared to the price of imported commodities has been ignored. The development of a synthetic rubber industry in the USSR in the early 1930's — a decade before World War II forced the United States to construct this industry — is indicative of the length to which Soviet leaders have gone to attain their objective of autarky.

3. The Soviet Union's industry has been technologically transformed, so that by 1954 it was one of the most advanced in the world, being in some cases up to or little behind the technological level of the United States. Manufacturing and mining processes employed in the USSR in 1928 were generally primitive and backward. Much of the existing industrial equipment was old, obsolete, and in poor shape. In the years since that time modern techniques and processes of all kinds have been introduced on a wide scale, while obsolete equipment has been replaced by far superior machinery. This technological progress has not proceeded at an even rate in all industries, and even by 1954 not all of Soviet backwardness had been eliminated. True, much of this technological advance has been scored by taking over gains made in other countries — sometimes through purchase or other commercial fashion, sometimes by disregard of patent rights, and sometimes through military or economic espionage — but the evidence suggests strongly that these borrowings have been assimilated by large numbers of workers and technicians who can apply them effectively. Frequently, however, this mechanization has been most uneven, being concentrated mainly on direct production operations. Subsidiary service functions in many plants, including such important work as loading and unloading of products and internal plant transport, are often mechanized only poorly or not at all, requiring large numbers of manual laborers working at low levels of productivity.

4. The geographic distribution of all Soviet industries — manufacturing, mining, electric-power generation, and others — has undergone a most radical change in the past quarter century. In the early years of the Soviet regime, industry was overwhelmingly concentrated in the western areas, particularly in the Ukraine and Moscow and Leningrad provinces. As late as 1930 these three regions together accounted for from 60 to 80 per cent of all Soviet electric power, coal, iron and steel, machinery, iron ore, and basic chemicals. At this time the Western Siberian Territory produced

these commodities only in small quantities or not at all. The Urals produced insignificant quantities of electric power, coal, and machinery, and only a quarter or less of all Soviet iron and steel, iron ore, and basic chemicals.[2] The geographical distribution of industrial production did not change drastically during the 1930's. The great bulk of this output continued to be produced in the area west of the Urals, though very striking and most important gains were also made in the Urals, Siberia, and Central Asia. The data in the following table show the change in the distribution of large-scale industrial production between 1913 and 1937.

TABLE 10. Gross Output of Large-Scale Industry in the USSR by Regions, 1913 and 1937.

Region	Output Million 1926–27 Rubles 1913	Output Million 1926–27 Rubles 1937	Output Per Cent of Total 1913	Output Per Cent of Total 1937	Ratio of 1937 to 1913 Output
WESTERN AREAS					
European North	201	1,624	1.8	1.8	8.0
Northwest and Central Regions	5,568	45,343	50.6	49.6	8.1
North Caucasus and Crimea	464	4,736	4.2	5.2	10.2
Ukrainian SSR	2,226	16,152	20.2	17.7	7.2
Belorussian SSR	119	1,733	1.1	1.9	15.4
Volga Region	687	4,809	6.3	5.3	7.0
WESTERN TOTAL	9,265	74,397	84.2	81.4	8.1
EASTERN AREAS					
Urals and Western Siberia	675	7,726	6.1	8.5	11.5
Eastern Siberia and Far East	211	2,928	1.9	3.2	13.9
Azerbaidzhan SSR	398	2,297	3.6	2.5	5.2
Georgian SSR	53	909	.5	1.0	17.0
Armenian SSR	17	214	.2	.2	12.6
Turkmen SSR	35	264	.3	.3	7.6
Uzbek SSR	284	1,512	2.6	1.7	5.4
Tadzhik SSR	1	157	*	.2	157.0
Kazakh SSR	60	841	.5	.9	14.0
Kirgiz SSR	1.2	139	*	.2	116.0
EASTERN TOTAL	1,735.2	16,987	15.8	18.6	9.8

* Less than one-tenth of one per cent.
Source: Adapted from Balzak, et al., Economic Geography of the USSR, p. 206.

[2] Narodnoye Khozyaistvo SSSR, Statistichesky Spravochnik, 1932, pp. 76–83.

World War II brought a far more drastic change in the geographic pattern of industrial production. As German forces occupied the area west of the line connecting Leningrad-Moscow-Stalingrad, some 1,300 plants were evacuated eastward. During the war these were put into operation at new locations, while other factories and mines in the east were expanded and new industrial installations were built. When the western areas were regained by Soviet forces, most factories, mines, and electric power installations had been completely ruined or damaged. Under these conditions, the distribution of Soviet industrial output in 1945 gave the Urals and the area east of the Urals a far greater relative importance than this region had had before the war. Since 1945, the war-ravaged Western areas have benefited from the great rebuilding efforts sponsored by the Soviet government, efforts which by 1954 had permitted the production of these areas to surpass even the 1940 levels. From 1945 to 1954, too, the expanded industry of the Eastern regions was still further increased. In 1954 there was a much more nearly even distribution of industrial output between Eastern and Western Russia than had existed in either 1940 or 1945. According to one Soviet source, industrial output in the Eastern USSR in 1952 was three times as great as in 1940. This area is said to have produced one-third of Soviet industrial output in 1951 — as compared with under 19 per cent in 1937 — including over half of all Soviet production of steel and rolled metal, almost half of all Soviet coal and oil, and over 40 per cent of all Soviet electric power.[3]

Capital Investment

The industrial progress achieved under the Soviet regime has been made possible by huge capital investments devoted to building and equipping factories, mines, and other productive installations. Complete data are not available for the entire period since 1928. The published figures that are available are somewhat misleading, since they are in terms of current prices and hence reflect the price inflation that has taken place. In the table below an effort is made to show the growth of industrial capital investment in the 1930's in terms of current prices and in "real" terms. Deflation of the data in current prices has been accomplished by use of an index of construc-

---

[3] *Planovoye Khozyaistvo*, No. 4 (1953), p. 15.

tion cost and must be considered as only roughly accurate, since this index may not adequately reflect the changing cost of industrial equipment.

TABLE 11. Capital Investment in Industry in the USSR 1928–38, in Current Prices and in "Real" Terms.

Year	Investment in Current Prices (BILLION RUBLES)	Index of Cost of Construction (1929 = 100)	Investment in "Real" Terms (BILLION 1929 RUBLES)
1928	1.9	111	1.7
1929	2.6	100	2.6
1930	4.1	98	4.2
1931	7.4	106	7.0
1932	10.4	161	6.5
1933	8.9	187	4.8
1934	10.6	218	4.9
Average for 1934–1938	14.6	294	5.0

Source: Investment in current prices from *Sot. Stroi.*, p. xxxiv and *Sot. Stroi. (1933-38)*, p. 113. Index of cost of construction from M. Gardner Clark's Ph.D. thesis, *Some Economic Problems of the Soviet Iron and Steel Industry*, p. 49. The figure for the 1934-38 average is estimated on the basis of Clark's 1935 figure, modified in the light of his remarks on cost rises in 1936 on page 50.

There is a striking discrepancy between the figures in current prices and those in "real" terms. The former show that the money value of investment in current prices increased more than seven-fold between 1928 and the average of 1934–38. If our deflating index is at all accurate, however, it would seem that the physical volume of resources devoted to industrial investment reached its peak for the period considered in 1931, at a level little more than four times that in 1928. It fell slightly in 1932 and then over the years 1933–38 declined to a stable level less than three times the 1928 volume. The most rapid application of capital to expansion of industry, apparently, took place in 1931 and 1932, years of rationing for urban consumers and of hunger in some major areas of the countryside.

The allocation of industrial capital investment between heavy industry producing means of production and light industry producing consumer goods in the mid-1930's greatly favored the former. Heavy industry received about 83 per cent of the total investment from 1934 to 1938; consumer goods industries only about 17 per cent.[4]

---

[4] *Sot. Stroi. (1933–38)*, p. 113.

Shaping Industrial Development

In planning industrial development since 1928, Soviet leaders have had to answer a number of key questions, the answers arrived at playing major roles in shaping the character of this development. What volume of production should be aimed at for each major commodity? What should be the rate of increase in output sought? Where should new plants and new industries be located? How large and how specialized should these new plants be? Put in other terms, the crucial decisions have been those regarding future volume, speed of growth, locational pattern, specialization, and scale of operation. During the rehabilitation period before 1928, the Soviet regime had attempted to restore production to the highest levels attained before World War I. But thereafter they were striking out into new ground, and required other models and experience to guide them.

In all these matters they were profoundly influenced by the economic history of the leading capitalist nations, particularly the United States and Germany. Questions of volume were apparently decided with the aim of reaching and surpassing the total output of key industrial commodities in France, Germany, and England. Later, per capita outputs in some of these countries were regarded as goals for Soviet per capita output. In 1939, at the Eighteenth Congress of the Communist Party, both Stalin and Molotov discussed comparisons of per capita Soviet output with that in other countries, indicating their desire eventually to surpass the highest American per capita output up to that time, that of 1929.[5] On questions of the rapidity with which increases could be achieved, Soviet leaders initially could probably do little more than guess. But as their experience increased and they accumulated basic data for future projections, they could make realistic estimates that were more likely to be attained, at least in the field of heavy industry, to which they were willing to sacrifice the interests of light industry whenever necessary.

In determining the geographical pattern of Soviet industry, the USSR's planners had to take many considerations into account. Some of these were economic. Soviet leaders were aware of the

---

[5] *The Land of Socialism Today and Tomorrow*, pp. 22, 23, 114–16. Moscow: Foreign Languages Publishing House, 1939. Clark, *Some Economic Problems of the Soviet Iron and Steel Industry*, p. 15.

desirability of establishing industry at locations and in locational patterns that would help to minimize production costs. Nearness to raw materials and to markets, availability of labor and transportation, costs of utilizing different sources of the same raw material, these are illustrative of the economic factors involved. Among the noneconomic considerations taken into account, two seem to have been most influential: the desire to lessen the vulnerability of the USSR's industry to destruction by attack from the west, and the desire to provide additional industry in particularly backward areas, such as Central Asia. In this locational planning, the force of noneconomic factors seems often to have overridden that of the cost considerations, a situation apparently aided by the consistent underestimation of transport costs during much of the 1930's. In particular, much of the development of the Urals and Western Siberia during the 1930's resulted in the construction of plants far from consumer markets. Moreover, the most celebrated feature of this eastern development — the marriage of Magnitogorsk iron ore with Kuznetsk coal as the basis of integrated iron and steel industries at both locations — required large shipments of bulky commodities over a distance of more than 1,300 miles, at high real cost. It is significant that Soviet transport authorities protested against the Magnitogorsk-Kuznetsk combine in the early stages of its planning, but were overruled by the industrial management authorities, who secured subsidies in the form of especially low freight rates for this development.[6]

The disproportions that arose because of the decisions taken may be illustrated by the following comparison of the cost of producing a ton of pig iron in different parts of the USSR, in terms of freight haulage required and actual man days of labor.[7]

	Cost		
	(TON-KILOMETERS OF		
Region	FREIGHT HAULAGE)	+	(MAN DAYS)
Ukraine and other Southern Plants.....	700	+	2–3
Central European USSR.............	900	+	3½–4
Magnitogorsk and Kuznetsk.........	4,500	+	2
Urals Charcoal Works	100	+	12

This example represents an extreme case of the results to which

---

6 Clark, *op. cit.*, pp. 207–8.
7 Cited in Clark, pp. 218–19.

underestimation of transport costs led in the early and mid-1930's. It does not fully expose these unfortunate results, however, because it does not take into account the very long hauls required for much of Magnitogorsk and Kuznetsk steel production in order to bring it to consumers. It cannot be entirely unrepresentative, however, for since the later 1930's there has been a violent swing in the other direction. Soviet industrial location policy now apparently takes the minimization of transport requirements as a basic desideratum. Molotov, reporting to the Communist Party Congress in 1939, put this new policy in these terms:

> In keeping with the best interests of the state, industry should be brought nearer to the sources of raw material and the consuming districts. This will help to do away with irrational shipments and shipments carried over inordinate distances. It will also be instrumental in the further advance of the economically less developed districts of the USSR. In the *main economic districts* of the Soviet Union we must secure a comprehensive economic development, which means that in each of these districts we must organize a fuel industry and the production of commodities like cement, plaster of Paris, chemical fertilizer and glass, as well as mass consumption goods of the light and food industries in sufficient quantity to meet the needs of these districts. . . . We must strictly forbid the construction of new plants in Moscow, Leningrad, and a number of other major industrial centers.[8]

In keeping with this policy, the utilization even of poor-quality raw materials — such as the inferior Moscow and Urals coal and the troublesome Kerch iron ore — has been and is being greatly expanded. To the extent that regional self-sufficiency can be attained, of course, the vulnerability of the USSR to industrial disruption from military attack will be lessened, and there will be benefits resulting from the diminution of demands made on railroad transport. A striking example of what has been accomplished along these lines is provided by the Kuznetsk iron and steel combine, once totally dependent on Magnitogorsk iron ore. In 1949 it was meeting 70 per cent of its iron ore requirements by employing locally produced material, though this was acknowledgedly poorer than that of Magnitogorsk. In 1940 the percentage was only 32.6.[9]

It should not be inferred from the above discussion that all Soviet industrial location during the 1930's, before the change in policy,

8 *Land of Socialism Today and Tomorrow*, p. 134.
9 *Pravda*, June 12, 1950.

ignored transportation considerations and emphasized development in the east. As Table 10 above has indicated, great development took place in the older industrial regions as well, building on the abundant raw material, labor, and transport resources there. Locational planning resulted from a tug of war between those who favored still more rapid development of the western areas, particularly the Ukraine, than actually occurred, and those industrial leaders who wished large amounts of resources diverted to the Urals, Siberia, the Far East, and Central Asia. The former group's arguments, about 1930, emphasized the force of transport and related factors whose full importance was not taken into account in policy-making until almost a decade later.[10]

With regard to problems of specialization and scale of facilities, Soviet development during the 1930's was similar to that in the area of location policy. Soviet policymakers tended to base themselves upon American and German experience, but to ignore the significant differences between their situation and that of foreign countries. The USSR was poor in capital and skilled labor compared with the United States and Germany, and also had a much smaller consumer market at the time. Soviet economists and planners at first tended to ignore or underestimate the importance of the law of diminishing returns and to be contemptuous of the "bourgeois" theory of the optimal size of firm or plant. Here, too, underestimation of the importance of transport costs played a significant role.

The result of this attitude was that much of the industrial development during the 1930's took the form of building large-scale and very specialized plants for different products. There was relative neglect of small and medium-sized plants and of plants producing a wide variety of related commodities, such as different types and forms of steel. An extreme example of this policy is the production of rolled-steel wheels for railroads, of which virtually all Soviet production in 1938 was concentrated at one mill in Dnepropetrovsk Province in the Ukraine. From there the wheels had to be shipped to railroads all over the vast expanse of the USSR. Similar lengthy hauls for other products also resulted, helping to intensify the railroad overloading, to which locational policy had

---

[10] Clark, *op. cit.*, pp. 205–7. Cf. also Dobb, *Soviet Economic Development Since 1917*, pp. 386–406, for a fuller discussion of Soviet industrial location policy, from a somewhat different point of view than that adopted here.

also contributed. Large specialized plants, appropriate for the United States with its large and rich markets in many areas, were uneconomic under Soviet conditions, where the output of one or two plants of each commodity or small group of commodities had to be shipped all over the country.

Recognition of the mistake came in 1938. A decree of February 26, 1938, declared that "the biggest shortcoming in planning and construction is gigantomania." The policy of overspecialization was now blamed on "the enemies of the people, the Trotskyite-Bukharin and bourgeois nationalistic diversionaries and spies." Sometimes the very men who had championed this policy attacked it, after the change of policy, as a mistake born of the application of "the principles of capitalist economy." Only by such vituperation, which would protect the "infallible" Stalin and his colleagues, could a mistake be recognized publicly and a reversal made. The extent of the change in policy was indicated by Molotov in the 1939 speech referred to above:

> Lastly, in the construction of new factories and mills we must prohibit such narrow specialization as would make the whole country dependent upon one special factory for the supply of any given product. Our plans still err in this respect. We must resolutely put an end to this absurd schematism in construction plans.[11]

Military considerations probably also played a part in this policy shift. If the USSR were dependent for the supply of a vital product upon the output of a single plant only, it could be deprived of that commodity by the capture or destruction of one plant, with serious consequences for all users of the particular product involved.

Study of the way in which industrial development took place in the 1930's seems to indicate clearly that over-all planning in that period fell far short of providing proper centralization and coordination of the numerous decisions made. Regional planning was most deficient, leading to irrational location of plants. Many particular people's commissariats and chief administrations made decisions in the light simply of their own departmental interests,

---

[11] *Land of Socialism Today and Tomorrow*, p. 134. The preceding discussion of specialization and scale has been based on Clark, *op. cit.*, Part II, pp. 56–114. Though this discussion by Clark deals specifically only with the iron and steel industry, the principles discussed are general, and applied to other branches of heavy industry developed during the period.

ignoring other branches of the economy. The coordination sought was frequently that which would serve the purpose of making the best record for the particular agency involved, even though this might be at the expense of the transport system or of some other economic administration.[12]

It seems clear that Soviet economic development in the 1930's — and more recently as well, though less material is available on which to base judgments — was a frenzied process, in which many costly mistakes were made. The sacrifices imposed on the Soviet people in terms of material deprivation and personal discomfort were huge. Yet it must be realized that those who directed this development had enormous human and material resources with which to work. Even employing them at far less than 100 per cent efficiency, much could be and was accomplished. In the material that follows, we shall trace briefly the development of the more important Soviet industries, in order to obtain a clearer and more detailed picture of the progress achieved. The specific industries we shall consider are those producing raw materials — electric power, coal, iron and steel, nonferrous metals, and chemicals — and machinery, armaments, and consumer goods.

Coal

Coal is by far the most important single component of the USSR's fuel supplies. Its increasingly predominant position among Soviet fuels is indicated in Table 12.

TABLE 12. Relative Importance of Major Fuels in the Centralized Consumption of the Soviet Union.

Fuel	1932	1940	1950 Goal
		(PERCENTAGE)	
Coal	59.4	71.9	75.6
Wood	19.9	13.9	9.7
Peat	3.7	6.2	6.2
Oil Fuel	17.0	7.9	6.3
Natural Gas	—	—	1.4
Shale	—	.1	.8

Source: *Planovoye Khozyaistvo*, No. 2 (1946), p. 101.

12 *Planovoye Khozyaistvo*, No. 1 (1939), p. 62; and No. 11 (1940), pp. 42–44.

The growth of Soviet production of coal since 1913 is shown by the following data, in millions of metric tons: [13]

Year	Production	Year	Production
1913	29.1	1950	260.0
1920	7.2*	1952	300.0
1927–28	35.5	1953	318.0
1934	93.9	1954 Goal	346.0
1940	166.0	1955 Goal	372.0
1945	149.3		

* Census industry.

This is an impressive record of growth over a period of forty years which included two world wars and one civil war. Between 1913 and 1950, Soviet coal production grew about ninefold. Output in 1953 was almost twice that of 1940. However, these figures exaggerate somewhat the real Soviet gain in this field since the data lump together both high quality hard coal and lignite with a low caloric content. If Soviet production of different quality coals is converted into units of a standard coal having a fixed caloric content per ton, the increase shown above is reduced somewhat. Dr. D. B. Shimkin has calculated that in terms of fuel having 7,000 calories per kilogram, Soviet production grew from a total of 31,500,-000 tons in 1913 to 213,100,000 tons in 1950.[14] This is less than a sevenfold increase over this period, as against the ninefold gain shown by the data above which make no allowance for the great increase of low quality lignite production in the Soviet period.

In 1913 the Donets Basin produced almost all the coal of the area that is now the USSR, about 25 millions tons of the 29.1 million ton total. During the Czarist era and the early years of the Soviet regime, therefore, Donbas coal had to be shipped over long distances to most of the industrial areas of the country, even as far as Turk-

[13] Data for 1913, 1927–28, and 1934 from *Sot. Stroi*, pp. 100–101; data for 1920 from *Narodnoye Khozyaistvo SSSR* v. *Tsifrakh*, p. 67; 1940 figure from Fourth Five-Year Plan; 1945 output calculated on basis of *Trud*, March 20, 1949 and government economic reports for 1946–48; 1950 output based on *Pravda*, April 17, 1951; 1952 output—*Ibid.*, October 6, 1952; 1953 figure based on *Pravda*, January 31, 1954; 1954 goal based on *Pravda*, April 27, 1954; 1955 goal calculated from percentage gain over 1950 called for by Fifth Five-Year Plan Directives in *Pravda*, October 12, 1953.

[14] D. B. Shimkin, *Minerals – A Key to Soviet Power*, p. 177. Cambridge: Harvard University Press, 1953.

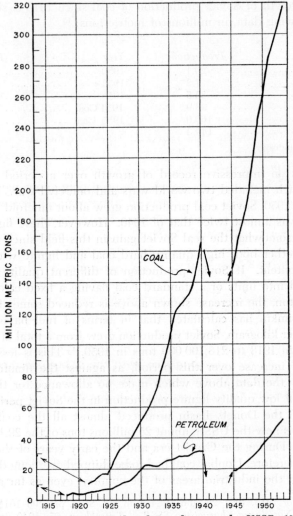

FIGURE 2. *Production of Coal and Petroleum in the USSR, 1913–53.*
Sources: Official Soviet publications and author's estimates.

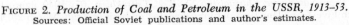

estan in Central Asia, at great expense.[15] The opening up of new
coal fields and the expansion of the Donbas and other old fields
were therefore an indispensable prerequisite for the general growth

15 J. S. Gregory and D. W. Shave, *The USSR: A Geographical Survey*, p. 288.
London: Harrap, 1944.

of industry and for the development of new industry in the eastern regions. Fortunately for the USSR, high-quality coal deposits were available in the Kuznetsk Basin in Western Siberia, in the Karaganda Basin in Kazakhstan, and in other places. The large brown-coal deposits of the Moscow Basin are rather poor because of their low heat and high ash content per unit weight, but this area too has been rapidly developed because of its nearness to many of the major coal-consuming plants and power stations of the USSR.

During the Fourth Five-Year Plan, the coal industry made very substantial progress. The Moscow coal basin achieved its 1950 goal in 1948 and then got a new program for still greater expansion.[16] The Donets Basin, which produced only about half its pre-war volume of coal in 1945, exceeded 80 per cent of the 1940 output in 1948,[17] and in the fourth quarter of 1949 reached the average 1940 quarterly production.[18] The Karaganda Basin's coal output in 1949 was 45 per cent over that of 1945 and equaled the desired rate for 1950 by July 1949.[19]   G. M. Malenkov reported in March 1950 that in the last quarter of 1949 the Ministry of Coal Industry's mines had reached the level planned for 1950.[20] Since this ministry produces the overwhelming amount of coal mined in the USSR, this would indicate that output in the last quarter of 1949 was equal roughly to the average level planned for 1950, that is, 62,-500,000 metric tons, as compared with the 41,500,000 metric tons produced quarterly on the average in 1940.

The expansion of coal production in major areas is indicated in Table 13.

The rapid rise of Urals coal production during the war is one of the most striking features of Table 13. This rise was undoubtedly motivated in part by the desire to restrict the load on the transport system that would otherwise have resulted if the sharply expanded coal needs of Urals industry, particularly for armaments and met-allurgy, had had to be met from Kuznetsk and Karaganda. In the late 1930's coal production in the Urals met only half of that area's needs.[21] Even after the expansion in Urals coal production during

---

[16] *Moskovsky Bolshevik,* February 9, 1950.
[17] *Planovoye Khozyaistvo,* No. 1 (1949), p. 56.
[18] *Pravda,* March 10, 1950.
[19] *Ibid.,* April 30, 1950.
[20] *Ibid.,* March 10, 1950.
[21] Balzak, *et al.. Economic Geography of the USSR,* p. 214.

TABLE 13. Growth of Coal Production in Major Soviet Coal Basins, 1913–52.

Year	Donbas	Kuznetsk	Moscow	Urals*	Karaganda	Others	Total
			(MILLION METRIC TONS)				
1913	25.3	.8	.3	1.2	—	1.5	29.1
1921–22	7.3	.9	.6	1.0	—	1.5	11.3
1929	31.0	3.0	1.3	2.1	—	2.7	40.1
1934	61.5	11.5	4.6	5.5	1.8	9.0	93.9
1940	85.5	19.0†	10.2†	12.0	6.5†	32.8†	166.0
1945	36.7	27.0†	18.0†	26.1†	11.0†	30.5†	149.3
1949	80.0†	‡	26.5†	‡	15.9†	‡	236.9
1950 goal	88.0	31.9†	24.6†	31.6†	15.1†	58.8†	250.0
1952	100.0†	40.0†	34.0†	‡	17.0†	‡	300.0

* Includes Kizel, Chelyabinsk, and other Ural fields.
† Estimated.
‡ Data unavailable.
Sources: 1913—1934—*Sot. Stroi.*, pp. 100-101, and *Sot. Stroi.* (*1933-38*), p. 47; 1940—1950—firm data and estimates based on data in Fourth Five-Year Plan, both general and republican sections; *Planovoye Khozyaistvo*, No. 2 (1946); *Izvestia*, May 23, 1946, and January 1, 1947; N. A. Voznesensky, *The Economy of the USSR During World War II*, pp. 26-27; *Trud*, March 20, 1949; *Moskovsky Bolshevik*, February 9, 1950; *Pravda*, December 28, 1949, and April 30, 1950; *Izvestia*, May 19, 1950; Schwartz, *Russia's Postwar Economy*, p. 30; 1952—estimated on basis of fragmentary data in *Pravda*, October 12, 1953; *Pravda Ukrainy*, September 25, 1952; *Kazakhstanskaya Pravda*, December 16, 1951.

the 1940's, Magnitogorsk still depended heavily upon Kuznetsk and Karaganda coal in 1949.[22] Similar transport considerations are undoubtedly behind the very rapid development of the Moscow coal basin, situated in the heart of the Central Industrial Region. This region imported 15,000,000 tons of Donbas coal annually in the late 1930's. The expansion of Moscow production during World War II and the first years thereafter was apparently inadequate to meet the Central Industrial Region's needs fully. A further increase in this output, to 50 per cent over the 1948 level, was then ordered for the years 1949-53.[23] Since 1948 output of this basin was about 24 million metric tons, this indicates a 1953 goal of about 36 million tons.[24] To meet the needs of Leningrad and its surrounding industrial area, long a major importer of Donbas coal before World War II, the Pechora coal basin in the north received intensive development during and after that conflict. In the future the Pechora basin is planned to be the source of coal for a large met-

[22] *Pravda*, October 4, 1949.

[23] *Ibid.*, December 7, 1948.

[24] *Planovoye Khozyaistvo*, No. 1 (1949), p. 56, gives basic percentage data for this estimate.

allurgical industry in the Leningrad region. Throughout the USSR emphasis is being placed upon development of local coal deposits to meet local needs, so far as possible.

Along with the rise in production and its rapid geographic spread, coal output under the Soviet regime has undergone a major technical revolution. In the 1930's, primitive methods of coal mining relying heavily on manual labor gave way to mechanization, as large numbers of new coal-mining machines were installed in both old and new shafts. By 1938, the USSR claimed that 99.1 per cent of its coal was mined by mechanical methods, principally coal-cutting machines and related equipment. Much of this machinery in the Donbas was destroyed during the general destruction of this area's major industry during World War II, but after the war Soviet writers claimed that the mines were being rebuilt with even more modern equipment than before, including many coal-digging combines with far greater productivity than the older machinery. On the other hand, much of the work of cutting new tunnels, loading, hauling, and other laborious aspects of coal mining continues to be done manually, requiring the employment of large numbers of workers, who could be replaced by machinery.[25] Immediately after the war material in the Soviet press indicated that much of the coal-mining equipment in use in such important areas as the Kuzbas and Karaganda fields was worn out and remained idle much of the time because of lack of spare parts. As Soviet industry returned to production of coal machinery of all types after the war, large numbers of new machines were produced, both to replace worn out equipment and to mechanize operations formerly done by primitive methods. All this permitted a significant improvement in coal-mining productivity, but Soviet officials continued to complain that much machinery was used poorly and that certain types of key operations were still done by hand.[26] In late 1949, the head of the Soviet coal industry commented:

> It must be recognized that what has been done in the field of mechanization is only the beginning of the great work which lies ahead of us to be fulfilled in the years immediately ahead in order to equip the coal industry with new, still more finished machines and

25 *Ibid.*, No. 2 (1946), p. 103.
26 *Ibid.*, No. 1 (1949), pp. 56–59.

mechanisms, and to achieve full mechanization of all processes of coal mining at all mines.[27]

A significant development in Soviet coal mining in recent years has been the rapid growth of open-cut coal mining from coal deposits on or near the surface, as compared with the older system of underground shafts. Such open-cut coal production began in Russia in 1913, but in 1940 only 3.8 per cent of all Soviet coal, or only about 6 million tons, was obtained in this way. By 1945, 11.9 per cent, or almost 18 million tons, of all Soviet coal was produced in this manner, a threefold growth during the war years. Most of the increased supply of open-cut coal came from the Urals during the war years, particularly the major Volchan site in Sverdlovsk Province. Later, two large open-cut coal sites were opened at Karaganda and one in the Khabarovsk territory in the Far East. The great advantages of this mode of mining are the increased productivity, lower cost of production, and the greater speed with which open-cut works can be built as compared with conventional mines. Soviet experience indicates that labor productivity in open cuts is roughly three times that in mines, while the cost of a ton of coal obtained in this fashion is approximately one third that of a ton mined conventionally.[28] In the future, Soviet utilization of this technique is to grow more rapidly than the general growth of coal mining. In 1954 or 1955, output of open-cut coal is planned to be two to two and one-half times the 1950 level.[29] This goal in absolute terms is probably equal to about 60 million metric tons, since the 1950 planned output of open-cut coal was 27 million tons.

The future perspectives of the Soviet coal industry are indicated by Stalin's statement in 1946 that by about 1960 the USSR plans to produce 500 million tons of coal annually, about 60 per cent more than the actual output in 1953. The Fourth Five-Year Plan laid the groundwork for this expansion by requiring the surveying of 765 sites for mines and open cuts with a total annual output of 361 million tons. In late 1949 the head of the Soviet coal industry declared that, to achieve Stalin's goal on schedule, the USSR would

---

[27] *Pravda*, September 1, 1949.
[28] *Planovoye Khozyaistvo*, No. 4 (1948), pp. 37–40.
[29] *Ibid.*, No. 2 (1950), p. 26.

have to raise the annual increment in coal output by at least 50 per cent over that of the preceding years. By about 1960, therefore, it seems likely that the USSR hopes to have an annual increase in coal output of 30 million tons or more, as against the roughly 20 million ton annual increase, on the average, achieved during 1946–49.[30]

While seeking to raise their coal output rapidly, Soviet authorities are keenly conscious of the need to raise the quality of their product. The Fourth Five-Year Plan provided for a large-scale program of constructing coal-concentration plants, and declared that "all newly-built pits must have concentration and screening installations," so as to eliminate rock and other impurities and provide more uniform sizes and qualities of coal. But the continuance of complaints regarding poor coal quality, lack of uniformity in grades, and the need for further reduction of ash content of coal suggests that this work of quality improvement is attended by many difficulties.

Efforts to improve Soviet coal technology during the early 1950's concentrated upon two directions of effort. First, the "cyclical" method of coal mining was being introduced as rapidly as possible under pressure from Moscow. In this system each 24-hour period of work is accomplished by the rotation of three shifts, two of them actually mining coal and the third preparing the mine face and tunnels for the next day's mining. Second, the production of mining machinery, particularly of improved postwar models, was pushed as rapidly as possible. With regard to mechanization, increasing attention was being given to the mechanization of the work done on the surface above the actual mine, particularly to loading and unloading. Mechanization of such work has lagged far behind mechanization of actual mining operations, so that large numbers of auxiliary manual laborers have been required on the surface. Press reports indicated that there was still abundant room for improved efficiency, particularly in the use of machinery and the organization of labor. In early 1952 the growth of open-cut coal mining was reported to be disturbingly slow, 5 per cent less than the annual growth of regular shaft mining. The Fifth Five-Year Plan's pro-

---

[30] *Pravda,* September 1, 1949.

jected increase of over 110,000,000 metric tons in coal production between 1950 and 1955 was scheduled to be made possible mainly by the opening of new mines, mostly in the old coal fields though some new coal areas were to be opened during the period.[31]

Inefficient use of equipment is apparently a major problem in the Soviet coal industry, as well as in other branches of Soviet industry. Premier Malenkov, speaking in April 1954, said that in 1953 and during the first quarter of 1954, over 40 per cent of all coal combines and coal-cutting machines, about half of all coal-loading machinery, and over 30 per cent of rock-loading machinery were idle.

Petroleum

The history of Russian petroleum as an industry in the modern sense started about 1870, when foreign interests — first the Nobel brothers and then the Rothschilds — began developing the Baku and nearby Caucasian oil fields. From a maximum of 42,000 tons annually before 1870, oil production rose to a peak of 11,500,000 tons in 1901, a year in which Russia produced over half the world supply and exported more than 1,000,000 tons. The rich Baku area was a focal point of international intrigue and struggle immediately after the Bolshevik revolution, and not until 1920 did the Soviet government finally seize complete control of the area. From the low point reached at the beginning of the 1920's, Soviet petroleum output expanded rapidly until the outbreak of World War II. During these years production rose rapidly at Baku, Grozny, and Maikop, the chief sources of oil in Czarist times, and at major new petroleum fields opened for exploitation east and north of the Caspian Sea. Production dropped sharply during World War II, but increased rapidly after 1945. The statistical picture of production growth follows, in millions of metric tons.[32]

---

[31] *Ugol*, Nos. 1 and 3 (1952); *Pravda*, September 19, 1950, June 6, 1951, February 12, March 20, and October 8, 1952; *Izvestia*, May 23, 1952.

[32] Data for 1913, 1927–28, and 1934 from *Sot. Stroi.*, p. 113. 1921 data from *Narodnoye Khozyaistvo SSSR*, p. 6. Data for 1940 and 1945 from A. Bergson, J. H. Blackman, and A. Ehrlich, "Postwar Economic Reconstruction and Development in the USSR," *The Annals*, May 1949, p. 56. Data for 1950–55 calculated from earlier figures and percentages or absolute figures given in *Pravda*, April 17, 1951, October 6 and 12, 1952, August 9, 1953, and January 31, 1954.

Year	Production	Year	Production
1913	9.2	1945	19.4
1921	4.0	1950	37.8
1927–28	11.5	1952	47.0
1934	24.2	1953	52.6
1940	31.0	1955 Goal	69.7

The geographic pattern of production and its changes over the years are shown in Table 14.

TABLE 14. Major Sources of Soviet Petroleum Production, 1913–50.

	1913	1927–28	1940*	1945*	1950 Goal*
			(MILLION METRIC TONS)		
Azerbaidzhan†	7.7	7.7	21.8	11.3	17.0
Grozny	1.2	3.7	5.1	.1	4.0
Maikop	.1	.1		1.3	
Kazakhstan‡	.1	.25	.7	1.0	1.2
"Second Baku"§	—	—	1.9	2.9	9.0
Uzbekistan	**	**	.2	.4	1.1
Turkmenistan	.1	**	.6	.7	1.1
Other	**	**	.7	1.7	2.0
Total	9.2	11.75††	31.0	19.4	35.4

* Estimated.   † Primarily from Baku.   ‡ Primarily from Emba Basin.   § Includes sources in the Bashkir ASSR and Kuibyshev, Molotov, and Chkalov Provinces. ** Very small.   †† Includes 277.000 tons of gas.
Sources: Data for 1913 and 1927-28 from *Sot. Stroi.*, p. 113. Data for 1940, 1945, and 1950 goal estimated on basis of information in the Fourth Five-Year Plan; *American Review on the Soviet Union*, August 1946, p. 6; *Planovoye Khozyaistvo*, No. 2 (1946), pp. 70, 85; and No. 3 (1946), pp. 12-19.

The rapid increase in Baku's output was the outstanding feature of Soviet oil development during the 1930's. This increase was accomplished by opening rich new oil areas, drilling new wells, and improving the technology of production. Nevertheless, exploitation of Baku petroleum resources during this period was wastefully and poorly done. Geological prospecting and drilling of exploratory wells was at a rate well below that required to insure continued high production in the future. Reliance was placed almost entirely upon natural underground pressure to force up petroleum. When this pressure declined, wells were permitted to become inactive, though more oil could have been obtained by modern techniques of artificially increasing underground pressure. The importance of small producing wells was underestimated, and repair work on them was neglected, so that 8,000 to 10,000 fewer tons of oil were obtained from these wells annually than might have been. Directors of oil-producing enterprises tended to focus their resources primarily upon achieving their current production goals, neglecting work necessary to maintain or increase their output in the future.[33] These deficiencies of exploitation technique in the 1930's were important contributory causes to the subsequent sharp decline of Baku output during World War II.

In the same period substantial beginnings were made in developing production in the "Second Baku" as well as in the Emba Basin and other Eastern sources. In 1940 the western areas of the USSR accounted for 88 per cent of all oil produced.

The position of the Soviet oil industry on the eve of the German invasion of June 1941 is perhaps best indicated by the 1941 regional oil production plan of the Soviet government. In this plan, which was originally classified "not to be published" and became known to the outside world only after it was captured during the war, the total planned 1941 output of 34,000,000 metric tons was to come in the main from the following sources: [34]

Azerbaidzhan (mainly Baku)	23,000,000 tons
Grozny	2,770,000 tons
Maikop	2,770,000 tons
"Second Baku"	2,677,000 tons
Kazakhstan (mainly Emba Basin)	900,000 tons
Turkmenistan	800,000 tons
Ukhta-Pechora	250,000 tons
Ukraine	350,000 tons
Far East	750,000 tons

During World War II, Baku's output fell catastrophically. Large numbers of skilled personnel as well as trucks and tractors were taken by the army. New drilling virtually ceased for several years, and production of many wells was halted, in part because of the need to "cannibalize" parts from some wells to replace parts worn out on others. All petroleum machinery factories in Baku were shifted to producing military supplies and armaments, so that newly produced equipment and spare parts became unavailable. Not until 1943 was drilling and prospecting renewed at Baku, and not until after the end of 1944 was the production of oil machinery in this

---

[33] *Planovoye Khozyaistvo*, No. 1 (1947), pp. 44–45.

[34] *Gosudarstvenny Plan Razvitiya Narodnogo Khozyaistva SSSR na 1941 god.*, American Council of Learned Societies Reprints: Russian Series, No. 30.

area fully restored. Despite the effórts taken to repair some of the earlier damage, Table 14 indicates that in 1945 Baku output was only about half that of 1940.[35] Such expansion or production as took place during the war occurred in the eastern regions, particularly in the "Second Baku," but the output rise there only partially offset the Baku decline.

Detailed statistical information on the fate of different Soviet oil-producing areas since World War II has been scanty, but enough has been released to make the main trends apparent. By 1950 the devastated Western oil areas, the Ukraine, Grozny, and Maikop, had been largely restored and technically re-equipped. Baku production grew as drilling began again and as intensive efforts were directed toward procuring petroleum from offshore sites under the Caspian Sea. The Eastern areas, particularly the Second Baku region, increased production steadily. The result of these trends was that by 1950 the Western oil areas produced 56 per cent of all Soviet oil — about 21,200,000 metric tons — and the Eastern areas 44 per cent, or about 16,600,000 tons. In 1940 the Western areas had produced about 27,300,000 tons — 88 per cent — as against only 3,700,-000 tons — 12 per cent — in the Eastern areas. It seems likely that in 1950 the Baku area produced less than the 17,000,000 tons originally required by the Fourth Five-Year Plan, while the "Second Baku" probably gave more than 10,000,000 tons, an amount well over its original plan goal.[36]

The year 1952 seems to provide a historic landmark in Soviet oil as the first year in time of peace when the Eastern oil fields produced more than half the national petroleum output. According to official data, the Volga-Urals oil region, or "Second Baku," alone accounted for 40 per cent of all Soviet oil production, or about 18,800,000 tons. Other Eastern areas provided more than ten per cent of total oil output. If we estimate roughly that the Western oil areas contributed about 48 per cent of all Soviet petroleum in 1952, this is equivalent to about 22,200,000 tons, little more than the 1950 total for this region given above.[37]

This last indication that Baku has lagged seriously in the early 1950's is strengthened by the published complaints appearing in

---

[35] *Planovoye Khozyaistvo, op. cit.,* pp. 39–41.

[36] This discussion based mainly on data in *Pravda,* April 17, 1951.

[37] Based on N. K. Baibakov's speech quoted in *Pravda,* October 11, 1952.

mid-1952. The necessary conditions had not been created at Baku for increasing oil output from wells under dry land, and slow drilling was a major bottleneck, it was charged. A major purge of Baku production executives apparently took place in the late summer of 1952, reflecting effort to improve this situation.[38]

Although the geographical dispersion of Soviet oil production increased sharply before 1941, the great predominance of Caucasian oil among Soviet petroleum resources imposed heavy transport costs on the USSR. With the expansion of industry and the use of machinery throughout the country's vast territory, petroleum products were required throughout this area, and most of them had to come from the Baku-Brozny-Maikop triangle. The average length of haul for oil products increased sharply as a result, the average distance for such hauls by rail rising from under 400 miles in 1913 to over 700 miles in 1937. In the late 1930's and even a decade later, the Soviet oil-transportation system was far inferior to that of the United States, being much more dependent upon railroads and making relatively little use of cheap pipeline movement, as shown below: [39]

	Percentage of Oil Transport	
Means	UNITED STATES	USSR
Railroad	2.2	42.7
Water	26.6	45.9
Oil pipeline	71.2	11.4

Only two pipelines existed in Czarist Russia. The number of such lines and their carrying capacity have been sharply increased under the Soviet regime, particularly in the "Second Baku" and other eastern fields since the mid-1930's. The sharp changes in the relative importance of different oil fields brought about by World War II and later developments have done much, probably, to make the geographical pattern of petroleum output coincide somewhat better with the pattern of consumption, so as to reduce the average transport haul for each ton of this product and its derivatives.

The oil industry went through a technical revolution during the 1930's. Improved methods of drilling were introduced, along with better tools and much more extensive use of electric motors. These

---

[38] *Bakinsky Rabochi,* September 24, 1952.
[39] Balzak, *et al., op. cit.,* pp. 220–21.

and other changes are reported to have cut drilling costs to half the 1913 level by the early 1930's.[40] Methods of oil extraction were also sharply improved. Pumping of oil from under the ground replaced bailing, and electricity replaced steam power, so that oil-extraction costs dropped to less than half their former level. Nevertheless, even in 1946, a Soviet petroleum industry head complained that oil-extraction technology was behind that of the United States and was not yet applying sufficiently modern scientific techniques for maximizing the percentage of petroleum reserves obtained and lowering costs.[41]

Helped significantly by American petroleum technicians and modern American machinery, the USSR greatly modernized and expanded its oil-refining industry between 1928 and 1940. In 1928 the USSR did not have a single petroleum-cracking unit for refining purposes and depended primarily upon direct distillation to obtain gasoline, lubricating oils, and other valuable components of crude petroleum. By 1937 almost 60 per cent of the USSR's greatly expanded production of gasoline was obtained by the cracking process.

The speed of technological progress has been great during the postwar period. Such advanced techniques as turbine drilling for wells dug as deep as 15,000 feet into the ground, slant wells for obtaining oil from under the sea, and catalytic cracking have been widely introduced. A synthetic oil industry has been created and is growing, though its precise magnitude is cloaked in secrecy. Pipelines have been greatly expanded. On the other hand, as late as 1952 or 1953, available evidence indicated that there was much inefficiency in drilling activity, slow progress in introducing secondary methods of oil production, and shortages of essential machinery. As of 1950 it seems likely that crude oil production had or was threatening to outrun refinery capacity, for the Fifth Five-Year Plan called for a doubling of Soviet refinery capacity by 1955. The inadequacy of Soviet pipelines — said to have attained "tens of thousands of kilometers" by 1952 — is indicated by ambitious plans to increase the volume of pipeline transport work five times between 1950 and 1955. That existing pipelines were not being

---

[40] Alcan Hirsch, *Industrialized Russia*, pp. 145–46. New York: Chemical Catalog Co., 1934.

[41] *Ibid.*, pp. 146–47. *Planovoye Khozyaistvo*, No. 3 (1946), pp. 12–19.

used fully is suggested by the complaints about the lack of high-pressure pumps needed for pipeline operation.[42]

The rapid progress of Soviet oil production since 1945 has permitted petroleum consumption to rise far above previous standards, while the Soviet Union had even become a net oil exporter by 1953. Simultaneously, however, there has been continued government backing of drastic petroleum economy measures — such as the encouragement given to the use of solid fuels and other non-petroleum fuels for trucks and tractors. There is no surfeit of oil in the Soviet Union, nor will there be such even if Stalin's original goal of 60,-000,000 tons is reached before 1960, as now seems likely.

Electric Power

From the very beginning of the Soviet regime, the rapid development of electric-power production has been a primary objective. The GOELRO plan adopted in 1920 looked forward to the development of Soviet industry and transportation on the basis of a rapid rise in the available supply of electric power. To Lenin and other Soviet leaders, electricity appeared almost as a magic instrument, which would permit them to free their country from its technological backwardness and would enable the Soviet Union to achieve high levels of industrial production and efficiency. They looked with disdain upon the comparatively small amount of electrification achieved in Czarist Russia, where even in 1913 the availability of electric power was concentrated mainly in a few large cities, particularly Leningrad and Moscow.

The objective of a rapid increase in electric-power capacity and energy production has been achieved during the Soviet regime. The statistical record of that achievement is given in Table 15.

The rapid development of electric-power generating capacity and production between 1928 and 1940 completely altered the former character of the Soviet electrical economy. As late as 1926, two thirds of all Soviet electric power was produced in small municipal and industrial power plants serving small areas, only one third coming from large plants. By 1935 these proportions had been more than reversed, and over three quarters of all electrical energy was produced by large regional power stations and major industrial

---

[42] *Izvestia*, October 3, 1952, and *Pravda*, October 11, 1952.

TABLE 15. Electric-Power Generating Capacity and Production in the USSR since 1913.

Year	Capacity (MILLION KILOWATTS)	Production (BILLION KILOWATT-HOURS)
1913.................	1.1	1.9
1921.................	1.2	.5
1928.................	1.9	5.0
1934.................	6.3	21.0
1940.................	11.3	48.3
1945.................	10.7*	43.2*
1950.................	24.0*	90.5
1951.................	27.0*	104.0
1952.................	31.0*	117.0
1953.................	34.0*	133.0
1954 Goal...........	40.0*	147.5
1955 Goal...........	48.0*	163.0

* Estimated.

Sources: 1913-1934—Sot. Stroi., pp. 82-83; 1940-1945—Abram Bergson, et al., op. cit., p. 56; 1950-55—see note 32 above.

power plants. In 1926, large generating plants had produced only about 1.2 billion kilowatt hours; in 1935 they produced 19.5 billion kilowatt hours. In the late 1930's a reaction occurred against such super stations. Their builders were denounced as guilty of "gigantomania," and were told to give more emphasis to small and medium-sized stations.[43]

A revolution was wrought in the nonagricultural areas of the Soviet economy as the ever-increasing availability of electric power provided the essential foundation for creation of new industries and technical reconstruction of old ones. Electrical drives replaced mechanical drives on a large scale, and electro-thermal and electrolytic processes began to be employed far more frequently than ever before. The extent of the transformation in different branches of the economy may be indicated by comparing their electric-power consumption in two years less than a decade apart.[44]

	1926	1935
	(MILLION KILOWATT-HOURS)	
Industry	2,430	17,970
Transport	90	570
Municipal and household use	660	3,760
Agriculture	30	190

It is clear from the above that industry was by far the main bene-

[43] Planovoye Khozyaistvo, No. 10 (1939), pp. 26-33.
[44] Electric Power Development in the USSR, p. 31. Moscow: 1936.

ficiary of this rapid electrification process, though transport employment of electricity rose sharply, as did urban consumption for lighting and other uses. Up to the present, agriculture has been least affected and benefited by electric power, though some efforts have been made in the postwar period to increase the employment of this energy in rural production and consumption.

It has been estimated that electric-power generating capacity of 5,000,000 kilowatts, 44 per cent of the 1940 Soviet capacity, was destroyed during World War II.[45] Nevertheless, so energetic was the construction of new generating capacity in the unoccupied eastern area and so quickly was part of the damaged western capacity rehabilitated that by the end of 1945 both capacity and production had virtually regained prewar levels.

The development of electric-power production and capacity since World War II has been one of the most remarkable phenomena of Soviet economic history. In 1953 both output and capacity were more than three times the levels of 1945; the goals planned for 1955 are roughly quadruple the 1945 figures. Without such rapid expansion the general postwar upsurge of Soviet industry would have been impossible, the need being greatest in such heavy power-consuming processes as the production of nuclear weapons (both atomic and hydrogen bombs), aluminum, and magnesium. One authoritative Soviet source has indicated that the longer-range goal, for 1960 or thereabouts, is 250,000,000,000 kilowatt-hours production annually, roughly six times the 1945 output and almost three times the 1950 level.[46]

Since World War II the devastated electric-power facilities of the formerly occupied western areas have been rebuilt and expanded beyond prewar levels, while much further expansion has taken place in the never-occupied areas east of the Leningrad-Moscow-Stalingrad line which marked the furthest German advance. Indicative of the steady rehabilitation in the West is the report that in the Ukraine, electric-power production in 1948 was only 75 per cent of the 1940 mark, but by 1951 was 140 per cent of the 1940 figure.[47] Progress in the eastern region from the Volga River Valley to the

---

[45] Bergson, et al., op. cit., p. 54.
[46] Izvestia, September 10, 1952.
[47] Pravda Ukrainy, September 25, 1952.

Pacific Ocean may be judged from Malenkov's statement that in 1951 this area produced more than 40 per cent of all Soviet electric power.[48] This percentage indicates that this vast eastern region produced about 42,000,000,000 kilowatt-hours in 1951, an amount almost 90 per cent as great as the power production of the entire country in 1940.

Despite this vast expansion of electric-power output, there was much evidence of continued power shortages during the early 1950's. In November 1952 stringent limitations on electric-power use during evening hours were announced in Moscow; a strained power situation was said to exist in Kazakhstan; Uzbekistan was reported to have an inadequate reserve of steam power stations, so that industries receiving hydroelectric power in the summer had great difficulties during other periods of the year; Latvian factories were said to be inadequately supplied with electricity; and the power supply in the Ukraine was officially declared inadequate for the area's needs.[49] Judging by United States experience with the vast electric-power requirements of nuclear weapons production, it seems reasonable to conclude that the corresponding drain on the Soviet power supply played an important role in producing at least some of the shortages complained of in the areas mentioned above.

Hydroelectric-power development received the greatest publicity in the postwar period, but the available data seem to indicate clearly that ordinary steam power plants, employing coal, oil, and other fuels, accounted for most of the expansion of power production between 1945 and 1953. In mid-1952 it was reported that over 80 per cent of Soviet power came from steam, or thermal, plants.[50]

The Soviet government has announced that on June 27, 1954, it opened a 5,000-kilowatt atomic power plant, a plant actually producing electricity for industrial and agricultural needs. It added that Soviet engineers were working on 50,000- and 100,000-kilowatt atomic power plants. The Soviet government would seem to have made an important advance in *experimentation* regarding atomic power for civilian needs. The 5,000-kilowatt station is obviously

---

[48] *Pravda*, October 6, 1952.

[49] *Vechernaya Moskva*, November 27, 1952; *Kazakhstanskaya Pravda*, September 21, 1952; *Pravda Vostoka*, September 23, 1952; *Pravda*, October 8, 1952; *Pravda Ukrainy*, September 25, 1952.

[50] *Pravda*, July 20, 1952.

too small to produce electric power economically, though it should be valuable as a pilot plant for larger future operations.

In 1950, total Soviet hydroelectric production was 18.3 per cent of all electricity generated, or about 16,000,000,000 kilowatt-hours, as compared with about 5,000,000,000 kilowatt-hours from this source in 1940.[51] By 1955, the Fifth Five-Year Plan called for hydroelectric capacity three times that of 1950. If this capacity were to be attained and production were to rise correspondingly, Soviet hydroelectric output would be about 48,000,000,000 kilowatt-hours, or about 33 per cent of the total electric power goal for that year. Whether these figures will actually be attained remains to be seen.

The most famous Soviet hydroelectric station is that on the Dnepr River near Zaporozhe, which had a capacity before World War II of over 500,000 kilowatts, and which had to be completely rebuilt after suffering great destruction during the war. Other important waterpower stations built before the war were at Volkhov and on the Svir River, both near Leningrad; at Shcherbakov and Uglich on the Volga; at Chirchik and on the Chu River in Central Asia; and on the Tuloma, Niva, and Suna Rivers in Karelia and the Kola Peninsula in the Northwest. The largest Soviet hydroelectric station announced publicly to have begun power output since 1945 is the Ust-Kamenogorsk station on the Irtysh River in Eastern Kazakhstan which began operation in July 1953. Work had begun on this plant in 1948 or earlier, and it was said to be the biggest hydroelectric station in the area east of the Urals, being often compared to the Dnepr station.[52]

Among the most significant hydroelectric projects scheduled for completion by 1955 or shortly thereafter are the following: at Kuibyshev on the Volga River a station with 2,000,000 kilowatts capacity and average annual output of 10,000,000,000 kilowatt-hours; at Stalingrad, also on the Volga, a station with 1,700,000 kilowatts capacity and 10,000,000,000 kilowatt-hours annual average output; a 250,000 kilowatt station at Kakhovka on the lower Dnepr River with annual output of over 1,000,000,000 kilowatt-hours. Together these stations are scheduled to produce anually over 21,000,-000,000 kilowatt-hours of electric power. Both the Kuibyshev and

---

[51] *Izvestia*, September 10, 1952.
[52] *Pravda Ukrainy*, November 27, 1952, and *Pravda*, July 3, 1953.

Stalingrad stations will be far larger than the Dnepr power station built in the 1930's. Much of their power will be moved at high voltage over a long distance to Moscow. In their case, at least, the former policy on "gigantomania" has apparently been reversed. The large Mingechaur hydroelectric station in Armenia had already begun at least partial operation by 1954.

The ambitious nature of future Soviet plans for hydroelectric development was indicated by the Fifth Five-Year Plan. This called for starting work before 1956 on new large stations at Cheboksary on the Volga, Votkinsk on the Kama, Bukhtarma on the Irtysh, and others. By early 1954 work had begun on the first of a series of large hydroelectric stations on the Angara River in Eastern Siberia. The first of these stations, near the city of Irkutsk, was reported planned to have a capacity more than twice as great as that of the Dnepr station, that is, over 1,000,000 kilowatts.[53]

A major feature of Soviet electrical development has been the rise of a number of large regional power systems combining the power generated by a number of different stations located within a given area. The Moscow system, for example, produced in 1936 more than 5 billion kilowatt-hours, and is one of the largest and most powerful electrical systems in the world. Other major power systems in the USSR at the end of the 1930's included the Leningrad, Gorky-Ivanovo, Dnepr, Donets Basin, Baku, Urals, and Kuzbas power systems. Most of these major concentrations of electric-power capacity and production exceeded individually in 1938 the total capacity and production of prewar Russia. In addition, the USSR has developed many smaller, localized high-voltage power networks for less important individual areas. The eventual goal of the Soviet regime is the creation of one unified national power system, so that electric power can be shifted from area to area in response to the varying requirements imposed by changes in supply and demand in different parts of the country. An indication of the postwar growth of Soviet regional electric-power systems is given by the fact that the Moscow system at the end of 1949 had one third more capacity than in 1940.[54]

---

[53] *Pravda*, October 12, 1953, and February 22, 1954.

[54] Balzak, *et al., op. cit.*, pp. 234–36. *Moskovskaya Pravda*, February 21, 1950.

A number of key facts about the Soviet electric-power industry were revealed by Deputy Premier M. G. Pervukhin in his speech published in the Soviet press April 27, 1954. The most important were:

1. The cost of electric-power generation was 10 kopeks per kilowatt-hour in thermal stations of the Ministry of Electric Power Stations and about 2 kopeks per kilowatt-hour at hydroelectric stations. These costs, however, presumably do not include interest on investment. Mr. Pervukhin implied that there had been a dispute between the backers of thermal and the supporters of hydroelectric power. His attack on those who believed that hydroelectric power always required more capital investment than thermal power, and his assertion that one should take into account capital investment in the coal industry necessary for generating electric power in thermal stations, suggested that the supporters of hydroelectric power held the ascendancy at the time he spoke.

2. He revealed that there had been great growth in the large electric-power networks of the country. The central electric-power system, including the power systems of Moscow city and province, and Tula, Ivanovo, Vladimir, Yaroslavl, and Gorky provinces, had twice the 1940 capacity. The Urals system, embracing Chelyabinsk, Sverdlovsk, and Molotov provinces, had 3.7 times the capacity it had in 1940. The sharpest capacity gain, 13 times, had taken place at the Karaganda power system, while even the restored Southern (Dnepr-Donbas) system had 1.7 times as much power as in 1940. After completion of the Kuibyshev and Stalingrad hydroelectric stations, he said, "there will be created the united power system of the European part of the Soviet Union, the greatest such system in the world."

3. At the time he spoke, there were being built or expanded 711 electric-power stations, which at their completion would provide additional electric-power-generating capacity equal to 75 per cent of existing capacity. In the future, he seemed to imply, there would be greater concentration on hydroelectric power than in the past.

That the Soviet government is keenly pushing research aimed at the generation of electric power economically from atomic energy would seem to be indubitable. As noted above, the Soviet regime claimed to have begun producing electric power on June 27, 1954, from a 5,000-kilowatt atomic power station. A clue to Soviet thinking on this subject seems to have been provided by the head of the Academy of Sciences, Academician Alexander Nesmeyanov, writing in *Kommunist*, No. 6, 1954:

Theoretical studies on the structure of the atomic nucleus, nuclear forces, and radioactivity have laid the foundation of the Soviet atomic industry. Our scholars must try to discover ever newer ways of receiving nuclear energy, fuller means of utilizing the energy of nuclear processes so as to make atomic energy accessible for wide utilization in industry and transport.

The advance of atomic energy into broad peaceful employment is undoubtedly a matter of an entire epoch, and old means of producing energy will coexist with atomic energy just as the steam engine does with the electric motor.

Iron and Steel

Iron and steel are in many ways the foundation metals of our industrial civilization, being used widely for many different purposes, including construction, machinery, transport equipment, and so on. In time of war, of course, steel is absolutely essential for the production of guns, munitions, tanks, and other military essentials. It is not surprising, therefore, that a major Soviet objective throughout the industrialization period has been the development of iron and steel production.

The statistical record of iron and steel production under the Soviet regime is shown in Table 16.

TABLE 16. Iron and Steel Production in the USSR since 1913.

Year	Pig Iron (MILLION METRIC TONS)	Steel
1913	4.2	4.2
1920	.1	.2
1927–28	3.3	4.3
1934	10.4	9.7
1940	15.0	18.3
1945	9.2*	11.2*
1950	19.3	27.3
1951	22.0	31.4
1952	25.1	34.5
1953	27.4	38.0
1954 Goal	30.0*	41.2
1955 Goal	34.0	44.2

* Estimated.

Sources: 1913-1934—*Sot. Stroi.*, p. 133; 1940—Fourth Five-Year Plan; 1945—Bergson, *et al.*, *op. cit.*, p. 56; 1950-53—Soviet government economic reports for 1950-53; 1954 steel goal based on *Pravda*, April 27, 1954; 1955 goal—Fifth Five-Year Plan percentage targets applied to 1950 output.

A serious possibility exists that the steel data for 1950 and afterward are not precisely comparable with the earlier figures. Up to late 1950, foreign investigators had based their estimates of Soviet steel production on the basis of data released in a technical Soviet publication issued in 1947. This, together with official percentage data released for later years, suggested that 1950 steel production was about 25,000,000 metric tons. But the November 1950 speech of Politburo member N. A. Bulganin and the official report on the completion of the Fourth Five-Year Plan both gave data which indicated 1950 Soviet steel production was over 27,000,000 metric tons. This substantial discrepancy has never been fully or satisfactorily explained. One American investigator has suggested that the difference arises because the Soviet government has redefined steel production so as to include cast iron which was not formerly included in the steel figure. If so, then the figures for 1950 and later given above should be reduced by several million tons each year in order to make them comparable with the earlier data as well as with Western steel statistics.[55]

Expansion of iron and steel production during the prewar five-year plans was accomplished both by the reconstruction and expansion of the old plants built in pre-Soviet times, particularly in the southern region, and by building new plants in various parts of the USSR, particularly in the Urals and Siberia. In 1940 more than 80 per cent of the total production of ferrous metals in the USSR came from plants entirely reconstructed or built during the Soviet regime. Among the largest new steel plants built in the 1930's were those at Magnitogorsk and Novo-Tagil in the Urals, at Kuznetsk in Siberia, and at Zaporozhe in the Ukraine; the Elektrostal plant in Moscow; and others. Many of the new iron and steel plants, as well as those reconstructed and expanded, are really large metallurgical and chemical combines. They engage not only in the output of iron and steel but also in the production of coking coal and of chemicals that are by-products of the coking process. In 1936 the Magnitogorsk plant produced 1,557,000 metric tons of pig iron and the Kuznetsk combine turned out 1,363,000 tons. Since then the capacity and output of both establishments have increased substantially.

---

[55] Cf. D. B. Shimkin, *Minerals — A Key to Soviet Power*, p. 36.

From the locational point of view, the most striking development of the 1930's was the creation of a giant modern iron and steel in-

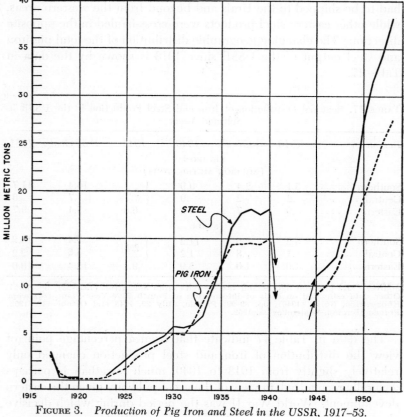

FIGURE 3.   *Production of Pig Iron and Steel in the USSR, 1917–53.*
Sources: Official Soviet publications and author's estimates.

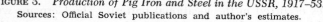

dustry in the east — at Magnitogorsk and elsewhere in the Urals, in the Kusnetsk basin of Western Siberia, and at Komsomolsk in the Far East. We have noted above that the Kuznetsk-Magnitogorsk development was originally founded on the basis of an exchange of coal and iron ore over the long distance separating the two areas. The subsequent tendency has been for each of these giant combines to become less and less dependent on each other, utilizing, more and more, nearby supplies, as well as coal from the intermediate Karaganda Basin in Kazakhstan. In the 1930's, the eastern metallurgical base did not produce a complete rounded assortment of iron and steel products, so that even in 1940 large amounts of steel products had to be shipped to the Urals and beyond from the western areas, while other eastern steel products were cross-hauled in the opposite direction. The changing geographic distribution of the total pig-iron and steel output of the USSR since 1913 is shown by the data in Table 17.

TABLE 17. Regional Distribution of Iron and Steel Production in the USSR in Selected Years.

Region	1913	1927–28	1940	1945	1950 Goal	1951
			PIG IRON (MILLION METRIC TONS)			
Southern	3.1	2.4	9.9	} 2.6	10.4	11.7
Central	.2	.2	.9		.7	.6
Eastern	.9	.7	4.2	6.6	8.4	9.7
			STEEL			
Southern	3.2	2.5	11.2	} 2.1	9.4	13.2
Central	.1	.8	1.2		3.6	2.2
Eastern	.9	1.0	5.9	9.1	12.4	16.0

Sources: 1913 pig iron figures and 1927-28 data from *Sot. Stroi. (1933-38)*, pp. 56-57. Other data estimated on basis of information in Fourth Five-Year Plan; *Planovoye Khozyaistvo*, No. 2 (1946), pp. 89-99; *Pravda*, July 29, 1948 and October 13, 1952; *Pravda Ukrainy*, September 25, 1952.

The data in Table 17 indicate that from a percentage point of view the distribution of iron and steel production changed only relatively slightly from 1913 to 1940, much less than is perhaps generally recognized, in view of the great publicity given the eastern development. World War II was the period during which decisive changes occurred in the locational pattern. The Germans were responsible for the destruction of 62 blast furnaces and 213 open hearth furnaces in the area they occupied. In the eastern area, during 1943 and 1944, however, 13 blast furnaces capable of producing 2,300,000 tons of pig iron, 70 steel furnaces capable of producing 2,800,000 tons of steel, and 28 rolling mills with an annual capacity of 1,700,000 tons of finished steel began operation. These developments completely altered the old geographical production pattern.

As is evident from Table 17 above, between 1945 and 1951 the Soviet Union succeeded simultaneously in rebuilding its war-devastated southern (mainly Ukrainian) iron and steel industry to a production level beyond the prewar peak, while expanding the eastern (mainly Urals and Kuzbas) industry still further. The production pattern in the early 1950's, therefore, was far more balanced than it had been in the prewar era, when the South predominated, or in 1945, when the East was dominant. Yet the Soviet steel industry continued to be concentrated in a relatively few areas. Chelyabinsk Province in the Urals, which includes Magnitogorsk among other plants, was reported in 1952 to have "long ago" exceeded the pig iron and steel output of all Czarist Russia in 1913, that is presumably to have an output well over the 4,200,000 metric tons of pig iron and the same amount of steel produced in that prewar year. For comparison it may be noted that fifteen years earlier, in 1937, Chelyabinsk produced only about 1,700,000 metric tons of pig iron and probably little more than 2,000,000 tons of steel.[56] Similar rapid growth at the Kuznetsk Combine in Western Siberia is indicated by the report that in the early 1950's this complex was producing 40 per cent more pig iron and 25 per cent more steel than before World War II.[57] This suggests that the Kuznetsk Combine alone was producing over 2,000,000 tons each of pig iron and steel annually in 1952.

Coincident with the expansion in the amounts of pig iron, steel, and rolled metal produced, there occurred a great diversification in the assortment of output. By 1940 the USSR supplied itself with virtually all types of carbon and alloy steels, as well as a wide variety of steel shapes and forms. Thus the Soviet iron and steel industry was able to meet the increasingly diverse and severe demands of the rapidly expanding machinery, construction, and other industries. One indication of this increasing technological self-sufficiency is the fact that the USSR's ferrous metals imports fell from about 1,200,000 metric tons in 1931, 22 per cent of the country's consumption at that time, to 97,300 tons in 1940, only .7 of one per cent of consumption.[58] But as noted above, this greater variety of output was not properly distributed over the country, leading to transport difficulties.

---

[56] *Pravda*, October 11, 1952, and *Sot. Stroi. (1933–1938)*, pp. 56–57.

[57] *Trud*, April 3, 1952.

[58] I. P. Bardin and N. P. Banny, *Chernaya Metallurgiya v Novoy Pyatiletke*, p. 9. Moscow-Leningrad: 1947.

The efforts being made by the USSR to achieve a more rational distribution of the output of finished steel products may be illustrated by the data below for steel-tubing output in different areas as a percentage of the national total: [59]

Region	1940	1950 Goal
Ukraine	71.9	44.0
Caucasus	—	18.0
Center	20.3	13.0
Eastern	7.8	25.0

Great strides have been made in the technological level of Soviet iron and steel production since 1928. As new plants were built and old ones reconstructed, Soviet leaders sought to introduce the most advanced equipment and techniques available. One of the most significant trends has been toward increasing the size of basic production units such as blast furnaces and open-hearth furnaces. An illustration of the changes that have resulted may be given by citing the fact that in 1900 Russia had 302 small blast furnaces, which produced 2,900,000 tons of pig iron. In 1940 the USSR had 92 blast furnaces, which produced 15,000,000 metric tons of pig iron. During the whole period, 1928 to 1940, the average productivity of a Soviet blast furnace increased fivefold.[60] Similarly, intensive work has been done on making it possible for all stages of iron and steel production to be automatically regulated; on introducing modern methods of rolling, including the continuous strip mill technique; and not least, on increasing the relative importance of scrap iron and steel in the industry's raw material base. In the past the Soviet Union has been badly deficient in scrap metal, so that pig-iron output often exceeded steel production. As late as 1935 the USSR produced 12,500,000 tons of pig iron and only 12,400,000 tons of steel. Progress in the direction of freeing steel output from complete dependence on pig-iron production was already substantial in 1940, however.

The main technical trends of the Soviet iron and steel industry in the postwar period may be summarized as follows:

First, continued development of very large plants. In 1951 about 60 per cent of all Soviet iron and steel mills were capable of produc-

---

[59] *Ibid.*, p. 123.
[60] *Ibid.*, pp. 71-72.

ing over 1,000,000 tons of iron or steel a year, as against only 39 per cent which had this much capacity in 1940.[61]

Second, continued progress in more intensive use of existing physical capacity. The amount of steel produced per square meter of open hearth furnace increased 42 per cent between 1940 and 1952. Facilitating this more intensive use was the introduction of improved equipment and methods. Particularly stressed have been the use of automatic controls in blast and open-hearth furnaces, and in rolling mills, as well as the use of pure oxygen in steel smelting.[62]

Third, great progress has been achieved in making iron ore available from sources near the main consuming plants. Counterbalancing this has been the problem of depletion of best quality ores. Thus the Kuznetsk iron and steel combine in the early 1950's secured 80 per cent of its iron ore from nearby sources rather than depending primarily upon Magnitogorsk ores from more than 1,000 miles away, as formerly. It did so, however, only at the cost of using poorer quality ores. How serious the over-all iron ore situation has become is evidenced, at the extreme, from the fact that Soviet metallurgists are studying the possible use of some ores having as little as 20 or 30 per cent iron content, roughly half the iron content considered normal for good ore before World War II. With the depletion of the richest ores at Krivoi Rog, the southern iron and steel industry is being forced to turn increasingly to the troublesome Krivoi Rog and Kursk iron quartzites and to the difficult brown ores of the Kerch Peninsula, ores with harmful impurities that are difficult and expensive to remove.[63]

Fourth, the problem of sufficient ferrous scrap has become troublesome since about 1950. The vast reserves of wartime scrap were largely exhausted by 1950 or 1951, while the demands of steel production for scrap grew greatly. This scarcity is apparently the motive for the higher percentage production increase scheduled for pig iron than for steel during the Fifth Five-Year Plan period.

Fifth, the basic line of Soviet iron and steel development is apparently to be the further expansion, through semi-duplication,

61 *Pravda*, October 13, 1952.
62 *Ibid.*
63 *Pravda*, September 7, 1953. I. Bardin, "Razvitiye Metallurgicheskoi Bazy Narodnogo Khozyaistva v Pyatoi Pyatiletke," *Planovoye Khozyaistvo*, No. 2 (1953), pp. 24–31.

of the great combines now existing in the Ukraine, the Urals, and the Kuzbas. The primary motivation here seems to be economy of construction cost, though this policy works counter to the previously enunciated policy of more equitable geograpic distribution of industry. Iron and steel plants built or being built in new areas, as in Georgia in the Caucasus and near Leningrad, are to play a secondary role up to 1955 at least. Small plants working on scrap or converting pig iron from other sources into steel are to be set up in different parts of the country to meet the needs of local consumer goods producers for galvanized iron and the like.[64]

Nonferrous Metals

The nonferrous metal industry of the USSR is engaged in the mining and refining of copper, lead, zinc, aluminum, tin, and other metals. To the extent that some nonferrous metals occur together in complex polymetallic ores, such as those containing lead, zinc, silver, and other metals, various parts of the nonferrous metal industry are intimately related with one another. Other branches, on the other hand, such as the aluminum industry, which produces its final metallic product from bauxite and other ores, are independent.

Quantitatively, each of the nonferrous metals is produced in only relatively small amounts, and even the aggregate of their production is far below that of pig iron or steel. These metals, however, play a vital part in modern industry. The rapid industrialization of the USSR during the late 1920's and thereafter brought with it a sharply increased need for these metals. Most important nonferrous metals had been produced only in relatively small quantities during the Czarist era or not at all, as in the case of aluminum and tin. Before the middle 1930's, a high percentage of Soviet requirements was met by relatively large imports from abroad.

Determined to make the Soviet economy independent of other nations in this as well as other fields, Soviet leaders projected and carried through a very large expansion of the production facilities and actual output of these metals. One indication of the success of this effort is the fact that between 1929 and 1935 the total imports of six major nonferrous metals — copper, nickel, aluminum, tin, lead, and zinc — dropped from about 117,000 metric tons to less

[64] Bardin, *op. cit., passim.*

than 79,000 metric tons. This drop occurred as the result of rising production, which more than made up for the increased Soviet need for these metals. But even in the late 1930's the USSR was still not completely independent of foreign nonferrous metals. Large imports of nonferrous metals were secured by the USSR under the Lend-Lease and Mutual Aid programs of World War II. In the postwar era this need continues.

The German successes in World War II in occupying so much of the western region of the Soviet Union resulted in heavy loss by the Soviet nonferrous metals industry, particularly the aluminum, zinc, and manganese branches. A number of the major mines and refining works of this industry were located in the area occupied by the Germans, so that their production was lost for part of the war. Presumably, these facilities were severely damaged or destroyed before the Soviet Union regained them. In the postwar period a major effort is being made to increase sharply the production of these metals. Expansion is taking place in the never-occupied areas, which had already increased production substantially during World War II. In addition the destruction in the formerly occupied territory has been repaired, and production is increasing there.

Copper. Copper production began in Russia during the era of Peter the Great, being concentrated in the Urals. By the middle of the eighteenth century, Russia was one of the world's great copper producers and had become a major exporter. In the late nineteenth century, Urals production was supplemented by that in the Caucasus, where new copper deposits were exploited through the efforts of foreign investors. Copper production in Russia in 1913 consisted of about 31,000 metric tons of blister copper and 16,700 tons of electrolytic copper. By 1929 this had increased to 35,500 tons of blister copper and 22,800 tons of electrolytic copper. Less than ten years later, in 1938, production of blister copper had increased just about threefold, to 103,200 tons, while electrolytic copper output had risen to over four times that of 1929, to 97,800 metric tons.[65]

In 1937 over 84 per cent of all copper smelted in the USSR was smelted in the Urals; almost 10 per cent in Kazakhstan; and 6 per cent in Armenia. This distribution of smelting was far from proportional to the distribution of reserves. The Urals had less than

---

[65] Balzak, *et al., op. cit.,* p. 257; and *Sot. Stroi. (1933–38),* p. 62.

16 per cent of all Soviet copper reserves at that time, while Kazakhstan had more than 50 per cent of Soviet reserves. The rapid expansion of copper production in Kazakhstan was a major objective of the Third Five-Year Plan, begun in 1938.

Since none of the major Soviet sources of copper was located in the area occupied by the Germans, this industry may not have experienced the sharp drop in production that so many other Soviet industries did. It seems not unlikely, however, that some reduction in copper output resulted at the beginning of the war because of the calling up of workers and specialists for military service. An important change that had taken place by 1942 was the increased importance of the Kazakh copper production as compared with that in the Urals. In 1942 Kazakhstan accounted for 40 per cent of all copper mined in the USSR; in the same year the Urals accounted for 46 per cent, a sharp change from the ratios prevailing in 1937. The amount of copper smelted at the Balkhash Copper Refinery in Kazakhstan doubled during the war.[66] The provisions of the Fourth Five-Year Plan called for the output of copper in 1950 to be 60 per cent above that in 1945. This plan required increase in the capacity of copper mines, concentration plants, and refineries. It called for completion of the first section of a new copper refinery in the southern Urals. It also provided for the erection of a new electrolytic copper plant, location unspecified.

Comparatively little has been published about the progress of copper production in the postwar period, so that we must rely upon estimates by foreign observers. A Department of Commerce tabulation estimates that crude copper output fell from 161,000 metric tons in 1940 to 141,000 tons in 1945, but that by 1950 this had risen to 256,000 tons.[67] D. B. Shimkin has estimated that been 1945 and 1950 copper output may have risen from 160,000 metric tons to 292,000 tons, though he is not certain that these figures pertain entirely to primary copper.[68] The Fifth Five-Year Plan calls for 1955 copper production, in terms of refined metal, 90 per cent over the 1950 output, equivalent to roughly 500,000 tons or more in terms of the above estimates. These are impressive rates of growth, but as late as December 1953 *Pravda* complained that the copper

[66] *Entsiklopediya,* cols. 256–57, 828.

[67] Data from the files of the European Division of the Department of Commerce.

[68] Shimkin, *op. cit.,* p. 113.

output of the Urals lagged behind the national economy's requirements. The same article indicated that refining capacity in the Urals had far surpassed the area's ore production so that it had to operate in large part on imported ores, presumably from Kazakhstan. Mechanization of copper mining in the Urals had apparently progressed slowly and unsatisfactorily in the postwar period.[69] The opening of the Ust-Kamenogorsk hydroelectric plant in Kazakhstan in July 1953 presumably helped ease the power shortage which has hindered copper production in this area during the postwar period.

Lead. Lead smelting began in Russia in 1704, during the reign of Peter the Great, in the Nerchinsk region of Eastern Siberia. By the end of the nineteenth century, however, the usable lead reserves in this area were exhausted, and dominance passed to the North Caucasus, where the Sadon deposit was most important. In 1913 the North Caucasus produced 96 per cent of all Russian lead, and the Urals virtually all the small remainder. Only 1,500 tons of lead were smelted in Russia in 1913. Lead production fell sharply after 1913, as a result of World War I and the civil war. In 1923 only 300 metric tons were produced in the USSR.

Data on lead production during the Soviet regime are sparse, but it is known that the goal for 1937 output was 115,000 metric tons. That this goal was actually reached by that date seems doubtful, in view of complaints that in 1935 the lead-production plan was fulfilled by only 72 per cent.[70] Nevertheless, it is clear that by 1940 very substantial advances had been made in lead production, as compared with the paltry 1,500 tons output of 1913. Soviet efforts to increase lead production have emphasized development of Kazakhstan, where 74 per cent of all Soviet lead was smelted in 1937. The Chimkent lead plant in southern Kazakhstan was apparently the largest single producer in the USSR in 1937, followed by the Ridder plant in the Altay mountain region of east Kazakhstan. The North Osetian Republic in the North Caucasus, and the Maritime Territory in the Soviet Far East also produced more than 10 per cent of all lead smelted in the USSR in 1937.[71]

Shimkin reports that Soviet lead production reached 62,500 metric tons in 1937, and that at the most generous estimate this output

69 *Pravda*, December 15, 1953.

70 *Narodnokhozyaistvenny Plan na 1936 god*, p. 117. Moscow: 1936.

71 Balzak, *et al.*, *op. cit.*, pp. 262–63.

may have grown from 60,000 tons in 1945 to 143,600 tons in 1950.[72] The Fifth Five-Year Plan calls for 1955 lead production to be 2.7 times that of 1950, or about 388,000 tons if this percentage rise is applied to Shimkin's estimate, which he labels "probable maximum," for 1950.

Zinc. Zinc production is closely allied with that of lead, because both metals frequently occur together in polymetallic ores. In 1913, Russian zinc production was only 2,900 metric tons, and Russia imported over 28,000 metric tons from abroad.[73] In 1923 only 200 tons of zinc were mined in the Soviet Union.[74]

Zinc production expanded in the Soviet period much as did lead output. The Second Five-Year Plan set a zinc-production goal for 1937 of 90,000 tons. It is not known whether this was realized, although substantial progress was undoubtedly made. In 1937, 42.5 per cent of all Soviet zinc was extracted in the Kazakh Republic, and over 23 per cent in Novosibirsk Province in Siberia. The North Osetian Republic in Caucasus, Chelyabinsk Province in the Urals, and the Maritime Territory in the Far East each contributed more than 10 per cent of all Soviet zinc mined. In North Osetia, where 15.5 per cent of all zinc ore was mined in 1937, about 36 per cent of all ore was smelted, much of it from distant regions such as the Altay mountains. In the late 1930's a large zinc distillation plant operated at Konstantinovka in the Ukraine, using zinc concentrates from the Far East and the Altay mountains, hauled over thousands of miles. In Novosibirsk Province the newly constructed Belovo zinc distillation plant used raw materials from the Salair polymetallic deposits. Electrolytic zinc was produced at the Chelyabinsk plant from waste products of the Urals copper-smelting plants.

The Konstantinovka plant in the Ukraine was presumably lost during the German occupation of that area in World War II, and the Caucasian zinc output in North Osetia must have been seriously affected as well.

For 1937, Shimkin estimates Soviet zinc metal output at about 65,000 metric tons. He calculates that, because of the loss of Ukrainian and North Caucasian sources, 1943 production fell to

---

[72] Shimkin, *op. cit.*, pp. 121–24.

[73] *Entsiklopediya*, col. 257.

[74] Balzak, *et. al., op. cit.*, p. 258.

about 38,000 tons, rising thereafter to 52,000 tons in 1945 and to 128,000 tons (plus or minus 10 per cent) by 1950.[75] The Fifth Five-Year Plan calls for zinc output by 1955 to be 2.5 times the 1950 level, or about 320,000 tons if Shimkin's 1950 estimate is correct. He notes that Poland's relatively large zinc output probably provides an important Soviet source of imports.

Aluminum. Aluminum production in the USSR is entirely a product of the Soviet era, and as late as 1929 this metal was not produced in that country. By 1933, 7,000 metric tons of aluminum had been produced; and in 1938 production had reached almost 57,000 metric tons.[76] The 1938 output, however, was still substantially below the 80,000 metric ton goal for 1937, which had been set by the Second Five-Year Plan.[77]

The first Soviet aluminum was produced in 1933 at the Volkhov aluminum plant near Leningrad, which used bauxite from Tikhvin and electric power from the Volkhov hydroelectric power station. A second aluminum plant was built at Zaporozhe, using Tikhvin bauxite and electric power from the Dnepr dam. Availability of electric power is extremely important for aluminum production, since the output of one ton of aluminum requires only two tons of aluminum oxide, the raw material, but up to 20,000 kilowatt-hours of electric power. In the late 1930's a new large aluminum plant was built at Kamensk-Uralsk, in the Chelyabinsk Province of the Urals, to utilize the large Urals bauxite deposits. Other aluminum plants were scheduled to be built during the Third Five-Year Plan period, that is, by 1942, in the Kuzbas and at Kandalaksha in the Kola peninsula. The latter plant was scheduled to operate on a new aluminum raw material, nepheline. Large quantities of nepheline are available in the Kola peninsula, as the result of the extensive production of apatite there — nepheline is a waste product of apatite-processing.

Both the Volkhov and Dnepr plants were lost during the German invasion early in World War II. As a result, the center of gravity of Soviet aluminum production shifted to the Urals and to the Kemerovo plant in the Kuzbas. The Krasnoturinsk plant northwest of

---

[75] Shimkin, *op. cit.*, pp. 136–38.
[76] *Sot. Stroi. (1933–38)*, p. 62.
[77] *Second Five-Year Plan*, p. 208.

Serov in the Urals began operation shortly after World War II. In 1945 the Urals accounted for 96 per cent of all bauxite produced in the USSR. The Fourth Five-Year Plan called for the doubling of aluminum production in 1950 as compared with 1945. It also provided that bauxite mines, two aluminum plants, and an alumina plant (alumina is aluminum oxide, an intermediate product derived from bauxite and required for the final production of aluminum) were to be restored during the Fourth Five-Year Plan period. Two new aluminum plants were to be built. The capacity of aluminum plants in the North Urals and in the Kuznetsk Basin was to be increased, while the first section of an alumina plant in the Azerbaidzhan Republic was to be finished and put into operation.

A Department of Commerce tabulation has estimated Soviet primary aluminum output in three key years to have been as follows: 1937 — 37,700 metric tons; 1940 — 59,900 tons; 1945 — 86,300 tons. Since the 1950 goal was set at twice the 1945 output, this suggests an objective of 172,600 tons for that year. Shimkin gives the following estimates for 1939 to 1946, in thousands of metric tons:

1939	49.8	1943	67.2
1940	56.7	1944	82.7
1941	63.4	1945	88.9
1942	42.6	1946	89.4

He estimates that of the 1946 total of 89,400 metric tons, the great bulk, 70,900 tons, came from Northern Urals sources. On the basis of his 1945 estimate, the 1950 goal would seem to have been almost 180,000 tons. He indicates that there is reason to believe 1950 Soviet aluminum production was larger than the actual goal, a reasonable hypothesis in view of the military importance of aluminum and the attendant high priority probably given it. It does not seem unlikely, therefore, that 1950 Soviet production may have been approximately 200,000 tons.[78] The Fifth Five-Year Plan called for 1955 aluminum production to be at least 2.6 times as great as in 1950, or about 520,000 tons on the basis of the above estimate. Assuming that progress on this program has been more or less on schedule, it would seem that in 1953 the Soviet Union may have produced as much as 400,000 or 420,000 tons of aluminum. If so,

---

[78] Shimkin, *op. cit.*, p. 102.

this would have been roughly half the 1951 production of the United States, which was about 800,000 tons. One indication that the aluminum production program is going well in the first half of the 1950's is the plan to produce 90,000 tons of aluminum kitchenware in 1954 and 107,000 tons of such kitchenware in 1955. Such amounts require aluminum in quantities far exceeding total Soviet production until less than a decade earlier.[79]

The Chemical Industry

A wide variety of products is produced by the Soviet chemical industry. Among them are basic chemicals such as sulphuric acid, nitric acid, chlorine and soda ash, as well as agricultural fertilizers and insecticides, synthetic rubber and rubber products, plastics, artificial fibers, photographic materials, aniline dyes, paints, varnishes, and other protective coverings, and numerous pharmaceutical and medical preparations — from aspirin and bicarbonate of soda to penicillin.

The chemical industry of Czarist Russia before World War I was extremely backward, producing only a small number of chemical products and relying heavily upon imported raw materials. Plants producing heavy chemicals, such as acids, alkalis, and salts, were small and for the most part used antiquated apparatus unsuitable for large-scale production. Many of these plants were destroyed or worn out at the end of the civil war, so that the Soviet government had to start almost from scratch in building up the chemical industry.

Development of Soviet chemical production during the past three decades has been built on the discovery and exploitation of the USSR's vast deposits of basic chemical raw materials, the building of many new plants using modern techniques and equipment for chemical production, and the initiation and growth of many important branches of this industry that did not exist at all before the Soviet era. In this process American, German, and other foreign technicians played an important role, as did large imports of machinery and equipment during the late 1920's and early 1930's.

Official Soviet data claim an almost fifteen fold growth in the physical volume of chemical production between 1913 and 1938,

---

[79] *Pravda,* October 28, 1953.

most of which occurred after 1928. These conclusions are drawn from output data calculated in 1926–27 prices and probably exaggerate this growth, particularly because of the great importance of new products introduced after 1926–27. Nevertheless substantial gains were undoubtedly made in this period, as the data in Table 18 indicate.

TABLE 18. Gross Production of the USSR's Chemical Industry and Output of Selected Products, 1913–38.

	Unit	1913	1929	1933	1938*
Gross Output	million 1926–1927 rubles	457	645†	2,301	6,809
Soda Ash	thousand tons	160	231	325	532
Sulphuric Acid	thousand tons	110	265‡	627	996**
Fertilizers §	thousand tons	§	247§	715§	2,610§
Aniline Dyes	thousand tons	4	13	16	35
Synthetic Rubber	thousand tons	—	—	2	26**
Plastics	thousand tons	—	—	4	8**
Iron Pyrites	thousand tons	76	301	415	978
Tires	thousands	19	142	672	3,548

* 1938 data preliminary. † 1928. ‡1928-29. ** 1935.
§ Includes superphosphates, ammonium sulphate, and potassium chloride. Figure for 1929 is 1927-28 actual, for 1933 it is 1932 actual, and for 1938 it is 1938 preliminary. Data for 1913 unavailable.
Sources: *Sot. Stroi.*, pp. 175-79. *Sot. Stroi. (1933-38)*, p. 67; Jasny, *The Socialized Agriculture of the USSR*, p. 495; *Entsiklopediya*, cols. 819-20; Hirsch, *Industrialized Russia* p. 70.

Before 1935 the USSR had already instituted a number of major branches of chemical production that had never existed in Czarist times. These included output of the following major commodities: synthetic ammonia and related chemicals, including nitrates and nitric acid; coke by-products; synthetic resins; rayon; potassium salts; phosphate fertilizers from apatite; methanol; butanol; acetone; synthetic rubber; many pharmaceuticals; and so on.[80] Since then other important new branches of chemical production have been initiated, as the Russians have striven to keep abreast of modern technology and attain maximum self-sufficiency. Among the more recent branches of chemical production are the manufacture of sulfa drugs and anti-biotics such as penicillin, and the whole field of radioactive chemistry.

---

[80] Hirsch, *op. cit.*, p. 71.

Soviet determination to achieve self-sufficiency in chemical — as well as other — products is probably best exemplified by the history of Soviet synthetic rubber production. As early as 1925, the Soviet government announced a contest open to scientists of all countries. Contestants were asked to produce a five-pound sample of synthetic rubber, to explain the process by which it was made, and to furnish data from which a factory to manufacture this rubber might be planned. The objective sought was the best method for commercial output of synthetic rubber. Professor Lebedev, of the USSR, and an assistant won the contest with a process based on passing ethyl alcohol over a catalyst so as to produce butadiene, the so-called divinyl process. By 1929 a small pilot plant was producing over two pounds of rubber daily, and on July 7, 1932, the first large Soviet synthetic rubber plant began production. The subsequent progress was rapid. Synthetic rubber output reached 26,000 metric tons by 1935, and was vastly increased thereafter. At the beginning of 1950, annual Soviet output of synthetic rubber was estimated to be above 200,000 metric tons, second only to that of the United States, whose synthetic rubber industry had been built up feverishly during World War II.[81]

Chemical plants have been built in many parts of the Soviet Union, frequently near sources of raw materials. Production of ammonium sulphate, benzol, toluol, and other coke by-products was integrated with the Soviet metallurgical coke industry at various iron and steel plants, particularly that at Magnitogorsk. The latter, for example, has a series of Koppers coking batteries with 69 ovens to a battery, as well as a large and up-to-date by-products plant and facilities for manufacturing 2,100 tons of ammonium sulphate monthly.[82] Synthetic rubber plants using the Lebedev process were located in potato-growing areas, since the basic alcohol employed is made from potatoes. Before World War II such plants were built at Yaroslavl, Voronezh, Yefremov in Tula Province, and Kazan. Another synthetic rubber-producing establishment, making "Sovpren," a synthetic rubber based on limestone as the initial raw material, was built at Yerevan, capital of the Armenian Republic.[83]

[81] *Ibid.*, pp. 95–97. *New York Times*, January 6, 1950.

[82] Louis Ernst, "Inside a Soviet Industry," *Fortune*, October 1949, p. 118.

[83] Balzak, *et al.*, *op. cit.*, pp. 289–90.

Among the major fertilizer plants built in the 1930's were those at Voskresensk in Moscow Province and at Konstantinovka in the Donbas, and the Neva Chemical Combine in Leningrad, producing superphosphates; the Solikamsk potassium works in the Urals; and the nitrogenous fertilizer plants producing ammonium sulphate in the major iron and steel centers of Donbas, Kuzbas, Magnitogorsk, and other areas.[84] The plastic industry, producing bakelite, celluloid, and other plastics, was more consumer-oriented in its location, and was concentrated before World War II in and around Moscow, Leningrad, Vladimir, and Kalinin. Pharmaceutical production of all kinds, before 1940, took place for the most part in Moscow, Leningrad, Kharkov, Kiev, Baku, and Chimkent, the latter being in Kazakhstan.[85]

World War II wreaked heavy damage upon the chemical industry. Many chemical plants were located in German-occupied areas and were destroyed or seriously damaged, though some of those most important for armaments output were successfully evacuated eastward. What remained of the chemical industry was concentrated virtually exclusively upon meeting military needs. The nitrogen industry, producing ammonia and nitric acid for explosives, received the greatest development. As a result, 252,000 metric tons of concentrated nitric acid were produced in eastern areas in 1942 and 342,000 tons in 1943, as compared with 232,000 tons produced in the entire USSR in 1940.[86] Fertilizer output was one of the chief casualties of the conflict, production having fallen to 20 per cent less than the 1938 level in 1940 and to probably less than one third of 1938 output at the lowest point of the war.[87] Large quantities of pharmaceuticals and other chemical products had to be imported during World War II from the United States, Great Britain, and Canada, under the Lend-Lease and Mutual Aid programs.

The official Soviet government report on the fulfillment of the Fourth Five-Year Plan claimed that 1950 Soviet chemical production was 80 per cent above the prewar level, far better than the original goal. It asserted that great progress had been made in

---

[84] *Ibid.*, pp. 285–87.
[85] *Ibid.*, pp. 291–92.
[86] Voznesensky, *op. cit.*, p. 44.
[87] Jasny, *The Socialized Agriculture of the USSR*, pp. 495–96. *Pravda,* April 3, 1947.

production of synthetic fibres, plastics, paints, pharmaceuticals, dyes, and fertilizers, as well as in synthetic rubber output, but it gave few data. For the year 1955, the Fifth Five-Year Plan called for increases of about 80 per cent for some key products such as soda ash and caustic soda as against the 1950 levels. The 82 per cent production increase called for in synthetic rubber would result in 1955 output of over 350,000 tons if our earlier assumption — that over 200,000 tons were probably produced in 1950 — is correct.

Discussion in the Soviet press in 1953 made it clear, however, that chemical output of some essential products was still inadequate and often of poor quality. Thus, in 1953 it was reported that dye output was 74 per cent over that of 1940. Many complaints were registered that most of this was production of the most primitive sulphur-base dyes and that little high-grade indigo dye was produced. Existing dyes, it was revealed, faded when clothing on which they were used was exposed to light or washed. Uniform dyeing of clothes was often difficult because of the form in which dyes were produced and made available.[88]

The deficiency of mineral fertilizer production was a major topic of discussion in September 1953 when a program for improving crop yields was published. Though Soviet agriculture was scheduled to get about 6,000,000 tons of this fertilizer in 1953, more than double the 1940 amount, major increases were ordered to meet full needs of farmers. The government ordered that by 1959 about 17,-000,000 tons of fertilizer capacity be available; by 1963 this capacity is to be raised to between 28,000,000 and 30,000,000 tons. Similar inadequacy of insecticide supplies was suggested by the order that 1955 output be double that of 1953.[89]

The Machinery Industries

Since 1928 the development of Soviet machine-building industries of all types has been the central facet of industrial growth in the USSR. Measured in 1926–27 rubles, machinery output in 1940 was 54 times as great as in the Russia of 1913, though gross production

---

[88] *Pravda,* August 13 and September 12, 1953.
[89] *Pravda,* September 3 and 13, 1953.

of large industry increased only 12 times.[90] In 1913 the value of all machinery built was 900,000,000 rubles at 1926–27 prices, less than 6 per cent of gross industrial output. In 1940 the production of machinery was valued at about 45 billion rubles in 1926–27 prices, or almost one third of all gross industrial output.[91] Even after allowing for the inflationary bias of the 1926–27 ruble valuation and for the fact that these figures probably include the value of armaments, it is clear that this branch of the Soviet economy has been developed tremendously. In the late 1920's and early 1930's the USSR had to import large quantities of machinery of all types for installation in the new plants, mines, and railroads being built, as well as for use on collective farms. Since the late 1930's, however, the USSR has become much more independent of foreign machinery supplies and has provided the great bulk of its requirements through its own manufacture. By 1954 the Soviet Union had become a significant exporter of machinery required by its satellites in Europe and Asia, though the quantities involved were probably not very large. Even in 1954, however, the USSR declared it would be glad to purchase large quantities of some types of machinery and equipment in the United States and other Western nations, if the latter had been willing to permit such exports in the quantities and types desired.

In this section our attention is focused upon the wide range of civilian and indirect military types of machinery and equipment whose production has been greatly expanded or initiated during the Soviet era. These include, among others, machine tools of all types; electric motors; precision instruments and control apparatus; boilers and other power-generating equipment; motor vehicles; tractors and other farm machinery; production equipment for many different industries, such as mining, chemicals, metallurgy, printing, textiles; construction machinery; and rolling stock for railroads and other transport equipment. As in the case of chemicals, the history of production development in this area of the economy has been marked by growing diversification of output and continued striving for technological improvement, based upon the results of domestic and foreign experience and research. The production of machine

---

[90] *Planovoye Khozyaistvo,* No. 4 (1946), pp. 4 and 18.
[91] Calculated on the basis of preceding data and *Sot. Stroi. (1933–38),* p. 22.

tools offers a graphic example of this trend. During the Second Five-Year Plan, 1933–37, about 200 types and sizes of machine tools were produced in the USSR. By 1940 there were 500 types and sizes. During the Fourth-Five-Year-Plan period, 1946–50, the USSR was scheduled to produce about 2,300 different types and sizes of machine tools.

In the First Five-Year Plan, American and other foreign industry not only supplied much of the machinery for hydroelectric, steel, aluminum, and other major production units, but also much of the foundation for Soviet machine-building. Hundreds of American machine tools went into the first great Soviet tractor factories, a number of which were planned by an American firm. The Ford Motor Company and other American concerns gave the USSR the technical assistance it required to build the major automobile and truck factory at Gorky. Foreign engineers served as technical advisors and supervised construction and operation of many new machinery plants, frequently modeling them after the most efficient plants abroad.[92] But as Soviet machine tool and machinery factories increased their output and as Soviet engineers mastered advanced foreign technology, the USSR's imports of machinery and technicians from abroad could be and were reduced.

The Soviet machinery industry was profoundly affected by World War II. Many important plants were destroyed or badly damaged in the occupied western areas, though the equipment of others was successfully evacuated eastward. Factories were converted, so far as possible, to the production of direct military supplies – tanks, planes, guns, and the like. A major factor that permitted this conversion to go as far as it did was the receipt by the USSR of large quantities of machinery of many different types from the United States and Great Britain during the war. This equipment aided materially in permitting the opening of new factories, mines, and power stations in the unoccupied part of the country. Soviet output of arms would have been materially lower if the USSR's factories had had to turn out the trucks, ships, machine tools, and similar complex equipment obtained from the Western allies.

At the end of World War II, faced with the necessity of re-equipping large numbers of devastated productive installations as well

---

[92] Heymann, *We Can Do Business With Russia*, pp. 8–61.

as building new ones, the USSR required large quantities of new machinery. Part of this need was satisfied by large-scale seizures of equipment of all types in areas occupied by the Red Army. The machinery industry was partially reconverted to peacetime production, but in the early postwar period its output in many branches climbed only slowly toward prewar output marks. The USSR desired to make important purchases of machinery abroad to supplement that available from the first two sources, but the amount actually obtained was well under that wanted, as the result of high domestic demand in the United States followed by the imposition of a virtual embargo on machinery exports that could increase the USSR's military potential.

Since World War II, great efforts have been made to incorporate technical production advances achieved in building military equipment during that struggle into the practice of the nonmilitary machinery industry. Mass-production techniques involving the use of assembly lines and conveyor belts have been introduced into many different branches of machine-building that before the war operated on more primitive levels. Serious efforts have been made to encourage development of the specialized manufacture of parts and semifabricated products so as to create integrated systems of plants, consisting of suppliers and final assembly units.

Much progress has apparently been made in these directions, but serious difficulties have also appeared. Assembly-line techniques, for example, require a smooth flow of all component parts and materials in pace with the speed of assembly. Such finely articulated cooperation is difficult to achieve under any circumstances and has been particularly difficult under the strains and shortages of the Soviet economy since 1945. As a result frequent stoppages and interruptions have occurred in assembly-line output because of the uneven rhythm of material and parts supply.

The supply difficulties sketched by the director of the Molotov Auto Plant in the city of Gorky in late 1953 are probably far from unique. He told of suppliers' frequent failures to meet deadlines and specifications; of the many shortages of spare parts which caused assembly line interruptions. In 1952 his plant had spent 3,000,000 rubles above planned costs merely to pay for shipping small parts by air or as baggage on express trains in the effort to minimize such interruptions.[93]

Proper specialization, and cooperation among different plants producing related products, have also encountered difficulties of a serious order. Plants asked to make nonstandard parts for others frequently tend to give such output low priority on their work schedules, regardless of the effect upon the purchasing plant. Factories turning out standard parts required by plants belonging to different industries and chief administrations frequently tend to favor plants in their own administrative organization, and to show bureaucratic disregard of the requirements of plants in other ministries or chief administrations.[94] The poor geographical distribution of specialized producers of parts and semi-fabricated products frequently requires, apparently, shipment of such items as stampings, forgings, gears, and other items over long distances. Thus one Urals machinery plant was reported in mid-1950 as receiving forgings and stampings from Barnaul, 1,200 miles away. This seems a somewhat extreme, but by no means unusual, case.[95] Unable to find adequate suppliers for parts and semifabricated products they require, many Soviet assembly plants find it necessary to manufacture for themselves relatively small quantities of such essential products, even though such manufacture is usually done in a primitive manner and at far higher cost than in specialized plants. In May 1950 one Leningrad plant director complained bitterly in a newspaper article that his plant had to produce its own optical instruments, electric lamps, electric motors and transformers, and steel forgings, although the city was well supplied with specialized plants producing these items, which did not always work at capacity.[96] Such complaints of poor coordination among plants and their suppliers were very frequent in 1946 and 1947, when Soviet industry was in the difficult throes of reconversion. Their persistent continuance even after 1950 suggests that very much remains to be done in modernizing and improving the work of machinery construction industries.[97]

---

[93] *Pravda,* October 14, 1953.
[94] *Planovoye Khozyaistvo,* No. 5 (1949), p. 42.
[95] *Pravda,* July 19, 1950.
[96] *Ibid.,* and *Leningradskaya Pravda,* May 12, 1950.
[97] Schwartz, *Russia's Postwar Economy,* pp. 35–40.

In the paragraphs below we shall consider briefly the development of production and the geographical distribution of plants in some of the chief branches of Soviet machine-building.

Farm Machinery. Soviet production of tractors, combines, tractor and horse-drawn implements, and other items of farm machinery grew very rapidly in the early and middle 1930's, as many large new plants were built and put into operation. In the late 1930's production of tractors, and probably some other major items, was sharply reduced, as some of this industry's plants were converted to military production well before the German invasion of the USSR. Soviet production of new farm machinery during World War II seems to have been very small, the result both of losses of plants in the western area and the almost complete military conversion of those remaining under Soviet control. The statistical picture of tractor and combine production is shown in Table 19.

TABLE 19. Output of Tractors and Combines in the USSR.

Item	1913	1927–28	1936	1940	1945	1949	1950
			(THOUSANDS)				
Tractors	0	1.3	116.1	31.0	7.7	87.3	107.3
Grain Combines	0	0	42.6	10.0	.3	29.0	46.0

Sources: 1913 and 1936–40. *Let Sovetskoy Vlasti*, p. 27. 1928—*Sot. Stroi.*, pp. 160, 162. 1940—estimated from data in Voznesensky's speech of March 15, 1946. Data for 1945, 1949, and 1950 estimated by the United States Department of Commerce.

From 1946 to 1950 the production of tractors and grain combines grew rapidly, particularly after reconversion of farm machinery plants from wartime military output was completed. Nevertheless, the goals for 1950 set by the Fourth Five-Year Plan were not fulfilled. Instead of the planned 112,000 tractors, only 107,300 physical units were produced. Similarly, instead of 60,000 grain combines, only 46,000 were manufactured.[98] The actual 1950 tractor output was still below the 1936 prewar peak of 116,100.

Though a partial statistical blackout on production of tractors and combines was instituted in 1951 and 1952, the available data suggest strongly that tractor production was reduced in both those years and combine production was cut in 1952, presumably to re-

[98] The combine target for 1950 was given in *Vestnik Mashinostroyeniya*, No. 11 (1947), the U.S. Department of Commerce has noted.

lease labor and materials for weapons required to supply Chinese Communist and North Korean forces fighting in the Korean War. The data on which this inference is based are the following official figures on tractors and combines delivered to agriculture during 1950–1953. The tractor figures given below are in terms of uniform 15 horsepower units, and hence are larger than the number of physical units produced, since the average horsepower of a Soviet tractor is well above 15. The data follow: [99]

Year	Tractors	Grain Combines
1950	over 180,000	46,000
1951	137,000	53,000
1952	131,000	41,000
1953	139,000	41,000

The Fifth Five-Year Plan called for tractor production in 1955 to be 19 per cent higher than in 1950, that is, about 127,700 physical units, little more than the original, but unfulfilled, goal for 1950. Tractor production in 1952 may have been only about 70,000, judging roughly by the horsepower data given above. In September 1953, as part of the general program to raise agricultural production, the Soviet government ordered that in the three and one-third years between January 1, 1954, and May 1, 1957, Soviet agriculture be supplied with 500,000 tractors in terms of 15 horsepower units, or at about the same average rate as indicated above to have held for the period 1950–52 inclusive. In addition, 250,000 cultivating tractors for row crops are to be supplied during this period.[100]

Among the major farm machinery plants built in the USSR during the 1930's were the tractor factories at Stalingrad, Kharkov, and Chelyabinsk; the combine plants at Zaporozhe, Rostov, Saratov, and Lyubertsy (Moscow Province); and the giant agricultural machinery factory at Rostov. Much of the equipment of the Kharkov plant was moved eastward to Rubtsovsk in Altay Territory, where a new tractor plant was built during the war. Other new postwar tractor plants have been constructed since 1945 at Lipetsk, Vladimir, and Minsk; and the ruined Stalingrad and Kharkov factories have been

---

[99] *Pravda,* January 26, 1951; *Planovoye Khozyaistvo,* No. 1 (1952), p. 8; *Pravda,* January 23, 1953 and January 31, 1954. In 1953, Soviet farms also received 18,000 cultivating tractors for row crops.

[100] *Pravda,* September 13, 1953.

restored and put into operation again. Similar expansion and re-habilitation have taken place in other farm machinery factories, so that by 1950 the USSR's productive capacity in this area probably substantially exceeded that of 1940. The lag in production behind the highest marks of the 1930's, however, suggested either that part of this capacity was being employed for military rather than farm output or that shortages of materials and parts were keeping output down.

Postwar Soviet tractor production has emphasized the manu-facture of diesel and caterpillar tractors, of a larger variety of tractors including small garden-type machines. Grain combines produced have included many self-propelled machines, while the production of sugar beet combines, cotton pickers, power mowers, hay stackers, and related machinery has increased greatly.[101]

Motor Vehicles. Data on production of motor vehicles in the USSR will be considered in more detail in the chapter on Transporta-tion and Communications. We may note here, however, that Soviet motor vehicle output increased from about 1,400 in 1929 to over 200,000 in 1938, probably the prewar peak. Truck production ac-counted for the great bulk of this output. Only about 20,000 pas-senger cars were produced in 1938, as against almost 180,000 trucks. The prewar peak of automobile and truck production was regained and exceeded in the late 1940's. The main Soviet passenger cars, the small *Moskvich,* medium *Pobeda,* the larger *ZIM,* and the large, luxurious *ZIS,* are largely modeled after foreign cars such as the German Opel and the American Ford and Packard. During the late 1920's the small AMO assembly plant in Moscow was renamed the Stalin plant and greatly expanded. Other major automobile plants were built at Yaroslavl, Gorky, and Rostov.[102]

In the postwar period, automobile plants in Moscow, Gorky, Yaroslavl, and Miass (in the Urals) are being or have been expanded; and new plants are being built at Dnepropetrovsk, Kutaisi, Ulyanovsk, Minsk, and Novosibirsk. Postwar truck models are scheduled to have carrying capacities varying from 2 tons (GAZ-63) to 5 to 7 tons (YAZ-200), and will have either diesel motors or more efficient gasoline engines, though there are also some gas generator models using hard fuels. Among new automobiles the ZIS-110

---

[101] *Ibid.,* August 9, 1953.
[102] Balzak, *et al., op. cit.,* pp. 280–81.

produces 140 horsepower and a top speed of over 80 miles an hour. The *Pobeda* model has a 50 horsepower motor and a top speed of over 60 miles an hour. The small *Moskvich* has a 23 horsepower motor and a top speed of under 60 miles an hour.[103]

Machine Tools. The production of metal-cutting machine tools of all types has been one of the most actively developed branches of machinery construction, because of the fundamental importance of these products for creating and maintaining modern industrial output. In 1928 the USSR produced about 1,800 machine tools; but ten years later, in 1938, about 53,900 were produced, and a goal of 70,000 had been set for 1942. The latter goal was not reached, because of the German invasion in 1941; but in the postwar period there has been a renewed drive to make up the losses suffered during the war. Production of machine tools in 1950 was scheduled to be 74,000, of which 12,300 were planned to be aggregative and special types. By that year the USSR was scheduled to have in operation a total of 1,300,000 machine tools.[104]

Before World War II machine tool plants were built in Moscow and Leningrad, and in the Ukraine and the Urals, where skilled labor and high-grade metal were available. Turret lathes were made in Moscow, milling machines in Gorky, gear-cutting tools and combination lathes in Sverdlovsk, automatic machine tools in Kiev, and so on.[105] During the years 1946–50 eighteen machine tool plants destroyed in the formerly occupied western areas were scheduled to be rebuilt. In addition, five new plants, two making heavy machine tools and three making multiple unit and special purpose types, were also scheduled for construction.[106]

After World War II machine tool production expanded greatly to meet the needs for re-equipping devastated plants and for equipping the many new plants called for by the Fourth Five-Year Plan. The official report on the fulfillment of that plan stressed that the postwar assortment of Soviet machine tools was far more varied and productive than had been true earlier. The new types included about 250 kinds of general purpose metal-cutting machine tools,

[103] *Planovoye Khozyaistvo*, No. 4 (1946), pp. 23–24. Full technical data on Soviet motor vehicles of all kinds are given in V. A. Korobov, *Traktory Avtomobili i Selskokhozyaistvennyye Dvigateli, passim.* Moscow: 1950.

[104] *Ibid.*, p. 22.

[105] Balzak *et al., op. cit.,* p. 273.

[106] *Planovoye Khozyaistvo*, No. 4 (1946), p. 23.

over 1,000 types of specialized and aggregative machine tools, as well as various other automatic and semiautomatic tools. The growth of production may be estimated as follows, but it should be borne in mind that the weight and capacity of postwar machine tools exceeded on the average those of the prewar models: [107]

Year	Number of Machine Tools	Year	Number of Machine Tools
1937	48,873	1949	69,000
1940	50,000	1950	80,000
1945	23,000	1951	82,500
1946	31,000	1952	85,000
1947	47,000	1953	96,900
1948	58,000		

At the end of 1950, Soviet sources claim, the USSR had more than twice as many machine tools as in 1940, a claim that seems credible in view of the impressive production growth shown above.[108]

Other Machinery. In addition to the products discussed, Soviet machinery plants produce a large variety of power, transport, and industrial equipment. The growth of this output has roughly paralleled that of the commodities discussed above. The number of locomotives produced, for example, increased from 479 in 1927–28 to 1,214 in 1937, while the 1950 goal was 2,720 railroad locomotives. Plants producing industrial equipment were distributed about the country, usually in close proximity to the industries they served. The major centers for all types of machine building were in the Ukraine, the Urals, and in and near Moscow and Leningrad. In the postwar period the relative importance of machinery plants in the Volga area and further east is considerably above what it was in 1940, though many of the plants destroyed in the west, particularly in the Ukraine, have been restored to production. New plants built since the war have been located in many different parts of the country, including the Baltic States and other western areas incorporated in the USSR since 1939, with the object of securing a more widely dispersed location pattern for this industry.

[107] Figures for 1937–1950 are estimates by the U.S. Department of Commerce based mainly on data in *Izvestia*, April 20, 1951, and in annual postwar government economic reports; 1951 estimate based on *Izvestia*, January 30, 1952; 1952 and 1953 estimates based on Ministry of Machine Tool increases shown in *Pravda*, January 23, 1953, and January 31, 1954, respectively.

[108] *Pravda*, October 16, 1951.

In late 1952, one of the chief Soviet machine-building executives, V. A. Malyshev, boasted:

> The staff of the machine-building industry can now report to Comrade Stalin that they are able to produce all machinery whatsoever that is needed by the national economy, that they can achieve assembly line production of such machinery and meet our country's needs for it.

He pointed out that in the postwar period more than 220 machines for mechanizing labor had been put into serial production, including the 1,250-ton walking excavator with a 14-cubic-meter bucket, capable under ideal conditions of moving more than 2,500,000 cubic meters of earth annually. "In 1951 alone 5.8 times as many dump trucks, 4.2 times as many mobile cranes and 21 per cent more excavators were manufactured than during the three prewar five-year plans combined." He put steam turbine production in 1951 at 2.9 times that of 1940, electrical equipment output 3.6 times as much, and petroleum equipment output almost five times as much.[109] In absolute terms the steam turbine percentage, for example, means that as against turbines with a capacity of 940,000 kilowatts produced in 1940, 1951 output of turbines had a total capacity of over 2,700,000 kilowatts.[110]

Yet there was a darker side to this picture. The large Soviet excavator drew many complaints because of the poor quality of many parts and defects in its construction, which caused it to break down frequently and stand idle, as was true also of other earth-moving machinery.[111] The progress made in heavy industrial machinery was often at the cost of failure to fulfill plans for making shoe, textile, and other consumer goods machinery.[112] Malyshev himself declared, in the speech quoted earlier, that "our designers do not always take into account the latest advances of science and technology when developing new machinery. They fail to make adequate study of the experience of machinery and equipment users. In some instances the heads of ministries and enterprises have shown inadmissible speed in putting new machinery into mass production without testing it thoroughly in advance."

---

[109] *Ibid.*, October 13, 1952.
[110] The 1940 figure is estimated by the U.S. Department of Commerce.
[111] Cf., for example, *Izvestia*, March 23, 1951, and September 14, 1951.
[112] *Pravda*, August 11, 13, and 14, 1953.

The main areas of quality weakness and quantitative production inadequacy in the Soviet machinery industry as of early 1954 seem suggested by the purchase offer for different types of machinery made to British businessmen who visited Moscow in February 1954. The Soviet Union offered to buy from Great Britain large quantities of power equipment, forging and pressing equipment, machine tools, textile and food processing machinery, railway equipment, steam boilers, rolling mill equipment, and hydraulic presses.

The Armament and Nuclear Energy Industries

For those skeptics who may have been unconvinced of the high quality and great magnitude of the Soviet arms capabilities by the demonstration of World War II, the events of 1949–53 provided what should have been convincing evidence. The explosion of the first Soviet atomic bomb in 1949 came far earlier than had generally been expected in the West, as did the explosion of the first Soviet thermonuclear weapon (presumably a fusion device of the hydrogen bomb type, though probably also containing other fusible material such as lithium) in August 1953. The Soviet weapons used by the Chinese Communist and North Korean forces during the Korean fighting of 1950–53 also were of high quality, particularly the MIG jet fighter which, published accounts indicate, was technically at the same high level as the primary United States jet fighter used in that war. The giant Soviet jet bomber — apparently in the same category as the United States B-52 — demonstrated in public on May 1, 1954, gave further evidence of Soviet capabilities.

In keeping with its policy of secrecy regarding military matters, the USSR has released extremely little information about all branches of its armament industry. It has made no secret of the fact that it sought to create modern plane, tank, gun, munitions, and other related factories during the 1920's and 1930's, as well as to build up the ship construction industry required to produce various types of naval vessels, including both surface ships and submarines. Much of the industrial development since 1928 has been aimed at providing the raw materials and machinery needed to equip and supply this armament industry from domestic sources alone. When the great test of these preparations came, during World War II, the losses of western plants proved so great that domestic Soviet arms production — even though expanded through conversion of many factories formerly making civilian equipment — proved inadequate, and large shipments of military items were required from abroad. Nevertheless there seems little reason to doubt that the USSR produced the great bulk of its World War II arms and munitions itself.

A few figures have been released regarding production of some items during World War II. In the last three years of the conflict, Soviet industry manufactured an annual average of over 30,000 tanks, self-propelled guns, and armored cars; about 40,000 planes; almost 120,000 artillery pieces of all calibres; nearly 450,000 light and heavy machine guns; over 3,000,000 rifles; and about 2,000,000 sub-machine guns. During 1942–44 an average of 100,000 mortars was produced annually. In 1944 over 240,000,000 shells, bombs, and mortar shells, as well as 7,400,000,000 cartridges, were produced.[113] Most of these figures are averages, so that they hide the actual sharp growth of output during the war, which is revealed by the following Soviet statement:

> During the war years airplane production in the USSR grew 4 times, tank production 7–8 times, artillery 6–7 times, mortar armament almost 8 times, military supplies almost 4 times. To the end of the Patriotic War the quantity of weapons in our army increased more than 5 times in comparison with the beginning period of the war, the quantity of airplanes 5 times, the quantity of tanks of contemporary models 15 times. . . .[114]

These high rates of growth taken in conjunction with the averages cited above suggest that at its peak during World War II Soviet industry probably turned out in one year more than 50,000 planes, 40,000 tanks, and 150,000 artillery pieces.

An offiicial summary of the tempo of growth of Soviet armaments production during the 1930's is provided by the following statement:

> During 1933–38 the military industry of the USSR increased by 286 per cent; the production of the aviation industry rose 5.5 times during five years.
>
> During the period from 1930 to 1939 the Red Army's supply of tanks increased 43 times, of airplanes 6.5 times, artillery equipment 7 times, tank and anti-tank artillery 70 times.[115]

Prof. M. G. Clark has made a careful study of the distribution of Soviet iron and steel consumption by different industries in the

---

[113] *Entsiklopediya*, cols. 827–28, and text of Fourth Five-Year Plan.
[114] *Voprosy Ekonomiki*, No. 5 (1950), p. 15.
[115] *Planovoye Khozyaistvo*, No. 1 (1946), p. 63.

1930's and has concluded that all munitions production is concealed in these statistics under the title "Miscellaneous Machine Building." On the basis of this analysis the data indicate that as early as 1932, production of arms and munitions of all types consumed almost 22 per cent of all Soviet iron and steel, and that this had increased to over 29 per cent by 1938. The absolute amounts used for that purpose rose in the same period from 1,646,600 metric tons to 4,986,200 metric tons. Steel used for munitions construction rose from 252,000 metric tons in 1932 to 880,000 tons in 1938. In 1932 munitions plants accounted for almost 46 per cent of all iron and steel used in construction of machine tool plants. By 1938 virtually all other machinery plant construction must have ceased, for iron and steel used in munitions construction accounted for 94.3 per cent of all that consumed in machine-building construction.[116]

Prof. Clark's statistical conclusions on the growth of Soviet munitions production during 1932–38 are presented in Table 20.

TABLE 20. Consumption of Iron and Steel in Munitions Industries of the USSR, 1932–38.

	1932	1933	1934	1935	1936	1937	1938
Total tonnage, Thous. Metric Tons	1646.6	1378.1	2204.6	2667.9	2873.3	4019.1	4986.2
Munitions as % of Machine Building	40.4	32.6	38.2	38.0	35.4	47.1	57.5
Munitions as % of All USSR Consumption	21.8	17.5	17.5	19.3	17.4	23.2	29.2
Munitions as % of Machine-Building Construction	45.8	65.9	72.8	73.4	82.5	84.5	94.3
Munitions as % of All USSR Construction	17.1	12.8	11.3	13.5	21.8	24.7	30.6

Source: M. G. Clark, *Some Economic Problems of the Soviet Iron and Steel Industry*, p. 42.

Though there are no official Soviet data, the available fragmentary evidence suggests that the course of the Soviet armament production effort since 1945 — excluding nuclear weapons output treated below — has been as follows. In 1945 and 1946 weapons output dropped sharply from the wartime high as industry was partially reconverted to civilian production. But this decline, it seems likely,

---

[116] Clark, *op. cit.*, pp. 41–42.

was not so great as to prevent the continuance of a relatively high level of weapons output in terms of prewar standards of such years as 1935 and 1936. From 1946 to mid-1950, the rapid recovery of the Soviet economy as a whole made available increasingly great supplies of materials and machinery for arms output, while experimentation went ahead rapidly on many fronts so that new weapons and new, improved models of old weapons were put into production in ever-increasing amounts. Guided missiles, jet and rocket planes, long-range bombers, snorkel-equipped submarines, radar-controlled anti-aircraft guns, and surface naval vessels, particularly cruisers and destroyers, received priority in this period, it seems likely.

After the outbreak of the Korean War and United Nations intervention in that struggle, it seems likely that there was a speedup in Soviet arms production. Reference has been made above to the evidence that in 1951 and 1952 some items of civilian machinery, particularly tractors, motor vehicles, and railroad equipment, were cut back in production, thus freeing materials and factory space for arms production. Presumably the pattern of this partial conversion to increased war production was somewhat similar to that of 1939–40, but the impact on the economy was less because of the much greater supply of resources available in the early 1950's as compared with the late 1930's.

One study has estimated that from 1945 to early 1953 the Soviet Union produced about 40,000 military airplanes, or twice the comparable United States production, with output in early 1953 running at the rate of about 10,000 planes annually.[117] Such an estimate cannot, of course, be considered precise, but the general order of magnitude does not seem unreasonable in the light of what is known regarding Soviet World War II production, the importance Soviet leaders attach to air power, and the numbers of Soviet planes seen in action during the Korean War.

The official published information on Soviet nuclear weapons progress has been confined to the announcements between 1949 and 1953, by the Soviet government and by the United States Atomic Energy Commission, of various Soviet atomic bomb explosions and one hydrogen bomb explosion. A knowledge of the physics of such

---

117 "The Red Air Forces," *Fortune*, February 1953, p. 120.

explosions, and of the magnitude of the United States effort required to produce these weapons, suffices to permit the drawing of important conclusions regarding the magnitude and nature of the Soviet atomic weapons industry.

The ability to explode these bombs implies that the Soviet Union has the vast industry required to produce the basic fissionable (atomic bomb) and fusable (hydrogen bomb) materials required by these weapons. To construct the corresponding United States industry has required the investment of well over $5,000,000,000. The Soviet industry is presumably not as large as this country's, but it would seem indubitable that this industry must represent an investment of at least several billion dollars in American prices. That this must have imposed a great strain on the much more limited Soviet economy seems self-evident, even if allowance is made for the scientific gains of successful espionage and also for the economies resulting from study of the earlier United States experience as described in the official *Atomic Energy for Military Purposes.*

The need for a vast industrial complex is evident from the nature of the materials required for nuclear explosions. An atomic bomb consists basically either of uranium 235 or plutonium. The former is a rare light form (isotope) of ordinary uranium 238. Uranium 235 occurs as only one part in 140 of ordinary uranium, and even ordinary uranium rarely occurs in rich ores. Even after ordinary uranium has been obtained, an expensive and time-consuming process, the separation of uranium 235 from uranium 238 is a complex and lengthy process requiring vast plants such as the giant diffusion and electromagnetic separation complexes at Oak Ridge, Tennessee. To produce plutonium, the more plentiful common isotope of uranium, uranium 238, is bombarded by neutrons in a nuclear reactor, also a process requiring expensive and complex production facilities.

The essential materials of the hydrogen bomb are the two forms (isotopes) of heavy hydrogen, hydrogen 2 (deuterium) and hydrogen 3 (tritium). Deuterium is relatively "cheap" as nuclear materials go since it occurs in nature and can relatively easily be isolated as in heavy water, that is, water whose hydrogen content is not ordinary hydrogen 1, but hydrogen 2, deuterium. Tritium, however, is a completely different matter since it does not occur in nature and must be most laboriously and expensively obtained by the neutron bombardment of lithium in nuclear reactors such as those built since 1950, at the cost of hundreds of millions of dollars, by the Atomic Energy Commission in this country.

From this brief excursion into nuclear physics, we can infer that the Soviet atomic and hydrogen bomb explosions represent undeniable evidence that the Soviet Union now has a major and most expensive atomic materials industry. This consists of large scale uranium mining facilities — within the USSR itself and at uranium deposits in East Germany and Czechoslovakia and perhaps elsewhere — as well as large separation plants for uranium 235 and large reactors for the production of plutonium and tritium. This obviously also implies that the Soviet Union now has a vast stock of engineering and scientific knowledge regarding nuclear energy, large numbers of personnel familiar with the problems of this field, and — because of the time span since the first atomic bomb explosion in 1949 — an appreciable stockpile of nuclear weapons.

Confirming this view is the fact that Soviet publications during 1953 and the first half of 1954 referred to these, among other, civilian applications of atomic products: the use of radioactive isotopes in agricultural and medical experimentation and in metallurgical control processes; the dating of organic remains by means of the radio-carbon technique; the creation of artificially radioactive substances for medical and other uses. A number of reports in early 1954 indicated, in fact, that the Soviet Union's production of radioactive substances had increased to the point where it could and did export such products to its Eastern European satellites.[118] The Soviet government claims a 5,000-kilowatt atomic power plant began operating June 27, 1954.

Consumer-Goods Industries

As noted earlier, consumer-goods output has usually been the neglected area of Soviet economic life, being slighted in comparison to the enormous resources devoted to expansion of all branches of heavy industry. Official statistics that purport to show greatly increased output of these commodities as compared to Czarist times or to the late 1920's are suspect because of the frequent noncomparability of data. The large fraction of this production that was

---

[118] An excellent summary of Soviet scientific progress in this and other fields is A. Nesmeyanov, "Dostizheniya i Zadachi Estestvennykh i Tekhnicheskikh Nauk," *Kommunist*, No. 6 (1954), pp. 60–77.

once turned out by individual craftsmen and their assistants does not appear to be taken adequately into account, and much of the increased production shown nominally by published data reflects merely the shift from artisan output to production in large government plants. In addition, the rapidly increasing urbanization of the Soviet population has resulted in a shift from household production of commodities such as bread to factory production, and the former type of output is not reflected in the data. It may well be that in the best periods of Soviet consumer-goods production, a larger total was turned out than in 1913 or 1928. But whether any such increase was proportionally much greater than the population rise is difficult to determine with the inadequate and unsatisfactory data available.

Consumer-goods production in the USSR takes several forms: output of large-scale state industry under various ministries; output of industrial and consumer cooperatives; and output of small-scale republic and local industry. In 1937 about one third of the output of consumer goods came from light industry, more than one third from different branches of the food industry, and somewhat less than one third from industrial cooperatives manufacturing a wide variety of food and nonfood products.[119] While large-scale plants predominate in some branches of this section of the economy, others consist primarily of small and medium-sized work shops that seek to utilize such local materials as are available or base their operations upon waste products of heavy industry. Also, some fraction of consumer-goods output is accounted for by heavy-industrial plants, which may produce such commodities as sidelines of their main production.

Over the years since 1928, consumer goods have usually been in none-too-abundant supply, and the usefulness of products available has been diminished by the low quality frequently characteristic of such Soviet output. Readers of the Soviet press in the 1930's and 1940's learned time and again of dresses that shrank catastrophically in the first rain, of shoes that fell apart after brief wearing, and of similar trials suffered by Soviet consumers. In the conditions of shortage that have been characteristic during most of the Soviet regime, many managers of consumer-goods plants and enterprises have apparently felt little compulsion to meet consumer desires as

---

[119] Balzak, et al., op. cit., p. 308.

regards quality and variety of output.[120] The low priority given these branches of production has also resulted, in all probability, in their getting the least desirable workers and managerial personnel on the whole, for rewards to talented persons have been higher in heavy industry. The fact that in May 1950, when heavy industry had reached an all-time output peak, it was difficult to buy furniture in Moscow is indicative of the situation in this area.[121] Shortages of consumer goods were most severe in the early 1930's and during World War II. The virtually complete concentration of output upon military needs during the latter period created clothing and food shortages and other difficulties of the most extreme sort. Improvement from the lowest levels took place in the middle 1930's and after 1945, but even the best conditions ever enjoyed by Soviet consumers would be considered deplorable by one accustomed to American standards, even during World War II. The level of material abundance at which Soviet citizens live is suggested by the fact that throughout the Soviet regime annual production of leather shoes has only rarely exceeded one pair per person, and has frequently been far below that poor level.

The much publicized 1953 program for increasing consumer-goods production substantially during 1954–56 had two facets of particular interest. First, it seemed to mean a government policy aimed at assuring production of such commodities in accordance with plan, in contrast with earlier years when consumer goods production usually fell well below plan targets because of the low priority given these industries in allocation of scarce material, machinery, and labor. Second, for the first time this program promised the Soviet people that there would be appreciable production of some durable consumer goods such as household refrigerators, washing machines, television sets, and the like. Though the quantities of such goods promised are small in comparison with the Soviet population — so that only the wealthiest and most influential groups in the country can expect to have such "luxuries" by 1956 — nevertheless, these promises opened up a vista that had virtually been unknown earlier. Whether the announced production goals will be achieved and, if they are, whether there will be still

[120] Cf. the typical complaints on this subject in *Izvestia*, August 4, 1949, and *Pravda*, September 13, 1949.

[121] *Moskovskaya Pravda*, May 8, 1950.

further production increases set beyond 1956 remain to be seen. *Textiles*. The statistical history of Soviet production of textiles is shown by the data below:

TABLE 21. Production of Soviet Textiles since 1928–29.

Year	Cotton Cloth	Wool Cloth	Linen	Silk Cloth‡
	(MILLION LINEAR METERS)			
1928–29	2,996	100.6	176.8	13.0
1940	3,886	120.3	272.2*	77.9
1945	1,605	61.7	†	†
1950	3,815	167.4	250.0§	126.0
1953	5,300	205.0	270.0§	388.0
1955 Goal:				
a. Fifth Five-Year Plan..	6,142	257.8	†	†
b. 1953 Revision	6,267	271.0	406.0	573.0
1956 Goal	6,500	335.0	†	635.0

* 1938. † Data unavailable. ‡ Includes synthetic fibres such as rayon and nylon. § Very rough estimate.
Sources: 1928-29 and 1938 (linen) — *Sot. Stroi.* *(1933-38)*, p. 73. 1940 — Cotton, *Tekstilnaya Promyshlennost*, No. 10 (1947); Wool, *Ibid.*, No. 11 (1947), p.35; Silk, Malenkov's speech of October 5, 1952. 1945 — Cotton, same as 1940; Wool, *Pravda*, December 21, 1949, and official economic reports for 1946-49. 1950 — Cotton and Wool, application of annual official percentage increases during 1946-50 to 1945 base; Linen — rough estimate taking account of statement in *Pravda*, October 28, 1953, that in 1953 linen output was still below 1940; Silk, Malenkov 1952 figure reduced by official percentages for output increase in percentages during 1951 and 1952. 1953 — *Pravda*, August 10, 1953, and January 31, 1954, plus linen statement referred to above. Original 1955 goals from Fifth Five-Year Plan directives. Revised 1955 goals and 1956 goals from consumer goods decree in *Pravda*, October 28, 1953.

As is clear from the data above, cotton cloth is the basic textile material in the Soviet Union. In Czarist times the bulk of cotton and other textile production was overwhelmingly concentrated in the Central Industrial area, the largest centers being Moscow, Ivanovo, and St. Petersburg (Leningrad), which received their raw materials from domestic sources such as Central Asia or from abroad. Soviet government development of cloth production was based upon intensive efforts to increase domestic cotton and other raw-material output so as to reduce or eliminate the need for large-scale imports from abroad. Old factories were reconstructed and a number of new factories were built, but the latter tended to be very large enterprises that took a long time to construct, typical of the "gigantomania" that afflicted Soviet industrial planning before the late 1930's. An effort was made to achieve a more even geographical pattern of production by building new plants in Western Siberia, particularly at Barnaul, and in Central Asia near the major cotton-growing areas.

In the development of the 1930's, however, a serious disproportion arose between spinning and weaving capacity, the shortage of the former preventing the utilization of all Soviet cotton output as well as the operation of weaving and hosiery mills at full capacity. During this period the cotton-textile industry consistently failed to achieve its production plans, a situation blamed officially on "saboteurs" and "wreckers," but probably really attributable to poor planning and the low priority of this industry.

During World War II, about 33 per cent of all Soviet spindles and 20 per cent of the country's looms were probably destroyed, while in unoccupied areas production was stopped in many plants to conserve manpower, fuel, and other resources.[122] From 1946 to 1950 cotton cloth output more than doubled as old factories were reopened and plants which had been destroyed were rebuilt, but the Fourth Five-Year Plan goal for 1950, 4,786,000,000 meters, was not reached, presumably a result reflecting once again the low priority of the textile industry. The original Fifth Five-Year Plan directives called for 1955 output 61 per cent above that of 1950, and in the early 1950's cotton cloth production finally exceeded the prewar levels. The cotton mill construction program for 1950–55 called for the construction of some of the largest cotton textile plants in the world at sites nearer the centers of cotton production in the southern and eastern parts of the country. The Kamyshin Cotton Combine, for example, is scheduled to have a daily production capacity of 1,000,000 meters of cloth, and other similar large plants are being built in Barnaul, Kherson, Stalinabad, Krasnodar, and Engels.[123] The 1953 revision of the cotton cloth goal for 1955 increased it only slightly, but stressed the need for more production of better quality types of cloth as well as the importance of a more varied assortment of textiles. In 1953, Moscow and Ivanovo Provinces each produced about one-third of all Soviet cotton cloth.[124]

The data above show that by 1950 wool and silk cloth had substantially exceeded prewar output levels, while linen production had failed to attain the prewar mark even in 1953. The speed-up in textile output ordered in 1953 resulted in the original Fifth Five-Year Plan goal for silk output in 1955 being reached approximately

[122] Bergson, et al., op. cit., p. 55.
[123] Pravda, October 13, 1952.
[124] Pravda and Izvestia, August 27, 1953.

in 1953, whereas the original wool cloth goal for 1955 was ordered reached in 1954. The largest factor in the very rapid rise of silk textile production was the rapid burgeoning of synthetic fibre production, which is included in the Soviet silk total. Such synthetic fibres were scheduled to reach by 1955 a production level 4.7 times as great as in 1950 and almost 11 times as great as in 1940. The 1941 Soviet economic plan provided for the output of about 32,000,000 meters of artificial silk.[125] If we assume that 1940 output was about 30,000,000 meters, the percentages cited above suggest that 1950 production of synthetic fibres may have been about 70,000,-000 meters and the 1955 goal about 330,000,000 meters.[126] The gross failure of linen output to reach prewar marks by as late as 1953 seems to be largely the result of the failure to achieve satisfactory levels of flax production.

Clothing and Knitwear. Before the Bolshevik revolution clothing and knitwear production in Russia was mainly on a handicraft basis, the work being done mostly by artisans, individually or in groups. Factory production was concentrated mainly in and around Moscow and St. Petersburg (Leningrad), near the sources of cloth and thread. Development under Soviet rule in the 1920's and 1930's consisted of a substantial shift from artisan to factory production, as new plants were built in many parts of the country, though the old concentration of output was not entirely ended.[127] Development of these industries was hindered, however, by the low priority given them in the securing of new capital and additional labor. The result was that output lagged far behind demand, and that quality of production was low. Indicative of the inadequate production was a government survey, made in 1936; it found that demand of consumers was for 967 million pairs of hosiery and 231 million pieces of knitted underwear. Planned production for that year, however, was for only 420 million pair of hosiery and 96 million pieces of knitted underwear, less than half the demand in each case.[128] The quality of Soviet output in this field is perhaps best indicated by this 1939 statement of Politburo member A. I. Mikoyan:

Are not the leaders of light industry ashamed when, for instance, a woman cannot wear a good pair of stockings without people saying

---

[125] *Gosudarstvenny Plan . . . na 1941 God, op. cit.*, p. 161.
[126] Basic percentages given in *Pravda*, October 13, 1952.
[127] Balzak, *et al., op. cit.*, pp. 317–18.
[128] *Trikotazhnaya Promyshlennost*, No. 6 (1936), pp. 1–3.

they must be imported? Why can't we produce more good stockings? Or take ties—if they are attractive, people say they must be imported. . . . Why should not good stockings and good ties be Soviet-made, not imported; why should not consumer goods be on a par with or superior to the best foreign make? [129]

How little this situation had changed more than 14 years later is indicated by the complaint voiced in Malenkov's speech of August 9, 1953:

> To the shame of our workers in industry, consumers often prefer to buy foreign-made articles simply because they are more attractive. Yet we have every opportunity to produce appealing textiles of good quality, smart and well-made clothing, durable and elegant footwear.

The growth of factory production of three important items of clothing during the period of Soviet rule is shown below: [130]

Year	Hosiery (MIL. PAIR)	Knitted Underwear (MILLION UNITS)	Knitted Outerwear
1933	250.9	36.1	17.2
1938	440.0	120.0	50.0
1941 Plan	538.0	132.4	55.1
1945	83.0	*	*
1950 Goal	580.0	*	*
1950 Actual	431.6	*	*
1955 Goal	777.0	382.0	88.0

* Data unavailable.

It is clear from the above that if the 1955 goals are actually achieved, then Soviet consumers will have more of these, and probably also other, types of clothing than ever before. But even the 1955 goals are equivalent on a per capita basis to annual production of only 3½ pairs of stockings, less than two suits of underwear, and less than one-half sweater or other knitted outer garment. Such levels are still far from affluence, though far above what Soviet consumers have historically had available.

---

[129] *Land of Socialism Today and Tomorrow*, p. 369.

[130] Sources: 1933 and 1938 — *Sot. Stroi. (1933–38)*, p. 73. 1941 Plan — *Gosudarstvenny Plan . . . na 1941 God*, p. 71. 1945 — H. Schwartz, *Russia's Postwar Economy*, p. 23. 1950 Goal — Fourth Five-Year Plan. 1950 Actual — *Pravda*, April 17, 1951, gives percentage relation between 1950 and 1945 hosiery output. 1955 Goal — *Pravda*, October 28, 1953.

Shoes. Before World War I, Russian shoe production was concentrated mainly in the hands of artisans working individually or in groups; shoe-manufacturing factories produced only about 8 million of the 50 to 55 million pairs produced annually.[131] The industry depended upon foreign sources for much of its raw materials and machinery. Development in the USSR before World War II was in the direction of building shoe factories; the private handicraft industry was wiped out. In addition, all branches of leather production were developed, in an effort to make the country independent of foreign supplies. The inadequacy of domestic leather supplies could not be remedied, however, because of the inadequate size of Soviet livestock herds, particularly after the great losses of the early 1930's. To make up this deficiency, production of leather substitutes as raw materials for shoes has been pushed vigorously. The old shoe-production factories in Moscow and Leningrad were rebuilt and expanded, and new ones were built in different parts of the country. Like other branches of consumer-goods production, shoe output fell catastrophically in the years of World War II.

After World War II, leather shoe production increased rapidly but the 1950 goal of the Fourth Five-Year Plan was not fulfilled, in part probably because the slow increase of livestock herds prevented the acquisition of adequate leather supplies and even the growing output of leather substitutes failed to make up for the deficiency in natural leather. The statistical history of factory shoe production under the Soviet regime is shown below: [132]

Year	Million Pair	Year	Million Pair
1929	48.8	1950	206.0
1940	205.0	1953	242.0
1945	64.5	1955 Goal	318.0

It seems likely that in 1951 and 1952 Soviet shoe production was on a plateau of about 250,000,000 pair whereas in 1953 it dropped

[131] *Vestnik Kozhevennoy Promyshlennosti i Torgovli*, No. 11 (1927), pp. 399–401.

[132] Sources: 1929 – *Sot. Stroi.* (1933–38), p. 73. 1940 – *Legkaya Promyshlennost*, No. 3–4 (1946), p. 2. 1945 – *Izvestia*, March 26, 1946. 1950 – *Pravda*, April 17, 1951. 1953 – *Ibid.*, August 8, 1953. 1955 Goal – *Ibid.*, October 28, 1953.

slightly to 242,000,000 pair. The 17 per cent increase reported for 1951 output over 1950 was adequate to make 1951 production about 250,000,000 pair, the figure predicted for 1952 in Malenkov's speech in October of that year. This hypothesis is strengthened by the failure of the 1952 economic report to give any percentage increase over 1951 for shoe production. The suspicion that leather shoe output actually declined in 1953 is also supported by the fact that the government economic report for 1953 claimed only a 4 per cent increase in production of leather shoes by the Ministry of Consumer Goods, saying nothing about total shoe output or about the large fraction of shoe production turned out by industrial cooperatives. This lack of progress during 1951–53 seems clearly related to the government's livestock difficulties, one reflection of which was the drop in cattle numbers during 1952.

Durable Consumer Goods. One of the major distinguishing features of Soviet economic development has been the lack of correspondence between the rapid growth of metal production and the failure of consumers to receive any analogous increase in durable consumer goods made of metal. Soviet production of passenger cars, refrigerators, vacuum cleaners, washing machines, and the like has been incredibly low when measured against the country's available metal supply. The reason, of course, was that this metal was needed for armaments and heavy industrial machinery, and consumers' wishes had little influence upon government allocations of available resources. The government's lack of interest in such items was further apparent from the frequent practice of assigning production of these items as sidelines for plants producing arms or heavy machinery. Plant managers given such assignments often regarded them as nuisances which drained off scarce resources from the primary production tasks of these plants, on the satisfactory fulfillment of which depended the managers' advancement or demotion. In this setting there can be little surprise in the fact that many of these sideline assignments were not fulfilled, while much of the little production received was of poor quality and high cost.[133]

The change of policy enunciated in 1953 after Stalin's death had already been foreshadowed in the public discussion regarding the

---

[133] Cf. the typical complaints in *Trud,* October 25 and December 8, 1950, and in *Izvestia,* December 27, 1951.

Fifth Five-Year Plan directives issued in 1952. Thus Mikoyan, speaking in October 1952, said that output of household refrigerators in 1955 would be ten times that of 1951. In the light of later data, this suggests that as late as 1951 Soviet annual refrigerator production, for a nation of over 200,000,000 people, was at most 33,000 units! [134] What the 1953 announcements did was to set up sharply higher production goals for a wide variety of consumer durable goods and to make clear that the attainment of these goals had high priority in the allocations of labor and materials. But there is little evidence even in the published material on the 1953 program that the Soviet government contemplated setting up a large network of plants for durable consumer goods. Rather, many of the assignments were given to such ministries as those concerned with armaments, aviation, metallurgical, and heavy machinery production. The "sideline" nature of these assignments for these ministries would seem plain, thus increasing the probability of difficulties similar to those experienced in the past. Nevertheless, the emphasis put upon these assignments in government announcements would seem to suggest that enough pressure will be exerted to secure substantial progress, barring some major change in the international situation in 1954 or 1955.

In the following compilation an effort has been made to bring together some of the fragmentary data on actual and planned Soviet production of these durable consumer goods: [135]

Commodity	Prewar	1950	1954 Goal	1955 Goal
Bicycles	385,600*	655,000	2,510,000	3,445,000
Sewing Machines	502,500*	800,000‡	1,335,000	2,615,000
Electric Irons	483,700*	486,000	3,550,000	4,375,000
Refrigerators	1,500†	20,000‡	207,000	330,000
Vacuum Cleaners	§	§	243,000	483,000
Washing Machines	§	§	111,000	296,300
Watches	635,000*	7,200,000	16,000,000	22,000,000
Radios	202,400*	1,000,000	2,861,000	3,767,000
Television Sets	none	100,000	325,000	760,000
Phonographs	843,500*	§	921,000	1,125,000
Cameras	207,500*	§	765,000	1,000,000

* 1938. † 1941 Plan. ‡ Rough estimate. § Data unavailable.

[134] *Pravda*, October 12, 1952, and October 28, 1953.

[135] Sources: 1938 — *Sot. Stroi. (1933-38)*, p. 141. 1941 Plan — *Gosudarstvenny Plan . . . na 1941 God*, p. 171. 1950, and 1954 and 1955 goals — given in or calculated from Mikoyan's speech in *Pravda*, October 25, 1953, and the consumer goods decree in *Pravda*, October 28, 1953.

These data make plain that a very impressive increase in the output of these goods is sought by 1955. But bearing in mind that the Soviet population will be not far from 220,000,000 persons in that year, it is apparent that the 1955 levels, even if attained, will permit only the upper groups of Soviet society to have vacuum cleaners, washing machines, refrigerators, television, and the like.

Cooperative and Local Production. As noted above, production of consumer goods by local state industry and by industrial cooperatives covers a wide range of commodities. Enterprises in this category can be thought of as the Soviet equivalent of the old handicraft and domestic industries of Czarist Russia. The government's intention in sponsoring this decentralized type of organization is presumably to permit maximum flexibility in adjusting production to demand and to encourage local initiative in developing output on the basis of local raw materials and the wastes and surpluses of large plants in other fields. But this type of organization also probably reflects government unwillingness to sponsor the growth of consumer-goods output with the same high capital investment as has been devoted to heavy industry. Cooperative and local industry production before World War II was concentrated in Moscow, Leningrad, Kiev, and Kharkov, while such output was small or insignificant in the area from the Volga River to the Pacific.[136] In the postwar period, the same concentration of local industry and industrial cooperatives has persisted. In 1947 almost half of all production by local industry in the RSFSR came from Moscow, while production in the regions of the Volga, Urals, Siberia, and the Far East was only 13 per cent, equal to only about one quarter of the output in Moscow alone.[137]

During World War II, these small consumer-goods enterprises were either wiped out or converted entirely to subcontracting for military production. Apparently disturbed by the slow revival of state-operated consumer-goods plants, the Soviet government took decisive action in late 1946 to stimulate industrial cooperatives toward much greater production of consumer goods, giving them the incentives and privileges discussed in the previous chapter. The 1947 goals set for these enterprises included production of about 30,000,000 pairs of shoes; 40,000,000 pairs of hosiery; 54,-

---

[136] *Planovoye Khozyaistvo,* No. 9 (1939), p. 113.
[137] *Ibid.,* No. 4 (1948), p. 56.

000,000 meters of cotton cloth; and so forth.[138] The government
drive to encourage cooperative production apparently had some
significant results, but as late as mid-1949 the record for the first
half of that year was summarized in this fashion:

> Enterprises of industrial cooperatives substantially underfilled pro-
> duction plans for construction materials, iron, enamel and glass
> utensils, shoes, linen and silk cloth. The quality of a significant part
> of goods produced is still unsatisfactory, the assortment is limited,
> and prices are high in a series of cases.[139]

In addition, however, such cooperative output was reported to exceed prewar levels and to have improved considerably over earlier
postwar years.[140] A lengthy description of the very important local
industry in Moscow Province as of May 1950 painted a picture of
chaotic disorganization, great shortages of material, poor planning,
failure to utilize capacity fully, and inadequate production.[141]

A government decree issued in late 1953 indicated that the
many deficiencies of local industry and industrial cooperatives continued to exist at that time. It spoke of their "regular failure to
meet the government output plan for many goods and the low
quality of the products manufactured" by them. It gave this description of their physical facilities: [142]

> Many local industry and industrial cooperative enterprises occupy
> residences and basements unfitted for production. . . . Most enter-
> prises are poorly mechanized, have outmoded equipment with low
> productive capacity. They are not provided with qualified personnel
> so that labor productivity is low and manufacturing cost high.

Conditions were so bad that there had apparently been much
Soviet speculation that the industrial cooperative system might be
abolished. This at least seems a fair conclusion from the lengths
to which Mikoyan went in August 1953 to assure cooperative officials that their organizations were an integral part of the Soviet
productive system and would be continued and strengthened. He
boasted that their output had risen in value from 28,000,000,000
rubles in 1940 to 42,000,000,000 rubles in 1952 and would be worth

138 Schwartz, *Russia's Postwar Economy*, p. 44. *Izvestia*, November 12 and
14, 1946. *Pravda*, December 29, 1946.
139 *Izvestia*, August 6, 1949.
140 *Ibid.*, June 1, 1949.
141 *Moskovskaya Pravda*, May 8, 10, 12, and 17, 1950.
142 *Pravda*, October 28, 1953.

47,000,000,000 rubles in 1953. In the next two or three years, he said, they would double their marketed output.[143] The head of these cooperatives had revealed earlier that there were 16,000 such organizations over the country employing 1,800,000 workers.[144]

The government program revealed in the decree quoted above provided for extensive capital investment in local industry and industrial cooperatives so as to provide them with needed machinery, assembly-line equipment, premises and the like. Soviet banks were ordered to provide loans of up to 500,000 rubles to different local and cooperative enterprises in order to facilitate the improvement and expansion of their output.

---

[143] *Pravda*, August 26, 1953.
[144] *Izvestia*, August 8, 1953.

CHAPTER VIII

THE ORGANIZATION OF AGRICULTURE

TWICE DURING THE YEAR after Stalin's death, in September 1953 and February 1954, the first secretary of the Communist Party of the Soviet Union, Nikita S. Khrushchev, made major speeches surveying the state of Soviet agriculture. The picture of Soviet farm economics he painted had both bright and dark spots, but complaints and admissions of failure overshadowed boasts of success. Besides attesting to incompetence, carelessness, poor planning, and similar reasons for poor performance, his speeches made it clear that the ancient struggle between the Soviet government and the millions of Soviet peasants was still far from ended, but continued as one of the basic dynamic forces in Soviet society. No one can read these speeches without concluding that the failure of Stalinist agricultural policy has created one of the great weaknesses — perhaps *the* greatest economic weakness and point of political vulnerability — of post-Stalinist Russia.[1]

Soviet agriculture as described by Khrushchev consisted of 94,000 collective farms, 8,950 Machine Tractor Stations (MTS) and Machinery Stations for Livestock (MZhS), and over 4,700 state farms. This is a complex far different from the aggregate formed by the roughly 25,000,000 small peasant farms which had existed three decades earlier. In this chapter, the present organization of Soviet agriculture will be considered against the background of its evaluation from 1917 to 1954. An attempt will be made in this consideration to take into account both the nominal forms of this or-

---

[1] Khrushchev's speeches appeared in the Soviet press, September 15, 1953, and March 21, 1954. For English translations, cf. *The Current Digest of the Soviet Press,* November 7, 1953, and May 5, 1954.

ganization, and the realities underlying the changes in these forms over time.

The Agricultural Plan

Like other parts of the Soviet economy, agriculture is directed by the national economic plan, but the extent and effectiveness of planned control are significantly weaker here than in other productive areas. Nature bows not to the planner's dictum. The fluctuations of climatic conditions produce unpredictable variations in harvests. The very nature of agriculture is such that the human beings engaged in it are dispersed over large areas. Control over them, even on a collective farm, is far more difficult than similar control over workers concentrated by the hundreds or thousands in the limited area of a factory. These and other differences between farming and other occupations have not been adequate to prevent a significant degree of planned control and development in Soviet agriculture, but the hopes of the planners have often been frustrated by nature or by the recalcitrance of the human beings ordered to turn plans into reality.

Agricultural objectives set down in the five-year plans cover such matters as acreages to be planted in different crops, average yields to be attained for each crop, the growth of livestock herds, expansion of farm machinery, the extent of irrigation projects, and so on. Similar but more detailed national objectives, prepared by the ministries concerned with agriculture and the State Planning Committee, are set down in the plans for each year. Special plans governing particular aspects of agricultural activity are published from time to time as need arises. The long-range program for afforestation and other antidrought measures, published in the fall of 1948, are examples of this more specialized type of state planning.

The comprehensive national programs are broken down through the chain of geographical administrative units, first the Union Republic, then the province and smaller areas, until finally the plan influences the activity of each farm and other productive unit in Soviet agriculture. In this way the transition is made from the national goal to plant, for example, 100 million hectares [2] in grain and the final decision by a particular farm to sow 100 hectares of

---

[2] A hectare is approximately 2½ acres.

its land in various grain crops. It is no simple task to allocate correctly the national agricultural objectives among different areas. Errors in such allocations cause difficulties at times, suggesting that the problems involved are by no means all solved.

The actual work of raising crops and livestock is carried on by three kinds of farms. The most important are the collective farms (*kolkhozy*), which produce the great bulk of agricultural output. The state farms (*sovkhozy*) produce a much smaller fraction of farm produce but are extremely important in some specialized products. Least important are the few remaining small peasant farms, which produce only a very small portion of all Soviet food. A fourth major unit important in production is the Machine Tractor Station (MTS), which works closely with the collective farms.

Most of Soviet agriculture relating to collective farms is directed by the Ministry of Agriculture, which has an elaborate central organization in Moscow and an extensive field apparatus. Its agents are to be found in every part of the Soviet Union. The ministry and its agents supervise the execution of the collective-farm plan and the day-to-day progress of agricultural activity. It collects a huge volume of agricultural statistics, almost none of which, however, are made public. Not the least of the ministry's functions is its research activity, carried on in almost a thousand agricultural research institutions of many kinds.[3] Most state farms are directed by the Ministry of State Farms, which exercises complete control over these state-owned and -operated units.

Aside from the general Communist control of the Soviet state and economy, the Communist Party plays a major role directly in the farm areas. In one speech referred to above, Khrushchev revealed that 76,000 out of 94,000 collective farms had party units, and there were more than 1,000,000 party members in the countryside, along with over 2,000,000 members of the Young Communist League. In addition each MTS has a party group attached to it with the duty of exercising direct control over farm work in the area served by the MTS.

The magnitude of the bureaucracy required to exercise state and party control may be inferred from Khrushchev's statement that there are between five and six officials for each collective, that is,

---

[3] Eric Ashby, *A Scientist in Russia*, pp. 30–34 and 212–15. New York: Penguin Books, 1947.

over 500,000 supervisors, aside from the communists on the collective farms. He blamed the defects of this bureaucracy for much that was wrong with these farms. This is his scathing description of the Soviet agricultural ministry:

> The bureaucratic structure is very unwieldy, including many administrations and divisions which duplicate each other and often do little or nothing. It is not surprising that the ministry fails to show maneuverability and accuracy in directing local organs, permitting bureaucracy and red tape in solving urgent problems. The Ministry . . . is poorly linked with practical work and is isolated from the collective farms and MTS. Not knowing the true state of affairs in each locality, the ministry nevertheless tries to regulate from the center all aspects of the activities of local farm agencies, collective farms, and MTS, giving instructions for which there is often no need in the localities.

The Collective Farm

In theory a collective farm is a democratic, cooperative association of farmers who have pooled their land and capital to form a large enterprise, which they operate in common, sharing its net proceeds in proportion to the quantity and quality of work they do. It is claimed that these large farms make for more efficient and bountiful production, since they avoid the inefficiencies and wastes of small peasant farming. In addition it is said that only by their formation was it possible to secure the use of modern agricultural techniques, particularly those associated with the use of tractors and other agricultural machinery. In the United States, however, machinery and scientific techniques are employed on family farms much smaller than the average collective farm.

Initially, during the 1920's, three major types of collectives were experimented with: the *toz,* the *artel,* and the *commune.* Today the *artel* is the standard type of collective farm.[4] The *toz* or "Society for Joint Land Cultivation," was simply a production cooperative. Farmers joined together to work their land and to buy and use expensive machinery. Each owner retained his rights to his own plots of land and to the harvest on this land, as well as to his livestock and tools. The *commune* was at the other extreme. All

---

[4] In 1933, 96.3 per cent of all collectives were *artels;* 1.9 per cent *toz;* and 1.8 per cent *communes.* Cf. Naum Jasny, *The Socialized Agriculture of the USSR,* p. 320. Stanford, California: Stanford University Press, 1949.

production capital — livestock, machinery, implements, barns, and so on — was owned by the group, whose members used it cooperatively in working the land. Members lived in community dormitories; their food was cooked in community kitchens; and their children were cared for in community nurseries. It is not surprising that the poorest peasants, who had no or virtually no private property, composed the bulk of commune members.

The *artel* is intermediate between those two forms. In it, most production is carried on collectively, and most means of production are owned by the *kolkhoz* (singular of *kolkhozy*); but some private production is carried on separately by each member family. Each farmer owns some agricultural capital such as livestock and simple tools. But he also shares in the result of the collective work in which he has participated. He thus receives both a collective and a private income, which he and his family can consume as they wish. Obviously this is a compromise between fully socialistic and fully individualistic production. As we shall see, many of the problems of *kolkhoz* agriculture have arisen from the instability of this compromise.

The Kolkhoz *Charter*

Each collective farm has a charter, or constitution, which defines its organizational structure, the responsibilities of collective farmers, and similar important matters. The present charter is largely the same as that drawn up by the government in 1935, which modified earlier practices. The description of collective farm organization that follows is based upon that charter and subsequent changes made in it.[5]

The collective farm's land is an aggregate area to be used for the profit of the collective farm as its needs dictate. The land itself belongs to the state, but the *kolkhoz* has the right to permanent use, a right confirmed by a government certificate that also indicates the boundaries of this area. This land may not be sold, bought, or leased. Each peasant family belonging to the *kolkhoz* has the right to a garden plot, varying in size in different areas from one quarter of one hectare to one hectare, which the members of the peasant

---

[5] An English translation of the charter is given in Hubbard, *The Economics of Soviet Agriculture,* pp. 131–47, and Gsovski, *Soviet Civil Law,* Vol. 2, pp. 441–62.

family may cultivate as they see fit. None of the *kolkhoz* land may be given to a member who withdraws, and the area is, in general, inviolate.

Despite these charter provisions, the later history of collective farms has revealed many instances in which *kolkhoz* land has been alienated illegally: by *kolkhozniki* (collective farmers) wishing to expand their private gardens beyond the legal maximum, by government organizations wishing to raise foodstuffs for their employees, and so on. At various times — as in 1939 and 1946 — the government has had to step in to restore large areas to the collective farms.

The *kolkhoz* owns all means of production save large machinery required to operate its enterprise. The means include cattle, simple implements, farm buildings, flour mills and other initial processing equipment, seed, fodder, and the like. The *kolkhozniki* may use privately, that is, own, their dwelling houses, garden tools, private livestock, and the buildings necessary to house these livestock. The number of animals a peasant household may own is rigidly limited, the actual quantity depending upon the area. In regions primarily devoted to crop-raising, for example, the limits are one cow, two calves, one or two sows (depending upon the discretion of the farm administration) and their progeny, up to ten sheep or goats, an unlimited number of poultry and rabbits, and up to twenty beehives.

The *kolkhoz* is obligated to carry on its work on the basis of an annual operating plan. This plan is drawn up by taking into account the government agricultural plan and the collective's obligations to the state under it. Farm operations must be carried on properly, and the farm must be operated so as to maximize production and conserve *kolkhoz* assets. It is the obligation of the collective also to improve the technical proficiency of its members and to provide them with amenities such as newspapers, books, barber shops, and clean streets.

Under the charter the general meeting of members is the highest authority on the collective farm. It elects all officers; decides on the acceptance of new members and the expulsion of old ones; and approves all budgets, plans, and other basic documents and decisions prepared by the administrative officers. Between general meetings, management of the farm is in the hands of the managing committee, consisting of five to nine committeemen (depending upon the collective's size), elected by the members at the general assembly. The highest official in the collective farm is the chairman, who is also, in theory, democratically elected by the general assembly.

With a few exceptions all collective farm work must be done by its members. Specialists may be hired if needed, and extra help may be taken on during harvest or other rush seasons. Otherwise the *kolkhozniki* and members of their families are the entire labor force of the farm.

Labor organization on each *kolkhoz* is obtained by means of division of the membership into a number of brigades. Each brigade is in theory composed of 50 to 100 members assigned to work in it for a period of time equal to the period of the crop rotation involved, that is, three or more years in most cases. The brigade is equipped with the necessary machinery, livestock, and other equipment to perform its task. It is headed by a brigadier, who is in complete charge of its activities. Many brigades are further subdivided into small work squads, usually composed of a dozen or fewer persons. This work squad is called a *zveno*, or link. A major problem of collective farm organization over the past two decades has been the turnover in membership of brigades and links. For best results the Soviet government has sought to obtain relatively constant membership in these organizations from year to year. The thought behind this has been that workers who do the same task and work on the same ground or livestock for several years will become most proficient at their task. Moreover, as we shall see below, this problem of constant membership of work teams, whether brigades or links, is closely connected with the question of increasing the incentive of collective farm members for maximum production. Although collective farm charters have provided for constant membership of these work teams since 1935 at least, this problem is still a matter of concern at the present.

Labor on the collective farm is measured in terms of an arbitrary unit, the work day. A work day is not a chronological day. Rather, it is a measure applied to the performance of a certain norm of work. For example, a worker who weeds an acre of onions may be given one-half a work day credit for his activity. On the other hand, a cotton harvester who has picked two acres may be given two-and-a-half work days credit. Under a reform adopted by the Soviet government in early 1948, there are nine different work-day rates for different tasks. These range from one-half a work day, the compensation for the least skilled and least arduous type of work, to two-and-a-half work days, the compensation for the most skilled and most arduous type of work. By use of this measure the Soviet government attempts to obtain a means of payment that reflects both the quantity and the quality of the work of each collective farmer. In particular, in the postwar period, the work-day method of payment has been modified to obtain a measure of payment related to the output received for the work expended. Each brigade and link receives a one per cent addition to the number of work days it has earned for each per cent by which its production exceeds the planned output. Conversely, for each per cent by which its crop or livestock outputs falls below the plan, one per cent of the work days it has earned is deducted, with a maximum deduction of 25 per cent. The intention here is obviously to reward those workers who do the best work and to penalize slackers. It is clear that such bonuses and deductions can only be applied effectively if the same workers are responsible all through the crop year or the livestock period for a particular portion of the work. It is for this reason that the Soviet government is now extremely anxious to obtain constancy in the membership of brigades and links engaged in collective farm work.

The similarities between this method of compensation for agricultural work and industrial wage rates are clear. The work-day unit permits the application of piece rates to agriculture. In addition, the rewards and deductions dependent upon amount of output permit greater inequality between workers — inequality, of course, determined by their production. All this is the application in agriculture of principles that have for a long time been dominant in the payments to industrial workers.[6]

The annual production and income of a collective farm are disposed of in a rather complicated fashion. The state has first claim upon production and receives a large share of all crop and livestock products. Most of the state's share is obtained in three ways. The first is the tax in kind, levied on all farm production. For grains, oilseeds, potatoes, vegetables, and certain other crops, this tax is computed as a delivery quota of a certain amount per unit of arable land. For cotton, sugar beets, flax, and some minor crops, contracts

[6] *Sotsialisticheskoye Selskoye Khozyaistvo,* July 1948, p. 8.

are drawn up between government agencies and collective farms indicating the amounts to be delivered. Obligatory livestock product deliveries are calculated on the basis of fixed amounts per unit of all agricultural land. These tax deliveries are paid for by the government, but usually at very low prices per unit, amounts far less than the same products could be sold for in the open market. Delivery quotas vary among regions and farms, depending upon differential fertility. Although the Soviet government nominally does not charge collective farms rent for their land, the state's profit on these obligatory deliveries is clearly an analogous type of income. An important economic consequence of this tax in kind is the shifting of the full burden of crop and livestock output fluctuations resulting from bad weather, insect infestation, disease, and so on to the collective farm, since the tax must be paid regardless of rises or falls in production. If crops are poor, the collective farm and its members get less, because the state's demands are usually unaltered. If crops are very good, the state usually gets more than originally planned, paying somewhat higher prices for above-plan deliveries. Collective farmers are constantly admonished that their "first commandment" is to provide the state with obligatory deliveries to meet this tax. Great pressure is exerted to assure that they do so and to guard against any holding back or concealment of products demanded by the state.

In addition to the tax in kind, the state receives another significant fraction of crop production as payment for the services performed by the equipment of Machine Tractor Stations. Third and relatively minor are the repayments each year of seed loans and other borrowings in kind from the government.

Since Stalin's death, the contracting system has assumed greater importance than before. In early 1954 it was being applied not only to industrial crops (cotton, sugar beets, flax, hemp, jute, oil seeds) and citrus fruits and tea, but also to purchases of grain, meats, milk, and other foods by government agencies securing farm surpluses left over after the tax in kind has been paid to the government and payment in kind has been made to Machine Tractor Stations. In the case of industrial crops, contracts are made with farms for the delivery of certain amounts of each raw material, the government contracting organization providing a great deal of technical direction and other aid and supervision during the entire period from soil preparation to harvest. As work on the crop progresses, the state agency pays advances to the collective farm. Prices paid the farms for a given crop depend in part on quality, but also in part on the degree to which the farm succeeds in exceeding the originally planned delivery total or the planned yield per hectare. Bonuses for high excess deliveries rise sharply. In addition farms are paid by being sold needed goods at very low prices. Thus in 1953 Uzbek cotton farms were able to buy quantities of butter and sugar for roughly one-third the normal retail prices, the amounts so puchasable being determined by the amounts of cotton delivered. The entire emphasis in making contracts is to provide farms with the maximum income stimulus to increasing production and contract sales to the government.[7]

After the government's demands have been met, various portions of the farm's production are reserved for seed, for fodder, for reserve against future crop failure, and for funds for special purposes, such as that for subsistence of those unable to work — that is, invalids, the aged, and others.

The remaining production of the farm is divided into two parts, on the basis of the decision of the general assembly of collective farm members. One part is sold, either to the government, to co-operative organizations, or on the open market. It is from these sales that the farm usually receives the bulk of its monetary income. A relatively small amount of produce sold freely in this fashion brings in much more income usually than a much larger amount of produce delivered in payment of the tax in kind to the government. The prices received are highest on the free markets, where sales are made directly to consumers, but production may not be sold on these markets until all obligations for delivery to the state are met.

The rest of the collective farm production is distributed among the members as payment in kind. The work days earned by all members during the year are totaled and then divided into the output to get a value per work day for each type of production. Thus a work day on a particular farm may be found to be worth two kilograms of grain. A farmer who has earned 150 work days during the year will therefore get 300 kilograms of grain as part of his

[7] Cf. the valuable description and data in M. Moiseev, "Printsip Materialnoi Zainteresovannosti i Kontraktsiya Selskokhozyaistvennykh Produktov," *Sotsialisticheskoye Selskoye Khozyaistvo,* No. 3 (1954), pp. 44–66.

earnings for the entire year. In computing the number of work days, percentage adjustments upward and downward are made to allow for overfulfillment or underfulfillment of output plans, as indicated above.

The disposition of the grain crops raised by collective farms during 1937, 1938, and 1939 is shown in Table 22.

TABLE 22. Distribution of Grain Crops of Collective Farms in the Soviet Union, 1937–39.

Item	1937 %	1938 %	1939 %
A. Deliveries to the state:			
1. Obligatory deliveries	12.2	15.0	14.3
2. Payments in kind to MTS.............	13.9	16.0	19.2
3. Return of seed loans	1.5	2.0	4.0
Total	27.6	33.0	37.5
B. Sales to the state and on free markets........	4.8	5.1*	4.0
C. Collective requirements and reserves:			
1. Seed requirements and reserves........	16.3	18.6	18.2
2. Feed requirements and reserves........	12.7	13.6	13.9
3. Reserve for aiding those in need........	1.1	0.8	0.8
4. Other expenditures	1.6	2.0	2.7
Total	31.7	35.0	35.6
D. Distributed to collective farmers on the basis of "work days" worked	35.9	26.9	22.9
Grand Total	100.0	100.0	100.0

* A statement was made that the 1.0 per cent designated for sale was unsold at the "beginning of the year," presumably of 1939.
Source: Lazar Volin, "The *Kolkhoz* (Collective Farm) in the Soviet Union," *Foreign Agriculture*, November-December 1947, p. 150.

It is worth noting in Table 22 that the government took a much larger fraction of the crop in the relatively poor production years, 1938 and 1939, than in the very good year, 1937. The diminution of the amount of grain distributed among collective farmers in 1938 and 1939 as compared with that they received in 1937 was thus accentuated far beyond the drop resulting merely from the decrease in production.

The monetary income of the collective farm is divided in rather similar fashion. The state income tax on collective farms has first claim upon this income. Money must be used also to pay for insurance on the property of the collective farm. Between 10 and 15 per cent of the money income must be set aside for inclusion in the indivisible fund, that is, the capital fund, of the collective farm, which is used to finance capital construction and repair on the *Kolkhoz*. Monetary income is also used to pay for any outside labor, services, and materials that a collective farm buys during the year. The remaining monetary income is divided among collective farmers, in proportion to the number of work days earned.

Around this matter of the division of the collective farm's production and income rages one of the fiercest struggles of Soviet life. Historically, the government's ability to take large quantities of the farm produce at extremely low procurement prices and then to resell this produce at far higher prices has been one of the most important domestic sources of the vast capital required for Soviet industrialization. The price for this has been paid by the collective farm members, whose consequent low returns for their work on the collective fields are discussed in a later section. Increasingly since World War II the Soviet government has learned that if it wishes to get higher production of vital farm products, it must increase the price it pays to the collective farms. This was done with respect to cotton in the late 1940's, with gratifying results. One of the most important steps taken in September 1953 in the effort to improve the collectives' livestock output was the substantial raising of procurement prices as well as the increase in prices paid for purchases above the obligatory delivery norms. In the spring of 1954, prices were increased also for flax and hemp deliveries. This central conflict between the government's desire for cheap farm produce and the peasants' desire for adequate prices was one of the major themes of Stalin's last major theoretical article regarding the economic problems of socialism. It seems significant that shortly after his death his proposed solution, the gradual but inexorable institution of a system of barter with the farms receiving industrial products directly for their crops and livestock, was rejected as a matter for the distant future. Instead the steps taken in September 1953 emphasized the increase of collective farms' monetary incomes through higher prices and reduced quotas of obligatory deliveries which are paid for at the lowest rates.

Khrushchev's September 1953 speech illuminated another aspect of this problem when he pointed out that, in practice, local officials often used the system of obligatory deliveries as a sort of progressive income tax in kind. Instead of applying equal quotas — based on acreage — to all farms, these local authorities often forced more prosperous farms to deliver much higher procurement quotas than poorer farms, thus depriving the better collectives of part of the fruits of their more efficient labor.

Postwar Organizational Developments

In early 1950, there were 254,000 collective farms in the USSR.[8] This figure represented an increase of 32,000 over the number reported in April 1947.[9] This increase was attributable mainly to the rapid collectivization of peasant farms that took place during 1948 and 1949 in the Baltic States, Eastern Poland, the Carpatho-Ukraine, and other areas annexed by the USSR since 1939. Most of these areas had gone through a land reform that had broken up large estates and parceled their land and property out among many peasant families. The beginnings of collectivization had been made in these areas before World War II, but were wiped out during that conflict so that the process had to begin anew after 1945. The pace of this collectivization may be illustrated by the case of Estonia, which had 47 collective farms in April 1948,[10] and over 3,000 a year and a half later in November 1949.[11] That such speedy transformation of the agricultural structure in these areas could have taken place without considerable government coercion and pressure, similar to that which took place in the USSR in the early 1930's, seems most unlikely.

The progress achieved in collectivizing the formerly independent areas is indicated by Table 23.

The number of peasant families belonging to all collective farms in 1940 was 19,200,000.[12] Later data have not been published. The corresponding number in 1950 may have been approximately the same if, as is perhaps not unlikely, wartime losses of collective farm population had been offset by postwar collectivization in the newer Sovietized areas. In 1938, collective farms had almost 90 per cent of the sown area of the USSR and accounted for almost 85 per cent

---

[8] *Pravda*, March 11, 1950.
[9] *Ibid.*, April 11, 1947.
[10] *Izvestia*, April 20, 1948.
[11] *Ibid.*, November 25, 1949.
[12] *Problemy Ekonomiki*, No. 1 (1941), p. 35.

TABLE 23. Collectivization in Soviet Territories Acquired since 1939, Based on Data for Late 1949 and Early 1950.

Area	Number of Collectives	Number of Peasant Families Collectivized	Per Cent of Peasant Families Collectivized
West Ukraine	over 7,000	1,200,000	95
West Belorussia	4,000	200,000	*
Latvia	4,035	*	over 95
Estonia	3,015	*	80
West Moldavia	1,743	*	over 80
Lithuania	6,300	*	over 75
Kaliningrad Province.	452	*	*
South Sakhalin	69	*	*
Tannu Tuva	100	*	*

Sources: West Ukraine—*Pravda Ukrainy*, March 7, 1950; West Belorussia—*Pravda*, October 30, 1949; Latvia—*Bolshevik*, No. 20 (1949), and *Pravda*, June 19, 1950; Estonia —*Izvestia*, November 25, 1949; West Moldavia—*Pravda*, December 6, 1949; Lithuania— *Pravda*, January 28, 1950, and June 16, 1950; Kaliningrad Province—*Pravda*, February 26, 1950; South Sakhalin—*Komsomolskaya Pravda*, August 2, 1949; and Tannu Tuva— *Izvestia*, October 11, 1949.

of all gross agricultural production. By 1950 the corresponding percentages may not have been very different.

The average size of collective farms has varied widely among different areas of the USSR in the past, but recent trends have been toward achieving greater uniformity by combining small collective farms into larger aggregates. In the USSR as a whole in 1938, the average collective farm had 78 families working about 3,800 acres of land, of which about 1,200 acres were sown to crops.[13] This average of about 15 acres sown to crops per peasant family is of course several times smaller than the corresponding sown acreage per farm family in the United States and is indicative of the greater pressure of population on the arable land in the USSR.

The variation in the size of collective farms in the USSR before World War II is strikingly indicated by data for January 1, 1938, regarding the distribution of farms by number of peasant families. About 25 per cent of the *kolkhozy* had 30 or fewer families; almost 43 per cent had between 31 and 80 families; and little more than 20 per cent had between 81 and 150 families. The remainder, about 10 per cent of all collectives, had over 150 families each, though only 2 per cent had more than 300 families.[14]

[13] Lazar Volin, "The *Kolkhoz* (Collective Farm) in the Soviet Union," *Foreign Agriculture*, November-December 1947, p. 158.
[14] Jasny, *op. cit.*, p. 319.

Different population densities and agricultural conditions in different areas accounted for these variations. Collective farms were often formed on the bases of existing villages, which in turn traced their origin and size back to the serf villages of the feudal era. In many areas, therefore, the collective farm pattern before 1950 reflected historical influences that had determined the earlier pattern of rural settlement, rather than any planning by Soviet authorities. In the late 1920's some Soviet authorities, impressed by the possibilities of mechanized agriculture, had looked forward to creating giant farms, some of them with as much as 250,000 acres in crops.[15] But lack of sufficient equipment and experienced and trained personnel, and the rapidity of collectivization in the early 1930's, all combined against any experimentation with a significant number of extraordinarily large collective farms at that time. On the contrary, many small and moderate-sized collective farms continued to exist throughout the 1930's and 1940's. In early 1950 in Moscow Province, for example, two thirds of all farms had less than 500 acres of arable land, and 45 per cent of them had 30 or fewer peasant families.[16]

The gross inequality of size between different collective farms before 1950 is most vividly illustrated by available data for 1939 on the distribution of *kolkhozy* in terms of arable landholdings. These data are probably typical of the size distribution that prevailed from the mid-1930's to early 1950. They are shown in Table 24.

TABLE 24. Distribution of Soviet Collective Farms in 1939 by Size of Arable Land Area.

Area (HECTARES)	Percentage of All Collective Farms	Percentage of Total Arable Land
50 or less	3.2	0.6
51–100	8.8	1.0
101–200	18.4	4.1
201–500	29.6	14.5
501–1,000	20.0	21.2
1,001–1,500	9.3	16.8
1,501–3,000	8.1	24.4
over 3,000	2.6	17.4
Total	100.0	100.0

Source: *Voprosy Ekonomiki*, No. 5 (1950), p. 48.

[15] *Ibid.*, pp. 26–29.
[16] *Pravda*, April 25, 1950.

Perhaps the most striking comparison of the inequalities shown by these data may be made if the first three and the last three categories are considered separately. Almost 60 per cent of all collective farm arable land was owned by the 20 per cent of all *kolkhozy* having 1,000 hectares or more (roughly over 2,500 acres). The smallest 30 per cent of all collective farms had less than 6 per cent of all arable land. In 1940 about 72,000 collectives were in this smallest group, having no more than 200 hectares (under 500 acres) of arable land each. They were concentrated mainly in the central, northwestern, and northern regions of the USSR. Half of them were not served by Machine Tractor Stations and their equipment.

The Communist Party and Soviet government moved against small farms in early 1950, instituting a national campaign to combine them into larger units having thousands rather than hundreds of acres. Great pressure must have been placed upon collective farmers to decide "voluntarily" to amalgamate their farms with neighboring ones, for the pace was swift. In Moscow Province, there were 6,069 *kolkhozy* at the beginning of 1950. By June 20, 1950, these had been amalgamated into 1,668, fewer than one third the original number.[17] In Leningrad Province the number of farms was reduced from over 2,000 at the beginning of 1950 to 600 four months later. The number of collectives in Novgorod Province fell from 3,653 to 792. In Belorussia, a progress report revealed, 9,782 collective farms had been combined into 3,480, though the task of unification had not been completed at the time of the report. The enlarged Belorussian farms averaged over 1,000 hectares of plowland each, three times the average of the farms from which they had been formed.[18] The initial impact of this drive at the beginning of 1950 was felt in the Moscow-Leningrad area, where farms tended to be smaller than elsewhere, but by late spring and summer the drive had obviously become national in scope. Not until this campaign was well under way was it publicly revealed that it had been initiated by a government decision ordering amalgamation of small farms in provinces, territories, and republics having a significant number of them.[19]

---

[17] *Ibid.*, June 23, 1950. An indication of how pressure for farm unification was exerted in Moscow Province is given in *Bolshevik*, No. 12 (1950), p. 49.

[18] *Leningradskaya Pravda*, April 23, 1950, and August 10, 1950. *Komsomolskaya Pravda*, August 4, 1950.

[19] *Pravda*, June 18, 1950.

The nominal reasons behind the 1950 campaign to enlarge collective farms were stated to be the following. Large farms use resources more efficiently than small farms, particularly because mechanized equipment can be employed more economically on them. Farms of several thousand acres and several hundred families can economically construct and utilize barns, warehouses, and other productive or communal structures that are beyond the financial capacities or effective use of small farms. Relatively, administrative expenses of large farms are lower than those of small farms. Government propaganda stressed statistics comparing highly productive and highly profitable large collectives with relatively unprofitable and rather unproductive small *kolkhozy*. It revealed that many small farms had more labor than they could use, while others had too few workers. By merging collective farms, large numbers of chairmen, bookkeepers, and other administrative officials could be released for field work or for transfer from agriculture, it was argued. Large collective farms could easily engage in efficient specialization requiring large amounts of capital. Some of these arguments are undoubtedly correct up to a point, but the propaganda involved strikingly ignored the real problems of the economics of the scale of agricultural enterprises and failed to suggest that there might be some optimum large size beyond which diseconomies outweighed economies. Politburo member N. S. Khrushchev, who spearheaded this campaign, admitted publicly that cases could be found where small collectives had done well and large ones had done poorly. Instead of trying to analyze the factors behind these "exceptions," however, he dismissed them, saying that they had no great significance.[20]

It seems likely that an important supplement to the stated reasons for this major reform was the fact that it permitted strengthening Communist Party and government control of the collective farms. In part this resulted from the substantial reduction in the number of collective farms achieved by the reform. Moreover, press reports indicated that in territories affected by this campaign the percentage of farms having Communist Party units increased sharply. Where

---

[20] *Moskovskaya Pravda*, April 25, 1950. An abridged version of Khrushchev's speech, omitting some significant points, appeared in *Pravda* the same day and is available in English translation in the *Current Digest of the Soviet Press,* June 10, 1950, pp. 3–6.

Communist Party members had formerly been scattered in small numbers on many small farms, the effect of the reform was to create large farms having enough members to form an effective working unit.

In early 1950, too, the same trend toward enlarging the size of basic agricultural work units showed itself in a change in the government attitude toward internal collective farm labor organization. In the post-war period until then, government policy had clearly favored the development of the small *zveno*, or link, work teams, in the effort to link each worker's reward as closely as possible to his own production. Working in small groups whose work-day credits were raised or decreased percentagewise in proportion to their overfulfillment or underfulfillment of the production plan, collective farmers belonging to links approximated most closely the individual piece-work wage system used in most of Soviet industry. This type of government encouragement, plus the great shortage of farm machinery on Soviet farms during and immediately after World War II, led apparently to widespread superseding of the large-brigade system of organization by the smaller link teams, the latter often being assigned to no more than 10 to 25 acres.

This government policy was dramatically reversed in February 1950 with the publication in *Pravda* of an article attacking Politburo member A. A. Andreyev for supporting the use of links rather than brigades. Though the article cited Kursk Province only, to show the allegedly evil effects of the link system, later material in Soviet newspapers indicated that this was a national phenomenon. *Pravda* argued that small work teams were completely unsuitable for large-scale mechanized agriculture, particularly in grain production, by far the most important area of Soviet farming. It accused Communist Party and government officials who had fostered the system of organization by links of having an anti-machine attitude and of being complacent toward the resulting idleness of equipment that accompanied the division of farms into *zveno* plots tended by small groups of farmers. In typical Soviet style, the editorial was followed by a swift campaign over the country to break up the links as the basic unit and to reinstate large-scale brigades of 50 to 100 or more workers, with their own equipment and large plots of land, as the primary form of collective farm labor organization. In the ensuing reaction, collective farmers were for the first time permitted to complain that local authorities had forced the link system on them against their will.[21] The link system was apparently retained for some industrial crops.

Study of the *Pravda* editorial and the subsequent reaction to it suggests that there was another reason beside that cited for the sudden and dramatic shift in farm labor organization policy. In Kursk Province, for example, complaints were voiced that the link system had led to increases in private incomes from collective work.[22] The link system clearly tended to divide a collective farm in effect into a number of small farms, each worked by a few individuals, whose incomes were basically determined by the output from the small acreage they cultivated. This must have often seemed to the peasantry as a masked revival of the old private farming for profit. With few or no machines to aid them, their technique of cultivation during and immediately after World War II must have deteriorated to the old peasant standard, except that far fewer horses were available on farms in the 1940's than in the 1920's.

The progress of the amalgamation drive after 1950 can be traced as follows. From 254,000 collectives at the beginning of 1950, the number was reduced to 123,000 by early 1951, to 97,000 by October 1952, and to 94,000 by September 1953. This drastic reduction makes it plain that not only small collectives, but also medium and even large ones were unified into what may be termed "supercollectives." Khrushchev revealed in late 1953 that as a result of this consolidation the average amount of arable land per collective farm had risen from about 1,500 acres to about 4,200 acres (in original units, from 589 hectares to 1,693).

Such a radical change vastly complicated the administrative problems of collective farms, for these now became much larger enterprises, each employing many more people and far more land than originally. Moreover, the typical "supercollective" consists of several villages usually miles apart, so that coordination is difficult, especially in view of the lack of telephones and the scarcity of motor transport on many farms. The problem of finding adequate trained

---

[21] *Pravda*, February 19 and March 22, 1950; *Sotsialisticheskoye Zemledeliye*, March 29, 1950; *Sotsialisticheskoye Selskoye Khozyaistvo*, No. 4 (1950), pp. 3–14.

[22] *Pravda*, March 22, 1950.

personnel to handle these giant farms was recognized from the beginning when a campaign was launched to replace working farmers serving as collective-farm chairmen with farm technicians who were supposed to be brought in from the outside. The failure of this campaign, three years after it had begun, may be gauged from Khrushchev's statement that only 16,600 collective farms had chairmen with university or secondary specialized education. "On most collective farms," he said, "the chairmen are people with elementary education." By the end of 1953, certainly, there was little indication that this drastic reorganization had brought about any corresponding great improvement in Soviet agriculture. On the contrary, the poor condition of Soviet agriculture, as described in Khrushchev's September 1953 and February 1954 speeches, seemed to suggest the amalgamation campaign had dismally failed to achieve the results hoped for.

An even more radical change had originally been proposed by Khrushchev in early 1950 at the same time as he initiated the amalgamation program. This was the formation of "agro-gorods," or farm-cities of around 5,000 people each. These, he urged, could be formed by moving the houses of farmers living in the scattered villages of each "supercollective" to a central point. This, he believed, would make for greater efficiency and flexibility in the use of labor, as well as permit the provision of more urban amenities for the population of each large agro-gorod. He urged that attention be given to building small apartment houses in such larger towns to replace the small traditional peasants' huts. And perhaps most sensitive of all, he spoke of moving the farmers' small private gardens from their individual backyards into a large common area apart from the farmers' dwellings, a change making the farmers' evasion of collective work in favor of work on his private plot more easily detectable by local authorities.

These suggestions were advanced during 1950 and early 1951, but apparently aroused enough peasant resistance to have them swiftly repudiated by the party high command. At the Nineteenth Communist Party Congress in October 1952, Malenkov dealt with these proposals in a critical fashion: [23]

---

[23] *Pravda*, October 6, 1952.

. . . it should be noted that certain of our leading officials have employed an incorrect approach, a consumer-oriented approach, to questions of collective farm development, particularly as related to the consolidation of small collective farms. They proposed forcing the pace of mass integration of villages into large farm settlements, proposing that all the old farm buildings and collective farmers' homes be pulled down and large "collective farm settlements," "collective farm towns," or "agro-cities" be built in new places. They saw this as the most important task in strengthening the farms organizationally and economically. These comrades' mistake was in overlooking the collective farms' primary tasks—the production tasks—and putting first the derivative, consumer tasks of organization of everyday living on the farms. . . . The Party acted in time to overcome these mistaken trends in the sphere of collective farm development.

Malenkov's use of the phrase "forcing the pace" of forming farm-cities seems to imply that while Khrushchev's proposal has been rejected for the time being — it was not mentioned by him in his reports of late 1953 and early 1954, either — the basic objective has not been discarded, and more may be heard of it in the future.

Problems of Kolkhoz Operation

The basic problem in the operation of the collective farm arises from the inefficiency of these farms and the low incomes that work in the collective fields gives the collective farmers. The low level of these earnings is indicated by an estimate prepared by Dr. Naum Jasny. This estimate indicates that in the years 1937 and 1938, the average payment per work day received by a collective farmer was 20 cents. This amount includes allowance, not only for the *kolkhoznik's* money income, but also for the value of income in kind received for his work in the collective fields.[24] The same writer describes the collective farmer's return also in these terms:

> In the last prewar years his daily reward averaged roughly six pounds of grain, a few pounds of potatoes and vegetables, and a little forage (mostly straw), and the equivalent of about one kilogram of coarse bread or half a kilogram of white bread in money. By 1946 it had dropped to possibly half this.[25]

---

[24] Naum Jasny, "The Plight of the Collective Farms," *Journal of Farm Economics*, May 1948, p. 315.

[25] Naum Jasny, *The Socialized Agriculture of the USSR*, p. 37. One kilogram is approximately 2.2 pounds.

The reasons for these low incomes are many and varied: the low yields generally received in Russian agriculture; the significant percentages of crop and livestock production taken by the government at very low prices; and so on.

The results of these low incomes are these. First, most collective farmers are forced to work their individual garden plots intensively in order to meet even the minimum needs of themselves and their families. Second, because any excess production from the garden plots and from the privately owned livestock of the collective farmer can usually be sold on the open market at relatively high prices, a great incentive is created for the farmer to neglect his duties on the collective land in favor of work on the small plot and the few livestock permitted him under the *kolkhoz* charter. Third, as Khrushchev said in September 1953, "if work in the communal economy does not give the collective farmer the necessary income for his work day, if his individual interests in his subsidiary private garden are infringed, then the collective farmer easily finds another area for the application of his labor. He leaves for the city, for factory production. Here are the causes for the reduction in the personal economies of the collective farmers and the drift of the rural population from the backward collective farms."

By 1939 the practice of doing little or no work for the collective farms had become so widespread that the Soviet government felt it necessary to end the pretense of universal voluntary participation in the *kolkhoz*. It issued a decree instituting an annual obligatory minimum number of work days on collective farm crops or livestock that must be earned by all members. The minima were raised in 1942 to between 100 and 150 work days annually, the number depending upon the region. The 1942 order established a required minimum of 50 work days for collective farm youngsters 12 to 16 years old. The same decree required that *kolkhozniki* must work at least a minimum number of days during each season of the year. The latter provision aims at preventing evasion of the objective of the act through concentration of all compulsory work time in one season, leaving the farmer free to work his own acres the rest of the year. A collective farmer who fails to work the required minimum time for the *kolkhoz* must be punished under the law by being forced to work for six months on his collective. During this period 25 per cent of his earnings are forfeited.[26] These provisions have remained in effect in the postwar period.

Dr. Naum Jasny has attempted the most detailed calculation of the relative returns to a collective farmer between work on the collective fields and work on his own small plot. He concludes, for the late 1930's: ". . . the income of the *kolkhozniki* from work on his own farm enterprises returned 125–130 kopeks per day. This is . . . about two-and-one-fourth times as much as their total receipts per work day from their *kolkhozy*." [27]

The relatively low returns from work on the collective farm fields explain many defects in collective farm operation that are frequently denounced in the Soviet press. Thus many farmers apparently seek to make money by evading or violating collective farm rules. Products owned by the *kolkhoz* are often not sold on the free market for the farm's account, but are sold instead to collective farmers at extremely low prices. The farmers then sell these products for much higher prices in the free market and pocket the profit. In both 1939 and after World War II, investigation by the Soviet government revealed that hundreds of thousands of farmers were illegally cultivating larger plots of garden land than permitted them by the kolkhoz charter. In each individual case, the amount of excess land cultivated privately was small, but in the aggregate appreciable amounts of land were involved. The techniques used to evade regulations were thus described in a 1939 state decree:

> The diversion and dissipation of the collectively held fields of collective farms for the benefit of the individual farming of the members includes various kinds of unlawful additions to house-and-garden plots which increase them beyond the size provided for in the Charter, [such as] where a household fraudulently obtains an additional house-and-garden plot for members of the family who pretend to be separated. . . . In a number of collective farms the practice is in reality to transform the house-and-garden plot into a private property of the household. . . . There is a large number of pretended collective farmers who either do not work at all in the collective farms or do only sham work and spend most of their time on their own personal farming . . . [which] results in an artificial shortage of labor on the collective farms although in reality there is a surplus of labor in the majority of regions of the USSR.[28]

[26] Gsovski, *op. cit.*, Vol. 2, pp. 484–86.
[27] Jasny, *The Socialized Agriculture of the USSR*, p. 699.
[28] From the May 27, 1939 decree of the Central Committee of the Communist Party and the Council of People's Commissars.

Many similar violations of the collective-farm charter were found in a national checkup during 1952. In South Kazakhstan Province, for example, 10,000 cases of illegal seizures of land totalling about 6,500 acres were found, while in only six counties of this province 2,000 farmers did not work the required minimum number of days in the collective fields. In Uzbekistan numerous violations were found, with frequent cases of action by local officials to protect violators. These same officials themselves often showed a penchant for taking farm produce for nothing. Some collective farms in this area, it was reported, distributed farm income without taking account of work days earned by different farmers. In 1951 in the Altay Province of Siberia, 65,000 acres of collective-farm land were found to have been stolen. The head of the Azerbaidzhan party organization denounced numerous "pseudo-*kolkhozniki* and idlers" and complained that large numbers of farmers tried to avoid work in the cotton harvest. Similar examples could be multiplied by reports from other Soviet areas.[29]

Not all Soviet collective farms are poverty-stricken, of course, and there is great variation of income and wealth among them. One Soviet report cites a farm in Uzbekistan which had a monetary income of almost 9,000,000 rubles in 1947, pointing out that in the same year many farms in Omsk Province received less than 25,000 rubles.[30] In his September 1953 speech Khrushchev compared two farms of roughly equal area in the same county of Kostroma Province. One of them had a monetary income in 1952 of 2,109,000 rubles, or 2,113 rubles per hectare of land. The other's income was only 151,000 rubles, or 167 rubles per hectare.

Differences in size partly account for differences in collective farm income — the result of the amalgamation program of 1950 was, of course, automatically to increase the number of "millionaire" collective farms because of this factor alone — but other important factors include differences in quality of soil, in quality of work by the *kolkhozniki,* and in the kinds of crop and livestock products produced, since sharply different price levels are paid by the government for different types of produce.

Seeking to justify an increased government price for livestock

---

[29] The cases cited are from *Kazakhstanskaya Pravda,* December 23, 1952; *Pravda Vostoka,* September 14, 1952; *Sotsialisticheskoye Zemledeliye,* May 29, 1951; and *Bakinsky Rabochi,* September 24, 1952.

[30] *Sotsialisticheskoye Selskoye Khozyaistvo,* April 1949, pp. 26–29.

products, Khrushchev in September 1953 gave this comparison of returns to collective farms from government procurements and purchases. The data are in terms of rubles per work day devoted to a particular activity:

Activity	Rubles per Work Day
Cotton—Central Asia............	17–36
Sugar beets—Ukraine	12
Industrial crops—USSR	18
Grain—North Caucasus..........	8–14
Livestock—USSR	5
Livestock—Ukraine	4

The differences are obviously marked. In reality they are probably even greater than Khrushchev indicated, for he did not give a figure for work on grain in the country as a whole. His figure on grain in the North Caucasus refers to a highly mechanized area where favorable soil conditions permit unusually high yields. It may be surmised that his reticence is probably based on the fact that the corresponding national grain ruble figure would have been even lower than the lowest figure shown above. Grain, of course, is the dominant crop in the Soviet Union. Its culture occupies many more people and much more land than any competitive farm activity.

The variation in the incomes of collective farmers is probably even greater than the variation of collective farm incomes. At least four factors determine the *kolkhozniki's* returns: the number of work days they earn each year, the value of the work day on their collective farm, the amount of production they can secure from their own garden plots, and the opportunities they have of selling their own production – plus part of their incomes in kind from the collective farm – at high prices. In addition some collective farmers work part time at lumbering, fishing, and other nonfarm jobs to augment their incomes.

Data are lacking on many of these points, but some information is available. In 1937 over 20 per cent of all collective farmers earned 50 or fewer workdays, while the highest 20 per cent earned over 300 work days.[31] The great variation of the value of a work day on

---

[31] Volin, *op. cit.*, p. 152.

different farms is clearly indicated by the data above on the variation of incomes received by different *kolkhozy*. Few figures are available on the amount of production in the private enterprises of *kolkhozniki*, but these perhaps tend to counteract the inequality suggested by the factors cited earlier, since some of the collective farmers who earn few work days more than make up for this by intensive cultivation of their private plots. High prices prevailing on urban free markets provide substantial additional income for those able to sell their produce in these markets. Collective farms and farmers nearest to large cities are in the most favorable positions, but many *kolkhozy* are very distant from such lucrative markets and must accept far lower prices for their surplus production.

In 1939 the average money income of a collective farmer from sources other than the collective farm, that is, primarily earnings from sales of the farmer's own produce, was only 1,132 rubles. The lowest 20 per cent of *kolkhozniki* averaged 488 rubles that year, while the top .2 of 1 per cent averaged 4,882 rubles, about ten times as much as the lowest group. The actions taken by the Soviet government in 1939 to discourage private farming by these peasants were felt most fully the next year, with the result that the corresponding 1940 money incomes were appreciably lower. This is indicated by the following percentage distribution of collective farmers' money incomes from noncollective farm sources in 1939 and 1940.[32]

Income Group	1939	1940
RUBLES	%	%
0–700	21.8	29.1
701–1,000	19.8	23.0
1,001–2,000	51.2	44.7
2,001–3,000	6.3	2.8
3,001–4,000	.7	.3
4,001 and over	.2	.1

The data cited above suggest that while the great mass of collective farmers are very poor, a small fraction of them do have relatively high incomes — from either their collective farm work or their private enterprises or both. This is confirmed by isolated reports in the Soviet press of some collective farmers' buying automobiles,

[32] Data from A. K. Suchkov, ed., *Dokhody Gosudarstvennogo Byudzheta SSSR*, pp. 139–43. Moscow: Gosfinizdat, 1945.

motorcycles, and other articles far out of reach of the average peasant.

One recent major study of Soviet agriculture argues that differentiation among the peasantry today is greater than ever:

> In 1927 only 3.9 per cent of all peasant households were classed as *kulaki* (well-to-do). . . . Moreover, the wealth and income of this group were considerable only in comparison with the distressing poverty of the bulk of the peasantry. In consequence of the thorough reorganization of agriculture, the percentage of persons in agriculture with higher incomes than that of the ordinary peasant was greatly increased.
>
> The former *kulaki*, actually the more energetic, harder-working peasants, are now replaced by the army of chairmen of the *kolkhozy*, tractor drivers, combine operators, and the like. These workers both number and earn relatively more than did the *kulaki*. The increase was particularly large in the number of persons with incomes several times that of an ordinary *kolkhoz* peasant. . . . The incomes of the rank-and-file peasants were below the average by only 3 per cent before collectivization and by about 15 per cent around 1938. [33]

The background of collective-farm and farmer poverty sketched above enables us to understand why the drift from the collective farms assumed such large proportions, particularly after World War II and particularly in the case of the better trained and better educated farm people who could hope for higher-paying jobs in the non-agricultural economy. Those who worked on the collectives after World War II were primarily the women, the old, the very young, and the men who, because of lack of education or of ambition, were content to remain and accept the poor lot that was theirs. It was this shortage of personnel, and particularly of technically-trained and managerially-competent personnel, which in part caused the failures and debacles of Soviet postwar farm policy in such key areas as livestock, potatoes, vegetables, and flax.

What distinguishes the new farm policy announced in September 1953 from the similar comprehensive program of February 1947 is the recognition that the situation can be righted only by making agriculture more attractive financially, both to the specialist and to the ordinary peasant. As early as the summer of 1953 the onerous income tax on the *kolkhoznik's* private garden production was cut roughly in half, and the government made it clear that it would no longer tolerate the former practice by local party and government

---

[33] Jasny, *The Socialized Agriculture of the USSR*, p. 75.

officials of seeking covertly to eliminate these garden plots. This was a major and historic concession. The increased prices for livestock, potatoes, and vegetables announced in September 1953 were in the same spirit, as was Khrushchev's attack on those local officials who sought to reduce the number of livestock owned privately by the collective farmers. Khrushchev failed to mention that this last attitude had its genesis in official policy going back at least to 1939. But whether these and other concessions will suffice permanently to lure technicians back from cities to farms, to stimulate farmers to work better on the collective fields, and to stem in part the migration to cities remains to be seen. It is conceivable that the concessions to farmers' private property instincts will simply increase their agitation for further concessions and for further relief from the collective-farm shackles.

"Democracy" on the Kolkhoz

The collective farm is in theory a democratic association of farmers governed by elected officers, with ultimate authority for farm policy resting in the general meeting of members. There is abundant evidence that the reality behind this façade is far different. Much material published in the Soviet press, particularly in the fall of 1946 when the government put special emphasis upon the problem, indicated that very frequently collective farm officials were appointed or removed arbitrarily by local Communist Party or government officials. Government exposés told of large numbers of farms where general membership meetings were not held for long periods, or, if held, were confined merely to approving arbitrary decisions of farm officials or of party or government officials. In many areas during and immediately after World War II, local authorities often regarded collective farms as sources of wealth to be looted for their own personal benefit, sometimes openly, sometimes in crudely veiled fashion. Theft of money, livestock, food, and other property was apparently common, while collective farmers were powerless to defend their interests against predatory officials. The major campaign initiated against such practices in September 1946 may well have been inspired by government fears regarding the consequences of this situation upon farmers' morale and productive effort.[34]

[34] *Pravda,* September 20, 1946; Volin, *op. cit.,* p. 155; Jasny, *op. cit.,* pp. 329–34.

To combat these and other abuses the government in the fall of 1946 created the Council for Collective Farm Affairs, headed by Politburo member A. A. Andreyev. This body was to exercise continuing supervision of collective-farm operation, to report abuses, and to suggest additional legislation required. Concurrently all collective farms were required to hold general membership meetings by February 15, 1947, to elect officials and set policies. These and other moves undoubtedly improved matters greatly, but the persistence of the basic problem was evidenced frequently, even after this major effort, in press reports from different parts of the country complaining of abuses precisely similar to those exposed in 1946.[35]

The abuses complained of by the state and the efforts which the latter directed against them must be viewed in proper perspective. Mass collectivization was instituted in a totalitarian fashion against the wishes of large numbers of those affected; collective farms must operate as directed by the government plan regardless of members' wishes; collective farm administrations are expected to follow the "suggestions" and "advice" of the Communist Party in operating their farms. The collective farm system, in short, is thoroughly authoritarian, and the scope of collective farmers' free choice is narrowly restricted. The government's campaign has not been directed toward altering these basic characteristics. Rather, it has sought to end corruption that robbed farms without enriching the state, and it has sought to eliminate the most flagrant and crude types of intervention by party and government officials in collective farm life. The state has chastised local party units that have arbitrarily named collective-farm chairmen, for example, but collective farmers have no right in any case to elect chairmen who will actively combat the party and press for farm independence against state orders. Put most simply, the government campaign against undemocratic practices on collective farms has aimed at putting a velvet glove on the iron fist of party control. The brusque rapidity of the twin organizational revolutions in 1950 — one suddenly amalgamating thousands of collective farms and the other drastically changing the internal labor organizations of tens of thousands of collectives — are eloquent evidence of how undemocratic the Soviet idea of farm "democracy" is in practice.

---

[35] Cf. the typical complaints in *Pravda*, March 27 and May 11, 1950; *Izvestia*, April 28 and May 6, 1950; *Pravda Ukrainy*, March 21, 1950.

The Machine Tractor Station

The Machine Tractor Station works closely in conjunction with the collective farm in producing most Russian agricultural output. These stations own most of the tractors, combines, and other complex agricultural machinery used in the Soviet Union. The use of these machines on the collective farm is governed by the terms of a contract signed between the *kolkhoz* and the MTS. These contracts provide for the types of work to be done by the machinery, the time at which each operation is to be performed, qualitative indexes to be maintained, and, not least important, the payment to be made for rental of the machinery. This payment, as noted above, is a share of the crop, the precise percentage being determined by government decree. In 1940, 7,069 Machine Tractor Stations served 200,000 collective farms, their machines working 110,700,000 hectares of sown land, or 94 per cent of the 117,600,000 hectares sown that year by all collective farms.

In part, the reason for the existence of these Machine Tractor Stations is purely technological, that is, the machinery they own can be used advantageously to cultivate several collective farms. It is therefore more economical to have a central point from which these machines can be dispatched to their areas of work. At this central point, moreover, can be maintained the workshops and the technicians required to keep this machinery in good operating condition.

The Machine Tractor Stations are owned and operated by the state. Historically, they have been concerned primarily with providing machinery for crop cultivation and harvesting. In the postwar period some special stations emphasizing provision of machinery for haying and other activities related to livestock work (MZhS) have been set up, as well as some experimental Electric Machine Tractor Stations working with electric-driven tractors.

In late 1953, each of the 8,950 MTS served on the average between ten and eleven *kolkhozy*, a far cry from the 30 *kolkhozy* served on the average at the beginning of 1950, that is, before the amalgamation movement. The latter reorganization certainly made the great bulk of collective farms large enough to use modern farm machinery economically and thus tended to remove one of the original reasons for putting these machines on the MTS rather than directly on the farm. In early 1952 two Soviet economists dared to suggest to Stalin that the state should sell the MTS machinery and equipment to the collective farms. Stalin's answer was a furious rejection. He argued that the collective farms could not afford such expensive equipment, ignoring the fact that much smaller private farms in the non-Soviet world have much expensive equipment. But his more basic reason was hinted at when he pointed out that if the farms did own the equipment they would be in a privileged position, since virtually all other productive equipment in the country is owned by the state. Yet it seems significant that thirty-five years after the Bolshevik Revolution politically faithful communist economists should propose a measure which, as Stalin saw, would tend to strengthen the non-governmental area of the economy and increase rather than reduce the influence of market forces in the planned economy.[36]

Basic also is the fact that the MTS provide the Soviet state with a major instrument for controlling the collectives. This control is exercised in a number of ways. First, any attempt by the kolkhoz to deviate from its plan can be easily observed and checked by the MTS officials who supervise the plowing, sowing, cultivation, and finally the harvesting for the great majority of collective farms in the Soviet Union. Secondly, the government, of course, wishes to make sure above all else that it receives its share of the crop first. Since the Machine Tractor Station's harvesting machines gather much of the collective farm crop, the government has an accurate check on how much has been harvested and is available for delivery.

During much of the 1930's and the 1940's, large numbers of MTS personnel were government political supervisors in rural districts. In the middle 1930's this task of supervision was performed by the so-called political division of the Machine Tractor Station, staffed primarily by loyal urban communists sent to the countryside for that purpose. After World War II, this function was performed by the so-called deputy director of the Machine Tractor Station for the political section, a functionary perhaps best compared to the political commissars who have from time to time been attached to Soviet military units. Political matters in the Soviet Union, Hubbard points out, can be made to cover almost anything. As a result these personnel of the Machine Tractor Stations have sometimes

---

[36] Leo Gruliow, ed., *Current Soviet Policies*, pp. 18–19. New York: Praeger, 1953. This debate is part of Stalin's "Economic Problems of Socialism," a full translation of which is given in this source.

had supreme power in their individual districts, fully able to override the decisions and wishes, not only of the collective farm members, but of the collective farm officials and even of local government and party bureaucrats.[37]

A decree of the Communist Party's Central Committee in September 1953 concluded that party control over farm work had been unsatisfactory. It abolished the post of MTS deputy director for political affairs and set up what appears to be a more stringent control mechanism. It ordered that every MTS have assigned to it a group of Communist Party workers headed by a secretary of the local county party committee. These are to provide the political guidance and supervision which the former deputy directors had apparently failed to provide adequately. In late 1953 and early 1954 thousands of urban communists were sent to the countryside to provide additional personnel needed for this new control organization.

Until the end of 1953, the MTS were paid in kind for their work on the collective farms in accordance with a sliding scale varying proportionally with the size of the harvest. Thus in the 1930's, the MTS received 10 to 20 per cent of a farm's grain crop, depending upon the yield, for using MTS machinery to plow, seed, cultivate, and harvest the crop. In September 1953 this method of payment was ordered abolished and replaced by a system of fixed rates differentiated according to geographic zones, with a bonus to be paid for high yields actually gathered and put in the barn. Khrushchev justified this change by pointing out that harvest yields depended not only on MTS work but also on the quality of seeds, amount of fertilizer employed, and the like. To require farms with higher yields to pay the MTS more was to penalize them for their efforts along other lines, he argued. But it is equally clear that a uniform payment system such as has been introduced penalizes the farm with low yields, a penalty the government probably desires introduced as an incentive.[38]

The many deficiencies of the MTS were described by Khrushchev in these biting words:

... many MTS ... violate the rules of agronomy, prolong the work time, till the soil badly, and conduct sowing poorly, which inevitably

[37] Hubbard, *The Economics of Soviet Agriculture*, p. 157.
[38] Cf. paragraph 79 of the MTS decree in *Pravda*, October 1, 1953.

reduces the harvest. Last year more than half the MTS did not fulfill their work plans. More than 20 per cent of the spring and winter sowing work was carried out late. Such important work as haying, accumulating silage for feed, and plowing of fallow is also done badly. Significant losses are permitted in gathering the harvest. This occurs because a significant part of the tractors and other machines stands idle during the period of field work. Only 34 per cent of all tractor drivers fulfilled their shift norms in 1952. . . .

One of the basic causes of this situation is the MTS' lack of qualified mechanically skilled personnel. The rich and complex equipment of the MTS requires able working hands. But this equipment is in the hands of seasonal workers assigned by the collective farms during the time of field work. The tractor driver is really not subordinate to the MTS director. If he wishes, he goes to work; if he does not go, it is hard for the director to influence him. Today he works on a tractor, but tomorrow he will return to the collective farm or leave for industry. . . . Tractor brigades lose 30 to 35 per cent of their drivers annually and in many of them the staff of equipment operators changes several times a year. . . .

It is urgently necessary to change the system of training tractor drivers, combine operators, and other large skilled groups. To this time these personnel have been trained badly. A fellow takes a 2–3 month course; they lead him around a tractor several times; then the steering wheel is put in his hands—and the tractor driver is ready. In the spring this tractor driver somehow drives out to the fields, and if the machine stops he sits helplessly by the tractor and waits for the mechanic because he does not know what to do.

Khrushchev described also the general lack of technically trained personnel in the MTS, the failure of existing wage rates adequately to stimulate the best performances by MTS personnel, and other faults of these stations, including their utter lack of equipment for properly repairing the complex machinery entrusted to them. On the basis of his diagnosis, the decree published October 1, 1953, ordered the strengthening of MTS with additional trained personnel, provided for increased capital investment in repair equipment and garage facilities, and required that much larger permanent staffs of equipment operators be maintained by these stations. But the MTS are still to continue to recruit workers on specialized machines, such as grain combines and cotton pickers, from seasonal workers provided by the collective farms.[39]

A report by the Minister of Agriculture, appearing January 26,

---

[39] *Ibid., passim.*

1954, in *Izvestia,* indicated that some — but far from enough — progress had been achieved since September 1953 toward remedying the MTS weaknesses described above. A total of 10,813 engineers, 10,601 technicians, and 104,644 agronomists and livestock technicians had been transferred to the MTS, many of them from urban occupations. This had permitted gains in raising the educational levels of the officials running these installations. He reported that as of the time he spoke 39 per cent of MTS directors and 73 per cent of their chief engineers had higher education, as against 22 per cent of the directors and 14 per cent of the chief engineers who had had higher education when the drive was initiated. The official Soviet economic report for 1953 revealed that at the end of that year the total number of permanent MTS workers was 1,400,000 greater than it had been a year earlier, a change reflecting the earlier-announced new policy of attaching permanently to MTS staffs far more of their key workers than had previously been customary.

State Farms

A state farm, or *sovkhoz,* is entirely the property of the Soviet government, which operates it with hired labor directed by managers responsible to the government ministry having control of the particular farm. These farms are literally "factories in the field," being operated in the same spirit and with as close adherence to the government plans — subject to the vagaries of climatic conditions — as any urban factory in the Soviet Union. Like the collective farms, the *sovkhozy* are usually large by American standards — frequently exceeding 5,000 acres in size.

Administrative direction of the state farms has varied from time to time. In late 1953 over 2,000 of them were under the control of the Ministry of State Farms, and most of the rest were under the direction of the Ministry of Food Industry or the Ministry of Foreign Trade. Some other Soviet ministries also had a few such farms under their control.[40]

In 1938, there were almost 4,000 state farms with 12,400,000 hectares under cultivation, roughly 10 per cent of all the sown area

---

[40] A good description of the development of the state farms during the 1920's and 1930's is given in Wolf Ladejinsky "Soviet State Farms," *Political Science Quarterly,* March and June 1938, pp. 60–82 and 207–32.

in the USSR. The total acreage of the more than 4,700 state farms existing in late 1953 has not been disclosed, but some notion of these farms' importance can be gauged from the fact that it was planned that these farms would provide the state in 1954 with about 15 per cent of all meat, 14 per cent of all milk, and about 16 per cent of all wool procured or purchased by the government.[41] State farms are also important in the production of grain, sugar beets, cotton, vegetables, and other products.

Over much of Soviet history the state farms have been particularly favored by the regime. Very large amounts have been invested in them, and during the early 1930's they were receiving tractors and other farm machinery more adequately than the collective farms; by the end of that decade virtually all basic crop operations capable of being done by machinery were being so performed. All this equipment belonged to each state farm on which it was used, and the *sovkhozy* were not dependent on Machine Tractor Stations.

As owner and operator of the farms, of course, the government receives all their net production, so that a very high percentage of their output goes to the state. In the late 1930's, for example, over 75 per cent of the grain production on state farms specializing in this crop went to the state,[42] as against the one third of the collective farm crop taken over by the government. On the other hand, the government naturally had to meet all expenses of state farm production, including wages, so that by no means all the production delivered to it represented net gain.

If agriculture were operated as is industry, almost all agricultural production would be conducted by state farms rather than predominantly by collective farms, as is actually the case. At various times the Soviet government and important figures in it have considered the possibility of making the state farm the dominant or exclusive production unit in agriculture, but the history of these farms has not been so bright as to encourage the implementation of this policy.

State farms have gone through several quite different stages of development. During the first decade of the Soviet regime, these

---

[41] *Pravda*, November 17, 1953, gives 1954 planned state farm deliveries as 654,000 tons of meat, almost 2,000,000 tons of milk, and 38,000 tons of wool. Total planned procurement give in paragraph 18 of livestock products decree in *Pravda*, September 26, 1953.

[42] *Bolshevik*, No. 5 (1947), pp. 23–24.

farms were organized primarily on the basis of large estates that had previously belonged to private, church, or state owners. These were usually very specialized — like, for example, the sugar-beet state farms — and were intended, in part, to act as model farms for the education of the surrounding peasantry. During this decade many of these farms worked at a loss, and during the middle 1920's their area was considerably reduced.

The second major period of their development stretches roughly from 1928 to the early 1930's. This period began when the Soviet government experienced extreme difficulty in making necessary grain collections from the individual peasants. In a speech in 1928 Stalin proposed, not only that collectivization be extended much more widely than it had yet been, but also that large numbers of huge state farms be formed in order to increase the amount of grain produced for the government itself. Between 1928 and 1932 the number of state farms increased from 1,400 to 4,337, while the sown area of these farms rose from 1,700,000 hectares to 13,400,000 hectares.

The high hopes held by those who had sponsored this rapid expansion were not fulfilled, however, for while production on the farms increased sharply as the result of the rise in their numbers and acreage, the gains to the state in terms of delivered grain were not nearly so great as had been hoped for. It was found, moreover, that production on the state farms was extremely expensive. Large numbers of them operated at substantial losses. These difficulties arose because they were often far too large for efficient management, and too specialized to permit balanced agricultural technique to be applied. Many of them had been established in relatively unpopulated areas with inadequate labor available, and where there were also difficulties because of the lack of water supply. For these and other reasons, a policy change took place. In the middle 1930's the size of many state farms was reduced drastically. A large number of the most unprofitable ones were liquidated, and their land and property in many cases transferred to collective farms. By 1938 the number of state farms had dropped below 4,000, and the sown area was 1,000,000 hectares less than in 1932. After the annexation of Eastern Poland and other western areas after 1938, however, state farms were formed there.

Since the late 1930's, an effort has been made to operate the state farms along more nearly conventional lines, to diversify their operations and to make a profit with them. The war dealt them a serious blow, however, reducing their supply of machinery, their sown area, and their livestock herds. In early 1947 A. A. Andreyev criticized the state farms sharply in his report to the Central Committee of the Communist Party. He castigated the one-sided character of many of them and their over-specialization, and reported that a high labor turnover rate continued to plague them and to reduce their efficiency. To remedy the latter difficulty, the government announced that each worker on a state farm would be permitted to have one-half hectare of ground for a garden plot that he might cultivate himself. Government credit was made available at low interest to finance building a home.[43] Andreyev's report and the subsequent resolution of the government ordered that first priority be given to increasing the livestock holdings of the grain and other crop-raising state farms. The expansion of crop-raising activities on those state farms that had hitherto specialized in the raising of livestock was also ordered.

Two years later, official decrees of the Soviet government indicated that not all the difficulties enumerated in 1947 had been solved, revealing that the work of making the farms better-rounded enterprises was not going so well as desired. In early 1949, it was ordered that most of the livestock state farms belonging to the Ministry of Meat and Milk Industry be transferred to the Ministry of State Farms, in order to improve the administrative direction of these enterprises. The Minister of State Farms, N. A. Skvortsov, reported in both 1949 and 1950 that many state farms continued to operate poorly and unprofitably, although he was able to report successes in over-all crop and livestock output, made possible by the priority given these farms in the receipt of farm machinery of all kinds.[44]

Published reports in the second half of 1953 indicated that the state farms still had many serious deficiencies. Khrushchev complained of their high production costs for grain, meat, milk, and other products. Results on different farms, he indicated, vary considerably with the variation in the quality of managerial personnel.

[43] *Pravda*, February 28 and March 7, 1947.
[44] *Izvestia*, March 13, 1949, and *Pravda*, June 19, 1950.

He pointed out that 31 per cent of the heads of farms under the Ministry of State Farms lacked even secondary specialized farm training, while 93 per cent of the subordinate specialized personnel had no specialized training at all. A later review of the state farms in *Pravda* complained of the poor use of state farm machinery, with tractors idle 30–40 per cent of the time in some areas. The article indicated that state managers often tend to use resources carelessly, feeling confident that state subsidies for their losses will always be forthcoming.[45]

The organization of labor on state farms somewhat resembles that on collective farms, that is, the work to be done is distributed among several brigades, each of which is headed by a brigadier or foreman. Payment of labor on the state farms, however, is on the basis of straight piece-work wages, with the hectare the basic unit of crop-work measurement. As has been true in other areas of Soviet wage policy, the trend has been increasingly toward adjusting the wages and earnings of state farm workers so that they reflect to the maximum extent possible the variation between high and low productivity. Workers who get the best harvests and the most production from their livestock have the highest incomes, and conversely.

The labor problem on the state farms has been a serious one. It has been one of the chief factors forcing a change to diversified farming. On the specialized state farms producing, say, grain or sugar beets, specialization has resulted in a labor demand curve having sharp peaks at certain times during the year. To satisfy the requirements imposed by this curve, the Soviet government has had to provide large numbers of temporary laborers for the period of peak need. On the other hand, since the number of permanent workers cannot be adjusted simply to the minimum needed during the farm year, there has been much idleness among workers on these farms during the wintertime, although these workers were still paid by the government. A more diversified pattern of crop and livestock enterprises on one farm helps to iron out the peaks and troughs of labor demand and thus to eliminate or at least substantially ease this problem of labor force. During much of the

45 *Pravda*, November 17, 1953.

1930's the labor force employed on state farms aggregated about one and a half million.

It seems likely that poor living conditions on state farms have tended to make for high labor turnover, and consequently for lowered efficiency. A government decree in late 1953 ordered the Ministry of State to carry on a large construction program during 1954–56 in order to build housing, schools, hospitals, nurseries, and similar facilities "for keeping cadres on the state farms." [46]

Great persistence has been shown by the Soviet government in maintaining the state farms despite the unsatisfactory experience it has had with them. To some extent, perhaps, this persistence is explained by their usefulness as demonstration farms and as experimental units. But a more fundamental consideration seems involved too. The stated Soviet objective is to put rural life on a parity with that in the cities. Clearly the nominally cooperative character of collective farms is sharply at variance with the employer-employee relationships of urban branches of the economy. The state farms, therefore, may well represent the ultimate universal pattern planned for all Soviet agriculture.

A new stage of state farm policy appears to have begun in early 1954 with the announcement of government plans to form many new state farms in Kazakhstan and other areas in which it was planned to expand grain acreage by over 30,000,000 acres through the sowing of virgin and fallow lands. Though part of this increased acreage was to be obtained on collective-farm land, the bulk was apparently in government land reserves, which were to be formed into state farms staffed by 100,000 young people recruited in cities and farms in European Russia. It seems obvious that this new move resembles closely — and probably has disadvantages similar to — the steps taken during 1928–32 when, as pointed out above, large numbers of new state farms were formed to produce grain in similarly distant areas. Whether this reversion to the policy that had proved a failure two decades earlier will have any greater success in the 1950's remains to be seen. During the first half of 1954 alone, 124 new state farms, with over 6,000,000 acres of arable land, were set up in the new farm areas.[47]

---

[46] *Ibid.*, September 26, 1953.
[47] *Pravda*, June 27, 1954.

Peasant Farms

By the beginning of 1938 the number of uncollectivized individual peasant farms in the USSR had been reduced to 1,300,000. These constituted only 6.5 per cent of all peasant households at that time, and they cultivated under 2,500,000 acres of crop land, an amount less than 1 per cent of the Soviet total. But the government found the number and "wealth" of these remaining nonconformists still too high for its comfort, and acted against them in both 1938 and 1939. In the former year, very heavy taxes were levied on horses owned by such peasants. (Only one in three even owned a horse.) In 1939, the maximum amount of land that could be occupied by such a farm was decreed to be under three acres generally, and less than that in special areas. The upper limit in irrigated regions was less than half an acre.[48]

The acquisition of the Baltic States, Eastern Poland, Bessarabia, Northern Bukovina, and other areas by the Soviet Union after the outbreak of World War II brought large numbers of peasant farmers under Soviet rule again. Initially the Soviet regime acted in these areas to liquidate the larger landowners and others assumed to be against its rule, carrying out a widespread land reform to divide large and medium-sized holdings among small peasants and those who had no land. Soviet control of these areas was wrested away for a time by Nazi occupation, but after reoccupying these territories the Soviet leaders began once again to shape the agricultural organization there as they saw fit. In 1946 over 3,000,000 peasant farms existed in the USSR, most of them in the area annexed after January 1, 1939.[49] In late 1948 and throughout 1949 vigorous collectivization drives were carried on in these western areas, and by 1950 the great majority of these formerly individualistic peasants had been collectivized and forced into the same mold as almost all other Soviet farmers. The individual farmer had become once again a rare and almost negligible element in the Soviet farm economy, except in a few special areas.

---

[48] Jasny, *The Socialized Agriculture of the USSR*, p. 314.

[49] G. Maryakhin. "Selskokhozyaistvenny Nalog v 1947g," *Sovietskiye Finansy,* No. 3 (1947), p. 21.

CHAPTER IX

AGRICULTURAL PRODUCTION DEVELOPMENT

TECHNOLOGICALLY, the peasant agriculture of the Soviet Union in 1928, on the eve of the period of mass collectivization, was far behind that of Western Europe and the United States. The two- and three-field systems of medieval farming were still widely employed, and the authority of the village community exercised great influence upon what millions of farmers grew and the timing of their crop operations. Habit, custom, and tradition were strong forces among the overwhelming mass of illiterate and semiliterate rural folk, to whom the doctrines of modern scientific agriculture were little known, if at all. But even if these doctrines had been known, few, if any, of the peasants would have been able to apply them in practice. Without significant amounts of capital, and tilling only small plots, the great bulk of these millions had little choice but to continue employing an agricultural regimen based upon the horse as the main source of draft power and natural manure as the main or only source of fertilizer. It is true that in the last years of the Czarist regime there had been rapid advances in the introduction of simple farm machinery, use of selected seed, and employment of chemical fertilizers. But after the setback of World War I and the civil war that followed it, Soviet agriculture had had little opportunity to progress beyond those beginnings. The wealthier farmers, who might have accumulated enough capital to make significant advances in their technology, knew in the late 1920's that the NEP period of grace was drawing to a close. They had no great incentive for investment in productive machinery or the like. A horse pulling a wooden plough might well be considered symbolic

334

of Soviet farm technology in this period.[1] Even so, much progress was made between 1923 and 1928.

The mass collectivization of the early 1930's had as one goal the abolition of the antiquated technology of the peasant agriculture it destroyed. Soviet leaders looked forward to the creation of enormous farms, operated with the help of tens or hundreds of machines and producing vastly increased amounts of crop and livestock output. Farms were to approximate agricultural factories, running in accordance with government plans and utilizing scientific techniques much like steel mills or coal mines. Battling against enormous opposition from the peasantry, mass destruction of agricultural capital, and shortages of trained personnel, by 1941 the Soviet government had nevertheless worked great changes in the technology of farming. Though the results of the enormous investment made here had fallen far below expectations, yet considerable progress had been achieved and high hopes were held for the future.

World War II dashed these hopes for the time being. Major areas of the richest farmland in the country were occupied by German armies and then looted of agricultural capital before being devastated by fire and shells. In the unoccupied areas of the country, little or no new farm machinery was made available, while old equipment broke down and spare parts became scarce or unavailable. Millions of farm workers went into the armed forces or the mines and factories, leaving women, old men, and children to operate the farms.[2] Under these conditions most of the technological gains achieved in the 1930's must have vanished, and much of the peasantry must have reverted to the practices prevalent before 1930. It was against this background that reconstruction of agriculture began in 1945, a reconstruction the objective of which was to exceed by far the best prewar levels of technology, output, and productivity. In the process, much that was done in the 1930's had to be duplicated in the late 1940's, but the road was easier because the active opposition that had blocked the way in 1928–32 no longer existed.

Farm Mechanization

The most publicized aspect of changes in farm production tech-

---

[1] Timoshenko, *Agricultural Russia and the Wheat Problem*, pp. 196–240.
[2] Voznesensky, *The Economy of the USSR During World War II*, p. 50.

niques during the Soviet era has been the mechanization of certain crop-production operations. Mechanization of livestock-raising and exploitation — milking cows, preparing feed, delivering water for livestock, and so on — has been little developed up to the present. In large part the disproportionate emphasis upon the mechanization of crop production reflects the much greater importance of this aspect of agriculture in a country as poor as Russia. In addition, many of the most important devices needed to mechanize livestock work require electricity, a power source available on only a small percentage of all Soviet farms.

The most striking feature of farm mechanization in the USSR in the 1930's was the rapid and widespread displacement of the horse as the primary source of power and transport for agricultural production by tractors, trucks, and other sources of mechanical power. This displacement is summarized below:[3]

Year	Horses	Tractors	Trucks
	(MILLION)	(000)	(000)
1928	33.5	26.7	.7
1933	16.6	210.9	26.6
1938	17.5	483.5	195.8

By 1940 the number of tractors in the country had risen to 523,000.[4] The picture presented by the data above was by no means entirely a planned development, however. Much of the reduction in the number of horses between 1928 and 1933 was the result of the slaughter of horses by peasants fighting or fearing collectivization or of the poor care of horses during the first confused period when collective farms had been set up wholesale. One student of the situation estimates that by 1938 the total amount of power available to Soviet agriculture had only about reached the 1928 level. But in 1938, 57 per cent of this power was accounted for by mechanical sources; in 1928 only 2 per cent of the total power supply had come from these sources.[5]

The mechanization of grain harvesting during the 1930's was sought through the large-scale introduction of combines, which both

---

[3] *Sot. Stroi. (1933–38)*, p. 88. *Sot. Stroi.*, pp. xxiv–xxv.

[4] N. A. Voznesensky, *The Growing Prosperity of the Soviet Union*, p. 25. New York: Workers Library Publishers, 1941.

[5] Jasny, *The Socialized Agriculture of the USSR*, p. 458. *Planovoye Khozyaistvo*, No. 12 (1940), pp. 49–67.

cut and thresh cereal crops, to replace the simpler tools, the sickle, and the scythe, used earlier. In 1928 the USSR had practically no such combines, but by 1940 it had 182,000.[6] Large numbers of tractor-pulled cultivators, seeders, plows, and related implements were provided to agriculture during this decade. In 1928 only 1 per cent of spring plowing was accomplished by tractor-plows; by 1938, 71.5 per cent of the work was done by these tools. In 1928 only .2 per cent of all spring grain was seeded by tractor-drawn equipment; by 1938, 56.7 per cent of this work was so done.[7] Similar rapid shifts from the use of hand tools and horse-drawn equipment to tractor-drawn and other machinery took place throughout most major branches of Soviet crop-raising, though animal husbandry, as we have noted before, was much less affected. But even in 1940 many important crop operations, such as picking cotton and harvesting sugar beets, were still being done manually in the main, because satisfactory machinery for performing these tasks had not yet been developed.

There is much evidence that initially, at least, there was a good deal of naivete in Soviet leaders' expectations of the benefits to be derived from mechanization.[8] There is nothing about a tractor that makes tractor plowing, for example, necessarily cheaper or more conducive to high yields than plowing with a horse-drawn implement. In the North Caucasus in the early 1930's the German farm concession firm, Drusag, found it more economical to plow with oxen rather than tractors, because wages and animal costs were so low.[9] Tractors *will* help produce higher yields if they permit agricultural operations to be done at the right time and if they permit higher quality of work than other means. But if the tractor seeds too late or plows too superficially — as is too often the case in the USSR, Soviet papers frequently complain — then low yields will result. Under the proper conditions of wages and prices, mechanization of farm operations can do much to cheapen farm costs, but for this there must be an adequate number of machines, a labor force competent to use the equipment and keep it in good repair, and the appropriate conditions of soil and climate. Throughout most of the

---

[6] Voznesensky, *The Growing Prosperity of the Soviet Union*, p. 25.

[7] *Sot. Stroi. (1933–38)*, p. 92.

[8] Jasny, *op. cit.*, pp. 26–30; and L. E. Hubbard, *The Economics of Soviet Agriculture*, pp. 260–63.

[9] Hubbard, *op. cit.*, p. 260.

past two decades the USSR has not had enough farm machinery; it has only slowly developed the necessary technically qualified operating and mechanical personnel in the agricultural areas; it has incurred huge costs because of poor use of the farm machinery; and it has often attempted to use mechanical equipment under inappropriate conditions. As a result the gains of such mechanization in terms of output and of reduction in labor needs and costs have been far more modest than was expected when this agricultural revolution began.[10]

Farm mechanization in the USSR has had at least two clear and major effects, however, which must be noted. First, it has drastically altered the structure of agricultural costs and greatly increased the dependence of farmers upon the nonagricultural sector of the economy. Instead of relying primarily upon horses produced on the farm and fed from farm-grown produce, mechanized farms must pay for industrially produced machinery and spare parts, and for petroleum products that fuel and lubricate the machinery. In the total financial balance sheet of agriculture, fixed overhead costs play a prominent role. The individual collective farm, of course, does not buy the machinery the government turns over to the Machine Tractor Stations, but those who direct the economy as a whole take into account the cost of this equipment initially and the cost of its maintenance thereafter in setting the amounts to be charged by the Machine Tractor Stations for its use. Second, as we have noted before, the fact that the collective farms are dependent upon the Machine Tractor Stations for the equipment required to till their fields places them at a disadvantage. It permits the latter to exercise a powerful influence upon the actual conduct of farm operations and to help assure that the government actually receives its high share of farm produce immediately after harvest.

During World War II, the level of mechanization of Soviet agriculture dropped sharply. Large numbers of tractors and trucks were requisitioned for the armed forces; much machinery was destroyed or stolen in the areas occupied by the Germans; virtually no new farm equipment was produced in the USSR and little was imported from abroad. Soviet agriculture emerged from the war period with much less mechanical equipment than it had had at the beginning, a situation aggravated by the fact that virtually all

---

[10] Jasny, *op. cit., passim,* especially chs. xviii and xix.

the machinery available was obsolete and badly worn. It could be used further only by dint of expensive repair work between harvest and spring time, and by large-scale replacement of parts that had worn out or broken.

From 1946 to 1950 the supply of farm machinery grew substantially but at a slower pace than had been projected by the plan. For example, Soviet agriculture received only 536,000 tractors (in terms of 15-horsepower-unit equivalent) instead of the 720,000 tractors (in the same equivalent) required by the plan. In the period 1946–52 inclusive Soviet agriculture received 804,000 tractors (in terms of 15-horsepower units) and 167,000 combines.[11] As of January 1954, the Machine Tractor Stations alone (not taking account of machinery on state farms) had over 1,000,000 tractors (in 15-horse-power units), about 80 per cent more than before the war, and 270,000 grain combines, or about 76 per cent more than before the war. In October 1952, Malenkov had reported that the capacity of tractors on MTS and state farms together was 59 per cent greater than the prewar level, while their combine capacity was 51 per cent greater.[12] In addition, of course, agriculture received many additional types of farm machinery from 1946 to 1953, so that by early 1954 it was probably substantially better mechanized than in 1940. Not all of the gain in tractor power mentioned above was a net addition to the power supply of agriculture, for, in part, tractors and other mechanical power sources had to make up for the decline in horses. Where Soviet agriculture had had 21,000,000 horses at the beginning of 1941, it had only 15,300,000 horses at the beginning of 1953.

The unevenness of Soviet mechanization of farming was indicated by Khrushchev. On the one hand he reported that 98 per cent of cotton sowing, 95 per cent of sugar beet planting, and 97 per cent of fall plowing on collective farms were performed by machinery. On the other hand he also reported that only 14 per cent of *kolkhoz* potato planting and less than 6 per cent of their potato harvesting was done by machinery. The general tenor of Soviet comment on mechanization of livestock work indicates that up to mid-1954 at least this was very little advanced. The need for

---

[11] *Pravda*, April 17, 1951, and January 23, 1953. *Planovoye Khozyaistvo*, No. 1 (1952), p. 8.

[12] *Pravda*, October 6, 1952, and March 6, 1954.

further substantial mechanization of Soviet agriculture was one of the main themes advanced in the official discussion during September 1953. Government decrees issued then ordered both the production of large numbers of tractors during 1954 to early 1957 and great stress upon increased mechanization of the most laggard types of farm work such as haying, potato and vegetable production, and livestock care. On June 27, 1954, *Pravda* reported that that fall Soviet agriculture would have available over 350,000 grain combines, about 33,000 flax harvesters, 11,000 sugar beet combines, over 24,000 cotton picking machines, and about 10,000 potato picking combines for the 1954 harvest.

Electricity as a source of light and power has increased greatly in importance on Soviet farms since the end of World War II. It was a negligible factor in Soviet farming in 1940, when only 10,000 collective farms — only about 4 per cent of the total — and 2,500 Machine Tractor Stations had electricity available to them.[13] World War II brought a setback in this field too, and by 1945 even fewer agricultural production units could avail themselves of electricity. Rural electrification grew with moderate speed after World War II. By April 1954 some 21,600 collective farms, or about 23 per cent of all *kolkhozy*, as well as most Machine Tractor Stations had electricity available. Soviet agriculture employed over 75,000 electric motors with a general capacity of 400,000 kilowatts, and agricultural consumption of electricity in 1952 was about four times as much as before the war, aggregating perhaps 1,500,000,000 kilowatt-hours of electric power annually, or less than two per cent of the national total.[14]

The lack of electric power on almost 80 per cent of Soviet collectives obviously poses a serious obstacle to the mechanization of many farm operations, particularly in the care of livestock. For the future the Soviet government apparently looks forward to continued increase in electricity supply to agriculture, and already experiments are being made on electric-driven tractors and related equipment.

Fertilizers

A sharp increase took place in the amount of chemical fertilizers utilized on Soviet farms in the 1930's. The amount of phosphatic,

[13] *Sotsialisticheskoye Zemledeliye,* May 31, 1950.

[14] *Pravda,* April 27, 1954. *Sotsialisticheskoye Selskoye Khozyaistvo,* No. 1 and No. 7 (1953). One third of the collective farms having electricity in 1954 used it only for home illumination.

nitrogenous, and potassium fertilizers used rose more than twelve-fold, from 259,000 metric tons in 1927–28 to over 3,200,000 tons in 1938. Counter-balancing this, however, was the sharp drop in the amount of manure available. This drop resulted from the great decline in livestock during the early 1930's. Jasny has estimated that the annual loss between 1928 and 1938 from this cause amounted to 225,000 tons of nitrogen, potash, and phosphoric acid, equivalent in plant-food value to almost 1,000,000 tons of commercial fertilizers.[15] Chemical fertilizers have been applied primarily to increase yields of sugar beets, cotton, and flax, and the amounts employed for these crops far exceed the quantities used in the era of peasant agriculture. On the other hand, relatively little has been applied on the vast areas north of the steppe, where grain and potatoes are the chief crops and where the loss of manure was felt severely.

The Soviet chemical industry began its conversion to war work relatively early. By 1940 the output of chemical fertilizers appears to have dropped about 20 per cent from the 1938 level. During the war itself fertilizer production fell very sharply. Even in 1946 probably only about 1,500,000 tons of the basic fertilizers were produced. By 1953, Khrushchev reported a sharply improved situation with agriculture scheduled to get 6,000,000 tons of mineral fertilizer. During most of the earlier postwar period, however, it is evident that the relatively low supply of mineral fertilizers, together with the deficient supply of manure resulting from the slow recovery of livestock herds, created great difficulties in the way of improving crop yields. Khrushchev recognized the importance of manure by saying that by 1955 Soviet agriculture should be able to obtain about 400,000,000 tons of manure, theoretically equivalent to 20,000,-000 tons of mineral fertilizer. However, the need for far greater amounts of mineral fertilizers was explicitly recognized in the order to triple such production by 1959 and to extend it even further by 1963. Obviously one of the motivations for this large scale fertilizer production increase is the desire to provide fertilizer not only for industrial crops — cotton, sugar beets, and the like — as at present, but also for grain, the basic food of the Soviet people.

Many expedients have been employed to increase the area of usable crop land: irrigation of arid regions, drainage of swamps, and clearing of cut-over and lightly wooded areas have been resorted to.

15 Jasny, op. cit., pp. 495, 497.

Over 6,000,000 acres, primarily in Central Asia, were irrigated between 1928 and 1941, but large areas were abandoned during World War II because they had become too saline or had been reduced to swamps. The Fourth Five-Year Plan called for restoring deteriorated irrigated land and irrigating new areas totaling about 1,500,000 acres. About 20,000,000 acres were made available for agriculture between 1928 and 1938 by clearing land in the forest areas and draining swamps, the latter primarily in White Russia. Significant losses of reclaimed land took place in the latter area during the war, when it was occupied by the Germans. The Fourth Five-Year Plan required that about 1,500,000 acres be drained between 1946 and 1950, much of this being land once reclaimed that had become swamp again during the conflict. The plan to plow up and sow to grain during 1954 and 1955 over 30,000,000 acres of virgin and fallow land in Kazakhstan, Siberia, the Urals, and the Volga Valley seems to be the most ambitious Soviet effort in the direction of expanding the sown area.

With a view to raising yields of grain and other crops, the Soviet government has sought to improve the farming practices of the collective farms. Some of the measures urged by the state are of undoubted value, but others are more questionable. The quality of seed sown improved greatly during the 1930's. It declined sharply during World War II and immediately thereafter, when there was shortage of any seed at all for planting. Great stress was laid upon introducing complex crop-rotation systems in different areas during the late 1930's, with particular emphasis upon the inclusion of grass crops in rotations. The gains made in this area during the 1930's appear to have been largely lost during the war that followed, so that the work has had to be redone to a large extent in the postwar period. The government has sought to have the ground prepared for seeding as well as possible. It has urged that fallow land be carefully cultivated to remove weeds, that plowing be deep, and that as much land be plowed in the fall as possible, since the draft power available has usually been inadequate to plow all the land for spring seeding in the early spring. Prof. T. D. Lysenko's "yarovization" technique of treating seeds to speed up ripening has been widely applied with government aid, though foreign experts have found it of extremely limited value. Perhaps more important than any specific measure has been the government's provision of a large force of agronomists throughout the countryside to help farms solve their technical problems.

A large land drainage program was called for by the Fifth Five-Year Plan which provided that the area of drained land be increased by over 40 per cent between 1951 and 1955. The most spectacular individual project provided for was the draining of the Polessye Lowland area in Belorussia and the Ukraine. In the former region alone over 3,500,000 hectares of marsh and swampland were to be reclaimed.[16] In 1954, there was evidence this program was lagging.

With regard to such matters as crop rotation, the supply of good quality seed, and the provision of agronomical advice to collective farms, Khrushchev indicated in September 1953 that much needed to be improved. On the first topic, he declared, "The introduction of crop rotation and its development on many collective and state farms has been badly organized." Though he did not mention the matter it seems likely that the amalgamation program of 1950 disorganized earlier postwar crop rotation efforts by suddenly changing the area within individual collective farms worked and planned. He commented on the lack of grass seed and complained, "There is among us unfortunately a negligent and at times criminal attitude toward potato seed." Many other comments in the Soviet press have indicated that collective farms often fail to put aside and store properly adequate amounts of high quality seed, and not merely grass and potato seed. With regard to farm specialists, he pointed out that there was only one such specialist for each five collective farms. He explained this by saying that only 5 per cent of the country's 350,000 agricultural specialists actually worked on the collectives. Most farm technicians, he indicated, had either left farm work altogether for more attractive urban occupations or were employed in the government bureaucracy engaged in "writing orders, directives, and instructions." To correct this situation the government ordered that by the spring of 1954 there should be at least 100,000 specialists working on the MTS, so that at least one full-time technician could be assigned to each collective farm. This order seems to have been fulfilled.

---

[16] *Pravda*, October 7, 1952.

Combating Drought

Many of the USSR's major agricultural regions are periodically subject to drought. The problem of finding ways and means of combating such calamities has received a great deal of attention from Soviet scientists and the Soviet government. The planting of forest shelter belts and the accumulation of snow were employed in the 1930's to help conserve moisture in dry land areas. From 1931 to 1937 collective farms planted trees on 1,500,000 acres to aid moisture retention, but the mortality rate among trees planted was high. World War II brought combat destruction in the western areas and gave other matters higher priority, so that large losses of forest land and shelter-belt area took place.[17] The severe drought of 1946 immediately after the war re-emphasized the gravity of the problem and undoubtedly played a major role in prompting the comprehensive program of antidrought measures announced by the USSR in late 1948.[18]

This comprehensive plan for combating drought was to be carried out from 1949 to 1965. It provided for the planting of eight huge state forest shelter belts and of great numbers of trees around the fields of 80,000 collective farms and 2,000 state farms. The area covered by this huge program stretches from the western borders of the USSR to the Ural Mountains. It is south of a line drawn from Kiev to Moscow to Magnitogorsk and is roughly equal to the combined size of England, France, Italy, Belgium, and Holland. The Soviet government will create major forest shelter belts along the banks and on the watersheds of the Volga, Don, Northern Donets, and Ural rivers. These will extend almost 3,300 miles, and their total area will be almost 300,000 acres. The bulk of new trees planted, however, will be on the collective farms, which, together with state farms, are scheduled to create windbreak tree plantings covering about 14,000,000 acres. To aid this work the Soviet government is scheduled to create 570 forestry stations having 22,000 tractors and 5,000 specialized machines for planting seedlings and taking care of them. Most of the work involved will be done by collective farmers, who will be paid in work days, that is, with a share in the output of the crops on the farms to which they belong.

---

[17] Jasny, *op. cit.*, pp. 489–90.
[18] *Pravda*, October 24, 1948, gives the full text of this decree.

MAP (SCHEMATIC)
LOCATION OF STATE FOREST PROTECTIVE BELTS AND OF FIELD SHELTERBELT PLANTINGS

Land Economics

SHELTERBELTS ON FIELD OF COLLECTIVE AND STATE FARMS

STATE (GOVERNMENT) PROTECTIVE BELTS

AFFORESTATION OF SANDS

EXISTING FOREST

SCALE
0   100   200 KM

V. SOVIET AFFORESTATION PLANS ANNOUNCED IN 1948

This will require the collective farms to finance this capital investment program out of current earnings, though the benefits, if any, of the program will presumably not be felt for some years. Ten-year loans to collectives are provided for to help them bear the burden of this work. Along with the afforestation aspects of the program, the plan provided for the creation of 44,000 ponds and water reservoirs on collective and state farms during 1949–55. It also called for the introduction by 1955 of crop rotations emphasizing use of grass for restoration of fertility on 77,509 collective farms and all state farms in the area. By these colossal measures the Soviet government hoped to retain moisture in the soil; curb the hot drying winds blowing west from the Caspian, which have frequently played so much havoc with crops; raise yields very substantially; and check soil erosion.[19]

If carried through, this gigantic program might well have contributed toward alleviating some of the most pressing drought and erosion problems of the steppe and forest steppe areas. That it could actually succeed in ending the drought menace entirely and permanently raising yields very substantially seems more doubtful. Solomon M. Schwarz has put one aspect of the matter succinctly:

> Shelterbelts mitigate the effect of drying winds, delay the melting of snow, slow down the water course, diminish evaporation from the soil, and thus contribute to a more even and complete use of the available water resources. But they cannot increase the resources. Moreover, forests, too, consume and evaporate considerable amounts of water. According to American experts, woods do not normally grow where precipitation is below 15 inches. . . . A glance at the precipitation map of the USSR shows that a considerable part of the territory envisaged by the plan for forest planting does not meet this demand. In particular, in the lower course of the Volga, from Stalingrad down, and in the greater part of the basin of the Ural river . . . it is perhaps possible to create shelterbelts right along the rivers partly at the expense of the flowing water. But at some distance from the rivers the creation is a dubious project, and the large expenditures of money and labor may go with the wind.[20]

---

[19] For further details on the plan, see the original text, *ibid.* A useful summary of some major features is provided in the *Current Digest of the Soviet Press*, June 7, 1949, pp. 11–15, and following. For two opposing evaluations of the plan, cf. Solomon M. Schwarz's articles in the *New Leader*, January 1 and 8, 1949, and William Mandel, "Remaking our Planet in Fifteen Years," *Soviet Russia Today*, December 1948, pp. 10–11, 29–30.

[20] *New Leader*, January 1, 1949, p. 15. Cf. also the symposium on this subject in *Land Economics*, November 1949, pp. 333–64.

The head of the USSR's Chief Administration of Erosion Control Forestation has pointed out that a large proportion of Soviet tree seeds do not sprout and acclimate themselves. At the extreme only 11 per cent of pine plantings survive. To plant the billions of oaks required for this program and have them survive, hundreds of tons of a special fungi-bearing earth are required, and no such amounts of this earth are available as yet. Other major technical problems must be solved too, he points out.[21] The rotation systems emphasizing the use of perennial grasses, which this program envisages introducing throughout the affected area, have not been successful in tests on dry land areas in the United States. There would seem reason to wonder whether these rotations will prove adequate on such land in the Soviet Union.[22] In short, the basic question is clearly that of whether the huge effort to be exerted and the great expenditures of resources to be made for fulfillment of this program could be justified by the perhaps only moderate benefits it would bring. It is characteristic of the Soviet system that the program placing such obligations and costs upon the peasantry was imposed upon them by the state, without any public discussion or debate.

In late 1952 Malenkov reported that about 6,500,000 acres of trees for shelterbelts had been planted during the preceding three and a half years.[23] In 1953, after Stalin's death, however, there seemed to be no stress put on this afforestation program, and it went unmentioned in the great discussion of measures to improve agricultural production which was conducted in September 1953. It seems likely, therefore, that much of the official pressure behind this program has been dropped and the program may have been largely abandoned. Some such decision seems likely since the emphasis of the new 1953 farm policy was on measures to increase farm production quickly and, at best, the benefits of the shelterbelt program, if carried out, would be received only after a comparatively long time. Moreover, by occupying land that might otherwise be planted to grain and other crops, the shelterbelt program seems to conflict with the 1954–55 effort to expand grain acreage quickly.

[21] *Current Digest of the Soviet Press,* June 7, 1949, p. 11.
[22] Jasny, *op. cit.,* pp. 490–91.
[23] *Pravda,* October 6, 1952.

Measures for the Future

In August and September 1950, the Soviet regime announced a number of major projects aimed at further combating the impact of drought upon Soviet agriculture. These included a complete reconstruction of the existing irrigation system and the creation of vast new irrigation and water supply systems in the desert area east of the Caspian Sea, in the areas east and west of the Volga River, in the Southern Ukraine and in Northern Crimea.

The order for revamping the existing irrigation system, which was published August 18, 1950, revealed that the USSR had about 11,000,000 acres of irrigated land, including almost 4,000,000 acres in the Uzbek SSR; about 1,500,000 acres in the Kazakh SSR; and about 1,250,000 acres in the Kirgiz SSR. This decree condemned the existing irrigation system on these grounds: excessive density of canals resulted in nonutilization of 4 to 12 per cent of the land available; small fields common in irrigated areas hindered proper use of farm machinery, resulting in the loss of up to 5 per cent of output on these fields; existing irrigation canals were often focal points of weed and insect infestation with resultant damage to crops on adjacent land; cleaning of the dense canal network required high labor costs annually.

To remedy these difficulties, the decree ordered that by 1953 the existing networks of permanent feeder canals be filled in. After this is done, new temporary feeder canals will be dug each spring and filled in after the harvest is gathered each year, though main irrigation canals will be maintained permanently. In setting up temporary canals, attention is to be focused upon minimizing their number and increasing the average size of fields so as to facilitate the use of farm machinery and to increase the amount of land available for crop use. The government ordered the provision of large numbers of earth-moving machines for this work. Collective farms in affected areas will pay 60 per cent of the cost, the government paying the remainder.

The drastic measures ordered by this decree suggest strongly that the irrigation system in the areas affected, built up laboriously over many years, must have operated very poorly. Digging and filling in temporary canals each year in the future will obviously be very expensive and have to provide substantial improvements in output to justify the cost. The available evidence is inadequate to

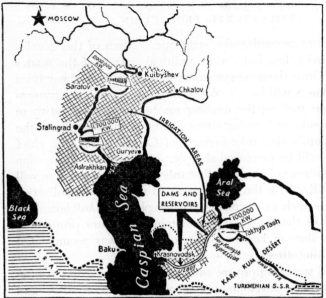

Kuibyshev Power Station
Capacity. 2,000,000 kw.
Output 10,000,000,000
kw-hr. per year.
To be completed in 1955.

Stalingrad Power Station
Capacity....1,700,000 kw.
Output ...10,000,000,000
kw-hr. per year.
To be completed in 1956.

Chief Turkmen Canal
Length .. 683.5 miles.
Will irrigate 3,212,300
acres.
May have been abandoned.

Kakhovka Power Station
Capacity .. 250,000 kw.
Output ...1,200,000 kw-hr.
per year.
To be completed in 1956.

South Ukrainian Canal and
North Crimean Canal.
Combined Length....
341.7 miles.
Both canals
will irrigate. . . .
3,706,500 acres
and water an additional . . .
4,200,700 acres.
May have been abandoned.

VI. SOVIET HYDROELECTRIC AND IRRIGATION PROJECTS
ANNOUNCED IN 1950

permit conclusions regarding the economic wisdom of this revolution in Soviet irrigation, but certain political aspects of the matter are apparent. Once the new system of temporary canals has been established, farmers will be completely dependent upon the government stations controlling the digging machinery, for unless these provide new canals each spring there will be no harvest. Thus the government's domination over farmers of Central Asia — the chief area affected — will be increased sharply. Moreover the dislocation of customary patterns of land use that this new system requires will probably be utilized by the government to root out anticollective farm practices — such as excessive private plots for *kolkhozniki* — that may exist in these areas. Here again a measure profoundly affecting the welfare of large numbers of people was promulgated without consulting them.

Irrigation and water supply are among the major objectives of the hydroelectric power developments scheduled at Kuibyshev and Stalingrad on the Volga, and at Kakhovka on the Dnepr River in the Southern Ukraine. The Kuibyshev station, scheduled for full operation in 1955, is to provide electricity for irrigating about 2,500,000 acres in the Trans-Volga area. In connection with the Stalingrad project, there is scheduled to be built by 1956 a gravity-flow canal and water supply system providing water to about 15,000,000 acres of land in the Caspian depression between the Volga and Ural Rivers. Electric power from the new Stalingrad hydroelectric station is to operate irrigation systems serving almost 4,000,000 acres of land between the Volga and Ural Rivers, north of the region served by the water supply system mentioned earlier. In addition, canals and water supply systems are to be built to irrigate and bring water to about 14,000,000 acres of land in the Sarpinsk depression, the Nogaisk Steppe, and the Black Lands area.

These are obviously very large and impressive projects with great potentiality for improving agricultural production. They will require huge capital investment and an enormous amount of labor. Not least significant is the fact that many of the new irrigation and water supply facilities to be provided in the future, if these plans are realized, will be in the areas included within the shelterbelt program discussed above. These Soviet plans are implicit admission that the shelterbelt program by itself cannot solve the problem of drought in the vast area west and north of the Caspian Sea. They seem impressive confirmation of the objections raised by Solomon Schwarz in the quotation above.

Several major projects announced in 1950 appear to have been abandoned or greatly slowed down after Stalin's death. One is the Chief Turkmen Canal which was scheduled to be built east of the Caspian Sea from Takhia-Tash on the Amu Darya through the Kara Kum Desert, terminating at Krasnovodsk on the Caspian Sea. This 700-mile canal was supposed to divert a large part of the Amu Darya from the Aral Sea. By this means it was hoped to provide water for irrigation of about 3,200,000 acres of desert land, most of which it was planned to turn into a highly-productive cotton area. The complete absence of any mention of this project in the central Soviet press after Stalin's death suggests that this construction work may have been dropped or deferred in order to free resources for other purposes. The amnesty decree adopted in late March 1953 may have played a role in such a decision by reducing the available supply of forced labor, which was probably intended to be a major source of labor supply for the work under the very severe desert conditions. A decree published April 23, 1954, and dealing with cotton growing in the Turkmen Republic, seemed to imply that the Chief Turkmen Canal had been replaced by the much more modest Kara Kum Canal project.

Similar evidence suggests that the South Ukrainian and North Crimean canals, also announced in 1950, have been abandoned since Stalin's death. This project aimed at irrigating 4,000,000 acres and providing water-supply facilities for an additional 4,000,000 acres. The Kakhovka hydroelectric project announced in conjunction with this canal scheme appears to be in process of construction, however, judging by Soviet press reports.

Total Agricultural Production

Any attempt to evaluate the influence upon production of the institutional and technical changes wrought by the Soviet regime in the agriculture of the USSR is made difficult by the untrustworthiness of the data published by that regime. Data have been suppressed for some years. There have also been changes in definition of what is being measured and in methods of computation, so as to make comparisons over time misleading if they do not allow for these changes.

In measuring total agricultural production, the Soviet government prepares a statistical series that purports to represent changes in the physical volume of farm production by valuing all crop and livestock products at average prices prevailing in 1926–27 over the USSR as a whole. The picture presented by these data for the years in which they have been published is given in Table 25.

TABLE 25. Gross Production of Agriculture in the USSR for Selected Years.

Year	Total*	Crops	Livestock Products
	(BILLIONS OF RUBLES AT 1926–27 PRICES)		
1913	12.6	8.0	4.6
1929	14.7	9.1	5.7
1930	14.0	9.6	4.4
1931	13.9	9.9	4.1
1932	13.1	9.8	3.3
1933	14.0	11.1	3.0
1934	14.6	11.3	3.3
1935†	16.1	12.2	3.9
1937	20.1	15.1	5.1
1940	23.2	‡	‡
1950 plan	29.5	‡	‡
1950 actual	26.5	‡	‡
1952	25.5	‡	‡

* Some total figures do not add up to sum of crops and livestock products because of rounding. † Preliminary. ‡ Unavailable.
Sources: 1913 and 1937—*Sot. Stroi. (1933-38)*, p. 84. 1929 to 1935—*Sot. Stroi.*, p. 232. Figures for 1940 and 1950 calculated from percentages in N. A. Voznesensky's speech of March 15, 1946, and from *Voprosy Ekonomiki*, No. 8 (1953), p. 55, 1952—*Pravda*, September 15, 1953.

Taken at face value, the data in Table 25 indicate a rather remarkable growth in the physical volume of all agricultural production. By 1940 this production is indicated as being almost twice the 1913 level. Crop production is shown to have been at almost twice the 1913 volume by 1937. Livestock production is indicated to have been very sharply cut during the early 1930's, but then to have almost regained its 1929 level by 1937. These official data cannot however be accepted as giving a full picture of the fluctuation of agricultural production under the Soviet regime for a number of reasons:

1. No comparable data have been published for the bulk of the

years of the 1920's; nor for the years 1936, 1938, and 1939, when there is good reason to believe that crops were relatively poor. compared with 1935 or 1937; nor for the war and postwar years until 1949–52. It seems obvious that in the past two decades, at least, these statistics have usually been issued only when they did not present too bad a picture of farm production, that is, propaganda objectives have governed and still govern their availability.

2. The data for different years in Table 25, though often freely compared by Soviet officials, are not comparable, since they cover different territories. The USSR was significantly larger in 1940 than in 1937, having absorbed Eastern Poland, the Baltic States, and smaller areas. After World War II it added the Carpatho-Ukraine of Czechoslovakia, part of East Prussia, southern Sakhalin, and other small areas. Between 1939 and 1945 the USSR gained 670,000 square kilometers of territory, with a prewar population of 24,300,000 persons and a substantial agricultural production.[24]

3. There have been important changes in the definition of agricultural production and the coverage of these indexes. Until 1933, the grain crop was reported on the basis of what had actually been harvested and put into the barns, that is, exclusive of substantial losses in harvesting and moving crops from the fields. Beginning in 1933, the grain crop was calculated on the basis of what had grown in the fields — the so-called "biological crop" — usually minus some inadequate small discount for losses. Beginning either in 1937 or 1939, all discounts for losses were ended, so that what was reported was substantially greater than what was available for use, since it included waste and losses of all kinds. In July 1939 this method of accounting was extended to the principal nongrain crops, so that in the case of cotton, for example, the cotton production reported and included in the index of total farm production included all cotton harvested, all cotton that fell on the ground, and all cotton that remained on the plant. By this device the output of agriculture was increased at the stroke of a pen, though no more and no less physical volume of crops became available for use.[25] Additionally, in 1937 and after, the output of farm products raised in the "victory gardens," as we should call them, of urban workers was included in

---

24 Balzak, et al., Economic Geography of the USSR, p. 544.
25 Cf. the full discussion of this matter in Jasny, op. cit., Note G, pp. 725–36.

the figures on total agricultural production. In 1937 this source accounted for almost one billion rubles worth of farm production, about 5 per cent of the total. In more recent years this figure has probably increased sharply, because of the great expansion of food-raising by urban workers that occurred during the war and postwar years.[26]

The fallaciousness of the practice of calculating harvests in terms of mythological biological yields was finally admitted after Stalin's death by both Malenkov and Khrushchev, who employed language strongly resembling that used earlier by Western economists in condemning this practice. Thus Malenkov said in August 1953: [27]

> . . . it is necessary to end the incorrect practice of calculating the results of the collective farms' work in producing grain and other crops not by the actual harvest but by the apparent harvest yield. It must not be forgotten that our country and our collective farms can be wealthy only in crops actually stored in the barns, not in crops still out in the fields.

Khrushchev spoke in the same vein a month later:

> It is necessary to end the incorrect practice of evaluating the results of the production of grain and other products by the apparent yield rather than by the actual harvest. This practice is not capable of increasing the harvest of farm products and even hinders the fight against harvest losses, which are still great in the collective farms. . . . We must organize accounting of the harvest gathered in the barns and pay bonuses in relation to the harvest which has been gathered so that MTS workers will be directly interested in the actual grain and other farm product harvests.

Neither of these Soviet leaders made any mention of the fact that for many years preceding these confessions the highest Soviet leaders had been deceiving world public opinion by quoting harvest statistics exaggerated by the disingenuous statistical trick termed the "biological yield."

An attempt to obtain a more accurate picture of changes in Soviet farm production has been made by Dr. Jasny. He has calculated the value of this agricultural production in 1928, 1932, and 1937, in the same prices as the official index but taking account of

---

[26] *Sot. Stroi. (1933–38)*, p. 84, shows explicitly that such production was not earlier included in the index. The subsequent inclusion of this output is testified to by *Slovar-Spravochnik po Sotsialno-Ekonomicheskoi Statistike*, p. 105.

[27] *Pravda*, August 9 and September 15, 1953.

that index's deficiencies. He has also calculated what output might have been expected to be in 1938 and 1940 on the pre-1939 territory of the USSR if the weather had been normal. Throughout these calculations he has accounted for production on the basis of the crops actually harvested, that is, without the waste and losses now included in Soviet calculations. His results follow: [28]

Year	Weather	Vegetable Products	Animal Products	Total
		(BILLIONS OF RUBLES AT 1926–27 PRICES)		
1928	Almost normal	9.5	6.0	15.5
1932	Almost normal	8.7	3.3	12.0
1937	Excellent	13.4	5.1	18.4
1938	Assumed normal	12.1*	5.3*	17.4*
1940	Assumed normal	12.4*	5.4*	17.8*

* Estimates of what the value of income from agriculture might have been with normal weather; *not* estimates of actual income.

The same writer has also attempted to compute the income available from agriculture, that is, the value of gross production as given above minus depreciation charges and the value of materials of nonfarm origin used in farming. Both depreciation charges and the value of nonfarm commodities used in agriculture increased sharply over the 1930's because of increased capital investment in this area of the economy and because of the vastly greater expenditure for gasoline and other fuels, lubricants, fertilizers, insecticides, and so on. Dr. Jasny's conclusions on the income from agriculture follow (in billions of rubles at prices of 1926–27): [29]

1928	9.2
1932	6.9
1937	10.5
1938	9.5*
1940	9.7*

* Estimates of what the value of income from agriculture might have been with normal weather; *not* estimates of actual income.

If Dr. Jasny is correct in his calculations — and the evidence suggests that his figures are much nearer the truth than those officially published by the Soviet government — then the net income of agri-

---

[28] Jasny, *op. cit.*, p. 673. A slightly revised set of total values is given on p. 682, but without the breakdown between vegetable and animal products.
[29] *Ibid.*, pp. 676–82.

culture in the USSR fell about 25 per cent between 1928 and 1932. By 1937 it was about 15 per cent above 1928. In 1938 and 1940, if weather had been normal, it would have been little more than in 1928. Dr. Jasny's estimates of the development of gross agricultural production given earlier suggest that the rise in this output that did occur between 1928 and 1940 (about 2.3 billion rubles, assuming normal weather in 1940) was almost entirely eaten up by the rise in depreciation charges and the cost of nonfarm production materials for agriculture during the twelve-year period. The increase in the net contribution of agriculture to the economy over this turbulent and revolutionary period was very slight, unless, of course, one includes the additional output of areas annexed in 1939 and 1940.

Dr. Jasny adds this melancholy information regarding the course of Soviet production during World War II:

> A marked decline in farm output followed directly upon the first shot; one can even rightly speak of "collapse." The decline in the uninvaded territory during the whole war (including 1945) was probably more than three times as large, in percentage terms, as the decline in Russian farm output during the war of 1914–18.[30]

As we shall see below, the output of a number of the most important Soviet crops in 1945 was half that of 1940 or less. In 1946 Soviet authorities announced that the country had been hit by the worst drought in fifty years, so that the production of grain, sunflower seeds, and sugar beets declined appreciably below that of 1945, though cotton production in 1946 did rise substantially over that of the preceding year. An emergency program to improve the quality of farm work and increase the amount of machinery and other resources available to agriculture was adopted by the Central Committee of the Communist Party in February 1947. In 1947, 1948, and 1949, official communiqués reported increased agricultural output in each of those years for particular crops, and — in 1949 — for livestock products, but no summary data on over-all farm production had been released through the end of 1949.[31]

In September 1953 Khrushchev revealed that in 1952 gross agri-

---

[30] *Ibid.*, pp. 69–70.

[31] Cf. the communiqués of the State Planning Committee and later the Central Statistical Administration of the Council of Ministers of the USSR released quarterly during 1947, 1948, and 1949. The brightest report on agricultural output was made public in the communiqué published in the Soviet press on October 15, 1949.

cultural output had been only 10 per cent above that of 1940. In terms of 1926–27 prices, this indicates that 1952 output was valued at 25,500,000,000 rubles, well below even the Fourth Five-Year Plan goal for 1950 of 29,500,000,000 rubles. The 10 per cent gain in 1952 over 1940, small as it is, loses even more of its significance when it is recalled that in 1952 the Soviet population was probably 10 per cent or almost 10 per cent larger than in 1940, while the geographic limits of the Soviet Union were somewhat bigger in 1952 than they had been twelve years earlier. At best these figures seemed to indicate that from 1946 to 1952 Soviet agriculture was able to repair the great damage of World War II and keep pace with the increase of population, but no progress had been made toward increasing output rapidly enough to improve the quality and quantity of the Soviet diet above the poor level prevailing in 1940. While this record can hardly be termed complete failure in view of the great wartime losses, neither can it be considered at all commensurate with the glowing claims made by communist propaganda for the "enormous advantages of socialist agriculture." It may be noted that 1952 gross farm production was even less than that of 1950. In 1950, that production had been 14 per cent more than in 1940, as compared with only 10 per cent more in 1952.

Grain Production

Grain production is the most important section of Soviet agriculture, since bread and cereal products provide by far the overwhelming bulk of calories available to the Soviet people. Grain is also most important as a livestock feed. Soviet statistics of grain production include primarily wheat, rye, oats, corn, buckwheat, millet, barley, rice, and dry legumes. Grain crops are produced throughout all the major agricultural areas of the country and occupy the great bulk of the USSR's total crop area. In recent years few data have been published regarding acreage, yields, and production of individual grain crops, so that the analysis below will be primarily in terms of grain production as a whole.

As indicated in the discussion above, these data must be interpreted with great caution, both because of the increase in the area of the Soviet Union since 1939, and because of the changes in the method of calculating yields and production since 1933. Much

TABLE 26. Acreage, Yield, and Production of Grain in the USSR as Indicated by Official Statistics and Statements for Selected Years.

Year	Acreage (MILLION HECTARES)	Yield (TONS PER HECTARE)	Production (MILLION METRIC TONS)
1913	94.4	.85	80.1
1928	92.2	.79	73.3
1932	99.7	.70	69.9
1935	103.4	.87	90.1
1937	104.4	1.15	120.3
1938	102.4	.93	94.9
1940	111.0*	1.07	119.0
1945	85.3*	.78	66.5
1946	†	†	61.0
1947	†	†	97.0
1948	†	†	115.0
1949	102.5*	1.21	124.5
1950 goal	105.8*	1.20	127.0
1950 actual	102.5*	1.21	124.5
1951	†	†	121.3
1952	99.1*(?)	1.31	130.0
1953	107.2*	1.11	129.0‡
1955 goal	†	†	174.3–186.8

* Enlarged post-1939 territory. † Data unavailable. ‡ Estimated.
Sources: 1913—*Sot. Stroi.*, pp. xxiv, xxv. 1928-38—Jasny, *op. cit.*, p. 793. 1940—*Planovoye Khozyaistvo*, No. 2 (1946), p. 125. 1945 — *Pravda*, March 7, 1947. 1946-51 — Official Soviet communiqués. 1952—Calculated on basis of Malenkov's October 5, 1952, speech. 1953—Production estimated on basis statement in *Pravda*, January 31, 1954, that 1953 harvest almost reached 1952 level. Acreage and yield calculated on basis *Pravda*, March 6, 1954, statement that 1953 grain acreage was 3,800,000 hectares below that of 1940. 1955 goal calculated on basis Fifth Five-Year Plan Directives.

of the apparent increase in yield and production shown above from 1928 to 1937, in 1938, and in 1940 is attributable to these two factors, rather than to any great improvement in agricultural efficiency brought about by collectivization and mechanization. Dr. Jasny has estimated that to make the production data for the late 1930's comparable with those of 1932 and earlier, when only the crop actually put into barns was counted, deductions of 20 per cent and more must be made from reported grain yield and production figures for those years given in Table 26 above. The year 1937 was one of exceptionally good weather, and resulted in an excellent harvest. A comparison of the official figures and Dr. Jasny's corrected figures throws this light on production progress.[32]

[32] Jasny, *op. cit.*, p. 548.

Grain Production
(MILLION METRIC TONS)

Year	Official	Jasny
1928............	73.3	73.3
1937............	120.3	96
1938............	94.9	76
1939............	106.5	82

If these corrected estimates represent the situation adequately, then grain production in the late 1930's in the USSR was about 15 per cent higher than in 1928, most of this increase being accounted for by the rise of about 10,000,000 hectares, or over 10 per cent, in the area sown to grain.

The data for 1945 above show vividly the impact of war upon Soviet grain-raising, even though production in 1945 was probably much higher than in earlier war years. Between 1940 and 1945 acreage declined almost 25 per cent, and yield fell almost 30 per cent, so that total output was only little more than half that of 1940. The drought of 1946, the lack of farm manpower and other production essentials, the organizational weaknesses of the collective farms, which had revealed themselves during the war — all these reduced grain output even below that of the previous year. The Soviet government claimed a 58 per cent rise in grain production in 1947 over 1946, a rise so sharp as to be almost unbelievable. It seems likely that the new system of government crop inspectors introduced that year to check acreage and yield figures prevented the under-reporting of production that had taken place earlier and resulted in more over-reporting than usual even in modern Soviet crop statistics.[33]

From 1949 to 1952, the data in Table 26 suggest, Soviet grain production remained essentially stationary, the gain in 1952 little more than offsetting the decline during 1951. In 1953, the economic report published on January 31, 1954 revealed, the grain harvest was somewhat below the 1952 level. The 1955 goal of raising grain production 40 to 50 per cent above the 1950 level was pronounced unrealistic by foreign observers when this objective was first announced in August 1952. In early 1954 there seemed no evidence to justify a change in this opinion, especially in light of the fact

---

[33] Cf. *ibid.*, p. 736, and *Sotsialisticheskoye Zemledeliye*, July 11, 1947, for an account of the new system of government supervision over determination of crop acreage and production.

that the September 1953 Soviet discussion of agricultural policy made no reference to this goal. The omission seemed a tacit admission of that goal's unrealistic nature.

Just how much importance should be attached to the apparent 20 per cent gain in grain yield between 1940 and 1952 is uncertain. Much of it may simply be the result of a greater degree of exaggeration of yields in 1952 than existed in 1940, but at least part of it may well be an actual gain resulting from improved weather, some improvement in farm work and the like. It must be remembered, however, that the yield is estimated on the basis of an uncertain acreage estimate. Actually the apparent increase in grain yield may be entirely illusory since Dr. Lazar Volin has estimated that total 1952 grain acreage was 107,300,000 hectares, substantially more than estimated in Table 26.[34] If Dr. Volin is correct, there was no significant gain in grain yields from 1940 to 1952.

As among different grains, wheat has been most favored in the postwar period. Khrushchev noted that in 1953 the area sown to wheat was 8,100,000 hectares greater than before the war. This contrasts sharply with the substantial reduction of over-all grain acreage from 1940 to 1952 shown in Table 26. But correspondingly, therefore, the area sown to other grain crops — particularly feed grain in all probability — must have declined very greatly. The need to feed the greatly increased Soviet urban population has undoubtedly been a major factor in the government's concentration on raising wheat production. Wheat accounted for 30 per cent of 1938 Soviet grain production. In 1952 the corresponding percentage would seem to have been substantially higher.

The above conclusion was confirmed on March 6, 1954, when the Central Committee of the Communist Party disclosed that the 1953 area sown to grain crops other than wheat and rye was 8,900,-000 hectares below the analogous 1940 area, though the total 1953 grain acreage was only 3,800,000 hectares below the 1940 level. Judging by the sweeping program announced on that date for raising grain production, the disappointing 1953 grain output must have been quite a blow to Soviet leaders. The 1953 result seemed to make unattainable the 1955 grain production goal, unless drastic

---

[34] Lazar Volin, "The Malenkov-Khrushchev New Economic Policy," *Journal of Political Economy,* June 1954, p. 197.

steps were taken in 1954 and 1955. The nature of these steps will be discussed below.

The pattern of grain utilization showed important changes in the late 1930's as compared with the years before World War I. If one compares the pattern of 1913 with 1938, the most striking shift is the great reduction of grain exports and the increase in the amount of grain consumed for food, the latter phenomenon being primarily the result of increased population. On the other hand, use of grain for livestock feed was less in 1938 than in 1913, even though it was already well above the low point of 1932 following the heavy loss of livestock during the great collectivization struggle.[35] If any substantial improvement is to be achieved in the diet of Soviet citizens in the future, livestock products — meat, milk, eggs, and so on — must be consumed in greater quantity. To produce one pound of meat usually requires feeding of five to ten pounds of grain. Hence improvement in the Soviet peoples' consumption of livestock products obviously will require substantial increases in the amount of grain fed to livestock, increases that are out of the question unless a substantial rise is achieved in grain output as a whole.

Perhaps the most striking change in the pattern of grain distribution under the Soviet regime before World War II was the increased share of the crop procured directly by the state and distributed by it. From the 73,300,000 metric tons of grain produced in 1928, the Soviet regime obtained 10,800,000 tons, or less than 15 per cent. The 1939 grain crop, on a comparable barn basis, is estimated by Jasny to have been 82,000,000 metric tons. Of this the state obtained 35,000,000 tons, or over 40 per cent.[36] Most of this grain obtained by the state, as pointed out in the previous chapter, was secured at prices far lower than it could have been sold for in the free market. Only the government's complete domination of the peasantry through the collective farm system made this sharp change in the amount of grain obtained possible. In consequence, the government had sufficient grain in the late 1930's, not only to feed the rapidly rising urban population and the armed forces, but also to export about 1,000,000 tons of grain annually. Most important, the high government grain procurements in this period before the German

---

[35] Jasny, *op. cit.,* p. 794.
[36] *Ibid.*

invasion of June 1941 probably permitted the accumulation of a substantial grain stockpile, which proved invaluable when production was cut drastically after that invasion. Jasny indicates that the Soviet government's grain stockpile may have increased by 10,000,000 tons in the late 1930's.[37] Other estimates have put the figure substantially higher. In the postwar period there have been indications that the Soviet government has followed the same practice of requiring high grain deliveries to the state to build up its food stockpile against war or other emergencies.

Khrushchev has revealed that the Soviet government obtained 40,000,000 tons of grain, through procurements and purchases, from the 1952 crop as against the 10,300,000 tons obtained from the 1926 crop. In 1926 the Soviet grain harvest was 72,600,000 tons, so that after government purchases are allowed for, there remained to the peasants 62,300,000 tons for seed, livestock feed, peasant food consumption, and reserves. In 1952, if we deduct 20 per cent to convert the biological harvest into the actual harvest, the Soviet production of grain was 104,000,000 tons. After deducting the 40,000,000 tons taken by the government, this left the peasants 64,000,000 tons, less than 2,000,000 tons more than in 1926. In 1926 the rural population was 120,700,000; in 1952 the rural population was probably over 130,000,000, if we take into account the probability that the Soviet Union's population in the early 1950's was over 210,000,000 in all. As for the urban population, Malenkov revealed that in 1953 it was 80,000,000. We may summarize this analysis as follows:

Year	Urban Population	State Grain Supply (Tons)	Rural Population	Peasant Grain Supply (Tons)
1926–27	26,314,000	10,300,000	120,713,000	62,300,000
1952–53	80,000,000	40,000,000	130,000,000+	64,000,000

This comparison shows clearly that over this 26-year period the Soviet government succeeded in increasing the grain supply available to it at the rate needed to feed the rapidly growing urban population; but this was accomplished only at the expense of substantially reducing per capita grain supplies for the rural — mainly peasant — population. In the face of these heavy grain procurements, there need be little wonder that the number of Soviet cattle

---

[37] *Ibid.*, p. 560.

dropped by 2,000,000 during 1952. Soviet peasants, like people everywhere, put their own food needs ahead of those of livestock.

In October 1952 and August 1953, Malenkov's speeches tried to deny or evade the fact that the grain shortage was an urgent Soviet problem. In the former speech he went so far as to declare: "The grain problem, which in the past was regarded as our most acute and gravest problem, has thus been solved, solved definitely and finally." The highly disappointing 1953 harvest apparently forced the Soviet leaders to face the grain problem publicly. The Central Committee decision on grain published in March 1954 stated the matter in this fashion:

> . . . the presently existing level of grain production, both as regards the gross harvest, and also its marketed portion, does not cover the growing needs of the national economy. There has arisen a disproportion between the quantity of grain becoming available for government disposition and the growth of state requirements. The quantity of grain remaining in the collective farms after these have fulfilled their requirements to the state also does not cover all the requirements of communal economy of the collectives. In many collective farms little grain is paid to collective farmers for their work-day earnings, particularly little feed grain, without which a sharp expansion of livestock is impossible.

Even by squeezing the collective farms, in short, the government had been unable to get all the grain it needed.

The program made public in March 1954 pinned its hopes on a general increase in the area sown to grain throughout the country, but particularly on the sowing to grain of 13,000,000 hectares (about 32,500,000 acres) in Kazakhstan, Siberia, the Urals, the Volga Valley, and the North Caucasus. These new acres were to come from land previously left untilled, and it was hoped that by 1955 the additional acreage would supply about 18,000,000 metric tons of additional grain, of which 70 to 80 per cent might be marketed. Top priority was given to this program, with large numbers of tractors and combines being assigned to its execution. The recruitment of 100,000 young people to do the manual labor required was ordered, as well as the transfer of thousands of technical personnel. Presumably additional grain can be raised if these millions of additional acres are sown. But presumably too, these new acres are largely marginal lands with poor soil, uncertain rainfall, or both. Hence unless nature is very kind with respect to rainfall, these new lands are likely to give low yields with the result that the additional grain obtained will be disappointing as well as expensive. The fact that there had been no hint of this grandiose program in the extensive official discussion of farm policy in September 1953 suggested that this move was an improvisation prepared hastily after the unsatisfactory 1953 grain harvest results became known.

The Communist Party Central Committee report published June 27, 1954, claimed a very substantial rise in 1954 spring grain plantings over 1953, 6,429,000 hectares. Of this it claimed that grain plantings on virgin and fallow lands accounted for 3,583,000 hectares as compared with the 1954 goal of 2,300,000 hectares of grain plantings on such lands. But this report of the new program's first substantial success was marred by the same document's revelation of the confusion and chaos that had marked the effort to settle and plant these new lands, defects that must have made this effort very expensive indeed.

Probably more important, however, was the announcement of an important concession to grain farmers, one equivalent to raising the price paid for their grain. The Central Committee ordered grain requisition quotas, paid for at very low prices, reduced, thus leaving more grain to be sold the government at the higher state "purchase prices."

Industrial Crops

The Soviet Union produces a wide variety of industrial crops to meet food, fibre, and other needs. These include cotton for textiles and cottonseed oil; sugar beets, which provide almost all the country's sugar; flax for fibre, oil, and export; sunflower seeds for vegetable oil; hemp; soy beans; tobacco; kok-sagyz and other rubber plants; and so on. The production of most of these crops was highly localized before World War II, each being produced chiefly in a few areas. During and since that conflict there has been significant further dispersion of the growing areas for these crops. Nevertheless even in 1950 each of these crops tended to be concentrated mainly in a few areas where climatic and soil conditions were particularly favorable for it. In considering the data of Table 27, the qualifications mentioned earlier must be borne in mind in evaluating changes in yield and output.

TABLE 27. Official Data on Acreages, Yields, and Production of Major Industrial Crops for Selected Years, 1913–55.

Year	Acreage (MILLION HECTARES)	Yield (TONS/HECTARE)	Production (MILLION METRIC TONS)
		UNGINNED COTTON	
1913	.688	1.08	.74
1928	.971	.85	.82
1932	2.172	.59	1.27
1937	2.09	1.2	2.58
1940	2.1	1.29	2.7
1945	1.2	1.03	1.2
1946	1.3	1.28	1.6
1947	1.467†	*	1.9
1949	*	*	over 2.7
1950 goal	1.7	1.84	3.1
1950 actual	2.3	1.63	3.75
1951	*	*	3.95
1952	*	*	over 3.95
1955 goal	*	*	5.8–6.2
		SUGAR BEETS	
1913	.649	16.8	10.9
1928	.770	13.2	10.1
1932	1.538	4.3	6.56
1937	1.193	18.3	21.86
1940	1.2	17.5	20.9
1945	.8	10.6	8.9
1946	.938	*	*
1947	1.058†	*	*
1949	*	*	22.2
1950 goal	1.4	19.0	26.0
1950 actual	1.26	18.6	23.4
1951	*	*	27.4
1955 goal	*	*	38.6–39.8
		FIBRE FLAX	
1913	1.0	.33	.33
1928	1.4	.24	.32
1932	2.5	.20	.50
1937	2.1	.27	.57
1940	2.1	.27	.57
1945	*	*	*
1946	.9	*	*
1947	1.3†	*	*
1950 goal	2.0	.40	.80

TABLE 27 (Cont'd).

Year	Acreage (MILLION HECTARES)	Yield (TONS/HECTARE)	Production (MILLION METRIC TONS)
		SUNFLOWER SEED	
1913	.969	.76	.74
1928	3.9	.54	2.1
1932	5.3	.43	2.3
1937	3.3	.64	2.1
1940	3.5	.94	3.3
1945	2.9	.63	1.8
1946	3.0	*	*
1947	3.1†	*	*
1949	*	*	3.8
1950 goal	3.7	1.0	3.7
1950 actual	3.6	.86	3.1
1955 goal	*	*	4.7–5.0

* Data unavailable. † Planned goal.

Sources: Table compiled mainly from data in *Sot. Stroi.*, pp. xxiv, xxv, 280, 339, and 345; Jasny, *The Socialized Agriculture of the USSR*, passim; *Itogi Vypolneniya Vtorogo Pyatiletnego Plana*, pp. 92-94; N. Anisimov, *Selskoye Khozyaistvo v Novoy Stalinskoy Pyatiletke*, pp. 39-53; *Pravda*, April 10, 1946, February 28 and March 7, 1947, April 17, 1951, August 20 and October 6, 1952; and *Sot. Stroi. (1933-38)*, pp. 95-98.

Cotton. Cotton is the most important textile fibre of the Soviet Union, as well as the source of much cottonseed oil. Before the Soviet revolution about half of the cotton utilized in Russian textile mills was imported from abroad. Imports exceeding 100,000 tons annually were also required during the 1920's. Determined to make themselves independent of foreign supplies of this important raw material, Soviet leaders ordered acreage expanded sharply during the 1930's. Increased fertilizer supplies helped raise yields significantly. Domestic production rose quickly, permitting imports to be slashed from 115,000 metric tons in 1929 to 58,000 tons the following year and only 16,500 tons in 1938.[38] In later years before World War II the Soviet Union was able to stockpile large amounts of the important fibre, though the textile needs of the Soviet people had not been fully met.[39]

Cotton-raising requires a warm climate and abundant moisture. Most Soviet cotton is raised on the irrigated land of Central Asia, particularly in Uzbekistan, which accounted for 60 per cent of all USSR cotton output in 1937. Large investments in irrigation works have been required for expansion of cotton-growing in these areas. During the 1930's Soviet leaders also sponsored the expansion of cotton-growing into new, unirrigated areas, including the southern

[38] Baykov, *Soviet Foreign Trade*, Appendix Table VI.
[39] Jasny, *op. cit.*, p. 567.

Ukraine, the Crimea, and the North Caucasus, where the plant grows relatively far north and with relatively little moisture, so that yields have been quite disappointing. These new areas accounted for 23.9 per cent of all land sown to cotton in the USSR in 1937, but produced only 9.1 per cent of the gross production.[40]

World War II wrought enormous damage upon cotton production. In the nonirrigated western areas, production dropped catastrophically or vanished entirely under the impact of German occupation. In the irrigated areas of Central Asia, large sections of cotton land were diverted to the growth of grain crops, which provided needed food and required less labor. Cotton cultivation declined in quality and was without the aid of any large quantities of commercial fertilizer, so that yields fell sharply.[41]

After the war the Soviet government took energetic measures again to expand cotton production rapidly, offering farmers special inducements in the form of more grain, consumer goods, and priority upon fertilizers and farm machinery to increase their output. Cotton farms were also relieved of indebtedness to the state arising from past failure to make required deliveries of farm produce.[42] Nevertheless production improved only slowly in the early postwar years, and the Soviet press complained that much of the irrigation system was being used improperly, crop rotation was being introduced unsatisfactorily, agronomical requirements were being violated, and so on.[43]

Apparently dissatisfied with the progress achieved in cotton production through 1948, the Soviet government issued a new decree on February 4, 1949, to speed the expansion of cotton output. To increase farmers' interest in growing cotton, despite high labor requirements, delivery prices paid by the government were more than doubled.[44] Cotton growers were permitted to buy bread at special low prices and were given other economic advantages. Uzbekistan's farmers were told that if they met the government's 1949 cotton delivery plan they would receive over 5,000,000,000 rubles, as compared with only 2,000,000,000 rubles for 1948 deliveries. In

[40] *Entsiklopediya,* col. 903.
[41] Jasny, *op. cit.,* p. 568.
[42] Schwartz, *Russia's Postwar Economy,* p. 59.
[43] *Pravda,* April 3, 1947.
[44] *Pravda,* March 3, 1949.

addition this decree provided for increased delivery of machinery
to cotton growers, expansion of irrigation works, and development
of the cotton-ginning industry.[45]

The efficacy of these measures is indicated by the Soviet claim
for 1952 which indicates that, on a biological yield basis, cotton
output was about 4,000,000 tons, far above the prewar record. The
appropriate discount for harvest losses was apparently indicated
by Malenkov's statement that in 1952 the state had actually received
3,770,000 tons of cotton, 70 per cent more than in 1940. Apparently
both the increased acreage and increased yield per acre played a
part in securing these results.

Judging from published information, Uzbekistan was still the
largest single cotton-producing area of the Soviet Union in the
early 1950's. The Ukraine had the second largest cotton acreage,
next to Uzbekistan, in 1952, but since this is planted primarily on
low-yielding nonirrigated land, the Ukraine was not the second
largest cotton-producing area. That distinction apparently belonged to Tadzhikistan, which in 1952 had the largest acreage yield
of cotton of any Soviet republic and was the second largest cotton-
producing area.[46]

Frequent reports in the Soviet press have indicated that despite
the impressive gains made in cotton production there is still much
poor work in this area. The increasing numbers of cotton-picking
machines are apparently used poorly and stand idle much of the
time. Collective farmers in cotton areas are often accused of seeking to evade work in the fields when they are needed for the
arduous work of cotton-picking by hand, still apparently the dominant harvest technique. Losses of cotton in the harvest are often
substantial.[47]

In seeking to achieve the 1955 cotton-production goal of about
6,000,000 tons (biological yield basis), emphasis is apparently being
put primarily upon increasing yields through better quality field
work, provision of more fertilizers and insecticides, and related
measures.

---

[45] *Sotsialisticheskoye Zemledeliye,* March 22, 1949.

[46] *Pravda Ukrainy,* September 25, 1952. *Kommunist Tadzhikistana,* November 22, 1952.

[47] Cf. the typical complaints in *Pravda,* October 3, 1951, July 20, 1952, and
October 9, 1952. *Izvestia,* September 30, 1952. *Pravda Vostoka,* December
3, 1952.

For the longer-run expansion of cotton production beyond the planned level of 1955, the Soviet leaders had originally pinned their hopes on the great expansion of cotton acreage in Turkmenistan and the Ukraine. This was to be made possible by the irrigation of large areas after the completion of the Chief Turkmen Canal and the South Ukrainian and North Crimean Canal. The apparent abandonment of these projects, however, seems to have forced a drastic change of plans toward renewed concentration on growth of cotton production in Uzbekistan, in accordance with a comprehensive plan made public in the Soviet press, February 12, 1954. The over-all objective of this plan is to increase cotton production in this region from 2,400,000 metric tons in 1953 to 4,200,000 tons in 1958. It is uncertain, however, whether these figures are biological yields or are in terms of harvested crops. Though additional supplies of fertilizers, insecticides, mechanical equipment, and trained personnel are counted upon to help raise the yield per hectare from a planned 2.5 metric tons in 1954 to a planned 2.9 metric tons in 1958, the greater reliance is upon increasing area sown to cotton by over 25 per cent. This increase is to be achieved by planting an additional 600,000 hectares (about 1,500,000 acres) of irrigated land to cotton. A little more than half of this land is to be obtained by extending the irrigation network, while the rest is to come from sowing to cotton irrigated land which was not so sown before 1954. About 40 per cent of the capital investment required is to be paid for by the collective farms, the rest by the government. A somewhat similar program for Turkmenistan was published April 23, 1954.

A general increase in the acreage sown to cotton in all areas of the Soviet Union capable of raising this crop was ordered by the March 1954 farm decision of the Central Committee of the Communist Party. This decision's comments indicated that despite all past efforts the condition of Soviet irrigated lands still left much to be desired. The first success achieved by this acreage increase program was the 354,000 hectare gain in cotton-planted area in 1954 as compared with 1953.

Sugar Beets: Virtually all the sugar consumed in the Soviet Union is obtained from sugar beets. Production of this crop before World War II was largely concentrated in the Ukraine, where almost three quarters of all production was raised in 1935. The bulk of the remaining production came from Kursk and Voronezh Provinces north of the Ukraine. The rest of the output was scattered in small amounts over the rest of the country.[48]

By 1928 the Soviet sugar-beet industry had exceeded the pre-revolutionary acreage but was still below it in yield and total output. Sugar-beet production was hit very hard by the disorder of the collectivization period and the forced expansion of sown acreage. In 1932 one third of the sharply higher acreage went unharvested, and total output was much less even than in 1913.[49] By 1937 substantial improvement had taken place as the earlier confusion was ended and more fertilizer and other resources were available. During the 1930's too, production was extended eastward into the Volga Valley and Asia.

The war brought about a catastrophic decline in Soviet sugar output. Almost all major Soviet sugar-beet-growing areas, including the Ukrainian Republic and Kursk and Voronezh Provinces, were occupied by the Germans and held for a considerable period of time. By 1945 sugar-beet production, even when accounted for on the inflated biological crop basis, was well below that of either 1913 or 1928, while acreage was one third below that of 1940.

In 1946 drought sent production down even below that of 1945, so that the actual amount of sugar beets available may have been approximately as low as in 1932, though the 1946 population of the USSR was far above that of a decade and a half earlier. Energetic measures taken to increase the supply of fertilizers and machinery and to organize production more effectively succeeded in improving the situation substantially, so that in 1947 the production of sugar beets increased 190 per cent over the very low level of 1946. This probably raised production above the 1928 level but still left it well below the 1940 mark. It seems significant that the government economic report for 1949 made no claim that the prewar level of sugar-beet output had been equaled or exceeded. Sugar-beet production in 1950 was officially announced as having been 2,500,000 metric tons more than output in 1940. This is obviously equal to about 23,400,000 metric tons, almost triple the crop grown in 1945, but below the 1950 goal of 26,000,000 tons.

In 1952, Malenkov announced, the Soviet government received for processing about 22,000,000 tons of sugar beets. This is ap-

[48] *Sot. Stroi.*, p. 346.
[49] Jasny, *op. cit.*, p. 583.

parently over 20 per cent less than the implied biological yield for 1952. Khrushchev indicated that the 1953 sugar-beet acreage was 28 per cent more than that of 1940, or about 1,576,000 hectares. He placed the goal for the actual, as distinguished from the biological, harvest in 1955 at 35,000,000 metric tons, a 13,000,000 ton gain over 1952. This was to be obtained, he said, by increasing sugar-beet acreage in old areas raising this crop, extending sugar-beet growing to new regions, and, chiefly, by raising yields.

By 1952, the Ukraine had apparently regained its prewar position as the dominant sugar-beet area of the Soviet Union, having planted over 900,000 hectares to this crop, or well over half the national total.[50] Complaints of high losses during harvesting, poor use of sugar-beet harvesting combines, and the like suggested that in the Ukraine and elsewhere much improvement could still take place in sugar-beet farming.[51]

In August 1953 Malenkov reported that production of refined sugar that year would be 3,600,000 tons, almost 70 per cent more than in 1940. The sugar production goals for 1954, 1955, and 1956 respectively are: 5,800,000 tons, 6,600,000 tons, and 7,100,000 tons.

The March 1954 farm decision of the Communist Party Central Committee ordered that during 1954–56 Soviet sugar-beet acreage be increased by 300,000 hectares in the areas most suited to this crop.

Sunflower Seed: Sunflower seed is one of the USSR's most important sources of vegetable oil for food, soap, and other industrial uses. In the mid-1930's most of this crop was grown in the Ukraine, North Caucasus, and adjoining areas, though output in Kazakhstan and Western Siberia was on the increase. The acquisition of Bessarabia from Rumania before USSR entry into World War II added an important sunflower growing region to the USSR.

Production of sunflowers grew sharply in the 1920's, before collectivization of Soviet agriculture. A large increase in acreage also took place between 1928 and 1932, but was accompanied by a significant decline in yields, so that output as a whole increased little. By 1940 a record amount of sunflower seed was reported produced, in part because of the acquisition of Bessarabia and in part because of the artificial increase in reported production resulting from the shift to accounting in terms of "biological crop." Sunflower acreage in 1945

---

[50] *Pravda Ukrainy,* September 25, 1952.
[51] *Sotsialisticheskoye Zemledeliye,* October 9, 1951, and November 1, 1952.

was much nearer 1940 levels than in the case of the major industrial crops, but the yield had fallen a third, so that output was below that of 1928.

The data in Table 27 suggest that Soviet sunflower-seed output exceeded that of 1940 in 1949, but fell well below it in 1950. In 1953 Khrushchev said that the collective-farm sown area of oil cultures had exceeded the prewar level, but he complained sharply of the low yields of sunflower seeds, suggesting that this major source of vegetable oils was still in unsatisfactory shape eight years after World War II had ended. His speech of February 1954 called for increasing the area planted to sunflowers and other oil seed plants by 500,000 to 600,000 hectares.

Fibre Flax: The USSR has long been one of the world's major producers of long fibre flax, the raw material for the important linen industry and at times a major export item. In 1938 about half the acreage of this crop was concentrated in the western and north-western areas, from Kalinin Province to Belorussia. There was also significant acreage in Molotov Province in the Urals and in Western Siberia.[52] Fibre flax production requires a great deal of manual labor, though machinery has been developed and introduced in recent years to reduce the hand labor needs. Acreages devoted to this crop in the 1930's were usually twice as great as in 1913, but the yield per hectare obtained was sharply lower, as the data of Table 27 show. Because of its high labor requirements and the great food shortages of the war years, both acreage and yield of this crop were catastrophically low in 1945, so that the Soviet government was faced with a very difficult task of rehabilitating production. Many complaints appeared in the Soviet press during the first few postwar years regarding the poor quality of work being done in rehabilitating this branch of agriculture. High losses in harvesting, poor quality of product, and unwillingness of farmers to participate in harvest work were among the deficiencies publicly condemned.[53] To provide greater incentives for increased production and improved quality, a government decree, apparently adopted in early September 1948, made a number of significant concessions to growers. Instead of being one of the crops farmers

---

[52] *Entsiklopediya,* column 906.

[53] *Pravda,* September 17, 1948; *Izvestia,* August 10, 1949; *Sotsialisticheskoye Zemledeliye,* August 13, 1949.

must deliver for extremely low prices in fulfillment of tax obligation to the state, flax became one of the crops delivered to the state under the contract system, presumably under much more advantageous price terms. Farms delivering flax also were guaranteed the right to purchase quantities of wheat and textiles under advantageous conditions and in proportion to amounts delivered, with bonuses for deliveries in excess of plan. Similar changes were effected in the delivery system for hemp, apparently also to stimulate higher production.[54] This may have helped overcome previous backwardness, for the 1949 output of flax was announced to have exceeded prewar levels.[55] A competent observer has expressed skepticism at this claim, pointing out no similar claim was repeated for 1950.[56] At any rate Khrushchev's withering statement regarding this crop's situation as of September 1953 leaves no doubt about the poor situation as of that date:[57]

> Such important technical crops as fibre flax and hemp require attention. Conditions conducive to their development have been created. . . . But despite the great aid shown by the state during the postwar period to MTS and *kolkhozy* in the flax and hemp regions, the condition of production of these crops continues to be extremely unsatisfactory. . . . The sown area of these crops has not only not been restored to the prewar levels, but has greatly decreased during the past three years as compared with 1950. Yields and quantities marketed of these crops remain low. Little concern is shown for providing collective farms with their own fibre flax seeds.

He blamed the low degree of mechanization of work on these very labor-intensive crops for this situation, and said much of the flax is lost after being raised because it cannot be harvested and given primary processing in good time. The March 1954 farm decision of the Communist Party Central Committee revealed that in the previous three years the area sown to flax had actually fallen 35 per cent. The May 12, 1954, decree on raising fibre flax and hemp production aimed to provide greater incentive to farmers raising these crops by increasing sharply prices paid by the government for deliveries of these crops. It set the following goals for 1955–57.

[54] *Izvestia*, September 15 and October 2, 1948.
[55] *Pravda*, January 18, 1950.
[56] Lazar Volin, *A Survey of Soviet Russian Agriculture*, p. 147. Washington: U. S. Department of Agriculture, 1951.
[57] *Pravda*, September 15, 1953.

	1955	1956	1957
Sown Area (000 hectares)	1,400	1,750	2,000
Fibre Delivered to State (000 tons)	210	288	350

Other Crops

The USSR produces many other crops beside those mentioned or considered in detail above. Potatoes are important for food, animal feed, and alcohol output, and are produced widely throughout the country, both on farms and in small "victory gardens" worked by millions of urbanites each growing season. A wide variety of vegetables is grown in the USSR, as well as fruits and berries of all kinds, though the consumption of these supplementary foods per capita is far below that customary in countries with higher-quality diets. Tea-growing has been traditionally concentrated in Georgia, along with citrus-fruit-raising, but efforts have been made in the postwar period to expand the numbers of areas in which such specialty crops are grown.

The fact that 18 to 19 million urban workers have had to cultivate potato and vegetable gardens in the postwar period is a revealing indication of the inadequacy of farm production of these foods to meet the country's needs. The importance of this type of output is indicated by the fact that urbanites produced over 14 million metric tons of potatoes and vegetables in 1948. The number of such "victory gardens" grew from 5 million in 1942 to 19 million in 1948.[58] Far from being a temporary measure of the war and immediate postwar periods, mass gardening by millions of Soviet urbanites has been put on a long-time permanent basis. A Soviet government decree issued February 24, 1949, provides that workers be permanently assigned garden plots on unoccupied land in and near cities and towns. Workers receiving this land, however, must commit themselves to remain employed at their place of work for five years thereafter. Workers are being encouraged even to plant fruit trees, which do not begin to bear until after several years, as well as to plant potatoes, green vegetables, and other food crops.[59]

The chronic vegetable and potato shortage of the Soviet Union was finally publicly recognized and acted upon after Stalin's death. Khrushchev diagnosed the situation, somewhat disingenuously, in these terms in September 1953:

[58] *Trud,* March 4 and September 3, 1949.
[59] *Professionalniye Soyuzy,* September 1949, pp. 16–18.

Demand for potatoes and vegetables has risen so that their current production level must be recognized as completely insufficient. In recent years yields and gross harvests of these crops have fallen rather than increased. Areas sown to vegetables have declined by 250,000 hectares as against 1940. Areas sown to potatoes have increased for the country as a whole . . . but there has been permitted a decline in yield in many areas which has brought about a decline in the gross potato harvest.

The decline in the gross potato harvest and the insufficient production of vegetables hinders us from seriously improving delivery of these products to the workers of cities and industrial centers.

He followed up by prescribing a program for increasing potato and vegetable production through increasing incentives for such output — by means of higher government prices — and by means of increasing the supply of machinery, greenhouses, irrigated land, and other necessities for these crops.[60] The continued shortage of potatoes and vegetables eight years after the war was best summed up by the newspaper *Trud* on April 7, 1954. It revealed then that in 1953 over 18,000,000 urbanites had tilled gardens from which they gathered about 10,500,000 tons of potatoes and vegetables.

Livestock

As a consequence of the primitive state of their agricultural production, the Soviet Union's people feed primarily upon grain foods and other vegetable products. The number of livestock per capita in the USSR is relatively small, and the productivity of these livestock, in terms of meat, milk, wool, eggs, and other livestock products, is rather low. Soviet per capita consumption of the major foods and raw materials obtained from livestock is very low compared to the United States or other countries having high standards of living. An increase in livestock numbers and improvement of their productivity have been among the major goals of Soviet agricultural plans for two decades and more, but these plans have often gone unrealized. In actuality, the number of livestock in Soviet herds has fluctuated very violently, in response to the mighty forces that have acted upon Soviet agriculture in the past three decades and more. This is indicated in Table 28.

---

60 The government decree reciting measures to be taken for increasing potato and vegetable output appeared in *Pravda*, September 29, 1953. An English translation appears in *Current Digest of the Soviet Press*, November 18, 1953.

TABLE 28. Numbers of Horses, Cattle, Hogs, and Sheep and Goats in the USSR
for Selected Years, and Goals for the Future.

Year	Horses JAN. 1	JULY 1	Cattle JAN. 1	JULY 1	Hogs JAN. 1	JULY 1	Sheep and Goats JAN. 1	JULY 1
			(MILLIONS OF HEAD)					
1913		35.5		60.3		20.3		112.0
1916	38.2		58.4		23.0		96.3	
1928	36.1	33.5	66.8	70.5	27.7	26.0	114.6	146.7
1932		19.6		40.7		11.6		52.1
1934	15.4	15.6	33.5	42.4	11.5	17.4	36.5	51.9
1938	16.2	17.5	50.9	63.2	25.7	30.6	66.6	102.5
1941	21.0		54.5		27.5		91.6	
1946	10.5		47.0		10.4		69.4	
1951	13.7		57.2		24.1		99.0	
1953	15.3		56.6		28.5		109.9	
1956 goal ..	15.2		67.5		35.5		159.0	

Sources: *Pravda*, September 15, 1953. Fifth Five-Year Plan directives and standard
Soviet statistical yearbooks and economic communiqués.

The data above are presented in two variants, for January 1 and
July 1, because the times at which livestock censuses have been
taken in the USSR have varied. It will be seen clearly from the
figures above that data for these different times cannot be compared
directly because of the great seasonal variation in livestock numbers
during each year.

Comparing the data for July it can be seen that, by the eve of
mass collectivization in 1928, herds of cattle, sheep and goats, and
hogs had been increased well above the 1913 levels, despite the
heavy losses of World War I and the civil war following it. By the
middle of 1932, however, the struggle over collectivization and
the confusion reigning on the hastily organized *kolkhozy* had resulted in the loss of roughly 40 per cent of all horses, over 40 per
cent of all cattle, over half of all hogs, and almost two thirds of all
sheep and goats, an agricultural catastrophe without parallel in
peacetime. By 1938 the number of hogs had recovered to more
than the 1928 level, but the numbers of horses, cattle, and sheep
and goats were still far below precollectivization levels. This recovery was the result of the consolidation of the collective farm
system and of the permission given to the individual collective
farmer to own and raise livestock.

World War II resulted in huge numbers of livestock being destroyed, and though some recovery took place in 1944 and 1945, the data for the beginning of 1946 show that the number of horses was only about half the prewar total;[61] and the number of cattle was about 15 per cent, the number of hogs some 60 per cent, and the number of sheep and goats 25 per cent, under the 1941 totals. By early 1946, too, significant numbers of livestock seized in the areas of Eastern and Central Europe occupied by the Red Army had arrived in the USSR and were included in the totals, so that these figures understate the degree of war loss.

The bad grain harvest of 1946, which lowered feed grain supplies particularly, and the postwar disorganization of Soviet agriculture were both reflected in the failure of livestock herds to increase at all during 1946. Cattle, horse, and sheep and goat numbers dropped slightly during the year, and the number of hogs — animals particularly dependent upon grain feed — dropped by almost two million, or over 15 per cent, to a figure close to the worst in all Soviet history. The three-year program for agricultural development adopted in February 1947 by the Central Committee of the Communist Party set up new detailed goals for the expansion of livestock numbers and the increase of meat, milk, wool, and other livestock product output. The goals set up by this plan are shown in Table 29.

TABLE 29. Livestock in the USSR on January 1, 1941, 1947, and 1951, and Goals for 1948–49.

	Cattle		Hogs		Sheep and Goats	
	ALL FARMS	COLLECTIVE FARMS	ALL FARMS	COLLECTIVE FARMS	ALL FARMS	COLLECTIVE FARMS
Year			(MILLIONS OF HEAD)			
Jan. 1, 1941, actual ·	54.5	20.1	27.5	8.2	91.6	41.9
Jan. 1, 1947, actual ·	46.8	15.8	8.6	2.4	69.1	39.1
Jan. 1, 1948, goal ··	52.0	18.4	13.4	4.6	84.7	46.0
Jan. 1, 1949, goal ··	56.1	21.2	20.3	6.3	97.8	53.7
Jan. 1, 1951, actual ·	57.2	28.1	24.1	12.2	99.0	68.3

Sources: Table 28, *Pravda*, February 28, 1947, and *Bolshaya Sovetskaya Entsiklopediya*, Vol. 16, p. 113.

The analysis of the livestock situation presented by the Central

---

[61] But this may exaggerate the decline in the total number of horses in the USSR, since these figures do not include army horses, whose numbers were probably substantially higher in early 1946 than in early 1941.

Committee before it adopted the program of Table 29 emphasized the lack of feed on many farms, the carelessness in handling much of the livestock, the low rate of natural increase among the livestock, and the large number of animals slaughtered to provide meat for collective farms. The latter phenomenon was blamed in large part upon the fact that a significant number of collective farmers did not even have a cow, so that their needs for meat, milk, and other livestock products had to be met from the animals belonging to the collectives as a whole.[62]

Livestock numbers increased sharply in 1948. The planned goals set for attainment by the beginning of 1949 were not attained, however, although collective farms did exceed the prewar numbers of cattle and sheep and goats. A decree of the Soviet government published in April 1949 presented this analysis of the livestock situation:

> . . . as a result of underestimation by local party, government, and agricultural agencies of the need to develop collectivized animal husbandry, the increase in livestock and its productivity lags behind the requirements of the national economy. Thus far not all collective farms have provided themselves with cattle and sheep divisions, and a large number of collective farms do not have hog or poultry divisions. The fixed minimum number of livestock for the collective farms at present is insufficient and retards the further development of communal animal husbandry . . . [many] collective farms are not taking the requisite measures for further growth of the collective herds. In addition, collectivized livestock suffer large losses annually from murrain and barrenness of the breeding stock, and have low productivity as a result of poor feeding and upkeep of the stock in many collective farms and also poor care for the animals . . . much poorly-fed stock is slaughtered so that collective farms give up too large a number of head of livestock in fulfilling the obligatory deliveries of meat to the state and thereby undermine the possibility for quicker growth of livestock numbers. To this time violations of the charter of the agricultural artel are still allowed in collective farms and the practice of squandering livestock from the cattle farms of the collectives has not been overcome. An excessively large number of collectivized animals in the collective farms are used for so-called internal needs.

This decree ordered that energetic measures be taken to end these deficiencies. It declared that the primacy of collective and state

___
[62] Cf. Politburo member A. A. Andreyev's speech in the Soviet press, March 7, 1947.

farms in animal husbandry must be assured by increasing the number of their livestock and raising these animals' productivity. Existing legal minimum numbers of livestock must be raised, and all collective farms were required to have cattle, sheep, hog, and poultry divisions.[63] On collectives failing to attain the minimum numbers of livestock and to organize the livestock-raising divisions required by this decree was imposed a 10 per cent rise in obligatory meat, milk, and wool deliveries to the state, beginning in 1950.[64] Other provisions called for rapid expansion of feed-growing on collective farms; a greatly increased rate of mechanization of farm operations connected with livestock, such as feed preparation, milking, sheep-shearing, water supply, and so on; and the building of great numbers of barns and other livestock buildings. The increase of livestock on collective farms provided by this decree is indicated in Table 30.

TABLE 30. Livestock Holdings of Collective Farms, January 1, 1949 and 1953, and Goals for 1950, 1951, and 1952.

Year	Cattle	Hogs	Sheep and Goats	Poultry
		(MILLIONS OF HEAD)		
Jan. 1, 1949, actual	20.9	5.3	50.7	unknown
Jan. 1, 1950, goal	24.0	10.0	62.4	65.0
Jan. 1, 1951, goal	28.0	13.0	73.0	120.0
Jan. 1, 1952, goal	34.0	18.0	88.0	200.0
Jan. 1, 1953, actual	30.3	16.1	77.2	unknown

Sources: Goal figures from *Pravda*, April 19, 1949. January 1949 data calculated on basis of figures in *Pravda*, March 24, 1950. 1953—*Pravda*, September 15, 1953.

During 1949 collective farms increased their livestock holdings substantially. By January 1, 1950, they had about 25,500,000 cattle; 9,500,000 hogs; and 60,300,000 sheep and goats.[65] These figures indicated that they had exceeded the goal figure for that date with respect to cattle but had fallen substantially below the objectives for hogs and for sheep and goats. Reports published in the Soviet press told of substantial progress in creating livestock divisions on collective farms and in building barns and other structures required

---

[63] Except for collective farms not raising grain, which need not raise poultry, and others having unsuitable conditions for hogs.

[64] The quotation and these provisions are from the decree published in the Soviet press, April 19, 1949.

[65] Calculated on basis of data in *Pravda*, March 24, 1950.

for animals. Many complaints were voiced, however, that progress
was slow in creating the feed base necessary for increasing livestock
numbers, and that much improvement was still required in the
future to permit attainment of the goals for 1951 and 1952. It should
be noted that part of the increase in collective-farm livestock registered in 1949 represented merely the fact that many individual
peasants in the western areas of the USSR were collectivized during
that year. The actual net increase of livestock on these farms, therefore, was probably substantially less than is indicated merely by a
comparison of the 1949 and 1950 data.

One of the most important pieces of information released in the
decree of April 19, 1949, was a set of statistics on the livestock holdings of various groups of private individuals. Since similar data
exist for the number held by these groups on January 1, 1938, in the
smaller territory included in the USSR then, a conditional comparison can be made — as in Table 31.

TABLE 31. Livestock Holdings of Collective Farms and Groups of Private Owners
in the USSR, January 1, 1938, and January 1, 1949.

	Cattle		Hogs		Sheep and Goats	
	1938	1949	1938	1949	1938	1949
Group			(MILLIONS OF HEAD)			
Collective Farms	14.8	20.9	6.3	5.3	22.8	50.7
Collective Farmers ...	25.1	19.1	12.8	3.7	30.7	18.5
Individual Farmers ..	1.5	3.9	0.6	1.9	2.4	2.8
Nonfarm Persons	4.2	7.0	1.9	1.6	2.4	5.2

Sources: Table 30, decree of April 19, 1949, and *Sot. Stroi.* (1933-38) p. 103.

These data show conclusively that the outstanding feature in
the changing pattern of livestock ownership from 1938 to 1949 was
the tremendous decline in the livestock holdings of the collectivized
peasantry, particularly in hogs. Simultaneously the collective farms
increased the number of cattle and sheep and goats they owned
very substantially, while suffering only a relatively nominal drop
in the number of hogs. If it is remembered that there were probably close to 3,000,000 individual peasants in the USSR on January
1, 1949, the figures above are put in proper perspective. The increase
registered for this category between 1938 and 1949 reflected only
the addition to the USSR of these peasants from the western areas

annexed after 1938. The growth of the cattle and sheep and goats owned by nonfarm persons is explained by the great growth of urban "victory gardens" and related farm activities resulting from the food scarcity of the war and postwar years. The number of hogs owned by such persons on January 1, 1949, was less than the number owned by this category on January 1, 1938, when such large cities as Lwow, Tallin, Vilna, and Riga were not in the USSR.

The poverty of the individual livestock holdings of collective farmers in 1949 may be seen in the figures given in the table above are divided by the number of such farmers. On the average, it would seem likely that each collective farmer may have had about one head of cattle and one sheep or goat; only one in four or five had a hog. Of course, some collective farmers had more than one head of cattle or more than one sheep or goat, suggesting that at the beginning of 1949 many others had no livestock at all, not even a cow to provide milk for their families. This situation was in part the result of war losses, but even before the war, in 1939, the government had begun to follow actively a policy of reducing the individually owned livestock of collective farmers by requiring them to sell large numbers of animals to the collective farms. In the postwar period the government continued this policy of favoring collective-farm livestock herds over individual collective-farmer ownership. It is noteworthy that the decree of April 19, 1949, provided for compulsory sales of collective farmers' cattle to collective farms. The objective of this policy was clearly to prevent the livestock holdings of the *kolkhozniki* from rising to the extent of permitting them to get appreciable income from this source and tempting them to withhold their labor from the collective farms in favor of working with their own livestock.

The complex postwar livestock policy described above produced some significant results. Between January 1, 1946, and January 1, 1953, as Table 28 shows, the number of Soviet horses grew by about 50 per cent, cattle over 40 per cent, hogs 25 per cent, and sheep and goats well over 100 per cent. These were no mean achievements, but the total reached fell far short of the Soviet Union's needs. Moreover, since much of the gain was made by the collective farms at the expense of keeping down the private livestock holdings of the collective farmers, serious tensions were created which made for considerable difficulties. These facts were finally openly recognized after Stalin's death. The Central Committee of the Communist Party described the Soviet livestock situation in these terms in September 1953: [66]

> . . . the rise in the number of head of socialized livestock and the level of its yields are completely inadequate. The number of cows in the country has fallen 3,500,000 below the prewar level and 8,900,000 below the 1928 figure. During 1952 the total number of cattle in the whole country was allowed to fall 2,200,000 and the number of cows 550,000 . . . the number of horses has fallen by 60 per cent as compared with the prerevolutionary period and 27 per cent compared with 1940. Correct management of the economy would have permitted a large rise in the numbers of productive livestock following the fall in horse numbers. But this did not happen. Year after year the state plans for increasing livestock numbers are not met. Yields in animal husbandry remain very low because livestock receive poor care. Recently the milk yield, wool clip, and some other qualitative indexes for livestock farming have been falling on collective farms. The collectives suffer great losses of livestock every year from disease and do not get a large number of young animals because female livestock are sterile. Instead of organizing work so that livestock divisions of collective farms assure the needed multiplication of socialized livestock, many directors of collective farms . . . continue to make large-scale purchases of livestock from collective farmers. . . .
>
> The unsatisfactory situation . . . results primarily from the lag in the procurement and production of feed. On many collectives grass planting is poorly developed, grass yields are extremely low, and the growing of feed root and melon crops as well as of corn and sunflowers for silage is neglected. . . .
>
> Numerous collective farms give a large portion of their animal products to the government as obligatory deliveries, but the present procurement prices for meat, milk, butter, and eggs have not created the necessary interest to induce collective farms and their members to develop socialized livestock-raising.

Khrushchev, in his speech before the Central Committee meeting which adopted the resolution quoted from above, added this revealing item of information:

> Compared to the prewar level, the number of individually owned livestock has fallen by 6,500,000 head. The number of collective-farm families which do not have their own cow has increased to 45 per cent of the total.

[66] *Pravda,* September 13, 1953.

He then enunciated this sharp reversal of policy:

... local Party, Soviet, and farm agencies must wholly end the wrong practice of infringing upon the personally owned livestock of the collective farmers. Only people who do not understand the policy of the Party or the policy of the Soviet state see any threat to the socialist system in the presence of individually owned productive livestock on a collective farmer's private holding within the limits set by the Collective Farm Statutes.

The time will come when the development of socialized livestock will have attained such a level that the personal requirements of the collective farmers for livestock products will be entirely satisfied by the communal economy. Then it will be disadvantageous for the collective farmers to have personal livestock. But while we do not have such a situation . . . the existence of livestock individually owned by collective farm families is not a hindrance but an aid to the communal livestock. . . .

A complex decree was adopted to effect changes deemed necessary to improve the situation. Government prices for procurement of livestock were raised sharply; the amounts of livestock products collective farms are required to deliver to the government at low procurement prices were cut substantially; collective-farm arrears in delivering livestock products were forgiven; collective-farm live-stock-product deliveries to the state were put upon a uniform basis for the country, and officials were forbidden to require greater de-liveries from more prosperous than from less prosperous farms in one area; acreages devoted to feed crops were ordered increased substantially; Soviet industry was ordered to supply agriculture with larger quantities of machinery needed for feed crop cultivation and for labor-consuming tasks in livestock-raising, such as milking cows. The decree also ordered that hereafter the Soviet livestock year is to begin October, rather than January, 1st. It set up these livestock goals (in millions) for October 1, 1954: [67]

	Total	Collective Farms	State Farms	Collective Farmers and Other Private Owners
Cattle	65.9	35.0	4.8	25.7
Cows	29.2	11.5	1.6	16.0
Pigs	34.5	21.5	4.3	8.5
Sheep	127.4	99.0	13.0	15.0
Goats	17.0	5.0	.1	11.9

[67] The decree appeared in *Pravda*, September 26, 1953. An English translation appears in the *Current Digest of the Soviet Press*, November 7, 1953.

These targets were apparently based upon an overly-pessimistic evaluation of the Soviet livestock situation as of the fall of 1953. This is indicated by the fact that the census of livestock conducted on October 1, 1953, found that in two categories, pigs and sheep and goats, the Soviet Union actually had more animals than these targets called for the country to have by October 1, 1954. The actual figures found on the 1953 date — as revealed in the official economic report for that year — were 63,000,000 cattle (including 26,000,000 cows), 47,600,000 pigs, 138,500,000 sheep and goats, and 16,200,000 horses. It may be that the more liberal policy toward private livestock announced two weeks before the 1953 census was held induced peasants to report their livestock holdings more fully and accurately than in earlier periods, when there was good reason for them to try to hide part of the livestock from the government census-takers. In any case the revelation of this unexpected situation was accompanied by a state declaration that the October 1954 goals had been raised beyond the original levels, so as to take account of the actual 1953 situation.

Khrushchev's speech of February 23, 1954, gave some evidence that the policy of encouraging the private ownership of livestock had had some success in 1953. He gave these data on the growth of these holdings during that year. Cows: 630,000 or 4 per cent. All cattle: 1,375,000 or 6 per cent. Sheep and goats: 2,690,000 or 12 per cent. Hogs: 6,130,000 or 77 per cent. These gains represented improvement, but hardly solved the problem of peasant poverty.

Livestock Products

As the result of the sharp variations of livestock numbers in the USSR over the past several decades, the output of meat, milk, eggs, leather, and other livestock products has also fluctuated very much. This is indicated by the data in Table 32.

Table 32 indicates that the struggle over collectivization reduced Soviet output of the major livestock foods to little more than one third of the 1927–28 level in the case of eggs, and to about half of the 1927–28 level in the case of meat and milk. Even by 1938 the pre-collectivization production levels had not been reached, although there had been a significant rise in population over the decade. The

TABLE 32. Production of Meat, Milk, and Eggs in the USSR in Selected Years.

Year	Meat (MILLION METRIC TONS)	Milk (MILLION METRIC TONS)	Eggs (BILLION)
1927–28	3.6	30.1	10.5
1929–30	4.5	28.0	*
1933	1.7	18.8	3.6
1934	1.5	20.2	4.2
1938	3.3†	28.9†	8.5

* Unavailable.
† Preliminary. Jasny believes that milk production in 1938 could not have exceeded 26 million tons.
Source: Jasny, *The Socialized Agriculture of the USSR*, p. 798.

1938 egg production, it may be noted, would have permitted on the average a consumption of about one egg weekly by each citizen of the Soviet Union. The meat production would have permitted average per capita Soviet meat consumption of less than one pound a week.

Not only did the Soviet Union pay a heavy price in the loss of livestock as the result of the collectivization struggle, but it has continued to suffer because of the poor handling and feeding of the remaining livestock. One indication of this is the decline in average slaughter weight per animal slaughtered. In 1925–26, the average weight of each head of cattle slaughtered was 376 kilograms; in 1938 it was only 275 kilograms. For hogs, weight declined from 104 kilograms to 89 kilograms, while for sheep it fell from 37 to 36 kilograms over the same period.[68] To get the same amount of meat, therefore, more animals had to be slaughtered, a factor that consequently hindered the growth of the size of herds.

World War II sharply reduced the supply of livestock products available for domestic consumption, a fact confirmed by the large amounts of American meat, dairy products, eggs, and related commodities taken by the USSR under Lend-Lease — about one billion dollars' worth of animals and edible animal products were sent to the USSR from the United States during 1941–44.[69] Accounts published in the Soviet press during February and March 1947 gave clear evidence that yields of milk, meat, and other products from Soviet livestock were far below prewar levels because of the

[68] Jasny, *op. cit.*, pp. 640–42, 798.
[69] "United States Trade with Russia (USSR) during the War Years," U. S. Dept. of Commerce, *International Reference Service*, December 1945, p. 4.

shortage of feed and the poor handling of stock.[70] Jasny estimates that perhaps 2,000,000 tons of meat may have been produced in the larger USSR of 1946, one third less than was produced in 1938 within the narrower borders and for the smaller population of the Soviet Union at that time. The production would have been even lower that year if the shortage of feed had not forced the slaughter of animals that could not be fed over the winter of 1946–47.[71]

The growth of collective farm livestock during 1947 and 1948 permitted substantial increases in deliveries of meat, milk, and milk products to the state, so that by the beginning of 1949 prewar deliveries of milk and butter had been exceeded and the 1940 level of meat deliveries almost equaled.[72] Egg supplies were probably far below the prewar figures because of the low number of poultry in collective farm flocks. The fact that deliveries of meat and milk to the state had equaled or almost equaled prewar figures does not necessarily mean that total production of these commodities has regained 1940 levels. The concentration of livestock in collective farm herds and the great decline in the number of animals owned by collective farmers between 1938 and 1949, shown above, suggests that consumption of meat and milk by the rural population has fallen greatly and that the latter has borne the brunt of the failure to increase livestock herds and livestock productivity to the prewar level.[73]

A government and party decree issued May 26, 1949, declared that "supplies of animal products still do not meet the growing requirements of the national economy." It called for the increase of deliveries of such products to the state by 50 to 100 per cent over the following three years. Quotas were set by the government providing for greatly increased deliveries by collective farms and state farms during 1949–51. Collective farms and farmers were warned that underweight animals would no longer be accepted by the

---

[70] *Pravda,* February 28 and March 7, 1947.

[71] Jasny, *op. cit.,* p. 647.

[72] *Pravda,* May 26, 1949.

[73] Jasny points out that in about a decade the amount of meat available for farmers' consumption fell from 2.39 million tons in 1927–28 to 1.24 million tons in 1938, while marketing of meat for the urban population and other groups fed by the government rose from 1.22 million tons in 1927–28 to 2.06 million tons in 1938. *Op. cit.,* p. 647.

government, and that they might no longer substitute other types of meat for required pork deliveries.[74] To prevent losses of leather because of careless handling of hides after slaughter on the farm, the decree prohibited barnyard slaughter in areas served by slaughtering centers. State prices on some products were raised, and additional incentives were provided for deliveries of animal products in excess of minimum requirements.

Data on the production of livestock products have been scarce for the postwar period, but some data regarding government procurements and purchases are available for the early 1950's. These data are compared with prewar procurements below: [75]

Year	Meat	Milk	Wool
	(THOUSAND METRIC TONS)		
1926–27	520	1,700	29.4
1930–31	2,343	1,200	50.5
1935	1,056	3,983	52.8
1940	2,000	6,000	121.0
1952	3,000	10,000	182.0
1954 Plan	4,100	14,300	230.0

The immediately preceding discussion clearly indicates that the level of livestock numbers in the early 1950's was proportionately far less above the level of 1940 than were the meat and milk procurements shown above. The explanation for the government's ability to get so much more livestock products in 1952 than in 1940 would seem to lie primarily in the reduction of rural consumption. In the case of meat, however, an additional factor was probably the large-scale slaughter of cattle during 1952, which resulted in cattle numbers declining by over 2,000,000 that year as noted above. Khrushchev revealed in September 1953 that at the beginning of that year the Soviet Union had 3,500,000 fewer cows than at the end of 1940. The Soviet government's ability to get 60 per cent more milk procurements and purchases in 1952 than in 1940 must, therefore, have meant a drastic reduction indeed of milk consumption on Soviet farms.

As regards butter, Malenkov reported in August 1953 that in-

---

[74] *Pravda*, May 26, 1949.

[75] Sources: Volin, *op. cit.*, p. 166. *Pravda*, August 9, 1953, and September 26, 1953.

dustrial production that year, excluding farm-churned butter for farmers' use, would be 400,000 tons that year. A Department of Commerce estimate is that only 369,000 tons of butter were actually produced in 1953. The gross inadequacy of 1953 butter production was shown by the unusually large butter imports bought that year. Soviet butter production annually during 1954–56 is scheduled to reach these levels: 1954 — 476,000 tons; 1955 — 560,000 tons; 1956 — 650,000 tons.

CHAPTER X

TRANSPORTATION AND COMMUNICATION

THE DEVELOPMENT OF transportation and communication facilities under the Soviet regime is closely linked with the growth of industrialization. The present economic organization of the USSR would be impossible without these means of coordinating the work of thousands of different enterprises located at many different places over the country's vast area. Kuzbas coal and Magnitogorsk iron ore are brought together to make steel for Chelyabinsk's tractor factory. The tractor in turn may be sent to the Ukraine, Central Asia, or the Far East for employment in agriculture. Each of these areas must receive petroleum products from Baku or other distant sources if the tractors are to operate. The food grown with the help of these tractors must be sent to storage warehouses and cities hundreds or thousands of miles away to feed the swollen army of Soviet industrial workers and their families. All this intricate cooperation of many different parts of the economy rests upon the existence of a transport system capable of moving the large volume of variegated freight required to hold together the complex pattern of production and consumption. Similarly, communications facilities are indispensable for the daily operation of the centrally planned economic system. Under Soviet conditions, consumer use of transport and communications facilities — for recreational travel or personal telephone chats with friends or relatives — is a very minor factor.

Lenin and his colleagues inherited the transport system of Czarist Russia, suffering at the time from the effects of three years of war. Transport facilities deteriorated further during the following years

389

of civil war and foreign intervention, but railroads and other means of transport recuperated rapidly during the years of the New Economic Policy in the 1920's. After 1928, however, they had to cope with the great new burdens created by the gigantic construction and production programs of the first three five-year plans. Soviet economic policy in the early 1930's treated the transport system less generously than heavy industry. It sought to minimize the allocations of new resources to railroads by sharply intensifying the use of existing equipment. When this policy threatened to paralyze the economy, it was hastily reversed. Under the leadership of Politburo member Lazar Kaganovich, capital investment in transport and the efficiency of railroads were sharply raised in the mid-1930's.

World War II brought the destruction of much of the dense transport network of the USSR in the western areas occupied by the Germans, though expansion took place in the unoccupied east during the war. The years since the war's end have been devoted to repairing the destruction of 1941–45 and to new expansion to meet the still growing needs of the economy.

Certain major fundamental factors have shaped the transport policy both of the Czarist and of the Soviet regime. Most of the Soviet Union is a relatively flat plain offering few serious obstacles to the builders of railroads. Most Soviet rivers, on the other hand, are frozen and unusable from three to nine months of the year. Moreover, many of the most important rivers are located in areas having little population. Railroads, however, can be built where needed and operated in all kinds of weather. Until recently, the USSR has had only a relatively small number of automobiles, trucks, and other motor vehicles, so that there has been little need for long paved highways such as are common in the United States. The overwhelming majority of its road are still made of packed dirt. Coastal maritime traffic in the USSR is of relatively minor importance because the great bulk of population and resources is located far from the coasts. The long northern sea frontier is frozen most of the year, requiring extraordinary effort and expense to permit navigation even during the brief period of open water.

Under these conditions the markedly uneven distribution of population and exploitable natural resources over the country has created a pattern of transportation need that can be satisfied most cheaply by large-volume land transport capable of working throughout the year regardless of the temperature or other climatic conditions. Railroads, therefore, perform the great bulk of transport service in the USSR. The predominance of railroads is clearly shown in Table 33, which measures freight volume, the most important single component of the service provided by the Soviet transportation system. In 1950 railroads accounted for 84.5 per cent of all freight turnover in the country. By 1955 it is hoped to reduce this to about 80 per cent.

TABLE 33. Freight Volume of Major Forms of Soviet Transport in Selected Years.

Year	Rail	River	Maritime	Truck
		(BILLION TON-KILOMETERS)		
1913	65.7	37.2	‡	‡
1922–23	23.5	12.9	‡	‡
1929	112.9	18.4	10.4	‡
1932	169.3	25.1	18.2	1.1
1940*	415	36	23	9
1945*	314	18.5	‡	‡
1950*	601	45.4	38.0	20.7
1952*	733	57.6	36.8	28.6
1953*	784	60†	40.1	32.3
1955* goal	811–841	79–82	59–61	37–38

* Expanded territory. † Estimated. ‡Data not available.
Sources: *Narodnoye Khozyaistvo SSSR 1932*, pp. 194, 216, and 443; *Sot. Stroi. (1933-38)*, p. 107; *Entsiklopediya*, col. 951; *Second Five-Year Plan*, p. 600; *Pravda*, April 17, 1951, January 29, 1952, October 6 and 12, 1952, and January 31, 1954.

The Soviet Railroad System[1]

Study of the railroad map of the Soviet Union immediately reveals an extremely uneven distribution of this means of transportation. In the western areas of the country, particularly west of a line connecting Leningrad, Moscow, and Kharkov, the number of railroad lines is large. Eastward, between this imaginary line and the Urals, the number of railroad routes thins out but is still substantial. East of the Urals the great bulk of Soviet territory is uncrossed by railroad lines except for those leading from the southern Urals to the Soviet Far East and penetrating into Central Asia and Kazakhstan. (See map.)

[1] The most comprehensive study in English of the Soviet railroad system is Holland Hunter, *The Economics of Soviet Railroad Policy*. Cambridge, Mass.: Harvard University, March 1949 (hectographed). It is the source of much of the material in this section. Cf. also his "Soviet Railroads Since 1940," in *Bulletins on Soviet Economic Development*, No. 4 (September 1950), pp. 10–20.

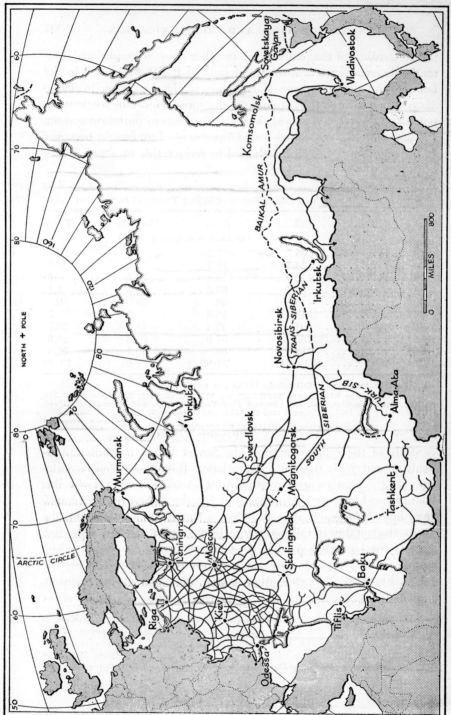

VII. THE SOVIET RAILROAD SYSTEM IN 1950

The reasons for this uneven distribution of rail transport facilities are to be found both in history and in the location pattern of Soviet population and resources. The Czarist regime built most of the many rail lines it constructed in the west, where the overwhelming majority of the country's population and the great bulk of resources being exploited were located. In addition, the building of railroads in the area west of Moscow was dictated by the desire to create optimum transport conditions for moving grain and other exports to European customers either over land or through ports on the Baltic or Black Seas. Military considerations also favored construction of an extensive network of rail lines on which troops and supplies could be shifted easily and rapidly throughout the western positions of Czarist Russia.

The Soviet Union inherited this rail network. Its energies at first were directed toward restoring the extensive sections of track and the large portions of rail equipment that had been damaged and made unusable during the years of civil war and foreign intervention. It also undertook the completion of many of the projected rail lines first laid out in Czarist times but not completed before the revolution. In the 1930's, as production grew in many areas, some of them old (such as the Donbas in the Ukraine), and others new (such as Magnitogorsk in the Urals and the Kuzbas in Siberia), the USSR built additional roads to meet new needs. About one half the increase in railroad track length between 1926 and 1935 was located in the Urals, Siberia, and Central Asia. During World War II much of the railroad trackage in the western USSR was destroyed or damaged as the result of combat and of deliberate destruction. At the same time some new roads were built in the areas immediately behind the battle lines, in order to speed the movement of troops and supplies. Some additional expansion also took place in the Urals, Central Asia, and Western Siberia, to service expanded industry there. In the postwar period the building of new lines has continued, and further work has been undertaken directed toward full rehabilitation of the railroad system demaged during the war. It should be borne in mind that, in the reoccupation of western areas as German invaders were driven out, restoration of rail lines had first priority. Upon the speed of this restoration depended the ability of the Soviet government to ease the transport problem involved in supplying and reinforcing its advancing armies.

The statistical picture of the development of the Soviet railroad system during the USSR's history is shown below:

TABLE 34. Length of Soviet Railroad System First Main Track in Selected Years.

Year	Total	Urals, Siberia, and Central Asia (KILOMETERS)	Per Cent in Eastern Area
1913	58,549	14,540	24.9
1917	63,252	†	†
1919	31,494	†	†
1926	75,721	23,062	30.5
1935	84,367	26,839	31.8
1940	106,102*	†	†
1945	112,868*	†	†
1949 .... Almost	118,000*	†	†
1950 goal	123,200*	†	†

* Includes lines taken over in occupied territory, including Eastern Poland, the Baltic States, and so forth.
† Data unavailable.
Sources: Hunter, *The Economics of Soviet Railroad Policy,* pp. 86 and 150; Hunter, "Soviet Railroads Since 1940," pp. 14, 15.

Among the most important individual rail lines built or completed by the Soviet Union have been: the five-hundred-mile route from Kazan on the Volga to Sverdlovsk in the Urals, completed in the early 1920's; the almost nine-hundred-mile Turkestan-Siberian railroad, finished in 1931, connecting the Trans-Siberian with Alma-Ata in southern Kazakhstan; a third trunk route between Moscow and the Donbas, strengthened and extended in the 1930's; and the 960-mile rail line linking the rich northern Pechora coalfields with the rest of the country, completed in 1943. Other new lines strengthened the connections between Magnitogorsk, the Kuzbas, and Karaganda, facilitating exploitation of the rich iron ore and coal deposits in the eastern USSR. Several links of a projected northern Trans-Siberian line, the BAM, or Baikal-Amur road, were finished, while the original Trans-Siberian route was made a double-track line throughout, thus substantially increasing its carrying capacity.[2]

During the First Five-Year Plan the Soviet government sought to

[2] The present stage of construction of the Baikal-Amur Road is not known. Some reports from former Soviet citizens tell of its completion and operation. This is doubted by many American specialists because of the absence of references to this road in published Soviet material. Cf. *The New York Times,* August 11, 21, and 26, 1950.

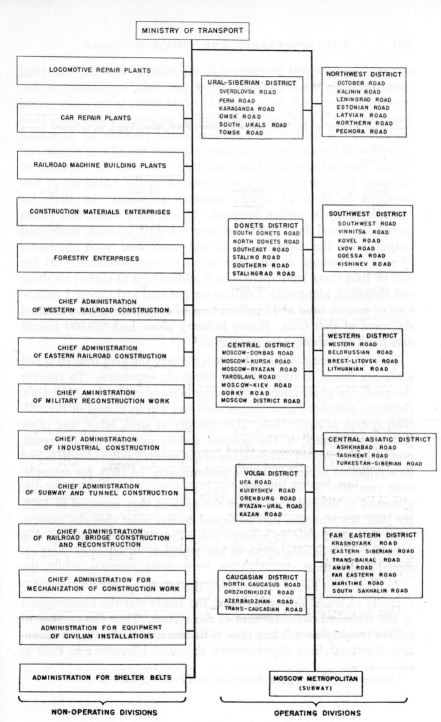

MINISTRY OF TRANSPORT

Non-Operating Divisions:

LOCOMOTIVE REPAIR PLANTS

CAR REPAIR PLANTS

RAILROAD MACHINE BUILDING PLANTS

CONSTRUCTION MATERIALS ENTERPRISES

FORESTRY ENTERPRISES

CHIEF ADMINISTRATION
OF WESTERN RAILROAD CONSTRUCTION

CHIEF ADMINISTRATION
OF EASTERN RAILROAD CONSTRUCTION

CHIEF AMINISTRATION
OF MILITARY RECONSTRUCTION WORK

CHIEF ADMINISTRATION
OF INDUSTRIAL CONSTRUCTION

CHIEF ADMINISTRATION
OF SUBWAY AND TUNNEL CONSTRUCTION

CHIEF ADMINISTRATION
OF RAILROAD BRIDGE CONSTRUCTION
AND RECONSTRUCTION

CHIEF ADMINISTRATION FOR
MECHANIZATION OF CONSTRUCTION WORK

ADMINISTRATION FOR EQUIPMENT
OF CIVILIAN INSTALLATIONS

ADMINISTRATION FOR SHELTER BELTS

Operating Divisions:

URAL-SIBERIAN DISTRICT
SVERDLOVSK ROAD
PERM ROAD
KARAGANDA ROAD
OMSK ROAD
SOUTH URALS ROAD
TOMSK ROAD

NORTHWEST DISTRICT
OCTOBER ROAD
KALININ ROAD
LENINGRAD ROAD
ESTONIAN ROAD
LATVIAN ROAD
NORTHERN ROAD
PECHORA ROAD

DONETS DISTRICT
SOUTH DONETS ROAD
NORTH DONETS ROAD
SOUTHEAST ROAD
STALINO ROAD
SOUTHERN ROAD
STALINGRAD ROAD

SOUTHWEST DISTRICT
SOUTHWEST ROAD
VINNITSA ROAD
KOVEL ROAD
LVOV ROAD
ODESSA ROAD
KISHINEV ROAD

CENTRAL DISTRICT
MOSCOW-DONBAS ROAD
MOSCOW-KURSK ROAD
MOSCOW-RYAZAN ROAD
YAROSLAVL ROAD
MOSCOW-KIEV ROAD
GORKY ROAD
MOSCOW DISTRICT ROAD

WESTERN DISTRICT
WESTERN ROAD
BELORUSSIAN ROAD
BREST-LITOVSK ROAD
LITHUANIAN ROAD

CENTRAL ASIATIC DISTRICT
ASHKHABAD ROAD
TASHKENT ROAD
TURKESTAN-SIBERIAN ROAD

VOLGA DISTRICT
UFA ROAD
KUIBYSHEV ROAD
ORENBURG ROAD
RYAZAN-URAL ROAD
KAZAN ROAD

FAR EASTERN DISTRICT
KRASNOYARK ROAD
EASTERN SIBERIAN ROAD
TRANS-BAIKAL ROAD
AMUR ROAD
FAR EASTERN ROAD
MARITIME ROAD
SOUTH SAKHALIN ROAD

CAUCASIAN DISTRICT
NORTH CAUCASUS ROAD
ORDZHONIKIDZE ROAD
AZERBAIDZHAN ROAD
TRANS-CAUCASIAN ROAD

MOSCOW METROPOLITAN
(SUBWAY)

NON-OPERATING DIVISIONS   OPERATING DIVISIONS

FIGURE 4. *Organization of the Soviet Railroad System in 1950.*

economize on capital investment in the railroad system. The total length of main track grew by only 7 per cent, approximately, between 1928 and 1933; the volume of freight traffic in the same period increased 82 per cent, and the volume of passenger traffic more than tripled. Much of this increase was made possible by improved operation of the railroads and more intensive use of equipment and tracks. Nevertheless the increased load exceeded the capacity of the most heavily used lines and resulted in the piling up of tremendous backlogs of freight awaiting shipment. In 1933, for example, a Soviet writer declared, "Mines, steel works and plants in the light and food industries were choked up with unshipped output . . . the railroads could not even deal with shipments of rails, fastenings, or pipe, the needs of transport itself." At the end of 1934 there were more than 3 million tons of timber awaiting rail shipment, along with 2 million tons of coal and almost 1 million tons of ore. A total of 15 million tons of cargo, altogether, awaited shipment at that time. Heavy industry alone had 650,000 freight cars piled up awaiting transportation.[3]

This inadequacy of the rail system to carry the load desired posed a serious threat to futher Soviet economic expansion. To counter this peril, the government took energetic measures in the mid-1930's. Politburo member Lazar Kaganovich was put in charge of the railroad system in early 1935. The quantity of steel, labor, and other resources allocated to the railroad system was sharply increased, permitting improved maintenance of the existing railroad system and its equipment as well as better performance. In 1935, for example, over one fifth of all the iron and steel produced in Russia was allocated to the railroads, twice the amount they received in 1932. By 1937 the situation had improved to the point that the government felt itself able to remove the railroad system from the top priority list. The allocations of key resources to railroads were reduced at that time.

An important factor in increasing the efficiency and load-carrying capacity of Soviet railroads during the 1930's was the improvement of the technical characteristics of the system. Thus the number of miles of multiple-track line (line with two or more tracks) in operation increased from about sixteen thousand kilometers in 1929 to

---

[3] Hunter, *The Economics of Soviet Railroad Policy*, pp. 104–5.

almost twenty-five thousand in 1940. About 40 per cent of the trackage was re-equipped with heavier rails, which, however, were still lighter than those used in other European countries and the United States. More powerful locomotives and larger freight cars capable of moving heavier loads were introduced. Some particularly important stretches of track — totaling about 1900 kilometers by 1940 — were electrified, making possible important fuel economies and improved service. Automatic brakes were introduced widely toward the end of the 1930's, as were automatic block-signal devices. All this significantly raised the technical level and carrying capacity of the Soviet railroad system. Yet in August of 1940 Kaganovich complained that the railroad system still had many deficiencies, pointing particularly at the low level of maintenance and the frequency of accidents. Throughout this period, too, the problems of running trains on schedule and in undiminished number under the difficult conditions created by the severe winter climate of most of the USSR were not solved satisfactorily.[4]

During the Second World War tremendous damage was done to the Soviet railroad system in the western areas. According to the official report of the Soviet government, the Germans put out of commission, entirely or partially, some thirty-four railroad lines, destroying 65,000 kilometers of track, 13,000 railroad bridges, 4,100 stations, 317 locomotive depots, and 129 repair centers, as well as thousands of locomotives and hundreds of thousands of cars. From 1941 to 1943 the length of railroad track in use in Soviet territory diminished by 40 per cent, while the total number of locomotives decreased by 15 per cent and the number of freight cars by 20 per cent. Nevertheless, by following a policy of giving first priority to restoration of railroad lines in re-occupied territories, the total length of trackage in the USSR at the end of 1945 exceeded that at the end of 1940, as seen above. This includes of course, the 11,000 kilometers of new track built during the war, a greater length than was built during the entire period 1928–39.

At the beginning of 1946, the USSR had in operation 113,000 kilometers of main track, 21,000 kilometers of second track, and some 1,700 kilometers of electrified line. The Fourth Five-Year Plan provided for reconstruction and construction of about 11,000 kilo-

---

[4] William Mandel, "Soviet Transport, Today and Tomorrow," *The American Review on the Soviet Union*, February 1941, pp. 29–35.

meters of main track, 12,500 kilometers of second track, almost 5,700 kilometers of electrified line, and over 10,000 kilometers of track equipped with automatic block protection. The most important new line projected was the so-called South Siberian railroad, a line roughly paralleling part of the existing Trans-Siberian Railroad. The South Siberian is intended to give a direct connection between Magnitogorsk and the Kuznetsk Basin, while to the west Magnitogorsk is to be linked to the Volga.

Measured in terms of freight turnover, the Soviet rail system recovered much more rapidly than planned during 1946–50. Total freight turnover on railroads had been 415 billion ton-kilometers in 1940 and 314 billion in 1945. In 1950 it had attained about 601 billion ton-kilometers or 13 per cent more than the original 532 billion goal. Average daily carloadings had been 97,900 cars in 1940 and only about 61,000 in 1945. In 1950 average daily carloadings were 118,500, or 3 per cent more than the 115,000 figure planned for originally. A good deal of progress was made in constructing new lines, but the five-year plan target for such construction was not met, so that in 1950 the total length of Soviet rail lines was presumably under the goal of 123,200 kilometers set for that year. Some rail lines in the Urals, Trans-Caucasus, and Krivoi Rog areas were electrified, as were some suburban lines serving Moscow, Leningrad, Riga, Kiev, Baku, and Tallin.[5]

Two key factors may be singled out as particularly important in making possible the rapid increase in Soviet railroad freight volume during the postwar period. First has been the USSR's ability to increase rapidly the number of freight cars in use. Professor Hunter has estimated the number of freight cars available as rising from 675,000 in 1945 to 852,000 in 1949, the latter quantity being well in excess of the original 800,000 goal for 1950. Second has been the policy of enforcing mercilessly strict discipline throughout the railroad system. Martial law for all railroad employees was introduced in 1943, during World War II, but has been continued into the postwar period. In addition, in January 1949 "Political Departments" were set up in all branches of the railroad system to intensify communist propaganda among workers and to apply additional pressure for exemplary labor discipline among the approximately 3,000,000 employees of Soviet railroads.

---

5 *Pravda,* April 17, 1951.

The Fifth Five-Year Plan called for an increase of rail freight turnover by 35-40 per cent by 1955 over 1950, a relatively small percentage increase as against that provided for other forms of transport, but still a very large amount absolutely. Its construction program was very ambitious, apparently seeking to make up for the failures of the earlier postwar period. The plan called for 2.5 times as much new rail track to be laid during 1951–55 as during 1946–50. The new lines to be built included the important Abakan-Akmolinsk section of the South Siberian, essentially the direct connection between the Karaganda Coal Basin and the Kuznetsk Basin; the Chardzhou-Kungrad line connecting the Aral Sea with the main east-west rail line of Soviet Central Asia; as well as several smaller lines of lesser importance. (See Map VIII.) Further progress was also called for in improving the technical conditions of Soviet railroads as well as increasing their supply of rolling stock, though no specific numerical goals for the latter were given.

Malenkov reported in late 1952 that rail freight turnover that year would be 80 per cent more than in 1940, indicating further gains since 1950. By the end of 1953 the following were reported to be fully completed: the 438-kilometer Mointy-Chu line which provides a direct north-south rail connection between Karaganda and Central Asia, cutting out the previous long detour around Lake Balkhash;[6] the short Urgench-Chardzhou line in Central Asia;[7] the Barnaul-Kulunda and Akmolinsk-Pavlodar sections of the South Siberian[8] as well as some subsidiary lines.

The dominant theme of Soviet rail transport policy over the past two decades has been that of maximizing the volume of services provided by the railroads while devoting the minimum possible amount of resources to them. This has been accomplished by increasing the density of traffic on the most important roads far above that customary in Western Europe and the United States. Moreover, substantial government pressure has been placed upon railroad clients to plan their operations in such a way as to minimize the amount of railroad transport service required by them. Soviet industries have been directed to eliminate cross hauls, that is, to prevent the shipment of the same material in different directions, so that steel, say,

---

[6] *Pravda*, October 27, 1953.
[7] *Ibid.*, August 2, 1953.
[8] *Izvestia*, January 16, 1954.

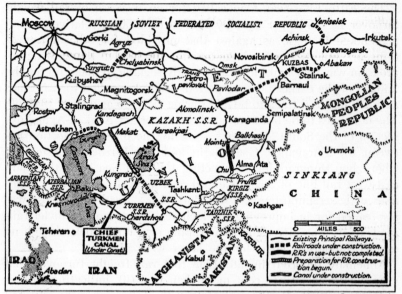

New York Times, September 2, 1952

VIII. RAILROAD CONSTRUCTION PROGRAM OF FIFTH FIVE-YEAR PLAN

shipped from the western producing areas to the east should not cross shipments of similar steel sent from eastern producers toward the west. A deliberate effort is also being made to plan the location of industry so as to reduce the length of haul required. In this connection the decision was made in the late 1930's to base Soviet industrial location policy in the future upon the principle of making the entire economy eventually consist of a series of more or less self-contained major geographic regions. One of the strongest motives for this is the desire to reduce the amount of interregional rail transport required, and thus to reduce the over-all amount of transportation service required of the railroads. By this step the economies of regional specialization are, of course, lost to some degree, perhaps substantially. Nevertheless, Soviet leaders seem to feel that the loss of production efficiency and the increase of cost that this may entail will be offset by the lessened strain put upon the transport system, and particularly its major component, the railroad system. Between 1930 and 1938, the average length of freight haul on Soviet railroads rose from 561 to 718 kilometers, a factor which must have underscored the need for the shift toward regional self-sufficiency adopted as state policy in 1939.

The volume and composition of freight carried by the Soviet railroad system in 1940 are summarized by the data in Table 35.

TABLE 35. Composition of Freight Volume of Soviet Railroads in 1940.

Type of Freight	Ton Kilometers (BILLION)	Freight Originated (MILLION TONS)	Average Length of Haul (KILOMETERS)
Total	415	592.6	700
Coal and Coke ...	106.8	152.5	701
Petroleum	36.4	29.5	1,234
Ores	19.7	35.2	562
Iron and Steel ...	26.2	27.1	966
Building Timber..	43.6	42.8	1,019
Grain	32.8	44.6	736

Source: Hunter, *The Economics of Soviet Railroad Policy*, pp. 198, 204.

One quarter of the total freight volume of Soviet railroads in 1940 was accounted for by the transport of coal and coke. The very high average distance over which building timber and petroleum products had to be moved give them second and third place, respectively, when volume is measured in terms of ton-kilometers, although in actual weight the amount of each was substantially below that of grain. To reduce the railroad load in the future it will obviously be most important to obtain petroleum, timber, and coal nearer the area of consumption.

Adequate analysis of Soviet freight rates by a foreigner is at present impossible because of the failure of the government to publish these rates. We do know that three major reforms have been carried out in the past two decades — in 1930, in 1939, and at the beginning of 1949. The trend in all these reforms has apparently been in the direction of making the rate charged for the movement of each type of goods more and more equal to the actual cost of the transportation service performed. Inasmuch as wages and other costs in the Soviet Union have gone up substantially since 1930, the general trend of freight costs and therefore rates must have been significantly upward. The principle of charging freight rates on different commodities in accordance with their "ability to pay," that is in relation to the value of the different commodities given the same service, is obviously in disfavor in the USSR.

In general, rates are apparently now being set at levels equal to the cost plus planned profit, as is the case with prices in other branches of the Soviet economy. Some goods, however, apparently still get lower rates than would be justified by actual cost, while others are still charged some excess rates as the result of government policy aimed at encouraging or discouraging the utilization of these commodities. The structure of Soviet freight rates in relation to distance carried is said to have been planned with two ends in view. The relative cost of short transport hauls has apparently been set rather high since the beginning of 1949, with a view to encouraging shippers to shift from railroads to truck transport for short hauls. For longer distances the rates decline, most often up to five hundred or a thousand kilometers, and increase thereafter. The purpose of this increase in rates for long-distance shipments is avowedly to discourage excessively long hauls and to encourage utilization of local or nearby resources by purchasers of commodities. The increase of rates brought about by the 1949 reform has apparently also aided the differentiation between the cost of short and very long hauls. Thus, for example, before the 1949 reform the difference in cost for moving a ton of coal one hundred kilometers, as against fifteen hundred kilometers, was twenty rubles and sixty-four kopeks. After the rates had been changed at the beginning of 1949, the difference became thirty-eight rubles and forty-four kopeks, thus almost doubling the extra cost of moving coal over fifteen hundred kilometers as against using local coal within one hundred kilometers' distance of the place of consumption.[9] At the beginning of 1950, railroad freight rates were slightly reduced.

Several reports published in the early 1950's indicated that despite the substantial improvement of Soviet railroad operation after 1945, there were still serious weaknesses. Thus *Pravda* noted in 1951 that while delivery time for rail freight had been cut by 20 or 30 per cent, many trains were late and there was poor discipline in some sections of the rail network. Steps had been taken, it reported, to eliminate duality in administrative leadership of railroads as well as to introduce the uninterrupted 8-hour working day for

[9] *Voprosy Ekonomiki*, No. 9 (1948), pp. 17–33. Cf. the fuller discussion of Soviet freight rates in N. Jasny, *Soviet Prices of Producers' Goods*, Chap. III.

I 952

rail employees generally.[10] A year later *Izvestia* pointed out that the speed of Soviet trains had increased relatively little and remained unsatisfactory. It looked to electrification of railroads as a solution, but complained that the existing electric-rail lines were exploited poorly.[11]

The remarkable speech by First Deputy Premier L. M. Kaganovich, published in the Soviet press April 27, 1954, gave a picture of the great tension under which the Soviet transport system, particularly railroad transport, was operating then. Though the average kilometer of track carried only 7,000,000 tons annually, on some stretches this reached 30–50 million tons. Despite all efforts to reduce the average distance of rail hauls, this figure had increased over the prewar 700 kilometers to 722 kilometers in 1950 and 748 kilometers in 1953. Kaganovich implied that the effort to obtain regional self-sufficiency had failed in large measure and gave this illuminating table on the extent to which the average rail haul for some key commodities had increased from 1940 to 1953:

Commodity	1940	1953	Increase
		(KILOMETERS)	
Lumber	1,019	1,193	174
Grain	736	949	213
Ferrous Metals	966	1,101	135
Cotton	1,814	2,375	561

He characterized the situation in these words:

> Railroad transport, which accounts for almost 85 per cent of all the freight turnover of all kinds of transport, still is forced to carry much surplus freight, to make extraordinarily long hauls, cross hauls, and other uneconomic shipments on which great sums are expended. Unfortunately, shippers and receivers of goods are little interested in how their goods move; they don't ask how much its transport will cost; they ignore joint rail-water shipment; they are not interested in rates; they don't protest against very high distance—all they want is to get the goods regardless of increased expenditures and higher cost of goods.

He placed the quantities of goods irrationally transported at these levels: 4,600,000 tons of oil, 13,000,000 tons of coal, and 4,500,000

---

10 *Pravda*, August 5, 1951.
11 *Izvestia*, September 27, 1952.

tons of lumber, among others. Up to 10,000,000 tons of coal have to be shipped annually from Kuzbas and Karaganda to Moscow. Movement of oil to the Far East costs over 1,000,000,000 rubles annually. He pleaded for more local production of many goods, and then made a comment which would seem applicable to a far wider circle of Soviet administration than that merely involved in railroad problems:

> We rightfully fight against bureaucracy, against the flood of paper, but part of this paper flood goes because each one waits to find out what the center will give him. He does not simply wait, but writes papers, and they write him from the center.

A second major Kaganovich speech, published in *Pravda*, May 24, 1954, reviewed the technical condition of Soviet railroads and concluded confidently that transport was not the "Achilles heel" of the Soviet Union. He revealed that six railroads – the Donets, Sverdlovsk, South-Urals, Tomsk, Stalinsk, and Omsk lines – performed 33 per cent of all Soviet rail freight carriage, having a 1953 freight turnover 80 per cent above that of 1940, but having only slightly increased carrying capacity. It is obviously these roads that work under the greatest tension. Kaganovich boasted that 82 per cent of all railroad work had been done in 1953 by locomotives built since 1935, but he admitted for the first time that in the preceding few years deliveries of railroad rolling stock had been reduced. Accidents still posed serious problems, he indicated, while expressing dissatisfaction with the slow progress of railroad electrification, which by 1960 is scheduled to be 10 times the prewar level.

Kaganovich predicted that by 1960 the volume of rail freight would grow by 50 or 60 per cent, but he gave no indication of any large new government investment program for railroads. Instead he emphasized better utilization of existing equipment.

Railroad Passenger Traffic

Passenger traffic forms a relatively small portion of Soviet railroad volume. This is true despite the fact that the Soviet Union has no such large network of bus lines and widespread ownership of personal cars as does the United States. The reason, of course, is that the average Russian does far less traveling each year than the average American. A large portion of Soviet railroad passenger traffic is accounted for by daily movement of workers living in the suburbs to and from their places of work in or near large cities. During the early 1930's the total volume of passenger traffic actually decreased for a number of years as the government authorities limited availability of resources for this purpose in order to ease the strain on a railroad system already seriously overburdened by more important freight volume. The statistical record of the development of Soviet passenger traffic is given in Table 36.

TABLE 36. Soviet Passenger Traffic in Selected Years.

Year	Volume of Traffic (BILLIONS OF PASSENGER KILOMETERS)	Number of Passengers (MILLIONS)	Average Length of Trip (KILOMETERS)
1913	25.2	184.8	136
1923	13.9	121.8	114
1929	32.0	365.2	88
1932	83.7	967.1	87
1935	67.9	919.1	74
1940†	98.0	1,343.5	73
1945†	66.2	843	78.6
1947†	95.1	*	*
1950 goal†	98.0	1,350	72.6
1951†	*	over 1,300	*
1953 goal†	*	over 1,500	*

* Data not available.
† Expanded Soviet territory.
Sources: Hunter, *The Economics of Soviet Railroad Policy*, p. 215; Hunter, "Soviet Railroads Since 1940," p. 16; *Bolshaya Sovetskaya Entsiklopediya*, Vol. 15, p. 630; *Pravda*, August 2, 1953.

By 1945, substantial improvement must have occurred over the lowest level of passenger traffic reached during World War II. Passenger traffic increased sharply in 1946 and actually declined slightly in 1947. It is noteworthy that the 1946 total volume of passenger traffic virtually equaled that planned for 1950 in terms of passenger kilometers. Presumably this was the result of the tremendous volume of passenger movement required to return soldiers demobilized from the army to their homes. The fact that the 1950 goals were roughly equivalent to the 1940 totals may indicate plans to shift more of the postwar passenger load to buses than was the case before the war. The opportunity to do this is illustrated by the fact that in 1940 suburban traffic accounted for 25 per cent of all passenger kilometers on railroads and 75 per cent of the passengers carried.

Soviet passenger train rates vary, depending upon distance traveled and the kind of accommodation employed. Some typical rates on important runs are shown below. The two columns indicate, first, rates in early 1948 and, second, rates in effect after a change took place late in that year.

		Old Rate	New Rate
Route	Accommodation	(RUBLES)	
Moscow–Leningrad	2-person compartment		
	(international car)	718	816
	Reserved soft seat	139.1	169
	Reserved hard seat	83.8	96
Moscow–Kiev	Reserved soft seat	166.75	189
	Reserved hard seat	100.3	108
Moscow–Vladivostok	2-person compartment		
	(international car)	2,642	3,016
	Reserved soft seat	938.5	1,075
	Reserved hard seat	559.15	643

River Transport

River transport in the Soviet Union is used primarily for carriage of bulky freight such as lumber, coal, cement, and salt. Cargo is carried both on self-propelled boats and on rafts and towed barges. The great advantage of water-borne freight movement is its lower cost as compared with railroad carriage. On the other hand, it is much slower than rail movement, but with proper planning that defect should not overcome the substantial cost advantage. Though the volume of river-carried freight grew substantially in the 1920's and 1930's, and has also grown since 1945, the progress in this area has never been satisfactory to the Soviet authorities. The latter have sought steadily to increase both the absolute and the relative proportion of freight carried by this means, but for a variety of reasons the progress achieved has not been satisfactory. The statistical record of development of Soviet river ways is shown in Table 37.

Before World War II about half of all the freight volume carried by the Soviet river transport system was carried on the Volga River; it consisted chiefly of lumber moved south and petroleum, grain, coal, salt, and fish moved northward. About one third of the total

TABLE 37. River Traffic in the USSR in Selected Years.

Year	Length of Waterways (KILOMETERS)	Freight Tonnage (MILLION TONS)	Freight Volume (BILLION TON-KILOMETERS)
1913	72,000	48.1	37.2
1928	71,600	18.3	15.9
1932	77,600	46.9	25.1
1940 .... over 105,000	66.6‡	36
1945	*	*	18.5
1950 goal	*	91.5	49.3
1950 actual	*	*	45.4
1951 .... over 128,000	*	*
1952	*	*	57.6
1953	*	*	60†
1955 goal	*	*	79–82

* Data not available. † Estimated. ‡ 1938.
Sources: *Narodnoye Khozyaistvo SSSR 1932*, p. 216, *Sot. Stroi.*, pp. 444, 462. *Entsiklopediya*, cols. 963, 983. *Pravda*, April 17, 1951, October 6 and 12, 1952, and January 31, 1954.

freight volume was carried over rivers in the northwest and northern areas of the USSR, including the northern Dvina, Pechora, and other northern waterways, over which the main commodity was lumber. About 10 per cent of the total volume of freight traveled over the Dnepr, Don, Kuban, and other rivers of the southwest area, with the Dnepr River accounting for the largest part. About 12 per cent of the total volume of river transport was carried over the rivers of Siberia and Central Asia, including the Ob, the Irtysh, the Lena, the Amur, and others.[12]

The distribution of different types of freight over the river ways is indicated generally by data for 1935. These show that out of 64.7 million tons of freight carried, more than half, 38.1 million tons, consisted of lumber. In the same year over 7 million tons of petroleum products and almost as much mineral construction materials were transported, as well as 4.6 million tons of grain. The only other items amounting to more than 1 million tons were salt and coal, the amount of each being roughly 1½ million tons.[13]

Great seasonality marks the work of the river transport system, since freezing of the waterways prevents their employment during part of the year throughout the country and over most of the year

[12] *Entsiklopediya*, col. 965.
[13] *Sot. Stroi.*, p. 444.

in some areas. This may be illustrated by data for 1935 given below:

Month	Million Tons[14]
January	Insignificant
February	Insignificant
March	Insignificant
April and May together	13.4
June	11.3
July	11.1
August	11.0
September	8.8
October	6.8
November	2.0
December	.1

An important diseconomy of the Soviet river transport system arises from the fact that on many routes the volume of freight to be carried in one direction is far greater than the volume of freight to be carried in the other direction. As a result much of the equipment is utilized for moving freight in one direction only and must return in the other empty or only partially loaded. The differences in density of traffic upon different rivers and in opposite directions on them may be illustrated by the following data for 1935: [15]

River	Upstream (THOUSAND TONS PER KILOMETER OF ROUTE)	Downstream (THOUSAND TONS PER KILOMETER OF ROUTE)
Volga	3,794	1,820
Kama	245	1,804
Neva	123	4,032
Svir	89	3,477
Moscow	923	96
Northern Dvina	25	2,488
Southern Bug	8	94

Soviet efforts to increase the volume of traffic on the river waterways of the country during the 1930's took a variety of forms. New and more powerful ships capable of carrying greater freight loads were added to the fleet. River routes were improved through increased use of dredges to deepen waterways, and means of illumination were installed to permit traffic by night as well as by day. Important canals such as the White Sea-Baltic and Moscow-Volga were

[14] *Ibid.*, p. 448.
[15] *Ibid.*, p. 454.

dug to make possible passage from one river system to another and thus increase the length of uninterrupted river carriage possible in key areas of the country. Port facilities and loading and unloading equipment were improved, with stress placed upon the use of more mechanical devices. In addition pressure was exerted upon directors of industrial enterprises and mines to induce them to use the river system more fully. Nevertheless the frequent complaints of the Soviet press and of Soviet leaders gave ample evidence that the progress of the river transport system, both absolutely and in relation to its success in taking part of the burden from the railroad lines, was far from satisfactory.

These difficulties with the proper functioning of Soviet river transport apparently still continue in the postwar period. Writing in early 1948, a Soviet specialist on the subject complained that many directors of enterprises who could use river transport prefer to use railroad transport, and listed the following reasons for this attitude: slower delivery of river-moved goods as compared with railroad-moved goods, made worse by the repeated failure of the river transport system even to meet their schedules; bad utilization of the river transport fleet, as a result of which its carrying capacity is below what it should be, making it necessary to shift goods to the railroads; lack of a sufficient effort by the Ministry of River Fleet to attract goods for river transport; higher river freight rates than rail rates for some goods; lack of sufficient transfer points for shifting goods between river vessels and railroads.[16]

Many of these difficulties apparently continued to exist in the early 1950's, despite much expansion of the river fleet and its work as well as the construction of increased facilities. Typical complaints voiced in 1952 told of many ships standing idle, of freight waiting on wharves for two, three, or more weeks awaiting shipment, poor use of port equipment and lack of wharves in the case of many factories on river banks, poor labor discipline among port and river boat workers, and the like.[17]

The most important development in Soviet river transport during the early 1950's was the opening of the Volga-Don Canal in June 1952, an event realizing a dream many centuries old. This canal unites 18,000 miles of waterways along the Volga River and the

---

[16] *Planovoye Khozyaistvo*, No. 2 (1948), pp. 20–30.
[17] Cf. *Izvestia*, March 20, May 21, and October 29, 1952.

rivers of northwest Russia with almost 8,000 miles of waterways in the basins of the Dnepr and Don Rivers. It provides direct water connections between the Black and Caspian Seas, while at times of the spring flood tide, when the Volga is navigable along its full length, the canal unites the southern seas bordering the Soviet Union with the northern seas. This has been emphasized by Soviet boasts that Moscow is now a Port of Five Seas. The volume of river transport should grow greatly as the result of this canal. Oil and lumber movement by river boats will apparently increase greatly because this canal will remove the need for transshipping these products by rail in the case of many shipments of these products. But this canal does not solve all the problems of cheapening freight movement, since it is closed during the winter months and the Volga River is still not navigable by larger vessels over important stretches during the summer and fall.[18]

Almost two years after the Volga-Don Canal had been opened, on April 17, 1954, *Izvestia* revealed that the canal was being used far below capacity and that Soviet leaders were bitterly disappointed at the failure of freight movement over this expensive waterway to reach the levels anticipated originally. In his speech printed in the Soviet press ten days later, Kaganovich gave this enumeration of the defects of the Soviet river transport system as of the spring of 1954:

> Water transport is badly utilized for moving freight which can be moved by this means, particularly materials other than ores, timber, coal, grains, consumer goods which are moved over long distances on roads paralleling waterways. We have many rivers such as the Chusovaya, Angara, Vychegda, Mezen, Sozh, Upper Yenisei, the Northern Don, and others which are not used for ships or are used only along short stretches. The new canals are insufficiently employed. . . . The water transport of fish, fruits and vegetables, textiles, and other consumer goods has still not regained the prewar level. The fault here lies primarily with the workers of water transportation themselves, who do not strive enough to secure freight, who move the freight they do get slowly, who badly safeguard these goods, and who utilize the available ship tonnage at a low level of productivity.

Transport of passengers forms only a small portion of the work

---

[18] *Sotsialisticheskoye Zemledeliye,* September 5, 1950, and *Izvestia,* July 10, 1952.

of the Soviet river fleet, usually amounting to less than 10 per cent of rail passenger traffic. Between 1929 and 1938, the number of passengers on Soviet river boats rose from around 21,000,000 to 68,100,000, as compared with almost 1,200,000,000 rail passengers in 1938. In 1935, out of a total of almost 2,900,000,000 passenger kilometers provided by the river fleet, over 10 per cent was suburban and intracity ferry travel. More than a third of all passenger kilometers that year was provided by boats traveling the Volga River; another 20 per cent was accounted for by boats on the Kama River. In the area of Moscow, there were about 5,000,000 ferry-boat passengers in 1935, one fifth of all ferry-boat passengers in the entire USSR.[19]

Automobile Transport

Soviet use of motor vehicles for passenger and freight transport is relatively far less important than in the United States or Western Europe. This is the result of the proportionately small number of cars, buses, and trucks in the USSR when compared to its population and the size of its territory, as well as of the relatively primitive and undeveloped road network available. Long-distance movement of passengers or freight by motor vehicles is of negligible importance in the Soviet Union. There are few facilities comparable to our national and regional bus and truck organizations. In many cities and their suburbs, however, local buses handle a significant proportion of passenger traffic and trucks carry a large volume of short-haul freight, thus supplementing the rail and river transport systems. Private passenger-car ownership is confined to a very small fraction of Soviet citizens, and taxicabs, too, are far less common than in the United States.

Nevertheless substantial progress has been made in developing this area of transportation since the Bolshevik revolution. At the end of 1937 there were about 760,000 motor vehicles in the USSR, the great majority of them trucks, as compared with about 9,000 in the Russia of 1914 and the 19,000 in the USSR at the start of the First Five-Year Plan.[20] During World War II, many motor vehicles were lost to the enemy or destroyed in combat, but the USSR received about 375,000 trucks of all kinds from the United States.

[19] *Sot. Stroi.*, pp. 450–51.
[20] Balzak, *et al., op. cit.*, pp. 494–95.

At the end of the war, Soviet troops confiscated large numbers of cars in Eastern Europe and other areas they occupied and brought many of them back to the USSR. These factors, plus the recovery of domestic production of motor vehicles after World War II, suggest that by 1954 the USSR had well over 2,000,000 cars, buses, and trucks in operation, the highest number in its history. The growth of Soviet motor-vehicle production is depicted by the data below:

TABLE 38. Soviet Motor-Vehicle Production in Selected Years.

	1929	1938	1940	1945	1950 Goal	1950 Actual†	1955 Goal
Total	1.4	211.4	147	87.7	500	397.3	476.8
Trucks ...	1.3	184.4	*	*	428	369.2	424.0
Others ...	.1	27.0	*	*	72	28.1	52.8

* Data unavailable. † Estimated actual.
Sources: 1929-1938—*Sot. Stroi (1933-38)*, p. 63. 1940—E. Lokshin, *Promyshlennost SSSR v Novoi Stalinskoi Pyatiletke*, p. 40. 1945-1955—Estimates by U. S. Department of Commerce based on Soviet sources.

The data above make it plain that in 1950 the Soviet Union produced a record number of motor vehicles, though the number fell far short of the original goal for that year. There is reason to believe that in 1951 and 1952, at least, motor-vehicle output was below the 1950 level because of diversion of resources to the needs of the Korean War and Soviet military preparation. This view is supported by the fact that the Fifth Five-Year Plan set a 1955 motor-vehicle output goal which was only a modest 20 per cent above the 1950 actual production.

In the extensive program announced in late 1953 for increased production of consumer durable goods, there is no mention of any sharp increase in the production of passenger cars. Mikoyan reported that in 1953 nine times as many cars would be sold to the public as in 1950 and that there was in October 1953 a six-months backlog of orders for cars.[21] We have estimated above that in 1950 only about 28,000 passenger cars were produced in the Soviet Union. Since the overwhelming majority of these undoubtedly were transferred to government ownership for the use of officials, probably only a few thousand cars were sold to private citizens.

[21] *Pravda*, October 25, 1953.

Mikoyan's comparison therefore, does not suggest a surfeit of passenger cars for Soviet citizens. More illuminating probably is the fact that no explicit goal for passenger car production is given in the special 1953 decree on increased output of consumer goods. Along with the increased output and supply of motor vehicles, the Soviet Union has added materially to its road network. This network has been and is quite inadequate — both in extent and in quality — for the needs of this huge country. New roads have been built during the Soviet regime and others improved, but the great majority remain ordinary dirt paths, entirely unpassable by wheeled vehicles because of rain or snow during large periods of the year. The paved-road network is moderately well developed in the western USSR, where many of the larger cities are connected by such all-weather links. East of the Urals the network of paved roads is grossly inadequate, so that many important areas are without adequate motor linkage. But even in the western area, most of the roads are unsurfaced.[22] The primitive character of Soviet roads is indicated by the fact that most road repair is done by millions of peasants conscripted for this labor annually. In the postwar period, a start has been made toward establishing a network of road repair and construction stations equipped with modern road-building machinery. The changing composition and extent of Soviet roads before World War II is shown by Table 39.

TABLE 39. Roads of the Soviet Union, 1913, 1928, and 1938.

	1913	1928	1938
		(THOUSAND KILOMETERS)	
Total	*	*	1,354.8
Natural-Dirt	*	*	936.4
Graded-Dirt	0	1–1.5	330.9
Hard-Surfaced	23.5	31.3	87.5

* Data unavailable.
Source: Balzak, et al., op. cit., pp. 495-96.

At the end of 1950, it was reported that 21,000 kilometers of hard-surfaced roads had been built during 1946–50. Whether this was much more than the length of hard-surfaced roads destroyed during World War II is doubtful. At the end of 1950, the Soviet government claimed that the length of improved roads was 2.5

22 Cf. the road maps of the USSR, Balzak, et al., op. cit., pp. 497, 499.

times as large as in 1940, and two years later Malenkov said that the length of improved roads was 3.1 times as much as in 1940. These latter figures suggest that the greatest emphasis in the postwar period has been put upon increasing the length of graded dirt roads, the main type apparently referred to as "improved." During 1951–55, 50 per cent more hard-surfaced roadway is to be built and reconstructed than during 1946–50. This will be a substantial gain if achieved, but still far short of the needs of a country the size of the Soviet Union. Until late 1953 the building and maintenance of major roads was a responsibility of the Ministry of Interior (MVD). After the purge of L. P. Beria, however, this function was assigned to a new Ministry of Highway Transport and Highways, which also is in charge of truck and bus movement.

In 1937 about 56 per cent of all freight moved in the USSR, measured by weight, was carried by trucks. But since these trucks were used almost exclusively for short distances, the total volume of freight movement by trucks — in ton-kilometers — was only 2 per cent of the national total for that year. In 1940 trucks carried 1,000,000,000 metric tons of freight as against only 600,000,000 tons carried by railroads, but the average length of truck haul was only one-seventieth of the average rail haul.

Truck freight carriage increased sharply from 1946 to 1950, but in the latter year the record 20,700,000,000 ton-kilometer freight turnover was still less than three per cent of all rail, water, and truck freight turnover. By 1955, the volume of truck freight turnover is to be near 38,000,000,000 ton-kilometers, almost twice the 1950 level, but still less than 4 per cent of all rail, water, and truck freight turnover. (See Table 33.)

Since World War II limited beginnings have been made toward a system of long-distance truck freight and bus service. In mid-1950 intercity truck freight service linked Moscow with Leningrad, Ryazan, Tula, Kaluga, Smolensk, and other communities in this general area. A Moscow-Tula bus service, using ZIS limousines, began in late 1950, and in August 1951 daily bus service was inaugurated between Moscow and the cities of Simferopol, Kharkov, and Yalta. In early 1952 the existence of Orel-Moscow, Simferopol-Kharkov, Kursk-Kharkov, and Orel-Kursk bus lines were noted, while later in the year bus service was reported available connecting Kiev with other leading Ukrainian cities and with Gomel in Belorussia.[23] Presumably this network of intercity truck and bus lines will expand over time, but by early 1954 these services still were of comparatively minor importance and limited coverage. One factor apparently inhibiting such long distance motor service is the lack of gasoline stations on the roads. In late 1951 it was pointed out that trucks moving between Moscow and Kiev had to leave Moscow with sufficient gas for the round trip, so that gasoline occupied one-third of their total carrying space! [24]

Soviet utilization of trucks and cars has been greatly hampered by the poor care given these vehicles and the great shortage of proper facilities for their repair and maintenance. In 1938, for example, only 43.1 per cent of all trucks available in the country were put to work each day. At the end of 1938 only two thirds of all machines were in movable condition, and less than half were in technically correct order. About 40 per cent of all machines required large or medium-sized repair jobs. The effects of poor current maintenance were aggravated by the lack of sufficient numbers of garages and repair shops. In 1939 there were reported to be only seven service stations in the Soviet Union, as compared with 90,000 in the United States. The lack of spare parts also crippled the work of motor transport, forcing widespread "cannibalization" of trucks and automobiles to keep part of the vehicle supply moving. Scarce supplies of gasoline and lubricating oils were wastefully used.[25] Similar complaints about the poor technical care of vehicles, excessive idleness of trucks resulting from spare-parts shortages, lack of repair and vehicle service facilities and the like were still frequently voiced in the early 1950's, though presumably the much larger number of vehicles available in the Soviet Union by 1953 or 1954 had been at least partially matched by some increase in facilities for taking care of them.[26]

Maritime Transport

Despite the long coastline of the USSR in the north, east, and

---

23 *Moskovskaya Pravda*, July 29 and December 9, 1950. *Pravda*, August 20, 1951. *Izvestia*, March 28, 1952. *Pravda Ukrainy*, November 22, 1952.

24 *Izvestia*, September 29, 1951.

25 *Planovoye Khozyaistvo*, No. 10 (1939), pp. 72–90.

26 *Pravda*, March 9, 1951. *Izvestia*, March 1, March 8, and September 10, 1952.

south, the Soviet Union — and Czarist Russia before it — has never been a major maritime power. Many of the country's maritime ports are frozen for three to nine months each year, creating problems similar to those faced by the river transport system. In addition much of the northern and eastern coast of the USSR is far from any large concentration of population requiring transport service. However, the desire to become a significant maritime power has been a significant force in Soviet transport development, and the opportunities for achieving this goal have become brighter in the past decade with the acquisition of the key Baltic ports of prewar East Prussia and the formerly independent Baltic States.

The development of Soviet maritime transport is shown below:

TABLE 40. Soviet Maritime Transport in Selected Years.

	Unit	1929	1938	1940	1950	1955 Goal
Freight......	Billion ton-km.	10.4	33.7	23	38	59–61
Passengers ...	Million	1.5	3.1	*	*	*

* Data unavailable.
Sources: *Sot. Stroi (1933-38)*, p. 107. *Entsiklopediya*, col. 951. *Pravda*, April 27, 1951 and October 12, 1952.

The great bulk of freight and passenger traffic carried by the Soviet merchant marine is moved between ports of the Soviet Union. Soviet ships participate also in international maritime commerce, though their role has been minor up to the present. Trade with overseas countries is rather small. Relatively few persons travel to and from the Soviet Union at all because of the restrictive Soviet policy toward foreign travel and visitors from abroad; and ships must compete with the USSR's rail connections both with European countries to the west and through China to Asia in the Orient. The chief maritime ports of the USSR in 1935, in order of the freight volume they handled, were: Baku, Astrakhan, Makhach-Kala (an oil port on the Caspian Sea), Batumi, Leningrad, Odessa, Mariupol, Novorossiisk, Archangel, and Vladivostok, each of which handled 2,000,000 or more tons of freight that year.[27] In the postwar era, such major Baltic Sea ports as Kaliningrad (formerly Königsberg), Riga, and Tallin, which have been acquired since 1935, would probably have to be added.

[27] *Sot. Stroi.*, p. 470.

In the postwar period, the USSR has pushed an extensive program of rebuilding its leading ports — particularly those in the west destroyed or damaged during the war. It has emphasized improvement of freight-handling facilities in these ports through installation of mechanical loading and unloading equipment, as well as the provision of adequate warehousing space. By 1950 the number of deepwater piers was scheduled to be 1.7 times as many as in 1940, and ship repair yards on the Baltic and Black Seas were to be completely restored. Ship-building facilities were to be greatly increased during 1946–50, partially through the building of two new shipyards, one on the Baltic and one on the Black Sea. The Fourth Five-Year Plan called for the building in 1950 of twice the ship tonnage constructed in 1940. The acquisition of ships from former enemy states, particularly the German liner *Patria* now called the *Rossiya*, has aided the USSR's maritime fleet in the postwar period. Much of the USSR's merchant marine freight-carrying capacity during the past decade has been provided by American vessels borrowed during World War II. The USSR has been slow to return these vessels, perhaps because of inadequate new building.

A major objective of the first postwar five-year plans has been the conversion of the Northern Sea Route into a normal waterway. This route was first developed in the early 1930's. The objective has been to provide a direct sea path from Leningrad and other northwestern ports to the basins of the Ob, Yenisey, and other Siberian rivers, as well as to the ports of the Soviet Far East. This waterway through the Arctic Ocean offers some of the greatest challenges in the world to navigators, since the period of navigation may vary from 70 to 120 days. Ice conditions in different parts of the area vary greatly and change frequently. To make this route passable, much effort and expense have been required to provide lighthouses, ice breakers, weather information, and other aids to navigation. The Third Five-Year Plan set 1942 as the time for routine functioning of this route, but the war made that goal unattainable, forcing its postponement to 1950 or later.[28]

As of January 1, 1949, the USSR had 423 sea-going ships of 1,788,000 deadweight tons, little more than the prewar figure of 1,600,000 deadweight tons. More than half the 1949 Soviet fleet was

[28] Trevor Lloyd, "The Northern Sea Route," *Russian Review*, April 1950, pp. 98–111.

twenty or more years old, with a speed of less than twelve knots an hour. By 1950 the USSR hoped to have a maritime fleet totaling 3,200,000 tons. This goal was not attained. In 1953 the entire Soviet bloc — primarily the USSR and Poland — had a seagoing merchant fleet with a gross tonnage of 2,500,000 tons, against 81,000,000 tons in the fleets of the free world.[29]

Soviet dissatisfaction with the size of its maritime fleet was indicated by the energetic efforts made during 1950–54 to place orders for ships in foreign shipyards. Yet the limited beginnings made in the early postwar period toward establishing Soviet luxury international passenger service were given up around 1950. In mid-1951, it was reported that the large ocean-going passenger liners, Rossiya, Gruzia, and Ukraina had been converted to domestic-cruise liners making ten-day tours of the Black Sea from Odessa to Batumi.[30]

Indicative of the progress being made on the Northern Sea Route was the 1952 report of a successful voyage by a fleet of Soviet ships which travelled 12,000 kilometers from the Volga River to Yakutsk, 8,000 kilometers of this journey being along the Northern Sea Route.[31] Further efforts to improve ocean ports, increase the tonnage of the maritime fleet, and increase the capacity of Soviet shipyards were called for in the maritime transport provisions of the Fifth Five-Year Plan.

In May 1954 the Soviet Army newspaper, Red Star, printed the fullest progress report on the Northern Sea Route. This indicated that the entire Arctic sea coast of the Soviet Union had been systematically explored, that an elaborate network of reporting stations had been set up to facilitate safe movement, and that the transport work done over this northern waterway was at record levels.

Air Transport

Air movement of passengers, mail, and freight has grown rapidly in the USSR since the late 1920's, owing to the speed with which

[29] American Merchant Marine Institute Study reported in New York Herald-Tribune, July 31, 1949. East-West Trade Trends, Report to Congress of the Foreign Operations Administrator, May 17, 1954, p. 25.
[30] Ogonyok, No. 26 (June 1951).
[31] Izvestia, September 28, 1952.

the great distances between major cities in European and Asiatic parts of the country can be covered in comparison with train or other surface transportation. Moreover, many important areas of the USSR are not connected by rail or by good roads with the rest of the country. For these relatively isolated regions, air transport provides an important means of communication without the necessity of investing large sums in building railroads or hard-surfaced automobile roads, investments that are as yet unjustified by the volume of passenger and freight traffic to and from these areas.

The length of route covered by Soviet air lines grew from 18,500 kilometers in 1929 to about 140,000 kilometers in 1939. It was scheduled to attain 175,000 kilometers in 1950. The volume of freight service performed grew from 400,000 ton-kilometers in 1929 to 30,300,000 ton-kilometers in 1938. The number of passengers carried increased from only 9,300 in 1929 to over 300,000 a decade later.[32] Before the war, Moscow was the single major hub of the Soviet civil air network, the major lines connecting it with all important regions of the country — the Far East, Leningrad, the Ukraine, North Caucasus, and Central Asia. More recently, apparently, Leningrad has become a secondary major hub, having connecting lines to Siberia, Central Asia, the Urals, the Ukraine, the Baltic States, and other areas. In Central Asia, Yakutia, the Caucasus, the Far East, and the Far North, areas where surface transportation is relatively poorly developed, local and regional airlines have been developed to help make up for the deficiencies of alternative transport facilities. In addition to purely domestic air routes, Soviet airlines in the postwar period maintain routes to the capitals of many of the border countries in Eastern Europe and Asia. Soviet planes make regular flights to Poland, Czechoslovakia, Hungary, Rumania, Bulgaria, Finland, Austria, Afghanistan, China, Mongolia, and Korea.[33] A significant development in late 1953 was the agreement reached between the Soviet civil airlines organization, Aeroflot, and the Scandinavian Air Lines. Under terms of this agreement, the facilities of the Soviet and Scandinavian lines are joined so that a passenger may board a Scandinavian plane any-

---

[32] *Sot. Stroi., (1933–1938)*, p. 108, and *USSR Information Bulletin*, April 22, 1949, pp. 264–65.

[33] *USSR Information Bulletin, op. cit.*, p. 264; *Entsiklopediya*, cols. 973–74. *Izvestia*, July 18, 1950.

where the line reaches as the beginning of a flight anywhere into the area served by the Soviet line, Scandinavian doing the booking in the non-communist world. Connections with and transfers to Soviet planes are made at Helsinki. A similar Soviet-French air agreement was signed in June 1954.

Although the airplane industry and the airlines of the USSR have made great advances technically since the late 1920's, there seems good reason to believe that they lag behind those of the United States. Not until 1948 was regular night flying introduced on a number of major air routes in the USSR, though in this country night flying — which requires extensive radio installations to guide planes — was common almost a decade earlier. Formerly, too, rigorous winter conditions forced maintenance of a much more limited schedule of flights than in summertime, but in 1948 it was reported that the winter schedule would be almost as extensive as that of summer. The frequency of long flights has also been increased sharply. In 1948 the Moscow-Vladivostok run took place only ten times a month, but in the summer of 1949 it was being conducted daily.[34] Over 500 routes were reported operating in June 1948; a year later the number of routes and the frequency of flights were said to have been increased substantially.[35] At the end of 1949, the volume of Soviet civil air transport service was reported to be eight times that of 1940. The length of fleet route was claimed to exceed that of the United States, a claim apparently based to some extent on duplicated mileage of different routes. Soviet airlines in 1950 were also claimed to be carrying more freight than the airlines of any capitalist country.[36]

The most recent set of absolute figures concerning Soviet civil air transport is from the Soviet economic plan for 1941. For 1941, Soviet civil air transport was scheduled to move 48,000,000 ton-kilometers of freight and 387,000 persons.[37] The Soviet radio has announced that in 1952 the Soviet civil air fleet's freight turnover was nine times that of 1940, suggesting that the actual figure may have been about 400,000,000 ton-kilometers. By 1955 the freight

---

[34] New York Herald-Tribune, June 9, 1948; Trud, June 8, 1948; Pravda, October 6, 1948, and June 1, 1949.

[35] Trud, June 8, 1948, and Pravda, October 6, 1948.

[36] Izvestia, July 18, 1950; Pravda, July 16, 1950; New York Herald-Tribune, February 6, 1949.

[37] Gosudarstvenny Plan Razvitiya . . . na 1941 God, p. 478.

turnover of the civil air fleet is to be at least twice that of 1950, or probably in excess of 600,000,000 ton-kilometers. New air passenger lines opened in 1953 included Moscow-Murmansk, Moscow-Barnaul, and Leningrad-Chelyabinsk.[38]

Communications

The Soviet communications system ties together the complex and geographically dispersed economy of the USSR. Without it the planned coordination and operation of this economy would be impossible. In addition, part of this communication system serves as a major vehicle for government propaganda and education. The transmission of personal messages for individuals is also part of the assignment of Soviet communications facilities, but probably a relatively smaller part than is the case in the United States because of limited availability of telephones for general use.

Soviet writers divide their communications system into the following major branches: the postal system, the telegraph system, the intercity telephone network, intraurban telephone systems, and radio broadcasting. Radio-telegraphy, teletype transmission, wire-photo transmission, and television are also branches of Soviet communications. All this vast communications network is owned and operated by the government as an essential part of the over-all national economy. Most of this network is administered directly by the Ministry of Communications. A number of branches of the economy, such as railroads, airlines, and the weather forecasting service, have their own radio, telegraph, and telephone networks to meet their own needs, but the technical condition and development of these are also under the general control of the Communications Ministry. The ministry charges for the services of its facilities through the sale of stamps for postal deliveries and through telegraph, telephone, and related charges, as in other countries.

Over the past three decades and more, the Soviet government has vigorously pushed expansion and technical improvement of communications facilities. The Czarist regime did have a mail delivery system, a telephone and telegraph system, and the beginning of radio broadcasting. In keeping with the concentration of economic activity and population in the western areas, there was a

[38] Soviet Home Service, August 4, 1953.

similar concentration of communications facilities in the same regions, though as early as 1861 there was telegraph service to Irkutsk near Lake Baikal. The Soviet government has done much to increase the availability of postal and electrical communications throughout the country, particularly from the Urals to the Pacific, where they were least developed before 1917. In the past two decades, there has been much effort, too, to bring the telephone and radio into the rural areas, but this has been hampered by the fact that most Soviet farms lack electricity. Battery-operated radios are therefore often used.

The state of the Soviet communications system before the German invasion of June 1941 is indicated by the following goals assigned by the government economic plan for 1941: [39]

Mail System: 2,580,000,000,000 letters; 48,000,000 parcels; 104,-000,000 money orders; 50,669 postal stations.

Telephone System: 1,816,800 kilometers of long-distance lines; 997,000 kilometers of local telephone lines; 1,088,800 urban telephone numbers; 80,600,000 inter-city and international telephone calls.

Telegraph System: 16,116 telegraph sending units; 144,000,000 telegrams transmitted.

In 1947 there were 51,000 post-office branches over the USSR, backed by an elaborate system of automobile, train, and plane transport, with final delivery by letter carriers. Besides letters of all kinds, the postal system distributes huge numbers of Soviet newspapers — some 6,600,000,000 copies in 1940 alone. Air mail is carried on all major lines as well as on local aviation systems in areas where surface transport is poorly developed. Mechanization of the handling and sorting of mail has been pressed and continues to be emphasized in the drive for greater efficiency and speed in the postal system.[40] Occasional complaints in the Soviet press about slow delivery of letters and newspapers suggest that the mail system is still somewhat primitive and slow in some areas, despite the undoubted advances over the past several decades. The 20,000 post-office branches destroyed during World War II were reported to have been all restored by the end of 1945.

About 31,500 telegraph offices operated in the USSR in 1947 as

[39] *Gosudarstvenny Plan Razvitiya . . . na 1941 God*, pp. 480–81.
[40] *Entsiklopediya*, cols. 992–94.

compared with 5,100 combined mail and telegraph offices operating in 1913. There were 175,000,000 telegrams sent in 1946, almost five times the 36,000,000 sent in 1913. By 1938 some 96 per cent of all cities and rural district centers had telegraphic connections with the capitals of their provinces, suggesting that the telegraph system covered virtually all the inhabited areas of the USSR. The growth of both the telegraph and telephone system of the USSR is indicated by the fact that the total length of lines for these facilities has grown from about 500,000 kilometers in 1913 to around 2,400,000 kilometers in 1938, an almost fivefold increase. Soviet specialists have introduced improved telegraph transmission systems, teletype communication, and radio telegraphy to speed this branch of communications.[41]

The USSR has a comprehensive system of telephone communications connecting Moscow with all provincial centers and, through them, with the centers of smaller regions. Similarly the capitals of each of the Soviet republics are connected with their provincial and district centers. The number of telephones installed grew from about 330,000 in late 1929 to 1,272,500 at the end of 1938. The extension of the telephone network before the war made it possible by 1940 to call Vladivostok from Moscow, as well as to establish radio-telephone communication between Moscow and San Francisco. Before World War II, the USSR had made substantial gains in raising the quality of its telephone system, installing increasingly automatic exchange equipment and other technical improvements as well as increasing the capacity and coverage of the system. Nevertheless, the number of telephones was so limited that at the end of the 1930's the Soviet Union was seventh among the countries of the world in this respect, lagging behind Canada, which has less than one tenth of the USSR's population. During World War II, most of the lines going through the areas occupied by the Germans were destroyed, so that 130,000 kilometers of telephone-telegraph wires had to be restored during 1943–45. A great deal of aid was received from the United States during the conflict, including more than 850,000 miles of field-telephone wire and 275,000 field telephones for the Red Army.[42]

---

41 *Ibid.; Sot. Stroi.*, p. 504. *Sot. Stroi.* (*1933–38*), p. 109.

42 *Ibid.*, and A. J. Steiger, "Communications: Railways, Highways, Air," in E. J. Simmons, editor, *USSR, A Concise Handbook*, pp. 284–85. Ithaca: Cornell University Press, 1947.

The intra-urban and rural telephone networks of the USSR exist primarily for business purposes, the use of phones for personal business being minor. The extension of telephone service throughout the country has apparently permitted virtually all cities of any significant size to have local systems. By 1947 telephones had been provided for 75 per cent of all rural governmental units and 90 per cent of all Machine Tractor Stations. Great damage was inflicted during World War II on the local systems of all communities in the areas occupied by the Germans, stations having a capacity of 325,000 numbers being destroyed. Much of this destruction had been repaired by the end of 1946, however, and this rehabilitation has presumably been continued since that time.[43]

Soviet radio broadcasting is a major means of spreading government propaganda, news, educational material, and entertainment to the domestic audience. The USSR also has a very extensive foreign broadcasting program for propaganda purposes. By 1940 it had 126 large urban transmitters, as against only 41 in 1929. In addition there were about 2,000 local rural radio transmitters. Radio reception is provided, for the most part, through loudspeakers in homes and public places, all wired to a central receiver. In 1940, there were some 5,500,000 listening posts connected with 10,000 wired networks of this type.[44] In 1948 it was reported that there were 7,000,000 such listening points, and that the USSR had 100 large radio stations, a number scheduled to increase by 28 by 1950. Production and utilization of individual receiving sets have increased greatly in the postwar period, but they remain few in number and high in price, so that they are out of the reach of most Soviet citizens. In May 1947, individual radio sets were estimated to have numbered only 1,300,000, about 18 per cent of all receiving equipment in operation.[45] A *Pravda* editorial late in 1948 complained sharply of the lack of individual radio receivers and of the poor quality of many of those produced. It reported a severe shortage of radio tubes and other spare parts, which, it said, kept many receiving units and some stations out of commission for ex-

---

[43] *Entsiklopediya*, cols. 995–96.

[44] Steiger, *op. cit.*, p. 286.

[45] *New York Herald-Tribune*, May 7 and June 11, 1948; Alex Inkeles, *Public Opinion in Soviet Russia*, p. 251. Cambridge: Harvard University Press, 1950.

tended periods.[46] Although similar complaints have been repeated frequently since then, the lack of radio parts did not prevent the USSR from inaugurating in 1949 a comprehensive program for jamming American and British broadcasts to Russia. These jamming activities indicated clearly both the high level of Soviet radio technique and the availability of large supplies of equipment and replacements.

In early 1953 it was reported that the Soviet Union's network of radio receivers was almost twice as large as in 1940, and that the number of receiving installations — presumably both individual sets and loud speakers wired to a central receiving unit — would be 30,-000,000 by 1955.[47] The rapid rate at which the number of radio receivers is to grow is indicated by the announced production goals of 2,861,000 radios in 1954 and 3,767,000 radios in 1955.[48] But even if these production goals are achieved and there are 30,000,000 or more radio receivers in 1955, this will still be equivalent to only about one receiver for every seven or eight persons, suggesting that large numbers of Soviet people, particularly in rural areas, will still not have their own radio reception.

Television transmission in the USSR began in 1938, was suspended during World War II, and was resumed thereafter. By the middle of 1954, regular Soviet television stations were being operated or being built in ten cities, Moscow, Leningrad, and Kiev, the most important of them. Television receivers were still very expensive, even though most had only small screens, 4 inches by 5 inches or somewhat larger. The number of television receivers installed by the middle of 1954 was probably little if any greater than 250,000, though for 1954 to 1956 the government promised rapid growth in television-set production with the following goals set: 1954 — 325,000; 1955 — 760,000; 1956 — 1,000,000. Color television was still only experimental in early 1954. There has been some indication of government plans to institute a system of TV screens wired to a single receiver as the basis for mass television.

[46] *Pravda*, November 22, 1948.
[47] *Izvestia*, May 7, 1953.
[48] *Pravda*, October 28, 1953.

CHAPTER XI

TRADE, HOUSING, AND SERVICES

THIS CHAPTER will deal with those areas of the Soviet economy that provide consumers with the goods and services they enjoy: the distributive system, the organization of housing, and municipal and other services. Earlier chapters have pointed out that satisfaction of consumer wants in the USSR's economic development has usually been secondary to the requirements of heavy industry, transport, and the armed forces. Even at the low average standard of living of the USSR, however, consumption normally takes substantially more than half of the gross national product or national income, both goods and services being included in these totals. A large and complex network of organizations is required to serve consumers. Both the size and range of functions of this network have tended to expand with the increasing urbanization and economic specialization of the Soviet population.

Soviet consumers form a large and heterogeneous mass of people composed of many groups, each with its own wants and needs. The requirements of a peasant family in a remote Siberian village differ sharply from those of a Moscow worker's family in which all adults have regular jobs. There are substantial income differences in the Soviet population, with corresponding sharp differentials in standards of living. A successful author may have a house in Moscow, a summer home in the Crimea, two cars, servants, and imported clothes. His way of life is an upper extreme far removed indeed from the customary consumption patterns of most Soviet citizens, yet the Soviet government has the problem of providing the goods and services high income groups expect as well as the more modest requirements of the majority.

426

Soviet Living Standards

Throughout Soviet history—as well as under the Czarist regime—the average standard of living in the USSR has been low compared with that in Western Europe and the United States. The Soviet diet has been predominantly composed of bread and other grain crops; meat, eggs, milk and dairy products, fruits, and most vegetables have been a minor part of it. Before World War II, after recovery had been achieved from the low levels of the early 1930's, the average Soviet citizen consumed around 2,800 calories daily, about as much as the average Bulgarian. Roughly two thirds of these calories were accounted for by bread and other grain foods; only about 10 per cent were obtained from meat and milk. In the same period the average American consumer received over 3,200 calories daily, of which well under one third were secured from grain products; meat and milk together contributed even more calories than grain products. A similar contrast is shown for this period between the Soviet diet and that of Great Britain, Denmark, Germany, Canada, Argentina, and Australia, though the differences are smaller.[1]

The general nature of the Soviet diet is indicated by the 1947 food ration schedule that prevailed in Moscow. This schedule, shown below, was supplemented by potatoes and vegetables grown

TABLE 41. Basic Monthly Food Rations in Moscow, January 1947.

Food	Heavy Workers	Other Manual Workers	Clerical Workers	Dependents*		Children
			(POUNDS PER MONTH)			
Bread†	42.0	36.0	30.0	18.0	0	21.0
Grits	4.4	4.4	3.3	2.2	2.2	2.6
Meat and Fish	4.9	4.9	2.6	1.3	0	1.3
Fats	1.8	1.8	.9	.4	0	.4
Sugar	2.0	2.0	1.1	.9	.9	1.1
Salt	.9	.9	.9	.9	.9	.9
Tea	.1	.1	.1	.1	0	.1

* Dependents were grouped into two categories.
† 30-day month basis.
Source: *Monthly Labor Review*, July 1947, p. 29.

[1] John D. Black and M. E. Kiefer, *Future Food and Agricultural Policy*, p. 40. New York: McGraw-Hill, 1948.

by workers themselves, by restaurant meals in factories, and by food purchased outside the ration system. The level of food consumption has been better than this at other times. Nevertheless the predominance of grain products and the relatively small quantities of protein foods such as meat and fish in these rations have been characteristic of the pattern of food consumption in the USSR throughout its history.

In the field of consumer goods, a corresponding situation exists. The average Soviet citizen still has little chance to own consumer durable goods such as automobiles, refrigerators, washing machines, television sets, and the like, though phonographs, bicycles, and sewing machines are owned by an appreciable minority. A revealing picture of the low supply of clothing available to the Soviet population is provided by a January 1936 survey made by Soviet statistical authorities among 7,000 young workers in the largest enterprises of nine major Soviet cities, including Moscow, Leningrad, and Kharkov. The group surveyed was probably relatively well-to-do, but the findings are from from impressive.

TABLE 42. Clothing and Footwear Inventories of Young Workers in Nine Soviet Cities in January 1936.

Men	Average Number of Items	Women	Average Number of Items
Overcoats and Topcoats	1.3	Overcoats and Topcoats	1.8
Suits	0.9	Wool and Silk Dresses	1.2
Trousers	2.1	Cotton Dresses	3.2
Shirts	3.9	Skirts	2.4
Changes of Underwear	3.6	Jackets	0.7
Leather Shoes	1.5	Blouses	3.4
		Changes of Underwear	4.4
		Leather Shoes	1.5

Source: *Planovoye Khozyaistvo*, No. 5 (1938), pp. 84-85.

As we shall see in more detail below, inadequate and poor-quality housing has been and is one of the worst features of the Soviet standard of living. The rapid expansion of urban population during the 1930's far outstripped the growth of housing facilities, so that great overcrowding became the rule in Soviet cities. The enormous destruction of rural and urban homes in western areas during World

War II forced millions to live in dugouts, caves, and similar make-
shift quarters. In the eastern areas beyond the furthest limit of
German penetration, city populations increased greatly during the
war, while only minimal resources were allocated for housing. Substantial progress was achieved in building new housing during the
Fourth Five-Year Plan, but even in 1950 this was one of the worst
areas of ordinary Soviet life.

Interesting light on the Soviet standard of living is given by the
pattern of consumer expenditures before World War II shown
below.[2]

	1934	1938
Expenditures	(PERCENT OF EXPENDITURES)	
Goods and Restaurant Meals	77.3	79.6
Services of All Kinds	10.5	9.6
Direct Taxes	4.2	3.2
Savings, Government Bonds, Insurance, etc......	8.0	7.6

Discussing the significance of these figures, a Soviet economist
pointed out the great discrepancy between Soviet and American
expenditure patterns with respect to services. Quoting an estimate
that in the United States 26 per cent of consumer expenditures go
for services, he declared that the Soviet figure of less than 10 per
cent in 1938 was much too low, even if allowance is made for the
free medical service available in the USSR.[3] Behind this statistical
difference is the great paucity of service and recreational facilities
in the USSR, so that it is frequently none too easy to obtain even
laundry, dry-cleaning, or good shoe-repair service.

The Soviet standard of living has not been static of course, but
has fluctuated sharply upward and downward at different periods
since 1917. The worst years were those immediately following the
Bolshevik revolution, 1917–21, during most of the First Five-Year
Plan, 1930–33, and during and immediately after World War II,
1941–45. The best years from the point of view of consumers, were
those around 1928, 1938, and 1950–54. Even taking these drastic
fluctuations into account, however, it seems correct to say that
throughout the era of the Soviet regime most Soviet consumers have

2 N. S. Margolin, *Balans Denezhnykh Dokhodov i Raskhodov Naseleniya*, p. 9.
Moscow-Leningrad: Gosplanizdat, 1940.
3 *Ibid.*, p. 10.

been ill-fed, ill-clothed, and ill-housed by western standards. Soviet consumers, of course, have little knowledge of western standards and do not use them in evaluating their own lot. They are probably much more impressed by the ups and downs they themselves experience. Nevertheless, there is no reason to believe that they have been content with the poor standard of living the Soviet regime has been able to provide them at the best of times. It is significant that in their public utterances in peacetime, Soviet leaders have always been careful to express their determination to improve the living standards of their people.

The Distribution System

Since the outlawing and elimination of private merchants in the early 1930's, the Soviet distribution system has been composed of three sectors: the state trading network, the cooperative trading network, and the free farm markets. The organization and functioning of this distribution system have varied from time to time. From 1930 to 1935 and from July 1941 to December 1947 rationing was general throughout the USSR; from 1936 to June 1941 and since the end of 1947 nonrationed distribution has prevailed. Since 1930 the scarcity of goods has been such that a seller's market has usually prevailed, with marked effects upon the efficiency and operation of the distributive system. Both the state and the cooperative sales networks are considered part of socialist trade and are governed fairly closely by the annual economic plan. In the farm markets located in cities or at railroad stations, collective farms, collective farmers, and individual peasants may sell whatever produce is left after their government delivery obligations are met. Prices on these markets are determined by supply and demand, and planned government control over them is indirect rather than direct. In 1940 about 216,000,000,000 rubles' worth of goods were sold through the distributive system. Of this, 128,500,000,000 rubles, almost 60 per cent, were accounted for by the state distribution system; 46,600,000,000 rubles, somewhat more than 20 per cent, by the cooperative stores; and 41,200,000,000 rubles, a little less than 20 per cent, by the farm markets.[4]

The state trading system embraces a large variety of organizations

---

[4] M. M. Lifits, *Sovetskaya Torgovlya*, p. 33. Moscow: Gospolitizdat, 1948.

at both the wholesale and the retail level. These serve the urban population primarily, as well as some special groups, such as the armed forces, whose *Voyentorg* is the equivalent of the American Post Exchange. The Ministry of Trade—a union-republican ministry —is the central organization here, but other ministries are also active in this field, either as suppliers or as both suppliers and retail distributors, with stores selling to the population. Each year the government's economic plan determines the volume of goods to be made available to the population and the prices to be charged in government stores. For major commodities such as textiles and shoes, the quantities to be sold are determined explicitly; the same thing is true of the relatively small numbers of consumer durable goods such as automobiles and radios. In planning domestic trade an effort is made to link the planned financial resources of the population — that is, money income from wages, pensions, sales by farmers, and so on — with the volume of goods and services that will be available, taking account of the amounts that will go for taxes, for purchase of government bonds and savings, and for other non-consumptive uses.[5] The Ministry of Trade is the main government planning and administrative agency in the distribution field, and other ministries exercise similar control over their subordinate trading organizations. Coordination of the entire distributive system is achieved through the State Planning Committee and the Council of Ministers.

At the wholesale level, the most important state organization is probably the Ministry of Requisitions, which procures agricultural products delivered to the state by collective farms and farmers in fulfillment of their compulsory delivery obligations and also in payment for Machine Tractor Station services. The Chief Administrations for Sales of the various industrial ministries sell that portion of their product destined for retail sale to the trading organizations, the importance of such sales depending in each case upon the nature of each ministry's output. In late 1953 the Ministry of Trade took over, from the ministries producing consumer goods and foods, the wholesale distribution agencies charged with selling these commodities to retail distribution organizations.[6] Actual wholesale distribution of industrial goods is organized around a

[5] Margolin, *op. cit.*, pp. 20–23.
[6] *Pravda*, October 25, 1953.

large system of warehouses, the *Prombazy*, which receive goods from factories and deliver to large stores and to state and cooperative retail trading organizations. These are independent enterprises subordinate to either a particular chief administration or to the state trading organization in a particular republic or province.[7]

The *Torg* is the main retail sales unit of the Ministry of Trade. This enterprise usually has subordinate to it a chain of stores in a particular city or locality selling a specified group of products. Each *Torg* is managed by officials appointed by the Ministry of Trade in the republic where it is located. It has staff departments for purchasing at wholesale, managing retail stores, planning, finance, and so on. A *Torg* may have under it large stores, each with its own budget and a relatively great degree of freedom in making purchases; or small stores headed by a director or manager who has little latitude in running operations. The stores within the *Torg* system supply the main bulk of necessities to most urban customers, but there are other stores that cater to demands of the higher-income groups for better quality and more diversified merchandise. The large *Univermag* or department store in each of the major cities has the largest variety of goods. In late 1953, in Moscow, a sort of super department store, the GUM (State Department Store) was reintroduced with a very wide selection of goods and services offered to consumers, similar to those offered in large American department stores.[8] In addition to the retail establishments subordinate to the Ministry of Trade, there are other stores subordinate to various specialized ministries and selling their products. Drugstores are operated by the Ministry of Health. In 1944 the Ministry of Trade's retail establishments accounted for 39 per cent of all retail sales exclusive of those on the farm markets, while the stores of other ministries accounted for another 6 per cent of the total.[9] A mail-order merchandising organization, *Soyuzposyltorg*, began operation in 1949.

The organization of state trade described above is that which has existed in the periods when rationing was not in force, from 1936 to mid-1941 and since December 15, 1947. A greater complexity existed during the periods of rationing, 1930–35 and 1941–47. The bulk of goods then were sold to the urban population in accordance

---

[7] L. E. Hubbard, *Soviet Trade and Distribution*, pp. 80–81.

[8] *Ibid.*, pp. 81–88; *Pravda*, October 25, 1953.

[9] Ryauzov and Titelbaum, *op. cit.*, pp. 64–65.

with ration schedules. In addition, commodities of all kinds could be bought without ration cards in so-called "Commercial stores" at much higher prices than those charged for goods obtained on rations. In this way an outlet was provided for the surplus incomes of Soviet citizens. In the early 1930's there were also *Insnab* stores, which sold to foreigners only, and *Torgsin* establishments, where goods could be bought only for foreign currencies and precious metals. During both periods of rationing, goods available to the Soviet population were differentiated according to the group into which each person fell. Highest rations were given to manual workers in the most important industries — and also to high government officials — and the lowest rations were allocated to adults not engaged in productive work outside the household, such as housewives. During both periods a large fraction of retail trade was handled through Departments of Worker Supply (O.R.S.) attached to different factories and other enterprises. These ran factory restaurants and sold scarce consumer goods to workers, frequently obtaining food supplies by operating their own farms.[10] In 1944, O.R.S. establishments accounted for 23 per cent of all retail trade turnover exclusive of farm market sales.[11] Despite the improvement of supply conditions after World War II, the work of these factory stores has apparently continued, and they are still important in key industries.

Cooperative Trade

Soviet cooperative trade is dominated by the large network of consumer cooperatives throughout the country, though industrial cooperatives and cooperatives of invalids also maintain stores. From the mid-1930's to 1946 the activities of consumer cooperatives were confined entirely to rural areas, while state establishments concentrated on urban markets. From late 1946 to 1949, however, notable expansion of consumer cooperative retail stores and restaurants took place in cities throughout the USSR as the result of a government order, one announced objective of which was to improve the operation of state stores by giving them more competition. The urban consumer cooperative network was liquidated in the summer of 1949. Thereafter, apparently, the pre-1946 semi-monop-

---

[10] Hubbard, *Soviet Trade and Distribution*, p. 39.
[11] Ryauzov and Titelbaum, *op. cit.*, pp. 64–65.

oly of the state trading system in the cities has been re-established, while the consumer cooperative distributive apparatus has concentrated solely upon the task of serving rural areas.[12] The magnitude of consumer cooperatives' operations, even when confined to rural areas, is obvious from the fact that at the beginning of 1953 these cooperatives operated over 254,000 retail outlets in which more than 1,000,000 employees worked. The number of cooperative members was put at 33,000,000 in mid-1953.[13]

All consumer cooperatives in the USSR are part of a central organization called *Tsentrosoyuz*, which performs somewhat the same functions in relation to the cooperative distributive system as does the Ministry of Trade for the corresponding state apparatus. The basic unit of *Tsentrosoyuz* is the village cooperative or *Selpo*. Different *Selpo* in a particular district are united in a district federation of cooperatives known as the *Raysoyuz*, and there is further integration into provincial and republican organizations as well as into the national *Tsentrosoyuz*. A *Selpo* may have from several hundred to several thousand shareholders, who elect the president and other officials as well as delegates to the *Raysoyuz*. The latter in turn elect delegates to the next higher body, the provincial cooperative union. In accordance with the Rochdale cooperative tradition, Soviet cooperatives are nominally democratic organizations with ultimate power in the hands of the members. But as in other Soviet institutions, the democratic façade conceals an organization that is controlled and directed by the state and the Communist Party in all essential matters.[14]

The village cooperative or *Selpo* operates the shops that supply the needs of that village, the number and character of these shops depending upon the size of the village, its prosperity, and other relevant characteristics of the community. The *Selpo* is frequently an independent enterprise that does not limit its functions to retail sales but also purchases goods from various industrial wholesale suppliers. In addition it frequently acts as an agent for its members

---

[12] The transfer of consumer cooperatives' urban stores to the Ministry of Trade in August 1949 was largely unannounced at that time, but was finally acknowledged in *Voprosy Ekonomiki*, No. 5 (1952), p. 21. The official reason given was the successful operation of the Ministry's stores, implying that competition was no longer necessary.

[13] *Izvestia*, June 23, 1953, and *Pravda*, July 4, 1953.

[14] Hubbard, *Soviet Trade and Distribution*, pp. 76–77.

in selling surplus farm produce to both cooperative and state purchasing organizations. The higher links in the hierarchy of the consumer cooperatives, such as the *Raysoyuz* and organs superior to it, concentrate on wholesaling functions and on supervising and controlling subordinate bodies in the administrative pyramid. The district cooperative councils, or *Raysoyuz*, often maintain stores in larger towns to which consumers from surrounding villages can turn for a larger and more diversified stock of goods than that obtainable in village stores.

Free farm markets exist at many points in the USSR, in cities, towns, and at railroad stations, where peasants bring their surplus produce for sale. Soviet economists term this market "unorganized" because its prices are set by supply and demand rather than by government edict. For this reason, as we shall see below, prices in these markets have been very revealing indicators of inflationary pressures on the Soviet economy in various periods. Those collective farms and collective farmers who are near an urban community or a railroad station where they can sell any appreciable amount of their produce are fortunate. The fraction of their output disposed of there is sold for higher prices than those paid by the government for obligatory deliveries to it, or paid by Soviet institutions for their "decentralized" purchases. But many collective farms are located in areas where the lack of urban communities or the poor condition of roads makes it difficult or impossible for them to sell any surplus on this free market. Farms and farmers in such a geographically disadvantageous position relative to urban markets benefit most from the purchasing activities of consumer cooperatives. These cooperatives buy surplus food and agricultural raw materials for sale in the cooperative stores or to state agencies, paying market prices prevailing in the rural localities. These quotations are usually well below urban market prices.

One of the reforms instituted in the fall of 1953 was a system of commission purchases of collective farm surpluses by the consumer cooperatives. The intention of this reform was that the cooperatives would move these surpluses to urban areas for sale at the higher prices prevailing there, receiving a commission for this service and returning the remainder of the sales price to the farms. A major reason for this change was the discovery that 500,000 collective farmers were engaged in selling on free markets, thus depriving the collective farms of a substantial work force. Mikoyan indicated in April 1954, however, that up to that time relatively little advantage had been taken of this new arrangement. One reason may have been farmers' distrust of the cooperatives and fear that they would not benefit as much financially as if they continued to market their own produce in the free markets. As of September 1953, there were about 8,500 of these free markets operating in cities and towns and at railroad stations and the like. They accounted for tens of billions of rubles of food product sales annually.[15]

Operation of the Distribution System

Compared to the United States, the Soviet Union has a very small domestic trade network serving a much larger population. In 1953 somewhat more than 3,000,000 persons worked in the state and cooperative distributive systems, serving a population of more than 210,000,000 persons.[16] In 1948 the roughly comparable figure for the United States was the 9,300,000 persons employed in retail and wholesale trade, serving a population numbering less than 150,000,-000 persons.[17] Similarly, we may compare retail outlets in both countries. At the beginning of 1938, the USSR had about 327,000 stores and retail selling points of all kinds. In 1939, the United States Census of Business found 1,770,355 retail stores in this country, almost six times the number in the Soviet Union, serving a population almost 20 per cent less than that in the USSR. The distribution system of the Soviet Union contracted substantially during World War II, and then began to expand again after the conflict. But at the end of 1949, Politburo member A. I. Mikoyan revealed, there were only 85 per cent as many food stores and only 83.3 per cent as many stores selling manufactured goods as there had been in 1940. He labeled this shortage of retail outlets a major deficiency of the Soviet postwar distributive system. According to Mikoyan, in 1953 total retail trade turnover was 79 per cent higher than in 1940, in comparable prices, but there were only 14 per cent more retail sales

---

15 *Izvestia*, September 9, 1953, and April 27, 1954.
16 *Pravda*, October 25, 1953.
17 *The Economic Almanac 1953–1954*, pp. 174–76.

units of all kinds, including restaurants.[18] The relative poverty of the Soviet trading system, both in personnel and in number of outlets, undoubtedly means that consumers are put to greater inconvenience in seeking to supply their wants than they are in countries devoting relatively greater resources to this sector of economic activity. The low standard of living prevalent in the USSR, of course, means that the quantity of goods that has to pass through the distribution system is proportionately less than in countries where consumers are more adequately supplied.

On the whole, the Soviet distribution system operates at a far from satisfactory level, though examples can probably be found of almost every level of service quality. At one extreme, for example, the Central *Univermag* in Moscow is probably one of the outstanding department stores in the world. Its 2,500 employees sell an average of 4,500,000 rubles' worth of goods daily to between 100,000 and 150,000 customers, virtually every type of consumer goods made in the USSR being available there. The staff is under strict supervision in an effort to insure that it treats customers intelligently and courteously. The store makes laboratory tests on goods where necessary to check on their quality. Even the Moscow *Univermag* cannot overcome the deficiencies that characterize Soviet consumer-goods production, such as the lack of variety among products, but obviously a great effort is made here to come close to western standards.[19]

Study of Soviet discussions of the domestic trading system, however, suggests that the above is a very unrepresentative example. Much more frequent are quite different conditions. Stores are often dirty, have limited assortments, and frequently lack even essential common goods. Personnel in stores are often poorly trained, discourteous, and have little or no knowledge of the goods they sell. The competence of even the managerial and supervisory staffs of the trading system is often assailed in the Soviet press.[20] The Soviet mail-order organization, *Soyuzposyltorg*, apparently also operates

[18] *Pravda*, March 11, 1950 and April 27, 1954. *Itogi Vypolneniya Vtorogo Pyatiletnego Plana Razvitiya Narodnogo Khozyaistva Soyuza SSR*, p. 63. Moscow: Gosplanizdat, 1938.

[19] *Bloknot Agitatora*, Moscow, No. 20(1949), pp. 31–39.

[20] Cf. for example the typical complaints in *Zarya Vostoka*, November 24, 1949; *Trud*, November 16, 1949; *Moskovskaya Pravda*, February 26, 1950; *Leningradskaya Pravda*, February 2, 1950; *Izvestia*, April 4, 1950; *Pravda Ukrainy*, March 23, 1950; *Trud*, December 19, 1948.

poorly, so that customers frequently cannot purchase goods that have been advertised, get products they did not order, or have to wait long periods before their orders are filled.[21]

The major inadequacy of Soviet distribution appears to be its frequent inability to supply customers with the goods they want when they want them and where they want them. Items are frequently unavailable in stores though warehouses are packed with them. When customers go to look for spring clothing, they often find only winter clothing, and vice versa. Selection of goods is often very limited. These and related deficiencies are apparently due to at least two factors. First, during more than half of the years between 1930 and 1950, Soviet customers were subjected to rationing. Those in charge of distribution became habituated to the relatively simple requirements of distributing goods in accordance with ration schedules, without any attention to the desires of consumers. Second, those in managerial positions in the trading system often have little knowledge of consumer demand in the areas over which they have jurisdiction, and their estimates of what will be required in each period in their localities are often wide of the mark. It is significant that more than thirty-two years after the Bolshevik revolution, A. I. Mikoyan found it necessary to declare in March 1950:

> It is necessary to organize scientific planning in trade organizations. Trade planning has its peculiarities, its specific features. This planning must take into account magnitudes which undergo frequent variations. It must take into account the relation of supply and demand, the needs of consumers, national and local peculiarities, climatic conditions.[22]

In October 1953, the highest Soviet authorities gave this evaluation of the operations of Soviet trade:[23]

> There are great weaknesses in trade organization, weaknesses that hinder further trade development and improvement of service to the public. Trade organizations do a poor job of studying consumer demand and make serious errors in distribution and delivery of goods. In many areas trade in all the goods demanded by consumers is still not organized. Even merchandise available in adequate quantity is not always available for sale. Trade organizations put little pressure on industry to increase production and improve the quality

[21] *Izvestia*, March 25, 1950. *Komsomolskaya Pravda*, April 30, 1950.
[22] *Pravda*, March 11, 1950.
[23] *Ibid.*, October 23, 1953.

of goods desired by the public. . . . There are serious weaknesses in the organization and dispersal of the retail trade network. Trade enterprises are poorly provided with up-to-date trade and refrigerator equipment. They do not have warehouses needed to store and sort goods so that merchandise may be supplied the trade network in planned manner. . . . Many public restaurants show little care for improving service to their clients who must wait a long time to have lunch or get a snack. The menu is frequently monotonous and the quality of the food low. Restaurants are poorly supplied with equipment and refrigeration facilities. In many cases they lack good tableware and cutlery.

Trading officials, of course, are not responsible for all the deficiencies of their work, since what they have to sell and when they have it to sell depend upon the operation of producing organizations. As we have seen above, much consumer-goods production is of rather low quality, and this is reflected in the goods available for sale. In addition there is apparently very poor planning of production over time so as to anticipate seasonal fluctuations in consumer demand. Finally, it may be pointed out that Soviet wholesale and retail organizations have relatively little competition and enjoy in many cases monopolistic or semimonopolistic positions in relation to their customers. They do not have the spur to improvement that is provided by the sharp competition under which merchants generally work in capitalist countries. The Soviet consumer does not have the choice of many competing stores, all seeking his patronage, that the American consumer has, and the results are apparent in the differences in operation between the two distributive systems.

Prices Consumers Pay

The price a consumer will pay for a particular product in a given locality usually depends upon where he buys it — whether in a state store, a cooperative store, or on the free farm market. During 1932–35 and 1944–47 the price paid in state stores depended upon whether the commodity was bought on rations or whether it was bought outside the ration system in a "commercial" store, which charged much higher prices. In 1947 about 40 per cent of all clothing, shoes, textiles, and other industrial consumer goods, measured in value terms, were purchased by consumers at these commercial prices.[24] The

---

[24] Lifits, *op. cit.*, p. 114.

relationship among prices in these different retail outlets has varied greatly over the past two decades. Sometimes prices in all these stores have been roughly the same in a particular area. At other times there have been marked differences.

Prices charged by state stores for the most important goods are set by the government as part of its planning activity. The retail price consists of the cost of the commodity, plus the cost of distribution, plus the turnover tax, plus the planned profit of the retail enterprise. For most important food products, three price zones have existed in the USSR since 1947, prices differing from one zone to another so as to reflect transportation costs and different productive conditions in various regions. In the case of many major consumer goods, the same price is charged in all urban areas but a price usually about 10 per cent higher is charged in rural areas. Three groups of retail prices exist for goods sold in state stores: the first and largest group includes prices for the most important commodities, which are set by the Council of Ministers or the Minister of Trade of the USSR. Prices for a second group of less important commodities are set by the councils of ministers of union republics or by provincial authorities. The third group of prices covers the least important commodities for which the government sets only wholesale prices at the manufacturing level, permitting trading organizations to add their own markup and thus determine the retail price.[25]

Prices charged by cooperative stores are in part determined by the government and in part determined by supply and demand. In rural areas, manufactured goods bought from state enterprises are apparently sold at the schedule of prices established by the government for these areas. Locally procured farm produce, raw materials, and consumer goods are sold by cooperative stores at prices determined on the market.[26] These stores, of course, have a semi-monopoly in each locality.

On the free peasant market all over the USSR, food prices are determined purely by supply and demand considerations and may change from day to day or even from hour to hour. The prices obtaining in these markets are very sensitive barometers. Sellers in

---

[25] *Ibid.*, p. 91. Ryauzov and Titelbaum, *op. cit.*, p. 134.

[26] Henry H. Ware, "The Function and Formation of Commodity Prices in the USSR," in *Bulletins on Soviet Economic Development*, No. 4 (September 1950), p. 24.

these markets are in competition with the state and cooperative stores. If buyers can obtain all the food they wish in these competitive outlets, the prices charged there will be the upper limit for prices in the farm markets, and farmers may even have to reduce their quotations below the levels of their competitors to clear their produce. On the other hand, if consumers cannot get all the food they want in state and cooperative stores, prices in the farm markets may and do rise appreciably above those charged elsewhere. In times of extreme scarcity, such as during World War II, prices in these markets can rise enormously above state-set quotations. The government's influence over the prices farmers receive in these markets is indirect, but powerful. It is exerted through two channels. First, the supply of goods available in state stores and the prices charged for them are important factors influencing consumers' decisions whether or not to buy in the farm markets. Second, the government determines how much of farm production it will require for itself in the form of obligatory deliveries and payment for Machine Tractor Station services. Only the surplus left over after these compulsory deliveries are made may legally be sold at the much higher prices urban consumers are willing to pay. It seems likely, however, that some farmers at least seek to evade this restriction and to sell here some of the produce that should nominally go to the state.

The price policy of the Soviet government is the key factor in the structure of prices consumers pay in the USSR. This price policy is directly linked with the entire complex of political and economic objectives sought by the state and hence is subject to both economic and non-economic factors. Thus, if deemed necessary, prices might be reduced at a time when it was felt that national morale was low or at a time when striking affirmation of popular support for the regime was desired. The latter consideration may have been behind the timing of the drastic price cut announced for March 1, 1950, little more than a week before the elections for the Supreme Soviet of the USSR. Similar factors may have influenced the policy of maintaining prices for rationed goods unchanged all through World War II, though great inflation was clearly evident in prices charged for non-rationed goods in commercial stores and on the farm markets.

From the economic point of view, two sets of considerations seem to guide government price policy. The first or aggregative factor is the relationship between the volume of money at the disposal of the population and the value of the goods available for sale to them. After allowing for that portion of the population's expenditures that will go for taxes, savings, and services, the government estimates the amount available for purchasing goods. It seeks to price the goods that will be on sale during a given year so that the total value of these commodities will be equal to the amount the population is expected to want to spend for goods. At a given time, the government may find that the expected value of goods to be available during the next period is greater than the amount of money the population is expected to be able to spend. This disequilibrium could be corrected either by reducing prices or by raising the population's income through wage increases or similar measures. The disequilibrium could also be ended by reducing the planned production of consumer goods, but this solution would be politically undesirable for obvious reasons. The alternative case is that in which the value of goods expected to be available for sale is less than the amount the population is expected to wish to spend. The difference between the two quantities corresponds to what in this country has sometimes been called "the inflationary gap." It can be resolved either by raising prices, by reducing the population's income available for such purchases, or by diverting resources from other uses to the production of consumer goods. The latter choice, of course, would require diminution of the volume of capital investment. The Soviet government has rarely chosen that method, preferring to use the first two types of measures during and after World War II when this situation was encountered. It is in this way that the general level of prices is decided.[27]

The actual level of government prices for consumer goods is substantially above the level of cost to the government, including both production and distribution costs. The difference is mainly attributable to the turnover tax, a general sales tax upon food and consumer goods levied at different rates for different commodities. This device is used to equalize the total sales value of goods available for consumers and the total amount they are expected to wish to spend on goods. The magnitude of the turnover tax's role may be appreciated from a comparison between the total value of retail turnover and total government receipts from this tax. In 1940, the

[27] Margolin, *op. cit.*, pp. 20–23.

total retail turnover of state and cooperative stores was about 175,-000,000,000 rubles, while total turnover tax receipts were almost 106,000,000,000 rubles, of which probably about 90 per cent, or 95,000,000,000 rubles, was paid out of food and consumer-goods receipts. Almost 60 per cent of the value of retail turnover, therefore, was accounted for by this tax. The need for this device arises from the fact that the portion of Soviet consumer incomes diverted to nonconsumption uses such as savings and direct taxes is substantially less than the value of the resources allocated by the state for capital investment, defense, and other activities that do not contribute to the current available supply of goods and services.[28]

Whatever the general level of prices set by Soviet authorities may be, the latter still have the problem of setting prices for individual commodities. Working within the general framework discussed above, they are also influenced by a second set of factors, those relating to the supply of and demand for each commodity. As regards supply, they have for each future period estimates of the planned output and existing reserves of each major commodity. They recognize that consumers' demands for different commodities depend upon the changing level of income, the distribution of income, and relative prices. Taking these factors into account, they apparently attempt to set a price for a particular commodity at which the demand will be equal to the anticipated supply. In other words, they are aware of the concept of a demand function in which the quantity that will be bought is related to price and income factors. They also take into account the different elasticities of demand for different commodities, realizing that salt, bread, and shoe sales, for example, will respond differently to an equal percentage change in price. Few details have been published about how such estimates of demand are made, but apparently Soviet authorities rely upon past experience and also upon study of data regarding budgets and expenditure patterns of different groups in the Soviet population.[29] As the supply of a commodity changes, the price can be altered, regardless of whether or not its cost has changed, merely by raising or lowering the rate of turnover tax levied on that commodity. The substantial portion of the retail price of most commodities accounted

---

[28] The data on the size of the turnover tax receipts and the portion coming from consumer-goods prices are taken from the following chapter on the Soviet financial system.

[29] Margolin, *op. cit.*, pp. 100–107.

for by the turnover tax makes it unnecessary for Soviet price-setters to vary prices in proportion to costs, though they presumably pay some attention to this factor in reaching their decisions. Increased efficiency of production permits not only lowered costs but also greater output from the same quantity of resources as before and thus influences prices on the supply side. All these decisions are made on the basis of data for the economy as a whole. Executives of the distribution system have the problem of trying to estimate demand in their localities at the existing set of prices at any given time. This, the complaints cited above suggest, they do rather poorly.

The price cuts announced in April 1953 were, in some cases, there is reason to believe, more extreme than justified by any actual increase in the supply of particular commodities. Thus Mikoyan declared in late 1953:[30]

> We are lowering prices even of goods of which we still do not have enough, if these goods are of great importance to the mass consumer. It must be said that this arouses further demand and puts pressure on us to increase the output of deficit goods needed by the public.

He might have added that the setting of prices below equilibrium levels which would equate supply and demand also creates opportunities for shrewd Soviet citizens — whom the government denounces as "speculators" — to buy up such deficit commodities and resell them at a profit.

An interesting 1953 innovation in Soviet price policy was the drastic cut in prices for old merchandise, a reduction made in the second half of that year. This was, in effect, an old-fashioned sale such as is familiar in noncommunist countries, but which was an innovation for Soviet consumers in the postwar period.

The much more modest and limited set of price reductions announced in April 1954 was probably in part the consequence of the inability of the state to make available in 1953 adequate supplies of goods to satisfy demand at post-April 1953 prices.

Prices Since 1928

Since the year 1936, with rare exceptions, the Soviet government has followed a policy of minimal publicity for statistics on consumer

[30] *Pravda,* October 25, 1953.

prices. Study of the behavior of Soviet prices, therefore, must be based for the most part upon fragmentary data, particularly figures collected by foreign correspondents, diplomats, and visitors in Moscow that have been published abroad. As a result, most figures available apply only to Moscow, and it is not entirely certain that the trends shown apply to the entire USSR. Serious question also exists as to the comparability of some of these data for different years. Is the suit priced in 1936 of the same quality as a suit priced by someone else a decade later? This is a typical question that must be faced in evaluating much of the available information. Comparability of food price data is frequently simpler to determine because of the greater standardization, but even here there are uncertainties. Nevertheless, the volume of data available is sufficient in size and trustworthiness to permit us to draw broad conclusions about the main trends in Soviet consumer price behavior since the beginning of the First Five-Year Plan. An added complication arises, however, because there are several different levels of prices in the USSR — state, cooperative, and free market. Moreover during 1932–35 and 1944–47 there were two main sets of state store prices — for rationed and for unrationed goods.

The state multi-price systems that existed during both periods of rationing since 1930 were ended by roughly similar techniques. The initial situation in each case was that rationed goods sold for low prices relatively close to or equal to prices in the prerationing period, while unrationed goods sold for much higher prices. In each case the end of rationing was announced with the institution of a new unified state price system intermediate between the old ration prices and commercial store prices. Workers' wages were raised somewhat to compensate them partially for the higher level of prices as compared with the previous ration level. The adjustment was somewhat more complex in the postwar period because the degree of inflation that had taken place in the economy since 1941 was much greater than had occurred a decade earlier. Commercial store prices were lowered several times after these stores were opened in 1944. In September 1946 prices of rationed foods were roughly tripled to reduce the gap between them and commercial store quotations. At the same time workers were given a graded wage increase, the largest raises going to lowest-paid workers.

In December 1947 rationing was abolished. A new price system was set up at a level close to the prices for food existing after September 1946 and intermediate between the old commercial prices and ration prices for manufactured goods. The great excess of currency that had been accumulated during and after World War II was wiped out by issuing a new currency at the rate of one new ruble for ten old rubles in cash. Savings deposits, government bonds, and other similar assets were revalued simultaneously, but at more favorable ratios. Between December 1947 and May 1954 there were seven sets of price decreases for many commodities, the most important and comprehensive reductions taking effect on March 1, 1950 and April 1, 1953.

Available data are inadequate to permit the construction of a year-by-year index of all Soviet prices since 1928. The approximate trend of state food prices in Moscow is indicated, however, by the series shown in Table 43. This food price index has been constructed by combining two different indexes, one covering 1928–39 and the other covering January 1941 to March 1950. These indexes have been chained together to make a continuous series even though their internal compositions are not the same. The error introduced by this procedure would seem to be small in comparison with the over-all magnitude of Soviet food price fluctuations, 1928–50, so that the figures shown below are believed to give a reasonably accurate, though rough, representation of the fluctuations over this period of more than two decades.

TABLE 43. Index of Moscow State Store Food Prices, 1928–50.

(1928 = 100)

Year	Index	Year	Index
1928	100	1939	919
1932	201	Jan. 1941	1180
Oct. 1935	806	Jan. 1948	2954
1936	830	March 1949	2658
1937	835	March 1950	2068
1938	858		

Source: Derived by chaining together Prokopovicz's index for 1928 to 1939 in *Russlands Volkswirtshaft unter den Sowjets*, p. 306, with the index for January 1941 to March 1950 given by Kravis and Mintzes on the basis of November 1928 food expenditures in *Review of Economics and Statistics*, May 1950, p. 167.

This index minimizes the violence of food price fluctuations because it does not take into account the heights reached by commercial store and free farm market prices in the early 1930's and during World War II. Moreover, it makes no allowance for the impact of the currency and savings revaluation of December 1947. Nevertheless even this minimal depiction of the fluctuations shows clearly that great inflation of food prices has taken place since 1928. By the beginning of World War II, food prices were on the average almost twelve times as great as in 1928. In January 1948 they were almost thirty times as great, and the price reductions that took place up to March 1950 still left the average more than twenty times as high as in 1928 and almost twice as high as in January 1941.

Price reductions in each of the intervening four years between March 1950 and April 1954 cut the prices of foods used in the index of Table 43 by about one-third, reducing the index to about 1400 by the end of this period. At this lowest level, of course, food prices were only about 20 per cent higher than at the time the Soviet Union was invaded by Germany in mid-1941.[31]

Study of the price fluctuations of particular foods for which relatively full data are available permits us to see more clearly the effects of the inflationary and deflationary forces that have acted on the Soviet economy. These data are shown in Table 44. It should be emphasized, however, that the data for years after 1947 are official state prices, which fail to reflect the actual market situation for times when particular goods are scarce in state stores and consumers must turn to the free market instead. Thus Harrison E. Salisbury reported in the *New York Times* of March 11, 1954, that low quality potatoes were being sold in state stores at 45 kopeks a kilogram, while potatoes in the free market were selling for up to 2 rubles 50 kopeks a kilogram. Similarly, while onions in state stores were selling for 2 rubles 25 kopeks a kilogram, the free market price was 5 rubles a kilogram. Similar observations were made by Marshall MacDuffie in the fall of 1953, during his extensive trip through much of the Soviet Union. Confirmation of this differential was given by Emmet Hughes, who visited Moscow shortly after Mr. MacDuffie. The latter in fact argues that some of the price cuts announced in April 1953 were deceptive, since some items cut most

---

[31] Cf. the detailed data given in Edmund Nash, "Purchasing Power of Soviet Workers, 1953," *Monthly Labor Review*, July 1953.

TABLE 44. Prices of Major Food Commodities in Moscow, 1928–54.

Year	Market	Black Rye Bread	Potatoes	Beef	Butter 1st Grade	Lump Sugar	Eggs
			(RUBLES PER KILOGRAM OR PER EGG)				
1928	Cooperative	.08	.085	.87	2.43	.62	.20
1932	Ration	.125	.25	2.12	4.66	1.25	.10
1932	Commercial	*	*	*	16–18	2.50	*
1932	Farm	*	*	*	*	*	*
1933	Commercial	2.50	*	*	34.80–48.20	15.00	*
1936	State	.85	.30	8.00	42.00	4.10	.40
April 1940	State	.85	1.20	16.00	16.00	5.50	.85
Jan. 1941	State	1.00	*	14.00	23.00	5.50	.75
Late 1942	Farm	100.00	*	500.00	1100.00	1000.00	15.00
Late 1943	Farm	130.00	*	*	1100.00	1100.00	20.00
May 1944	Farm	80.00	*	450.00	800.00	800.00	27.00
Aug. 1944	Commercial	*	*	320.00	650.00	650.00	*
July 1945	Commercial	45.00	*	250.00	525.00	500.00	*
Sept. 1, 1946	Ration	1.00	*	14.00	28.00	5.50	*
Oct. 1, 1946	Ration	3.40	*	30.00	66.00	15.00	*
Nov. 1946	Farm	20.00–45.00	4.00–10.00	70.00†	180–200	80–120	5–6
Jan. 1948	State	3.00	*	30.00	70.00	15.00	1.40
Jan. 1948	Farm	*	3.5	35.00†	60.00	*	3.50
March 1950	State	2.00	.67	20.52	40.32	12.75	1.02
April 1953	State	1.11	.45	12.60	26.75	9.09	.69
April 1954	State	1.03	.45	12.60	26.75	9.09	.69

* Data unavailable.

† Average of several prices.

Sources: Modern Review, June 1948, p. 276; Baykov, Development of the Soviet Economic System, p. 244; Hubbard, Soviet Trade and Industry, p. 273; Prokopovicz, Russlands Volkswirtschaft unter den Sowjets, p. 305; Review of Economics and Statistics, May 1950, pp. 166–67; American Economic Review, December 1946, pp. 877–80; Labor Abroad, March 1950, p. 44; Monthly Labor Review, July 1953; New York Times, April 1, 1954.

sharply in price simply disappeared from the market, while redefinition of grades for meat made the most desirable meat cuts little if any cheaper. Their reports (in *Collier's*, March 5, 1954, and in *Life*, February 15, 1954) should be borne in mind in evaluating the data in Table 44, as well as the index changes shown in Table 43 and the accompanying discussion of those changes.

The explosive rise of farm market prices during the early years of World War II is probably the most striking phenomenon shown by the data above. The tremendous gap between these prices and the commercial store prices later in the war, on the one hand, and the very low ration prices, on the other, is an illuminating indication of the degree of inflationary pressure that existed in Soviet markets during this period. Consumer incomes had increased substantially because of increased working hours, while the amount of goods available had been reduced very greatly. Moreover, rations were not only quantitatively low but were also often unfulfilled, so that hunger was a potent force inspiring the competition for the scarce amounts of unrationed food available. Only the wealthiest Muscovites could have been regular customers for this very high-priced food, while farmers who had any significant quantities of food to sell in these markets must have accumulated much cash.

Any effort to trace the price of manufactured consumer goods over the years since 1928 is exceedingly difficult because of the paucity of data and uncertainties regarding the comparability of prices at different times. Perhaps all that can safely be said is that a substantial rise in the prices of the most important of these items has taken place since the five-year plans began. The case of leather shoes is probably representative. A pair of men's leather shoes of unknown quality cost 18 rubles in November 1926.[32] A pair of men's leather shoes, probably of rather poor quality, cost 270 rubles at the ration price of December 1946 in Moscow.[33] About the same time, unrationed shoes bought in Moscow commercial stores varied in price from 810 rubles for the lowest quality to 1,600 rubles for the best.[34] In November 1948, state stores in Moscow sold shoes for

[32] Hubbard, *Soviet Trade and Distribution*, p. 270.

[33] Irving B. Kravis and Joseph Mintzes, "Soviet Union: Trends in Prices, Rations, and Wages," *Monthly Labor Review*, July 1947, p. 35.

[34] Harry Schwartz, "Prices in the Soviet War Economy," *American Economic Review*, December 1946, p. 880.

100, 350, and 500 rubles per pair, depending upon quality. The cheapest shoes had rubber soles and heels and poor leather tops and were poorly sewn; the best were approximately as good as standard Montgomery Ward shoes in this country.[35] A similar picture arises from comparison of prices for a man's suit. An English visitor in the USSR in 1934 reported that a suit of undescribed quality cost 87 rubles.[36] The ration price for a man's suit in Moscow in December 1946 was 800 rubles.[37] The commercial store price for a suit about the same time varied from 1,600 to 4,000 rubles, depending on quality. In March 1950, the uniform state store price for a man's single-breasted wool suit was about 1,100 rubles.[38] These examples are not unrepresentative, examination of other available data indicates. It is worth remarking that by 1950 prices were so high relative to earnings that, on the average, it required more than a month's earnings to purchase a man's suit or overcoat, while it probably required almost two weeks' earnings, on the average, to purchase a pair of moderately good black calf shoes.

An Englishman who visited Moscow in April 1952 found these prices prevailing, in rubles per unit: medium to good man's suit, 1,000 to 3,000; medium to good man's overcoat, 900 to 4,000; cotton or rayon man's shirt, 75–300; medium quality man's gabardine raincoat, 1,000; men's socks, 10; man's leather shoes of medium quality, 200–400; woman's dress, 450–600; woman's blouse, 100–300; woman's shoes, 150–500; nylon stockings, 25–50; child's socks, 2.65; child's shoes, 40–50; radio sets, 350–800; television set (presumably very small screen), 800; bicycle, 500–1,000; motorcycle, 2,295–2,870; Moskvich motor car (like Crosley or Austin), 8,000–9,000; Pobeda car (like Chevrolet), 18,000.[39] Many of these prices were lowered in April 1953 by varying percentages, from 8 per cent for leather footwear to 14 per cent for ready-made women's dresses and other

[35] Information from the Bureau of Labor Statistics, U. S. Department of Labor.

[36] Colin Clark, A Critique of Russian Statistics, pp. 30–31. London: Macmillan, 1939.

[37] Kravis and Mintzes, op. cit., p. 35.

[38] Schwartz, op. cit., p. 880; Labor Abroad, March 1950, p. 44.

[39] Charles Madge, "Notes on the Standard of Living in Moscow April 1952," Soviet Studies, January 1953, pp. 233–34. A similar and somewhat more detailed price list is given in T. Schulz and P. Wiles, "Earnings and Living Standards in Moscow," Bulletin of the Oxford University Institute of Statistics, September and October 1952, pp. 321–22.

cotton outer garments and 20 per cent for hosiery. There were additional price cuts a year later.[40]

In the first half of 1954, the prohibitions maintained by Soviet censors in Moscow against cabling price information abroad were apparently dropped. This permitted the *New York Times* correspondent there to cable an abundance of such data to his newspaper. The following prices, prevailing in Moscow after April 1, 1954, are based on those dispatches:

Commodity	Price in Rubles
Black rye bread	1.03 per kilogram
Best white bread	2.95 per kilogram
Best beef	14.19 per kilogram
Steak	20.00 per kilogram
Soup meat	7.90 per kilogram
Calves liver	15.35 per kilogram
Pork chops	21.12 per kilogram
Milk	2.92 per liter
Nylon-type stockings	30.00 per pair
Women's shoes	200–468 per pair
Toilet soap	1.00 per small cake
Leica-type cameras (Kiev brand)	2,475–2,790 per camera
Skis	112.5 per pair (no fittings)
Kerosene	.66 per liter
Gasoline	1.00 per liter
Washing machines	405 per machine
Vacuum cleaners	405 per cleaner
Men's gold wristwatches	1,039 per watch
Tea	7.38 per kilogram
Coffee	36.11 per kilogram
Salt	.49 per kilogram
Radio-phonographs	450.00 per set
Radios	191–765 per set, depending on size
Television sets (5- by 8-inch picture)	2,250 per set
Refrigerators (about 7 cubic feet)	2,000 per unit
Small refrigerators (2 or 3 cubic feet)	680 per unit
Cheapest phonograph	220 per unit
Good quality men's suits	1,650
Good men's winter coats	1,750–2,340 per coat
Good men's spring coats	1,112–2,480 per coat

Deputy Premier Mikoyan, speaking in April 1954, gave some scanty data on over-all price movements. He claimed that between 1950 and the time he spoke the over-all Soviet price level had declined more than 25 per cent. He claimed a 56.7 per cent decline in prices between 1947 and mid-1954. Food prices in 1954, he said,

---

[40] *Pravda*, April 1, 1953, and April 1, 1954.

exceeded those of 1940 by 14 per cent, while for industrial goods the price excess was 27 per cent.

Against the background of the price fluctuations discussed above, the changes in the volume of retail trade may be appraised briefly. The relevant data are shown in Table 45.

TABLE 45. Volume of Soviet Retail Trade by Distributive Channels in Selected Years.

Channel	1922– 23	1926– 27	1928– 29	1932	1935	1938	1940	1947‡
	(BILLIONS OF RUBLES AT CURRENT PRICES)							
State	.5	2.4	3.0	14.5	63.1	99.9	128.5	251.6
Cooperative	.4	7.0	11.8	25.8	18.6	40.1	46.6	73.0
Private	2.7	5.2	2.7	†	†	†	†	†
Farm Market ...	*	*	*	7.5	14.5	24.4	41.2	*

* Data unavailable.
† Insignificant or nonexistent.
‡ Plan.
Sources: *Narodnoye Khozyaistvo SSSR*, p. 315; Lifits, *Sovetskaya Torgovlya*, p. 33; *Pravda*, April 21, 1947.

Since 1947, data on the volume of retail trade in current prices which could be used to supplement Table 45 above have in general not been published. Presumably, this is because the price reductions after that date prevented the volume of trade in current prices from increasing as rapidly as the physical volume of goods sold. Malenkov has stated, however, that the original plan for 1953 provided for 312,000,000,000 rubles worth of goods to be sold on the market from April through December. If converted to a full-year basis, this is equivalent to 416,000,000,000 rubles in terms of prices prevailing after the price cut of April 1, 1953. In addition, Mikoyan stated that an additional 37,200,000,000 rubles worth of goods would be sold during April to December 1953.[41] Taking into account also the fact that trade during January to March of 1953 was at the higher prices which prevailed during most of 1952, it seems likely that actual retail sales of state and cooperative stores, including also restaurants, totalled about 470,000,000,000 rubles. It is possible that this figure also includes sales in collective-farm free markets in cities and at railroad stations, but this is uncertain. In 1950 these free markets accounted for 12 per cent of all Soviet retail trade.[42]

[41] *Izvestia*, October 25, 1953.
[42] *Voprosy Ekonomiki*, No. 8 (1953), p. 129.

Some data have been released which, it is claimed, measure the growth of the physical volume of goods sold at retail in the Soviet Union. Thus between 1928 and 1940, the volume of retail trade expressed in comparable prices is said to have grown 4.6 times. From 1926 to 1953, another official statement asserts, the volume of retail trade grew almost eightfold expressed in comparable prices.[43] While there is no way to check these claims, there can be little doubt that the actual volume of Soviet retail trade has grown greatly with the rapid urbanization of the country and with the penetration of urban wants into part of the rural countryside. The Soviet citizen of 1954 bought much more of his daily needs, and produced himself far less of his daily needs, than did his father or mother a quarter of a century earlier. But this change should not be confused with an equivalent rise in the standard of living. Bread baked by a peasant woman in 1928 did not enter the retail sales figures. Bread baked by a government bakery in 1954 and eaten by that woman's children living in the city did enter the retail trade statistics, so that the latter data measure the increased urbanization of Russia as well as any possible increase in the actual volume of goods consumed, if there really was such an increase.

Urban Housing

The most consistently dark aspect of the Soviet standard of living has been and is housing. Initially, after the Bolshevik revolution, workers living in slums were encouraged to seize and move into the homes of the well-to-do. This proved only a temporary palliative, however. Soviet housing conditions were poor in the 1920's, both as regards quantity of space available and the quality of accommodations. At the beginning of the First Five-Year Plan about 75 per cent of all factory workers in the USSR had less than six square meters of housing space per capita, an area little larger than a rectangle measuring nine feet by six feet. Over 20 per cent of them had less than three square meters per capita. The authors of the First Five-Year Plan pointed to the deplorable state of urban housing as one of the worst features of the Soviet scene and projected an ambitious program of improvement.[44]

[43] *Pravda*, April 21 1947, and October 25, 1953.
[44] *Pyatiletny Plan Narodno-Khozyaistvennogo Stroitelstva SSSR Tom II*, pp. 281 ff. Moscow: Gosplan, 1930.

This improvement did not take place. In the late 1920's and the 1930's, urban populations grew far more rapidly than housing construction. Beset by shortages of materials, men, and machinery, the Soviet government cut its ambitious housing construction plans rather than restrict the flow of resources to industrial and transport construction. During the Second Five-Year Plan period, 1933–37, for example, 64,000,000 square meters of urban housing space were scheduled to be made available for occupancy.[45] In actuality only 26,800,000 square meters of housing became available during these years, about 40 per cent of the planned amount.[46]

The worsening of housing conditions in the late 1920's and early and mid-1930's is clearly indicated by a comparison of the growth of urban population and urban housing space in these years. The census of 1926 found 26,314,000 people living in urban communities. At the end of that year urban housing space in the USSR aggregated 159,000,000 square meters, so that per capita housing space was roughly 6 square meters. The census of January 1939 found 55,910,000 urban dwellers in the country. The amount of housing space available then is not known, but at the beginning of 1938 it was about 221,000,000 square meters.[47] If we assume that urban population was only 50,000,000 persons in 1938, a figure probably too low, we find that per capita housing space in cities and towns was less than 4.5 square meters, a reduction of over 25 per cent from the already low figure of 1926. Behind these bare statistics and averages is, of course, a degree of overcrowding so serious as to bring great discomfort and inconvenience to tens of millions subjected to it. Privacy was and is a rare privilege for those living in Soviet cities and town. Under these conditions, the typical housing available for a small or medium-sized family in a Soviet city was only one room, in an apartment containing three

---

[45] *The Second Five-Year Plan*, p. 50. New York: International Publishers, n.d.

[46] *Itogi Vypolneniya Vtorogo Pyatiletnego Plana Razvitiya Narodnogo Khozyaistva Soyuza SSR*, p. 63.

[47] V. L. Kobalevsky, *Organizatsiya i Ekonimiki Zhilishchnogo Khozyaistva SSSR*, p. 106. Moscow-Leningrad: Narkomkhoz RSFSR, 1940. The estimate for urban housing space at the beginning of 1938 is obtained by adding to Kobalevsky's figure of 195,000,000 sq. meters of housing space at the beginning of 1933 the 26,800,000 sq. meters put into use during 1933–37. From this, 800,000 sq. meters are deducted as an allowance for housing going out of use.

to six families, all sharing the kitchen and bathroom, if any.[48] Millions of single workers who flocked to the great new construction projects and factories during the 1930's had to live in barracks, often under the most primitive and difficult conditions.[49] The abysmally bad housing situation in many industrial centers was one of the major factors producing worker discontent and high labor turnover during these years.

Moscow, the capital of the USSR and one of its most important industrial centers, suffered severely in this period. In 1926 the city had about 10,400,000 square meters of housing space and about 2,000,000 inhabitants. Per capita housing space then was slightly more than 5 square meters. In 1939 the city had 17,400,000 square meters of housing space, a rise of roughly 70 per cent. But its population had more than doubled, to 4,137,000 persons. Consequently per capita housing space had fallen to little more than 4.2 square meters, a drop of about 20 per cent. Moscow must have been then and probably still is one of the most overcrowded major cities in the Western world. In 1912 the city had had 1,600,000 inhabitants and 11,900,000 square meters of housing space, a per capita average of roughly 7.4 square meters. Such "abundance" of housing was unknown in Moscow after the early 1920's, though the inequality of housing accommodations that existed there in Czarist times had been tremendously reduced under the Soviet regime. In 1912, almost 40 per cent of all Moscow apartments were considered overcrowded. In 1939 virtually all must have been.[50] This deterioration was not confined to Moscow by any means. In the city of Gorky, for example, per capita housing space fell from over 6 square meters in 1923 to under 4 square meters in 1937.[51]

Aggravating the discomforts and hardships arising from the lack of housing was its poor quality. Defective construction and lack of repair characterized much of it. Apartment houses and homes built in the 1920's and 1930's were often put up hastily by poor

[48] John N. Hazard, *Soviet Housing Law*, pp. 19–21. New Haven: Yale University Press, 1939.

[49] Cf. the picture of worker housing and life in Magnitogorsk in John Scott, *Behind the Urals, passim.* Boston: Houghton Mifflin, 1942.

[50] D. L. Broner, *Ocherki Ekonomiki Zhilishchnogo Khozyaistva Moskvy*, pp. 12, 13, 16, and 17. Moscow-Leningrad: Narkomkhoz RSFSR, 1946.

[51] Gordon, *Workers Before and After Lenin*, p. 199.

workmen using faulty materials and parts. The results soon became evident in the failure of central heating and other facilities, the cracking of plaster, the leaking of roofs, and similar evidences of shoddy workmanship and materials. In the rigorous winter climate characteristic of the USSR, these defects must have contributed substantially to making housing conditions intolerable for millions of workers. Little wonder that many migrated from job to job in the First and Second Five-Year Plan periods, hopefully seeking better living quarters and subsistence.[52]

World War II brought catastrophe to the housing of Soviet citizens. In the areas occupied by Germans, more than 50 per cent of all urban living space and about a quarter of all rural dwellings were destroyed or damaged.[53] In the areas to the east of the German advance, the already tight housing situation was aggravated as millions of refugees fled there from the west. The mobilization of many farm people to replace workers entering the armed forces and to work in evacuated, new, or expanded enterprises put further strain upon the already inadequate housing in eastern cities. The growth of population in some of these cities has been pointed out in Chapter I. It is clear that under wartime conditions the expansion of housing must have lagged far behind the expansion of population, further worsening the situation.

Faced by the greatest housing shortage of its history, the Soviet government allocated a large amount of resources to new construction. The Fourth Five-Year Plan called for the government to build or restore 72,000,000 square meters of city housing during 1946–50 and planned that individuals, aided by government loans in many cases, would build an additional 12,000,000 square meters. By 1950 it was hoped to have 25 per cent more state housing than before the war. Almost half of this new housing was to be built in the areas that had been devasted during the conflict.[54]

From 1946 through 1953, the total amount of urban housing space reconstructed or newly built was 183,000,000 square meters, whereas over 4,000,000 rural houses were built or repaired.[55] This first figure will help us to make an approximate estimate of the Soviet urban

52 Ibid., pp. 195–98.
53 Voznesensky, The Economy of the USSR During World War II, p. 87.
54 V. P. Maslyakov, N. L. Filatov, and V. V. Barmin, Finansirovaniye Zhilishchno-Kommunalnogo Khozyaistva, p. 7. Moscow: Gosplanizdat, 1948.
55 Izvestia, March 9, 1954.

housing situation as of the beginning of 1954. It was estimated above that at the beginning of 1938 total Soviet urban housing space was 221,000,000 square meters. Taking into account the little additional housing constructed thereafter and the amount of urban housing space in the areas annexed during 1939–40, it seems likely that the Soviet Union had about 250,000,000 square meters of housing space when Germany attacked in mid-1941. The amount of housing destroyed or damaged during the war has been put by a Soviet source at about 70,000,000 square meters.[56] Soviet housing space at the beginning of 1946, therefore, may have totalled about 180,000,000 square meters. By the beginning of 1954, as noted above, 183,000,000 square meters of housing space had been added by reconstruction and new building. Adding this to the amount estimated as available at the beginning of 1946, our rough estimate of total Soviet housing space on January 1, 1954, is 363,000,000 square meters. In this estimate we assume that the small amount of new housing built during World War II was balanced by housing that became unusable because of sheer age and neglect during 1946–53.

Malenkov revealed in August 1953 that there were then over 80,000,000 dwellers in urban communities in the Soviet Union. Dividing 363,000,000 square meters by 81,000,000 people gives an average housing space of about 4.5 square meters per capita, a figure the same as the almost 4.5 square meters calculated above as the average for 1938. This calculation is approximate, of course, but it seems doubtful that any errors involved could seriously affect the magnitude of the result. In fact we have confirmation from Malenkov himself that our conclusion is essentially correct. In October 1952 he said, "Despite the great volume of housing construction, there is still an acute housing shortage everywhere." [57] In August 1953, he repeated essentially the same statement. There can be little doubt but that the housing standards of the mid-1920's, considered then so abysmally terrible, still remain standards of spaciousness which are unlikely to be attained in the foreseeable future. No more serious economic problem faces the Soviet government, if it actually wishes to improve living standards as the post-

---

[56] *Kommunist,* No. 4 (1954), p. 55.
[57] *Pravda,* October 6, 1952.

Stalin regime insists, than to ease the intolerable crowding of Soviet cities.

Precise data on the postwar housing situation in major Soviet cities are most scarce, but available figures for Moscow and Leningrad are illuminating. Moscow, at the beginning of 1950, had about 5,100,000 inhabitants according to the election district data cited in Chapter I above. The total volume of housing space in that city then was probably only about 18,600,000 square meters, equivalent to a per capita average of about 3.65 square meters. This would be more than 10 per cent below the 4.2 square meters average of early 1939. Leningrad had about 260,000 apartments in early 1950, a time when election district data indicate its population was well over 3,000,000. The average number of residents per apartment then must have been more than twelve — crowded conditions indeed.[58]

While frankly recognizing the housing shortage, Soviet leaders apparently have no intention of increasing government capital investment in new housing construction to the level required if the situation is to be improved sharply. The alternative they intend to follow was indicated by A. I. Mikoyan in his major speech reported in *Pravda,* March 12, 1954:

> Housing requirements are so great and so much exceed our current possibilities that housing is inadequate despite the quick growth of housing construction carried out by government agencies. Therefore it is necessary also broadly to develop individual housing construction, housing construction cooperatives. To help ease the solution of the sharp problem here, which is connected with the welfare of the people, it is necessary to develop trade in building materials and parts, and also in pre-fabricated houses built by construction organizations to the order and for the account of citizens, as well as to help housing construction by credits and by bringing to it the savings of the population. And it is true that many citizens have the savings or can accumulate the savings so that in time they can pay the cost of either an individual house or of apartments in a cooperative apartment house.

[58] The number of apartments in Leningrad is calculated from the statement in *Leningradskaya Pravda,* May 31, 1950, that 117,000 apartments in that city, housing 45 per cent of the total population, were supplied with gas. The procedure for calculating total housing space in Moscow in 1950 was as follows: According to *Pravda,* February 3, 1949, Moscow's housing space had regained the prewar level. This was approximately 18,200,000 square meters according to Broner, *op. cit.,* p. 17. When 400,000 square meters for new housing built in the city during 1949 is added, the total given in the text is obtained.

That this is a "solution" which can benefit only the wealthier groups in Soviet society — who probably already enjoy the best and most spacious available housing — would seem to be obvious.

In 1953, however, the Soviet government did increase capital investment in new housing by 11 per cent over 1952. In addition it gave housing construction needs higher priority than earlier for scarce construction materials. But productivity of construction labor in 1953 did not rise as rapidly as hoped for, while poor quality construction, careless handling of materials, and the like continued to plague housing construction.

Urban Housing Administration

The organization of the Soviet housing economy has undergone many changes since the beginning of the Bolshevik revolution. The USSR has experimented with rent-free housing; small apartment houses managed by concessionaires; housing built and managed by cooperatives; and, since 1937, predominantly state-owned and -operated housing. Most Soviet urban dwellings today are state-owned and -managed, either by municipal governments or by economic enterprises and institutions. In the latter group, housing is reserved for employees of the particular enterprise or institution and must be surrendered when a worker leaves. In addition, there are privately owned dwellings and dwellings owned by the few cooperative housing groups that survived the reform of 1937. This measure ended most cooperative housing and transferred the buildings involved to the state.

In formulating its housing policy, the Soviet government has opportunity to and does exercise influence upon the welfare, standard of living, and incentives of its people. By giving enterprises control over a large portion of scarce housing facilities and making occupancy of this housing conditional upon continued employment in a given place of work, the government gives the directors of its plants a potent weapon against labor turnover. In the distribution of housing, preference is shown to Stakhanovites and others with outstanding production records — and also, of course, to those well-connected politically. Thus one's opportunity to have decent housing, even by minimal Soviet standards, often depends upon where one works and how well one works, and is often a most potent incentive for improved productivity. On the other hand, housing space has become one of the competitive lures enterprise directors can use in attracting workers, an important weapon in a country where wage competition is frowned upon though not unknown.

Soviet propagandists have often boasted about the low rents paid by Soviet citizens, pointing with pride to the fact that rent takes a much smaller portion of urban incomes than in the United States. Viewed superficially, this argument is valid. For the USSR as a whole, rent accounted for only 7.1 per cent of the average worker's budget in 1928 and only 5.4 per cent in 1936.[59] In Moscow, the percentage importance of rent in the average worker's budget fell from 9.2 per cent in 1927 to 2.4 per cent in 1943.[60] In 1935–36 American families with incomes of $1,750 to $2,000 spent an average of $302 for housing, or somewhat under 15 per cent of total income. At lower income levels the percentage was closer to 20 per cent.[61] Obviously, however, such comparison of the relative importance of rent in the USSR and the United States is meaningless, because of the great discrepancy in the quantity and quality of housing provided urban dwellers in the two countries. It seems not unfair to say that one has to look at the worst slum areas of American cities to find housing conditions comparable to those typical in the USSR.

The Soviet rent policy, established in 1928 and apparently continued at least to the late 1940's and perhaps even to 1954, was initially based upon the premise that rental income should cover the cost of current maintenance and amortization of housing facilities. In addition rents were planned so as to allow for differences in the qualities and conveniences of different housing facilities and so as to bear differentially upon persons receiving varying incomes. The inflationary rise in costs and wages since 1928, however, has apparently prevented the attainment of both objectives in recent years. In 1944 the cost of maintaining houses under Moscow's municipal administration was 228,700,000 rubles, while total rents received were only 142,300,000 rubles. A Soviet writer points out that during the war a worker in Moscow earning 200 rubles monthly

---

[59] Kobalevsky, *op. cit.*, p. 206.
[60] Broner, *op. cit.*, p. 104.
[61] National Resources Planning Board, *Family Expenditures in the United States,* Statistical Tables and Appendixes, p. 3. Washington, D. C.: Government Printing Office, June 1941.

and living with his family in a room with an area of 16 square meters paid 8 rubles and 48 kopeks monthly if the apartment had water supply and sewage facilities, and 6 rubles, 48 kopeks, if it had neither convenience, a difference far less than the worth of these facilities. Before the war in Moscow, 53 per cent of all housing was occupied by persons receiving over 400 rubles monthly, all paying the same maximum rate. This Soviet writer concluded his discussion by calling for a complete revision of what he considered to be the obsolete rental regulations, in the direction of raising them to meet actual maintenance and amortization costs as well as to permit proper differentiation of rents in correspondence with differences of housing quality and occupants' incomes.[62]

Soviet rents are based upon the number of square meters occupied by a family, this measurement excluding corridors, bathrooms, kitchens, and other ancillary facilities. The basic rate per square meter of housing space may vary from 30 to 44 kopeks, as set by housing authorities. From this rate certain deductions or additions are made to take account of the quality of the facilities and conveniences available. Thus 10 per cent is deducted if there are no sewage facilities in the house, and 5 per cent if there is no electricity; while 5 per cent is added if hot water is provided, 2 per cent if there is a bath, 3 per cent if there is gas, and so on. The rate determined in this way is then differentiated in accordance with the income of the occupant. In the RSFSR, for each 10 rubles of income received monthly above 145 rubles, an additional 3.3 kopeks per square meter must be paid. The maximum monthly rental rate, however, is 1 ruble, 32 kopeks, per square meter. There are special rates for some categories of persons, including a substantially lower schedule for military personnel. In addition to rent, occupants of Soviet houses pay charges for central heating and for public utilities, including water supply, sewage, electricity, radio, and other conveniences.[63]

The scarcity of urban housing described earlier has made the rationing of housing space a feature of Soviet life for many years. In theory, the nominal amount of housing space each Soviet citi-

[62] Broner, *op. cit.*, pp. 100–103.

[63] Maslyakov, *et al.*, *op. cit.*, pp. 115–23. A more detailed account of the Soviet rent system is given in M. F. Parkins, "Soviet Policy on Urban Housing and Housing Rent," *Land Economics*, August 1953, pp. 269–79.

zen is entitled to under the rationing system is 9 square meters. This
is roughly twice the 4 or 5 square meters per person which is the
actual average. Thus those in charge of allocating this scarce space
have great power, and there are many opportunities for abuses,
as the following—which seems a representative complaint—shows: [64]

> There are many workers living here in temporary barracks erected
> years ago when the Kuznetsk combine was built. These buildings,
> which disfigure Kuznetsk steelworkers' city should long ago have
> been demolished. Yet this task has been wretchedly handled, not
> because there has been little house construction, but because space
> has been thoughtlessly allocated. Often people in acute need of
> apartments remain on the lists for years, while those living in decent
> circumstances get new and even more convenient dwellings. . . .
> There are still times when crooks and opportunists, having infiltrated
> housing administrations, try to profit at the state's expense by carry-
> ing out shady deals. . . . Advanced production workers, other things
> being equal, must have first turn in getting new living space.

Public Utilities

In the area of public utilities, Soviet experience seems to have
been similar to its experience with regard to housing. Large investments were made in building new water supply, sewage, trolley,
gas, and electric supply systems and in expanding those that had
existed before the revolution. In 1913, for example, only 215 cities
had water supply systems; in 1938 this figure had risen to 411 cities.
The number of cities with sewage systems was more than six times
as great in 1940 as before the revolution, in the area within the
pre-1939 borders of the USSR.[65]

Despite these advances, however, the availability of these and
other conveniences was by no means satisfactory even in the best
era before World War II. The 1939 census listed 174 cities having
50,000 or more population. Yet in 1938 only 107 cities had sewage
systems and only 79 cities had trolley or trolley-bus systems. It is
indicative of the way in which Soviet planning seeks to hide deficiencies behind ornate show that the USSR built the artistically
beautiful and highly expensive Moscow subway in a period when
fewer than half of its large and medium-sized cities had even trolley
lines.[66] Another indication of the lack of essential utilities is pro-

---

[64] *Trud*, December 12, 1953.
[65] *Sot. Stroi. (1933–1938), op. cit.*, p. 136. *Entsiklopediya*, cols. 1005–6.
[66] *Sot. Stroi. (1933–1938)*, pp. 136–37.

vided by data on urban housing built in 1935. Of all this new housing, 32 per cent had no water supply, 38 per cent had no sewage facilities, 92.7 per cent had no gas supply, and 54.7 per cent had no central heating.[67]

The destruction and deterioration of housing during World War II was paralleled by similar losses to public utility facilities. In the list of partially or fully destroyed facilities were 251 water supply systems, 114 sewage systems, 46 trolley systems, and 362 municipal electric stations. In addition the utility systems in the never-occupied areas became more inadequate than ever to meet local needs as population rose in the cities there. The Fourth Five-Year Plan called for restoration or construction during 1946–50 of 40 water supply and 52 sewage systems. Indicative of the inadequacy of prewar facilities is the fact that this plan called for construction of water supply systems in such important eastern cities as Sverdlovsk and Chimkent, while new sewage systems were to be built in such major communities as Krasnoyarsk, Tomsk, Irkutsk, and Frunze, among others. Trolley lines were to be introduced into Krasnoyarsk, Barnaul, Tomsk, Karaganda, and Bryansk, and bus lines into Novosibirsk, Gorky, Tashkent, Minsk, Yerevan, and Sevastopol, among others. In the postwar period a great deal of work was scheduled to be accomplished in providing gas to residents in Moscow, Leningrad, Kiev, Kharkov, Lvov, Odessa, Baku, Saratov, Kuibyshev, and other cities where this useful cooking and heating fuel had formerly been available to few or none.[68]

Material appearing in the Soviet press during 1950–54 suggested that substantial, but inadequate, progress had been made during the postwar period with respect to public utilities. The common complaint running through accounts from many communities was that the expansion of urban population had outrun existing facilities built to serve much smaller numbers of people. In new workers' suburbs in many parts of the country, houses were often put up and people moved into them with little attention to provision of water supply, sewage facilities, electricity, and the like. The increasing pollution of Soviet rivers by factories on their banks tended further to complicate public utility problems in many areas.[69]

---

[67] Kobalevsky, *op. cit.*, p. 109.
[68] Maslyakov, *et al.*, *op. cit.*, pp. 6–8.
[69] Cf. the typical complaints in *Izvestia*, June 3, 1951, January 9, March 8, June 24, and August 19, 1952, and in *Trud*, April 19, 1953.

Medical Service

In few if any areas of the Soviet standard of living have such appreciable gains been made since the Bolshevik revolution as in the field of medical care. Eager to have a population capable of working at top productive capacity and physically fit for combat in war if need be, the Soviet government has recognized the importance of providing medical care and has devoted substantial resources toward that objective. The number of doctors and dentists in the Soviet Union increased from 19,800 in 1913 to 130,400 in early 1941 to almost 300,000 in early 1953. The number of hospital beds grew from 142,310 in 1913 to about 850,000 in early 1941 and to approximately 1,100,000 in 1951.[70] It is clear that the quantity of medical service received by the people of the USSR has increased enormously. This service is provided in the main through the system of socialized medicine under which costs are met by the state so that they are paid for by the people indirectly through the general tax and government revenue system rather than by direct payment of fees as in the United States. In addition the Soviet government has actively encouraged scientific research on medical problems and has sought the swift introduction into medical practice of new scientific advances in this field.

Despite the great advances made, however, it seems clear that much further improvement is required to bring the quantity and quality of Soviet medical service up to the level of more productive nations. Thus to serve the more than 200,000,000 people of the Soviet Union in the early 1950's there were fewer than 300,000 doctors and dentists and about 1,100,000 hospital beds as noted above. The United States, with a population roughly 25 per cent less, had approximately the same total number of doctors and dentists and over 1,500,000 hospital beds. The United States does not have the large number of intermediate medical personnel, known as *feldshers*, who are employed in the Soviet Union. The fact that such incompletely trained medical personnel are required, however,

[70] *Entsiklopediya*, cols. 1163, 1164, and 1178. *Gosudarstvenny Plan Razvitiya . . . na 1941 god*, p. 608. *Pravda*, October 6, 1952, gives the number of hospital beds in 1951 as 30 per cent above that of 1940. *Izvestia*, June 20, 1953, states there are also 900,000 *feldshers* and nurses.

is perhaps the best indication of the inadequacy of Soviet doctors for the requirements of that country's large population.

The quality of Soviet medical service is naturally open to question in view of the very rapid increase in the number of doctors and other medical personnel from the extremely low levels at which the Soviet regime began. There can be little doubt that at its best Soviet medicine is extremely good. However, the repeated complaints in the Soviet press about incorrect diagnoses, carelessness and rudeness in handling patients, lack of equipment, failure of doctors to keep up to date in their knowledge, scarcity of even common drugs, and similar faults, all suggest that the average standard of medical care leaves much to be desired.[71] The persistence of part-time private medical practice by doctors employed by the state is also indicative of the unsatisfactory quality of service in the socialized system. The same doctor may be consulted without charge in a government clinic, yet a significant number of patients apparently feel it worth their while to consult him at home and pay him to get what they consider better care. As one Soviet physician wrote in mid-1950: ". . . in the hospital or clinic we still work inadequately well if the sick are ready to pass us by on the way to doctors practicing privately."[72]

It is interesting to note that despite the government control of medicine the distribution and availability of medical personnel in the Soviet Union are highly unequal in different areas. The best situation apparently exists in Moscow, which had over 25,000 doctors and dentists and over 50,000 *feldshers* and nurses to serve its roughly 5,400,000 people in mid-1953.[73] If the same ratio of medical personnel to population had obtained in all the Soviet Union, the country would have had roughly 1,000,000 doctors and dentists and 2,000,000 *feldshers* and nurses, far above the numbers actually available at that time. Rural areas apparently have the least adequate medical service, in terms of personnel available, quality of personnel, and quality and quantity of facilities and medicines. The situa-

---

[71] Cf., for example, the typical complaints in *Trud*, December 26, 1948; *ibid.*, January 25, 1950; *Literaturnaya Gazeta*, April 15, 1950; *Leningradskaya Pravda*, June 29, 1950. Cf. also the translated material on this subject in *Current Digest of the Soviet Press*, September 9, 1950, pp. 13–17.

[72] *Literaturnaya Gazeta*, June 28, 1950.

[73] *Izvestia*, August 28, 1953.

tion in the rural areas of Central Asia is apparently particularly bad.[74]

Other Services

The provision of ordinary consumer services such as laundry, shoe repair, and the like is perhaps the most primitive and undeveloped section of the Soviet economy affecting the standard of living. Such services are apparently best developed in Moscow and Leningrad, though even in these cities they are by no means adequate. Elsewhere they are much less available. Consumer services are frequently performed by *artels*, that is, cooperatives of craftsmen who can be hired for fees to perform work in their line. The low standards in this area are suggested by the following quotation from a speech made by Politburo member A. I. Mikoyan in 1939:

> We must open more public laundries and dry cleaning shops, more shops for repairing shoes, pressing clothes, etc. Moscow and Leningrad already have quite a number of Americanized repair shops where—if they are properly organized, as we can and must make them—people can hand over their shoes to be repaired; the job is done in fifteen or twenty minutes and at the same time you can have your suit ironed while you sit reading the newspaper. (Laughter, applause.) [75]

The same Soviet official was saying the same thing eleven years later, in 1950:

> The work on organization of services for the population must receive especially great extent: organization of every kind of repair of shoes, clothes, household articles, laundering and dry cleaning of clothes, the work of *artels* engaged in building and repairing individual homes to the population's order. It is necessary to guarantee accurate, exact, conscientious work in all these cooperatives serving the population. Here is still a virgin field of work.[76]

The reality behind these complaints may be suggested by summarizing a few of the items on this subject that appeared in the Soviet press during 1948–50. Until early 1950 Moscow had no repair shops for metal articles.[77] In mid-1948 *Izvestia* printed a letter from

---

[74] *Trud*, December 16, 1953.
[75] *Land of Socialism Today and Tomorrow*, p. 368.
[76] *Pravda*, March 11, 1950.
[77] *Moskovskaya Pravda*, April 7, 1950.

a group of prominent intellectuals, including scientists and writers, complaining that there was nowhere to take automobiles for repair and pointing out that since their owners were incompetent to fix them, once cars broke down they remained out of use for long periods.[78] Leningrad, a city of over 3,000,000 persons, had only two automobile service stations in early 1950.[79] Moscow laundries do a very poor job of cleaning clothes and dislike to work for private citizens, preferring to contract with enterprises and institutions for large quantities of work. Their equipment is obsolete, and up to early 1950 there had been little progress in building new laundry equipment.[80]

Material in the Soviet press during 1951–53 suggested the situation was little changed almost a decade after the end of World War II. In mid-1952 the major city of Chelyabinsk, with over a half million people, had only one public laundry, and this handled mainly work for government institutions.[81] In Sverdlovsk, another major city, the work of shoe repair and tailoring shops was said to be so bad and to require so long a wait that consumers were better advised to buy new shoes or a new suit of clothes rather than expect to have their possessions repaired.[82] In late 1952, the Ukraine, a region with more than 40,000,000 people, had only 110 dry-cleaning shops.[83] The same year the newspaper *Trud* declared that the number of cleaning and clothing repair shops in the RSFSR, largest of the Soviet republics, was "a drop in the sea in comparison with demand."[84] Such examples could be multiplied indefinitely.

Mikoyan declared in October 1953: "It is necessary rapidly to increase the network of enterprises helping substantially to lighten the work of housewives, enterprises such as laundries, dry cleaners, clothing and shoe repair shops and other enterprises for everyday services." [85] Whether this declaration will have any more effect than earlier statements of a similar nature remains to be seen. Certainly there is great demand for an enormous expansion of service facilities.

[78] *Izvestia,* July 7, 1948.
[79] *Leningradskaya Pravda,* March 30, 1950.
[80] *Trud,* March 29, 1950.
[81] *Izvestia,* June 17, 1952.
[82] *Ibid.,* October 8, 1953.
[83] *Ibid.,* August 14, 1952.
[84] *Trud,* June 6, 1952.
[85] *Pravda,* October 25, 1953.

CHAPTER XII

THE SOVIET FINANCIAL SYSTEM

M ONEY AND THE financial institutions concerned with money play an important role in the Soviet economy. Along with the economic plan, they help to integrate and coordinate the functioning of the many different parts of the complex productive distribution mechanism in the USSR. The supply and distribution of money, the operation of the banking system, and other activities of Soviet financial organizations are all ruled by the economic plan. The planners utilize these parts of the Soviet economy as instruments to help them accomplish their basic production and other goals. The notion once held by some Soviet leaders that money would die out in a socialist economy has long since been repudiated by the present rulers of the USSR. They regard money and the accompanying system of financial institutions as indispensable for the operation of the USSR's complex economy.

Money performs many of the same functions in the Soviet economy that it does in the United States. It is a medium of exchange and a repository of generalized purchasing power. All personal incomes — whether of officials, ordinary workers, farmers, or others — are paid entirely or partially in cash. Individual owners of money may expend it as they please to purchase the commodities and services they desire. Money serves as a unit of account in transactions between different enterprises. All purchases and sales in the Soviet economy are expressed in money terms and are paid for either by actual currency or by some type of bank document such as a check. Money is also a repository and store of value in the

USSR. Money deposited in a savings bank will draw interest. It may be used to buy government bonds, which also bring in an unearned income. If a Soviet citizen wishes, he may hoard money at home and save it there until he needs it at some future date. There are two important uses of money in our economy, however, that are illegal in the USSR. Money may not be used to finance a private undertaking requiring the employment of others for private profit. It also may not be legally used by private individuals to buy commodities in order to resell them at a higher price. Such purchase and sale, normal from the point of view of a capitalist economy, are regarded as "speculation" in the Soviet Union.

The operation of the monetary aspects of the Soviet Union is governed by the financial plan. The financial plan, as we have seen in Chapter V above, is an integral part of the over-all economic plan. It parallels and is integrated with the production and distribution plans for each period of time. From the most general point of view, the financial plan provides in advance for the income and expenditure levels and patterns of all major portions of the Soviet economy. The three most important component parts of the financial plan include: (1) the government budget, which embraces a much larger portion of the national income in the Soviet Union than it does in any noncommunist nation; (2) the credit plan, which governs the granting of short- and long-term credits by the Soviet banking system to industrial and other enterprises during the period involved; and (3) the cash plan, which controls the supply of money in circulation. Through the financial plan, the Soviet government attempts to insure that the working of the monetary and fiscal aspects of the economy will be dovetailed with that of the other parts of the economy. In so far as possible, the Soviet government seeks to make certain that money and banking forces will not exercise any independent influence upon the course of events, that is, any influence at variance with the objectives of the over-all economic plan.

The present situation, in which money plays an important and indispensable role in the Soviet Union, is a far cry from that envisaged at the beginning of the present regime's hold on power. The attitude that existed in the first year or two after the October revolution is summarized by the following extract from a resolution adopted at the Eighth Congress of the Russian Communist Party in March 1919:

> During the early stage of transition from capitalism to Communism, while Communist production and distribution have not been fully organized, it is impossible to abolish money. Hence, during this period the bourgeois elements will continue to make use of money . . . for the purpose of speculation, gain, and the robbing of the toiling classes. Leaning upon the nationalization of banks, the Russian Communist Party aims to carry through a number of measures which will widen the sphere of moneyless settlements and which will pave the way for the abolition of money: the compulsory keeping of money in the People's Bank; the introduction of budget books; the displacement of money by checks, and short term tickets entitling one to products, etc.[1]

As late as May 1921 Soviet economists were busily engaged in drawing up a plan to wipe out money entirely and replace it by a labor unit of accounting to be called the "tred." [2] The Commissar of Finance, appearing before the first All-Russian Congress of the Council of National Economy in 1918 declared, "In a Socialist society finance is not supposed to exist, and therefore I beg to be excused for its existence and for my own appearance here." [3] But even in those early years, Lenin and others warned that money had important uses and that serious consideration had to be given to assuring that money was properly employed so that the economy might operate.

Soviet Inflation 1917-24

From 1917 to 1924 the Soviet Union underwent one of the classic runaway inflations of human experience. In this period, when production and trade were at relatively low levels, the printing presses operated almost incessantly to turn out a flood of paper money that drove the old ruble's value steadily downward while sending the price level soaring to astronomical heights. In these frantic years the value of the ruble often depreciated from hour to hour, and ordinary monetary calculations for business purposes became nightmarishly difficult. Barter exchanges and payments

---

[1] Quoted in Arnold, *Banks Credit and Money in Russia*, p. 106.
[2] *Ibid.*, pp. 107–8.
[3] Quoted in Arnold, p. 112.

in commodity form even for government taxes assumed major proportions. Recipients of currency sought to rid themselves of it as soon as possible before it had lost much of the value it had had when they accepted it. This of course helped increase the velocity of currency circulation, thus accelerating the inflationary pressures. Only the revival and rapid growth of production and trade after the institution of the New Economic Policy made it possible to lay the groundwork for, and finally accomplish the institution of, a relatively stable currency.

The statistical anatomy of this super-inflation is shown by the data in Table 46.

TABLE 46. Volume of Currency in Circulation and Price Level on Selected Dates, 1918–24 in Soviet-Ruled Area.

Date (FIRST OF EACH MONTH)	MILLION RUBLES	Notes in Circulation INDEX JULY 1 1914 = 1	PRICE INDEX 1913 = 1
Jan. 1918	27,650	17.0	21
Jan. 1919	61,326	37.6	164
Jan. 1920	225,015	138.0	2,420
Jan. 1921	1,168,597	716.7	16,800
Jan. 1922	17,539,232	10,757.6	288,000
Jan. 1923	1,994,464,454	1,223,597.8	21,242,000
Jan. 1924	225,637,374,014	138,427,836.8	5,457,000,000
Mar. 1924	809,625,216,667	496,702,886.9	61,920,000,000

Source: Arthur Z. Arnold, *Banks Credit and Money in Soviet Russia*, pp. 76, 91, 128–29, 186–87.

Merely to keep pace with the enormous numbers in which ordinary calculations had to be carried on during this inflation, the government had to devalue the ruble twice. A decree of November 3, 1921, ordered that one ruble of the 1922 issue should be equal to 10,000 rubles of earlier issues. On October 24, 1922, a ruble of the 1923 issue was declared to be equal to 100 rubles of the 1922 issue, that is, to 1,000,000 pre-1922 rubles.

The underlying cause of this inflation between 1917 and 1924 was the fact that the Soviet government operated throughout this period with enormous deficits. This budgetary deficit was the result of two factors. In the first place, many of the old sources of governmental income had been wiped out by the revolution. Pro-

duction was low and the Soviet government's ability to collect adequate revenues from its population was far below its needs to meet
its expenses. On the other hand, the Soviet government's requirements for money were far greater than those of the Czarist regime.
In the early years of war communism, it had to meet the great expense of fighting civil war and foreign intervention. In addition
the nationalized industries and railroads operated at large deficits,
which had to be made up from the government budget. The Soviet
government had little alternative but to turn to the printing press
to cover the difference. The relationship between Soviet government
incomes and expenditures during these early years is indicated by
the data in Table 47.

TABLE 47. Soviet Government Income, Expenditures, and Deficits, 1918–21.

Year	Income	Expenditure	Deficit	Deficit as % of Expenditures
		(MILLION RUBLES)		
1918	15,580	46,706	31,126	66.6
1919	48,959	215,402	166,443	77.3
1920	159,604	1,215,159	1,055,555	86.9
1921	4,139,900	24,471,900	20,332,000	83.1

Source: V. P. Dyachenko, *Sovetskiye Finansy v Pervoy Faze Razvitiya Sotsialisticheskogo Gosudarstva*, pp. 185, 307. Moscow: 1947.

From the beginning of the New Economic Policy in 1921, Soviet
authorities realized the necessity of creating a stable currency and
wiping out the inflationary disorder that so hindered economic
development in those years. The Soviet government acted vigorously from 1921 to 1924 and finally reached its objective. Among
the important early reforms were such measures as the separation
of state industry from the state budget, so as to make the latter no
longer responsible for the deficits of the former; the reform of the
tax system, with the objective of increasing the income of the government; and the attempt to institute a rigid policy of economy
in government expenditures, so as to decrease the need for further
issue of currency. However, as trade and output increased after
1921, the need for more currency also grew.

The first major monetary step toward a stable currency was taken
in October 1922, when the state bank was empowered by government decree to issue a new unit of currency, the *chervonets*, which
was declared equal to 10 czarist gold rubles. This new monetary

issue was to be fully secured, 25 per cent of the value to be covered by gold and foreign currencies and the remaining 75 per cent by short-term notes of various kinds and by easily marketable goods owned by the state bank. These *chervontsy* (plural of *chervonets*) were not made legal tender. They were declared to be acceptable in payment to the state or by the state in all cases where gold payment was required by law. The state bank could demand the repayment in *chervontsy* for all loans made in that currency. The *chervontsy* were issued in limited amounts and remained fully backed, in order that popular confidence in this currency might be kept as high as possible. From the time of the beginning of the issuance of the *chervontsy* to the final Soviet monetary reform in 1924, the USSR had two paper currencies consisting of the State Bank's *chervontsy* and the ordinary Soviet rubles issued by the government itself. These latter rubles were known as *sovznaki*. By October 1, 1923, *chervontsy* accounted for 75 per cent of the total value of all money in circulation, and the *sovznaki*, ordinary rubles, accounted for 25 per cent. The number of *sovznaki* in circulation, of course, far exceeded the volume of *chervontsy*, but the value of each ordinary Soviet ruble was now infinitesimal.[4]

By early 1924 all was ready for the final completion of the monetary reform, which was carried out by a series of decrees issued in February and March of that year. The Soviet government treasury was authorized to issue a new currency in units of 1, 3, and 5 gold rubles. These were decreed to be legal tender, that is, they had to be accepted for all purchases and in payment of all debts. The printing and issuance of the old *sovznak* currency was ordered stopped. On March 7, 1924, the redemption of the old *sovznak* currency was ordered, the rate being fixed at 50 thousand rubles of the 1923 pattern *sovznak* (equivalent to 50 billion rubles of the pre-1922 *sovznak* issues) for one of the new gold rubles. Redemption took place during April, May, and June 1924. Provision was made for the issuance of silver and copper coins of 10, 15, and 20 kopeks, and of half rubles in silver, as well as of copper coins of 1, 2, 3, and 5 kopeks. Beginning with July 1, 1924, the issuance of paper money to cover state budgetary deficits was ordered discontinued.[5]

---

[4] Baykov, *The Development of the Soviet Economic System*, pp. 89–90.
[5] *Ibid.*, p. 91.

Soviet Money 1924-47

From 1924 to 1947 the Soviet Union continued to have two major types of paper money, the *chervontsy*, each unit of which was equal to ten ordinary rubles and which were issued for the most part in notes of 1, 3, 5, and 10 *chervontsy*; and ordinary ruble currency, circulating in denominations of 1, 3, and 5 rubles. The *chervontsy* were technically issued by the State Bank and came to be called simply bank notes; the ordinary ruble notes were issued by the government treasury nominally, but actually were also governed by the State Bank. The bank notes were backed by gold, foreign currencies, and short-term notes owned by the State Bank. The treasury ruble notes were a purely fiat currency, that is, their value basically came from a government decree ordering their acceptance as money. The official Soviet position was that they were backed by all the property of the Soviet regime and therefore did not need any special reserves to give them intrinsic value. In addition, in 1946, bronze and nickel coins worth 1, 2, 3, 5, 10, 15, and 20 kopeks circulated (100 kopeks equal one ruble), as well as remains of earlier silver and copper coinage.[6]

No sooner had a relatively stable domestic currency been obtained than Soviet leaders became conscious of the fact that this stability was threatened by depreciation of the ruble on foreign monetary exchanges. The government in 1924 had arbitrarily set the parity between its own and foreign currencies at the prewar mint ratios, so that an American dollar was declared equal to 1.943 rubles, a pound sterling to 9.458 rubles, 100 francs to 7.616 rubles, and so on.[7] Ruble quotations on foreign exchanges abroad, however, gave the Soviet currency far less favorable quotations, as smugglers paid for their purchases abroad with large exports of bank notes. In this way foreign exchange markets reflected the fact that high prices existing in the USSR made the purchasing power of the ruble far less than that established by the official foreign exchange parities. It was these high domestic prices that created profit opportunities for smugglers, who could buy goods much more cheaply abroad even if they exchanged bank notes at less than official government rates for foreign money. The Soviet government, of course, could have supported the

---

[6] M. Boguslavsky, Y. Greben, and A. Proselkov, *Operativnaya Tekhnika i Uchet v Gosbanke SSSR*, p. 252. Moscow: 1946.

[7] Arnold, *op. cit.*, pp. 264, 447.

foreign exchange rate of the ruble by purchasing foreign-owned bank notes with gold or precious metals, but its supply of these commodities in the early 1920's was far too low to permit the extensive purchases that would have been required. A decree of July 9, 1926, therefore, forbade the export of bank notes, and the State Bank discontinued redemption of its notes owned abroad. For a time foreigners visiting the USSR were permitted to bring ruble notes in with them, so that there continued to be a foreign market for Soviet currency at substantial discounts from the official rates. To stop this, the government decree of March 21, 1928, prohibited the import as well as the export of banknotes, thus making the ruble a completely internal currency. In this way the ruble was protected from the more realistic valuations given it by foreign markets, but to do this the government for many years afterward had to conduct its foreign economic relations in other currencies.[8]

During the 1930's and 1940's the exchange rates between the ruble and other foreign currencies were set arbitrarily by the Soviet government, primarily for the purpose of providing a basis on which foreigners bringing their currency into the USSR could exchange it for rubles. The ruble was grossly overvalued as judged by any comparison of its purchasing power with the purchasing power of the nominally equal amounts of dollars, pounds, and so on. In general the Soviet government changed ruble rates so as to reflect changes in the value of freely fluctuating foreign currencies based on gold. Thus, when the American dollar was devalued by President Franklin D. Roosevelt, its ruble value was cut to 1.15 rubles as against 1.943 rubles earlier. In 1935 and 1936, however, the government made more adequate recognition of the great inflation of domestic prices that had occurred and devalued the ruble. Beginning April 1, 1936, fine gold was valued at 5.6807 rubles per gram, as against 1.29 rubles per gram earlier, a devaluation of 77.5 per cent. This resulted in new foreign exchange values of the ruble, including a rate of 5.06 rubles for the dollar. In 1937 the dollar was declared equal to 5.3 rubles, and the nominal ruble parity of other currencies was calculated by multiplying their dollar values by 5.3.[9] These new ratios also overvalued the ruble, however, the margin of overvaluation increasing as Soviet prices went up after 1936. During World War

---

[8] *Ibid.*, pp. 262–63.

[9] *Ibid.*, pp. 447–49. Boguslavsky, Greben, and Proselkov, *op. cit.*, p. 265.

II, official exchange rates remained unchanged, despite the great inflation of nonration Soviet prices. Some allowance was made, however, for diplomatic personnel, members of the American Embassy staff being permitted to get 12 rubles for an American dollar rather than the 5.3 rate maintained nominally. The changes in foreign exchange rates for the ruble put into effect during 1949–54 will be discussed later in this chapter.

The monetary reform of 1924 provided a much more stable currency than had existed earlier. In the years that followed, up to World War II, production increased many times, so that the volume of commodities that could be bought in the USSR with ruble notes greatly increased. However, the late 1920's and 1930's were also years of inflation in the USSR, although this inflation proceeded more slowly than during 1917–24. The tremendous industrialization program of the first three five-year plans required the diversion of much of the country's output of capital investment, while holding down the growth of consumer-goods production to a much slower pace. The catastrophic events in agriculture during the early 1930's sharply curtailed the availability of many important foods and agricultural raw materials. Meanwhile the number of industrial workers being paid money wages and relying on the market for the commodities they needed increased sharply. The severest impact of these forces before World War II was felt in the early 1930's, when the USSR had to impose stringent rationing upon its urban population in an effort to stretch supplies of food and consumer goods so that they would meet at least minimal needs. Concurrently the supply of money in circulation and the volume of credit grew rapidly. The increase of money in circulation is shown in Table 48.

TABLE 48. Currency in Circulation in the USSR, 1928–36.

Date	Bank Notes	Treasury Notes and Coins	Total Currency in Circulation
		(THOUSANDS OF RUBLES)	
Jan. 1, 1928	1,002,900	664,900	1,667,800
Jan. 1, 1930	1,501,000	1,272,000	2,773,000
Jan. 1, 1932	2,784,413	2,888,897	5,673,310
Jan. 1, 1934	3,342,502	3,429,046	6,771,548
Apr. 1, 1935	3,978,041	3,901,366	7,879,407
Apr. 1, 1936	5,934,994	Unavailable	Unavailable

Source: Arnold, op. cit., pp. 412–13.

The inflationary impact of these forces upon the prices of basic foods is indicated by the data in Table 49.

TABLE 49. Prices of Food Items in Moscow, 1928, 1936, and 1940.

	Rye Bread	Rice	Potatoes	Sugar	Beef	Butter	Eggs
	(RUBLES PER KILOGRAM)						(PER EGG)
1928....	.08	.48	.11	.62	.87	2.43	.19
1936....	.85	8.00	.30	4.10	8.00	16.00	.40
1940*...	.85	8.00	1.20	5.50	16.00	23.00	.85

* April 1940. Prices were raised later in the year.
Source: S. N. Prokopovicz, *Russlands Volkswirtschaft unter den Sowjets*, p. 305.

It is clear from Table 49 that prices of many basic foods rose tenfold or more between 1928 and 1940, a very substantial inflationary movement by any standard. To speak of the stability of the Soviet ruble after the monetary reform of 1924 is justifiable only if one has in mind a comparison with the much wilder gyrations of the ruble before that reform.

World War II and its aftermath completed the inflationary depreciation of the monetary system inaugurated in 1924. Production of consumer goods and food for market sale to civilians dropped precipitously during the war, both because much of the USSR's production capacity was lost to the Germans and because of government measures aimed at maximizing output for the needs of the armed forces. At the same time, the government had to renew printing of currency to meet its budgetary deficit, especially in 1942. The total volume of currency in circulation in the USSR increased by 2.4 times during three war years, thus increasing the inflationary pressure upon the greatly reduced supplies of commodities available for purchase.[10] The Soviet government attempted to keep a restraining hand on prices by instituting a rigid rationing system at the outset of the war and by draining off a larger part of the civilian population's income through higher taxes and large bond issues sold to the public. Goods sold under the rationing system were for the most part sold at the same prices as before the war. The pressure of inflationary forces expressed itself, therefore, in 1942 and 1943 primarily in the collective farm markets, where farmers could sell their surplus produce at any price they could get without requiring ration tickets. Prices prevailing in these free

[10] Voznesensky, *The Economy of the USSR During World War II*, pp. 73, 76.

markets, sometimes termed black markets—mistakenly, for these were legal transactions—soared far above the old prices, sometimes exceeding them by 100 times or more. In late 1943 rye bread, selling for 1 ruble per kilogram in the ration stores, cost 130 rubles a kilogram in the free market. In the same period sugar, which was almost unobtainable in the ration stores, where it cost 5 rubles a kilogram, sold for 1,100 rubles in the Moscow free market.[11] These are extreme cases, but they illustrate the magnitude of inflationary pressures existing in the early years of World War II.

From 1944 to 1947 the Soviet government sought to strengthen the value of the ruble by a number of different measures. "Commercial" stores were opened in 1944, at which goods could be bought without ration cards but at much higher prices. These prices were reduced a number of times in the years that followed, causing pressure for similar price reductions in the competitive farm markets where food was sold. Price reductions were made possible by the increasing supply of food and consumer goods that became available in the last year of World War II and after the end of hostilities. The price differential between the commercial stores and the ration stores was narrowed considerably in September 1946 by a government order roughly tripling the prices of foods sold under the rationing system, but this differential still remained substantial. The narrowing of the gap in prices between the same commodities sold under the rationing system and in the commercial stores, plus the greatly increased supply of food and consumer goods, provided the groundwork for the Soviet monetary and ration reform of December 1947, the most important government decree dealing with money since the reform of 1924. The severe 1946 ration price increases took place after the disastrous crop failure of that year.

The 1947 Monetary Reform

The decree of the Council of Ministers announcing the 1947 reform declared that the volume of money in circulation had increased greatly, both because of war needs and because invading forces had introduced large quantities of false ruble notes. It acknowledged that this increase in money supply, together with the decline in goods available for sale, had increased prices ten or fifteen times over

---

[11] Schwartz, "Prices in the Soviet War Economy," *op. cit.*, p. 877.

the prewar level. This admission, of course, understated the extreme inflationary peaks pointed out above. The decree accused "speculative elements" of using the gap between government ration prices and free market prices to enrich themselves. It made no mention of farmers, although those among them who had been able to sell significant quantities in the free markets had been the chief beneficiaries of the extremely high prices prevailing there. The purpose of the decree, it was declared, was both to establish a full-valued monetary system and to prevent the "speculative elements who enriched themselves during the war and accumulated considerable sums of money" from buying up goods after the abolition of rationing.[12] In other words the government sought to upset the distribution of purchasing power that had resulted from the war and early postwar price situation so as to penalize those who had benefited—the farmers primarily, though the decree did not mention them—and to improve the relative position of those who had been at a disadvantage earlier. This latter group consisted primarily of the urban population.

To achieve these objectives a complex set of measures was ordered. Rationing and the two-price system (commercial and ration prices) were abolished, and one system of state-owned stores set up, selling goods to all comers without ration tickets at one state-fixed level of prices. All cash owned by the population was ordered exchanged for new 1947 rubles at the rate of 10 old rubles for one new ruble. This very low exchange rate reflected the real depreciation of the ruble even after the recovery of 1944–47. It also affected primarily those who had hoarded cash, that is, farmers with little faith in banks or government bonds and speculators who kept cash for fear that depositing it in banks would make their profits known to the state. Accounts in government banks were also ordered revalued at a sliding scale. Accounts up to 3,000 rubles were maintained without change, that is, converted at a 1-to-1 ratio. All accounts of from 3,000 to 10,000 rubles were revalued at a 1-to-1 ratio for the first 3,000 rubles and at a rate of 3 old rubles for 2 new ones for the amounts in excess of 3,000 rubles. Accounts in excess of 10,000 rubles had the first 10,000 rubles revalued as indicated above and all sums over 10,000 rubles revalued at the rate of 2 old

---

[12] An English translation of this decree was printed in *The New York Times*, December 15, 1947.

rubles for 1 new ruble. Government bonds outstanding were ordered exchanged for new bonds at the rate of 3 old rubles for 1 new ruble, although two bond issues—those of 1938 and 1947—were handled somewhat differently. Current accounts of cooperative organizations and collective farms in Soviet banks were ordered devalued at the rate of 5 old rubles for 4 new rubles. All taxes, obligations to the state, wages, and other fixed obligations were ordered unchanged, to be paid at the same rates in new currency as in the past.

With one move, therefore, the Soviet government considerably altered the distribution of real wealth among its people, introduced a new currency, abolished rationing, and considerably simplified the distribution and price system for consumer goods and food. In a democratic society, such a far-reaching move affecting tens of millions of people would have been the subject of bitter parliamentary and public debate and controversy. In the Soviet Union, it was carried out by authoritarian government decree, with no consultation of either those who lost or those who gained from the move. Inflationary pressure was thus virtually wiped out for the time being by the expedient of declaring all paper money owned by the population worth only 10 kopeks on the ruble. The alternative of course would have been to raise prices almost tenfold, but this would have been bad from the foreign propaganda point of view and also would not have produced the internal social consequences that flowed from the differential rates of devaluation actually used. The reform is a good illustration of a dictatorship's ability to sugar-coat the bitter pill of currency confiscation by the sweet shell of ration-free trade.

The monetary system of the USSR since the 1947 reform has consisted of three elements: bank notes, treasury notes, and metallic coins with denominations under one ruble. This system is of course formally similar to the pre-reform system, despite the drastic devaluation caried out in December 1947.[13]

The "Gold Standard" Ruble

As pointed out above, the official value of the ruble in terms of foreign currencies for more than a decade after 1937 was deter-

---

[13] F. D. Livshits, *Bankovaya Statistika*, p. 401. Moscow: Gosfinizdat, 1948.

mined by the Soviet government on the basis of its unilateral declaration that 5.3 rubles were equivalent to one dollar. As other currencies fluctuated in terms of the dollar, their ruble values were changed on the basis of the 5.3 ratio. From 1937 to early 1950, foreigners visiting the Soviet Union and wishing to exchange their own currency for Soviet money had to accept this ratio of exchange, unless they were diplomatic personnel, who obtained a more favorable rate. The ruble did not serve as an actual medium of foreign exchange outside the USSR during this period, and its export or import continued to be forbidden. Soviet foreign trade continued to be conducted in foreign currencies, and Soviet trade agreements with other nations were usually expressed in terms of dollar amounts.

A decree of February 28, 1950, made important changes in this situation. The decree announced a comprehensive series of price cuts on consumer goods and food and declared that this and earlier price reductions had raised the actual value of the ruble above that indicated by prevailing foreign exchange rates. Moreover it declared that the American dollar had proved to be an unstable currency, so that the USSR could no longer base the ruble upon it but must shift to a gold base. The Council of Ministers ordered, therefore, on the basis of this reasoning that: (1) the gold content of the ruble should be declared equal to .222168 grams of pure gold; (2) the State Bank of the USSR should buy gold thereafter at a price of 4 rubles and 45 kopeks per gram of pure gold; (3) the official exchange rate between the dollar and the ruble should be changed from 5.3 rubles to the dollar to 4 rubles to the dollar; and (4) the exchange ratio of the ruble in relation to other currencies should be changed in the same ratio as in the case of the dollar, and that where foreign currencies fluctuated in the future their ruble exchange values should be altered accordingly.[14] At the same time diplomatic personnel in the USSR were informed that after June 30 they would no longer receive any preferential ruble exchange rate.

Although Soviet commentators hailed these changes as putting the ruble on the gold standard, this was not true. The Soviet government put an arbitrary gold valuation on the ruble and announced that its gold purchasing monopoly would pay a corresponding price for gold. But in a true gold standard situation, holders of a given

[14] *Pravda,* March 1, 1950.

currency must be able to obtain gold from the government at roughly the same price as that for which the government will purchase gold. The Soviet announcement of the new ruble "gold standard" made no mention of what ruble price it was willing to accept from those who wished to buy gold. Information on this point became available in March 1954 when it was reported that Soviet jewelry stores sold gold "in small wafer-size pieces at the rate of ninety rubles for one gram of gold of 916/1000 fineness" to persons who wished to have gold teeth instead of the stainless steel teeth usually provided by Soviet dentists. This is equivalent to 2,800 rubles a fine ounce of gold as against $35 a fine ounce in the United States. On the basis of the Soviet *selling price* for gold, the ruble is worth only 1.25 cents in United States money, not 25 cents as indicated by its *purchase price* for gold.[15] The Soviet claim that postwar price cuts had raised the exchange value of the ruble above its previous exchange rate ignored the fact that the government had made no revision of the exchange rate during the entire preceding period— particularly during World War II—when this rate overvalued the ruble tremendously. More important, the government gave no evidence of the ruble's supposed undervaluation. This was wise, since any comparison of the ruble's purchasing power with that of the dollar would have shown the falsity of the claim that even 5.3 rubles, let alone 4 rubles, were equal in purchasing power to one United States dollar. Since the 1950 reform, the Soviet government has maintained the ruble-dollar ratio constant. It has changed the ratio between the ruble and the currencies of other noncomunist countries besides the United States in proportion to world currency market changes (or official parity changes) in the relation between those currencies and the United States dollar. With respect to the currencies of Eastern Europe, the Soviet government has changed their ruble ratios since 1950 to correspond to the official relationship with the ruble set by the communist governments of those countries for their own currencies. The trend has been for these satellite regimes to declare their currencies based on the ruble. The official Soviet government ratios between the ruble and various foreign currencies shortly before the 1950 reform, immediately after it, and in early 1954 are shown in Table 50 below:

---

[15] *New York Times*, March 7, 1954.

TABLE 50. Official Ruble Foreign Exchange Rates, November 1, 1949, March 2, 1950, and February 1, 1954.

	Exchange Value in Rubles		
Foreign Currency	NOVEMBER 1, 1949	MARCH 2, 1950	FEBRUARY 1, 1954
U. S. Dollar	5.30	4.00	4.00
British Pound Sterling	14.84	11.20	11.20
Egyptian Pound	15.24	11.52	11.52
Canadian Dollar	4.82	3.63	4.12
100 Swedish Kroner	102.32	77.22	77.22
100 Swiss Francs	121.84	91.47	93.27
100 Albanian Leks	10.60	8.00	8.00
100 Afghan Afghani	31.55	23.66	19.05
100 Belgian Francs	10.62	8.00	8.00
100 Bulgarian Leva	1.86	1.40	58.82
100 Hungarian Forints ..	45.49	34.10	34.10
100 Dutch Guilders	139.29	105.26	105.26
100 Danish Kroner	76.59	57.91	57.91
100 Indian Rupees	111.83	84.30	84.30
100 Iranian Rials	16.43	12.40	12.40
1,000 Italian Lire	8.34	6.40	6.42
100 Mongolian Tugriks ..	131.40	100.00	100.00
100 Norwegian Kroner ...	74.20	56.00	56.00
100 Pakistan Rupees	160.76	121.05	121.05
1,000 Polish Zlotys	13.25	10.00	1000.00
1,000 Rumanian Lei	35.33	26.74	666.70
100 Turkish Lire	188.35	142.86	142.86
1,000 Finnish Finnmarks.	22.95	17.47	17.47
1,000 French Francs	15.15	11.46	11.43
100 Czech Crowns	10.60	8.00	55.56

Sources: *Izvestia*, November 1, 1949; March 2, 1950; February 2, 1954.

The consequences of this reform upon foreign trade will be discussed in a later chapter, but one more aspect of this reform requires attention. The Soviet move in putting the ruble upon a nominal gold base focused attention upon the possibility that the USSR might some day repeal restrictions upon ruble exports and imports and try to make the ruble an international currency. The possibility exists of course that the USSR may some day permit free purchase of gold by ruble holders at a price in line with the government's ruble purchase price for gold. This would require both a realistic foreign exchange rate for the ruble and a large stock of gold. The possibility that Soviet gold reserves may have reached very substantial amounts by 1950 cannot be ruled out, since gold production and reserve figures have not been published since before 1940. The belief that substantial Soviet gold reserves may exist is based upon information indicating very substantial output in the 1930's. In addition, when Henry Wallace visited the Kolyma gold area in 1944, he found that gold production had been continued there.[16] The magnitude of Soviet gold output before World War II is indicated approximately by the data of Table 51, which is based on estimates of the Director of the U. S. Mint.

TABLE 51. Estimated Gold Production in the USSR, 1918–40.

Year	Fine Ounces	Year	Fine Ounces
1918	554,588	1929	707,300
1919	173,610	1930	1,501,083
1920	73,945	1931	1,655,725
1921	65,907	1932	1,038,000
1922	191,614	1934	3,858,089
1923	305,425	1935	4,784,030
1924	546,550	1936	5,173,000
1925	632,390	1937	5,358,982
1926	760,605	1938	5,235,909
1927	688,492	1939	5,000,000
1928	385,800	1940	4,000,000

Source: From annual reports of the Director of the United States Mint for 1935 and subsequent years as cited in Chee Hsien-Wu, *Two Decades of Soviet Foreign Trade*, p. 237.

Available data on Soviet gold shipments abroad during the 1920's and 1930's indicate that a large fraction of the gold produced in the USSR, particularly in the 1930's, remained there, accumulating. With the addition of output retained since 1940, total gold reserves in the USSR may well be very substantial.[17]

As late as December 1953, a new set of Soviet customs regulations published in *Vneshnyaya Torgovlya*, official organ of the Ministry of Foreign Trade, retained the previous prohibitions on the export or import of rubles. Soviet gold exports during the last months of 1953, apparently exceeding $100,000,000 in value, aroused worldwide interest during the first year of the post-Stalin regime.

The Soviet Budget

The state budget of the USSR for each year consists of the pro-

---

[16] Henry A. Wallace, *Soviet Asia Mission*, p. 35. New York: Reynal and Hitchcock, 1946.

[17] Chee Hsien-Wu, *Two Decades of Soviet Foreign Trade*, p. 246. Cambridge, Mass.: Harvard University, 1947. Unpublished Ph.D. Thesis.

jected program of government expenditures and the planned volume of government revenues for that period. The Soviet budget provides funds for the country's armed forces, for social security needs, education, and the other usual functions of government. These expenditures are met in the main by taxes paid directly or indirectly by the population of the Soviet Union. The annual budget is prepared by the Ministry of Finance and presented for approval each year by the Finance Minister to the highest legislative body of the country, the Supreme Soviet. Once approved, the budget's execution is supervised by the Finance Ministry, which checks on expenditures by government organs and collects authorized taxes and other government revenues.

In the matters enumerated above, the Soviet budget and budgetary practice resemble more or less the United States budget and budgetary practice. A number of important differences exist, however, which deserve careful attention. These differences flow from the fundamental dissimilarities in political and economic organization between the Soviet Union and capitalist countries.

First, the Soviet budget governs a much wider area of the life in the USSR than is governed in the United States by our budget. All the Soviet economy is planned by the regime, and — with the major exception of the collective farms — almost all production is carried on by governmental quasi-corporations that own and operate industrial plants, mines, railroads, and other enterprises. The Soviet budget is the major source of funds for new capital investment and for the increase or replenishment of working capital. Accumulation and distribution of funds for this purpose through the state largely substitute in the USSR for private individual and corporate capital accumulation and investment in other countries. Moreover the USSR has a complete system of socialized medicine, which is completely financed through the state budget. There are no privately owned schools, theatres, newspapers, book publishing houses, art museums, or the like in the USSR. Consequently all educational and cultural institutions in the country are financed through the state budget, except in so far as they meet part of their costs through tuition fees, ticket sales, and the like. The almost all-inclusive functioning of the Soviet state is thus naturally reflected in the extensive area covered by its budget. On the other hand, the incomes and revenues of production trusts, combines, and other government quasi-corporations that have been set up on the basis of economic accountability (*khozraschet*) are not part of the state budget, though the latter draws upon their profits, if any, and may provide capital investment funds or working capital. In 1937, it has been estimated, Soviet government revenue was 36 per cent of the USSR's gross national product. The corresponding figure for the United States in that year was 17 per cent.[18]

Second, the Soviet budget is part of the country's over-all economic and financial plan for each year, not an isolated document. The budget's monetary allocations provide for the distribution and allocation of the country's resources in accordance with the production program outlined by the economic plan. In the process of executing the budget, officials of the Ministry of Finance are required to supervise simultaneously the execution of the economic plan by the enterprises and institutions with which they work. This integration of economic plan and government budget is an obvious necessity. Without such integration much confusion and waste would result. But, consequently, this means that Soviet legislatures cannot have the same independence in reviewing budgets and changing them as American legislatures. Any major change in the budget would require similar changes throughout the entire annual economic plan, a matter far outside the customary competence of the Soviet legislature. It is no surprise, therefore, that the budgetary review by the Supreme Soviet each year is little more than a formality, marked usually only by very minor proposals for changes with regard to either expenditures or revenues. Indicative of this absence of real legislative control over the budget is the fact that the Soviet budget is usually presented to and approved by the Supreme Soviet in February or March, or even later, well after the government has begun functioning on the basis of the new budget for that calendar year. Only large global totals of incomes and expenses are presented publicly to the Supreme Soviet.

Third, the Soviet budget is exceedingly centralized. The expenditures and revenues approved by the Supreme Soviet in Moscow cover not only those of the all-union government, but also those of the individual constituent republics and the complex of all lower

---

[18] Abram Bergson, "Soviet National Income and Product in 1937," *Quarterly Journal of Economics*, May 1950, pp. 236–37.

TABLE 52. Chief Soviet Budgetary Revenues and Expenditures in Selected Years.

	1938	1940	1942	1944	1946	1948	1950	1952	1953	1954*
					(BILLION RUBLES)					
Revenues										
Total Revenue†	127.5	180.2	165.0	268.7	325.4	410.5	422.1	497.7	539.7	572.5
Turnover Tax	80.4	105.9	66.0	94.9	190.9	247.3	236.1	260.7*	240.4*	234.3
Profit Tax	10.5	21.7	15.3	21.4	16.2	27.2	40.4	58.4	80.6*	92.6
Direct Taxes on Population	5.1	9.4	22.0††	37.2	22.7	33.2	35.8	47.4*	46.1*	45.7
State Loans and Gifts	7.6	11.5	17.5	37.5	24.7	23.9	31.0	36.3	16.7*	15.9
Social Insurance Levies	7.2	8.5	‡	9.0	‡	16.2	‡	‡	‡	‡
Expenditures										
Total Expenditures†	124.0	174.4	182.8	263.9	307.5	370.9	412.7	460.2	514.8	562.8
Military§	23.1	56.8	108.4	137.9	73.6	66.3	82.9	108.0	110.2*	100.3
National Economy	51.7	58.3	31.6	53.7	106.2	149.6	157.3	178.8	180.6	216.4
Social-Cultural Measures	35.3	40.9	27.8	51.3	80.0	105.6	116.8	122.8	128.8	141.4
Administration and Justice	5.4	6.8	‡	7.4	11.8	13.1	13.8	14.4*	14.3*	‡
Surplus (+) or Deficit (−)	+3.5	+5.8	−17.8	+4.8	+17.9	+39.6	+9.4	+37.5	+24.9	+9.7

* Plan.
† Totals include items not enumerated as well as those enumerated in table.
‡ Not available.
§ Includes only direct expenditures for armed forces.
†† Estimated.

Sources: K. N. Plotnikov, Byudzhet Sovetskogo Gosudarstva; Entsiklopediya; Finansy SSSR za XXX Let; N. A. Voznesensky, The Economy of the USSR During World War II; M. I. Bogolepov, Sovetskaya Finansovaya Sistema; Planovoye Khozyaistvo, No. 2 (1949); A. Zverev's budget messages for 1946-50; Bolshevik, No. 12 (1950); Bulletins on Soviet Economic Development, No. 3 (August 1950) and No. 7 (Series 2, December 1952); Izvestia, August 6, 1953; Pravda, April 22 and 28, 1954.

provincial, city, and rural governmental units. The budgetary system is hierarchical, so that the legislatures and authorities at each level of government have extensive powers over the budgets of all government units under their jurisdiction. The Supreme Soviet of the USSR approves the budgetary revenues and expenditures of the constituent republics and also the relationships between the budget of each republic and the total budgets of all local governmental units in that republic. Then in each republic — the Ukraine or the RSFSR for example — the same process is repeated downward, and so on through the entire hierarchical organization. The expenditures permitted each level of government depend upon the activities for which each is given primary responsibility. The all-union government, for example, has control of financing capital expansion of all major industry subordinate to it, while republican and local governments deal with less important industry and pay much more attention, relatively, to such matters as fire protection, medical care, and the like. The incomes that each independent budget below that of the all-union government may draw upon are also determined both in source and in amount by the integrated national budget. Local governments are consulted regarding their wishes, and they supply estimates of needs and incomes to the central authorities of the Ministry of Finance, who draw up the integrated national budget. But these local units have far less fiscal independence than states, cities, and counties in this country.

Fourth, for more than two decades the Soviet budget has usually been balanced with an excess of revenues over expenditures, except in the early years of World War II, when large-scale currency issue had to be used to cover deficits. This balance is in part only nominal, since Soviet budgetary practice lumps the revenue from government bonds sold to the population and to financial institutions along with tax income and other nonreturnable payments to the government (tuition fees in schools, license fees, and so on). In terms of United States practice, therefore, the Soviet budget has often been unbalanced, that is, it has had an excess of outgo over nonreturnable income. The need to resort to government borrowing to meet current revenue needs is of course the hallmark of a deficit in American public finance.

A democratic government's ability to balance its budget in a period of increased and heavy expenditure, such as war, is often impaired by popular and legislative resistance to higher taxes. The Soviet government has no fear of opposition to its tax program in the rubber-stamp Supreme Soviet, but it does have to take account of popular reaction. In World War II, for example, tax revenues fell far short of meeting expenditures. Before 1944 substantial deficits had to be met by printing money. The Soviet government could have raised taxes adequately to meet its expenditure needs, though administrative confusion early in the war may have been some obstacle. But sharply higher indirect (sales) taxes would have raised the price level substantially, creating popular discontent and perhaps endangering attainment of the goal of assuring the minimum subsistence needs of essential workers. To have raised direct income taxes adequately to meet revenue needs would have reduced the incentive effect of higher incomes as means of securing increased output. The Soviet government compromised, therefore, raising its revenue in part by issuing money and in part by increasing direct and indirect taxes. It also greatly increased the sale of government bonds, sources of unearned income for their purchasers and means of saving for future consumption. The impact of its fiscal policies upon morale and incentives is a factor in the Soviet government's calculations in time of peace as well as of war.

The inflationary pressures upon the Soviet economy during World War II are clearly indicated in the growth of government revenues and expenditures between 1938 and 1946. In 1946, when Soviet production was well below the prewar level, both income and outgo were about two and a half times as great as in 1938.

The Turnover Tax

The turnover tax is the most important single source of Soviet government revenue, often accounting for about 60 per cent of all income in time of peace and roughly 40 per cent even in the war year 1942. This tax is the basic weapon the Soviet regime employs to divert a large part of the national income from consumption to capital investment and other government objectives. It is essentially a differentiated sales tax imposed heavily but with differing rates upon all significant articles of consumption. Products of heavy industry were initially subject to the turnover tax but at low tax rates.

However, the trend over the past two decades has been toward free-ing nonconsumer goods from the tax or making its impact upon them negligible. The tax is levied upon commodities at the time of fabrication and upon government purchases at low requisition prices of peasant obligatory deliveries. The tax must be included in the price of the commodity thereafter, so that it is passed on fully to the final consumer. Because it is levied initially upon the manu-facturing enterprise (or, in the case of farm commodities, upon the government requisitioning organization), Soviet budgetary statistics list it as revenue from socialized production, though ultimately it is paid in full by consumers and is clearly a sales tax. The impact of the turnover tax is shown by the comparison of the relative impor-tance of different industries in relation to production and in relation to turnover tax payments given in Table 53.

TABLE 53. Importance of Major People's Commissariats in Production and as Sources of Turnover Tax Revenues, 1939.

Commissariat	Per Cent of Total Gross Output	Per Cent of Turn-over-Tax Revenue
Petroleum Industry	3.1	8.0
Meat and Dairy Industry	4.5	7.3
Food Industry	11.7	29.7
Textile Industry	10.2	13.0
Light Industry	7.9	2.6
Agricultural Requisitions	2.5	34.4
Other Commissariats, primarily in Heavy Industry	60.1	5.0

Source: A. K. Suchkov, *Dokhody Gosudarstvennogo Byudzheta SSSR*, p. 16.

It is apparent from the data above that food items and consumer goods were the source of almost 90 per cent of all turnover tax re-ceipts in 1939. The high proportion of this tax revenue paid by the People's Commissariat of Agricultural Requisitions is a measure of the success of the Soviet government in squeezing a substantial surplus out of agriculture. Farmers receive low prices for their ob-ligatory deliveries of some key foodstuffs and raw materials. The costs of these commodities as they go on to further processing and sale are much higher, since they contain the substantial turnover tax imposed.

The turnover tax was established by the tax reform of September

2, 1930, which wiped out a whole host of special taxes on commodities and on different stages of production, substituting for them the turnover tax and the profits tax discussed below.[19] Later changes during the 1930's were made to remedy weaknesses in the original enactment, aiming at such goals as defining precisely the production unit responsible for paying the tax and the value of goods to be used as a base for calculating the tax. As it now exists, the turnover tax is very complex, with many different rules of payment for a large variety of commodities. The tax may be imposed as a percentage of the selling price at retail, as a percentage of the wholesale price, as an absolute sum per unit of commodity, or on some other base. Rates of taxation on the same goods may vary from region to region and from selling place to selling place, that is, one rate may be established for cities, another for rural areas, and so on.[20] Rates are changed from time to time as deemed necessary by the Ministry of Finance, but their impact upon many important goods is indicated by the following list effective in 1940:[21]

Commodity	Tax Rate
Potatoes	48–62 per cent of retail price
Beef	67–71 per cent of retail price
Fresh Fish	35–53 per cent of retail price
Butter	60–66 per cent of retail price
Table Margarine	59–67 per cent of retail price
Sugar	73 per cent of retail price
Vodka	84 per cent of retail price
Soft Drinks	20 per cent of retail price
Cigarettes	75–88 per cent of retail price

(tax rate enacted in 1938)

The impact of the changes of economic policy announced in 1953 upon the budget for 1953 and 1954 is apparent from Table 52 above. For both years the turnover tax was planned to be only little more than 40 per cent of all Soviet government revenues, where formerly it had normally been more than 50 per cent in years of peace. The planned government receipts from the turnover tax in 1953 and 1954 were lower than the corresponding planned 1952 receipts. Two factors seem to explain this develop-

---

[19] *Finansy SSSR za XXX Let*, p. 44. Moscow: 1947.

[20] A. K. Suchkov, *Dokhody Gosudarstvennogo Byudzheta SSSR*, pp. 22 ff.

[21] Cited in Naum Jasny, *The Soviet Price System*, pp. 164–65. Stanford: Stanford University Press, 1951.

ment. First, the price reductions on different goods announced in April 1953 and April 1954 were probably made possible mainly by lowering turnover tax rates on these commodities. Second, the substantial increases of prices paid to farmers for livestock products, potatoes, and vegetables — as announced in September 1953 — narrowed substantially the difference between government procurement prices and government sales prices. This undoubtedly lessened the amount of "turnover tax" the government pocketed through its system of agricultural requisitions. As Table 53 shows, the turnover tax on agricultural requisitions was the largest single source of revenues from this tax in 1939, a situation that was probably little different during 1946–52.

The profits tax — or more precisely the deduction from profits for the government budget — was introduced by the tax reform of 1930, at the same time as the turnover tax. The tax rate applied differs from industry to industry and from year to year, so that the contributions of different industries to the state's income from this tax are not proportional to their profits. In setting profits tax rates, the government takes into account the needs of each industry for expanding its fixed and working capital. The state leaves relatively more of its profits to an industry or enterprise whose capital is to be expanded rapidly than to one whose capital is not to be so expanded. The disparate treatment given different branches of the economy in 1940 is shown below: [22]

Branch of Economy	Total Profit	Profits Tax	Rate of Tax
	(BILLION RUBLES)		(PER CENT)
Petroleum	.4	.14	35.0
Machinery	1.2	.77	63.8
Iron and Steel	1.0	.25	25.0
Chemicals	.59	.28	48.1
Light and Textile Industries	2.7	2.4	90.0
Food	4.2	3.6	84.1
Transport and Communications	6.4	3.3	51.9

The imposition of the profits tax upon a given enterprise is determined by the size of its profits, if any, and by whether or not the enterprise is scheduled to have capital investment expenditures or to increase its working capital. An enterprise for which it is not

---

[22] Suchkov, *op. cit.*, p. 86.

planned to increase the fixed or working capital surrenders to the state its entire planned profit, save for the amount going to the director's fund and other authorized deductions. In other cases the government takes the excess of profit over the enterprise's needs for its own capital expansion and for the director's and other funds. But in no case may the government receive less than 10 per cent of the profit. Before the last war even enterprises operating at a loss were required to pay the government a profits tax equal to 10 per cent of the profit planned for them, but this requirement was apparently suspended during World War II.[23] In this way the government is able to drain off profits from different enterprises and industries, for reinvestment in other industries and enterprises that may be making no profits or inadequate profits, or for other government expenditures.

Income Taxes

Income taxes are levied separately upon Soviet citizens, depending upon whether they work for wages, are independent artisans, writers, or the like; or are collective or individual farmers. As we shall see below, these income taxes have rate schedules and define taxable income in such a way as to aid accomplishment of government policy outside the fiscal field, as well as to provide budgetary revenue.

The income tax rates for different groups of the Soviet population — as these rates existed in mid-1952 — are summarized below: [24]

Workers and employees hired by the state, including executives: A person having one job only has the first 260 rubles a month of his pay exempt from taxation; one having several jobs pays the graduated tax separately on the income from each job, rather than adding all his incomes together and getting into higher tax brackets, but the 260 ruble exemption applies only to income from his basic job, presumably the one giving him the highest income. The rate is

[23] Ibid., pp. 86–89.
[24] A. M. Aleksandrov, Finansy SSSR, pp. 330–32. Leningrad: Gosfinizdat, 1952. It may be noted that additional income tax is required from unmarried adults and married persons having fewer than three children. Those having no children must pay a penalty tax of 6 per cent of their income; those having only one child pay 1 per cent; those having only two children pay ½ per cent additional.

graduated from 1.5 per cent of all income up to 150 rubles monthly (this obviously applies only to those having at least one outside job beside their basic work) to 13 per cent of all income exceeding 1,000 rubles per month. Persons having over three dependents receive a 30 per cent deduction from the tax normally applying to income from their basic job.

Workers and employees hired by industrial cooperatives pay a tax on their income from the cooperatives (wages plus their share of any profit) at rates 10 per cent higher than those paid by state-employed persons.

Writers and artistic workers pay the same taxes as state-employed persons on their basic salaries if they work for the state. On any honoraria they receive above ordinary wages they pay rates varying from 1.5 per cent on income up to 1,800 rubles annually to 13 per cent on income in excess of 12,000 rubles annually. There is no portion of their income from honoraria which is exempt.

Individual artisans working for themselves pay rates varying from four per cent on income up to 1,800 rubles annually to 81 per cent on that portion of their income, if any, exceeding 70,000 rubles annually. These rates also apply to the incomes received by persons in private professional practice, such as doctors who treat patients at home in addition to working in government clinics. For this group the first 600 rubles of such private income annually is exempt from taxation.

The relatively low rates of income tax paid by most Soviet citizens, as described above, should not lead to the mistaken conclusion that Soviet citizens pay relatively little of their incomes as taxes to the government. Actually if account is taken of both direct and indirect taxes, particularly the turnover tax, it turns out that Soviet citizens normally pay about 60 per cent of their income in taxes, a rate more than twice as great as that paid by United States citizens in such nonwar years as 1940 and 1949. The discrepancy between the two countries reflects, of course, the much more important role of state activities in the Soviet Union than in the United States.[25]

The system of taxation for collective farms as organizational entities is complex, involving taxation on the farms' incomes both of produce and money. The state does not tax the following

[25] F. D. Holzman, "The Burden of Soviet Taxation," *American Economic Review,* September 1953, *passim.*

items: sums received for compulsory produce deliveries to the state, for which the low prices paid are in a real sense already a reflection of a heavy tax; the portions of a farm's produce delivered to the MTS in payment for its services; some types of farm expenditures, such as feed used for livestock. The items taxed and the rates are as follows: [26]

1. The portions of a farm's produce used for nonexempt production purposes, such as seed grain — 6 per cent of this produce's monetary value in terms of the low government requisition prices.

2. The farm's income from sales of produce to the government at the higher prices paid for produce sold under contract or sold in excess of the amounts of compulsory deliveries — 9 per cent.

3. The part of the farm's produce distributed among the collective farmers as return for their labor-day contributions is valued at prices double those the government pays for deliveries in excess of compulsory delivery norms, and is taxed at a 12 per cent rate.

4. Other collective farm money income, particularly income from sales in the free collective market where the highest prices are received, is taxed at a 15 per cent rate.

All farm products received by Machine Tractor Stations from collective farms in payment for their services are handed over to the Ministry of Requisitions and credited at the low requisition prices. Hence much of the state's net income from these deliveries also appears as part of the turnover tax credited to this ministry.

A major change in the system of income taxes levied on collective farmers and on the relatively small number of remaining individual peasant (uncollectivized) farmers was instituted in mid-1953. Until that time the primary purposes of these income taxes had been to discourage collective farmers from spending too much time on their private plots at the expense of work on the collective fields, and to punish monetarily those peasants who obdurately remained outside of the collectives. The system of taxation was a complex one, in which the government imputed arbitrarily the taxable income supposedly accruing to such farmers per unit of land in their private plots, the imputed income being valued at relatively high prices in terms of those prevailing during 1950 to 1953, though perhaps more reasonable in the earlier war and post-

[26] Aleksandrov, *op. cit.*, pp. 315–17.

war years. Individual peasants had been further hit by being required to pay taxes at rates twice those paid by collective farmers. In August 1953, however, one of the first conciliatory moves of the post-Stalin regime toward the farmers was to scrap this long-existing income tax system and to substitute a simpler, less heavy, and less discriminatory system. The new tax system levies the same rates on collective farmers' private plots and on individual peasants' farms. Instead of being arbitrarily imputed on the basis of what crops or livestock are grown, the new rates are based on a given number of rubles per one-hundredth of a hectare, the rates being different in different localities. Thus in the RSFSR the tax rates vary from 3 to 14 rubles per one-hundredth of a hectare, with the average rate 8.5 rubles. The highest rates are applied in the Georgian Republic, where they may reach 25 rubles per hundredth hectare — presumably in the subtropical regions producing citrus fruit — and on irrigated land in Central Asia, where the rate goes up to 20 or 22 rubles per hundredth hectare.

The Soviet Finance Minister has stated that this not only simplifies the taxation system, but reduces its burden. In its first full year of application, 1954, tax revenue from this source is expected to be only about 40 per cent of the revenue from this source in 1952. To help collective farmers who do not have their own cow each to get one, tax rates for such farmers were cut 50 per cent in 1953 and 30 per cent in 1954. Among those otherwise subject to the tax, men over 60 and women over 55 are relieved of this levy if there are no persons capable of work in their family. Relieved of the tax too are doctors, teachers, agronomists, and similar professional people in rural areas, as well as rural families which have one or more members employed in such specially important industries as coal and other mining, forestry, and the like. But the tax is intended also to help increase pressure for strict labor discipline on collective farms. Any collective farm family having a member who does not work at least the minimum required number of days on the collective fields has its income tax automatically increased by 50 per cent.[27]

Government Bonds

Since the early 1920's the Soviet government has annually ob-

[27] *Pravda*, August 6, 1953.

tained a significant amount of income by selling bonds to its people and to banks and other institutions.

Although an individual's decision to purchase state bonds is nominally voluntary, there is strong pressure exerted on workers to make them subscribe three to four weeks' earnings annually for this purpose. Bonds issued to the general public in the postwar period have been mainly lottery bonds. Thus, bonds issued in 1950 gave their holders the right to participate in annual lotteries, which pay out prizes totaling up to 25,000 rubles, the total amount of prizes each year being equal to 4 per cent of the value of the bond issue. Over the 20 years of the issue's term, 35 per cent of all bonds will win prizes and be redeemed by the state. The remaining 65 per cent of the bonds will be redeemed at face value, their owners getting no interest at all. Before all Soviet bonds sold to the general public were made lottery bonds, they were issued in conventional form, each bond-owner receiving the required interest. In the early 1920's short-term bonds received 5 per cent interest. Later loans issued to help finance the industrialization program paid a rate of 11 to 13 per cent. The great volume of governmental bonds issued during World War II carried a nominal 4 per cent interest rate, but the Monetary Reform of 1947 ordered these exchanged for bonds paying only 2 per cent, the old bonds being exchanged for new ones at the rate of 3 rubles' worth of old bonds for 1 of the new conversion issue.

In 1953, after Stalin's death, the Soviet government virtually admitted that its former claims that bond purchases were voluntary were false. The 1953 government bond issue, carrying a reduced 3 per cent interest charge as the basis for lottery prizes, was announced together with the statement that workers would not be allowed to subscribe more than two weeks wages. Thereafter Soviet propagandists counted among the monetary savings the new regime had brought the Soviet people the reduction in bond sales in 1953 as compared with 1952!

Bonds are also sold to banks and other Soviet institutions, thus permitting the government to include in its budget the free funds of financial and other enterprises active in the economy. In 1939, over a quarter of all revenue from state bond sales came from enterprises and banks.[28]

---

[28] Suchkov, op. cit., p. 178.

Besides the major sources of income discussed above, the Soviet budget has a number of other sources of revenue, including local taxes on buildings (dwellings and plants), nonagricultural land, livestock owned by urbanites, and the like. Since 1938 the payments made by Soviet enterprises to social insurance funds have been included in budgetary revenues. Money deposited in savings banks is counted as a state revenue on a par with income from bond sales. Customs duties accounted for 3 billion rubles of the government's income in 1940, or 1.7 per cent of all revenues.[29] A fuller exposition of these tariff duties will be given in a later chapter.

From the review of the Soviet tax structure given above, it seems clearly apparent that taxes are levied not only to provide needed revenue, but also to help accomplish political and social goals of far wider scope than mere fiscal objectives. Thus it may seem strange at first that most Soviet citizens in urban areas pay graduated income taxes the progression of which stops at 13 per cent. This is in sharp contrast with income tax rates in the United States and Great Britain, where progressive rates at times exceed 80 per cent on the largest incomes. It would seem to be paradoxical that the Soviet government treats very large incomes more kindly than do the governments of capitalist states. The reason however is simple. The Soviet government long ago realized that high income-tax rates reduce the incentives for individuals to earn high incomes. Since, in the main, high incomes in the Soviet Union are the result of important service to the state — by industrial executives, scientists, successful authors, and the like — the Soviet government seeks to make sure that these individuals have undiminished incentive to make the exertions necessary to earn these incomes.

Income Division Among State Budgets

The balance of incomes and expenditures in the Soviet budget is primarily a balance for the comprehensive total budget. The latter includes the budgets of the all-union government, the different republics, and provincial, city, and other local governmental units. Different taxes and other revenues are usually designated as going primarily to particular levels of government — the great bulk of revenues going to the all-union budget. To obtain balance in the sub-

[29] Ibid., p. 129.

ordinate budgets — where expenditures usually substantially exceed the revenues going to them directly — the all-union government allocates part of its revenue to them. If necessary, direct subsidies may be given subordinate governmental units by higher units, but effort is usually made to assure balance by preallocation of certain percentages of different types of income.

In general the all-union budget receives the revenues from profits of major industry, trade, means of transport, communications, banks, insurance organizations, and other such sources. It also receives the incomes of Machine Tractor Stations, customs dues, almost all fines levied for breaking the law, consular fees, proceeds of state bond issues, and the income of social insurance organizations. Republican budgets receive the profits from industrial and trade enterprises under republican control. Local budgets receive directly the profits tax on industrial and trade enterprises under local control, rents of houses controlled by local authorities, incomes of municipal public service enterprises (water supply, trolleys, sewage systems, and the like), and the specifically designated local taxes mentioned above.

All basic national taxes are considered parts of the all-union budget, but some minor ones, such as taxes on cooperative enterprises, go directly to republican or local budgets. Fixed percentages of the major all-union tax revenues, however, are allocated to republican and local budgets to help make up the deficit between their planned expenditures and the incomes directly assigned them. This practice has the additional virtue in the Soviet view of enlisting the self-interest and cooperation of local authorities in collecting these taxes. Thus rural governmental units receive part of the turnover tax collected as the result of the government requisitions and purchases of farm products in their areas. In the case of the tax on horses owned by individual peasants, 25 per cent is allocated to the budget of the republic in which it is collected and 75 per cent to the budget of the province or territory in which it is obtained. A law of December 21, 1931, provided that republican and local budgets receive part of the turnover tax collected as the result of processing of cotton, tobacco, oil, and other products grown or obtained in their areas. Part of the government revenue from the mining of precious metals and the production of alcoholic beverages is similarly transferred to local budgets.

The most important device for insuring the balancing of subordinate governmental budgets is the practice of assigning proportions of major national taxes or revenue items to different provincial, city, and other local budgets. The percentages of the revenues from different taxes collected in a given area and allocated to that area's budget vary sharply from region to region, depending upon the budgetary problem encountered in each case. The diversity of practice followed is indicated by the following schedule, which lists 1950 percentage allocations of different items of major revenue to the budgets of several regions:[30]

Tax	Altay Territory	Khabarovsk Territory	City of Moscow	Novosibirsk Province	Tuvinian Autonomous Province
Farm Income Tax	25	100	100	30	100
Urban Income Tax ...	70	30	10	100	100
Tax on Bachelors, Childless Couples, and Small Families..	80	10	10	80	—
Machine Tractor Station Incomes	25	100	—	35	100
Forestry Income	30	50	50	100	100
State Bond Subscriptions	60	40	10	90	100
Turnover Tax	12	2.5	2.4	17.5	36.9

The division of Soviet government budgetary revenues among different levels of government for the year 1941 is shown in Table 54.

About 60 per cent of the all-union budgetary revenues came from the turnover tax, with the profits tax providing somewhat over 10 per cent of the total. In the republican budgets, the profits tax provided almost half the revenue and the turnover tax about 20 per cent. About a quarter of all local budgetary revenues came from the turnover tax and about 20 per cent from the profits tax, with the most significant other revenues coming from the direct taxes on the population and on various enterprises and organizations.

Budgetary Expenditures

In peacetime, the largest single group of Soviet budget expendi-

---

[30] *Pravda*, July 9, 1950. Rovinsky, *Gosudarstvenny Byudzhet SSSR*, pp. 41–48.

TABLE 54. Revenues of Soviet Governmental Units' Budgets in 1941.

	All-Union Budget	Republican Budgets	Local Budgets	Total
	(BILLION RUBLES)			
Turnover Tax	113.3	2.9	8.6	124.8
Profit Tax	19.2	6.3	6.2	31.7
State Loans	9.5	0.9	2.9	13.3
Taxes on Population	7.4	—	5.1	12.5
Local Taxes and Revenues ...	—	—	2.5	2.5
Customs Duties	3.0	—	—	3.0
Taxes on Enterprises and Organizations	1.3	—	3.9	5.2
Social Insurance Payments ..	7.7	2.3	—	10.0
MTS Income	1.9	0.3	0.4	2.6
Forest Income	—	—	0.7	0.7
Rental Income on Property of Local Governments	—	—	0.8	0.8
Other Incomes	7.2	0.5	2.0	9.7
Funds Available on Jan. 1, 1941	4.8	0.2	0.5	5.5
Total	175.3	13.4	33.6	222.3

Source: Rovinsky. *Gosudarstvenny Byudzhet SSSR*, p. 48.

tures are those aimed at financing the national economy. These appropriations cover a large fraction of the cost of new capital investment in productive facilities (plants, railroads, machinery) and also provide additional working capital for the economy. New enterprises receive fixed capital from the state when they begin operation, so that they may work in accordance with the principles of *khozraschet* (economic accountability); existing plants may receive additional working capital from the state if they are expanding their activities; enterprises that are running at a deficit may receive budgetary grants as subsidies to make up their losses, particularly if their losses were provided for in their financial plans. The distribution of government expenditures for the national economy among different branches is indicated in Table 55.

Budgetary appropriations are by far the most important source of funds for capital investment. In 1948, for example, the total capital investment of the USSR amounted to 86.2 billion rubles, of which 57.2 billion rubles came from budgetary appropriations. The rest came from the profits, amortization reserves, and other resources of economic enterprises and institutions. The growth of working

TABLE 55. Budgetary Expenditures for Financing the National Economy in Selected Years.

	1938	1940	1942	1944	1946	1948	1950*	1953*
					(BILLION RUBLES)			
Total	51.7	58.3	31.6	53.7	106.2	147.5	164.4	192.5
Industry	23.6	28.6	†	27.3	68.8	94.1	85.3	82.6
Agriculture‡	11.4	12.2	5.1	7.0	12.3	20.5	36.6	39.9
Transport and Communications	7.4	6.8	†	7.7	10.0	14.3	15.0	†
Trade and Requisitions ...	†	2.0	†	1.2	3.2	4.1	9.3	†
Municipalities and Housing	2.9	2.5	†	1.8	†	4.4	†	†

* Plan.
† Not available.
‡ Includes forestry in 1948 and afterward.
Sources: Same as Table 52.

capital over recent years has been substantially the result of budgetary appropriations too. In 1940, such appropriations provided 49.3 per cent of the increase in enterprises' working capital; in 1947, 68.6 per cent of the increase; in 1948, 62.3 per cent; while in 1949 it was planned to provide 42.9 per cent of the growth from this source.

As we have seen earlier, capital investment during any period is provided for in the capital investment plan, which lists specific projects. The budgetary appropriations for capital investment parallel and are coordinated with this part of the over-all economic plan. All major investment projects — defined as those exceeding certain minimum amounts in terms of estimated cost, the minimum in each case depending upon the branch of the economy — must be approved by the Council of Ministers. Thus the Soviet government keeps tight rein upon economic expansion, through both the capital investment plan and the budget.[31]

It may be added that for many years a significant percentage of the appropriations for financing the national economy has been devoted to military purposes. The production of armaments of all types is carried on by economic ministries, such as the Ministry of Aviation Industry. The building of armaments plants and their pro-

[31] *Planovoye Khozyaistvo*, No. 2 (1949), pp. 42, 45; Rovinsky, *op. cit.*, pp. 71–72.

vision with working capital have presumably been financed by this portion of Soviet government expenditures and are not counted in the direct military budget of the USSR. The rapid development of nonmilitary heavy industry, accomplished mainly through budgetary appropriations, has also obviously been a major factor in increasing Soviet military strength, though less directly.

The second largest component of Soviet government expenditures during the postwar period has been the financing of the so-called social and cultural measures. The categories included in this component, and the changing size of their appropriations since before World War II, are shown in Table 56.

TABLE 56. Budgetary Appropriations for Social and Cultural Measures of the Soviet Government in Selected Years.

	1938	1940	1946	1948	1950*	1953*
			(BILLION RUBLES)			
Total	35.3	40.9	80.4	105.6	120.7	129.8
Education	18.7	22.5	38.1	55.1	59.5	62.1
Health†	7.6	9.0	13.8	19.9	21.9	24.8
Social Insurance ···	6.0	5.4	7.3	8.7	‡	
Aid to Widows and Mothers of Many Children	‡	1.2	3.6	2.5	4.0	42.9
Social Security	‡	2.9	17.6	18.4	22.4	

* Plan.
† Includes physical culture work.
‡ Data unavailable.
Source: Same as Table 52.

The magnitude and composition of the items coming under the category of social and cultural measures reflect the tremendous social service functions of the Soviet state. Care must be taken in interpreting this portion of the budget, however, since not all categories are adequately described. The item labeled education is a case in point. This includes not only expenditures for schools of all types but also the cost of political propaganda, military academies, scientific research institutes, museums, expositions, all newspaper and book publishing, theatres, orchestras, and so on.[32] The health appropriation pays not only for medical personnel, hospitals, and the like, but also for the maintenance of some kindergartens, chil-

---

[32] Rovinsky, op. cit., p. 206.

dren's homes, and the like.[33] Social insurance expenditures provide for payments to persons unable to work because of illness, accident, or related cause; for funeral expenses; for pensions to permanently incapacitated or retired elderly workers; for maintenance of sanatoria, rest homes, parks, and so on. Social security expenditures are primarily those made to or for persons invalided during war or in military service. This explains the sharp rise in the appropriations for this purpose between 1940 and 1946. Other individuals, including victims of accidents or persons making outstanding contributions to the Soviet state in some capacity, for example, also may receive aid from social security funds. Invalids, if totally disabled, receive pensions; or they may be put into special homes for invalids. If possible, however, they are retrained so as to permit them to work and to earn a living despite their war injuries or other handicaps.[34]

The organizations engaged in the activities financed by the social-cultural appropriations of the budget are entirely controlled by the over-all economic plan and the financial plan, including the budget itself. The economic plan allocates to them personnel and other required resources, while the budget allocates the funds to pay for these resources. The institutions — hospitals, schools, rest homes, and the like — submit estimates of their requirements to higher authorities. The latter in turn make such changes as they deem desirable and finally approve the budgets and programs for each future period. All incomes received by such institutions — tuition fees in schools, for example — are turned over directly to the government; the institutions do not have the right to use their incomes for their own needs. This method of operation is aimed at assuring complete government control of their activities. Institutional budgets are set up on the basis of norms. Thus a hospital will be entitled to a quota of doctors and a particular allowance for wages and other expenses depending upon the number of beds it has, the average number of days a bed is occupied, and the location of the hospital.[35]

Little has been published on the detailed composition of the military section of the Soviet budget. The available evidence indicates that it covers only the direct costs of the land, sea, and air forces of the Soviet Union. The military organizations presumably pur-

---

33 *Ibid.*, p. 223.
34 *Ibid.*, pp. 230–40.
35 *Ibid.*, Chapter 14 and pp. 223–25.

chase their requirements of food, arms, and the like from other government organizations. Presumably, also, there is no turnover tax levied upon munitions and arms purchased by the armed forces. The buying power of the ruble used for such purchases reflects primarily the actual cost of production and hence is relatively greater in real terms than rubles used by ordinary customers to buy food, clothing, and the like. The relative value of military appropriations in real terms is therefore also higher than the proportion these appropriations are of total budgetary expenditures. Members of the armed forces are also paid wages in addition to receiving food, clothing, and equipment, as are military personnel of other nations.

The distribution of government expenditures among the different levels of government reflects the different functions assigned them. The all-union budget provides for the financing of most of the national economy and military expenditures. The republican budgets finance only those parts of the economy subordinate to them and are occupied much more with executing the social and cultural aspects of the budget. Local governments are primarily concerned with social and cultural measures. Thus in 1941 the all-union budget provided over 96 per cent of all budgetary funds for industry and transport, but only about one third for education and under 10 per cent for health services. Local budgets on the other hand provided over 96 per cent of all expenditures on municipal construction and housing, almost 55 per cent of all education expenditures, and almost 80 per cent of all health service spending.[36]

The Banking System

Financial transactions among enterprises, institutions, and other organizations in the USSR are conducted through the aid of a complex banking system. The central institution of the Soviet banking system is the State Bank *(Gosbank)*, an organization with about 5,500 offices all over the USSR and millions of clients. In addition there are four specialized banks occupied primarily with the problems of long-term investment. These are the Industrial Bank (*Prombank*), the Agricultural Bank (*Selkhozbank*), the Trade Bank (*Torgbank*), and the Municipal Bank (*Tsekombank*). There is also a national network of savings banks, in which individuals may keep their

---

[36] *Ibid.,* pp. 34–35.

own savings.[37] In addition there is the Bank for Foreign Trade (*Vneshtorgbank*), which plays a role in the Soviet government's foreign trade and credit transactions.

The State Bank is the basic source of short-term credit for all enterprises and institutions in the USSR, extending this credit in accordance with the credit plan for each part of the economy as approved by the Council of Ministers. All transactions between government enterprises and institutions requiring the transfer of money go through the State Bank's books by means of credits for sellers and debits for purchasers. The State Bank acts as the government's fiscal agent, receiving all taxes and other payments to the state and paying out budgetary appropriations to enterprises and institutions within the limits provided by the budget. The State Bank issues money and withdraws it from circulation, thus regulating the volume of currency available to individuals and organizations at any time in accordance with the Cash Plans approved by the Council of Ministers. All supplies of precious metals and foreign currencies owned by the Soviet government are entrusted to the care of the State Bank, which also handles settlements with foreigners through its accounts with correspondent banks abroad.

The Credit Reform of 1930 and subsequent legislation concentrated virtually all short-term credit operations in the State Bank by prohibiting the granting of credit by one enterprise to another, and by eliminating other banks — with minor exceptions — from the short-term credit field. The volume of credit rose rapidly during the 1930's, loans granted rising from 140,000,000,000 rubles in 1934 to 475,000,000,000 rubles in 1938. The volume of indebtedness of economic organizations to the State Bank grew from 3,800,000,000 rubles on January 1, 1930, to over 40,000,000,000 rubles on January 1, 1941.[38] Initially, short-term credit was conceived of as primarily important for the financing of seasonal peaks of operation in industry, trade, and other branches of the economy. It aimed at providing the funds needed to accumulate seasonal reserves of raw materials and other goods, to pay production expenses at times of maximum operation, and to bridge the time gap between shipment of goods and receipts of payment. In the late 1930's, however, the

---

[37] Boguslavsky, Greben, and Proselkov, *op. cit.*, p. 16; and *Pravda*, May 18, 1949.

[38] *Entsiklopediya*, col. 1058.

relatively nonseasonal heavy industries, such as machine construction, were brought into the orbit of the State Bank's operations by requiring them to finance a substantial portion of their current operations through credit from this source. State Bank credit is of major importance to trading organizations. As of early 1949, 70 per cent of all trading organizations' purchases were financed through the State Bank.[39] In general the Soviet government attempts to set the working capital granted economic enterprises free of charge at the minimum level possible, and to require these enterprises to meet their working capital needs in excess of this minimum by resort to the State Bank's credit facilities. This policy is motivated by the desire to make the area of the State Bank's control activities as wide as possible.[40]

Loans granted by the State Bank to enterprises are usually for specific purposes and for fixed periods; must be repaid; carry interest charges; and are within the maximum limit set by the enterprise's credit plan. Loans may be granted outside the enterprise's credit plan in case of unexpected emergency or other unanticipated situation, where such credit will aid accomplishment of the state's goals or their overfulfillment. Since the enterprise receiving the loan is paid by means of transfers to its State Bank account, the bank is able to receive payment at the time the purpose for which the loan was granted is accomplished and the resulting goods are sold. In this process the State Bank is required to keep a sharp eye on the actual operations of the plant, making sure that it is observing its physical production and financial plans and is using any credits granted it for the specific purpose intended. This "control by the ruble" makes the State Bank an overseer of the entire Soviet economy in all its ramifications and operations. Bank officials are praised if they fulfill their control functions properly and show initiative in aiding enterprises to improve their work and speed up their utilization of working capital and credit.[41] Enterprises that fail to fulfill their obligations to the State Bank punctually and properly may have sanctions applied to them, that is, they may be denied further credit; the commodities put up as security for loans may be sold by the bank; and so on. Enterprises estab-

[39] *Pravda*, May 18, 1949.
[40] *Planovoye Khozyaistvo*, No. 3 (1946), p. 52.
[41] *Pravda*, May 18, 1949.

lishing a good credit record may be rewarded by being granted additional credits at favorable terms to help them overfulfill their production or other plan.[42]

The total volume of credit the State Bank issues is determined by the Credit Plan approved by the Council of Ministers quarterly and covering the entire economy. The resources upon which the Bank draws in issuing credits are the following: the Bank has its own reserves, including its original charter capital, its accumulated reserves from profits, and other special funds; all the funds deposited in the Bank by the enterprises and institutions required to have accounts in it are also available as a base for credit operations; finally, as the currency-issuing authority of the country, the State Bank can increase its resources by printing additional money. Of these main sources, the chief is usually the total of deposits entrusted to it. The Bank's freedom to print money to increase its resources is checked by the fact that it is governed by the government's Cash Plan, which is worked out in concordance with the over-all Credit Plan. The State Bank can therefore never independently cause inflation by excess credits or currency issuance; it is purely a tool of higher authorities, limited to executing their instructions.[43]

From the point of view of Soviet enterprises, the activity of the State Bank as a financial transfer agent is most important, since all payments from buyers to sellers are effectuated by the Bank's bookkeepers upon receipt of orders from the appropriate authority, usually the seller's acceptance of his purchase. Because one bank does the whole job, there is no need for interbank clearing houses such as exist in the United States and other countries. The magnitude of the State Bank's operations, however, has led it to organize Mutual Clearing Bureaus in key areas of the country. These Mutual Clearing Bureaus arrange for settlement of accounts between concerns having frequent transactions with each other so that the volume of work involved can be reduced considerably. Each enterprise belonging to the Mutual Clearing Bureau has a clearing account in which are entered all its debits and credits. At the end of each period an enterprise receives the net credit or net debit to which

---

[42] *Finansy SSSR za XXX Let,* p. 128.

[43] V. M. Batyrev and V. K. Sitnin, *Finansovaya i Kreditnaya Sistema SSSR,* pp. 64–65. Moscow: 1945.

TABLE 57. Distribution of Short-Term Credits in the USSR, 1933, 1938, and 1941.

	Jan. 1, 1933	Jan. 1, 1938	Jan. 1, 1941
		(BILLION RUBLES)	
Heavy Industry	.9	4.7	10.0
Light and Textile Industries . .	.7	6.6	9.1
Food Industry	1.7	8.5	10.7
Requisitions Commissariat . . .	1.6	2.8	3.3
Lumber Industry	.5	1.3	2.5
Transport	.4	1.4	1.5
Agriculture	1.4	1.7	2.2
Trade	2.3	10.7	11.1
Foreign Trade	.3	.4	.9
Local Industry and Industrial Cooperatives	.5	.8	1.4
Other	.2	1.8	2.3
Total	10.5	40.7	55.0

Source: *Finansy SSSR za XXX Let*, p. 127.

it is entitled, the great bulk of the money value of its transactions having been canceled by the comparison of credits and debits. Although this system resembles somewhat the check-clearing organizations of the American banking world, it should be noted that checks — that is, negotiable paper instruments — are comparatively little used in the USSR. Accounts between enterprises are instead usually paid for by so-called giro-orders, which direct payment to only one recipient and cannot be transferred by endorsement, as checks can.[44] Aside from the reduction of labor, this system also reduces the amount of currency required in the economy while permitting strict control over all payments to, and payments by, economic organizations. The use of currency in the Soviet economy is thus confined largely to the payment of wages (including collective farmers' money receipts as shares of the farm's money income) and the consequent use of these money wages by the population for purchases of goods and services.

Savings Banks

The Soviet government encourages its people to save money for future needs. For this purpose there exists a wide network of State

[44] G. A. Shvarts, *Beznalichnyye Vzaimnyye Raschety v SSSR, passim*. Moscow: 1946.

Labor Savings Banks throughout the country. These had over 47,000 branches at the beginning of 1951. The motivation for personal saving is probably less strong, however, in the Soviet Union than in capitalist countries. A Soviet citizen has little fear of unemployment and has at least a minimal security arising from the widespread system of government pensions and aids for those who become disabled or too old to work. At the time of the German invasion of the USSR, total deposits in these banks totaled about 6,800,000,000 rubles. The volume of deposits grew rapidly during and immediately after the war, in part because of increased incomes during this period of great shortages of things to buy. Also, during the war, the Soviet government prohibited vacations and ordered, instead, that monetary compensation be deposited in blocked accounts in the savings banks. Over 30,000,000 such accounts were opened, but the money in them was not released until after the conflict. At the beginning of 1946 total deposits in savings banks were 9,000,000,000 rubles; by the middle of 1947 they exceeded 13,000,000,000 rubles. Presumably the total value of deposits fell below this level as the result of the conversion from old to new money — at rates of 1:1, 3:2, and 2:1, depending upon the size of the account — at the end of 1947. Whatever the magnitude of this reduction, it was soon made up. At the end of 1953 the total deposits in savings banks exceeded 38,500,000,000 rubles.[45]

In the late 1930's the interest paid on deposits of individual citizens, with the right of withdrawal at any time, was established at 3 per cent annually, while similar deposits of organizations received 1 per cent interest. In 1939 a system of time deposits was established, paying 5 per cent interest on savings left for six months or longer. For most depositors the interest on such savings is an insignificant source of income, since the great majority of accounts are extremely small. A sample study conducted on January 1, 1938, found the following distribution of these accounts: [46]

Size of Account	Per Cent of Depositors	Per Cent of Savings
Under 100 rubles	67	5
100–1,000 rubles	23	28
Over 1,000 rubles	10	67

[45] *Finansy SSSR za XXX Let,* pp. 307–14; *Pravda,* April 22, 1954. Soviet Home Service, April 20, 1951.

[46] Batyrev and Sitnin, *op. cit.,* p. 75.

The fact that 10 per cent of all savings depositors owned two thirds of the value of all deposits is an interesting commentary on the inequality of wealth in the USSR. During the war the average size of accounts probably increased, along with the over-all increase in the volume of savings in these banks. One indication of this probability is the fact that only 80 per cent of the accounts remained unchanged at the time of the monetary conversion in late 1947; [47] since accounts up to 3,000 rubles remained unchanged, this indicates that 80 per cent of all depositors must have been in this category, a substantially smaller percentage than that indicated by the data for January 1, 1938. During the war, savings bank deposits were solicited, with interest to be paid in the form of lottery prizes ranging from 50 to 200 per cent of the winners' total deposits. This lure apparently did not prove attractive; most depositors preferred to receive a straight interest return rather than accept a chance in a lottery.[48] In early 1951 there was indication that the system of lottery prizes for holders of savings deposits still existed or had been re-established. In that year drawings were scheduled for April and October, 25 winners to be chosen out of each 1,000 accounts. One winner got 200 per cent, two winners received 100 per cent, and 22 winners received 50 per cent of their average savings account balance for the previous half year.[49]

The functions of savings banks were expanded during World War II so as to make them agents for collecting taxes due the government from individuals. They also pay out pensions and government monetary awards to winners of medals and other honors. As noted earlier, the assets of the savings banks — consisting chiefly of the deposits made in them — are invested in government bonds, and the annual increases in these assets are treated as additions to the state's budgetary revenue, on a par with money received from the sale of bonds.

Investment Banks

The four major long-term investment banks are essentially concerned with making available to different economic organizations funds for capital construction. The great majority of these funds

[47] *Pravda*, February 1, 1948.
[48] *Finansy SSSR za XXX Let*, p. 310.
[49] *Sovkhoznoye Gazeta*, March 10, 1951.

are allocated to the banks by the government through the budget and are nonreturnable grants, not loans. The investment banks also have available obligatory amortization allowances accumulated by economic organizations, funds from the profits tax, and the capital funds of collective farms. Strict control over the execution, progress, quality, and financial discipline of construction projects is exercised by these banks. This control is usually far more detailed and closer even than that exercised by the State Bank over recipients of short-term loans.

The Industrial Bank (Prombank) — known more fully as the Bank for Financing Industrial and Transport Capital Construction — makes available government construction grants to industrial, transport, communications, and road-building organizations under different economic ministries. It also makes long-term credits available to local and provincial industrial enterprises to help them organize or expand output of consumer goods, food manufactures, construction materials, and fuel.

The Municipal Bank (Tsekombank) — known more fully as the All-Union Bank for Financing Municipal and Housing Construction — works with local municipal governments, giving them credits or nonreturnable grants for housing, public utility, and related construction. It also finances the building of entire new communities. In recent years this bank has also granted long-term credits to individuals to enable them to build or repair homes, as well as loans to demobilized soldiers, war invalids, families of dead soldiers, and needy families of persons serving in the armed forces. It cooperates with a system of local municipal banks.

The Trade Bank (Torgbank) — known more fully as the Bank for Financing Capital Construction of Trade and Cooperatives — provides funds for capital investment by cooperatives as well as by domestic and foreign trade enterprises and organizations of the Ministry of Requisitions. Cooperatives must repay credits from this bank, but government organizations receive nonreturnable grants, as in other areas of the economy.

The Agricultural Bank (Selkhozbank) gives long-term credits to collective farms for construction, repair of buildings, purchase of equipment or cattle, irrigation works, and so on. It also makes short-term loans of less than a year's duration to the collective farms for some capital expenditures. Long-term loans are made by this bank to collective farmers and to other individual borrowers, particularly invalids of the last war and families of soldiers. Government agricultural organizations, such as state farms, are also financed by this bank.

These banks can only finance construction projects that have been specifically authorized by the government, and usually, also, only those for which complete cost estimates and architectural plans have been prepared. Financing is provided only within the limits of the estimated cost for different types of work. The banks may refuse to provide funds if costs exceed estimates, or if they observe wasteful utilization of funds and resources made available for construction. The banks keep close check on the progress of each construction project, analyze the balance and other accounting records of each project, and inform responsible organs of economic control if they find any abnormality in the financial or economic situation of a project. To facilitate control over the cost and progress of construction work, such activity is usually not carried on by the enterprise that is finally to operate the new plant, mine, or other productive facility being built. Special construction organizations subordinate to construction agencies receive contracts to carry on the work and are supervised by the banks. Where an enterprise does carry on its own construction activity, all funds available for and expenditures required by this construction work are kept in separate accounts and are not intermingled with the financial record of the enterprise's normal activity, thus also facilitating direct control over the construction work.

The funds assigned to a given project are placed in an account maintained by the enterprise for whom the new facility is being built. This enterprise transfers to the contracting construction organization at the beginning of the work 15 per cent of the estimated amount to be spent that year on the project. Further financing of the contractor is made as each section of work is completed, payment being based on the estimated cost agreed on initially. The banks keep constant checks over the correctness of the prices paid and the accuracy of reports regarding the volume of work actually completed. One result of this system is that if the cost of construction exceeds that originally estimated, the additional cost must be paid out of the contracting organization's funds and not from the allocation given the enterprise to finance the project. This requirement is obviously aimed at stimulating the contractor's interest in doing the most economical job most expeditiously. Short-term credits may be granted construction organizations by the investment banks in order to help them make a seasonal accumulation of materials, fuel, and other resources. The expenditure of these short-term credits is also very closely controlled.[50]

Insurance

Insurance is a government monopoly in the Soviet Union. In part the Soviet government is the world's greatest self-insuring organization since its accumulation of reserves of food and other commodities is an effort to guarantee the country as a whole against the risks of drought, war, or other catastrophe. More conventional types of life and property insurance, similar to those existing in capitalist countries, are administered by the Chief Administration for State Insurance (*Gosstrakh*), which is a branch of the Ministry of Finance and has agents and agencies throughout the country.

By law some types of insurance are compulsory. These cover primarily the vast supply of housing owned by the state's agencies, as well as buildings, crops, and livestock owned by collective farms, collective farmers, and individuals. Voluntary insurance may be obtained by state organizations or enterprises and by private individuals on farm products, animals, household effects, means of transport, freight, and the like. Property insurance can be obtained covering risks such as fire, floods, explosions, storms, drought (in the case of some crops only), transportation accidents, and so forth. Life insurance is in general voluntary, except in some special cases, such as compulsory insurance for firemen. Life insurance can be bought — depending upon age and after a medical examination — on a term basis for a specific period of years or as insurance which terminates only with the insured person's death. Insurance against invalidism is also covered in the same way as life insurance.[51]

No over-all figures on the size of the Soviet Union's insurance

---

[50] Boguslavsky, Greben, and Proselkov, *op. cit.*, pp. 334–37. Batyrev and Sitnin, *op. cit.*, pp. 77–85. For discussions of the most recent trends in Soviet credit organization and practice cf. R. F. D. Hutchings, "Investment Regulations," *Soviet Studies*, October 1952, and R. W. Davies, "Short-Term Credit in the USSR," *Ibid.*, July 1953.

[51] Aleksandrov, *Finansy SSSR*, pp. 365–88.

operations seem to have been published in recent years. That they are large is indicated by statements that hundreds of millions of rubles annually are paid out to beneficiaries upon damage of their property or the death of insured persons. Hundreds of millions of rubles are also said to be used for such preventive measures as building fire depots, veterinary installations, and the like, the money coming from insurance funds.[52]

[52] M. Shermenev, "Strakhovye Fondy Sotsialisticheskogo Gosudarstva," *Finansy i Kredit SSSR*, June 1953, pp. 31–32.

CHAPTER XIII

HIRED AND PRISON LABOR[1]

ARTICLE 12 of the Soviet Constitution declares: "Work in the USSR is a duty and a matter of honor for every able-bodied citizen, in accordance with the principle: 'He who does not work, neither shall he eat.'" In theory this article is taken to mean that every physically able adult must engage in direct productive activity, unless supported by the earnings of a relative, as in the case of a wife maintained by her husband.

Workers in the USSR today fall into one of the following categories: members of collective farms, hired employees of the government, employees of industrial and consumer cooperatives, individual artisans who work alone, household servants — maids, cooks, chauffeurs, gardeners, and the like — employed by individuals, and involuntary laborers forced to work at particular jobs in the course of serving a penal sentence. The employment of workers for the profit of an individual employer is now forbidden, though it existed on a significant scale during the 1920's. Collective farmers have already been discussed in an earlier chapter. The number of household servants and individual artisans in the USSR is relatively very small, and almost no information is available about them as groups. Soviet labor statistics combine in one category those working for the state and those working for industrial or consumer cooperatives, so that we may think of these as forming the total hired labor group. Although the members of this last group work under

---

[1] Many of the topics treated in this chapter are discussed at greater length in Solomon Schwarz, *Labor in the Soviet Union*. New York: Praeger, 1952.

516

a number of severe restrictions on their liberty, they are also sometimes referred to as "free" workers in contradistinction to the unfree or forced laborers in the final category listed above. Most of this chapter will be concerned with the relatively free persons composing the hired labor group. The remainder will summarize the incomplete information available concerning prison labor.

The Supply of Hired Labor

During 1917–20 food shortages and economic disorganization in the cities forced a large-scale migration to the countryside. This, combined with the need for soldiers to fight the enemies of the Soviet regime, created a severe shortage of workers for industry, transport, and trade, a shortage that was combatted by the militarization of labor. Workers were mobilized and labor armies were put to work on urgent tasks of production and transportation under conditions of strict military discipline. With the relaxation and abolition of many government controls during the years of the New Economic Policy, labor conscription was abandoned. Demobilization of the armed forces and new migration from the rural areas to non-agricultural occupations provided the increased manpower required to raise the level of economic activity from the very low depth of 1920 back to and beyond that achieved before World War I. The number of workers in large industry had fallen from 2,885,000 in 1913 to 1,601,700 on January 1, 1922, the latter figure representing already some recovery from the lowest point. By 1929 there were 3,353,000 workers in these industries, over twice the number in 1922. Similarly construction workers increased from 194,000 in 1923–24 to 923,000 in 1929. Other urban areas of the economy experienced similar rises. In 1928 about 8,700,000 persons were employed in nonagricultural occupations of all kinds, exclusive of domestic servants. Of these about 7,400,000 worked for the government, almost 1,100,000 for cooperatives, and 349,000 for private employers. By 1930, the number privately employed was only 51,000 and became virtually zero soon thereafter.[2]

The First Five-Year Plan began in 1928 and inaugurated a period of unprecedentedly rapid economic development. Tremendous numbers of new workers were needed to build and man the new

---

[2] *Narodnoye Khozyaistvo SSSR*, pp. 410–13.

factories, mines, oil fields, railroad lines, and other productive enterprises, as well as to provide the administrative and other services required by the increasingly complex and growing economy. The growth that took place may be illustrated by Soviet data on the number of workers and employees in the national economy, that is, government employees predominantly,[3] plus those working in cooperatives. The average annual number of workers and employees in the national economy grew from 11,539,000 in 1928 to 23,681,200 in 1934 and 31,500,000 at the end of 1940.[4] Part of the 1940 figure is attributable to hired workers in the newly annexed territories of the USSR, the Baltic States, Eastern Poland, and other areas. Allowing for these, it is clear that the number of hired workers in the USSR increased by approximately 18,000,000 persons in little more than a decade, a rise of roughly 150 per cent. If we take into account the new workers who replaced the losses due to death and retirement, it seems likely that almost three out of every four hired workers in the USSR in 1940 had assumed that status after 1928.

Most of these new workers came from agriculture, the area of the economy where an excess supply of labor had been chronic and where birth rates were highest. The basic overpopulation of most rural areas had been intensified by the collectivization of many small farms to form a relatively small number of large farms and by the increasing mechanization of crop production, though the exact number of workers freed by these measures is difficult to measure. When abundant new employment opportunities opened outside of agriculture, many farm people flocked spontaneously to fill the new jobs, hoping thus to improve their standards of living. Others were recruited by the numerous agents sent into the countryside by enterprises needing labor to negotiate labor recruitment contracts with collective farms. The competition for surplus farm labor grew so intense that the central government had to intervene in 1938 and reserve particular areas exclusively for recruitment by particular industries.[5]

According to the Soviet government, unemployment in the USSR

[3] Government employees include not only those in industry, transport, trade, finance, and other nonagricultural work, but also those working on state farms and at Machine Tractor Stations.

[4] *Sot. Stroi.*, pp. 508–9; Voznesensky, *The Economy of the USSR during World War II*, p. 7.

[5] Baykov, *The Development of the Soviet Economic System*, p. 354.

disappeared at the beginning of the 1930's. In the latter half of the 1920's, about a million workers were usually registered on the rolls of the government labor exchanges as seeking work, the number in April 1929 being as high as 1,741,000, or almost 10 per cent of the total number reported employed in the national economy that year. These figures understate the actual number of unemployed at that time, since they do not include many young people looking for their first job. But as work on the First Five-Year Plan progressed, the earlier labor surplus was converted into a labor shortage. When the scarcity of workers became acute in 1930, the government decided it would cease supporting with unemployment insurance those who chose not to accept jobs offered them. Accordingly on October 11, 1930, the People's Commissar of Labor announced the end of unemployment insurance payments and ordered that all those registered as unemployed be compelled to accept any job offered them. Henceforth the only acceptable excuse for not working was to be sickness, which had to be proved by a medical certificate. The same month the labor exchanges were directed to register all workers without jobs, and all wives and older children in urban communities, even if they had no special training and had not worked before. All those registered were to be offered employment. If they refused, they were removed from the rolls and forbidden to accept a job for a fixed period. Thus administrative pressure was applied to force women and youngsters who did not want to go to work to become hired laborers.[6] One result of these and later measures was that the number of women workers and employees in the USSR increased from 3,900,000 in 1930 to over 11,000,000 in 1940, including many housewives who would probably not have worked if it had not been for government pressure.[7] These constituted over one third of the total hired labor force, and 41 per cent of all production workers in industry, in the latter year. The increasing disparity between wages and prices during much of the 1930's also provided a potent stimulus for women to add to family income by taking jobs outside the home.

Since the early 1930's the Soviet government has claimed that there is no unemployment in the USSR. This claim has been a valuable propaganda weapon, although it is largely a matter of

---

[6] *Ibid.*, pp. 212–13.

[7] *Entsiklopediya,* col. 1125.

definition whether the claim is to be accepted or rejected. All through the 1930's, for example, the Soviet press complained bitterly about the high rate of labor turnover in industry and transport. Millions of workers changed jobs annually. In the United States such workers would be recorded as unemployed in the period between leaving one employment and entering another and would appear in the statistics of unemployment. In the USSR this "frictional" unemployment was ignored. The Soviet claim, in short, is based upon a very narrow definition of unemployment, accompanied by the abolition of all statistics on the subject.

This criticism, however, should not blind us to the true state of affairs in the Soviet labor market since the early 1930's. Since that time there has usually been an over-all shortage of labor as the result of the steady production increase, which was interrupted only by the German invasion. Probably throughout the past two decades any Soviet citizen who wished a job could find one, though it might not be the job he really wanted and it might be in another community than that in which he lived. These conditions were approximated in the United States during World War II, when unemployment, including the "frictionally" unemployed discussed above, fell below the 1,000,000 mark. The Soviet Union has probably had what might perhaps be called "over-full" employment since the early 1930's, in the sense that many hired workers would have preferred not to work at all or to work only part-time and would have willingly accepted the corresponding income reductions if they had been permitted to do so. All this has been the result of the monopolistic government control of the Soviet economy, which has permitted steady development to take place unhindered by fluctuating consumer demand and other factors producing capitalist business cycles.

But whether it is termed "full employment" or "over-full employment," it is clear that for two decades Soviet hired workers have been free of the insecurity that rises from fear of prolonged involuntary unemployment, though they have been plagued by many other insecurities and fears. This state of affairs has had important repercussions on the labor market, on the stability of employment, and on labor discipline. In particular the Soviet worker's confidence that he can find a job relatively easily if he loses his present one has created attitudes toward work that the Soviet government has characterized as "irresponsible" and against which it has turned the force of penal regulations. These replace in part the pressures exerted in a capitalistic society by the fear of unemployment.

The expansion of the labor force did not occur uniformly in all fields, since growth of output and worker requirements was uneven among the different branches of the economy. This unequal development is shown by the data on the distribution of the hired labor force shown in Table 58.

TABLE 58. Workers and Employees in Principal Branches of the Soviet Economy, 1928, 1932, 1937, and Goal for 1941.

Branch	1929	1932	1937	1941 Goal
		(MILLIONS)		
Industry	3.1	8.0	10.1	11.1
Construction	.7	2.8	2.0	3.1
Railways	1.0	1.3	1.5	1.7
Waterways	.1	.15	.18	.21
Other Transport	.2	.6	1.1	*
Communications	.1	.22	.38	.46
Trade	.5	1.4	2.0	2.4
Communal Feeding	.06	.5	.4	.7
Education	.8	1.4	2.3	2.9
Health Services	.4	.6	1.1	1.6
State, Administrative, and Other Institutions†	1.2	2.2	2.5	*
Banking Institutions	.1	.13	.19	.28
Agricultural Institutions‡	1.7	2.9	2.5	2.1

* Data unavailable.
† Includes housing and municipal services after 1928.
‡ Employees of state farms, Machine Tractor Stations, etc. In 1928 included almost 1.3 million workers employed by private farms.
Sources: 1928—Sot. Stroi., p. 508; 1932 and 1937—Sot. Stroi. (1933–38), p. 138; 1941—Gosudarstvenny Plan . . . na 1941 God, p. 512.

In expanding its labor force during 1928–40, the Soviet regime had to contend with the problem of quality as well as quantity. The great majority of new workers recruited for nonagricultural employment during these years had never had any previous experience or familiarity with machines and their operation. They were not accustomed to the discipline required in a factory or on a railroad. At a higher level of competence, the newly expanded productive system required far larger numbers of engineers, chemists, metallurgists, accountants, executives, and other directing personnel than had ever been required in the Soviet Union before. Thus at all levels of the labor force an immense training program had to be undertaken. The primary education system was widely extended as well, in an effort to provide that basic literacy essential for almost all workers in an industrial society. In the decade between 1928–29 and 1938–39, the number of students in the Soviet primary and secondary schools of all kinds increased 2½ times, from 12.1 million to 31.5 million. The number of Soviet citizens studying in schools of all types, including extension-course students, reached 47.4 million in 1938–39, probably close to half the entire population if we exclude the aged and preschool children.[8]

Some notion of the rapid increase in the number of technically trained workers may be obtained by considering the growing enrollment of major types of schools during the First and Second Five-Year Plans. Thus the number of students in institutions of higher education grew from about 160,000 in 1928 to 516,000 at the beginning of 1936. Enrollment in secondary schools training technicians rose from 254,000 in 1928 to 754,000 at the beginning of 1932 and declined slightly thereafter. Enrollments in factory schools training skilled workers of all types increased from 178,000 students in 1928 to a peak of 975,000 in 1932, but fell sharply thereafter.[9] The frenzied educational drive of the 1930's, accompanied by the enormous increase in students and graduates, was quite naturally accompanied by an appreciable decline in the quality of training. University courses were cut to three years; some requirements were abolished; the supply of teachers competent to teach could not be expanded rapidly enough to cope with the influx; training became too specialized in many cases; all these factors contributed to the decline in quality.[10] Under these conditions many skilled workers, technicians, and directing personnel had to finish their education on the job, a costly process. In the late 1930's changes were made aimed at improving the quality of the educational system. Out of the confusion and frenzy of this period were born both the new labor force and the new technical-managerial force of the Soviet economy, both of which have been developed greatly since the early years of the 1930's. Without the millions of specialists graduated by secondary schools and higher educational institutions, realization of Soviet industrialization would have been impossible.

[8] *Sot. Stroi. (1933–38)*, p. 116.
[9] *Sot. Stroi.*, p. 572.
[10] Baykov, *op. cit.*, pp. 218-19.

Labor Discipline Problems

Another major facet of Soviet labor force development during the 1930's was the high rate of turnover and the frequently low discipline of the new army of workers. In the atmosphere of ever increasing labor demand and accompanying shortage, workers had little fear of unemployment and often shifted from job to job, their shifting usually being prompted by the hope of improving working and living conditions, both of which were frequently extremely poor. At the extreme, in 1930, all branches of large-scale industry hired during the year 176 per cent of the average number of workers employed in these branches, while 152 per cent of this average left their jobs during the year. Even in 1935, when a much greater degree of stability had been achieved, hirings were 91.6 per cent of the labor force, and workers leaving their jobs composed 86.1 per cent of the total. In 1932 the average worker in large-scale industry was absent from work almost six days without an acceptable reason. The high labor turnover and frequent truancy of workers raised major difficulties in the way of the smooth operation of production and slowed down considerably development of a trained work force.[11] Many workers left before they had even been trained for new jobs, and others left after having gained some experience, both groups disrupting the proper working of their enterprises.

To combat these destructive tendencies the Soviet government used many techniques, imposing increasingly tighter control upon workers and entrepreneurs in an effort to achieve stability, discipline, and faithful performance of duties. As early as 1930, an enterprise manager guilty of luring workers from other enterprises was liable to prosecution. Workers who evaded transfer to work ordered by the government or who changed jobs frequently were denied the right to be referred to industrial jobs for six months. Beginning in May 1930, engineers and technicians getting over 250 rubles a month could not get salary increases in most cases if they moved to another enterprise without getting the permission of their former employer. This move was obviously aimed at preventing "pirating" of badly needed trained workers by competing

[11] *Sot. Stroi.,* pp. 530–31.

plants. Before the end of 1932, plant managers were given the right to issue ration cards to employees, so that dismissal meant the loss of ration cards for food and consumer goods, as well as eviction from housing owned by the employing enterprise. A decree of November 15, 1932, ordered that workers absent for one day without an acceptable excuse be fired and deprived of their housing. No one could be hired without a certificate from his former employer giving the reason for his leaving his old job. Any managerial personnel failing to enforce government penalties for absenteeism were liable to prosecution.

These measures did not cause any immediate drop in labor turnover, which was almost as bad in 1933 as in 1932. But absenteeism declined sharply, falling in large-scale industry from 5.96 days per worker in 1932 to less than 1 day per worker in 1933. "Comradely production courts" were set up in 1931 and afterward in different enterprises and institutions to try workers for violating labor discipline or carelessly handling property. These courts could fine errant employees, suggest their dismissal to management, or propose their expulsion from their union for a fixed period.[12]

Nevertheless labor turnover remained high throughout the 1930's, while absenteeism and lateness to work continued to be problems. Under the conditions of labor shortage in those years, it is not surprising that many managers succumbed to the temptation to look the other way rather than to dismiss workers who were truant. In late 1938 a new campaign began against workers shifting from job to job or unjustifiably absent from or late to work, culminating in two major decrees. One, adopted December 20, 1938, required that all workers employed by the state or cooperative enterprise have labor books, giving their employment history, reasons for shifting from one enterprise to another, and any praise or honors won by them. This was intended as a type of passport for workers, hindering them from shifting around too much among jobs. Even more pointed was the decree of December 28, 1938. Workers late in reporting to work, leaving early for lunch, returning late from lunch, leaving their job early, or loafing on the job were to be punished by reprimand or transfer to a lower job for up to three months. Three such violations in a month or four in two months were to be

---

[12] *Ibid.*, and Baykov, *op. cit.*, pp. 214–15 and 228–29.

considered equivalent to absenteeism and therefore ground for automatic dismissal. Under the original statute, "tardiness consists in arriving for work not more than ten or fifteen minutes after work has begun, and if a worker comes later than that he is considered absent," and losses a day's pay. Nine days later, worker reaction had been so violent that the limit was raised to twenty minutes.[13] Workers dismissed for absenteeism lost all seniority rights and were ordered discriminated against in the granting of social insurance benefits such as pensions, disability allowances, maternity leaves, and the like.

The logical culmination of this legislation came with a decree of June 26, 1940, prohibiting workers from leaving their jobs without permission of their employers, unless for reasons of health or for enrollment in a university or vocational school. Violation was punishable by imprisonment for two to four months. Since workers desiring to leave their jobs might have deliberately absented themselves from work in order to be dismissed, the penalty for absenteeism was changed from dismissal to compulsory work in the same enterprise for up to six months. During this period 25 per cent is deducted from the worker's wages. A decree of October 19, 1940, gave the government the right to transfer skilled workers and technical personnel anywhere in the country, without regard to the employees' wishes.[14]

This tightening up of labor discipline seems clearly to have been inspired by the growing danger of war as Hitler advanced in the late 1930's, but all these regulations have been retained or made more stringent since then. The labor book, it should be mentioned, serves as an effective aid to enforcement of some of this legislation. The book is held by the employer and surrendered only if the employer consents to a worker's leaving his job. Under the law, the worker may not get a job unless he has his book. Unless a worker can find a new employer willing to violate government regulations his old employer has him at his mercy. But the chronic labor shortage in the Soviet economy offers great temptations to employers to accept workers without being too fussy about the legality of their position.

[13] Baykov, op. cit., pp. 350–51, and Manya Gordon, Workers Before and After Lenin, pp. 122–23.
[14] Gsovski, Soviet Civil Law, Vol. I, pp. 828–30.

In the late 1930's, the problem of skilled workers again became increasingly acute. In part this may have been a reflection of the inadequate flow of new laborers into the expanding nonagricultural sectors of the economy. In part, too, it seems likely that with increasing education of large numbers, many more young people were competent to hold, and wanted, white-collar jobs, rather than to do manual labor in the factories, mines, and railroads. Under these circumstances, the Soviet government felt it necessary to assure itself of a flow of new trained workers adequate to meet its plans for the future, even if this required sharp limitation of freedom of occupational choice for many. Accordingly, the decree of October 2, 1940, authorized the annual draft of between 800,000 and 1,000,000 boys between 14 and 17 years of age. Those 14 or 15 years old were ordered to enter trade and railroad schools for two years of training designed to make them skilled workers, while those 16 or 17 years old were ordered to take six months' training in factory schools preparing less skilled categories of labor. At the end of their training periods, these youths are required to work for several years at such places as ordered by the government, even if this means that they are sent far from their family and friends.[15] So far as possible the Soviet government attempts to get voluntary recruits for these schools, stressing that all students' expenses are paid during training. The deficit between government labor requirements and the number of volunteers is made up through the compulsory draft.

When this decree first appeared, many believed it was purely an emergency measure dictated by the threat of war. The State Labor Reserves, as this program is termed, has apparently become a permanent feature of the Soviet labor scene, however. During the war the draft was extended so as to cover girls 16 to 18 years of age for training in the factory schools. A decree of June 19, 1947, revised the earlier provisions somewhat, providing for the drafting of boys 14 to 17 and girls 15 and 16 years of age for trade and railroad schools, and of boys and girls 16 to 18 years old for industrial training schools. Boys up to 19 years of age may be drafted for work in the most important industries — coal and other mining, metallurgy, petroleum, and so on. Labor Reserve draftees need

---

[15] *Ibid.*, pp. 830–31.

not fulfill their compulsory military service term until after their training and their four years of obligatory assigned work have been completed. During World War II, over 2,000,000 young workers were graduated from the Labor Reserve Schools, providing what must have been a most vital addition to the nonagricultural labor force. The Fourth Five-Year Plan provided that 4,500,000 young skilled workers should be graduated from these schools during 1946–50, over 10 per cent of the number of workers and employees planned for the national economy in 1950. Graduates of universities and technical schools are also subject to compulsory assignment for several years after being graduated.[16]

In the early 1950's, the importance of the State Labor Reserves — as judged by the number of graduates of its schools — declined appreciably. From a record high of 1,000,000 graduates in 1948, the number of graduates fell to only 320,000 in 1953.

World War II brought major changes in both the supply of and demand for workers in the Soviet economy. The available supply was cut sharply by large-scale military moblization as well as by the loss of the population in the large western area occupied by the Germans. Requirements were cut, too, by German capture of productive resources — factories, mines, power plants, and the like — in the west, but requirements in the eastern areas free of German control rose sharply, since some 1,300 plants were moved there from the occupied zone. In addition, many new mines, factories, power plants, as well as some stretches of railroad, were built in the east during the war, requiring construction workers first and then manpower to operate the new installations. The repercussion of wartime events on the supply of workers is suggested by the available data on the number of workers and employees: 31.2 million in 1940; 19.3 million in 1943; and 27.2 million in 1945.[17] The changes that took place in the geographical distribution of the Soviet labor force during the first two years of World War II are suggested by the following data on the number of workers and employees in industry: [18]

---

16 *Ibid. Entsiklopediya,* col. 1130.

17 Harry Schwartz, "Soviet Labor Policy, 1945–1949," *The Annals of the American Academy of Political and Social Science,* May 1949, p. 75.

18 Voznesensky, *op. cit.,* p. 60, gives basic data for this calculation.

	1940	1943
	(THOUSANDS)	
Total USSR	10,920	7,527
Volga Area	327	563
Urals	927	1,538
West Siberia	436	675
Central Asia and Kazakhstan ..	382	600
Rest of the USSR	8,848	4,151

To meet the labor needs of the nonagricultural economy during the war, the Soviet government resorted to stern measures. A decree of December 26, 1941, declared that all those employed directly or indirectly in war industry were to be considered mobilized for the duration of the war and permanently assigned to their jobs. Unauthorized departure of those mobilized was to be considered desertion, to be tried by court martial and punished by imprisonment for five to eight years. Two decrees issued in 1943 placed all railroad, merchant marine, and river-craft workers under martial law. At the very beginning of the war, the chief areas of the country were placed under martial law, and military authorities were authorized to draft workers for work in connection with the war emergencies. Later, a decree of February 13, 1942, mobilized the able-bodied adult population of the cities for work "in industries and construction projects, primarily in the aviation and tank industries, in the armament and munitions industries, and in the metallurgical, chemical, and fuel industries." Later decrees in the same year mobilized urban adults and high school students for farm work. A labor draft for invalids even was enacted in August 1942.[19] The utilization of these measures is indicated by the fact that in 1943 some 7,609,000 persons were drafted for essential work, about half of them for agriculture—probably mainly during the harvest season —and the rest for industry, construction, and forestry.[20]

During the war, therefore, almost every able-bodied civilian in the cities could be assigned to any task where labor was needed, just as if he were in the armed forces. Many less essential activities —including production of consumer goods, operating stores of all kinds, maintaining service establishments, and so on—were closed down so that their workers could be shifted to more essential oc-

---

[19] Gsovski, *op. cit.*, Vol. I, pp. 832–34, and Vol. II, pp. 548–50.
[20] Voznesensky, *op. cit.*, p. 60.

cupations. Since the bulk of able-bodied Soviet manpower went into the armed forces, the role of women in the labor force increased sharply. Women had composed 38 per cent of all workers and employees in 1940; by 1942 they were 52 per cent of the total, and accounted for more than half the work force in industry, trade, communications, communal feeding, medical services, and government administration. The proportion of all workers under 18 and over 50 increased sharply between 1940 and 1942. A new wave of migrants came from the farms to fill urban jobs left vacant by men drafted for the armed forces as well as to provide workers for the many new enterprises built during the war. So far as possible, in short, every man, woman, and youngster capable of working was given a role in fighting or producing for the fighters.[21]

As the Red Army reconquered the western areas of the USSR, the resident population there was put to work again operating such enterprises as were fit to work and rebuilding those that had been damaged or destroyed. About 8,000,000 workers and employees were added to the total between 1943 and 1945. After World War II, demobilization of the armed forces sent large numbers back to urban and farm work. By the end of 1949 the number of workers and employees in the national economy exceeded 35,000,000, a total some 15 per cent higher than in 1940.[22] All through the postwar period, the Soviet government maintained constant pressure to get a maximum number of its citizens working. In late 1946 rations for nonworking adults, such as housewives, were reduced below their previously low level. The monetary reform of December 1947 was a blow to persons who had made their living buying and selling goods in the favorable atmosphere created by the previous two-price system. The bulk of their previous cash accumulations was largely wiped out and their opportunity for future gains became relatively very bad, so that they had to go to work in more conventional types of Soviet employment. By the spring of 1948, less than six months after the reform, a writer in *Pravda* was able to report that large numbers of additional city people were flocking to seek factory employment. The labor situation had improved so much,

---

21 *Ibid.*, pp. 60–61.
22 Based on Schwartz, "Soviet Labor Policy 1945–1949," *op. cit.*, p. 75; and *Pravda*, January 18, 1950.

he wrote, that many factory directors could now pick and choose among applicants for work, rather than having to accept all who came to their door.[23]

By the end of 1953, the Soviet government reported, the number of workers and employees in the national economy had grown to almost 45,000,000 persons, or about 17,000,000 more than the number in this category in 1945. The Fifth Five-Year Plan had provided that this number should increase to 45,100,000 by 1955, so that the actual increase during 1951–53 was obviously faster than foreseen even in late 1952, when the Fifth Five-Year Plan had been promulgated. Most of the increase during this three year period took place in 1953, the result apparently of three factors: the release of Soviet prisoners under the terms of the partial amnesty of March 1953; the mid-1953 release of military personnel who had served longer than their legally-stipulated compulsory service period; and the addition to the staffs of Machine Tractor Stations of more than a million persons in late 1953, most of them individuals who had formerly worked for the MTS only part time before the shift in policy that was announced in September 1953.

The discussion above testifies to the extremely rapid postwar increase in the nonagricultural labor force of the Soviet Union, a basic factor behind the country's rapid increase in industrial production between 1945 and 1953. The other side of the coin, however, was the fact that this increase took place at the expense of agriculture, which was drained of large numbers of workers, drained most seriously of large numbers of more skilled and able people. The discussion of the farm labor situation in an earlier chapter has already pointed to some of the measures the government took in September 1953 in an effort to redress the balance and to help provide the trained personnel needed if farm production were to increase at a better tempo than earlier in the postwar period.

Other important problems remained to be solved in the postwar labor situation. Millions of demobilized veterans had never held a peacetime job before and, except for their familiarity with military machinery, presented the same training problems as the millions of new workers from the farms had in the early 1930's. Large numbers of skilled workers, specialists, and technicians of all kinds had

[23] *Pravda*, May 28, 1948.

died during the war, so that the economy suffered from a great shortage of such personnel. Both these circumstances called for a major
effort in training new factory, railroad, mine, and other workers,
and also help explain the continued utilization of the Labor Reserve
draft technique in the postwar period. In 1949 alone, 723,000
youngsters graduated from Labor Reserve Schools, while 6,600,000
workers were trained or given new skills in on-the-job training
courses.[24] The educational system was rapidly rebuilt so as to
help it recover from the great ravages of war and enable it to turn
out the engineers, doctors, architects, and other professional workers
needed so badly if the country's economic plans were to be achieved.
Great efforts and progress were made toward solving these problems
during the first half-decade after the war's end. Yet even as late
as the spring of 1950, Pravda complained of the serious shortage
of engineers and technicians in the Donbas and suggested stripping
research institutes of young engineers to help meet the problem.[25]
It seems most unikely that the difficulty was confined only to this
area, the most important of Soviet coal fields.

The continued rapid rate of expansion of the Soviet economy
after 1950 made the need for trained technicians grow greatly even
while the number of new graduates in technical fields increased.
How rapidly the Soviet Union is turning out technicians may be
judged from the fact that Soviet schools graduated 54,000 engineers
in 1954, against 19,000 engineers graduated that year from United
States schools.

Labor discipline too was a serious problem, felt most severely
in the early postwar years. The strict legislation of 1940 remained
in effect, as did the imposition of martial law upon transport workers.
The use of the labor book as a means of reducing turnover proved
inadequate in the early postwar years. Many workers did not have
labor books, either because they had never been issued one during
the confusion of the war and early postwar years, or because their
books had been lost. Many employers, pressed by the need for
workers to meet their goals, simply disregarded the requirement
that they must not hire anyone lacking a labor book. The result
was that many workers could and did move freely from job to job,

---

24 Pravda, January 18, 1950.
25 Ibid., March 29, 1950.

without getting the consent of each employer they left, despite the
law's prohibition. The incentive for such turnover and shifting was
the same as for the similar phenomenon in the early 1930's. Conditions of work and life in the Soviet Union were hard, with food,
housing, clothing, and other necessities in short supply generally
but varying in availability from place to place. Under these circumstances workers naturally moved from place to place in response to
reports of better conditions at places other than where they worked.
The Soviet press warned factory heads repeatedly in 1946 and 1947
that to curb labor turnover they had to improve workers' conditions, but this was more easily said than done under the prevailing
scarcities. In the summer of 1946 a major effort was made to insure
that all workers had labor books and that the law authorizing use
of this device to cut down turnover was observed. But three years
later, complaints were still appearing in the press that many employers continued to hire workers who had no labor book, thus
facilitating their illegal departure from their previous employment.[26]

The amnesty decree of late March 1953, issued shortly after
Stalin's death, aroused hopes for an easing of Soviet labor discipline
laws, since it called for the submission by appropriate authorities
of proposals for liberalizing these and other disciplinary laws.
However, no further mention of this subject was made in the following year and in late 1953 material in the Soviet press indicated that
the old laws were still being enforced, in some cases by the imposition of jail sentences.

The Work Week

In the postwar period, the basic work week in the Soviet Union
has consisted of six eight-hour days, forty-eight hours in all. Sunday
is the common rest day for most workers. Individuals whose jobs
require them to work under specially dangerous or harmful conditions have a shorter labor day — four to seven hours — depending
upon the particular occupation. Legally, overtime work is usually
forbidden, except for those working in defense industries, or in case
of emergency, or where technical or natural conditions require it.
Overtime is paid for at a higher rate than normal working time.
Some categories of workers — including women in the fourth or

---

[26] *Ibid.*, July 27, 1946, and *Trud,* September 17, 1949.

later month of pregnancy, nursing mothers, invalids, persons with active tuberculosis, and the like — may not be required to do overtime work. Night work is defined as that done between 10 P.M. and 6 A.M. and consists usually of a seven-hour rather than an eight-hour shift. Where operations must be conducted continuously throughout all twenty-four hours, however, night shifts are the same length as those done during the day. Workers who have been employed in one enterprise for at least eleven months are entitled to two weeks' leave with pay each year.[27]

During World War II, the work week was considerably lengthened in an effort to compensate for the reduced civilian labor force. A decree of June 26, 1941, permitted enterprise directors to require up to three extra hours daily. Many workers labored eleven hours a day six days a week, or sixty-six hours weekly, receiving 50 per cent more than their base pay for the hours worked overtime. Youngsters under 16 years were required to work no more than ten hours daily under this decree, while women more than five months pregnant or in the first month of nursing a new baby were exempted from overtime. All vacations were abolished during the war, workers being paid for the unused leave, at first in cash and later in blocked bank credits, which were paid after the war. The two weeks' annual leave was reinstituted by a decree of June 30, 1945.

During the late 1920's and the 1930's, the seven-hour day was the standard in the USSR, but the work week varied. In order to get maximum utilization of productive equipment, a continuous work week was ordered, that is, enterprises operated every day of the week. At first a decree of September 1929 provided that most workers labor four days, rest the fifth day, and then begin again. Later this was changed to five days of work with the sixth day off. Thus, for an individual worker, the rest day might be Thursday during one six-day period, Wednesday the next time, and so on. Not until June 27, 1940, was the seven-day week, with Sunday as the common rest day, introduced. The same decree lengthened the work day from seven to eight hours. Although this move increased hours substantially, no compensating wage increase for workers paid on a time basis was granted.[28]

---

[27] N. G. Aleksandrov and D. M. Genkin, eds., *Sovetskoye Trudovoye Pravo*, pp. 175–84. Moscow: 1946. Gsovski, *op. cit.*, Vol. I, p. 826.

[28] Baykov, *op. cit.*, pp. 214, 351, and Gsovski, *op. cit.*, Vol. I, p. 826.

Labor Incentives

Ideally, a worker can be most useful in the production process if he works at top efficiency all the time, if he keeps his eyes open for ways to improve methods of work and shows initiative in suggesting such changes, and if he strives to improve his own knowledge and qualifications so as to help him increase his output or to enable him to move up to a more responsible job. The problem of how to induce the millions of Soviet workers to behave in such a manner, or at least to move toward this type of behavior, has preoccupied the makers of the USSR's economic policies for over two decades. The naive notion that workers in a socialist state would necessarily become maximally productive because they felt themselves the owners of all resources has long since been discarded. By the early 1930's, it had become clear to the top leaders of the USSR that self-interest and the desire for personal gain were still the primary factors in the individual worker's reckoning. Only by enlisting the worker's self-interest could productivity be increased. This meant, of course, that monetary and nonmonetary rewards had to be offered for those contributing most to production, in accordance with the formula: "From each according to his ability, to each according to his work."

Soviet wages policy, however, was at first greatly influenced by an egalitarian philosophy born of the widespread early belief that the revolution would wipe out great inequalities of income and welfare. Wage schedules established in 1918 and 1919 therefore provided for much smaller differentials between the earnings of the highest- and the lowest-paid workers than had formerly been prevalent. Under the pressure of need to improve production, a sharp reversal of attitude took place in 1920 and 1921, a government decree on wage policy in the latter year declaring that "any thought of equalitarianism must be discarded." In 1926 and 1927, a reverse turn in the opposite direction took place, epitomized by the declaration of M. P. Tomsky before the Seventh Trade Union Congress:

> The direction of our wage policy must be along the line of a leveling of wages, on the one hand of the low-paid workers of separate industries . . . and on the other hand, within the working class itself in the direction of a leveling of the increasingly incongruous gap be-

tween the wage of qualified labor and the wage of simple, unqualified labor . . . the difference between the pay of qualified and unqualified labor is of such a colossal magnitude as does not exist in Western Europe. . . . In the future we must reduce the gap in wages between qualified and ordinary labor.[29]

While Tomsky undoubtedly exaggerated the actual differentiation in earnings at the time, in 1927 the policy he urged was put into effect so that earnings inequalities were reduced substantially in the following two years.[30]

By 1931, the pendulum had once again swung in the other direction: a speech made by Joseph Stalin set the policy that has been followed in general ever since. Raising the question of the reasons for the great turnover and instability of the labor force, he said:

> The cause is the wrong structure of wages, the wrong wage scales, the "Leftist" practice of wage equalization. In a number of our factories wage scales are drawn up in such a way as to practically wipe out the difference between skilled labor and unskilled labor, between heavy work and light work. The consequence of wage equalization is that the unskilled worker lacks the incentive to become a skilled worker and is thus deprived of the prospect of advancement: as a result he feels himself a "sojourner" in the factory, working only temporarily so as to earn a little and then go off to "seek his fortune" elsewhere. The consequence of wage equalization is that the skilled worker is obliged to wander from factory to factory until he finds one where his skill is properly appreciated.
>
> . . . In order to put an end to this evil we must abolish wage equalization and discard the old wage scales . . . we must draw up wage scales that will take into account the difference between skilled labor and unskilled labor, between heavy work and light work. We cannot tolerate a situation where a rolling-mill hand in a steel mill earns no more than a sweeper.[31]

Here again the existing situation was decribed in exaggerated fashion, but the new direction Soviet wage policy was to take had been laid down unmistakably.

Wage Determination

In the 1920's trade unions played a very important role in setting

---

[29] Quoted by Abram Bergson, *The Structure of Soviet Wages*, p. 187. Cambridge, Mass.: Harvard University Press, 1944.
[30] *Ibid.*, pp. 188–89.
[31] Stalin, *Problems of Leninism*, pp. 371–72.

wage rates and schedules. The Central Council of Trade Unions, representing all unions, set the maximum number of wage categories and the maximum percentage difference between highest- and lowest-paid workers in all industries. The actual wages to be paid different groups of workers in all industry, within the limits set by the higher authorities, as well as the classification of the industry's employees were set by the union in that industry after consultation with the administrative personnel of People's Commissariats and enterprises. On this basis the earnings of individual workers were determined by collective agreements between unions and management or on the basis of individual employment contracts.[32]

In the late 1920's and early 1930's, however, the central government itself began to set more and more wage scales directly. Well before World War II, therefore, wages for virtually all types of employees were set by the central government as part of its comprehensive economic planning, all direct influence of unions on wages being eliminated. Since then wages have not been subject to bargaining between workers and employers. Collective agreements reached between the two groups merely incorporate the rates set by state authorities. The Council of Ministers may approve wage schedules directly or authorize the head of a particular Ministry or Institution to set them.[33] In its economic planning, therefore, the government is able to determine the wages total for the economy and its branches by multiplying the planned number of workers by the rates of wages it has set. Wages are changed as seems necessary to effectuate government policy and achieve particular production ends, rather than in response to direct pressure from workers. For example, in order to attract more workers to a given industry, wages paid by it may be raised while others remain static.

Most Soviet workers and employees are paid on the basis of a rate schedule consisting of several categories, each of which has a wage coefficient, that of the lowest category being one. The rate for a worker in any category is then obtained by multiplying the rate for the lowest category by the wage coefficient of the worker's group. Payment may be either on the basis of time worked or by piece rate, that is, per unit of product of work accomplished. Scales

<hr/>

[32] Bergson, *op. cit.*, pp. 170–71, and Gsovski, *op. cit.*, Vol. I, p. 807.

[33] Aleksandrov and Genkin, *op cit.*, pp. 211–12, 218, and Gsovski, *op. cit.*, Vol. I, pp. 806–9.

are usually set so as to make it possible for workers receiving piece-rate compensation to earn more than those paid on a time basis, since the Soviet government believes that payment on the basis of production results tends to stimulate output. This may be illustrated by the scale set for construction workers in 1940: [34]

Wage Category	I	II	III	IV	V	VI	VII
Wage Coefficient	1.0	1.17	1.40	1.71	2.15	2.75	3.66
Time Rate in Rubles/Hour	3.84	4.49	5.38	6.57	8.26	10.56	13.82
Piece Rate in Equivalent Rubles/Hour	4.96	5.80	6.94	8.48	10.66	13.64	17.86

The hourly piece rate is obtained in the following manner: each worker has an output norm setting the number of units of production he is to turn out per hour (or day, or week, as the case may be). This norm is multiplied by the payment per unit of output to get his hourly (or daily, or weekly) wage. Straight piece-work schedules give the worker a fixed payment per unit of product regardless of whether he falls below, equals, or exceeds his norm. Progressive piece-rate schedules pay a fixed amount per unit until the worker reaches his norm. Beyond that a higher rate is paid per unit of output, the higher rate sometimes ranging from a 10 per cent increase for small output in excess of the norm to perhaps a 100 per cent increase for exceeding the norm substantially. This progressive piece-rate system aims at creating a strong incentive for the worker to exceed his norm substantially. Under both the straight and progressive piece-rate systems, however, workers producing less than their norm receive proportionally less earnings.

The above discussion has focused on individual workers' piece rates, but collective piece rates also exist. These provide for a team or brigade of workers to receive a fixed total sum for the completion of some major task on which all are engaged. Piece rates were applied in Soviet industry in the early 1920's, and by 1928 about 58 per cent of all workers in large-scale industry were paid on that basis. By 1935 almost 70 per cent of all workers in large-scale industry worked for piece rates.[35] In 1949, V. V. Kuznetsov, the head of all Soviet trade unions, reported that the majority of Soviet workers received payment on the basis of piece rates, including 71

[34] Aleksandrov and Genkin, op cit., p. 218.
[35] Sot. Stroi., p. 526.

per cent of those making machine tools, 83 per cent making cotton textiles, 84 per cent in the woolen goods industry, and 92 per cent in lumber milling.[36]

Premiums and bonuses are also paid workers and employees in an effort to stimulate improved work. Bonuses may be paid periodically as part of the wages of workers who reach specified quantitative or qualitative production goals, who economize on the use of raw materials or fuel, or who help lower the cost of production. Premium payments may also be made to those who show special initiative at their work, who help introduce technical improvements, or who perform assignments not entering into their usual duties. Bonuses may be paid from the director's fund discussed earlier or from a special premium fund at the disposal of top economic directors, this special fund varying between ¼ and 2 per cent of the total wages fund for the institution or economic organization involved. Bonuses and premiums apparently have a particularly important role in the compensation of enterprise directors, engineers, technicians, and other supervisory officials who play a key role in seeking fulfillment or overfulfillment of state economic plans.[37] Somewhat similar to the bonus system in its incentive effect is the institution of "personal rates." Persons of outstanding ability entitled to such rates can negotiate for themselves salaries up to 150 per cent of the government-fixed salaries of ordinary specialists in their field.[38]

Since the beginning of the First Five-Year Plan, strong inflationary pressures have influenced the course of Soviet money wages and caused them to rise very substantially. Whether the sharp rise in average money wages has been accompanied by a corresponding increase in real wages seems dubious, in view of the rapid increase in prices for food and consumer goods during the 1930's and through 1946, as well as the scarcities of these commodities and housing during most of the past two decades. Among the forces making for the rise in money wages have been: competitive bidding for labor between plants; government efforts to attract workers to nonagricultural jobs; the institution of incentive wage-rate systems such as straight and progressive piece rates, bonuses, and so on.

---

[36] *Pravda*, April 21, 1949.
[37] Aleksandrov and Genkin, *op. cit.*, pp. 208–10.
[38] *Ibid.*, pp. 214–15.

These forces have usually combined to send wages up more rapidly than provided for by government plan, so that wages in turn have tended to act as an inflationary force upon other parts of the Soviet price system. Some increases in wages, as in the mid-1930's and in 1946, were instituted in order to compensate workers partially for sharp rises in prices of goods they bought as the state sought to end rationing and to institute a system of unlimited sale of goods at higher fixed prices. The change in average annual money earnings of workers and employees in the Soviet economy is shown by the data below, in terms of rubles:[39]

1928	703	1936	2,856
1929	800	1937	3,047
1930	936	1938	3,467
1931	1,127	1940	4,100
1932	1,427	1946	6,000
1933	1,566	1947	7,100
1934	1,858	1948	7,400
1935	2,269		

During the late 1940's and early 1950's, until the first months of 1954, virtually no information was published regarding over-all changes in average earnings of Soviet workers and employees. In January 1954, however, the economic report for 1953 reported a two per cent increase in average earnings over 1952. In April 1954, Mikoyan asserted that "the average money earnings of workers and employees of all industry, taken as a whole, has seriously increased and in 1953 was 219 per cent of the 1940 level." In May 1954, Transport Minister Beshchev reported that the "average earnings of the workers of railroad transport has grown more than twice in comparison with the prewar level."[40]

In the light of the above, as well as of some other fragmentary evidence, it does not seem that we will be far off if we assume the 1953 average annual earnings of Soviet workers and employees as being about 219 per cent of the 1940 average, 4,100 rubles. On this assumption the 1953 average earnings may be estimated as approximately 9,000 rubles. Since it is likely that nonindustrial wages did

---

[39] Sources: *Sot. Stroi.*, pp. 512–13; Abram Bergson, "A Problem in Soviet Statistics," *The Review of Economic Statistics*, November 1947, p. 236; Harry Schwartz, "Soviet Labor Policy 1945–1949," *The Annals of the American Academy of Political and Social Science*, May 1949, p. 80; *Itogi Vypolneniya Vtorogo Pyatiletnego Plana*, p. 105.

[40] *Pravda*, January 31, April 27, and May 19, 1954.

not rise quite as rapidly as industrial wages from 1940 to 1953, this estimate of 9,000 rubles is probably somewhat too high. In using it to study real earnings in the section below, therefore, the result must be regarded as giving an upper limit.

Real Earnings

The data on money earnings given above are very misleading guides to changes in the purchasing power of workers' incomes, since they do not take into account the great rise in prices since 1928. It is difficult to correct satisfactorily for these price changes because of the lack of adequate price data and because of the Soviet government's failure to publish a cost-of-living index for most of this period. A somewhat more satisfactory insight into changes in real earnings may be obtained, however, by employing the index of state store food prices in Moscow discussed in Chapter XI above. The great importance of food in Soviet workers' budgets suggests that it is not unreasonable to use an index of food prices as a crude measure of changes in living costs, particularly since changes in the most important ordinary consumer goods' prices have usually been in the same direction as food price changes. If we use the Moscow food price index to deflate the money earnings figures given above, we obtain the following interesting results:

TABLE 59. Money Earnings of Soviet Workers Deflated by Food Price Index.

Year	Average Annual Earnings	Food Price Index (1928 = 100)	Earnings in Terms of 1928 "Food Rubles"
1928	703	100	703
1936	2,856	830	344.1
1937	3,047	835	363.8
1938	3,467	858	404.1
1940	4,100	1,180*	347.5
1948	7,400	2,954	250.5
1953	9,000†	1,400	642.8†

* January 1941. † Upper limit.

Little precision can be claimed for the results above.

An elaborate study of real earnings in the Soviet Union, 1928–52, was published by Janet Chapman in the May 1954 issue of the *Review of Economics and Statistics*. Though presenting data for four years only, this study took into account a wide selection of food and nonfood commodity prices as well as the prices of key services. In addition the prices employed were weighted according to the relative importance of different goods and services in urban workers' budgets in 1928 and 1937. The latter procedure was used because of the sharp change between 1928 and 1937 in the composition of the standard of living of Soviet workers, a change that was primarily in the direction of a worse standard of living. This greater precision gives greater confidence in the results obtained by this study, though paradoxically two different sets of results emerged, the statistical conclusions differing with the use of 1928 and 1937 weights. Taking 1928 as 100, the measures of the cost of living obtained by this study were:

	1928 weights	1937 weights
1928	100	100
1937	701	495
1948	2152	1559
1952	1444	1005

Deflating annual money earnings by these cost of living indexes, the following indexes of real earnings were obtained with 1928 as 100:

	1928 weights	1937 weights
1928	100	100
1937	58	82
1948	45	62
1952	72	103

After making allowances for the portion of workers' earnings taken by taxes and by virtually compulsory purchases of government bonds, the following indexes of real earnings were obtained with 1928 as 100:

	1928 weights	1937 weights
1928	100	100
1937	57	81
1948	40	56
1952	63	90

The interpretation of these results in detail is obviously complex because of the differences resulting from the use of the two different weighting systems. Nevertheless a few major conclusions seem to emerge without difficulty, especially if we remember that 1937 was one of the relatively prosperous years of the 1930's and that by

1948 much progress had already been made toward lifting the standard of living and real earnings above the terrible levels of World War II.

First, after 1928 the level of real earnings in the Soviet Union plunged far downward, and not until a quarter of a century later — 1952 or 1953 — did real earnings come even moderately close to or at most equal the 1928 level.

Second, in the worst periods — the early 1930's and the years during and immediately after World War II — real earnings were probably half or even less than half the 1928 levels.

Third, from 1948 to 1953 real earnings rose consistently and sharply, the rise probably exceeding 50 per cent of the 1948 level. In part this resulted from increased production of food and consumer goods; in part too, however, this rise was made possible by the confiscatory wiping out of much of the population's savings by the Monetary Reform of 1947.

Differences in Earnings

Wage differentiation in the Soviet economy exists among industries and branches of the economy, as well as among various grades of workers in one industry or plant. The differentiation in average annual earnings among different branches of the economy and their changes over time may be illustrated by the following data in rubles: [41]

Branch of Economy	1928	1935
Large-Scale Industry	870	2,375
Construction	996	2,497
Transport	861	2,389
Agriculture	290	1,566
Forestry	395	1,525
Communications	776	1,944
Trade	783	1,851
Restaurants	623	1,552
Education	678	2,328
Medical Services	638	2,249
State Administrative Personnel	903	3,246
Banking	981	2,664
Entire National Economy	703	2,269

If we look at the most dynamic single branch of the economy during the 1930's, large-scale industry, we also find a rapidly changing pattern of wages marked by strong differentiation among par-

[41] *Sot. Stroi.*, pp. 512–13.

ticular industries. The trend of change among industries was such as to raise most sharply the earnings of workers in heavy industries, while those producing consumer goods found their wages lagging behind, as a reflection of the lower importance attached to them. Thus average wages of coal miners in 1928 were fourteenth in rank among seventeen branches of large industry; by 1935 they were fourth. On the other hand, printing workers' wages fell from second highest in 1928 to eighth in rank in 1935, while shoe workers' wages fell similarly from fourth to ninth place over the same period. In 1935 the ranking of industries by wages, from highest to lowest, was: petroleum, electric power stations, metal-working and machine construction, coal, iron and steel, iron-ore mining, chemicals, printing, shoes, fur and leather, woodworking, cotton textiles, paper, wool textiles, clothing, processed food, and linen textiles.[42] By the mid-1930's, therefore, the important wage advantage of heavy industry over light industry must have given the former a substantial edge in the competition for workers.

All the available evidence indicates that sharp differences exist among the earnings of different workers in the Soviet Union. These arise from differences in output and types of work performed. Presumably inequality of earnings has increased substantially since Stalin's attack on equalitarianism in 1931, but comprehensive data are lacking since the mid-1930's. In October 1934 the distribution of earnings for wage earners and salaried workers in Soviet industry was as follows: [43]

Monthly Earnings in Rubles	Per Cent of Wage Earners and Salaried Workers Receiving These Earnings
Less than 60.1	4.7
60.1 to 120.0	28.4
120.1 to 180.0	30.5
180.1 to 240.0	15.8
240.1 to 300.0	9.0
300.1 to 380.0	5.6
380.1 to 500.0	3.8
500.1 to 580.0	.9
580.1 to 660.0	.5
660.1 to 780.0	.4
780.1 to 940.0	.2
940.1 to 1100.0	.1
Over 1100.1	.08

[42] Ibid., p. 525.
[43] Bergson, The Structure of Soviet Wages, p. 228.

Prof. Bergson has pointed out that in October 1934 some Soviet workers earned less than 50 rubles while others received more than 1,420 rubles, indicating that at that time the highest-paid Soviet workers got more than 28.3 times as much as the lowest-paid ones. Comparing the wage patterns of Soviet industries in 1928 with those of American industries in 1904, Prof. Bergson found them remarkably similar, leading him to conclude that in both countries capitalistic wage principles had been paramount.[44]

Inequality of earnings probably increased during World War II. The progressive piece-work system was extended to more workers. In the case of railway train and dispatch crews, the rate of payment for fulfillment of between 100 and 110 per cent of the base quota was twice the base rate, while triple rates were paid for achievement above 110 per cent of the quota.[45] During the war, the monthly earnings of ordinary workers in all-union industry—primarily heavy industry—rose from 375 rubles in 1940 to 573 rubles in 1944, or little more than half. In the same period average earnings of engineering and technical workers rose from 768 rubles to 1,209 rubles. In the iron and steel industry in 1944, the average wage of engineering and technical workers reached 1,725 rubles, roughly three times the average for ordinary industrial workers.[46]

In the early postwar period, inequality of earnings was apparently reduced somewhat by the government decree providing for arbitrary increases in wages, the highest rise going to the lowest-paid workers. These increases were intended to compensate partially for the approximate tripling of ration food prices in September 1946. The results may be illustrated by the machinery industries. Before the reform, two wage payment systems existed in these industries, one giving the highest-paid worker 3.2 times as much wage as the lowest-paid, and the other giving him 3.6 times as much. After the reform, these ratios were reduced to 2.1:1 and 2.65:1 respectively, a fact deplored by a Soviet analyst. The same writer pointed out that the incentive functioning of the graded wage system in the postwar period was weakened by the unjustified upgrading of workers. He cited plants where few or no workers received the

---

[44] *Ibid.*, pp. 96, 129.

[45] A. E. Pasherstnik, "Problems of Legal Wage Regulation in Wartime," *The American Review on the Soviet Union*, May 1946, pp. 64–65.

[46] *Voprosy Ekonomiki*, No. 10 (1948), pp. 26–27.

lowest wage rates, while a more-than-justifiable number received a medium wage rate.[47]

Data on wages actually paid to individual workers in the postwar period are extremely fragmentary. Those published are usually selected to emphasize the heights to which wages can go for workers who show outstanding production results. Published data are not a random sample showing the full range of variation of all workers' earnings. Nevertheless these figures serve to point up the extremes of inequality of earnings during this period. It was indicated above that in 1948 the average annual earnings of all workers and employees were about 7,400 rubles or not quite 620 rubles a month. Reports made public in 1948 and 1949 told of outstanding skilled miners receiving incomes of 5,000 to 10,000 or more rubles monthly.[48] At the other extreme it seems most likely that some workers earn under 300 rubles monthly, so that the extreme ratio between the highest-paid industrial workers in the USSR and the lowest-paid may well be 30:1 or even higher. College teachers are reported to receive between 4,000 and 5,000 rubles monthly, while heads of research institutes receive 8,000 rubles monthly. A member of the Academy of Sciences receives 5,000 rubles a month just by virtue of his position. Since many academicians also head institutes or laboratories, their monthly earnings are apparently 13,000 rubles, supplemented in many cases by royalties, prizes, consultants' fees, and the like. Similar or higher earnings are received by top industrial and government officials, while authors of successful novels, plays, and other books probably receive even higher incomes than any of those mentioned above. Stalin Prize winners may get up to 200,000 rubles, over 50 times as much as the annual income of the lowest-paid Soviet workers.

Nonmonetary rewards and incentives also play an important role in spurring Soviet citizens on to increase their output and their qualifications. Outstanding workers are widely publicized and acclaimed as heroes who should be emulated. They are awarded decorations and honors, such as the Order of Lenin or the Order of the Red Banner. They are made Heroes of Labor. They are elected to the Supreme Soviet and other legislative bodies. Material rewards are given them, such as preference in allocation of housing space or — during the period of greatest shortages during and after World War II — priorities in receiving food and consumer goods. The outstanding worker is more likely to get the right to a vacation in the Crimea or other resort area than the one who merely fulfills his quota. On the other hand, the backward worker often finds his name posted on a plant bulletin board with the objective of shaming him into improving his performance. Also he is likely to fare worst in the sharing of scarce housing and other resources.

Appeals are made to the worker's loyalty to his factory or other production unit in order to increase productivity. Socialist competitions are held frequently between different plants, railroads, mines, or the like, the objective of these competitions being to attain the highest quantitative production, or the best quality output, or the lowest cost, or some similar goal. Cash prizes were introduced during the war for plants winning all-union socialist competitions. These prizes provided bonuses for managerial and production workers. During the war, plants engaged in armament or iron and steel production were paid first prizes ranging up to 700,000 rubles for plants having more than 30,000 workers. In 1949 it was reported that, during each quarter of the year, 1,000 Red Banners and 2,500 cash prizes were awarded to the victors in socialist competitions.[49] Such competitions may be called in honor of May Day or in honor of an anniversary of the Bolshevik revolution; or they may be initiated by one enterprise challenging all others of its type. The notion behind them is always that of utilizing the worker's team spirit to spur him on. Soviet press accounts often claim that these competitions arouse great enthusiasm among workers and spur them on to new achievements. At other times, however, the press complains that competitions are carried on only in the most formal sense, indicating that they sometimes mean little or nothing to the workers whom they are supposed to spur on to better performance.

The Stakhanovite movement has also been used as a means of raising productivity. It was initiated in 1935, when Alexei Stakhanov, a coal miner, set a new production record by reorganizing his own and his fellows' work technique. His achievements were publicized throughout the country, and soon similar outstanding and

---

[49] Aleksandrov and Genkin, *op. cit.*, pp. 210–11; *Pravda*, April 21, 1949.

phenomenal production records were being chalked up by Stakhanovites in many different industries. Often these production records
were made possible only by the creation of specially favorable
conditions of work and by placing strains upon equipment far
greater than those it was meant to stand, but in its propaganda the
Soviet government cited the Stakhanovites' production records as
examples of what could be attained if workers tried harder and
improved the organization of their daily routines. Work norms for
all workers were raised several times in the late 1930's, the increases
being justified in part on the basis of the much higher output
achieved by Stakhanovites. The output of these outstanding workers
is often many times the average of their fellows, many of whom lack
the strength or the skill to emulate the record achievements.[50] In
the postwar period more emphasis has been put upon creating
Stakhanovite work teams, but rewards to the large number of individual Stakhanovites remain high. Enterprise directors are constantly urged to base production quotas for all workers upon the
average of the best workers, rather than upon the simple average
performance of all workers, good and bad.

Speaking at the 1954 trade union congress, N. M. Shvernik, head
of the Soviet unions, gave this picture of the problems facing administrators of the Soviet wage system as of the date he spoke,
June 7, 1954: In some branches of industry, wage schedules were
obsolete in view of changed production conditions. In many industries wage scales offered workers little stimulus to improve their
skills since wages of the least skilled workers were too close to the
wages of the most highly skilled workers, while the differentials
for workers doing particularly unpleasant and heavy work were
only 15 to 20 per cent over the wages of workers working under
usual conditions. He centered attention on a particularly serious
problem in these words:

> The fact should also be noted that the planned and actual earnings
> of machinery construction workers are as a rule twice as high as
> the wage rates. Earnings steadily rise, but the wage rates in dif-
> ferent branches of production remain at the former level. Therefore
> in order to guarantee workers earnings in the range of average
> earnings, the administrators of factories bureaucratically establish
> deliberately lowered levels of output, norms which do not stimulate
> the growth of labor productivity. (Cf. *Trud,* June 8, 1954.)

---

[50] Gordon, *Workers Before and After Lenin,* pp. 171–76 and 406–9.

Elsewhere in his speech he hinted that this factor was at the root of the Soviet government's difficulty in having plant administrators adopt high output norms based on technological criteria rather than on average output. Where plants had been permitted to raise wage rates at the same time that they raised norms, he said, the percentage of technically-based work norms rose greatly. The absurdity of the existing situation, he pointed out, was illustrated by the machinery industry, where workers were accustomed to overfulfilling their work norms by 60 or 70 per cent as a matter of course, yet at the same time planned goals for raising labor productivity were not attained.

Productivity

At the beginning of the five-year plans in 1928, the productivity of Soviet nonagricultural labor was clearly far below that of workers in comparable occupations in the United States and Western Europe. Soviet equipment was antiquated, and the techniques employed were often obsolete. Hand workers predominated in many occupations that had been taken over by machinery in other countries, while the influence of modern time and motion studies and other rationalizing techniques had been scarcely felt in the Soviet Union. Since that time much effort and expense have gone into the task of improving productivity. Tens of thousands of new modern machines have been introduced in every production field. Time and motion studies and related techniques similar to those sponsored by Taylor and others in the Western world have been applied widely. Great pains have been taken to spur workers on to improve the intensity of their labor, to increase their skills, and to improve the quality of their performance. All these forces have undoubtedly done much to raise worker production per man-hour, although they have been applied under very difficult conditions. The great expansion of the nonagricultural labor force during the 1930's and the war and postwar convulsions in the labor market in the 1940's brought millions of untrained and unskilled new workers into factories, mines, and railroads. The speed with which productivity rose depended on the rate at which these new workers could be trained and assimilated into the work force.

Soviet data on the average productivity in the 1930's and the 1940's were obtained by dividing gross output in terms of 1926–27 prices by the number of workers. The deficiencies of these prices mentioned earlier in this volume apply equally well to the measurement of productivity as to that of gross production. In both cases they tend to exaggerate the actual increase achieved.[51] For this reason Soviet statements on productivity gains during the 1930's and 1940's are probably too high, though there is no question but that real gains of a substantial nature were made. The official claim is that between 1928 and 1940 productivity per worker in industry increased by more than 3.5 times, or at an average of about 11 per cent annually.[52] The initial impact of the Nazi invasion upon the Soviet economy, with its attendant confusion, disruption, and changeover from civilian to military goods, must have reduced productivity substantially below the 1940 level. During the war itself, however, substantial gains were made from the original low levels. The Soviet claim is that productivity per industrial worker rose about 40 per cent on the average during World War II, the sharpest gains being made in armaments production, where productivity is said to have risen 70 to 90 per cent.[53] This claim is no doubt also exaggerated, for the reasons indicated above, but it is clear that substantial if lesser gains must have been realized. Factories reconverted from, say, tractor to tank production undoubtedly produced much more efficiently in 1944 than in 1941. A similar gain occurred in this country during the years of World War II.

The Fourth Five-Year Plan called for labor productivity in industry in 1950 to be 36 per cent above the prewar level. Initially, however, labor productivity in 1946 fell, as the result of the difficulties experienced in reconverting from war to peace production. This decline seems confirmed by the failure of the State Planning Commission to mention any increase in productivity in its report on economic progress during 1946. Increases of 13, 15, and 13 per cent in average labor productivity were reported for 1947, 1948, and 1949, respectively, as against each preceding year, or a total increase by 1949 over 1946 of 43 per cent. Productivity in 1946 was substantially below the prewar level, and not until 1948 was the

[51] *Slovar-Spravochnik po Sotsialno-Ekonomicheskoi Statistike*, p. 218.

[52] Sh. Turetsky, *Proizvoditelnost Truda i Snizheniye Sebestoimosti v Novoy Pyatiletke*, p. 49. Moscow: 1947.

[53] *Ibid.*

prewar level of industrial productivity reported exceeded. Whether the prewar level would have been recorded as surpassed if a less inflationary measure of productivity had been employed is uncertain. At any rate, in 1946, in terms of the USSR's own indicator, industrial productivity was probably 20 per cent or more under that of 1940.[54]

Before World War II, Soviet economists calculated the per capita output of industrial workers in other leading countries in terms of rubles and compared these figures with the corresponding ones for the Soviet Union. They expressed the average productivity of Soviet workers in 1928, 1932, and 1937 as percentages of the average productivity of American, British, and German workers in those years, and got the following results:

	Soviet Industrial Productivity as Per Cent of		
Year	USA	GREAT BRITAIN	GERMANY
1928	16.2	55.3	44.6
1932	26.2	70.7	60.5
1937	40.5	103.1	97.0

Full details of these calculations have never been made public, so their accuracy has not been subjected to proper check. Nevertheless the conclusion that in 1937 Soviet industrial productivity per worker was still well below half that in the United States seems unquestionable. The comparisons with Great Britain and Germany seem more open to doubt.

Supplementing these data for all industry, Soviet economists also compared worker productivity in particular industries. Soviet coal output per worker-hour in 1937, they found, was 67.4 per cent of the American, 106.4 per cent of the British, and 76.9 per cent of the German level. Soviet pig-iron output in tons per worker-year in 1937 was 46.7 per cent of that in the United States, 128.2 per cent of the German level in 1935, and 142.6 per cent of the English level in 1936. Similar comparisons were found for other industries.[55]

Soviet studies of the reasons for lower productivity in the USSR than the United States focused attention upon the great number of workers required in their plants to supplement those directly

[54] Schwartz, "Soviet Labor Policy 1945–1949," p. 77.
[55] Planovoye Khozyaistvo, No. 3 (1939), pp. 152–54.

engaged in production. In the automobile industry of the USSR, for example, such ancillary service employees were 55.3 per cent of the total in 1937. In 1929, they formed only 29.3 per cent of the workers in the United States automobile industry. Surface workers in the Soviet coal industry formed 24 to 25 per cent of the total, but were only 14 to 18 per cent of those employed in the United States.[56] A comparison of the Soviet Kemerovskaya power station with the South Amboy station in the United States found that though the American installation produced somewhat more power and though both operated under much the same conditions, the Kemerovskaya station employed 480 men, 9.5 times as many as the South Amboy plant. In the case of an American coal mine producing three times as much as the Kizelugol Trust in the Urals, a study showed that the latter had eleven times as many technical workers, twice as many miners, three times the number of surface workers, eight times as many office workers, and twelve times the number of supervisory officials. The Inland Steel Company in this country employed 9,200 persons to turn out 1,500,000 tons of steel annually, while the Soviet Dzerzhinsky plant used 20,000 workers to produce 1,200,000 tons in 1939.[57] Commenting on productivity differences between American and Soviet workers, an American engineer who worked many years in the USSR has written:

> The unfavorable comparison of the productivity of the Soviet worker with that of his American colleague is in no way an expression of Russian laziness or lack of dexterity. The Russian worker as an individual does more physical work in his eight-hour shift than the American. But each department needs 50 to 100 per cent more men than a similar American department. The reasons are inferior quality or absence of automatic controllers for flows, pressures, etc., and of photoelectric and electronic equipment; inferior quality or absence of hand and machine repair tools; shortage of spare parts and materials; and inferior organization.
>
> The American engineer can hardly realize the difficulties facing his Russian colleague. Small tools, a reasonable stock of spare parts, and the ready availability of parts not in stock are taken for granted in the U. S. The Russian usually has machines and equipment from the most widely separated sources, and no spare parts at all. In Voroshilovsk, for example, in the by-products department, we had pumps from Skoda, run by motors from Germany's A.E.G., some on

[56] *Ibid.*, No. 9 (1939), p. 33.
[57] A. Yugow, *Russia's Economic Front for War and Peace*, p. 180.

Italian ball bearings and some on Swedish S.K.F. bearings. The steam pumps came from Worthington, in the U. S., while some small turbine pumps came from Britain's Metro-Vickers. Some relays came from G.E., and the motor controllers from Cutler-Hammer. No catalogues were available and, even if we had been able to select the necessary replacement or spare parts, currency was obtainable only under the most extreme circumstances.[58]

Soviet leaders are undoubtedly well aware of these weaknesses. Much of their current effort is directed toward raising productivity by improving the quality of equipment available to their workers as well as the efficiency of work organization. The increasingly wide introduction of assembly lines and related mass-production techniques in the past decade is illustrative of the moves being taken to improve industrial productivity both absolutely and relatively vis-a-vis the United States. Yet it is most significant that as late as September 11, 1950, *Pravda* found it necessary to print a long article complaining about the frequently low productivity in Soviet plants. In terms reminiscent of those employed a decade earlier, the article inveighed against the great dominance of hand workers in ancillary branches of production, such as loading and unloading, intra-plant transport, and the like. In many plants, the article revealed, such ancillary workers outnumber those employed in direct production, the same situation denounced before World War II.

In any consideration of Soviet productivity, it must be remembered that at any given time the level of output per worker differs considerably between different plants in the same major industry. The best and most modern plants in the USSR probably enjoy a very high rate of worker productivity, perhaps equalling or exceeding that of some plants in the United States, while far worse productivity is obtained in less modern and less well-run factories. A vivid example of the differences in worker productivity among Soviet plants is provided by the following data on per capita iron and steel output for workers on blast furnaces and open-hearth furnaces in various plants in 1939.[59]

---

[58] Louis Ernst, "Inside a Soviet Industry," *Fortune,* October 1949, p. 172.

[59] Bardin and Banny, *Chernaya Metallurgiya v Novoy Pyatiletke,* p. 166; a very illuminating analysis of such variation is given in *Voprosy Ekonomiki,* No. 6 (1950), pp. 30–40.

Plant	Pig Iron	Steel
	(METRIC TONS PER WORKER)	
Magnitogorsk Combine	2,840	1,168
Kuznetsk Combine	2,324	1,389
Krivoy Rog Plant	1,733	—
Zaporozhstal	1,579	1,074
Azovstal	1,642	664
Kirov Plant	2,102	523
Dzerzhinsky Plant	785	529
Petrovsky Plant	799	299
Kramatorsk Plant	725	293
Ordzhonikidze Plant	707	400
Frunze Plant	636	403

In the data above, pig-iron productivity at Magnitogorsk was more than four times as great as that at the Frunze plant. The variation in steel productivity between the Kuznetsk and Kramatorsk plants was almost five to one. Obviously, therefore, conclusions about Soviet productivity based on observations at one or a few plants may be misleading, while reliance on averages alone conceals the great differences between different plants.

By the early 1950's, the official Soviet claims on the growth of productivity implied that man-year output of the average worker in large-scale industry was roughly five times as great as in 1928.[60] That this must be regarded skeptically has been indicated above, although the fact of important productivity increase is of course indubitable. Prof. Galenson suggests that in 1950 Soviet productivity was probably only moderately — perhaps 5 or 10 per cent — above that of 1940. The Soviet level of productivity in 1950 he believes may have been at most 40 per cent of the United States level for that year. For the future the outlook seems to be for a more rapid increase of industrial productivity than in the United States since, among other reasons, there is much greater room for such improvement in the Soviet Union than in the United States. By 1970, Prof. Galenson suggests, Soviet productivity is likely to be somewhere between 49 and 65 per cent of United States productivity. The lower limit would result if, during 1950–70, Soviet productivity increases annually averaged only 3 per cent and United States 2 per cent; the upper limit corresponds to Soviet and United States

[60] Walter Galenson, "Industrial Labor Productivity," in Bergson, ed., *Soviet Economic Growth*, p. 195.

percentages of 4 and 1.5 respectively. Such projections are speculative, of course, but they do indicate the probable direction of future trends.[61]

An important caution in studying Soviet labor productivity arises from the possibility that the data involved may have been computed in a manner which may make the published results misleading, that is, the data may contain other faults besides those arising from the past use of 1926–27 prices discussed earlier. That this is actually the case at one level of labor productivity computation is clearly indicated by the following extract from a speech at the 1954 Congress of the Soviet trade unions, a speech published in *Trud,* June 13, 1954.

> In our view the existing manner of determining the level of labor productivity for an enterprise as a whole is incorrect. Now, when determining labor productivity, there are taken into account only workers belonging to industrial groups, while other categories of workers — clerical employees, service personnel, and the like, whose number is often as much as 35 per cent of the total number of workers at a plant — are not taken into account.

Labor Unions

Soviet labor unions differ in functions and objectives from similar groups in capitalist countries. They are completely creatures of the state, the employer of their members. As such their chief goal and purpose is to stimulate in every way possible the growth of production and worker productivity. They act as instruments of the state in administering social insurance legislation and helping to enforce legislation regarding industrial safety, housing, and other matters. Soviet unions are under the complete control of the same ruling Communist Party hierarchy that controls the USSR's government and economic system. Under these circumstances it is not surprising that strikes have been virtually unknown for over two decades, that wages are set by government order rather than by collective bargaining, and that some of the most repressive measures

---

[61] *Ibid.,* pp. 212–13. It is interesting to note that not until 1951 did labor productivity in the Soviet coal industry as a whole regain the prewar level. Even in mid-1954, moreover, the prewar level of productivity had not been regained in such important sections of the coal industry as the Kuzbas, the Karaganda Basin, and much of the Donbas. *Trud,* June 8, 1954.

now governing Soviet workers have been announced by the government as originating in response to union wishes. The Soviet justification for the "company union" character of these organizations
derives from the assumption that the USSR is a workers' state. It is
argued that there can be no basic difference of interest between em-
ployee and employer such as is normal in a capitalist economy. The
Soviet emphasis on trade-union stimulation of production is de-
fended on the ground that the real income of all workers can only
be increased if production rises. Since there is no unemployment
in the Soviet Union, it is argued, workers and their unions need
not be afraid that higher production or technological advance will
harm them, and therefore they need not follow the restrictionist
or anti-innovation policies of unions in capitalist countries. It is
impossible to tell whether ordinary workers in the USSR are con-
vinced by these arguments, since under the conditions of Soviet
life expression of contrary opinion is not permitted. The apparent
lack of opposition to this type of unionism need not necessarily reflect worker support or acceptance.

It took more than a decade of debate and controversy after the
1917 Bolshevik revolution, however, before the present philosophy
of trade-union role and function became formally dominant. In
the first five years after Lenin's seizure of power, several different
viewpoints contested the issue. Trotsky, in a 1920 pamphlet, took
a position similar to that which finally triumphed, arguing that since
workers now controlled the state, trade unions should be merged
with the government. He saw their new functions as centering
primarily about the creation of an "atmosphere of productivity" so
as to help the state gain its economic goals. He urged that Soviet
unions wage war against the spirit of "trade unionism" — by this he
meant the objectives and tactics of unions in a capitalistic society
where the interests of workers are considered opposed to those of
employers. At the same time, Mikhail Tomsky, head of the Soviet
trade unions, argued that unions must have a separate and independent existence apart from the state so that they could defend
workers against the government administrators who were their direct
employers. Lenin himself at times seemed to lean toward this latter
position, for he told the Tenth Party Congress in March 1921:

> Ours is a workers' government with a bureaucratic twist. Our pres-
> ent government is such that the proletariat, organized to the last

man, must protect itself against it. And we must use the workers' organizations for the protection of the workers against their government.[62]

At other times, however, Lenin argued that the unions must be the "faithful ally" of the employing state, and he envisaged them as "reservoirs of state power, a school of communism, a school of management."[63] By this he apparently meant that trade unions should concentrate on indoctrinating workers, rather than on actually taking over administration of the economy itself as had been urged in the 1919 program of the Russian Communist Party.

Under Tomsky's leadership during most of the 1920's, Soviet trade unions did do much to defend workers' interests, fighting particularly against excessive differentials between highest- and lowest-paid workers. The struggle between those who shared Tomsky's view that unions must emphasize the protection of the workers' interests as sellers of labor power, and those, like Stalin, who maintained that the unions must be instruments of the state emphasizing maximum worker productivity, came to a head in 1928 and 1929. Tomsky and his supporters were removed from their positions and replaced by men like N. M. Shvernik, who supported Stalin's policies, so similar to those Trotsky had advocated a decade earlier. The official evaluation of the sins committed by Tomsky and his cohorts was put in these terms:

> Instead of mobilizing all the forces of the working class for the development of an increased tempo in socialist construction, for the fulfillment of the Five-Year Plan . . . the old leadership of the trade unions gave precedence to the "defensive" work of the trade unions as against the problems of their participation in socialist construction. Through Tomsky the old leadership urged that "it is impossible at the same time to manage an enterprise on the basis of commercial cost-accounting and yet be the exponent and defender of the workers' interests." . . . This was an expression of narrow "trade unionism."[64]

The Sixteenth Congress of the Communist Party, held in 1930, set down the new conception of trade-union functions and objectives in these terms:

[62] V. I. Lenin, *Sochineniya*, 3rd edition, Moscow, vol. 26, p. 104.
[63] V. I. Lenin, *Selected Works*, vol. IX, p. 70. New York: International Publishers, 1943.
[64] *Pravda*, April 12, 1932.

Under the leadership of the party, the trade unions have now removed their bankrupt leaders and have begun a determined fight against the elements of "trade unionism" and opportunism in the trade union movement. Today the basic factor in energizing and improving the entire work of the trade unions must be Socialist competition and its offspring, the shock brigades. Socialist competition and the shock brigades must become the primary concern of all the constructive activities of the unions. The problem of the trade unions is the organization of the Socialist competition and the shock brigades.

Union Organization

Soviet labor unions are organized on the industrial principle, that is, a union in a given field will include all workers employed in plants in the industry or industries within the union's jurisdiction. Thus there is one union for all metallurgical workers, another for coal miners, another for employees in all branches of lumbering, and so on. The jurisdictional scope of different unions has varied sharply from time to time, with the result that there have been great fluctuations in the number of individual unions existing in different periods. In the fall of 1937, the existing 47 unions were broken up into 154 smaller groups. In the fall of 1945 there existed 168 unions in the USSR according to the report of the CIO group that visited there at that time. Thereafter another change in policy took place. The unions were reamalgamated, and in April 1949 there were only 67 individual unions. In general the number of unions has changed with changes in the number of government ministries. Thus, when many ministries were consolidated shortly after Stalin's death, many unions were again consolidated.

Nominally, trade-union membership is voluntary, and a small fraction of Soviet workers are nonmembers. There is undoubtedly much pressure on workers to join, however. In addition, members have certain advantages over nonmembers, such as the right to receive greater social insurance payments, preference in admission to rest homes and sanatoria, free legal aid, and so forth. New members pay an initiation fee of 1 per cent of their monthly wage. Monthly dues since October 1953 have been 50 kopeks per 100 rubles of earnings for workers earning up to 500 rubles; a somewhat smaller percentage of monthly earnings for those receiving between

500 and 700 rubles; and 1 per cent of earnings for those receiving 700 rubles or more.[65]

The growth of Soviet labor union membership has been roughly parallel to the growth over time of the number of nonagricultural workers in the USSR, and enrollment has varied between 65 and 90 per cent of those eligible for membership. In January 1918 Soviet trade unions had 2,532,000 members, a number which increased to almost 11,000,000 by 1928. The rapid industrialization of the country in the 1930's was reflected in the fact that by the beginning of World War II there were about 25,000,000 union members out of more than 30,000,000 wage earners. In the postwar period membership grew from 27,000,000 in 1947 to 28,500,000 in April 1949 and to 40,420,000 by January 1, 1954.[66] This represented a membership including almost 90 per cent of all 45,000,000 workers and employees in the Soviet economy then. Union leader Shvernik noted in June 1954 that the greatest percentages of eligible union members who did not actually belong were in the agricultural field (over 20 per cent), among lumbering and paper workers (15 per cent), and among construction workers, that is, all fields in which seasonal workers make up relatively very high percentages of the labor force.

No explicit data regarding the membership of particular unions seem to have been published for many years. An estimate of the membership of some unions can be made on the basis of the number of delegates they sent to the June 1954 trade union congress, assuming as seems likely that each delegate represented about 30,000 members. The largest Soviet union was that of agricultural and farm requisition workers, with about 4,000,000 members; the railroad workers' union had 3,500,000; the medical workers' union had 2,400,000; and unions with about 2,000,000 members each included the food industry workers', consumer goods industry workers', coal miners', and cultural workers'.[67]

The structure of Soviet trade unions is pyramidal. The primary unit is the shop or factory group, the former in large enterprises. The branches of a particular union are combined into district, regional, republican, and finally all-union organizations, the latter of course being the national union itself. The branch meeting of

[65] *Pravda,* October 19, 1953.
[66] *Entsiklopediya,* cols. 1753–54; *Pravda,* April 21, 1949; *Trud,* June 8, 1954.
[67] Based on data in *Trud,* June 10, 1954.

members is the primary source of authority at the local level, and its participants elect both a factory committee (or shop committee if it is a shop unit) and an auditing committee. The former attends to the local's business between branch meetings and the latter checks on the factory or shop committee's work. At the district, regional, republican, and all-union levels, conferences of elected delegates are held from time to time, and these elect corresponding district, regional, republican, and all-union committees to operate the organization, as well as corresponding auditing committees. Thus each national union's central committee is at the apex of a hierarchical pyramid whose broad base is the multitude of local branches throughout the country.

Integration of the different unions is also realized at all levels. The All-Union Trade-Union Congress — which under present rules must meet at least once every four years — includes delegates from all Soviet trade unions, and is nominally the ultimate source of power in general union policy. This Congress elects the All-Union Central Council of Trade Unions (AUCCTU), which functions between congresses as the directing and policy-making body for the entire union movement. In the postwar period republican, territorial, and provincial trade-union councils were formed to integrate union activities in each area of the country. Earlier experience had apparently shown that lack of such coordinating groups resulted in many deficiencies in trade-union work.[68]

Soviet trade unions are organized on the principle of "democratic centralism," by which is meant that all trade-union officials are elected by the membership or the membership's delegates, that decisions are made by majority vote, and that at any stage in the hierarchial pyramid the decision of a higher body (say, a republican organization or the all-union central committee of a union) is binding on all units subordinate to it. In actual practice control of the trade-union organization is highly centralized, but the adherence to democratic practices—as distinguished from merely democratic forms—has often been poor. Perhaps the most striking example of this was the failure to hold any All-Union Congress of Trade Unions for seventeen years, between 1932 and 1949, a period in which many major decisions were made and executed without any direct refer-

---

[68] *Pravda*, October 16, 1948.

ence to the membership's wishes. In 1935 the Soviet press raised a hue and cry about the lack of democracy in the trade unions, revealing that many officials were appointed rather than elected and that these officials often abused their power.[69] Reforms made then apparently did not end bureaucratic violations of trade-union democracy, for such complaints have frequently appeared in the Soviet press since then.[70] In any case, of course, the Communist Party leadership controls the trade unions and bends them to its will, and no effort is made to poll the membership before major decisions are taken. The Tenth All-Union Congress of Trade Unions, which finally took place in April 1949, saw no complaints voiced about the failure to meet for almost two decades. There was no free debate about union policy at this congress either. The eleventh congress met in June 1954.

Union Functions

The 1949 statutes and bylaws of Soviet trade unions set down nine categories of functions for these organizations, functions which were not essentially altered at the 1954 congress. These follow together with comment on them: [71]

    1. Organize socialist competition of workers and employees for fulfilling and overfulfilling state plans, increasing the productivity of labor, improving the quality and lowering the cost of production.

This, we have seen above, is the primary function. Not infrequently attention has been focused so single-mindedly upon this function that trade-union officials have neglected to protect the interests of workers.

    2. Participate in planning and regulating wages of workers and employees, in devising a system of wages guided by the socialist principle of pay according to amount and quality of labor; strive to introduce new progressive output norms; keep track of the correct calculation of labor and the application of piece-work and progressive bonus pay for labor.

It will be noted that there is no mention here of trade-union negotiation with employers regarding wages, but merely of participation

[69] Gordon, op. cit., pp. 110–13.

[70] See, for example, Trud, October 28 and November 16, 1948.

[71] Trud, May 11, 1949. An English text of these statutes and bylaws is given in the Current Digest of the Soviet Press, May 31, 1949, pp. 26–32.

in devising wage scales that will have maximum incentive effect. There is little information on the extent, if any, to which trade-union leaders actually influence Soviet government wage policy and act as advocates of workers' interests in the formulation of the economic plan that sets the over-all amount and division of total wages paid. It is clear, however, that in practice this provision is intended to spur union officials at the local level to be constantly alert for means of changing the wage payment system in particular enterprises so as to strengthen its incentive nature. In current practice, Soviet wage scales are set by the government agencies that employ workers in accordance with over-all government wage policy. Wages are not and may not be disputed by unions at the local level once they have been promulgated.

3. Help workers and employees to raise their production and business qualifications; spread the work-experience of leading workers and employees, the innovators in production and science, and assist in introducing progressive techniques in industry.

4. Conclude collective agreements with the administration of enterprises.

The collective agreements referred to in this paragraph are the Soviet equivalent of the agreements reached between free trade unions and employers. In the 1920's and early 1930's, these agreements were widely concluded between unions and enterprises throughout the USSR's economy. From 1936 to early 1947, however, collective agreements apparently vanished, a phenomenon explained by Soviet writers in these terms:

> Experience has shown that the restoration of the practice of concluding collective agreements is not expedient. *The collective agreement as a special form of legal regulation of labor relations of workers and employees has outlived itself.* [Italics in original.] Detailed regulation of all sides of these relations by normative acts of governmental power does not leave any room for any contractual agreement concerning one labor condition or another.[72]

In March 1947 the practice of concluding such collective agreements was resumed by order of the Presidium of the All-Union Central Council of Trade Unions, which listed the objectives and subjects to be covered by these agreements in the following order: increasing productivity of labor; improving the wage system as a

---

[72] Aleksandrov and Genkin, *op. cit.*, p. 106.

stimulus to higher production by substitution of piece rates for time rates and more intensive use of work norms based upon technical possibilities rather than average performance; programs for training workers and technical personnel; methods for improving labor discipline; measures to improve safety of working conditions; methods of improving plant recreational facilities.[73] The level and amount of wage rates are not a subject of negotiation in the making of these agreements, since rates fixed by the state are mandatory. Collective agreements have been concluded annually each year since 1947, unions assuming obligations for raising productivity and managements promising to improve various aspects of working and living conditions. Checkups on the observance of these agreements have frequently revealed failures to observe the obligations and promises made in them. In 1948, 40,000 collective agreements were concluded, covering some 17,000,000 workers and employees. In 1953, about 53,000 collective agreements were concluded, probably covering 20,000,000 or more workers.[74]

> 5. Carry out control over the condition of labor safeguards and safety techniques in enterprises and institutions; participate in settling labor disputes; conclude agreements with the management of enterprises regarding the method of expending resources on measures for safety techniques and labor safeguards.

Supervision of safety measures in enterprises of all kinds is performed by trade-union inspectors, whose duty it is to recommend changes and improvements where required. The above paragraph also indicates that labor disputes do occur in the USSR and have to be settled. Strikes as a means of settling such disputes are virtually unknown in the USSR. There is no legal prohibition against strikes, but severe punishment would undoubtedly be meted out to a union official or anyone else who called an unauthorized work stoppage. One of the few examples noted in the past two decades of an incident resembling a strike took place in early 1946. After two years of attempting to secure badly needed improvements in safety precautions, an inspector of the Electrical Workers Union ordered workers to walk out temporarily. But this demonstration may have been officially arranged so that it could be publicized as an example of Soviet workers' freedom to strike.[75]

---

[73] *Trud,* March 16, 1947.
[74] *Izvestia,* February 3, 1949, *Trud,* August 5, 1953.
[75] *The New York Times,* April 7, 1946; account based on an article in *Trud.*

Most labor disputes in the postwar period are said to arise over improper implementation of labor laws, factory rules, or collective or individual labor agreements, as well as over "unjustified demands of individual unscrupulous workers." Wage rates, hours, and working conditions are determined by law and are not subject to dispute. Workers having grievances submit them to their shop or factory committee, as the case may be, which investigates the matter. If the complaint is found to be justified, management is asked to correct matters. In this way, it is claimed, most disputes are settled. If management fails to mend matters, the dispute is usually taken to the shop or factory Rate and Disputes Commission (in Russian, this is termed the *Rastsenochno-Konfliktnaya Komissiya*, or RKK for short), which is usually composed of two representatives each of workers and management. The commission holds a public hearing on the matter and then reaches a decision, which must be unanimous if it is to be binding. If the commission disagrees, the dispute can be taken to public courts. A unanimous decision of the commission can be appealed to higher trade-union organs, which may confirm it or annul it; in the latter case the matter is directed back for reconsideration to the original commission or is sent to the people's courts. If the commission's decision is affirmed through all appeals procedure, management becomes subject to legal prosecution if it fails to carry out the decision.[76]

> 6. Direct state social insurance, determine and issue relief (payments) to workers and employees for temporary disability, strive for better organization of medical aid for workers and for safeguarding the health of women and children, build sanatoriums and rest homes, organize mutual loan societies, participate in allocating living space in housing belonging to enterprises and institutions, exercise mass control over fulfillment of plans for housing and cultural construction, the work of restaurants, shops, municipal welfare enterprises and transport.

In administering the complex system of Soviet social insurance, including disability payments, old-age pensions, and the like, trade unions act as agents of the government and distribute funds from the state budget appropriated for these purposes. The unions took over this function in the early 1930's, when the People's Commissariat of Labor was abolished. Using their own and government funds, Soviet trade unions build and operate numerous sanatoria, rest homes, and

---

[76] *Labor Abroad*, December 1949, pp. 36–40.

children's camps. Union inspectors check the work of the distributive system to help insure its proper operation. In conducting these activities, Soviet unions exercise a great deal of influence over the welfare of all workers, expending large sums and employing many persons in the process. This work is not always performed well, however, as complaints in the Soviet press testify.

    7. Help members of trade unions to raise their ideological-political and general-educational standards, spread political and scientific knowledge, conduct widespread production-technical propaganda, form clubs, houses and palaces of culture, Red corners and libraries, and develop among the workers and employees mass amateur art participation, physical culture, sports and touring.

In early 1949 Soviet trade unions operated 8,000 clubs, homes of culture, and palaces of culture; over 8,000 libraries; more than 5,000 movie units; and over 4,000 stadiums, gymnasiums, sports fields, swimming pools, and ski runs.[77]

    8. Draw women into state, industrial and social life; help workers and employees in the communist education of children.

    9. Appear in the name of workers and employees before state and social agencies on problems on labor, living conditions, and culture.

From this recital of Soviet trade-union functions, it is apparent that their activities are both more comprehensive in some directions and less comprehensive in other directions than those of unions in the United States. They are not independent organizations of workers. Their influence upon the centralized formulation of wage policy and the centralized decisions regarding the allocation of the national income is obscure, and presumably is never at variance with state policy. On the other hand, to the extent that they force enterprise managements to observe safety regulations and other measures protecting workers, they do exercise an important influence. As the administrative agency for state social insurance, trade unions perform functions confined to government agencies in capitalist countries. Their cultural and welfare activities resemble strongly functions undertaken by some unions in this country, such as the International Ladies Garment Workers Union. But in the forefront of Soviet union consciousness at all times is the obligation to spur production. When contradictions arise between the demands

[77] *Pravda*, April 21, 1949.

of increased production and workers' interests, it is the former that
frequently triumphs, as evidenced by union assent to such measures
as the higher postwar work week, strict labor book requirements and
other control over workers, and by many reports in the Soviet press
of union neglect of workers' safety or welfare. All too often, apparently, trade-union officials have looked the other way when
enterprise directors have required illegal overtime or Sunday work,
have failed to build promised housing, have not provided proper
rest or safety facilities, and the like.[78] It is a commentary on the
situation that the Soviet government has had to remind union officials
from time to time that they must protect workers as well as advance
output.

The thesis that a free trade-union movement devoted primarily
to the immediate interests of its members is incompatible with a
planned economy is one that the Soviet Union's experience would
seem to support though not necessarily to prove. What is clear is
that in the late 1920's Stalin and his supporters reached the conclusion that a worker-oriented union movement would be incompatible with the high rate of industrialization and the consequent
sacrifices in consumption toward which the five-year plans were
directed. The difficulties experienced by the British labor government in restraining union wage-increase demands in the postwar
period are probably indicative of the troubles that would have
plagued Soviet planners after 1928 if the union movement had
remained under Tomsky's control and had pursued an independent
policy reflecting workers' aspirations. As it was, deprived of the
ability to strike or otherwise take collective action in protest against
the low standard of living to which they were subjected in the
1930's, millions of individual workers showed their dissatisfaction
by moving from job to job, until state controls were made sufficiently
stringent to stop this unorganized type of resistance. Along with
collectivization of agriculture, therefore, the subjugation of the
labor unions and the application of coercive restrictions upon
workers' liberties have been most important factors in the rapid
economic development of the USSR since the late 1920's.

---

[78] Cf. the typical complaints in *Trud*, April 13, 1948; September 2 and October 16, 1949; *Pravda*, October 16, 1948; and *Trud*, June 8–15, 1954.

Prison Labor

We have seen above that there is an important element of coercion in all Soviet labor relations. A worker may not leave his job without his employer's permission; graduates of the Labor Reserve Schools and all universities and technical institutes must work for several years after their graduation wherever the Soviet government assigns them; large numbers of peasants are conscripted annually to do obligatory work in repairing roads; and so on. The ordinary Soviet worker must be punished if he is absent from work without a legally acceptable reason or if he is late to work, and there are other restrictions that severely limit his freedom. But these controls and limitations characterize what is normally termed the free hired-labor force in Russia. In addition to this group there are also a significant number of prison and forced laborers.

The topic of prison labor in the Soviet Union is probably the most controversial in the entire area of Soviet economics. It is also the subject on which reliable and comprehensive information is most difficult to obtain. The matter has been a cause for warm international dispute in the early 1930's and since World War II. In the former period efforts were made in a number of countries to secure prohibitions against imports of Soviet goods on the ground that these were produced by forced labor. In the more recent period the subject of prison labor in the Soviet Union has been hotly debated before the United Nations, and both official and unofficial demands have been raised for comprehensive investigation of the situation within the Soviet Union. These demands have been refused by the Soviet government. In the early 1930's some foreigners were allowed to inspect Soviet prison labor camps and came back with reports that the importance and nature of this type of labor had been much exaggerated and distorted abroad.[79] The reports of these observers have been challenged by some writers, who point out that it would have been simple for the Soviet authorities to alter true conditions in any area before the foreign delegation arrived there. As a result, it is alleged, these observations must be discarded entirely.[80]

---

[79] Joseph Freeman, *The Soviet Worker*, pp. 259–63. New York: Liveright, 1932.

[80] D. J. Dallin and B. I. Nicolaevsky, *Forced Labor in Soviet Russia*, pp. 224–25. New Haven: Yale University Press, 1947.

Because of the controversial nature of this subject, it seems wise to begin with an indication of the nature of the evidence upon which current belief that large numbers of prison laborers are used in the Soviet Union rests. It is known first, that Soviet law provides that the Ministry of Interior (formerly known in Russia by its initials NKVD and now known as MVD) has the authority to send individuals to prison in "camps of correctional labor," to exile them to a definite locality in the Soviet Union with or without confinement, or to prohibit residence in certain places.[81] The official Soviet position seems to be that these correctional labor camps are simply prisons in which law breakers are confined, given useful work to do under humane conditions, and thus re-educated into socially useful citizens. While no official statistics on the number of these prisoners have been published for many years, Soviet statements seem to imply that the number of prisoners is not excessive and compares relatively favorably to the number of prisoners in other countries, who are also required to do work of various kinds while serving their terms.

As against this official position of the Soviet government, there exists widespread belief that the USSR has millions of prison laborers who are put to work under extremely harsh conditions, with the result that many die or are permanently injured before they have finished their terms. Reports to this effect, which circulated abroad in the 1920's and 1930's, were to a large extent based on the accounts of individuals who had fled from the Soviet Union and who claimed to have been incarcerated in these camps. Some of these reports may have been exaggerated by groups interested either in stimulating dislike of the USSR or in limiting competition from Soviet exports. Nevertheless, from the present perspective it seems clear that many of these accounts were true in all essentials, though they were often received with incredulity by the outside world because of the difficulty in documenting them and because of the unbelievable character of the conditions described. Since World War II, however, the outside world has received a much more abundant stream of information about this aspect of Soviet life. Today both its existence and great importance seem beyond doubt. The evidence has come from literally thousands and tens of thousands of persons who spent some time as forced laborers in

---

[81] Gsovski, *op. cit.*, Vol. I, pp. 238–39. *The New York Times*, July 23, 1949.

these camps and then later reached the outside world. Many of these individuals were Polish nationals who were living in eastern Poland when it was taken over by the Soviet Union in 1939. At first sent to forced-labor camps, where they remained for some time, these individuals were freed after the Soviet Union entered World War II against Germany and concluded an agreement with the Free Polish Government providing for their release so that a Free Polish army might be formed in Iran.[82] In addition to the accounts of these Polish citizens, the outside world has received similar accounts in recent years from many Soviet citizens who had been imprisoned in forced-labor camps and who were able to flee the Soviet Union after the Nazi invasion of 1941.[83] There are also occasional references to forced laborers in Soviet publications that suggest they are a significant group. Thus a Soviet statistical dictionary has this reference:

> The wage fund is calculated, however, not only for hired workers and employees and cooperative artisans, but also for military personnel and other categories who are not free workers.[84]

The volume of this assorted evidence, combined with the blanket refusal of the Soviet government to permit outside investigation since World War II of the truth or falsity of these reports, raises a most strong presumption that forced labor is a significant factor in the USSR's economy.

The number of prisoner laborers in the USSR and changes in that number over past years are not known with any precision because of the natural reluctance of the government of the USSR to release statistics on this topic. Estimates by various observers in recent years have varied widely, ranging from one to two million to over 20 million persons. In some cases efforts have been made to estimate this figure by compiling lists of prison camps, on the basis of interviews with former forced laborers, and then multiplying the number of camps found in this fashion by some estimated number of prisoners per camp.[85] Another approach has been through analysis of

---

[82] The experiences of these Polish citizens is best summarized in the collective work, *The Dark Side of the Moon,* and also in such accounts of individual experiences as Gliksman, *Tell the West.*

[83] See the typical account in V. Petrov, *Soviet Gold, passim.* New York: Farrar, Straus, 1949.

[84] *Slovar-Spravochnik . . .,* p. 213.

[85] Dallin and Nicolaevsky, *op. cit.,* pp. 49–87.

Soviet data on wages and employment, utilizing the fact that published Soviet statistics on the total wage fund of the economy show that this figure is substantially above the product of the number of hired workers and employees and the average annual earnings. The difference between the wage fund and the product described above is apparently due to wages paid military personnel and unfree workers as indicated in the quotation cited above.[86] But these and other methods of estimation require that arbitrary assumptions be made at one point or another and are therefore incapable of giving more than very approximate results.

The prisoners sentenced to forced labor are apparently of three kinds: ordinary criminals, officials and others who violate Soviet economic laws, and political prisoners. The latter, who are usually alleged to be the great majority of these unfortunates, include persons who have expressed political opinions at variance with those approved by the Soviet regime, farmers who have resisted collectivization, members of nationality groups distrusted by the Soviet government, persons who carried on illegal religious activities during the period of violent government opposition to religion, and the like. Some sources claim that at various times the MVD has arrested large groups of people simply in order to augment its supply of forced laborers, though none of the arrested group was guilty of any crime, even in the broad Soviet concept of that term. In the postwar period an important component of the forced labor group has consisted of German, Japanese, and other prisoners of war, as well as dissident citizens of areas in Eastern Europe and Asia that were occupied by the Red Army at the end of World War II. Large numbers of Poles, Estonians, Latvians, and Lithuanians have also apparently been deported from their homelands in the postwar period and added to the ranks of this group.

A most important advance in public knowledge of Soviet slave labor took place in late 1950 when the United States government released a secret document, the 1941 economic plan of the USSR.[87]

---

[86] Harry Schwartz, "A Critique of 'Appraisals of Russian Economic Statistics.'" *Review of Economic Statistics*, February 1948, pp. 38–41.

[87] This document is the *Gosudarstvenny Plan Razvitiya Narodnogo Khozyaistva SSSR na 1941 God.* A photo-lithoprint reproduction has been published by the American Council of Learned Societies as No. 30 of its series of Russian reprints. An interesting, but not entirely convincing, effort to compute the number of Soviet slave laborers on the basis of data in this document was made by Naum Jasny in his article in the *Journal of Political Economy,* October 1951.

This material had been originally captured by German forces and then by western troops. It gave for the first time something approaching a comprehensive—though not complete—picture of the economic importance of the secret police agency, the NKVD (the Ministry of Internal Affairs now known as the MVD).

This plan revealed that, among other functions, the NKVD was responsible for about one-sixth of all new construction in the USSR during 1941, for about 11 per cent of all Soviet lumber production, over 20 per cent of all railroad ties made in the USSR, 40 per cent of all chromium ore, over 5,000,000 tons of coal or about 5 per cent of the national total, all production in the growing Ukhta-Pechora oil field in the Far North, much consumer goods output, and so forth. The plan did not give a full picture of NKVD activities since it did not contain data on armaments output or production of raw materials geared most closely to armaments, such as non-ferrous metals, where slave labor is known to be most important. The plan gave no information on gold output nor did it throw any light on the very large area of NKVD activity where it acts as a subcontractor and labor supplier for other agencies. Despite these gaps, however, this plan—which Soviet authorities never intended the outside world to see—provides the most conclusive evidence yet available from Soviet sources that slave labor is a major fundament of the USSR's economy.

During World War II and the early postwar period, the conditions under which prison laborers lived and worked were almost unbelievably bad. Numerous descriptions by persons who served as forced laborers during this period told of semi-starvation as chronic, of great brutality, of incredibly bad lodging, and the like. Under these conditions, the labor productivity of these workers was inevitably low, their mortality rate was high, and the system was most uneconomic from any point of view save as a device for punishing political malcontents. Beginning with 1948 conditions of food, lodging, and the like were apparently somewhat improved; much greater stress was laid on offering prisoners economic inducements for higher productivity; and the operation of the forced-labor system took much more into account the fact that these prisoners could represent an economic asset. How changed conditions became is evident from reports we have of a major strike conducted in the summer of 1953 by prisoners in the great Vorkuta coal area in northeastern European Russia.[88]

As late as June 1952 there was published indication of the continued importance of slave labor in the Soviet Union. When the Soviet government announced the distribution of awards to individuals who had played a major role in helping to complete the Volga-Don Canal, the published list showed that among the recipients of the highest awards were the leaders of the MVD, a circumstance hardly explainable except on the hypothesis that slave labor was employed on this project. The fact that the list of awards did not identify these individuals' connection with the MVD seems to strengthen this hypothesis.

The limited amnesty for Soviet prisoners announced in late March 1953 may have resulted in the release or the shortening of prison terms for some forced workers. The amnesty conspicuously omitted from its benefits those imprisoned for political opposition to the regime, the "counter-revolutionaries" whom all reports indicate are the main group of forced laborers. The softening of Soviet labor laws and of the harsh discipline they impose upon Soviet workers, farmers, and military personnel was promised in the original amnesty. But a year after this promise was issued publicly there was no indication that any such changes of the law had actually taken place.

Some reports from foreigners who left the Soviet Union after Stalin's death suggested that remaining forced-labor camps had been transferred from the Ministry of Internal Affairs and shifted to the Ministry of Justice as part of the shake-up following the purge of Lavrenti P. Beria in June 1953. There were also some other fragmentary indications of a shift of economic functions from the MVD to more normal governmental agencies. But as of the first months of 1954, the situation seemed obscure.[89]

[88] Cf. the articles by B. Gerland in the New York Herald-Tribune, March 1–3, 1954, and the extended interview with her in Sotsialistichesky Vestnik, February 1954. Her observations are substantiated also by Helmut Gollwitzer, Unwilling Journey. Philadelphia: Muhlenberg Press, 1954.

[89] An analysis of the forced labor situation in the Soviet Union by an observer who differs sharply with the conclusions suggested in this section will be found in Alexander Baykov, "A Note on the Economic Significance of Compulsory Labour in the U.S.S.R.," Bulletins on Soviet Economic Development, Bulletin 7 (Series 2), December 1952, pp. 30–41.

Two International Comparisons

The preceding discussion of the Soviet worker and his lot may be put in perspective by citing the conclusions of two studies comparing the position of the Moscow worker with British and American workers in the early 1950's. The first study, based on the observations of an Englishman who visited Moscow in the spring of 1952 and who carefully collected and analyzed many price and wage data, concludes as follows:[90]

> It will be asked: how do the many families with monthly incomes of 1000 rubles and less manage to live in present-day Moscow? Obviously unless they consist of only two or three persons, they will be quite unable to afford anything so "luxurious" as the very austere Moscow "human needs" diet outlined in Table I. However, take away from this diet all the foods that, for an English person, would make the diet at all edible . . . and replace the calories thus lost by the cheapest carbohydrate foods, and the cost of the diet is reduced by about two-fifths. Something of this kind is probably the remedy applied by the working class family with several dependent children and old parents. On the other hand, luxuries large and small are made and sold in Russia, and some of the minor ones are certainly quite within the reach of an exceptionally well paid worker with no or few dependents; but the masses are very poor by western standards, and the great luxuries are reserved—as everywhere—for the rich. The average working-class family can afford little family life; husband and wife will be working each their 48 hours per week in factories, while their children are being looked after in a creche, or, very often, by the grandmother living with the family. Even with both parents thus working, a Moscow family will rarely attain the standard of living enjoyed by an English working class family in which only the husband is the bread winner while the wife devotes herself solely to her family.

A Bureau of Labor Statistics study of the worktime required on the average—as of the spring of 1953—by workers in Moscow and New York, to earn enough to buy units of basic food and consumer goods, found that the Moscow worker had to work twice to 25 times as long to buy basic foods. For basic clothing items he had to work usually 8 to 20 times as long as the New Yorker.[91]

---

[90] T. Schulz and P. Wiles, "Earnings and Living Standards in Moscow," *Bulletin of the Oxford University Institute of Statistics,* September and October, 1952, pp. 324–25.

[91] Edmund Nash, "Purchasing Power of Soviet Workers, 1953," *Monthly Labor Review,* July 1953.

It may be noted that the British study cited above assumed that average Soviet earnings were somewhat higher than noted earlier in this book, while the Bureau of Labor Statistics assumed a somewhat lower earnings figure. Nevertheless the agreed conclusion—that the living standard and real earnings of Soviet workers are far lower than those of their British and American counterparts—seems clear beyond doubt.

CHAPTER XIV

FOREIGN ECONOMIC RELATIONS

Soviet foreign economic relations consist of many varied activities: foreign trade, international financial transactions, foreign loans and investments, collection of reparations, tourism, participation in international postal and other communications arrangements, and so on. The USSR is a signatory to various international economic agreements and a member of some international governmental organizations dealing with economic subjects.

The manner in which Soviet foreign economic relations are conducted and the objectives they serve reflect the political and economic structure of the Soviet Union. With insignificant exceptions, all these activities are conducted by agencies of the Soviet state. Foreign trade and financial transactions are integrated with the over-all economic plan of the USSR and are themselves carefully planned. A government monopoly of foreign trade was instituted in April 1918 and has been in effect ever since. Usually goods have been sold or bought abroad for government account or for the accounts of government-owned enterprises whose independence is merely a legal fiction, as pointed out in an earlier chapter. In making decisions on foreign economic policy, the Soviet government takes into account political as well as economic factors. As a result, the Soviet regime does not necessarily buy in the cheapest market or sell in the dearest market, as would an independent entrepreneur operating under capitalist conditions. Before World War II, these facets of Soviet foreign economic policy differed considerably from the corresponding arrangements prevalent in most other countries

574

of the world. These different arrangements raised complex problems for other nations and citizens of other nations doing business with the USSR. In more recent years, of course, state trading and direct government participation in foreign economic relations have become much more prevalent.

The reasons for centralized government dominance of this area of Soviet life are both ideological and practical. Foreign trade and related aspects of international economic relations have long been regarded as among the most important "commanding heights" that any socialist state must hold if it is to control its entire economy. In addition, it would obviously be most difficult to operate a domestic planned economy unless foreign trade were integrated with the domestic planning. For example, the foreign-trade monopoly is far more effective than any tariff system in assuring that government plans to develop high-cost domestic industries will not be hindered by cheap, competitive imports. Conversely, the monopoly's export policy can be based upon considerations deriving from the domestic plan rather than merely upon considerations of profitability in the light of fluctuating world market prices. Direct government control and operation of all foreign economic relations are therefore most important means of insulating the domestic economy so far as possible from the fluctuations of the world economy as a whole. It may be pointed out, however, that experience has shown that this insulation is by no means perfect.

When properly operated, this centralized system gives the Soviet regime important tactical advantages in dealing with foreign buyers and sellers. At any given time, the Soviet government knows its position in relation to the rest of the world and each foreign country separately, thus greatly simplifying formulation of policy. This has been particularly important in the past two decades, when foreign currencies have not been freely interchangeable, raising complex problems of currency control and clearing in foreign trade. It also facilitates the utilization of foreign economic relations for political objectives. There have been times, however, when the USSR has sold goods abroad on consignment, thereby exposing itself to unpredictable price fluctuations. As the sole buyer and seller of goods and services for the USSR, the Soviet government has a strong bargaining position as against competing buyers and sellers in other countries. There is no competition among Soviet buyers and sellers on the foreign markets to affect prices adversely from their point of view.

Its monopoly of foreign trade permits the Soviet government to insulate its domestic price system from prices prevailing in world markets. The prices at which the Soviet Union buys or sells goods abroad need not and frequently do not have any close relationship to the prices of the same commodities in the Soviet Union itself. In advancing its economic interests abroad, the Soviet government is able to back them with all its political, economic, and military might, giving it substantial advantages frequently over individual foreign enterprises or weaker foreign states. In formulating and executing its foreign policy, the Soviet regime is not under the pressure of conflicting domestic interests such as those that exert so powerful and contradictory a set of influences upon, say, the tariff policy of the United States. Where and when necessary, the managers of the USSR's economy can and do act against the interests of particular groups of Soviet producers and consumers in making decisions about foreign transactions.

On the other hand, of course, there are disadvantages too. The lack of competition among Soviet buyers and sellers may mean reduced initiative and less favorable results on occasion. The problem of coordinating all the manifold foreign economic activities of the USSR is no easy one, and confusion must sometimes affect operations. The fact that foreigners must do all their business through the Soviet government's agencies makes the USSR's foreign economic relations particularly vulnerable to political tensions between the USSR and other countries. As a result Soviet trade abroad has often been hindered by boycotts, blockades, embargoes, penalty rates, and other discriminatory restrictions arising from political causes. But whatever the advantages or disadvantages of the organization of Soviet foreign economic relations, it is clear that the USSR's regime regards that monopoly as an inseparable part of its planned economic system and has no intention of modifying it substantially in the foreseeable future.

Viewed most generally, the primary objective of Soviet foreign economic policy and activity has been the increase of the USSR's political, economic and military strength by the use of foreign resources on unilaterally advantageous terms. The specific means employed to further this objective have differed from period to period in Soviet history, depending upon the circumstances at each time. Two particular goals derived from this general objective deserve particular attention. In the economic sphere Soviet policy for more than two decades has been directed at establishing maximum self-sufficiency. The effort to achieve such autarky required the importation of large quantities of foreign materials, machinery, and technical knowledge. These had to be paid for regardless of the burden imposed upon the domestic economy. As the Soviet economy developed, goods formerly bought abroad were produced at home, and corresponding reductions were made in purchases abroad.

In following this policy the Soviet government has put little value on the advantages arising from international division of labor, prizing more highly the security advantages of maximal domestic production of all commodities considered essential. Soviet export policy for the most part — but not exclusively — has been dictated by the requirements for essential imports rather than by any desire to attain a maximum "favorable" balance of trade or payments. There are no private interests in the Soviet Union putting pressure on policy-makers to maximize exports and minimize imports; on the contrary, the pressures have been in the other direction for the most part. It is not surprising, therefore, that the Soviet Union has eagerly sought large quantities of goods in payment of reparations after World War II. This policy has differed sharply from that of many of the victor nations after World War I, when reparations in goods were in effect frequently refused because of the complaints of domestic interests adversely affected by such free imports.

Second, the Soviet government uses foreign trade and other aspects of foreign economic relations as weapons for increasing its political influence or domination in weaker foreign countries. Before World War II, this factor was most noticeable in the Soviet foreign-trade policy in Asia, particularly Iran, Afghanistan, Turkey, Mongolia, Tannu Tuva, and Western China.[1] The USSR utilized the advantages of its geographical position to absorb the surpluses of these nations and to make them dependent upon Soviet imports, dictating prices at which goods were exchanged and seeking to hinder eco-

---

[1] Violet Conolly, *Soviet Economic Policy in the East*, pp. 4–5. London: Oxford University Press, 1933.

nomic changes in these countries that might weaken Soviet influence. In the postwar period this policy has been extended to all of Eastern Europe under Soviet domination, North Korea, and Communist China.

The Soviet government also uses trade as a weapon in political disputes with foreign countries, as in the case of the reductions in Soviet purchases ordered at various times in the 1920's and 1930's during political disputes with Great Britain.[2] At times, too, it has conducted business with foreign countries in such a way as to aid local communist parties there. For example, in the spring of 1946, just before the French parliamentary elections, the USSR offered to sell 500,000 tons of grain to France, negotiating directly with Maurice Thorez, head of the French communist party and then a Vice-Premier in the French government.[3] The Soviet refusal to join with the Western European nations in the Marshall Plan in the period following World War II was obviously influenced, in part, by the fear that its influence in its Eastern European satellite nations would be threatened if the Soviet Union and its satellites were to receive American aid through the European Recovery Program. Soviet economic pressure upon Yugoslavia both before and after the latter country's break with the Cominform in 1948 illustrates this facet of the USSR's foreign economic policy. Yugoslavia's "hostile attitude" was cited by the Soviet government as the reason for reducing trade with that country in 1949 to one eighth of its former level.

Foreign-Trade Organization

The foreign-trade organization of the Soviet Union has undergone many changes over the more than three decades of that country's existence. We shall be concerned here primarily with the organization that has existed relatively unchanged since the mid-1930's.

Pyramidal organization is common in the Soviet Union. Foreign trade follows this pattern. At the apex is the Ministry of Foreign Trade, which has direct control over all these activities and exercises general administrative, planning, and coordinating functions.

[2] Stella K. Margold, *Let's Do Business with Russia*, pp. 140–41. New York: Harper's, 1948.

[3] Schwartz, *Russia's Postwar Economy*, p. 86.

Among the more important activities of the Foreign Trade Ministry are the following: it negotiates international trade agreements and other economic pacts with foreign nations; prepares the foreign-trade plan annually and quarterly, in terms of amounts and kinds of commodities, countries of sale and purchase, and financial balances; arranges for credits to be obtained from or given abroad; supervises the administration of Soviet customs; directs the activities of all Soviet export and import agencies abroad; directs and coordinates the activities of procurement and sales organizations in the USSR dealing with commodities to be exported or imported; formulates regulations and issues authorizations for all aspects of foreign-trade activity. At the head of the ministry is a Minister of Foreign Trade, who is a member of the Council of Ministers. The activities of the Ministry of Foreign Trade are, of course, subordinate to the Party Presidium, the Council of Ministers, and other higher organs of the Communist Party and the Soviet government. Its plans must be integrated with the general economic plan and approved by the government before they go into effect.[4]

Under the Foreign Trade Ministry there is a complex group of organizations that carry on the actual work required to realize the export and import plans of the Soviet government. The most important of these are the monopolistic export and import organizations and the trade delegations resident in foreign countries. Thus the ministry has a wide network of agents throughout the USSR and in virtually all foreign countries to transact its business. The monopolistic export and import corporations carry on the actual foreign trade of the USSR. As of the end of 1953, all but one of these corporations either export or import — or sometimes both export and import — specified groups of commodities to most countries of the world. One corporation, *Vostokintorg*, operates on a regional basis and handles all trade with Afghanistan, Outer Mongolia, and Sinkiang. In addition there are specialized organizations for shipping and tourism. Each organization handles all business falling within its jurisdiction, and foreign firms or individuals can effect transactions only with the appropriate Soviet state enterprise.

These monopolistic organizations conclude contracts at home and abroad for procurement and sale of the articles assigned to them, and

---

[4] Baykov, *Soviet Foreign Trade*, p. 24.

their representatives are to be found in many different countries. Since the end of World War II, most Soviet business has been transacted abroad, though more important and particularly sensitive transactions have been conducted in Moscow, and Soviet furs are sold at auction in Leningrad in July of every year. These corporations are nominally independent enterprises, having their own balance sheets and bank accounts and operating on a commercial basis in accordance with the principles of economic accountability (*khozraschet*). As of the end of 1953, the following organizations were active in different fields.[5]

Stankoimport. Exports and imports machine tools, ball and roller bearings, optical instruments, scientific equipment, and so forth.

Mashinoeksport. Exports mining, oil well, metallurgical, power, electrical, chemical, food-processing, light-industry, and construction machinery and equipment.

Mashinoimport. Imports power, electrical, oil field, mining, pumping, and related equipment and machinery.

Transmashimport. Exports and imports ships, rolling stock, and other transport equipment.

Tekhnoeksport. Provides technical aid and equipment for projects abroad in virtually all branches of heavy and light industry.

Promsyryeimport. Exports and imports a wide variety of ferrous and nonferrous metals and metal products.

Tekhnopromimport. Exports and imports equipment and machinery mainly for consumer-goods industries as well as for communications, laboratory, and medical purposes.

Raznoimport. Imports and exports nonferrous metals, rubber, cable goods, technical rubber articles, and other goods.

Raznoeksport. Exports clothing, durable consumer goods, tobacco, cement, and some other goods.

Soyuzpromeksport. Exports industrial chemicals, metallic ores, precious metals, fertilizers, nonmetallic minerals, and the like.

Soyuznefteeksport. Exports and imports petroleum and petroleum products.

Eksportlen. Exports and imports many different textile raw materials and textiles.

Prodintorg. Exports and imports food and alcoholic products of many kinds, including caviar, canned goods, and wine, among others.

Eksportkhleb. Exports and imports grains, grain seeds, grain products, oil seeds and cake, and the like.

Eksportles. Exports timber and timber products, newsprint, woodpulp, and pulp and paper products.

---

[5] Based on an official list released by the Soviet trade delegation in India.

Soyuzkhimeksport. Exports and imports chemical and pharmaceutical products and naval stores.

Mezhdunarodnaya Kniga. Exports Soviet publications and stamps. Imports foreign publications to the Soviet Union.

Soyuzpushnina. Exports furs and fur products.

Intourist. Handles all foreign travel arrangements in the USSR.

Sovfrakht. Charters foreign and Soviet ships abroad and in the USSR and fulfills orders connected with marine shipment.

Vostokintorg. Virtually monopolizes all Soviet trade with Outer Mongolia, Afghanistan, and Sinkiang Province of Communist China.

Soyuzvneshtrans. A foreign-trade service organization which handles transportation of commodities by all means of transport, as well as loading, storage, insurance, and customs clearance of goods moving in foreign trade.[6]

In foreign countries the Ministry of Foreign Trade is usually represented by a Trade Delegation. This is a fairly elaborate organization; it forms part of the Soviet Embassy and its three chief officials have diplomatic status. Organizationally the commission is a replica of the ministry. It represents the export and import corporations, acts as their agents, makes market surveys for them, and negotiates contracts with buyers and sellers for commodities offered or required by export-import organizations. In addition the trade delegations keep sharp watch over economic conditions and market opportunities in each country and supply information about Soviet foreign trade needs and requirements to foreign firms.[7] In the United States, the functions of a trade delegation are performed by the Amtorg Trading Corporation. Legally Amtorg is a regular commercial corporation formed under the laws of the state of New York. All its stock, however, is owned, through the frequently rotated chairmanship of the board of directors, by the Bank for Foreign Trade in Moscow. Like trade delegations in other countries, but without their official or diplomatic status, Amtorg negotiates and signs contracts with buyers and sellers for most Soviet commercial transactions in the United States. The personnel of Amtorg includes representatives of the various export and import corporations as well as representatives of several other economic ministries concerned with foreign trade. Amtorg officials were compelled in 1949 to register their corporation as an agent of the Soviet government.[8]

---

[6] For an earlier list of Soviet foreign-trade organizations as of 1947, cf. *Finansy SSSR za XXX Let,* pp. 119–20.

[7] Baykov, *op. cit.,* pp. 27–28.

[8] Margold, *op. cit.,* pp. 52–55. *The New York Times,* December 9, 1949.

Planning Foreign Trade

The annual and other foreign-trade plans of the Soviet Union consist of both material and financial balances somewhat similar to those composing the general economic plan of the country. It will be recalled that, in the general economic plan, material balances make allowances both for imports as part of the supply and for exports as part of the utilization of each commodity. Before World War II, the procedure seems to have been that the Soviet government first determined the irreducible minimum of foreign imports — of goods, technicians, technical information, and services — required to achieve its plans. In this way the quantities to be imported and their approximate cost were determined. A roughly equal volume of exports was then set by taking into account the fact that imports had to be paid for, except in so far as they could be financed by credits, gold shipments, or similar devices. The commodities to be exported, and the amounts of each to go to each country, were then determined in the light of the USSR's needs for its own production, also taking into account market conditions, prices, and demand abroad. For each commodity, therefore, the material balance of imports or exports would specify the amounts to be bought from or sold to different foreign countries, the total in each case being the total import or export item allowed for in material balances of the general economic plan. Even before World War II, however, political considerations were taken into account in determining these plans, as in the case of the systematic Soviet effort to obtain dominance in the markets of Middle Eastern and Asiatic countries.

Since World War II, political factors have become much more important. As early as 1949 it seemed most unlikely that foreign-trade plans were based primarily upon determination of minimum import needs and the selection of commodities to be exported in payment. Rather, Soviet interests in developing and dominating the satellite nations in Eastern Europe and Asia also undoubtedly played a major role in this planning.

Paralleling the material balances, foreign currency and other financial balances are prepared to shape the financial relationships between the Soviet Union, the rest of the world as a whole, and each individual country with which the Soviet Union does business. These financial plans take account of all currency receipts and expenses of the Soviet Union abroad, including not only those arising from merchandise and service transactions but also such items as the cost of maintaining Soviet representatives abroad, costs of borrowing, tourism incomes, and so on. The State Bank works closely with the Ministry of Foreign Trade in drawing up these financial plans. Before World War II, when Soviet foreign trade was largely of a multilateral character, financial planning was not directed at balancing Soviet expenditures in each country with its income from sales made in that country, but rather at obtaining an over-all balance with the rest of the world. This effort, of course, had to take into account the difficulties raised by the nonconvertibility of many foreign currencies. In the postwar period the increasingly bilateral nature of Soviet trade, as evidenced by the conclusion of many agreements providing for balanced annual exports and imports to and from particular countries, has narrowed the area in which a multilateral balance has been sought. Soviet postwar foreign financial planning has also had to deal with the extraordinarily complex currency conditions prevailing after World War II, particularly the non-convertibility of sterling and sterling-based currencies into American dollars.[9]

Since the prohibition of exports or imports of rubles was instituted in the late 1920's, all actual payments and receipts between the USSR and foreign countries have been made in foreign currencies. Until 1950, bilateral trade agreements drawn up between the Soviet Union and other nations used the American dollar as the unit of account for determining both prices and the aggregate value of trade, though no actual payments were required if a balance of trade was achieved. The ruble was an entirely domestic currency divorced from the fluctuations of prices and currencies in foreign markets. The arbitrary exchange value for the ruble set by the government from time to time had little or no practical significance, except for foreigners arriving in the Soviet Union who wished to convert their own currencies into Soviet money. From June 1937 to March 1, 1950, the ruble was officially valued in terms of foreign currencies by declaring 5.3 rubles equal to one dollar and then establishing the ruble values of other currencies in terms of their parities with the American dollar. This 5.3 ratio was main-

---

[9] Condoide, *Russian-American Trade,* pp. 34–38, 45–49.

tained all through World War II and the years immediately after it, when the domestic purchasing value of the ruble was lower than at the time this ratio was initially set. The resulting gross over-valuation of the ruble had no effect upon Soviet foreign trade be-cause the ruble was not utilized in foreign transactions and do-mestic prices were set by the Soviet regime without regard to the prices for similar commodities in other countries.

On March 1, 1950, the Soviet government announced a new gold value for the ruble, making it nominally equivalent to twenty-five cents. Instead of 5.3 rubles to the dollar, a new ratio of 4 rubles to the dollar was established. This move did not make the ruble a truly gold-backed currency, since gold cannot in general be ob-tained for rubles by private individuals in the Soviet Union. Nor did it remove the prohibitions against exporting or importing rubles. The immediate effect of this reform seems to be a tendency to use the ruble, not necessarily as the unit of account, but as the unit employed for public announcements of Soviet foreign relations with weaker nations, as exemplified by the Finnish trade agreement con-cluded in June 1950.[10]

To the extent that the USSR employs world prices, this "shift" from the dollar to the ruble merely requires multiplying dollar figures by four to put them in ruble terms. Several Eastern Euro-pean satellites maintain their foreign-trade accounts in terms of the ruble as a unit of measure though apparently not necessarily as a unit of transaction. The ruble is grossly overvalued in relation to Western currencies.[11]

All financial transactions involving foreign countries pass through the State Bank of the USSR. It has correspondent banks all over the world, which credit and debit its account as transactions occur. This centralized control of all financial transactions permits the

---

[10] *The New York Times,* June 14, 1950.

[11] The overvaluation of the ruble-exchange ratio introduced on March 1, 1950, is easily evidenced by translation of Soviet prices for important com-modities into other currencies, using the 4:1 ruble-dollar ratio. Thus, as pointed out in a United States State Department protest to the Soviet govern-ment in March 1950, a kilogram (2.2 lbs.) of butter cost $1.52 in Washington, D. C., but between $8.58 and $11.03 in Moscow at the official exchange rate. First-grade beef costing $1.39 a kilogram in Washington was $6.07 in Moscow. White bread costing $.26 a kilogram in Washington cost $1.40 in Moscow, etc. *The New York Times,* March 28, 1950. For a similar later comparison, cf. *Ibid.,* March 19, 1954.

Soviet State Bank to have an up-to-date picture of the state of its financial relationships with each country of the world. When necessary to balance accounts, it can shift convertible foreign currencies from one country to another. Alternatively, to reach a general balance with the rest of the world, it may export or import gold bullion or other precious metals or stones. This arrangement also permits the State Bank to act as a major control organization over the economic relations of the USSR with foreign countries, in somewhat analogous fashion to the manner in which it controls the activities of domestic economic enterprises borrowing short-term credit from it. Presumably, if a Soviet enterprise tried to import goods illegally, it would not receive authorization of payment from the State Bank; conversely, any illegal exports would be detected in the unexpected payments made to the State Bank in terms of foreign currencies.

Soviet Tariff Policy

Although the Soviet government determines directly the kinds and amounts of commodities to be bought abroad, it maintains a system of tariffs on most imports and some exports. Unlike tariffs in a free-enterprise society, Soviet customs duties do not play a significant role in determining the nature and volume of foreign trade. Tariffs paid by enterprises importing goods, for example, are, in reality, merely bookkeeping transactions between agencies of the same state. The tariff has real significance only for the very limited amount of goods brought into the Soviet Union through nongovernmental channels — for example, parcel post, goods brought in the luggage of visitors, goods imported by the diplomatic missions in Moscow, and the like. Soviet tariff rates are in general rather high, but they serve no real protective function as do high tariffs in a free-enterprise society. The Soviet system of monopoly of foreign trade is a much more effective barrier against imports of cheap foreign goods that might compete with domestic industry than any simple tariff or quota device such as is common in capitalist countries. From an accounting point of view, Soviet import tariffs may help equalize the cost of foreign commodities with the cost of those same commodities made domestically.

The latest available data on Soviet tariffs pertain to those in effect in 1945, rates that had apparently remained unchanged since early 1937. The rates were divided into four different groups. The first and presumably the most important group at that time covered all imports and exports from Western Europe and overseas countries. The second group consisted of special preferential tariff rates established for trade with eastern countries through Caspian Sea ports and also over the land border of the USSR from the Black Sea eastward covering goods from Turkey, Iran, Afghanistan, Mongolia, and Sinkiang. The third group of special tariffs was established for certain basic goods produced in Afghanistan and sent from there. A special fourth group of differential tariffs existed for goods brought in through the port of Murmansk. These were generally at a lower level than the tariffs applied in the first category, in order to make up for the higher transport expenditures required for goods coming through that port. Besides this, there were some special tariff rates established by agreements between the USSR and foreign countries.

The major group of tariffs, presumably applicable to the first group of countries indicated above, consisted of nine basic group-rates. Imports of food products were either duty-free or taxed at very low rates, at a fixed amount per unit of weight. Livestock entered duty-free, but livestock products were taxed at differing rates, ranging from 50 per cent of price for animal fats to 1 to 15 per cent for leather and related products. Lumber entered duty-free, but furniture of every kind paid a duty of 10 rubles per kilogram. Other wood products were taxed at a rate of 150 per cent of price. Mineral construction materials paid a duty of 150 per cent of the base price; graphite, 100 per cent; raw natural rubber, 100 per cent; and aspirin, 1 per cent. Metallic ores of all kinds were duty-free, but iron and steel were taxed at 50 per cent of the price; tin, 10 per cent; lead and zinc, 60 per cent; gold, silver, and platinum were duty-free. Optical, scientific, and medical instruments were taxed at 1 per cent of price; watches, 300 per cent; and typewriters, 200 per cent. Paper pulp was taxed at 40 per cent of the price; paper, 100 per cent; but newspapers and periodicals entered duty-free. Cotton and cotton-wool mixtures were taxed at 20 per cent of price; raw wool, 35 per cent; yarns and threads, from 100 to 200 per cent of price. Haberdashery raw materials were taxed at 400 per cent of price; precious stones, 150 to 300 rubles per kilogram; women's shoes, 150 to 350 rubles per kilogram.

Very few exported products are taxed, the most important of these being certain types of livestock, such as horses and karakul and merino sheep.

Customs duties are a relatively small source of Soviet government revenues. In 1939 they amounted to almost 2,100,000,000 rubles, or 1.3 per cent of all state budgetary income. In 1940 they amounted to about 3,000,000,000 rubles, or about 1.7 per cent of all state budgetary income.[12]

In countries where foreign trade is carried on by private interests, governments seek to influence the character and volume of their countries' foreign trade by the imposition of tariffs, import quotas, export subsidies, and the like. All these are designed to influence the transactions of private importers and exporters by affecting the price relationships they take into account or by setting limits to their activities. The Soviet control of foreign trade, on the other hand, is much more direct, and the tariff system has little real importance in determining import policy. This difference between Soviet and non-Soviet policy on foreign-trade control has raised problems. Illustrative is the case of countries wishing to conclude trade agreements with the USSR providing for reciprocal most-favored-nation treatment and barring discrimination. When concessions on tariff rates were extended to the USSR, its exports to the country reducing these duties were naturally aided, because private importers there responded to the changed price situation. But any Soviet tariff reductions need not have a corresponding influence on the other contracting nation's exports to the USSR. Similarly, efforts to ban "discrimination" in foreign trade could have little relevance to Soviet state trading organizations, which did not necessarily behave like private foreign traders and which did not have to expose the motivation for sales or purchase policy in public. To overcome these difficulties, a number of Soviet trade agreements concluded in the 1930's, including several reached with the United States, provided that the USSR would purchase at least a minimum amount of goods in the other contracting country during a fixed period in return for the concessions — tariff or otherwise — granted to ease entrance of Soviet goods. This provision helped assure that trade between these countries would increase, but it

---

[12] Suchkov, *Dokhody Gosudarstvennogo Byudzheta SSSR*, pp. 130–32.

evaded the problem of trade discrimination and may actually have fostered it. Thus the USSR may have had to purchase more goods in a given country to meet its obligation than it would have done if it had bought all commodities in the cheapest markets.[13]

Foreign Trade Before World War II

The volume of the USSR's foreign trade between the Bolshevik Revolution and the outbreak of World War II first grew and then declined. Starting off from the negligible levels of the first post-revolutionary years the volume of trade steadily increased until the early 1930's, imports playing a major role in accelerating the industrialization of the country. As the Soviet Union found it possible to produce more and more goods formerly imported, the volume of imports, and consequently of exports to pay for them, fell off after the early 1930's, up to 1938. In 1940, trade was at about the 1938 level despite wartime difficulties, because of Soviet efforts to stockpile deficit raw materials in fear of involvement in World War II and also because of the large volume of trade provided for in the Soviet-German economic agreement of 1939.

At no time in the 1920's and 1930's was Soviet trade large in comparison with the country's population and resources. Its maximum share of world imports before World War II was 2.7 per cent in 1931; the corresponding maximum for exports was 2.3 per cent in 1932. These percentages were on a par with those recorded for relatively small countries like Switzerland and Sweden having populations well under 5 per cent of that of the Soviet Union.[14]

In the early 1920's Soviet trade developed very slowly. Exportable surpluses were small or nonexistent in many of these years. In addition many of the major powers of the world sought to blockade the Soviet Union, and in particular refused to accept gold shipped from the USSR in payment for goods. In general the low level of foreign trade in the early 1920's reflected both the chaos and disorganization of this period internally, the political animosity of major capitalist nations, and the resentment engendered abroad by the Soviet re-

---

[13] Alexander Gerschenkron, "Russia and the International Trade Organization," *American Economic Review*, May 1947, pp. 626–27.

[14] Alexander Gerschenkron, *Economic Relations of the USSR*, p. 20. New York: Committee on International Economic Policy, 1945.

pudiation of the debts contracted by the Czarist and Kerensky regimes.

As production increased within the Soviet Union, more goods became available for export. At the same time foreign countries come to be reconciled to the existence of the USSR and began to reach credit arrangements with it, ending the former gold blockade and otherwise making arrangements to facilitate trade. As early as 1923 the USSR began to receive three-to-six-month credits from individual foreign firms for its purchases, and the volume grew rapidly thereafter. The credits received in these early years were guaranteed almost entirely by Soviet-owned gold deposited in foreign banks. Beginning with 1926, a number of countries, including Germany, Italy, Norway, and Austria, extended government guarantees for private credits given the USSR. These were mainly short- and medium-term credits for purchase of goods, ranging up to 39 months in duration and usually carrying extraordinarily high interest charges because of the risks believed to be involved in extending credit to the communist government. By adhering to a policy of scrupulously paying all its obligations in full and on time, the Soviet government soon improved its credit position and was able to receive more favorable terms. Soviet indebtedness abroad reached a maximum of 1,400,000,000 rubles in 1931, but by the end of 1935 this figure had been reduced to 120,000,000 rubles, largely as a result of the USSR's success in exporting more than it imported during 1933 to 1935. Soviet shipment of gold, silver, platinum, and precious stones abroad also helped provide the funds to pay for the great imports required during the early 1930's.[15]

The changing volume of Soviet foreign trade to 1938 is shown by Table 60.

The peak of Soviet imports was reached in the early years of the First Five-Year Plan, after the USSR had begun its rapid industrialization program. This period was also the time of the largest foreign-trade deficit. That deficit would have been even larger if it had not been for exports of a number of commodities, particularly grain, that Russia could ill afford to spare. Grain was exported in the early 1930's despite widespread famine conditions in the Ukraine. It was the Soviet misfortune that its need for extensive machinery

---

[15] I. S. Ginzburg, *Vneshnyaya Torgovlya SSSR*, pp. 110–60. Moscow: 1937.

TABLE 60. Soviet Foreign Trade, Prewar and 1918–38.

Year	Export*	Import*	Balance*
	(MILLIONS OF RUBLES)		
1909–1913 average	6,513.9	4,994.1	+1,519.8
1913	6,596.4	6,022.5	+ 573.9
1918	35.5	460.8	− 425.3
1919	0.4	14.0	− 13.6
1920	6.1	125.7	− 119.6
1921	88.5	922.9	− 834.4
1922	357.4	1,181.7	− 824.3
1923	954.8	627.2	+ 327.6
1924	1,476.1	1,138.8	+ 337.3
1925	2,664.4	3,620.9	− 956.5
1926	3,173.7	3,016.5	+ 157.2
1927	3,267.0	3,320.5	− 53.5
1928	3,518.9	4,174.6	− 655.7
1929	4,045.8	3,857.0	+ 188.8
1930	4,539.3	4,637.5	− 98.2
1931	3,553.1	4,839.9	−1,286.8
1932	2,518.2	3,083.5	− 565.3
1933	2,167.5	1,525.1	+ 642.4
1934	1,832.4	1,018.0	+ 814.4
1935	1,609.3	1,057.2	+ 552.1
1936	1,359.1	1,352.5	+ 6.6
1937	1,728.6	1,341.3	+ 387.3
1938	1,331.9	1,422.9	− 91.0

* These data are in terms of the constant exchange value of the ruble adopted April 1, 1936. The original data on which this table is based are in terms of current prices for 1925 to 1938; for the years 1918 to 1924, values were given in terms of prices of 1913. Up to September 1923 the figures of foreign trade apply to only the European frontiers of the USSR; for the remaining years they apply to all frontiers.
Source: *Finansy SSSR za XXX Let,* p. 318.

imports came at a period in world history when the "terms of trade" had turned against the USSR, that is, in this period world prices fell generally as a result of depression, but prices on industrial goods paid by the USSR fell significantly less than prices paid for Soviet raw materials exported abroad. As a result the USSR had to ship out much more in physical terms than it would have otherwise.

The desperate Soviet need for foreign currency and the low prices at which the USSR was willing to sell its products in order to meet that need led to widespread foreign charges of Soviet "dumping," and to efforts to prohibit the receipt of Soviet exports in a number of countries. Some opinion in this period held that the Soviet exports at very low prices were designed to ruin the

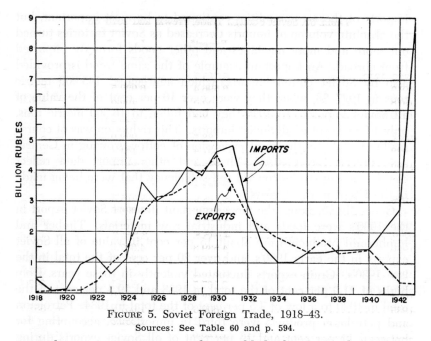

FIGURE 5. Soviet Foreign Trade, 1918–43.
Sources: See Table 60 and p. 594.

capitalist system. It seems much more likely that it was the pressing need for funds with which to meet its foreign obligations that explains the USSR's readiness to sell at extremely unfavorable prices; at other times and in other circumstances it has given abundant proof of a desire to receive as high a price as it can for its products.

As strictly programmed by the government, Soviet imports throughout these years were overwhelmingly composed of production goods. After 1925, production goods made up more than 80 per cent and sometimes more than 90 per cent of all Soviet imports, while consumption goods were usually under 10 per cent of the total after 1929 and were as low as 4.6 per cent in 1931. From 1925 to 1938 roughly two-thirds of Soviet exports consisted, usually, of industrial goods, including industrial raw materials; the remaining third consisted of agricultural commodities.[16]

Machinery of all kinds, iron and steel goods, nonferrous metals and products, and electrical equipment made up well over half of all Soviet imports in the early 1930's. In later years of the 1930's,

16 Baykov, op. cit., Appendix Table II.

imports of these commodities continued to be most important, but the absolute volume of imports decreased as Soviet factories turned out more and more machines and other goods formerly imported from abroad. An important example of the same trend is provided also by Soviet cotton imports, which aggregated 145,000 metric tons in 1927–28, when they were over 16 per cent of the value of all Soviet imports. In 1938 they had fallen to 16,500 metric tons, only 1.8 per cent of all Soviet imports. This reduction was of course made possible by the great expansion of cotton-growing in Central Asia during the 1930's.[17] These and other import data reflect clearly the big strides toward self-sufficiency that were being made in the USSR in those years.

Generally speaking, the most important items of Soviet export in the 1930's were foods and industrial raw materials. Timber and lumbermill products were about 15 per cent in value of all Soviet exports in the early 1930's, and over 20 per cent of the total in the late 1930's. Grain exports fluctuated violently in these years, from highs of 21.9 per cent of the total in 1938 and 19.4 per cent of the total in 1930 to a low of 4.5 per cent of the total in 1934. Petroleum and petroleum products were third in importance, accounting for between 11 per cent and 19 per cent of all Soviet exports during most of the 1930's. The Soviet government had to wage a fierce struggle with foreign oil companies before it could establish its position in the world petroleum market. Fur exports averaged roughly about 10 per cent of total Soviet exports in value during the late 1920's and 1930's, being particularly important in Soviet trade with the United States. Other major articles of Soviet export during these years included cotton tissues, flax and flax products, manganese ore, and coal. An important development in the middle and later 1930's was the increase of Soviet exports of machinery, iron and steel products, cotton, and some other products for which the USSR had formerly been greatly or almost entirely dependent upon imports and which had been formerly exported in small quantities or not at all.[18]

Soviet trade during the 1920's and 1930's was of a distinctly multilateral character. Deficits were incurred in some countries and credit balances in others, the two balancing off for the most

---

[17] *Ibid.*, Appendix Table VI.
[18] *Ibid.*, Appendix Tables IV and V.

part. From the middle 1920's to 1938 the Soviet Union had a favorable balance of trade every year with most Western European countries except Germany, where major unfavorable balances were frequently the rule. The Soviet Union bought more from the United States than it sold here in almost every one of those years. The USSR usually had an excess of imports over exports during this period with Czechoslovakia, Poland, the Scandinavian countries, and Iran, though only Iran among them usually accounted for more than 1 per cent or 2 per cent of the USSR's export or import trade.[19]

The over-all geographical pattern of Soviet foreign trade during the 1930's may be indicated by the data on its regional distribution given in Table 61.

TABLE 61. Regional Distribution of Soviet Foreign Trade in 1931 and 1937.

Region	Exports		Imports		Balance†	
			(MILLIONS OF RUBLES*)			
	1931	1937	1931	1937	1931	1937
Central Europe	599.1	136.6	2,039.2	229.5	−1,440.1	− 92.9
Western Europe	1,692.7	1,012.9	553.8	425.2	+1,138.9	+587.7
Northern Europe	126.7	63.2	194.7	24.5	− 68.0	+ 38.7
Balkan Countries	50.2	14.6	4.6	5.6	+ 45.6	+ 9.0
Near East ....⎫ Middle East ....⎬ Far East ....⎭	592.9	271.4	616.9	207.9	− 24.0	+ 63.5
American Continent and British Dominions...	113.4	139.2	1,062.8	346.7	− 949.4	−207.5
Baltic Countries	212.2	42.7	215.5	27.7	− 3.3	+ 15.0
Japan	86.8	11.7	55.5	54.4	+ 31.3	− 42.7
All Others	79.1	36.3	96.9	19.8	− 17.8	+ 16.5
Total	3,553.1	1,728.6	4,839.9	1,341.3	−1,286.8	+387.3

* Rubles used in this table are calculated on the basis of April 1936 exchange ratios.
† + = export surplus; − = import surplus.
Source: Gerschenkron, *Economic Relations of the USSR*, p. 33.

Trade During World War II

World War II resulted in a profound transformation of the Soviet foreign-trade pattern. The most summary view of this change is given by the data below:

[19] *Ibid.*, Appendix Table VII.

Year	Exports	Imports
	(MILLIONS OF RUBLES)	
1938	1,331.9	1,422.9
1940	1,412	1,446
1942	399	2,756
1943	373	8,460

It is believed that these data are in terms of 1936 rubles and are therefore comparable with the ruble data in tables above.[20] It is clear from the above data that while commodity imports in 1943 increased almost sixfold, commodity exports fell to almost one fourth of the 1940 level. It is likely that 1944 data, if available, would show a much larger rise in imports and little if any increase in exports.

This remarkable transformation in the pattern of Soviet foreign trade was the consequence of the tremendous military struggle inaugurated when the German army invaded the USSR in June 1941. Within a short time after the initial blow, German forces occupied many of the richest agricultural and industrial areas in the USSR west of Moscow, reducing sharply the economic resources available to the Soviet government and making normal economic life impossible. From the point of view of foreign trade alone, the German invasion cut the Soviet Union off from virtually all of continental Europe. At the same time the Soviet Union's need for supplementary production and resources of all kinds, from armaments to foods and medicines, increased greatly, yet it was virtually impossible for it to pay for any significant fraction of the required imports through exporting commodity surpluses since there was no really surplus production. The result was a revolutionary change in the pattern and volume of Soviet foreign trade.

To meet the desperate Soviet need for immediate outside aid, the American Lend-lease and the British and Canadian Mutual Aid programs were set up, under which the USSR received tremendous amounts of commodities of all kinds on the basis of special agreements and at no current cost to the Soviet Union. The Soviet foreign-trade pattern during World War II, in consequence, consisted of the importation of record volumes of goods, almost entirely from the United States, Great Britain, and Canada, and the simul-

---

[20] Voznesensky, *The Economy of the USSR during World War II,* p. 40.

taneous export of only very small quantities of goods. Almost
$13,000,000,000 worth of goods were received by the USSR from
the three major Western allies during World War II, of which
about $11,200,000,000 worth came from the United States.[21] This
is an average of about $3,000,000,000 annually. Both in quantity
and in value, these imports far exceeded even the peak of prewar
Soviet purchases, reached in 1931.[22]

About half the American Lend-lease shipments to the Soviet
Union during the war consisted of military items, including 14,500
airplanes, 7,500 tanks, and almost one billion dollars' worth of
ordnance and ammunition. The published figures on Soviet munitions production during the war suggest, however, that by far the
greater bulk of Soviet armaments was produced in the USSR itself.[23]
Relatively, the nonarmament component of Lend-Lease and Mutual
Aid shipments probably played an even greater role in meeting
vital Soviet needs than did the armament component. For example,
the United States sent the USSR over two million tons of food;
more than 475,000 trucks, and other motor vehicles; 30,000 machine
tools; 11 million pairs of boots and shoes; almost 2,000 locomotives;
well over 300,000 tons of aluminum, copper, and other nonferrous
metals and metal alloys; over 20 million yards of army textile material; and many other miscellaneous commodities. Great Britain
sent more than 100,000 tons of food; a similar quantity of rubber;
power plant equipment with total capacity of over 370,000 kilowatts; over 15,000 electric motors; over 100,000 tons of nonferrous
metals; and other miscellaneous products. Canada sent over 200,000
tons of wheat and flour; almost 100,000 tons of aluminum, copper,
zinc, nickel, and other nonferrous metals; over 13,000 tons of rails
and other commodities. Every sector of the USSR's military and
economic apparatus received vital equipment and raw materials
that eliminated bottlenecks and shortages and permitted the Soviet
war effort to attain the enormous magnitude it did.[24]

It seems clear that without this great aid from its three Western
allies the continued survival of the Soviet Union would have been
enormously more difficult during the dark days of the war, if it
were possible at all.

21 Schwartz, *op. cit.*, p. 15.
22 Baykov, *op. cit.*, p. 78.
23 See Joseph Stalin's speech of February 9, 1946.
24 Schwartz, *op. cit.*, pp. 15–16, and Baykov, *op. cit.*, p. 78.

The Soviet Union provided a small volume of goods and services as "return lend-lease" during the war. It made available bases for American planes in the Ukraine, food and other commodities and services for American personnel in the USSR, repair services for American ships in Soviet ports, and other miscellaneous free services. The Soviet argument is that the chief return for this Western aid was the tremendous Soviet war effort, which helped so vitally in defeating Germany.

In the later stages of the war, when the Soviet army had occupied Eastern Europe and entered into Germany and Austria, the USSR began to receive immediate tangible economic aid from these military victories. The Soviet army customarily lived off the country. USSR policy from the beginning in these areas was aimed at securing most speedy return of goods looted and stolen from the Soviet Union by the former invading forces, and also at seizing capital goods and consumer goods that would be of benefit to the Soviet economy. These trends in Soviet foreign economic relations matured more fully in the postwar period and will be discussed in the next section.

Postwar Foreign Economic Policy

Emerging as one of the two leading world powers in the postwar era, the Soviet Union has played a much more direct and far-reaching role in world economic relations since 1945 than ever before in history. The policies it has followed in its foreign economic relations have been determined primarily both by its bitter political struggle against the West, and particularly against the United States, and by the urgent needs for outside resources to help heal the enormous wounds of World War II. Initially in this period, the occupation by Soviet troops of an immense area, including all of Eastern and much of Central Europe as well as Manchuria and North Korea in Asia, permitted the USSR to derive important economic benefits. Subsequently the creation of communist-dominated satellite regimes in all the regions first occupied by Soviet troops, plus the conquest of China by the communist forces in that country, have further enhanced and consolidated Soviet influence, both economic and political, in a vast area of the earth embracing more than one third of all the peoples of the world. Conversely, in the areas free from Soviet or communist control, the increasing apprehension over the USSR's territorial and political ambitions has had serious restrictive effects upon the volume of trade and other economic relationships between the West and the Soviet Union.

In the latter period of World War II and shortly thereafter, high hopes were held by many in the Western world that cooperation with the Soviet Union could be continued in the postwar era. To help achieve continued economic cooperation between the Soviet Union and its Western allies, a number of important steps were taken in 1945 and 1946. The United States granted the USSR a credit of over $250,000,000, payable in thirty years with interest rate of 2⅜ per cent, to permit the latter country to receive Lend-Lease commodities that had been ordered or were otherwise earmarked for the USSR at the time of World War II's conclusion. The United Nations Relief and Rehabilitation Administration provided the Soviet Union with more than $200,000,000 worth of sorely needed food, textiles, seeds, farm machinery, and other commodities to help two of the most distressed areas of the USSR, the Ukraine and Belorussia. About $191,000,000 worth of this came from the United States. Soviet participation was invited in the formation of all international economic organizations in process of creation during 1944–46. Soviet delegates actually played a prominent part in the deliberations at Bretton Woods and at some other meetings for these purposes.

Yet these efforts came to naught. The USSR refused to join any of the independent international economic organizations, including the World Bank, the International Monetary Fund, the Food and Agricultural Organization, and others. When U. S. Secretary of State Marshall proposed his now famous plan for European recovery in June 1947, the Soviet Union was invited by France and Great Britain to join with them in helping to bring about European cooperation in order to make possible the enlistment of American aid to further European economic recovery. But after a short and unpleasant conference in Paris in July 1947, the Soviet Union refused to participate in what became the European Recovery Program and rather brusquely ordered two of its satellites to reverse their decision to participate. Behind these events, of course, was the sharp political antagonism between the Soviet Union and the

West, born of the West's suspicion that the USSR aimed for world domination through its communist fifth columns in every significant country of the world. The USSR for its own part apparently chose the road of non-cooperation with the West as the most advantageous of the alternatives open to it at the close of the Second World War. The high hopes held by many in 1945 were thus rudely shattered. The actual pattern of world economic and political relationships since then has been far different from that hoped for at the time of the common victory over the Axis nations.

In 1954 the Soviet Union did join the International Labor Organization, a body Soviet propaganda had often denounced earlier. In 1953 and 1954 increased Soviet activity was also apparent in United Nations economic groups dealing with international trade and economic development of undeveloped countries.

The main objective of Soviet foreign economic policy in the years 1945–48 seems to have been the acquisition of maximum foreign resources for its own needs, both to rehabilitate the devastated areas of the western USSR and to facilitate the further economic expansion projected by the Fourth Five-Year Plan. In addition, the Soviet policy has used economic weapons as a means of consolidating the USSR's influence and dominance in satellite countries and as aids in Soviet political warfare against the Western world. Since 1948 the Soviet Union has put great emphasis on seeking to shape and consolidate all its satellite nations into a closely knit economic group. These tendencies found their expression in such events as the formation in January 1949 of a Council of Mutual Economic Aid, consisting of the USSR and its Eastern European satellites; the signing of the Soviet-Chinese trade and loan agreement in February 1950; Soviet extension of loans to a number of countries, particularly Poland, Czechoslovakia, and China; and the wide publicity given to official assertions that the USSR's aid would be the primary outside force making industrialization of Eastern Europe and of China possible. In the same period the USSR and its satellites engaged in many forms of provocative behavior that antagonized the rest of the world, with resulting restrictions of economic relationships between the two groups of nations. Evidence of the USSR's success in creating an integrated economic bloc dependent upon it was the fact that in 1949, two thirds of the total foreign trade of the USSR was accounted for

by the "people's democracies" — the satellite nations. Before World
War II these nations probably accounted for only 10 per cent or
less of Soviet trade. Western Europe, the United States, and other
countries, who accounted for 90 per cent or more of Soviet trade
in 1938, accounted for only one third of it in 1949.[25] By 1953, the
evidence suggests, Soviet trade with other communist-ruled countries was probably close to 90 per cent of total Soviet foreign trade.

The postwar Soviet economic objective of securing a large surplus of imports over exports so as to facilitate reconstruction within
the USSR was achieved, as we shall see below. At the beginning
of 1945, Soviet policymakers undoubtedly realized that this goal
could be reached in one or in both of two fashions. They might
have relied primarily upon securing large long-term reconstruction
loans from Western countries and international economic agencies
such as the World Bank. One such loan of roughly a quarter of a
billion dollars was actually received from the United States to
finance receipt of Lend-Lease "pipeline" products. But on the whole
this method of making an import surplus possible was ruled out by
the political antagonism between the Soviet Union and those nations most likely to provide such funds. In particular, the Soviet
wartime request for a $6,000,000,000 loan and the American counter-
offer of a $1,000,000,000 loan never reached a compromise.

The alternative route, which actually played the most significant
role in making a large import surplus possible for the entire period
of 1945–49, was that of extorting enormous amounts of commodities,
services, capital equipment, and financial values from the countries
defeated or occupied by Soviet troops. The largest part of this
import surplus was probably made possible by German reparations
deliveries, almost entirely from the Soviet-occupied zone of Eastern
Germany. These were scheduled to amount to $3,658,000,000 by
the end of 1950,[26] but there is no certainty that this accounting includes all the capital equipment, food, and other commodities
taken by the Soviet Union from Germany or utilized for the support
of Soviet troops occupying that country. Eastern Europe also suffered large losses from Soviet takings in the first year of Soviet
occupation; thereafter reparations deliveries were regularized in
accordance with the peace treaties reached with those defeated
nations.

[25] *Pravda*, December 21, 1949.
[26] *Pravda*, May 16, 1950.

Soviet seizures of capital equipment and other resources in Manchuria in the latter half of 1945 were also very great. Edwin W. Pauley, chief American representative at the Moscow Reparations Conference of 1945, who visited Manchuria after it had been occupied by Soviet troops, declared upon his return: "On their arrival Soviet troops began a systematic confiscation of food and other stockpiles and certain complete industrial installations, the Soviets took by far the greater part of all functioning power-generating and transforming equipment, electric motors, experimental plants, laboratories and hospitals. In machine tools they took only the newest and best, leaving antiquated tools behind." Mr. Pauley charged that Russian removals and damage had caused a $2,000,000,000 loss to the Manchurian economy, though presumably the actual value of Russian takings for the Soviet Union was substantially less. *Izvestia*, denouncing Mr. Pauley's estimate, valued the industrial part of the war booty seized by the Soviet army in Manchuria at $95,000,000.[27]

On the basis of the evidence cited above, it seems clear that by the end of 1950 the Soviet Union had received in reparations from the former enemy or enemy-occupied countries more than $4,000,-000,000 and perhaps more than $5,000,000,000. These acquisitions were most substantial aids in permitting realization of the Fourth Five-Year Plan production objectives.

In its commercial trade relations with the rest of the world, the Soviet Union has practiced a much greater degree of bilateralism than before the war. Between 1945 and early 1954 it concluded one or more bilateral trade agreements, providing for balanced exports from and imports to another country during a given time period, not only with all of its Eastern Europe and Asiatic satellites, but also with a number of non-Soviet dominated countries, such as England, Sweden, Norway, France, India, and Argentina. Speculation on the motivation of this postwar shift from multilateralism toward bilateralism has centered about a number of reasons: The Soviet Union may feel that it can make a more favorable bargain by arranging for all purchases and sales with a particular foreign country at one time. In this way the predominance of Soviet economic, political, and military power may perhaps be used most advantageously. Second, the postwar fluctuations and nonconverti-

---

[27] Quoted in Schwartz, *op. cit.*, p. 106.

bility of many foreign currencies may have moved the Russians toward bilateral trade agreements, which eliminate or minimize the need for actual currency transactions. Third, as a country with a planned economy, the USSR may find it more convenient to fix at one time the amounts of goods it will sell to and purchase from a given foreign country, and the prices and values involved, rather than to keep its plans flexible all year around and purchase and sell wherever in the world conditions seem most advantageous at different times of the year. Whatever the reason, it is clear that Russia's flight from multilateralism has not been a short-term phenomenon, for in 1954 it was still pronounced.

Soviet Foreign Trade, 1946-54

It is difficult to give a fully satisfactory picture of the growth of Soviet foreign trade from 1946 to 1954 because of the paucity of data. The veil of Soviet secrecy over foreign trade statistics was lifted only occasionally between 1946 and early 1954, and such data as have been published have been very general as well as scanty. The Statistical Office of the United Nations, as well as some individual investigators, have sought partially to dispel this secrecy by compiling information on Soviet trade from the foreign trade reports of countries with which the Soviet Union does business. For most of this nine-year period, however, such efforts have necessarily produced incomplete results because of the secrecy of foreign-trade data maintained also by other communist-ruled countries which, as was noted above, account for the great bulk of Soviet foreign trade in the postwar period. With these cautions in mind, we may attempt to examine the available data and to draw such inferences as are possible from them.

Turning to official Soviet data first, we may note A. I. Mikoyan's statement in late 1949 that the USSR had more than doubled the physical volume of its foreign trade as compared with the prewar level. V. Nesterov declared in April 1952: "The Soviet Union's foreign trade, according to customs returns, now amounts to over 18,000,000,000 rubles and measured in comparable prices, it is roughly three times as great as before the war." For 1953, the Soviet government reported: "The foreign-trade turnover of the Soviet Union grew to 23,000,000,000 against 20,800,000,000 rubles in

1952, an 11 per cent gain. The foreign trade turnover in 1953 (in comparable prices) was almost four times more than the prewar level."[28]

The general upward trend of Soviet foreign trade from 1949 to 1953 would seem to be clear from these data. During the same period, as noted above, Soviet trade became more and more trade with its communist satellites and allies, the proportion of such commerce in the total rising from two-thirds in 1949 to 80 per cent in 1952 and probably close to 90 per cent in 1953. It was this phenomenon that led Stalin to write in 1952 of the disintegration of the world market into "two parallel world markets," one communist and the other noncommunist.

Stalin and lesser Soviet commentators blame this phenomenon on the capitalist "boycott" of the Soviet Bloc, meaning actually the restrictions on exports of strategic goods to communist countries imposed in 1949 and afterward. Such United States laws as the Battle Act sought to make these measures more effective by banning American economic aid to foreign countries shipping designated strategic goods — primarily munitions, weapons, and goods useful in the production of armaments — to the Soviet Bloc.

But even without these restrictions, it seems likely that the proportion of Soviet trade with communist countries would have gone up after 1949. Soviet economic policy has always aimed at maximum self-sufficiency and there is no real evidence that this objective has been abandoned, though the concept of self-sufficiency may have been modified somewhat to take into account the fact that the Soviet Union now leads a major bloc of nations. Moreover, the economic growth of Eastern Europe and of Communist China after 1949 has been rapid, making available more goods for shipment to the Soviet Union and creating greater needs in those countries for Soviet goods. The Soviet objective has also clearly been to tie the satellite economies in with its own.

The volume of trade between the Soviet Union and the noncommunist world from 1948 through 1953 is summed up in the following data: [29]

---

[28] *Pravda,* December 21, 1949. Committee for the Promotion of International Trade, *International Economic Conference in Moscow April 3–12, 1952,* p. 62. Moscow: 1952. *Pravda,* January 31, 1954.

[29] *East-West Trade Trends.* Mutual Defense Assistance Control Act of 1951 (The Battle Act). Fourth Report to Congress, Second Half of 1953, p. 89. Washington, D. C.: Government Printing Office, 1954.

	Free World Exports to the Soviet Union	Free World Imports from the Soviet Union
	(MILLIONS OF DOLLARS)	
1948	533	492
1949	437	272
1950	301	252
1951	386	397
1952	481	462
1953 (est.)	410	380

Interpretation of these data is complicated by the fact that after the outbreak of the Korean War in mid-1952 world prices rose substantially, whereas they fell somewhat when that war was near its truce point and afterward. Nevertheless, the conclusion would seem warranted that the volume of Soviet trade with the West was never cut so sharply as the most vigorous proponents of an embargo wished; although, conversely, the strategic commodities embargo did have some effect in reducing trade with the Soviet Union. The small proportion of total free-world trade which Soviet trade was during these years should also be noticed. Even in 1948, when trade restrictions first began to be imposed, Soviet exports were substantially less than 1 per cent of the world export total, excluding exports of communist nations to one another. The percentage was even lower in subsequent years.

Soviet trade with its chief trading partners among noncommunist nations from 1948 to 1953 is shown in Table 62 below. The 1953 data are preliminary, being based upon the annual rate as indicated by returns for the first half of 1953.

It is apparent from Table 62 that Soviet trade with noncommunist countries during this period was primarily trade with Western Europe and with a few countries in Asia and Africa. The Soviet Union imported from abroad ships, some types of machinery, nonferrous metals, natural rubber, cocoa beans, wool, long-staple cotton, prefabricated houses, paper and lumber products, and fish, for the most part. It exported outside its orbit feed grains, timber, manganese, furs, seafood, asbestos, bristles, and other products. In late 1953, when the Soviet Union's sterling balances were apparently dangerously low because of an unfavorable balance of trade with the Sterling Bloc — the group of countries whose economies are linked with the British pound sterling — the Soviet Union apparently shipped well over $100,000,000 worth of gold to Western Europe, particularly England, to make up its trade deficit.[30]

TABLE 62. Soviet Foreign Trade with Chief Noncommunist Trading Partners, 1948–53.

Soviet Exports to	1948	1949	1950	1951	1952	1953*
		(MILLION UNITED STATES DOLLARS)				
United Kingdom	109.2	51.9	95.8	168.3	162.7	57.6
France	11.1	4.9	4.8	13.6	18.0	14.6
Netherlands	3.4	21.5	2.3	13.9	25.6	11.6
Norway	27.2	22.0	10.3	10.2	11.4	7.0
Sweden	12.6	2.8	5.9	13.1	20.0	6.0
Italy	4.1	16.5	14.5	22.0	34.0	8.4
Finland	51.2	37.7	23.6	41.3	81.5	96.4
Egypt	46.2	2.4	16.8	20.2	31.1	27.2
Iran	.6	4.1	10.2	18.8	23.9	**
India	9.8	27.0	3.5	1.6	1.7	.6

Soviet Imports from						
United Kingdom	28.4	39.3	39.7	66.6	104.9	41.0
France	.2	.6	2.6	4.8	6.4	6.8
Netherlands	4.3	7.2	.5	1.6	4.8	4.4
Norway	19.4	20.5	8.0	12.1	10.2	11.2
Sweden	16.9	21.2	21.8	33.4	44.4	23.0
Italy	3.4	17.8	20.0	23.7	20.3	13.6
Finland	145.6	135.2	64.5	121.5	155.0	125.2
Egypt	49.8	12.1	25.2	7.2	28.7	20.6
Iran	2.8	–	–	–	22.0	**
India	16.2	12.6	2.9	13.6	4.2	.8
Malaya-Singapore	47.3	24.8	39.7	24.0	9.3	**
Pakistan	16.6	9.5	11.4	4.1	–	14.6
Australia	–	30.5	23.6	13.1	–	7.2
Gold Coast	10.0	6.1	4.9	9.5	11.7	16.0

* Preliminary estimate based on first half of 1953.
** Data unavailable.
Sources: *Direction of International Trade*, annual issue for 1953, pp. 170–73. *Ibid.*, February 1954, p. 79.

From 1949 through early 1954, the Soviet Union carried out an intensive propaganda and political battle against Western restrictions on strategic exports to the Societ Bloc. At the communist-inspired so-called World Economic Conference in Moscow in April 1952, Western businessmen were tempted by offers of billions of

[30] *New York Times*, December 30, 1953. *The Economist*, January 2, 1954, pp. 50–51.

dollars of trade with the Soviet Bloc if only the restrictions were lifted or disregarded. Before and after this meeting Soviet and communist propaganda had few qualms and little restraint in painting the prosperity that could come to the West if only Soviet and satellite orders were accepted regardless of their nature. The United States' allies were bombarded with pleas to break with the United States on this issue, being assured that only selfish American desires to strangle the economies of Western Europe and Asia were behind the embargo. An unwary observer of these tactics might well have concluded from the tone and content of this intensive propaganda that the Soviet Union's only objective was to save the capitalist world from depression through placing vast orders for every imaginable commodity.

The West's counter-arguments during this period were mainly these. First, the restrictions had been imposed because of fear of Soviet aggression, a fear which had been greatly strengthened by the communist invasion of South Korea in mid-1950. The Soviet Union was told in effect that if it cooperated in reaching a political settlement of major world issues, then the West might feel safer and loosen or lift the embargo. Second, it was pointed out that the glib Soviet talk of billions of dollars of purchases waiting to be made was always vague about how these purchases were to be paid for. Except possibly for gold, the Soviet Union gave little evidence of having such vast export surpluses that it could pay for the large imports it claimed to want. Third, an air of insincerity surrounded these Soviet trade offers because many of the commodities said to be desired — English textiles for example — were not embargoed and could be purchased without limit if the communist countries actually wished to. The reality seemed to be that the communists wished only tie-in arrangements, so that purchase of nonstrategic goods such as textiles was contingent upon permission to purchase strategic goods such as heavy machinery.

After Stalin's death, the drive to increase trade with the noncommunist world entered a new phase and showed new characteristics. First, the Soviet Union suddenly began to purchase much larger amounts of food and textiles from the noncommunist world. Thus in the last eight months of 1953 the Soviet Union bought $40,000,000 worth of butter, $22,000,000 worth of meat, $28,000,000 worth of textiles, and smaller values of lard, cheese, sugar, herring, and citrus fruit, presumably in order to obtain supplies needed for improving the lot of the Soviet consumer as promised by Premier Malenkov in August 1953. Such purchases fell far short of adding up to one and a third billion rubles, the value of consumer goods and food Mikoyan had said in October 1953 would be purchased outside the Soviet orbit, but the amounts were substantial by previous standards.[31]

A second change was the actual conclusion of several important trade agreements with noncommunist countries, the most important being agreements with Argentina and India. The Argentine agreement provided for a Soviet credit to Argentina up to $30,000,000 in value to finance purchase of Soviet capital goods. This credit provision was a major innovation which immediately aroused much comment. The bilateral trade provided for in the agreement called for the exchange of the following commodities during the twelve months following August 1953: Argentina would send the Soviet Union 20,000 tons of wool, 14,000 tons of cattle hides, 75,000 tons of linseed oil, 15,000 tons of quebracho extract, 13,000 tons of meat, and smaller quantities of lard, cheese, sheepskins, and miscellaneous products. The Soviet Union would send Argentina 500,000 tons of crude oil, $500,000 worth of petroleum products, 300,000 tons of coal, 50,000 tons of steel, 20,000 tons of pig iron, $1,000,000 worth of dyes, $500,000 worth of drugs and medicinal products, $500,000 worth of precision instruments, and varying quantities of tool steels, special steels, pipe, asbestos, carbon black, rails, axles, boiler plates, and so forth. The $30,000,000 credit was to be used for additional purchases of Soviet capital equipment for oil exploitation, coal mining, railroad transportation, farm machinery and equipment, and other machinery.[32] This emergence of the Soviet Union as a large-scale exporter of capital goods to the Western Hemisphere marked a drastic change from earlier experience.

The Soviet-India agreement of December 1953 provided for Soviet

---

[31] *New York Times,* February 22, 1954. Mikoyan had declared that a total of 4,000,000,000 rubles worth of consumer goods and food would be bought during 1953 from communist and noncommunist sources. This is equivalent to slightly more than one-third of Soviet imports in 1953, if it is correct to assume imports were about half the reported trade value.

[32] Data supplied by U. S. Department of Commerce.

purchase of Indian jute, tea, coffee, tobacco, shellac, pepper, spices, wool, hides, skins, and vegetable oils. The Soviet Union agreed to ship wheat, barley, crude oil and oil products, iron and steel manufactures, tractors and other farm machinery, and a wide variety of industrial equipment including machine tools, mining and road-building equipment, electrical equipment, machinery for the textile, shoe, and food industries, timber and paper, chemicals, dye stuffs, medicines, optical goods, films, and printed matter. The Soviet Union promised to provide technical assistance in connection with delivery of the capital equipment. Payment between the two countries is to be in rupees, though the Soviet Union may use sterling to settle any unfavorable balance it may accumulate.[33]

The largest trade volume mentioned in this campaign was announced in February 1954, when the Soviet Minister of Foreign Trade formally offered to buy about $1,100,000,000 worth of British goods during 1955 to 1957. This total included over $300,000,000 worth of cargo ships; almost $150,000,000 worth of electric-power equipment; almost $100,000,000 worth of forging and pressing equipment and machine tools; the same amount of textile and food-processing machinery; over $300,000,000 worth of raw materials, food, and consumer goods; plus two floating docks, railway equipment, rolling-mill equipment, and hydraulic presses. This purchase offer was conditional on Britain's purchasing equal values of unspecified Soviet commodities. In addition, of course, the offer assumed that the large fraction of the desired commodities classified as strategic would be shipped, in reversal of past embargo policy. Skeptical Western observers pointed out that such general trade offers were still far short from conclusion of contracts at agreed prices and with agreed specifications. In addition they noted that some of the goods the Soviet Union wished to buy from Great Britain were the same as goods the Soviet Union had agreed to supply India and other of its trading partners.[34]

Other developments in early 1954 included a small Soviet loan of gold and convertible currencies to Finland, an indirect Soviet offer to buy large amounts of United States surplus butter and cottonseed oil, and some increasing evidence — in the form of state-

---

[33] *New York Times*, December 3, 1953.
[34] *Ibid.*, February 5, 1954.

ments by Prime Minister Winston Churchill, Mutual Security Administrator Harold Stassen, and others — of sentiment for relaxing trade barriers between East and West. Though the Soviet offer for United States butter and cottonseed oil was rejected, there could be little doubt but that if economic conditions worsened in the noncommunist world, the pressure for more trade with the Soviet Bloc would increase.

Soviet-American Economic Relations

For the most part, Soviet postwar economic relations with the United States have been dominated by the bitter political struggle going on between these two nations. In the early postwar period, as pointed out before, trade flourished, as the United States provided credit for Soviet purchase of "pipeline" Lend-Lease materials as well as most of the goods sent to the USSR under the UNRRA program. It had been anticipated in 1944 and 1945 that the Soviet Union would be a very large customer of the United States in the postwar period, particularly if it could obtain credits to purchase large amounts of machinery and raw materials required for its reconstruction. At one point in the negotiations between the two countries, an American credit of $1,000,000,000 was offered the Soviet Union, provided that the latter permitted equality of economic opportunity in the Eastern European countries dominated by it. This offer was refused. Instead, as the "cold war" worsened, the United States, beginning March 1, 1948, introduced a comprehensive licensing system on exports to Europe and denied licenses for shipment to the USSR and its satellites of machinery and other commodities that might contribute to the Soviet war potential. In its administration of the Marshall Plan, too, the United States has exerted influence on the countries receiving American aid under the European Recovery Program to assure that none of the aid provided these countries would be turned into deliveries to the Soviet Union aiding that country's war potential. This selective American embargo on shipments of commodities most desired by the Soviet Union has resulted both in a sharp decline in the volume of trade, particularly in exports to the USSR, and in the emergence of a new trend in commodity exchange, namely, a systematic favorable balance of trade for the Soviet Union. Since 1947, Soviet exports to the

United States have exceeded their purchases here, in sharp contra-distinction to the previous years' experience. During 1950–53, United States exports to the USSR virtually ceased.

TABLE 63. United States Trade with the USSR, 1931–53.

Year	Exports	Imports
	(MILLIONS OF DOLLARS)	
1931–35 (average)	33.0	13.0
1936–40 (average)	57.9	24.2
1941	107.5	30.1
1942	1,425.4	24.7
1943	2,994.8	29.9
1944	3.473.3	49.6
1945	1,836.4	58.7
1946	357.9	100.6
1947	149.1	77.1
1948	27.9	86.8
1949	6.6	39.1
1950	.7	38.3
1951	.055	27.4
1952	.020	16.7
1953	.019	10.2

Sources: *Statistical Abstract of the United States, 1948,* p. 928, and data from the Department of Commerce.

The change brought about by the export restrictions imposed in 1948 may be seen from the fact that in 1947 Soviet purchases of machinery and vehicles in the United States amounted to $109,000,000; in 1949 the value of exports in this category was less than $500,000. Almost 70 per cent of the total value of merchandise exported to the USSR from the United States in 1949 consisted of raw cotton, a commodity not usually exported to the USSR in immediately preceding years. In 1949 more than one half of Soviet exports to the United States consisted of undressed furs of all kinds. Soviet exports of platinum, manganese, and chromium were reduced sharply as compared to preceding years, apparently in retaliation against the barriers imposed on Soviet purchases in this country. Soviet willingness to export more to the United States than was bought here resulted in all probability from the fact that surplus dollars earned in this country could be used by the USSR to purchase badly needed commodities in other parts of the world. It seems not unlikely that heavy Soviet purchases of wool and natural rubber in Southeast

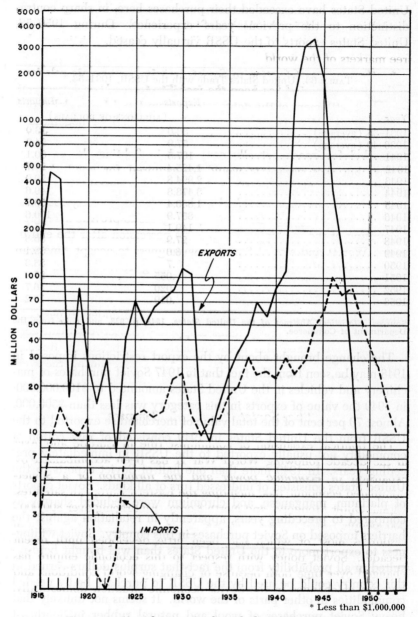

FIGURE 6. *United States Trade with the USSR, 1915–53.*
Sources: Condoide, *Russian-American Trade*, p. 91, and Table 63.

Asia and Australia in 1949 and 1950 were financed to a large extent by dollars earned in the United States and then converted into sterling at the relatively favorable dollar-pound ratios existing in the free markets of the world.

Another source of friction in Soviet-American economic relations in the postwar period has been the inability to reach an agreement regarding settlement of the debts arising from Lend-Lease deliveries during World War II. American policy, applied in negotiations with all recipient countries, has been that no payment would be demanded for goods actually consumed in fighting the common enemy, but that payments would be required for goods having peacetime use. Despite prolonged negotiations stretching over almost a decade, no agreement had yet been reached in early 1954, the result both of an apparent Soviet unwillingness to provide a detailed accounting of the remaining goods in its possession after the end of World War II and also of Soviet unwillingness to accept American estimates as to the amount of the debt arising from the Lend-Lease operations. One Russian offer for settlement of this matter was reported to be $240-$300,000,000 — less than 3 per cent of the total value of Lend-Lease sent to the USSR, and well under 10 per cent of the value of nonmilitary items shipped.[35] Soviet-American economic relations have also been similarly exacerbated by Russian failure to return merchant vessels lent the USSR during the war. By early 1954, not all these vessels had been returned yet.

The Soviet Economic Empire

The political expansion of communist rule in Europe and Asia in the decade following World War II has been accompanied by expansion of economic power and the formation of a Soviet-dominated economic bloc including the Eastern European satellites, China, Outer Mongolia, and North Korea. Embracing over 800,000,-000 people, one-third of humanity, this region is rich in natural resources most of which had been little developed until recent decades. Soviet policy with respect to this economic empire has changed over time both because of changing world conditions and because of changes in the Soviet economic situation domestically.

---

[35] *Foreign Aid Supplement,* U. S. Department of Commerce, December 1952, p. 23.

Between 1945 and 1954, this policy seems to have gone through three main stages:

In the first period — which may roughly be taken as 1945 to 1948 — the Soviet emphasis was upon maximum exploitation of this area to meet the internal needs of the USSR. This was the period of looting in Eastern Germany and Manchuria, heavy reparations collections, removals of capital equipment, and the like. In Germany and Austria the Soviet government seized hundreds of industrial and other firms and operated them for its own account. In Eastern Europe and North Korea, so-called "joint-stock companies" were formed to operate key economic areas of these countries. Nominally these were formed by contributions of equal amounts of capital by the Soviet Union and by the countries in which these enterprises are located. Actually the great bulk of the capital contributed by the Soviet Union for these companies in Eastern Europe consisted of former German assets in that area. Ownership of these assets had been vested in the Soviet Union by the Potsdam Agreement of 1945. In Hungary, for example, such joint companies were set up early in the postwar period to control bauxite production, petroleum and petroleum refining, coal output, power plants, electrical and agricultural machinery enterprises, chemical production, air and motor transport development, and so forth. This occurred also in Rumania and to a lesser extent in Yugoslavia. These joint-stock companies were guaranteed profits, given exceptionally favorable tax treatment, and generally occupied most exceptional positions.[36] That this policy of economic exploitation and imperialism was bitterly resented in the countries so affected was made clear by the defection of Yugoslavia from the Soviet Bloc, and it was also indicated by the later changes in Soviet economic policies toward its satellites.

The second stage of development of the Soviet economic orbit may be taken to encompass the years 1949 to mid-1953. In this period the Soviet Union began to grapple with the problem of longer-range exploitation of its satellites, while faced with the competitive example of the billions of dollars of economic aid given

[36] Preliminary Report 20 of the House Select Committee on Foreign Aid, *The Eastern European Economy in Relation to the European Recovery Program, passim.* Washington: Government Printing Office, 1948.

the Western European nations by the United States. The Soviet Union could and did forbid its Eastern European satellites to become eligible for American economic aid by participating in the Marshall Plan, but the American example had to be counteracted by a program that would at least seem to resemble a policy of economic aid. Moreover this period marked the emergence of Communist China as a major factor in the Soviet empire. From 1950 to 1953, of course, the Korean War was fought, raising additional economic problems for the Soviet Union. The official beginning of this second stage of economic policy may be taken to be the formation in January 1949 of the Council for Mutual Economic Assistance, consisting of the USSR, Bulgaria, Hungary, Poland, Rumania, and Czechoslovakia originally. The purpose of this organization was stated officially to be "the exchange of experience in the economic field, the rendering of technical assistance to each other, and the rendering of mutual assistance with regard to raw materials, food stuffs, machinery, equipment, etc." [37]

During this second period, the Soviet Union put greatest emphasis on the rapid industrialization of its Eastern European satellites. It provided machinery, engineers and technicians, and blueprints for new factories and mines in this area. For the most part this was paid for by conventional trade as discussed below, but some credits were given, notably the more than $500,000,000 granted Poland in two loans.[38] Communist China received a $300,000,000 credit in early 1950 to assist in rebuilding its nonagricultural economy from the low state to which the postwar civil war had reduced it. Three factors played a role in motivating this policy: the need to discourage Titoist defection and sentiment among the satellites; the possibility of long-range strengthening of over-all communist military-economic potential by industrialization of the USSR's allies; and the need to increase production within the Soviet orbit of materials and equipment denied the communist world by the Western embargo on strategic exports. As a result of this policy, trade between the Soviet Union and its satellites, as well as among the satellites themselves, grew rapidly.

---

[37] *New York Times,* January 26, 1949. Albania and East Germany joined later.

[38] The first Polish loan of $450,000,000 was announced in early 1948. On a per capita basis, taking into account Poland's much smaller population, this was a far more generous credit than the 1950 Chinese loan.

The high degree of trade integration that has been achieved between the Soviet Union and its satellite and allied countries may be shown by the following 1952 data on the percentage of these countries' trade that was transacted with other communist countries, and also with the Soviet Union alone: [39]

Country	Per Cent Trade within Bloc	Per cent Trade with Soviet Union
USSR	80	—
Albania	100	almost half
Outer Mongolia	100	no data
North Korea	100	no data
Communist China	72	53.5
Bulgaria	89	57
Rumania	85	58
Hungary	71	29
Czechoslavakia	71	35
Poland	67	32
East Germany	78	no data

The volume of Soviet trade with the countries of Eastern Europe has been studied in detail by Leon M. Herman. His estimates of the value of this trade (in millions of United States dollars) in the years 1947 and 1951 follow:

Country	1947	1951
Albania		
total	13.0	24.0
exports	6.5	12.0
imports	6.5	12.0
Bulgaria		
total	90.3	153.3
exports	45.6	86.4
imports	44.7	66.9
Czechoslovakia		
total	66.8	470.0
exports	38.9	247.5
imports	27.9	222.5
Hungary		
total	27.9	228.4
exports	14.5	111.2
imports	13.4	117.1

[39] N. Ivanov, "Ekonomicheskoye Sotrudnichestvo SSSR so Stranami Narodnoi Demokrati," *Vneshnyaya Torgovlya*, No. 11 (1953), pp. 13–26.

Country	1947	1951
Poland		
total	150.1	425.0
exports	79.5	235.0
imports	70.5	190.0
Rumania		
total	49.8	242.2
exports	29.9	122.5
imports	19.9	119.7
East Germany		
total	27.0	426.0
exports	11.0	250.0
imports	16.0	176.0
Soviet Bloc		
total	424.9	1,968.9
exports	225.9	1,064.6
imports	198.9	904.2

It will be noted that in 1951 three of these countries, Czechoslovakia, Poland, and East Germany, accounted for roughly two-thirds of satellite Eastern Europe's trade with the Soviet Union. This proportion has probably also held true roughly in 1950, 1952, and 1953.

It is probably a misnomer to speak of trade in connection with these economic relations, since trade implies some degree of equality in negotiation and bargaining power. Certainly for Eastern Europe, Outer Mongolia, and North Korea, there can be no degree of equality with the Soviet Union. Despite the talk of "equal trade," just prices which do not reflect the inequalities of capitalist markets, and the like, there would seem to be little doubt but that in relation to these countries the Soviet Union dictates to its partners what shall be traded and on what terms. There may be more of an approach to equal bargaining in the case of Communist China, but here too the economic advantage is with the Soviet Union.

In general, trade between the Soviet Union and other members of its bloc consists mainly of Soviet export of finished and semi-finished products, particularly all types of machinery and equipment, in exchange for satellite raw materials, foodstuffs, and consumer goods. There are, however, important qualifications to the above generalization. The more advanced of the satellites, particularly East Germany, Czechoslovakia, and Poland, supply the Soviet Union with some types of machinery and transport equipment. The Soviet Union also supplies many of the satellites with raw materials in which they are deficient, particularly iron ore, nonferrous metals, and cotton.

In addition, the Soviet Union has supplied its satellites with much of the technical assistance they have required for expanding their industries. Soviet engineers and technicians by the thousands have gone to Eastern Europe and China to supervise the building and operation of new plants, mines, and the like. Many of the new plants have been built on the basis of Soviet specifications and in accordance with plans drawn up in the Soviet Union, a factor which has helped the standardization of satellite industrial practice along Soviet lines.

Statements by communist spokesmen sometimes suggest that the goal of this trade, and more basically of the economic planning of the communist world, is creation of a fully integrated Soviet Bloc economy, dovetailing in all respects and maximally independent of the noncommunist world.[40] It is most doubtful that this degree of integration has actually been achieved or was even sought during the second period. The economic plans of the Eastern European satellites up to 1953 seemed to be mere replicas of Soviet economic plans, with the same emphasis on building up all possible branches of heavy industry, than parts of an integrated whole. Some statements by Czechoslovak communist leaders in early 1954 seemed to suggest that beginning in 1956 the economic plans of the Soviet Union and its Eastern European satellites would actually be integrated with more emphasis on division of labor and specialization among members of the bloc. Both Czechoslovakia and Hungary have delayed the beginning of their next five-year plan period until 1956 so that their plans can more easily be coordinated with a uniform five-year plan for the Soviet Union and Eastern Europe during 1956–1960.

During 1950 to 1953, of course, the Korean War posed great problems for Soviet economic policy toward its Asian allies. That large amounts of Soviet military equipment and supplies were delivered to the North Korean and Chinese Communist forces during this period has been testified to time and again by United States

---

[40] Cf. for example the statement by Hilary Minc in *Pravda*, September 25, 1951. This is quoted also in Harry Schwartz, "East-West Trade," in Bergson, ed., *Soviet Economic Growth*, p. 346.

and other United Nations spokesmen, who have exhibited captured Soviet material and have pointed to the large numbers of Soviet-made MIG fighters which made up the communist air force in this war. How these deliveries of war supplies were financed and to what extent, if any, they forced curtailment of planned Soviet deliveries of industrial equipment to Communist China has been kept secret. During this period the Soviet Union relinquished to the Communist Chinese the Soviet interest and participation rights in the Chinese Changchun railroad, thus complying with one provision of the February 1950 Soviet-Chinese agreement. Another provision of that agreement had called for Soviet restitution to China of all property "acquired by Soviet economic organizations from Japanese owners in Manchuria." When announcement of such restitution was finally made, it became obvious that only a small portion of the property seized by the Soviet Union in Manchuria in 1945 had been returned. The great bulk of this property — steel-making equipment, electric-power-generating machinery, industrial machinery, and so forth — was not returned, presumably on the legal ground that this had been seized by the Soviet armed forces as "war booty" rather than acquired by "Soviet economic organizations."

It should not be thought that the process of milking the Eastern European satellites was unimportant during this second period. A great volume of reparations flowed to the Soviet Union during these years, particularly from East Germany. The economic exploitation of Eastern Austria, an area occupied by Soviet troops, proceeded at maximum speed. Profits flowed to the Soviet Union from Soviet-owned enterprises in East Germany, Rumania, and Hungary. And in China the beginning of future profits was laid by the formation of three Soviet-Chinese joint-stock companies. One of these prospects for and produces oil and gas in Sinkiang Province. A second is similarly concerned with nonferrous metals in the same area, and a third flies civilian planes along the routes Peking-Chita, Peking-Irkutsk, and Peking-Alma Ata.[41] Viewed most broadly, of course, the basic economic exploitation of the Soviet satellite areas arose not from any specific takings by the Soviet government, but

[41] An early announcement of these enterprises is given in *Izvestia*, March 29, 1950. An account of Soviet economic penetration into and exploitation of China's Sinkiang Province will be found in *Foreign Affairs*, April 1954.

from the fact that Soviet puppets in each country directed economic development there along the lines ordered from Moscow, rather than as the inhabitants of each land might have desired if allowed to express their choices freely.

The third stage of economic policy considered here began in mid-1953 and was still continuing in the middle of 1954. The stage had been set for a new policy by the death of Joseph Stalin, the termination of fighting in Korea, and the decision made by the post-Stalinist regime to shift domestic economic policy somewhat toward greater emphasis on improving the Soviet standard of living. In addition the restiveness and resentment shown by the population of Eastern Europe — particularly in the June 1953 riots and demonstrations in East Germany and Czechoslovakia — also affected this policy.

As revealed during the first year of its execution, this modified economic policy toward the rest of the Soviet orbit included these elements:

1. The flow of economic aid from the USSR to Eastern Europe was decreased in order to permit an increase in the flow of such aid from the Soviet Union to China and Asia. In the summer and fall of 1953 announcements were made in the various Eastern European satellites that economic plans were being altered so as to reduce the former frenzied pace of and emphasis upon heavy-industrial development. One of the major reasons given for this slowdown in several of these countries was the lack of adequate raw material supplies, though earlier it had been taken as axiomatic that deficient raw materials would be supplied by the Soviet Union. On the other hand, in September 1953 substantial increases in Soviet economic aid to North Korea and China were announced. The Soviet government granted North Korea 1,000,000,000 rubles to cover Soviet help in rebuilding hydroelectric stations, ferrous and non-ferrous metal plants, chemical and cement factories, and other installations damaged or destroyed during the Korean War. According to the official announcement this aid will be provided "by means of planning work done by Soviet organizations, by supplying equipment and materials, by giving technical assistance in the process of restoration and construction, by handing over patents and technical documents . . . and by also training Korean personnel for these

enterprises." There was a hint in the announcement that in addition to the outright grant North Korea had received a credit for consumer goods, and for help in restoring transportation, agriculture, public utilities, and other areas of the economy.[42] About the same time Communist China received what is apparently a long-term credit, amount undisclosed, to help finance industrialization during its first five-year plan period. The Soviet Union will supply equipment and technical aid to build or to expand a total of 141 large plants producing iron and steel, nonferrous metals, coal, oil and oil products, machinery, automobiles, tractors, and electric power.[43]

2. Major economic concessions were made to Eastern Germany in the summer of 1953, concessions aimed in part at influencing the September 1953 elections in Western Germany. As a result the Soviet government ceased collecting reparations as of January 1, 1954, returned the last 33 major East German industrial concerns which had been run by the Soviet government in that territory,[44] accepted a limitation on occupation expenses in Germany so that these may not exceed 5 per cent of the East German budgetary revenue, gave East Germany a two-year credit of 485,000,000 rubles with interest at two per cent, and increased 1953 Soviet exports to East Germany by 590,000,000 rubles, roughly a 50 per cent rise in one year.[45] Thus Soviet economic policy in East Germany had turned through a full 180 degrees from the ruthless looting of 1945 to the generosity of 1953. This shift resulted, of course, from the rising importance of Germany in the struggle between East and West, the Soviet Union attempting through its more benevolent policy in East Germany to influence West Germany against ratifying the European Defense Community agreement and rearming as part of a Western coalition.

3. There were many signs in late 1953 and early 1954 that in this period the Soviet trade drive against the Western restrictions really sought to secure more East-West trade for Eastern Europe and China, as well as for the Soviet Union itself. To the extent that Eastern Europe and China do increase their trade with the West, of course, their economic dependence — though not necessarily

---

[42] *Pravda*, September 20, 1953.
[43] *Ibid.*, September 17, 1953.
[44] 66 East German plants had been returned in 1952.
[45] *Pravda*, August 23, 1953.

their political dependence – upon the Soviet Union will decrease. There seemed little doubt in early 1954 that this willingness of the Soviet Union to see its satellites increase their economic relations with the West was born of the inadequacy of Soviet resources for the simultaneous accomplishment of vital economic tasks at home and rapid building up of satellite economies abroad. Communist China, in particular, probably failed by a wide margin to be satisfied with the amount of Soviet resources allocated for Chinese industrialization during 1953–57. Even by 1959 when the Chinese factories being built or expanded with Soviet help, are scheduled to reach full production, China's output of the most important heavy industrial products is scheduled only to be at the 1932 Soviet level.

CHAPTER XV

RETROSPECT AND PROSPECT

AGAINST THE BACKGROUND of the preceding chapters, it seems fitting to attempt some evaluation of the complex saga of Soviet economic development. What has been accomplished and at what cost? What are the future prospects for Soviet economic development? The past is prologue to the future. If we are to have any hope of forecasting the future course and speed of Soviet progress, we must comprehend the nature of what has been done.

Among Soviet accomplishments, the first in importance has been the creation of a society and an economy based on noncapitalist institutions and principles. The abolition of private ownership of almost all means of production, the coordination of economic development through a unified economic plan, the collectivization of millions of peasant farmers — these are major and revolutionary achievements with profound consequences. The rulers of the USSR have created an integrated and viable state and economy which have survived successfully through profound crises. Soviet experience has become the model for economic development throughout Eastern Europe and communist-dominated Asia.

Second in the list of accomplishments, we may cite the at least partially successful harnessing of personal ambitions to coordinated and planned economic development. The private initiative and enterprise, based on the desire for gain and power, which built the economies of capitalist countries have been largely curbed in the USSR. Instead a system of incentives and punishments has been created calculated to enlist the energies of the tens of millions of adult Soviet citizens toward the realization of state goals. Nowhere else in the world have the "carrot and the stick" been so carefully joined together to direct the aspirations and energies of a major mass of humanity. Moreover, by intensive and unchallenged propaganda, the Soviet government has undoubtedly enlisted the enthusiasm and moral fervor of millions of its subjects in the work of realizing its objectives. One need not believe all Soviet claims about the "New Soviet Man" to understand that the accomplishments of the past decades would have been impossible if millions had not been persuaded that they were engaged in a crusade worthy of great exertions and great sacrifices. The youngsters of the 1930's who carved Komsomolsk out of a wilderness, and many others like them, were moved by an ideal and by a collective dream. In everyday Soviet life an army of agitators — aided by every possible medium of propaganda and communication — hammers away at the theme that the citizen who serves the government's interest is simultaneously serving his own interests.[1]

Third, and not least important, we may cite the great growth in production and the accompanying technological revolution. The Russia of 1914 stood in fifth place in the ranking of nations according to industrial production. Though it was advancing rapidly, its industry was far from commensurate with the relative importance of its population and of the vast area it covered. Its agriculture still showed important influences of the primitive technology that had been largely abandoned long before in Western Europe. With respect to productivity and technological level, its industry and agriculture were far behind such countries as the United States, Germany, and Great Britain. The USSR of 1954 is the second most powerful nation in the world, in large part because of the growth of industrial production that has provided the sinews of modern war. The bare skeleton of the accomplishment in the field of industry may be shown by the comparison given in Table 64.

In little more than a third of a century, despite the destruction of one civil war and two World Wars, coal output has been increased about tenfold, pig-iron production about sevenfold, steel about ninefold, petroleum almost sixfold, and electric power generated over sixtyfold. Along with this has gone the comprehensive development of every other branch of heavy industry: machine-building,

---

[1] Inkeles, *Public Opinion in Soviet Russia*, passim.

armaments, chemicals, and the like. On the other hand, the gains made in agriculture, though appreciable in some fields, have been of no such magnitude as those in industry, and the disproportions between industrial and agricultural growth have often caused difficulty.

TABLE 64. Soviet Production of Selected Commodities in 1913, 1928, 1940, and 1953.

Commodity	Unit	1913	1928	1940*	1953†
Coal	mil. metric tons	29.1	35.8	166.0	320.0
Pig Iron	mil. metric tons	4.2	3.4	15.0	28.0
Steel	mil. metric tons	4.2	4.3	18.3	38.0
Petroleum	mil. metric tons	9.2	11.5	31.0	52.0
Electric Power .	billion kwh	1.9	5.1	48.3	133.0

* Expanded territory. † Approximate.

In the process of development the technological level of most branches of Soviet production has been raised substantially. Engineers, physicists, chemists, and other technicians have been trained in numbers far greater than ever before. The most able of these specialists rank with the best in the world. The Soviet achievements in producing hydrogen and atomic bombs testify to the strides that have been made. These feats were accomplished sooner because of the treachery of Klaus Fuchs and others like him, but there can be little doubt that they would have come in any event. A country with scientists and mathematicians of the stature of Frenkel, Kolmogorov, and Kapitsa, to name but a few, has the intellectual personnel required to solve the problems, and Soviet economic development provided the material means that made possible the actual achievement of plutonium and tritium production and atomic and hydrogen explosions.

Less spectacular, but very important, has been the rise in labor productivity since 1928. Nevertheless, even in 1954 the supply of technically trained personnel in the USSR was still not adequate for all needs, and much remained to be done to bring labor productivity up to the best levels of the non-Soviet world.

The Soviet achievement in industry must be seen in perspective. The historical records show that the United States had reached the absolute level of Russia's 1913 production of the five commodities shown above in the middle and late nineteenth century, as early as 1867 in the case of coal and as late as 1899 in the case of petroleum. The 1953 output of these commodities in the USSR is for the most part at the absolute level attained by the United States about the time of World War I. Looked at in the large, the development of Soviet industry from 1913 to 1953 took roughly as long and covered somewhat the same ground as American industrial growth from, say, 1878 to 1918.[2] Of course, this analogy should not be pressed too closely, since the Soviet technological level of 1953 is far above the world level of 1918.

The Soviet achievement was made despite the physical destruction wrought during 1914–20 and 1941–45, destruction that has no parallel in the corresponding American experience. The growth of the USSR's economy, until the 1940's, had to be financed almost entirely from domestic resources without the inflow of capital from abroad such as aided economic development in the United States. Soviet heavy industry in 1954 was far more comprehensive than that of this country in 1918. It included, for example, a major and almost all-embracing atomic industry such as this country did not develop until World War II and afterward. On the other hand, American industrial development did not emphasize heavy industry so lopsidedly, at the expense of consumer goods and services. Finally, the Soviet progress was accomplished with the aid of a far larger population and a much more advanced world technology than were available to the United States in the comparable period of development. But taking all factors into account, the USSR's economic development has obviously been a remarkable achievement.

A satisfactory comparison between the pace of Soviet industrialization and that in the United States or other capitalistic countries should be based, of course, upon data regarding over-all industrial output. The inflationary character of Soviet statistics on this matter, based upon 1926–27 prices, has been pointed out before and makes conclusions drawn from them of uncertain value. Perhaps the closest analogues in capitalist experience for the Soviet development are to be found in the cases of Germany and Japan. Both of the latter emerged from technological backwardness compara-

---

[2] Bureau of the Census, *Historical Statistics of the United States 1789–1945. passim.* Washington, D. C., Government Printing Office, 1949.

tively late, and both were able to make very rapid initial progress in industrial output by drawing, as the Soviet Union has, upon the experience and advanced technologies of the countries whose industrialization had preceded theirs. The rapid industrial development of Czarist Russia after 1890 also provides a parallel for the Soviet experience, though accomplished in a radically different social, political, and economic setting. Some have argued that all of the feats of Soviet industrialization could have been accomplished under Czarist rule if World War I and the overthrow of that regime had not interrupted this earlier progress.[3] Like all speculations about what might have been in history, however, such arguments must rest upon assumptions whose validity is unverifiable.

One additional factor deserves mention. The extension of communist control over Eastern Europe and much of Asia has added appreciably to over-all communist and Soviet military-economic capabilities. With respect to Eastern Europe, the magnitude of this increment is shown by the following production data for 1952, in millions of metric tons and billions of kilowatt-hours as appropriate.

Country	Coal*	Pig Iron	Steel	Electric Power	Oil
Bulgaria	7.4	–	–	1.4	–
Czechoslovakia	53.6	2.4	3.6	11.6	.2
East Germany	157.2	.65	1.9	21.6	–
Hungary	18.7	.58	1.4	3.9	.6
Poland	90.6	1.8	3.2	11.9	.2
Rumania	4.3	.4	.7	3.0	8.4
Total	331.8	5.83	10.8	53.4	9.4

* Including lignite.
Source: United Nations, *Economic Survey of Europe in 1953*, pp. 271-76.

Assuming some increase in the above totals in 1953 over 1952, and taking account of Communist China's output as well as of Russia's in addition to the above, it seems likely that in 1953 the entire Soviet Bloc produced over 700,000,000 metric tons of coal and lignite, about 35,000,000 metric tons of pig iron, over 50,000,000 metric tons of steel, almost 65,000,000 metric tons of crude oil, and about 190,000,000,000 kilowatt-hours of electric power. These represent large resources not to be lightly dismissed.

---

[3] N. S. Timasheff, *The Great Retreat*, pp. 374–76. New York: Dutton, 1946.

The Cost Involved

Heavy costs have been paid for Soviet progress, both material and nonmaterial in character. They have been of a magnitude and a nature that find no counterpart in the comparable American experience. Only in time of war or the grave threat of war has this country undergone deprivations even remotely analogous.

From many points of view the most important cost has been the great loss of freedom suffered by those whom the Kremlin rules. The Soviet peoples are regimented peoples. Even the nominally free worker or peasant is under virtual military discipline—guaranteed employment and minimal subsistence as is a soldier, but like him completely subordinate to the state, which directs all productive activity. The trend of legal regulations has been ever more toward imposing greater control and limiting freedom of occupational choice. Legally the Soviet worker may not leave his job without his employer's consent, except in extraordinary circumstances. Hundreds of thousands of Soviet youngsters are drafted annually to be trained in vocations selected for them by the state. After their training they must go and work wherever in the vast Soviet Union the state orders them to go. The collective farm peasantry must plant those crops the state wishes; sow, cultivate, and harvest at state-dictated times; and regard its delivery obligations to the state as having first claim upon the product of its sweat and toil. The millions of slave laborers in the Soviet Union are merely the victims of Soviet coercion at its extreme, not an isolated and extraordinary group of unfortunates.

When the restrictions on political freedom, on the liberty of expression and on dissent are taken into account, the picture becomes even blacker. The Soviet economy and society of today are a far cry from the humanitarian visions of generations of socialist idealists. In the name of the working class, the Soviet state has fastened upon its workers chains so strong and so burdensome that they can only be compared with the worst abuses of peonage. No capitalist corporation in democratic Western countries would ever dare treat its workers as the Soviet government, the world's greatest single employer, has treated those who operate its factories, railroads, and mines.

The reader may wonder how these remarks square with the

earlier description of the enthusiasm generated by Soviet propaganda to aid accomplishment of its economic objectives, or with the statement about Soviet success in relating realization of personal ambition with accomplishment of government goals. This apparent contradiction may be resolved, however, if we think again of our analogy between Soviet society and an army The soldier has no freedom, but he may be enthusiastic about realization of the army's military goals and willing to lay down his life to help attain them. Anyone who has ever served in the armed forces knows, too, that within the framework of their constricting regulations there are incentives and punishments that work powerfully. The desire for promotion or fear of being restricted to quarters are potent stimuli for good or improved performance; their analogues are equally powerful in the USSR.

But for a fuller resolution of the conflict, it must be pointed out that the fund of enthusiasm on which the Soviet government could draw was probably much greater in the 1920's and 1930's than it has been since World War II. The very fact that since the mid-1930's the Soviet government has had to increase its coercive measures and to increase the economic and noneconomic incentives offered its people would seem to support that hypothesis. What need would there be in the postwar period for the dreary endless round of socialist competitions, begun on every pretext—such as May Day or the Korean conflict if the naive and unquestioning enthusiasm of the First Five-Year Plan had carried over to the Fifth Five-Year Plan? Would the directors of an economy whose members were moved primarily by hope of a glorious future have to explain that they abolished rationing because it was too egalitarian and did not provide sufficient incentives for greater production? Obviously the same factors and considerations do not move all of the Soviet millions, yet the system of Soviet incentives makes it clear that personal self-interest, not idealistic enthusiasm, is the primary source of motivation for the USSR's citizens.

The Standard of Living

The Soviet people bore the brunt of the cost of Soviet industrialization, as did their ancestors in the time of Peter the Great when a remarkably similar development took place. It is true that part of the USSR's development was made possible by utilizing more fully resources that had been unemployed, such as many mineral deposits, or that were seriously underemployed, such as agricultural labor. But the pace and the volume of economic development since 1928 have required far greater resources than these. In consequence the standard of living in the USSR fell seriously in the early 1930's. Its recovery thereafter to the end of the decade was at a far slower pace than would have been the case if resources had been employed in accordance with consumer wishes. In the late 1930's, moreover, rapidly increasing military expenditures added to the burden that had to be borne by the economy in general and consumers in particular.

The impressive production achievements of Soviet heavy industry are unmatched in those sections of the economy serving consumers, except for education and medical care, both fields directly related to production efficiency. Throughout the Soviet regime, the diet of consumers has consisted primarily of bread and cereals; they have had little in the way of clothing, and much of that has been of rather shoddy quality; and the housing of those who live in cities and towns deteriorated over most of the Soviet period—even before World War II—to a general slum level of overcrowding and poor quality. The immense efforts put forth in the USSR since 1928 and the enormous resources employed could have made possible a rise in the standard of living to heights far beyond any known before in that country. But the government put guns before butter and factories before homes, failing time and again to realize the glowing promises of improved conditions made to its people. We have quoted earlier Prof. Bergson's observation that around 1937 the real per capita disposable income available to consumers in the USSR was roughly equivalent to that in the United States during the decade 1869–78. At the same time the volume of Soviet production of chief industrial raw materials was at approximately the level of United States output of these commodities in the first decade of the twentieth century. The thirty-year gap indicated between consumption and industrial raw material output is a crude but significant measure of the differential impact of capitalist and Soviet economic development upon standards of living.

An aggravating factor increasing the cost that had to be paid for Soviet economic development between 1928 and 1940 was the fact that it was accomplished wastefully and with many errors. One would hardly expect such a frenzied concentration of resources upon an objective to be otherwise in character. When mistakes and waste came to light or were too heavy to be ignored, Stalin and his colleagues diverted the blame to "Trotskyite saboteurs and imperialist spies." They conveniently overlooked the fact that they had approved all phases of the development and encouraged many of the trends they subsequently denounced with terms such as "gigantomania." In addition, the centralized character of the Soviet economy and the constant fight against efforts to deviate from the plan have required a large bureaucracy and an army of watchmen of all kinds. The support and maintenance of these personnel have had to be borne in addition to the normal costs of economic development.

It may be argued that the sacrifices imposed upon the peoples of the USSR during 1928–40 were justified by the results of World War II. Without such frenzied industrialization, the USSR would presumably not have been able to stand up against the Nazi war machine and help so decisively in defeating it. There is undoubtedly much to be said on this side of the case. It is this interpretation of events that Stalin gave implicitly in his speech of February 1946. But this argument loses at least part of its force when we realize that a large part of the development during 1928–40 took place in the areas that the Germans occupied, regions lost in the first months of the war. The Donbas, the Dnepr hydroelectric installation, and many other major economic facilities built or expanded by the Soviet regime gave almost no help in winning the conflict. The Soviet Army, whose equipment with modern weapons had been so major an objective of economic activity in the 1930's, was forced back to the gates of Moscow by early December 1941. True, Soviet industry recovered and produced most of the armament to equip the new armies that ousted the invader. Yet one who studies the time table of events and evaluates the role of American Lend-Lease and British Mutual Aid deliveries may well wonder whether collapse could have been avoided had these resources not become available. The list of goods shipped the USSR during the war included almost every commodity needed in the struggle, from guns and planes to metals, aviation gas, rubber, machinery, shoes, and food of all kinds. If Soviet industry had had to produce all the trucks, ships, locomotives, and other commodities received from abroad, it could never have produced the volume of arms it did. The industry behind the line of furthest German penetration during the conflict was largely created during the Soviet regime and played an immensely vital role in obtaining victory. But the records of Lend-Lease and Mutual Aid help are the best proof that this alone was inadequate. If military considerations alone are to be used as the justification for Soviet industrialization in the 1930's, then they would seem to point also to inadequate preparation, particularly in the area of locational policy for the industry developed in those years.

Maurice Dobb has referred contemptuously to the "loose and ill-informed chatter in the West" about Soviet "industrialization promoted at the expense of the standard of life of the people."[4] The First Five-Year Plan, he argues, envisaged a rise in the absolute level of consumption during its term. Dobb concedes that " a fall in the standard of life occurred in certain of the 'tight' years of the First Five-Year Plan," but attributes this to extraneous and accidental factors. Yet this most sophisticated apologia for the cost of Soviet industrialization ignores the facts. All the Soviet five-year plans to date have promised far greater benefits to consumers than were actually realized. Promises are cheap and help morale, but the whole Soviet experience until Stalin died had been that when resources proved inadequate it was consumer goods and services that bore the cuts needed to assure fulfillment of goals for heavy industry. The First Five-Year Plan, for example, set a goal for cotton-textile production of 4,670,000,000 meters. Actual output was only 2,694,000,000 meters in 1932. The Second Five-Year Plan set a goal for cotton-textile output of 4,900,000,000 meters; actual production was only 3,447,700,000 meters.[5] Shoe production in the last year of the First Five-Year Plan was to be 145,000,000 pairs; it was only 94,500,000 pairs in 1932.[6] In the Second Five-Year Plan, it is true, the shoe-production goal was apparently fulfilled in 1937, but the benefits here must have been far outweighed by the debacle

---

[4] Dobb, Soviet Economic Development since 1917, pp. 25–26.

[5] Pyatiletny Plan Narodno-Khozyaistvennogo Stroitelstvo SSSR, Tom I, p. 213. The Second Five-Year Plan, p. 246. Itogi Vypolneniya Vtorogo Pyatiletnogo Plana Razvitiya Narodnogo Khozyaistva Soyuz SSR, p. 85.

[6] Pyatiletny Plan . . ., p. 221. Itogi Vypolneniya . . ., p. 85.

in housing. Instead of 64,000,000 square meters of housing becoming available during 1933–37, as planned, only 26,800,000 square meters were actually put into use.[7] Never since 1928 has the per capita housing available to urban residents come close to the goal set in the First Five-Year Plan for 1932–33.

We do not have adequate data to measure precisely the course of the Soviet standard of living, but the decline in the First Five-Year Plan was far sharper than Dobb indicates, and recovery took an extended period. The world depression that began in 1929 obviously cannot be blamed on the Soviet leaders and is therefore extraneous and accidental in Dobb's sense. But the bloody and costly struggle over collectivization was neither extraneous nor accidental, though it worked great hardship on consumption. If the government had not been able to bend the peasantry to its will, it could not have extorted the grain it needed to feed the urban masses and for export at ruinous prices in payment for foreign machinery. Collectivization was the cornerstone of the foundation that permitted the rapid industrialization of the 1930's, and its costs are properly chargeable against that advance.

One last point may be mentioned in this summing-up of negative aspects of Soviet economic development. This is the rise of new classes and new divisions in Soviet society as a result of the economic policies followed. The hierarchical structure of organization in every field of the USSR's society is paralleled by the hierarchy of persons. At the top is the Presidium of the Central Committee, an oligopoly whose like has perhaps never before been seen, measured by the vastness of resources controlled and the freedom of discretion enjoyed. Below the Presidium is a large and complex congeries of groups, each with its special privileges and favored position: the Communist Party bureaucracy; the managers of industry, trade, and transport; the officials of the collective farms; the successful writers, artists, and scientists, richly rewarded for putting their talents to work for the perpetuation of the ruling oligarchy's sway; the favored members of the secret police, whose incomes are high to assure their loyalty; the mass of Stakhanovites who set the pace for their fellows; the officers of the armed forces. In the aggregate these are a substantial number, totaling in the millions. Though many of them live

---

[7] Cf. Chapter XI above.

poorly, in comparison with a skilled American worker or small business man, they are the new nobility and the new bourgeoisie of the Soviet society. The bounty given some of these groups flows from their productive contribution and is properly chargeable against production. But the resources devoted to those who keep the Soviet people in thrall fall into quite another category.

Whether these groups total 5, 10, or even 20 per cent of the Soviet population, it is clear they form a small though most important minority. Their composition and numbers, their relative shares of the national income, their absolute level of well-being, these and other matters are hidden from both the Soviet people and the outside world by the statistical blackout that has prevailed for many years. Below them is the great mass of Soviet citizens, who bear the main portion of the cost of economic development and military preparations. To the extent that mobility still exists in Soviet society, talented members of the underprivileged majority can and do enter the ranks of the more privileged groups. The hope and possibility of such rise may perhaps be an important element in reconciling tens of millions to their lot. Yet neither this hope, nor the low standard of living that has always prevailed in what is now the USSR, is obviously adequate. Else why need the state spend so much energy in distorting and misrepresenting the facts about how ordinary workers and farmers live in the United States and elsewhere in the Western world? The tremendous impression made upon Soviet soldiers when they entered the far from prosperous areas of Eastern Europe at the end of World War II is a measure both of their poverty and of the false picture they had been given of life outside their country. Ironically, much of the huge cost of the vast propaganda machine constantly engaged in deceiving the Soviet people about the outside world is included under the "education" item of the Soviet budget! The size of this item is then trumpeted to the world as proof of the "welfare state" nature of the USSR.[8]

If we break away from Marxist shibboleths, it seems not unfair to characterize the Soviet economy in these terms: From the point of view of organization and objectives it is a military feudal economy based upon industry rather than agriculture and employing twentieth century technology for military, productive, and propaganda

---

[8] Rovinsky, *Gosudarstvenny Byudzhet SSSR*, p. 206.

tasks. In the last analysis, its internal stability and freedom from overt discontent are guaranteed by the repressive forces of the state and the Draconian measures they employ.

U.S. and USSR

In the current struggle for world mastery between the forces led by the Soviet Union and those led by the United States, comparison of the economic strength of the contending groups is of particular interest. For a full evaluation of the relative position of the two groups, the economic strength of all nations on both sides should be compared. We shall restrict ourselves here, however, to the two leaders, because of the limited scope of this volume. The industrial power of Western Europe, including Great Britain, is substantially more than that of Soviet-dominated Eastern Europe. On the other hand, the vast manpower of China is an important asset in the ballance sheet of communist strength, particularly if India remains neutral. China's manpower was a major factor that had to be reckoned with in the Korean struggle.

Comparison of two such disparate economies as the United States and the Soviet Union is beset with pitfalls, which must be taken into account in advance. In the first place, even during the Korean conflict and the ensuing partial mobilization, the United States was working at a level much further below capacity production than was the Soviet Union. The standard work week in the United States is 40 hours, against 48 in the USSR. Moreover, a larger fraction of the female population is employed in the USSR than in the United States. With existing capacity of plant and equipment, therefore, this country could, if necessary, increase its output more, proportionately, than the Soviet Union. Secondly, military production takes a far smaller fraction of American productive capacity in peacetime than it does of Soviet capacity. Even during the Korean war, United States production of durable consumer goods—automobiles, refrigerators, television sets, and the like—was at record or near-record levels, though these items are obviously most competitive with armaments in terms of raw materials, machinery, and skilled manpower. Under these circumstances the interval of time required for conversion of American productive capacity to full military production would probably be greater than that of the

Soviet Union by a substantial margin. But with conversion completed, the ratio of armaments output in the two countries would be much more nearly proportional to their productive capacities. With these factors in mind, the following comparison may be considered. In the following table, United States output in 1953 is compared with estimated Soviet output in that year for some key industrial commodities:

Commodity	Unit	U.S.	USSR
Coal	mil. metric tons	437	320
Pig Iron	mil. metric tons	69	28
Steel	mil. metric tons	101	38
Petroleum	mil. metric tons	323	52
Electric Power	billion kwh	514	133

The wide superiority of United States industrial production is evident from the above comparison. Given time, in any conflict in the near future American industry could far outproduce Soviet industry in weapons of war. Only in manpower does the Soviet Union have the edge, the comparable figures in 1954 being 210–215,000,000 persons in the USSR and about 160,000,000 in the United States. The comparison above omits agricultural products, but there too a similar picture would be shown, taking into account relative populations. The United States, it should be remembered, helped much to feed its allies in World War II, while at no time lowering American diets below relatively high nutritional levels.

The leaders of the USSR are well aware of their quantitative disadvantage in the event of a long-drawn-out conflict conducted along the lines of World War II. They have undoubtedly made plans to take this into account. Large-scale postwar Soviet purchases abroad of rubber, wool, tin, and other commodities in which the USSR is deficient suggest clearly that it is actively stockpiling raw materials, and probably also food. It is quite probable, in view of past Soviet preparations for World War II, that the USSR scrapped a far smaller fraction of its military equipment than did the United States. The USSR has undoubtedly been stockpiling arms from current production and arming its allies on a major scale. In the middle of 1954, all information indicated that the existing military force of the Soviet Union was at least as strong as that of the United States, with the conspicuous exception of naval forces. Moreover the central position of the Soviet Union with respect to both Europe and Asia facilitates any action it might take toward bringing its resources to bear upon anticommunist nations on both continents, especially in Western Europe and the Middle East. The United States by comparison has a much more difficult logistics task in bringing its resources to bear in Europe, across 3,000 miles of the Atlantic Ocean, or in Asia, across the more than 5,000 miles of Pacific Ocean. On the other hand the USSR faces the risk of large-scale obsolescence of much of its present vast store of military equipment in the next few years.

Nuclear weapons—including both atomic and hydrogen bombs —are an important factor in any evaluation of relative military-economic potential. Presumably the United States has a far larger stock of these weapons than the USSR, and this will probably continue to be the case indefinitely. At some date in the future, however, barring the outbreak of war beforehand, the USSR may have a sufficient stock of bombs, long-range aircraft, and perhaps guided missiles to allow it to hope to knock out the United States with a simultaneous attack on all major targets. Yet the Soviet leaders will have to take into account possible retaliation. Their industry is still highly concentrated in a relatively few areas, and the rail and road transportation network east of the Volga River is thin indeed. Soviet petroleum production would be severely strained in any war involving use of large masses of motor vehicles, tanks, and aircraft. Yet the largest single Soviet oil basin, that around Baku, is most vulnerable to attack from relatively nearby non-Soviet territory in the south.

The Party Presidium has undoubtedly also taken these facts into account. The relocation and new development of industry since 1940 have created a much more dispersed pattern of location than existed before World War II. The effort to develop the Soviet economy as a series of somewhat self-sufficient major industrial regions has apparently been intensified in the postwar era, though it was begun as early as 1939. To the extent that this program has been and will be successful, it will give the USSR greater assurance in the future against complete economic paralysis resulting from the breakdown of transport facilities. But the basic concentration of petroleum output in a few areas still remains a glaring weak spot, even though large reserves may have been accumulated in areas lacking significant production.

As far as the material factors are concerned, there seems little reason to believe that Soviet economic strength has yet reached such a point as to give the leaders of the USSR confidence of winning a protracted struggle against the United States. But we must not become overly complacent on this score in the light of the rude surprises the Soviet Union has given us since 1945 in the field of modern weapons. The rapidity with which the Soviet Union mastered production of atomic and hydrogen bombs, jet planes, and long-range bombers testifies clearly that the Soviet armed forces have highly capable scientists and engineers working for them. The hints released in late 1953 and early 1954 of sensational Soviet progress in long-range guided missiles—including perhaps even rockets capable of carrying on intercontinental warfare across the Atlantic Ocean—can be disregarded only at our dire peril. The swift pace of modern military technology and science is such that underestimation of one's opponent may well be disastrous.

Those charged with the planning of American strategy in relation to the Soviet Union have a twofold task. They must try to prevent the outbreak of a Soviet-American war as well as plan to win one should it occur. In both areas of such planning there is danger that non-military elements may be underestimated. Among the latter none is more important than the continued great poverty of the mass of the Soviet people, more than three decades after the Bolshevik revolution. As pointed out earlier, the rulers of the USSR have felt it vitally necessary for the preservation of their own power to conceal the true situation and to try to convince their people that, poor as their lot is, they are far more fortunate than workers in capitalist countries, particularly the United States. The Soviet government's fear of the truth on this matter is indicated by the expensive lengths to which it has gone to jam Voice of America broadcasts beamed to the USSR. A more imaginative approach is required to break through the fog of lies spread by the Soviet government on this score. If the Soviet peoples could be informed of the reality of life in the "bourgeois" countries and of our desire for peace, there would be no danger of war. But such knowledge would imperil the stability of Kremlin rule, by demolishing the foundation of lies on which it is built. There is no more important area to which American resources must be devoted if peace is to be maintained or war to be won.

The difference in economic organization between the United States and the Soviet Union could be an important factor in a war between them. The highly centralized control of production in the USSR discourages initiative at lower administrative levels in the making of major decisions. Directors of enterprises have little to say about the volume and nature of output as well as about the interconnections between enterprises at different stages of a productive process. The reliance upon a long-term plan to provide guidance of operations leads to different habits of thought from those that are customary among entrepreneurs who must gauge their work in the light of rapidly shifting market conditions and consumer preferences. These considerations suggest that there is a flexibility and adaptability in the American economy far superior to that in the USSR. Moreover, there is no one source of control in the American economy, comparable to the Party Presidium and the economic ministries, whose elimination or impaired opportunities for communications with subordinates would so impair over-all economic direction. On the other hand, the ability of the Soviet Union to convert to war production during World War II offered an impressive example of skill and flexibility in meeting combat needs under adverse conditions. These factors are all relevant to any calculation of how either the United States or the Soviet Union would react to such an ordeal from the air as Germany and Japan suffered during World War II. All rational men must hope that the world need never again know such a time. The strained atmosphere of our times, however, makes such speculations of vital importance.

In sum, it is not the quantitative strength of the Soviet economy as such that raises concern in comparison with that of the United States. Rather it is the concentration of that economy upon direct and indirect military production, in peace and even more in war. By such concentration the Soviet Union has produced nuclear weapons and large quantities of first-class planes, tanks, and guns. Yet at the same time it has been unable to guarantee the production of uniformly good-quality articles of common necessity, from shoes and dresses to bricks and clocks. In this evaluation of the two countries and their strength, it should be borne in mind too that the relatively low standard of living in the USSR has some military virtues. The shift from civilian to military life is far less of a change for the Soviet citizen than for his American counterpart. Under the harsh conditions of ground combat, the Soviet citizen can adjust more easily to making do on what is available than the American. The performance of North Korean troops in their offensive sweep of July and early August 1950 provides an indication of the military advantages gained from using personnel accustomed to a low standard of living. But the subsequent performance of American troops against them provided an equally illuminating insight into the value of American weapons. In the Soviet Army the ruggedness of the North Koreans is combined with armament of a level rivaling and sometimes surpassing that of the weapons at the disposal of our troops.

Economic Development to 1960-65

Any attempt to consider the future economic development of the Soviet Union must begin by recognizing the basic uncertainty posed by the threat of war between the two great power blocs of our time. That such a conflict would be enormously destructive of life and property on both sides seems certain. It seems fruitless to attempt to speculate here on the nature and economic consequences of such a holocaust. Instead we shall assume here that peace of some kind will continue to prevail, even if interrupted by peripheral outbreaks that do not involve the two major powers of the current world in direct conflict. On this assumption we shall examine Soviet intentions for future economic development for the period in which these intentions have been made most explicit, that is, to about 1960 or 1965. We shall also examine some questions of longer-run development, to 1970 and beyond.

At the Eighteenth Congress of the Communist Party of the Soviet Union in 1939, both Stalin and Molotov discussed the future goals of Soviet economic growth. They indicated that their objective was ultimately to attain production levels permitting the USSR to equal and exceed what was then the highest per capita industrial output of the United States, that attained in 1929. Molotov's estimate of how long it would take to do this was given in this sentence: "We need another ten or fifteen years at least, another two or three five-year plan periods." [9]

In other words, it was the Soviet hope to outstrip the most advanced capitalist nations by 1947 or 1952 or soon thereafter. Stalin

[9] *The Land of Socialism Today and Tomorrow*, p. 119.

indicated then that for pig iron an annual output of 50,000,000 to 60,000,000 metric tons would have to be attained. Writing in 1940, an outstanding Soviet economist spelled these longer-range goals out more specifically, indicating that steel production would have to reach 70,000,000 to 80,000,000 tons; coal output would have to rise to six times that of 1937, or to over 750,000,000 metric tons; and oil production would have to rise to five or six times that of 1937, to over 150,000,000 metric tons annually.[10]

World War II rudely interrupted these plans. From 1941 to 1945 much Soviet capital was destroyed and the USSR's production was sharply reduced, despite the wartime development of areas beyond the line of furthest German penetration. In the same years, capitalist nations snapped out of the stagnation of the depression-blighted 1930's. The United States, particularly, increased its production, both absolutely and per capita, substantially. Both of these factors put the goal of equalling and exceeding the best levels of per capita capitalist industrial production much further away than they had seemed in 1939. In describing goals for the future in his famous speech of February 9, 1946, therefore, Stalin omitted all reference to per capita comparisons with the capitalist world. Instead he phrased the objectives in this manner:

> As regards the plans for a longer period ahead, the Party means to organize a new mighty upsurge in the national economy, which would allow us to increase our industrial production, for example, three times over as compared with the prewar period. We must achieve a situation where our industry can produce annually up to 50 million tons of pig iron, up to 60 million tons of steel, up to 500 million tons of coal and up to 60 million tons of oil. Only under such conditions can we consider that our homeland will be guaranteed against all possible eventualities.

Stalin indicated that might take three or more five-year periods, that is, to 1960 or 1965 or thereabouts. His reference to guaranteeing his country against "eventualities" was obviously an oblique means of stating that the increase of military-economic strength would be the primary objective of future development. Aside from the implicit abandonment of the hope of outstripping capitalist nations in the foreseeable future, his speech is noteworthy because several specific goals given by it are less than those implied by him and

---

[10] *Planovoye Khozyaistvo*, No. 10 (1940), pp. 36–37.

Molotov in 1939. This is clearly shown by comparison of Stalin's target figures quoted above with those stated or implied in the article by the Soviet economist referred to earlier. It must be remembered that the territory and population of the USSR in 1946 were both substantially greater than at the time of the Eighteenth Communist Party Congress in 1939.

It is noteworthy that the specific production goals enunciated by Stalin are, in the case of pig iron, steel, and coal, roughly equal to the corresponding American output of these commodities in 1940 or 1941. In the case of petroleum, however, the 60,000,000 metric tons objective is only about one third of the American production in 1940. On a per capita basis, of course, Soviet production of even pig iron, steel, and coal would be far below that of the United States in 1940 or 1941 should these goals be reached by 1960 or 1965. The over-all goal for gross industrial production indicated by Stalin, triple that of 1940, is equivalent to about 400,000,000,000 rubles in 1926–27 prices. This is the same goal indicated by a Soviet source in 1939 as the future target to be attained — presumably by 1947 or 1952 — if the USSR were to equal per capita American industrial production in 1929.[11] In 1939, however, Soviet calculations were based on the premise that the USSR would have roughly 200,000,000 persons by the time the 400,000,000,000 ruble output objective was attained. By 1960 or 1965, assuming that all of Stalin's goals are attained then, there will be appreciably more than 200,000,000 persons in the Soviet Union. Hence even then the USSR will not have attained American 1929 per capita industrial production.

When Stalin enunciated his long-range goals in 1946, he presumably based them on the assumption that the objectives of the Fourth Five-Year Plan would be reached on schedule by 1950. An important insight into the thinking behind this long-range planning is obtained if we assume, as Stalin's economists may have, that the long-range objectives he stated might be reached by about 1962. The interval between 1950 and 1962 is the same as that between

---

[11] Y. A. Ioffe, *Ekonomicheskoye Sorevnovaniye Sotsializma i Kapitalizma*, p. 17. Moscow: Ogiz, 1939. Ioffe does not state specifically that the per capita production of the United States referred to is that of 1929. This seems likely, however, since his discussion is based on Stalin's speech at the Eighteenth Communist Party Congress.

1928 and 1940. While the absolute gains scheduled to be won in the later period are greater than those actually attained in the earlier period, it must be remembered that the Soviet economy begins from a much higher original level in 1950 than it did in 1928. The percentage gains scheduled to be made in the period after 1950 are substantially lower than those actually achieved in the earlier years of most intense economic development. This is shown in the table below.

	Percentage Growth in Production	
	1928–1940	1950–1962
Commodity	ACTUAL	PLANNED
Gross Industrial Output	642	195
Coal	464	200
Pig Iron	441	256
Steel	426	236
Petroleum	270	170

The relative modesty of the percentage gains scheduled to be attained after 1950 is apparent from this comparison.

The following seem likely to have been the most important factors in the considerations that preceded the setting of these long-range post-war goals. First, much of the rapid progress from 1928 to 1940 was obtained by utilizing more fully the initially existing stock of capital. The greatly increased burden placed upon the railroad transport system during this period is an outstanding example of this. Moreover, most earlier development took place in existing centers of population and was made possible by greatly increasing the crowding of existing housing. For future progress, however, Soviet planners must provide for the utilization of less accessible resources in thinly populated areas. More and more they will have to use inferior-grade raw materials formerly not required. New rail lines must be built, along with many more new cities and towns. The existing overcrowded stock of housing cannot be relied upon to hold many more people, so that urban housing construction will have to increase proportionally or more than proportionally to the future growth of urban population. It is significant that even before World War II the Soviet government announced a ban against building new productive enterprises in a number of the largest Soviet cities, including Moscow and Leningrad.

Second, it may be that Soviet planners have decided that other branches of the economy must receive a larger share of capital investment in the future. In the postwar period, railroad transport requires great reconstruction and substantial expansion. The road network of the USSR is most inadequate and requires substantial development if the economies obtainable from greater use of automobiles and trucks are to be secured. With the rapid growth of population likely in the future, agricultural output must be increased greatly. This requires not only heavy investment in such activities as irrigation and the major afforestation project begun in 1948, but also investment aimed at still further mechanizing and electrifying agriculture so as to increase labor productivity there. Only by such increased productivity can adequate numbers be released from the rural labor force to provide the workers needed for the expanding nonagricultural economy.

Third, Soviet planners have probably reckoned with the desire of their people for less future sacrifice and a higher standard of living. To meet this desire there must be increased production of food, housing, and consumer goods. In part this must be made possible by increased investment in, and allocation of labor to, the sadly neglected field of consumer services of all kinds. After the sacrifices and hardships of the years since 1928, the Soviet people can hardly be in a mood to sustain similar deprivation to 1960 or afterward. Intent upon remaining in power and minimizing internal dissent, Soviet leaders are probably quite sincere in their avowals that increasing the standard of living is high on the list of their future objectives.

Fourth, the problem of labor must hold a central place in Soviet planning for the future. The development of the 1930's was made possible by moving millions of underemployed workers from agriculture to nonfarm occupations, particularly industry. In the future, such huge mass migration from the countryside in such a short period will not be possible, since much of the slack of underemployment there has already been taken up. Natural population increase will continue to provide additional labor resources, but for the short run — from 1955 to 1965 — the number of young workers entering the labor market will reflect the reduced birth rate and high infant and child mortality of the hard years during World War II. To make their labor supply adequate for their future goals, Soviet leaders will have to, and obviously intend to, press for maximally rapid increases in labor productivity. The best levels attained by capitalist countries are their most obvious objective. But starting from the higher level of productivity existing in 1950, Soviet leaders cannot count upon making progress as rapidly as they did when they started from the abysmally low level of 1928. The frantic appeals for higher labor productivity published in the Soviet press in the spring of 1954 gave evidence of this problem's importance.

The above analysis of the probable future slowing down of the rate of Soviet economic growth was originally written in 1950. Since then it has become clear that Soviet petroleum production is likely to reach the long-term goal set by Stalin well before 1962, probably by 1955 or thereabouts. Moreover, as pointed out in an earlier chapter, the Soviet 1955 goal for gross industrial output, as set by the Fifth Five-Year Plan, is seemingly equivalent to about the 400,-000,000,000 rubles in terms of 1926–27 prices originally envisaged by Stalin for attainment in 1960 or later. The meaning of the latter fact is obscure because of the change in the method of calculating Soviet industrial output indexes which was introduced in 1952. Certainly the 1955 goals for coal, steel, pig iron, and electric power are well below the levels Stalin and his colleagues envisaged for 1960 in their early postwar planning.

Since 1950, too, many anxious voices have been raised in the Western world pointing to the seemingly much more rapid economic growth in the Soviet Union (and its satellites) than in the United States (and Western Europe and much of the rest of the free world). Concentrating their attention on the disparity between rates of growth of industrial output of eight to ten per cent annually in the communist sphere as against much smaller rates — usually under five per cent annually — in the United States, these observers warn that sometime in the future the Soviet Union must catch up and then surpass the United States. One of the most cautious of these observers, Mr. Peter Wiles, says ". . . the absolute level of American production, even allowing for its future growth, may well be attained by the Soviet Union before 50 years have passed." [12] More alarmist voices put the matter more strongly and more closely in

---

[12] Peter Wiles, "The Soviet Economy Outpaces the West," *Foreign Affairs*, July 1953, p. 578.

the future ahead of us. Certainly an extended period of major depression in the United States, with concomitant stagnation of investment and underutilization of resources, would permit the Soviet Union to narrow the gap rapidly.

The logic of this position is unassailable if it is supposed that past rapid rates of Soviet economic growth can be maintained little changed. Yet as argued above there is good reason to expect serious slowing down of the rate of Soviet industrial expansion. The measures taken by the regime of Premier Malenkov since Stalin's death represent a concession to the pressures discussed above for more rapid improvement of the domestic standard of living. This concession has taken the form of some reallocation of investment from heavy industry to light industry and agriculture. True, so far as could be judged by early 1954 the Malenkov regime is trying to keep such diversion as low as possible and does not contemplate, for example, any real attack on Russia's housing problem anywhere commensurate with the need. Yet the initial concessions may be far from the final ones, though the Malenkov regime's pronouncements indicate that it intends to push the development of heavy industry and armaments as rapidly as possible given the political situation at home.

It is in agriculture, however, that the issue may be decided. The failure of Soviet food production to keep pace both with the growth of population and with the desire of the Soviet population for improved quality of nutrition was the theme of Khruschev's remarkable addresses of September 1953 and February 1954. Recognition that the root of the difficulty was in the failure to expand grain production sufficiently came in early 1954 with the announcement of the semidesperate project of putting over 30,000,000 acres of marginal land under the plow by 1955 so as substantially to increase grain production. If this and other related measures fail, then much more capital investment will have to go into agriculture in order to raise yields very sharply.

Certainly no upper limit can be placed, a priori, on the possible levels of Soviet economic expansion. But the matter is more complicated than mere mechanical projections of past trends would suggest. Certainly in 1960 or 1965, the evidence suggests, Soviet industrial production is likely still to be below, say, the United States levels of 1952 or 1953. For the further future, there are the revolutionary possibilities of automation and atomic energy, the full import of which — for good or for evil — is unpredictable.

In the light of the considerations sketched above, we may note that it was not until March 1954 that a high Soviet leader followed the 1939 example of Stalin and Molotov by publicly discussing the economic backwardness of Russia on a per capita basis compared with advanced noncommunist countries. This discussion was given in the following remarks by Deputy Premier A. I. Mikoyan printed in *Pravda,* March 12, 1954.

> Instead of the armaments race, why should there not be competition between the two systems—socialist and capitalist—with respect to peaceful production and raising the living standards of the people. We are prepared for such a competition. With respect to some products, we know that some capitalist countries produce more of them per capita and often this production is of better quality than our's. This is connected with the fact that these countries took the road to industrialization earlier than we did, and did not suffer, as we did, such great war losses. The Soviet Union has already shown the advantages of its economic system with respect to both the tempo of economic development and the level of technical development.

These were certainly brave words. But they came at a time when the Soviet Union was frantically engaged in building nuclear and other armaments, when there seemed no foreseeable end to the housing crisis, and when extreme measures had been forced upon the government in its efforts to ensure even the nation's grain supply. These facts too must be borne in mind in evaluating Mikoyan's remarks.

The Geography of Future Development

The speculations above are partially confirmed by a rather detailed outline of the nature of future economic development given in October 1949 by the outstanding Soviet geographer V. F. Vasyutin.[13] He indicated that the great natural wealth of Siberia is to be the basis of much future development. Industry in this area is to be furnished large quantities of cheap hydroelectric power from the Angara and Yenisey rivers. New railroads must be built in

---

[13] *Izvestia Akademii Nauk SSSR Otdeleniye Ekonomiki i Prava,* No. 3 (1950), pp. 179–92. This discussion also takes into account various projects announced since Vasyutin delivered his paper, intended to realize objectives he mentioned.

Siberia, and new cities and industrial centers must be built along those lines. Kuzbas coal output must be tripled, presumably to about 90,000,000 metric tons annually. Industry is to be developed in this area up to the point where it will require about 75,000,000 metric tons annually, he implies. The Kulundinsk and Barabinsk steppe areas must be turned into great food-production regions to feed the expanded population of the area. Siberia is to become a major lumber, wood-chemistry, cellulose, and paper center of the USSR. The mineral and agricultural resources of the Minusinsk basin are to be intensively developed. Yakutsk and the Tuvinian autonomous province are also to be centers of substantial economic progress. In the Far East, emphasis is to be put upon developing metallurgical industry, both ferrous and nonferrous; expanding forestry activity; and making this area more nearly independent and self-sufficient with regard to food.

In the future development of Kazakhstan, the mineral resources of the Altay mountains and hydroelectric power from the Irtysh River are to be stressed. The region around Lake Zaysan in southeast Kazakhstan is to be developed as a highly intensive food production center and also as a major source of coal and shale. In central Kazakhstan, the nonferrous metallurgy in the neighborhood of Lake Balkhash will be further developed. In addition ferrous metallurgy is to be developed by combining Karaganda coal with iron ore from the Dzhezkazgan, Ata-Su and Karkoralinsk regions. The Ekibastuz coal basin is to increase its production. Great expansion of irrigation will be needed for agriculture in this territory, and the problem of providing water for industrial uses is also to be worked on intensively. In southern Kazakhstan, hydroelectric power will be obtained from the Ili River and from the numerous smaller mountain rivers there, while the agricultural potential of the area south of Lake Balkhash is to be developed. Metal mining and industry are to be of major importance. In western Kazakhstan exploitation of the petroleum and natural gas resources of the Emba-Urals area will receive priority along with increased production from local coal supplies.

The Fergana Valley of Central Asia is also to be a major center of future economic progress, which will be based upon increased exploitation of mineral resources and further growth of cotton production. As noted in Chapter I, uranium ore is found in this area and may be an important basis for present and future development.

Hydroelectric power and irrigation are key features of the development envisaged for the Caucasus. The water resources of the Kura, Araks, and Zanga Rivers, and of Lake Sevan, are central in these projects. Subtropical crops are to be further expanded in the Kolkhid (Colchis) and Lenkoran areas and on the Black Sea coasts of the North Caucasus and Crimea. Iron ore, petroleum, and natural gas production are to be focal points of attention on the Kerch Peninsula.

Future economic development in the Volga River region is to be based on hydroelectric power, irrigation, and increased oil output in the "Second Baku" region. In late August 1950, the Soviet government announced plans for construction of two of the largest hydroelectric stations in the world on the Volga River at Kuibyshev and Stalingrad.[14]

New industrial centers are to be created in the Urals on the basis of the iron ore there combined with coal from the Pechora Basin in the north. The Ukhta-Pechora region in the European north is to have forestry, wood-working, cellulose, and paper industries developed, along with an agriculture adapted to the extreme climatic conditions there.

In the Ukraine, the Donbas is to be further developed as a primary center of all kinds of industry. The Kakhovka hydroelectric station will be built on the Dnepr River, and the Carpatho-Ukraine will become an important industrial center. Future economic progress in Moldavia is to be based on exploitation of hydroelectric power from the Dnestr River.

The future economic pattern envisaged for the Moscow-Leningrad region will rest on intensive expansion of local coal and metallurgical production. Exploitation of the Moscow and other coal basins there is to be increased, as is the mining of iron ore from the Kursk Magnetic Anomaly. New metallurgical plants are to be built near Leningrad and in the neighborhood of Moscow.

In all this future development, apparently, it is intended to continue emphasizing the need for partially self-sufficient economic regions, capable of supplying their own requirements of food, consumer goods, and other commodities as far as possible. Vasyu-

---

[14] *Pravda*, August 21 and 31, 1950.

tin has declared, however, "We will always use the advantages of correct territorial division of labor between regions, combining specialization with the maximum possible and necessary all around development (literally, complexity)." Where the line is to be drawn between specialization and self-sufficiency is not clearly indicated. Vasyutin has defined the degree of complexity desired for each major region in these terms:

> The problem of complex development of a region is first of all to guarantee the specialized branches of national significance necessary raw materials, fuel, electric power, different raw materials and in the maximally possible degree satisfy the requirements of the region for fuel, metal, construction materials, chemical fertilizers, agricultural products, and consumer goods, in correspondence with the instructions of the 18th Party Congress.[15]

Prof. Khachaturov, the outstanding Soviet specialist on transport economics, has indicated that the reasoning behind this planned geographical pattern of development is the desire to have transport requirements grow more slowly than production. Writing in 1940 and looking ahead to 1947 or 1952, he argued that a more even distribution of industry in the future would permit reduction and elimination of many long hauls required before World War II. By the time the USSR had equaled 1929 per capita United States industrial production, he believed the volume of Soviet railroad freight turnover would be between 900,000,000,000 and 1,000,-000,000,000 ton-kilometers per year. This figure is only two and a half times the 1940 volume of 415,000,000,000 ton-kilometers, though the Soviet goals call for tripling 1940 industrial production. Khachaturov estimated that by 1947 or 1952, years now replaced by 1960 and 1965 as terminal points of present long-range planning, Soviet railroads would be carrying about 1,500,000,000 metric tons of freight with an average transport distance of 600 to 650 kilometers.[16] As indicated earlier, however, considerations of military strategy are probably also behind this planned localization of economic activity. The speech by First Deputy Premier Kaganovich, published in April 1954, indicated Russia still has far to go before it achieves regional self-sufficiency.

---

[15] *Izvestia Akademii Nauk SSSR, op. cit.,* p. 190.
[16] *Planovoye Khozyaistvo,* No. 10 (1940), pp. 37–38.

The Communist Future

At best the shape of the future is not clear, and it becomes dimmer the further we attempt to probe. As Soviet planners look beyond 1960 or 1965, the possibilities before them become more abundant, as do the alternatives among which they may choose. The avowed ultimate goal of Soviet development is the achievement of the long-promised state of communism. The people of the USSR have been told for over three decades that the sacrifices demanded of them are worth while because they are building a new society in which human nature will be far different from that existing at present and in which distribution can be in accordance with need rather than productive contribution as at present. Some facets of the problem of building a truly communist society are beyond the scope of this volume. Whether or not the great mass of human beings can be conditioned to work for the joy of working rather than to obtain the necessities and luxuries they want is a question for a treatise on psychology and perhaps on psychiatry. It may be remarked here, however, that the highly differentiated system of rewards and punishments now prevalent in the Soviet Union would hardly seem conducive to the development of that type of attitude toward work. The discussion will be limited here to the economic aspects of the requirements to be met for the attainment of communism.

Soviet leaders have scrupulously refrained from setting any very definite time by which they hope to attain communism, preferring ambiguity that would arouse hopes without committing the state to specific performance. Nevertheless, it seems pertinent to inquire whether it is likely that the USSR can achieve a state of abundance permitting distribution according to needs by 1970. Soviet leaders, like Marx before them, have been ambiguous as to the concept of the needs that would be met in a communist society. Skeptics may argue that since human wants are insatiable no society can ever hope to be sufficiently productive to give people all they want. But perhaps the term 'needs' could be interpreted as consisting of the goods and services comprising a level of high consumption. For exploratory purposes let us assume that Soviet leaders might be able to institute communism if by 1970 they could attain per capita production equivalent to that of the United States in 1953. This would require substantially higher absolute output than was achieved by the United States in that year, because of the more numerous Soviet population. Even the American postwar production level might be inadequate for communism, or at least this has been implied by one Soviet economist.[17]

We shall assume that by 1970 the Soviet Union will have about 260,000,000 people. This is derived from an assumed 1953 population of 210,000,000 and an annual increase of almost 3,000,000 persons in each of the following seventeen years. In Table 65, therefore, American per capita production of various key commodities in 1953 has been multiplied by 260,000,000 to secure a figure of what Soviet production would have to be in 1970 to give the minimum material base for instituting a communist system of distribution.

TABLE 65. Soviet Production Required in 1970 to Equal United States 1953 Per Capita Output of Selected Commodities.

Commodity	U. S. 1953 Per Capita	Required Soviet 1970 Output Equivalent	1953 Soviet Output
Coal	2,731 kg.	710 mil. metric tons	320
Pig Iron	431 kg.	112 mil. metric tons	28
Steel	631 kg.	164 mil. metric tons	38
Petroleum	2,019 kg.	525 mil. metric tons	52
Electric Power	3,213 kwh	835 billion kwh	133
Cotton Textiles	57.5 meters	15 billion meters	5.3
Leather Shoes	3.12 pair	812 million pair	242

The immensity of the task before the Soviet economy is implied clearly by the data above. To achieve 1953 United States per capita output by 1970, the Soviet Union would in 17 years have to double its coal, quadruple its pig iron and steel, multiply petroleum output ten times and electric power more than six times, triple cotton textile production, and more than triple shoe production. Even the above comparison minimizes the nature and magnitude of the progress that would have to be accomplished because it leaves out of account the far greater expansion of consumer services that would have to be made to attain the American standard in this field of consumption. In addition, the table above does not indicate the increase in agri-

[17] *Izvestia Akademii Nauk SSSR, op. cit.,* No. 3 (1949), p. 223.

cultural output that would have to be attained so that Soviet food production per capita might equal that of the United States in 1948. The latter is particularly important because of the fact that until now Soviet food consumption has been heavily based upon grain. Presumably in the future communist society consumers will wish a more diversified diet and one including much more in the way of meat and dairy products. To produce a pound of meat requires between five and ten pounds of grain fed to livestock. Any increase in meat and dairy output to American levels would consequently require a tremendous increase in grain production.

In the area of food production, therefore, the possibilities of raising Soviet per capita output to the American level may be considered on the basis of grain, which, as pointed out above, is also the basis for meat and dairy production. In 1946 American per capita output of six major grains, wheat, rye, barley, oats, corn, and rice, was 970 kilograms. Assuming 260,000,000 persons in the USSR in 1970, the equivalent level of per capita output would require production of 258,000,000 metric tons of grain in that year. Actually, to make the Soviet figures comparable with the American ones, allowance would have to be made for the fact that Soviet grain statistics are on an exaggerated field basis that does not allow for losses. This might perhaps raise the grain requirement, in terms of Soviet harvest statistics, to 280,000,000 metric tons. In 1953 the Soviet Union's biological crop of grain was less than 130,000,000 metric tons. Thus in the 17 years from 1953 to 1970, total Soviet grain output within the present boundaries must more than double in order to equal American per capita output in 1946. Whatever may be accomplished toward increasing sown area and yields per acre in the next twenty years, such a stupendous feat seems most unlikely of accomplishment. One student of Soviet agriculture has pointed out that even an increase of Soviet grain production by 1970 to 162.9 million metric tons will be most difficult to achieve, if it can be done at all.[18] The vastly greater amount required to achieve the standard indicated above seems out of the question. Faced by both an increasing population and a strong demand by their people for an improved quality of diet, it is clear that the Soviet leaders are under great pressure to

[18] Joseph J. Bulik, "USSR: The Fifteen Year Afforestation Plan," *Land Economics,* November 1949, pp. 358–60.

increase grain output in the future substantially, even if they cannot achieve the very high goal calculated as required for communism under the assumption made here.

As one surveys the enormous progress that would have to be made by 1970 to achieve even the minimum level of abundance that might make a communist system of distribution practical, it seems most unlikely that it can be done. The gains required to reach American 1953 output per capita in both goods and services will be difficult to achieve by 1980 or perhaps even later. When one takes additionally into account the insatiability of human desires, the increasing differentiation among Soviet consumers and income recipients, the great stratification of Soviet society and the official derogation of egalitarianism, it would not be surprising if the dream of communism in this century proved to be hollow, a vain hope placed before the poverty-stricken masses to impel them to great efforts and sacrifices.

It may be objected that future technological progress is likely to be great and that such developments as the harnessing of atomic power may make accomplishments that now seem far away more easily realizable. The dynamic scientific and engineering advance of recent generations lends point to this objection, yet it is difficult to see what technological advances would be sufficiently great to speed very substantially the attainment of contemporary American per capita production.

Soviet spokesmen, it is true, have boasted of their intention to use atomic power for peaceful purposes. It may be that the Soviet evaluations of the costs of atomic power and its relative economies are brighter than those made by American economists because investment calculation in the USSR does not take into account any explicit charge for interest, an important item in view of the high capital costs involved. There is also the possibility that Soviet calculations on this matter may envisage use of atomic power for very large-scale plants where economies of scale may reduce costs well below those estimated in the case of the 75,000 kilowatt plant, the plant that has been most carefully analyzed in this country.[19] Most serious technical discussion of future Soviet power expansion

---

[19] Walter Isard and Vincent Whitney, "Atomic Power and the Location of Industry," *Harvard Business Review,* March 1950, pp. 47–48.

published in the USSR has focused upon hydroelectric power projects, the most conspicuous examples being the huge Kuibyshev and Stalingrad stations announced in August 1950 and discussed above. For the next decade, however, it seems likely that economic factors will play a secondary role in determining Soviet policy on atomic power. The USSR announced on June 30, 1954, that it had put a 5,000-kilowatt atomic power plant into operation. This was obviously done regardless of expense, because of the political and propaganda prestige resulting from such an accomplishment. But such an advance, even if made before corresponding progress in countries where costs play a more decisive role, is still a long way from making atomic power a significant major element in economic expansion.

The pessimistic conclusions drawn above regarding the possibility of the attainment of sufficient abundance to permit a communist system of distribution in the foreseeable future should not be misunderstood, however. Given peace and stability, the USSR will continue to make substantial progress both in heavy industry and in standard of living, after the goals set by Stalin for 1960 or 1965 have been attained. Once these goals have been reached, there will probably be a further reduction in the rate of growth, to 100 or 50 per cent every ten or fifteen years, rather than the 200 per cent envisaged after 1950. This will still be very substantial progress. If we assume that Stalin's targets set out in 1946 are reached by 1962, then a 100 per cent further increase by 1974 would bring the *total* output of Soviet heavy industry at least to well above American levels before the Korean War. Steel output might rise to over 100,-000,000 metric tons; coal production to well over 700,000,000 metric tons; and so on. This is not to be construed as a prediction in any sense. Rather it is intended to point out that even substantial lowering of past rates of Soviet progress would bring its total industrial production much more nearly abreast of that of the United States twenty-five years from now than it is at present, assuming only moderate continued economic expansion of the more mature American economy. All this would be true even though per capita industrial production would still be far behind that in this country because of the discrepancy in population. The story in agriculture, of course, is far different, for no comparable rapid rates of growth are to be expected there. It is conceivable that rapid future Soviet population growth, if unmatched by corresponding improvement in crop and livestock yields and food supply, might result in serious pressure on the Soviet regime, forcing it to export capital equipment in exchange for food, or perhaps reinforcing other motives for imperialistic adventures. Such speculations about the possible situation two decades or more ahead of us must obviously be very inconclusive, especially in view of the grave problems that must be overcome in the near future in the international arena.

The future development of Soviet foreign economic relations will be influenced very greatly by the world political and military situation. If present strained relationships between East and West continue, as seems most likely, the world will certainly continue to be divided into two great trading blocs having relatively little to do with each other economically. In such a situation, the already substantial integration of the economies of the Soviet satellite countries with that of the USSR will increase. The vast area from the Pacific to the western borders of East Germany beyond the Elbe River will tend to became a single economic unit coordinated effectively from a single center, Moscow. This will be a latter-day colonial empire reminiscent of that created by Nazi Germany in the Balkans before World War II. As the core and chief power within this bloc of nations, the USSR is in a position to benefit from the economic development of its satellites. It can unilaterally impose terms of trade favorable to it; through present and future joint-development corporations operating in satellite countries, it can profit handsomely from their economic progress. The complete political subservience of its satellites provides abundant prerequisites for such economic exploitation.

China is a special case. The relationships between China and the USSR are and obviously will be far different from those between, say, Bulgaria and the USSR. The Soviet government can hardly look forward with pleasure to the rise of a strong and economically well-developed China on its southern border. Yet fear of Tito-like defection exerts strong pressure to accede to Chinese demands for economic aid. Even with the best of will, however, the Soviet government is not now in any position to give Mao Tse-tung and his associates anything like the volume of economic development assistance they want and need. In this area, surely, there is fertile soil for the seeds of rancor and discord. The area of Chinese-Soviet economic relationships both is influenced by and influences political relationships between the two countries. The course of those relationships in the years ahead will be one of the decisive factors of world history.

Whatever the future may hold for the Soviet economy, the lessons of its past are clear. Like other dictatorships before it, the Kremlin oligarchy has been able to accomplish great feats with the vast resources at its command, but only at enormous cost. Deprived of political liberty, the Soviet masses have received neither economic liberty nor a satisfactory standard of living. Deceived by lies and cowed by the secret police, they are powerless, as the fruits of their toil are diverted to support the new Soviet aristocracy and to maintain the largest military establishment in the world. The existence of freedom and truth anywhere in the world endangers the Kremlin's rule, for from them may come exposure of the colossal deception that is being practiced on the over 210,000,000 citizens under Moscow's rule. As the free world struggles to prevent further advances by Soviet totalitarianism, it will do well to remember that the poverty-stricken masses of the USSR can become our most valuable allies if the fog of falsehood and ignorance that obstructs their understanding can be swept away.

THE SOVIET ECONOMY 1954-1958

THE STORMY AND RAPID economic development of the Soviet Union during the first 37 years of that country's existence is described in detail in the main body of this volume. The developments in the years 1954–1958 have been such as to make the subject of Soviet economics of greater importance and concern to the world than ever before. In this appendix an effort is made to describe briefly the chief aspects of Soviet economic development in these latter years, an effort facilitated by the greater wealth of economic data released by the Soviet Government in recent years.[1]

Basking in the glow of the Soviet sputniks, Soviet sources have attempted to make it appear that the period considered here has been one of steady, rapid progress without significant setbacks. The fact of progress appears clear, but any objective evaluation of these years must take into account the fact of setbacks, for example the impact of the Hungarian Revolution and other forces which required the scrapping of the Sixth Five Year Plan in September 1957, well before its scheduled end in 1960.[2]

Four facets of Soviet economic development during 1954–1958 seem notable. They are:

1. The major changes in organization of industry, agriculture, and economic planning introduced in 1957 and 1958.

2. The substantial growth of industrial and agricultural production during this period.

---

[1] A description of the new wealth of Soviet economic statistics released during 1956 and 1957 is given in Harry Schwartz, "The Renaissance of Soviet Statistics," *Review of Economics and Statistics*, May 1958. Much of this data is presented in English in the following two publications: *Statistical Handbook of the U.S.S.R.* (A translation of *Narodnoye Khozyaistvo S.S.S.R.* with introduction, additional tables and annotations by Harry Schwartz) The Conference Board Studies in Business Economics Number 55, National Industrial Conference Board, 1957 and Harry Schwartz, *The Soviet Economy 1956-1958*, Conference Board Studies in Business Economics, Number 60, National Industrial Conference Board, 1958.

[2] *Pravda*, September 26, 1957.

A

3. The effort made to ease the rigors of Stalinist economic policy upon the Soviet people, and to make life more tolerable for them.

4. The emergence of the Soviet Union, together with Communist China and the other nations ruled by governments loyal to Moscow, as a significant force in the world economy. This development poses significant problems before the West.

Below, these four developments are considered in turn.

Reorganization of Economic Organization

A trend toward decentralization of industrial control was evident in 1954–1956. In 1956, for example, only 45 per cent of Soviet industrial output was accounted for by enterprises directly under the control of the national government as against 70 per cent in 1952.[3] This was largely the result of the transfer of many enterprises, particularly in light industry, to the control of the union republican, provincial, and local authorities.

In 1957, however, a much more drastic change took place. Industrial administration was largely shifted to a regional basis and almost all central ministries were abolished. More than 100 Councils of National Economy (*Sovnarkhozy*) were formed, each controlling most significant enterprises in its area. The economic administrative regions so formed usually embraced one province each, though some included several provinces and some, in the less industrialized union republics, were coincident with union republics. In making this change Soviet leaders denounced the inefficiency of the former centralized ministrial administration and expressed the hope that by shifting more control power closer to the site of production greater efficiency would be attained.[4] At the same time Soviet leaders expressed fear of the consequences of local officials using their expanded powers to put local interests ahead of national interests.

---

[3] *Narodnoye Khozyaistvo SSSR v 1956 Godu*, Moscow, 1957, p. 47.

[4] N. S. Khrushchev's major speech explaining this reorganization appeared in *Pravda*, May 8, 1957, and an English translation will be found in the *Current Digest of the Soviet Press*, June 12, 1957. Experience during the first year of this reform showed that the early fears of local officials putting local interests first were justified. To curb such activity, the Soviet Government in April 1958 issued a law providing prison sentences or lesser punishment for officials failing to meet obligations toward supplying other regions of the country. Cf. *Pravda*, May 19, 1958.

In agriculture, two fundamental organizational changes were made during the first half of 1958. The Machine-Tractor Stations were largely abolished and converted into local repair depots for farm machinery. The machinery owned by the M.T.S. was largely sold to the collective farms in a sharp turnabout from the position expressed by Stalin in 1952. The justification for this radical change was again the great inefficiency and unnecessary cost which had been created by the former dual system. But in addition it was claimed that the collective farms had become strong enough economically and their members sufficiently devoted to the Soviet system so that they could be entrusted with ownership and control of their basic means of production.[5] This move required the reorganization of the procurement system for farm produce since collective farms' payments in kind for the use of M.T.S. machinery had formerly made up a significant part of these procurements. The solution adopted was the wiping out of the former complex system under which the government had formerly obtained farm produce. This had included requisitions at very low prices, purchases at higher prices, and—for some agricultural raw materials—purchases under a contract system. Instead there was instituted a uniform purchase system with prices differentiated by regions of the country. Only the average prices to be paid farms in the country as a whole were published, along with the indication that these might be lowered in years of good crops and raised in years of poor crops. Use of such adjustments seemed obviously a surrogate for the fluctuations of prices on free markets where prices tend to fluctuate, other factors being equal, inversely to the size of crops.[6]

Other organizational changes in agriculture during this period included the following: A continued decline in the number of collective farms—partly because of the continuing merger of smaller farms into larger units and partly because of the conversion of some collective farms into state farms—from 93,300 at the beginning of 1954 to about 78,000 at the beginning of 1958. A continued increase

---

[5] *Ibid*, February 28 and March 1, 1958.

[6] This decree, published in the Soviet press on July 1, 1958, also altered the prices collective farms pay for goods required in production, putting them more nearly in a position similar to the favored state farms.

in the number, and particularly in the sown acreage, of state farms, primarily because of the predominant use of this organizational form in the exploitation of the virgin lands. At the beginning of 1958 there were about 5,800 state farms as against 4,857 four years earlier, while their sown acreage rose from 18,236,000 hectares in 1953 to 35,285,000 hectares in 1956, and even more afterward.[7] During this period, too, collective farms were given somewhat more freedom in running their own affairs—subject to government plans for delivery of produce. The rules requiring collective farmers to work at least a certain minimum number of days on the collective fields were tightened and the minima in general made higher. The size of farmers' private garden plots tended to be reduced, though farmers' compulsory delivery obligations to the state on the produce of these plots were removed effective the beginning of 1958.

With respect to economic planning, the abolition of most industrial ministries in 1957 tended to increase the importance and influence of the Gosplan, or State Planning Committee, which serves as the chief coordinating body in the economy. The Seven Year Plan, covering 1959–1965, was designed to substitute for the scrapped Sixth Five Year Plan and the scheduled Seventh Year Plan. Information available in mid-1958 indicated that the Seven Year Plan would cover a smaller number of indexes than customary earlier as part of an effort to put more emphasis on planning nearer the grassroots, at the level of union republics, provinces, major cities, and counties.[8]

Soviet Production Growth

The growth in output of key Soviet industrial commodities during 1954–1957 is shown below, along with the 1958 goals set by the plan for that year and the original 1960 goals set by the Sixth Five Year Plan. The latter presumably are no longer binding in view of the abandonment of that plan.

---

[7] *Ekonomika Selskogo Khozyaistva*, No. 2, 1958, p. 5 and *Narodnoye Khozyaistvo SSSR v 1956 Godu*, pp. 106, 146-147.

[8] On the new system of "perspective planning" cf. *Promyshlenno-Ekonomicheskaya Gazeta*, May 11, 1958 and the editorial in *Planovoye Khozyaistvo*, No. 6, 1958.

Commodity	Unit	1954	1955	1956	1957	1958 goal	1960 goal
Pig iron	mil. met. tons	30.0	33.3	35.8	37.0	39.1	53
Steel	mil. met. tons	41.4	45.3	48.6	51.1	53.6	68.3
Coal*	mil. met. tons	347.1	391.3	429.2	463.4	490.1	593
Oil	mil. met. tons	59.3	70.8	83.8	98.3	112.0	135
Gas	bil. cub. meters	8.8	10.4	13.7	20.2	30.6	40
Electricity	billion kwh	150.6	170.1	192	209.5	231.0	320
Fertilizers	mil. met. tons	8.1	9.6	10.9	11.7	n.a.	19.6
Machine tools	thousands	102.4	117.1	121.3	130.9	n.a.	200
Tractors	thousands	135.4	163.4	184	203.0	n.a.	322
Motor vehicles	thousands	403.9	445.3	465	495.4	n.a.	650
Trucks	thousands	300.9	329.0	358	371.6	n.a.	n.a.
Freight cars	thousands	23.9	34.4	40	38.3	n.a.	52
Grain combines	thousands	38.6	48.0	82	131.1	n.a.	140
Cement	mil. met. tons	19.0	22.5	24.9	28.9	n.a.	55
Cotton cloth	bil. meters	5.6	5.9	5.5	5.6	n.a.	7.3
Woolen cloth	mil. meters	243.2	251.0	268	282.1	291.5	363
Leather shoes	mil. pair	257.8	274.5	289.8	315	342.2	n.a.
Domestic refrigerators	thousands	94.0	151.4	224	308.7	n.a.	635
Washing machines	thousands		45.7	87.0	195	377	n.a.	528
Sugar	mil. met. tons	2.6	3.4	4.4	4.5	n.a.	6.5
Motorcycles	thousands	205.9	244.5	297	334	n.a.	395
Bicycles	millions	2.4	2.9	3.1	3.3	n.a.	4.2

* Includes lignite.   n.a. Not available.
Sources: 1954-1957 production data from annual official Soviet economic reports. Goals for 1958 from *Pravda*, Dec. 20, 1957 and for 1960 from *Narodnoye Khozyaistvo SSSR*, pp. 60-61.

The Malenkov program for raising the Soviet standard of living sharply by 1956 was not accomplished on schedule, being abandoned in early 1955 when he was forced to resign as Premier. Soviet industry, however, showed its rising capabilities in other fields during the period considered here by turning out some of the finest jet bombers and jet transport planes in the world, and, in 1957–1958, by its accomplishments in the fields of intercontinental ballistic missiles and earth satellites. But the strain the rapid tempo of advance imposed on the Soviet economy was suggested by the frequent evidence of capital shortage in the Soviet economy, for example the 1957 long term "postponement" of most Soviet government bond redemption and the decision announced in August 1958 to cut back on the very expensive hydroelectric program.[9]

In Soviet agriculture, substantial production gains were achieved

[9] *Pravda*, August 11, 1958. For earlier evidence of the problems posed by capital shortage cf *The New York Times*, October 20, 1957.

during 1954–1958. In large part these reflected the greater incentive provided Soviet farmers by higher government prices paid for their produce. In part too these gains reflected the partial success, in 1956 and 1958, of the Khrushchev virgin lands grain program, and of his later program greatly to expand Soviet corn plantings. The latter was a fiasco in many areas, but in other Soviet areas it succeeded in providing enough additional livestock feed to promote the growth of livestock herds and, particularly, to permit sharp increases in milk production. Data on farm output in this period follow:

Commodity	Unit	1954	1955	1956	1957	1960** Goal
Grain	million metric tons	83.9	103.2	125.5	102.1	180.0
Raw cotton	million metric tons	4.1	3.9	4.4	4.2	6.1
Sugar beets	million metric tons	19.8	30.6	32.4	35.4	47.1
Sunflower seed	million metric tons	1.9	3.8	4.1	n.a.	n.a.
Milk	million metric tons	38.2	42.2	49.1	54.7	84.2
Meat*	million metric tons	6.3	6.4	6.6	7.4	12.8

* Includes animal fats   ** As set by the Sixth Five Year Plan.   n.a.—Not available.
Sources: Based on official Soviet data.

Livestock numbers in the Soviet Union during this period grew as follows:

	Jan. 1, 1954	Jan. 1, 1955	Jan. 1, 1956	Jan. 1, 1957	Jan. 1, 1958
			(millions)		
Cattle	55.8	56.7	58.8	61.4	66.7
Cows	25.2	26.4	27.7	29.0	31.4
Hogs	33.3	30.7	34.0	40.8	44.3
Sheep	99.8	98.9	103.3	108.1	120.1

Source: *Vestnik Statistiki*, No. 4, 1958, p. 92.

Easing The Strain

From the point of view of the Soviet people, the most important economic developments during 1954–1958 were those which eased the strain they had worked under in Stalin's last years and improved their material position. Not all developments during this period were in this direction, of course, and the virtual cancellation of most government bonds in 1957 was an important step in the opposite direction. Nevertheless, it seems fair to conclude that by, say, the mid-summer of 1958 there had been significant improvement in many areas of Soviet life over the situation four or five years earlier. And the Soviet regime was committed publicly to a policy of further improvement.

The key developments in this area may be briefly summarized: Although no really significant price reductions were announced by the Soviet regime between April 1, 1954 and mid-1958, increased production of food and consumer goods permitted Soviet consumers to satisfy their demands more adequately than earlier. During these years the Soviet Government carried out an internal redistribution of income, raising the incomes of collective farmers, raising the minimum levels of wages and pensions, and reducing somewhat the most extreme inequalities among Soviet workers. The normal work week was reduced from 48 to 46 hours, and in 1958 some categories of workers—in such key areas as coal mining—began to be put on six or seven hour workdays, equivalent to workweeks of 36 or 42 hours. A very substantial increase of housing construction was ordered and began to be executed, with the goal set at ending the terrible Soviet housing shortage before 1970. Programs were announced to equal United States output of milk, meat, butter, clothes and shoes by the early or middle 1960's, and, as noted above, some increase in the output of these consumer commodities had been achieved by 1958.

The status of Soviet workers was significantly improved during this period by a series of measures which removed or alleviated a number of the worst evils of the preceding Stalinist period. Though no official statistics on the matter were issued, the available evidence indicates that the institution of forced labor was sharply reduced with the release of many Soviet citizens and foreigners who had been kept in prison for such work. The Soviet worker's right to change his job without permission of his employer was restored. Soviet labor unions were ordered to take more interest in defending workers' interests, though not to the extent of calling strikes. At least nominally, the authority of Soviet unions and of permanent production conferences of workers in Soviet factories and other enterprises were enhanced by decrees issued in late 1957 and mid-1958. At the time of this writing, it seemed difficult fully to assess the impact of these changes. But it seems clear that significant improvements have taken place in the status of the Soviet worker, though he still has far to go before enjoying either the freedom or the standard of living of his American counterpart.

International Economic Relations[10]

In 1957 and 1958, there was growing free world concern with the question of Communist, particularly Soviet, economic competition. Growing Soviet production gave a greater seriousness to consideration of Communist boasts that the Soviet Union would outstrip the United States. The Soviet Union turned to economic aid to underdeveloped non-Communist countries as a means of making political gains, and by mid-1958 it had promised about $2,000,000,000 such aid, mainly in the form of credits carrying low interest rates and easy repayment terms, to India, Egypt, Syria, Indonesia and a number of other countries. Soviet trade with the non-Communist world increased sharply during this period, and in some commodities—notably aluminum in late 1957 and early 1958—Soviet sales below market prices caused accusations of "Soviet dumping" to be voiced by some affected Western producers.

Free world trade with the Soviet Union grew as follows in this period:

	1953	1954	1955	1956	1957*
			(million dollars)		
Free world exports	423.5	576.7	601.6	784.1	999.7
Free world imports	381.8	500.4	640.3	814.3	1,041.6

* Preliminary data.
Source: *Statistical Review of East-West Trade 1956-57*, Government Printing Office, Washington, 1958, p. 2.

Total Soviet trade turnover, exports plus imports, rose from 23,-000,000,000 rubles in 1953 to 29,000,000,000 rubles in 1956 and 33,000,000,000 rubles in 1957. The great bulk of this trade, however, was with other Communist states. In 1956 Soviet foreign trade turnover with Communist China was 5,989,000,000 rubles, over one

[10] Helpful sources on the topic treated here are *The Sino-Soviet Economic Offensive in the Less Developed Countries*, Dept. of State Publication 6632, Government Printing Office, Washington, May, 1958, and the world survey of Soviet economic penetration in *The New York Times*, July 7, 1958.

fifth of all Soviet foreign trade, and with East Germany, 4,790,700,-
000 rubles. These two countries plus Czechoslovakia accounted for
nearly half of all Soviet foreign trade in both 1955 and 1956.[11]

The character of Soviet economic relations with other Communist
countries changed significantly during this period, particularly after
the Hungarian Revolution and the Polish near-revolution of October
and November 1956. Largely as a result of these disturbances, the
Soviet Union during 1956–1957 granted other Bloc members about
$1,500,000,000 in long term credits and grants. It also cancelled
debts, totalling over $1,500,000,000 they owed to the Soviet Union
and made other concessions as well.[12] In this period of late 1956 and
1957 the Eastern European satellites may have been a net drain on
the Soviet economy. In the years 1956–1958, a great deal more attention was paid to the Council for Mutual Economic Assistance,
and serious efforts were made to employ it as a vehicle for working
out coordinated economic plans based on a rational division of labor
among the Soviet Union, the other Eastern European members of
the Council, and—to a lesser extent—the Asian members of the
Bloc, particularly Communist China.

---

[11] *Vneshnyaya Torgovlya SSSR za 1956 god*, Moscow, 1958, pp. 7-9. This
was issued as a statistical supplement to the magazine *Vneshnyaya Torgovlya*.
[12] *The Sino-Soviet Economic Offensive. . . .*, op. cit., p. 17.

REFERENCE INDEX

657

GENERAL INDEX

A